Human resource management
in Australia

Human resource management
in Australia

robin **kramar**   peter **mcgraw**   randall s. **schuler**

3rd edition

LONGMAN
An imprint of
Addison Wesley Longman

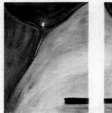

Cover design: Lyndell Board, incorporating the
painting *Over the obstacle* by Kim Bolitho,
reproduced by permission of Kim Bolitho.
© Kim Bolitho. All rights reserved.

Addison Wesley Longman Australia Pty Limited
95 Coventry Street
South Melbourne 3205 Australia

Offices in Sydney, Brisbane and Perth, and associated companies throughout the world.

Copyright © 1997 West Publishing Company and Addison Wesley Longman Australia Pty Limited

First published 1987 by Harper & Row (Australasia) Pty Ltd as *Personnel/Human Resource Management*, adapted from R. S. Schuler, *Personnel and Human Resource Management* (2nd edition) published by West Publishing Company, St. Paul, Minnesota, USA, 1984.
Reprinted 1988, 1989, 1990 (twice), 1991
Second edition 1992 by HarperEducational as *Human Resource Management in Australia*
Reprinted 1992 (twice), 1993, 1996
Third edition 1997
Reprinted 1997, 1998 (twice)
6 7 8 03 02 01

All rights reserved. Except under the conditions described in the Copyright Act 1968 of Australia and subsequent amendments, no part of this publication may be reproduced, stored in a retrieval system or transmitted in any form or by any means, electronic, mechanical, photocopying, recording or otherwise, without the prior permission of the copyright owner.

© Commonwealth of Australia 1997
All legislation herein is reproduced by permission but does not purport to be the official or authorised version. It is subject to Commonwealth of Australia copyright. The Copyright Act 1968 permits certain reproduction and publication of Commonwealth legislation. In particular, s.182A of the Act enables a complete copy to be made by or on behalf of a particular person. For reproduction or publication beyond that permitted by the Act, permission should be sought in writing from the Australian Government Publishing Service. Requests in the first instance should be addressed to the Manager, Commonwealth Information Service, GPO Box 84, Canberra ACT 2601.

While every effort has been made to trace and acknowledge copyright, in some cases copyright proved untraceable. Should any infringement have occurred, the publishers tender their apologies and invite copyright owners to contact them.

Designed by Lyndell Board
Set in 10/12 pt Sabon
Printed in Australia by McPherson's Printing Group

National Library of Australia
Cataloguing-in-Publication data
   Human resource management in Australia

   3rd ed.
   Includes index
   ISBN 0 582 81113 9.

   1. Personnel management - Australia. I. Kramar, Robin.
658.300994

The publisher's policy is to use paper manufactured from sustainable forests

contents

About the authors		vi
Authors' acknowledgements		ix
Acknowledgements		x
Introduction		xvi

Part 1 The HRM context — 1
chapter 1 HRM—History, models, process and directions — 2
chapter 2 Strategic human resource management — 44

Part 2 The external environment — 87
chapter 3 Industrial relations and enterprise bargaining — 88
chapter 4 Equal Employment Opportunity — 122
chapter 5 Occupational health and safety — 158

Part 3 The internal environment — 209
chapter 6 Human resource planning and career development — 210
chapter 7 Job analysis and design — 262
chapter 8 Recruitment, selection and placement — 304
chapter 9 Performance management — 352
chapter 10 Reward management — 408
chapter 11 Training and development — 462

Part 4 The international environment — 503
chapter 12 Cross-cultural management — 504
chapter 13 International human resource management — 538

Glossary — 587
Names index — 601
Subject index — 607

about the authors

Ed Davis is Professor of Management and Director of the Labour-Management Studies Foundation in the Graduate School of Management at Macquarie University. He holds a Master of Arts from Cambridge, a Master of Economics from Monash and a PhD from La Trobe University. During 1992 he held the post of Distinguished Academic Visitor at Queens' College, Cambridge. He is joint editor of the *Economic and Labour Relations Review* and author and co-editor of several books. His most recent books are *Making the Link: Affirmative Action and Industrial Relations* No. 7 (Canberra, AGPS) and *Managing Together: Consultation and Participation at Work* (Melbourne, Longman, 1996). The first was co-edited with Catherine Harris and the second with Professor Russell Lansbury.

Robert L (Bob) Kane is an Associate Professor in the School of Management at the University of Technology, Sydney, where he teaches HRM. He has published research and conceptual articles on various aspects of HRM in Australia and overseas. His current research projects focus on issues such as the relationship between HRM and organisational strategy and change programs and include the areas of human resource planning and career development.

Robin Kramar is a Senior Lecturer in Management (Human Resource Management) at the Graduate School of Management, Macquarie University. She has taught industrial relations and human resource management at a number of Australian universities for more than twenty years. She has published widely in the area of human resource management, labour market issues, equal employment opportunity and organisational change. She is currently Director of the Centre for Australasian Human Resource Management. She is also Book Review Editor for the the *Asia Pacific Journal of Human Resources* and is a member of the Editorial Boards of this journal, the *International Journal of Employment Studies* and the FT Law & Tax monthly publication, *Employee Relations Brief*. Robin has a BComm (Hons) and a MComm (Hons) from the University of New South Wales and a PhD from Sydney University.

David Lamond joined the Macquarie Graduate School of Management in 1990 following a successful career as a senior manager in the NSW public sector. David is a Senior Lecturer in Management and Deputy Director of the Asia-Pacific Research Institute (APRIM) at the MGSM. He consults extensively both locally and internationally. He was a Visiting Fellow in Management at the Cranfield University School of Management in 1994. His current research interests are in personality and managerial style and strategic human resource management.

Peter McGraw is a Senior Lecturer at the Macquarie University Graduate School of Management in Sydney, where he teaches human resource management. Originally from the UK, Peter graduated with a BA (Hons) from Leicester University and obtained his MA from Warwick University. Peter been an academic for thirteen years, and has published widely in areas concerned with management and employee relations. He has held visiting academic positions at Sydney University and IMD. Before becoming an academic Peter worked for trade unions and management associations in both the UK and Australia. His current research interests include human resource management strategy, international human resource management and employee involvement issues. Peter has extensive consulting/training experience in the management area and has consulted to numerous organisations in Australasia, Europe and Asia.

Lindsay Nelson worked in industry in the field of human resource management and industrial relations before becoming an academic. At present he lectures in topics related to human resource management and organisational behaviour in the Department of Management, University of Tasmania. He has formal qualifications in industrial psychology and is a registered psychologist. He has published in the areas of occupational health and safety and employee relations. His current research interests are in organisational change and enterprise bargaining.

Graham O'Neill has a BA (Hons) and a postgraduate Diploma in Applied Psychology. He is Director of Operations for the Melbourne Office of The Hay Group. He rejoined Hay from the ANZ Bank where he was Senior Adviser, Reward Planning. Prior to joining ANZ, Graham had spent some 15 years consulting to a range of Australian, New Zealand and overseas companies, with a special emphasis on reward planning, design and management. He is Editor-in-Chief of the John Libby & Co. bi-monthly R*eward Management Bulletin* and has edited 2 books, *Corporate Remuneration in the 90s: Strategies for Decision Makers* (Longman Professional, 1990) and, with Robin Kramar, *Australian Human Resource Management: Current Trends in Management Practice* (Pearson Professional, 1995). He is a previous editor of *Human Resource Management Australia,* now the *Asia Pacific Journal of Human Resources,* and remains on the editorial board of that journal.

Randall S. Schuler is Research Professor, Stern School of Business, New York University. His interests are international human resource management, organisational uncertainty, personnel and human resource management, entrepreneurship, and the interface of competitive strategy and human resource management. He has authored and edited over twenty-five books, has contributed over twenty chapters to reading books, and has published over seventy articles in professional journals and academic proceedings. Presently, he is on the Editorial Board of *International Journal of Human Resource Management, Human Resource Management, Asia Pacific Journal of*

Human Resources and *Organisation Science*. He is a Fellow of the American Psychological Association. Professor Schuler has been on the faculties of the University of Maryland, Ohio State University, Penn State University, and Cleveland State University. He also worked at the United States Office of Personnel Management in Washington, DC, and has done extensive consulting and management development work in North America, Europe and Australia.

Andrew Smith is Associate Professor in Human Resource Management and Head of the School of Management at Charles Sturt University. He is also Co-Director of the Group for Research in Employment and Training. Andrew has an Honours degree from Cambridge University, and MBA from Aston University. His doctoral studies were undertaken at the University of Tasmania. He has worked in academia for nine years. Prior to this, Andrew spent ten years working in a variety of Human Resource Management positions in the automotive and aerospace industries in the UK. Andrew's particular area of expertise is training and development. His research interests include the impact of training and development on organisational performance, the evaluation of training, organisational change and issues of skill formation at the enterprise level particularly in manufacturing. He has managed a number of large, national research projects in the area of training and development. His book, *Training and Development in Australia* was published by Butterworths in 1992.

Bruce Stening has over twenty year's experience as a management educator, consultant and trainer. His current appointment is as Professor of Management and former Director of the Australian National University's Managing Business in Asia Program. He has previously held professorial and other senior appointments at universities both in Australia and in various other countries including Japan, Finland, South Korea and New Zealand. He has acted as a consultant and trainer to numerous corporations both in Australia and abroad, in many instances in relation to issues of cross-cultural management. He is the author of three books and over fifty academic papers, published principally in journals of psychology and management. Many of those publications relate to the interaction of members of different cultures, usually in the context of multinational corporations. He has a PhD in organisational behaviour and is a member of several professional organisations, including the International Association for Cross-Cultural Psychology, the International Association of Applied Psychology, the Academy of Management, the Academy of International Business and the Society for Intercultural Education, Training and Research. He is a Fellow of the Australian Institute of Management.

authors' acknowledgements

We would to thank the many people who assisted us with the completion of the third edition of *Human Resource Management in Australia*, in particular Catherine Smith who reviewed the whole book and provided many thoughtful comments. We would also like to thank the following individuals for their invaluable comments on early draft chapters:

- Mike Lake, University of Ballarat
- Ann Brewer, University of Sydney
- Ann Lawrence, Deakin University
- Cec Pendersen, University of Southern Queensland
- Russell Lansbury, University of Sydney
- D'Arcy McCormack, La Trobe University.

The continued support and encouragement of Susan Lewis, Louise Ewan and Paul Watt at Addison Wesley Longman was much appreciated during the production stage. In addition, James Davidson and Marah Braye were instrumental in getting the project off the ground.

Robin Kramar
Peter McGraw
MGSM
Sydney

acknowledgements

We would like to thank the following for permission to reproduce copyright material.

ACTU, 'The future of unions in Australia', Report to 1995 Congress, Table 3.3, p. 10 and *Together For Tomorrow,* 1991, Congress, p. 109

Adler, N. & Bartholomew, B./*Academy of Management Executive,* Table 13.2, p. 564

Australian Government Publishing Service—Commonwealth of Australia copyright reproduced by permission: Affirmative Action Agency, *A Practical Guide to Affirmative Action: Towards a Better Workforce,* (1995), Figure 4.2, p. 139, Table 4.2, pp. 141–42; *Affirmative Action Annual Report 1994–1995,* pp. 148–49; Quality *and Commitment: The Next Steps* 1992, p. 146 and *The Triple A List,* pp. 150–51; Australian Bureau of Statistics, *Industrial disputes By Incidence, Employees Involved and Working Days Lost, 1980–95* cat. no. 6321.0, Table 3.4, p. 105, Callus, R., Morehead, A., Cully, M. & Buchanan, J. (1991), *The Australian Workplace Industrial Relations Survey,* Table 3.5, p. 522, p. 148; Carter, C., Nicholson, J. & Barlow, M. (1995), 'The Australian manager in the twenty-first century', in *Enterprising Nation: Industry Taskforce on Leadership and Management Skills,* Volume 2, Figure 2.7, p. 71, 74; Comcare Australia (1994), *Return To Work Policy & Guidelines,* p. 177; Department of Industrial Relations, *Benchmark,* May 1995, pp. 117–18; Department of Industrial Relations, *Enterprise Bargaining in Australia,* Annual Report 1994, Table 3.7, p. 112, Table 3.8, p. 114; Department of Industrial Relations, (1994), *The Workplace Guide to Work and Family, Work and Family Unit,* pp. 77–78; Economic Planning Advisory Council, (1991), *Improving International Competitiveness,* p. 108; House of Representative Standing Committee for Long Term Strategies (1995), *The Workplace Of Future Report,* Table 2.3, p. 73; Industry Commission, *Work Health and Safety Draft Report* (1995): *An Enquiry Into Occupational Health & Safety,* Table 5.2, p. 164, Table 5.3, p. 165, Figure 5.2. p. 166, Figure 5.3, p. 169; Karpin, D. S. (1995) *Enterprising Nation: Reviewing Australia's Managers To Meet The Challenges Of The Asia Pacific Century, Executive Summary,* Table 11.2, p. 486, Table 12.1, p. 507, Figure 13.2, p. 544, Worksafe Australia *Compendium of Workers Compensation Statistics,* (1994), *1991–1992,* p. 163

Allen Consulting Group (Melbourne), p. 494

Australian Business Limited (1995), *An Introduction,* Sydney, p. 102

Australian Centre for Industrial Relations Research and Teaching (ACCIRT) (1995), *Agreements Database and Monitor*, Table 3.6, p. 111

Australian Chamber of Commerce and Industry, 'Dulux Case Study' no. 1, in a series called *Integrated Workplace Change*, pp. 37–42

Australian Safety News (1994), pp. 182–83

Ayres, I. & Braithwaite, J. (1992), *Responsive Regulation Transcending The Deregulation Debate*, Oxford University Press, p. 175

Bagwell, S./*Australian Financial Review*, pp. 147, 154–55

Beer, M. & Spector, B. (1995),'Corporate wide transformations in human resource management', in *Human Resource Management Trends and Challenge*, Harvard Business School Press, p. 19

Beer, M., Spector, B., Lawrence, P., Mills, D. & Walton, R. (1985), *Human Resource Management: A General Manager's Perspective*, Free Press, Figure 2.2, p. 57

Beer, M./*Organizational Dynamics*, p. 385

Betts, Neville/*HRMonthly*, pp. 195–96

Brake, Terence, Walker, Danielle M. & Walker, Thomas (1995), *Doing Business Internationally: The Guide To Cross-Cultural Success*, Richard D. Irwin, Figure 12.1, p. 513, Figure 12.3, p. 522

Brooks, B. J./*Compensation and Benefits Review*, Table 13.6, p. 575

CCH Australia Ltd, pp. 135, 167, Figure 9.9, p. 376

Cipolla, Larry & Traffoed, Chris/*HRMonthly*, pp. 400–401

Collins, R. (1994), 'The strategic contributions of the personnel function', in A. R. Nankervis & R. L. Compton (eds), *Readings in Strategic Human Resource Management*, Nelson, p. 53, 57, Figure 2.3, p. 58

Cousens, Liz & Cousens, Ted/*Management*, pp. 354–55

Cox, M. & Blake (1991), 'Managing cultural diversity: implications for organisational competitiveness', *Academy of Management Executive*, pp. 26–27

Critchley, R./*HRMonthly*, Table 6.2, p. 239

Davis, Mark/*Australian Financial Review*, pp. 94–95

Dwyer, Paula/*Business Week*, pp. 527–28

Dyer, L. (1982), 'Human resource planning', in K. M. Roland & G. R. Ferris (eds), *Personnel Management*, Allyn & Bacon, p. 224

Edstrom, A. & Galbraith, J. R./*Administrative Science Quarterly*, Table 13.5, p. 569

Fastenau, Maureen/*HRMonthly*, pp. 124–26

Ferguson, Adele/*Business Review Weekly*, pp. 540–41

Field, L. & Ford, B. (1995), *Managing Organisational Learning: From Rhetoric To*

Reality, Addison Wesley Longman, Figure 11.4, p. 489

Forbes, Ronald/*Management,* pp. 391–93

Forman, David/*Business Review Weekly,* pp. 62–63

George, J. ACTU President, extract from address to 8th Women, Management and Industrial Relations Conference, 1996, Sydney, p. 116

Gittins, Ross, Economics Editor/*Sydney Morning Herald,* pp. 53–55

Gora, Bronwen/*Sunday Telegraph,* pp. 212–14

Hatfield, Louisa/*Sydney Morning Herald,* pp. 46–48

Heller, J./*Personnel,* p. 557

Hendry, C. (1990), 'Corporate Strategy and Training', in J. Stevens & R. Mackay (eds), *Training and Competitiveness,* Kogan Page, Figure 11.5, p. 491

Hooper, Narelle & Stickles, Georgi/*Business Review Weekly,* p. 128

Hooper, Narelle/*Business Review Weekly,* pp. 197–98

Huczynski, A. A. (1993), *Management Gurus,* Routledge pp. 16–17

Huselid, M. A., Jackson, S. E. & Schuler, R. S. (1995), 'The Significance of Human Resource Management Effectiveness for Corporate Financial Performance', Paper presented at the *Academy of Management Conference,* August 5–8 1995, Vancouver, Canada, p. 10

International Labour Organization (1990), *Environment and the World of Work,* Geneva Copyright © International Labour Organization, pp. 93, 129

Ives, Blake & Jarvenpaa, Sirrka (1996), 'Will the Internet revolutionize business eduction and research?', *Sloan Management Review,* pp. 23–24

James, David/*Business Review Weekly,* pp. 67–68

Kabanoff, B. (1993), 'An exploration of espoused culture in Australian organisations', *Asia Pacific Journal of Human Resources,* vol 31. no. 3, p. 52

Kane, R. L. & Stanton, S. (1994), 'Human resource planning in a changing environment', in A. R. Nankervis & R. L. Compton (eds), *Readings in Strategic Human Resource Management,* Nelson, Figure 6.2, p. 226

Kanter, R. M. (1989), *When Giants Learn To Dance,* Simon and Schuster, p. 23

Knauft, E. B. 'Construction and use of weighted checklist rating scales for tow industrial situations' *Journal of Applied Psychology,* Figure 9.3, p. 369

Kotter, J. P. 'Leading change: why transformation efforts fail', *Harvard Business Review* March–April 1995, © 1995 by the President and Fellows of Harvard College, p. 24

Krautil, Fiona/Esso Australia, pp. 380–81

Lawler, E. C. 'Human resource management: meeting the challenge', *Personnel Management,* p. 36

Lawson, Mark/*Australian Financial Review*, pp. 306–307, pp. 307–309

Ledford, G. E./*Organizational Dynamics*, Table 10.4, p. 427

Legge. K. (1995), *Human Resource Management: Rhetorics and Realities*, Macmillan

Limerick, D./*Asia Pacific Journal of Human Resources*, p. 239

Long, Stephen/*Australian Financial Review*, pp. 328–29

Marshall, Ray/*Australian Financial Review*, p. 113

McGhee, Karen/*Sydney Morning Herald*, pp. 254–55

McGregor, D. (1960), *The Human* Side Of Enterprise, McGraw-Hill, p. 228

Metal Trades Industry Association of Australia for *MTIA: the bottom line* pp. 101–102; The original version of this article was published in MTIAs newsletter in 1993. MTIA subsequently made minor variations to the article into the form it now appears. MTIA advises that whilst the article is correct and accurate in content, it merely expresses the intentions and policies of the Association at the time and is not to be construed as necessarily reflecting the present activities or policies of MTIA.

Mintzberg, H. (1988), 'Opening up the definition of strategy', in J. B. Quinn, H. Mintzberg, & R. M. James (eds), *The Strategy Process*, Prentice-Hall, Table 2.1, p. 50

Moore, Sir John 'Termination change and redundancy case' *Statement*, Melbourne, p. 96

Moss. Kanter R. (1977), *Men and Women of the Corporation*, 1977, Basic Books, p. 343

Naisbitt, John (1995), *Megatrends Asia: The Eight Asian Megatrends That Are Changing The World*, Nicholas Brealey, p. 508

National Occupational Health & Safety Commission (1993),*Worksafe Australia, Henderson's Automotive (SA): An OHS Led Recovery, OHS Building Best Practice,* Figure 5.1, p. 166, p. 180

O'Neill, G./*Asia Pacific Journal of Human Resources*, Figure 10.3, p. 416

O'Relly, Brian/*Fortune*, pp. 360–61

Pfeffer, J. (1995), *Academy of Management Executive*, vol. 9, no. 1, Figure 1.3, p. 14

Podsakoff, P. M., Greene, C. N. & McFillen, J. M. (1987), 'Obstacles to the effective use of reward systems', in R. S. Schuler & S. A. Youngblood (eds), *Readings in Personnel and Human Resource Management*, 3rd edition, West Publishing, Table 10.7, pp. 444–45

Rahim, A./*Personnel Journal*, Figure 13.3, p. 567

Roberts, Peter/*Australian Financial Review*, pp. 4–6, 25–26, 315–316, 319–20, 334–35

Russell, Matthew & Lamont, Leonie/*Sydney Morning Herald*, pp. 151–52

Russell, Matthew/*Sydney Morning Herald*, p. 143

Sathe, V. (1985), *Culture and Related Corporate Realities,* Richard D. Irwin, Table 12.3, p. 516

Saul, Dr Peter/Strategic Consulting Group *What Does Success Look Like?*, Figure 2.1, p. 51

Schein, E. H. (1978), *Career Dynamics: Matching Individual And Organizational Needs,* Addison Wesley Longman, p. 231

Schuler, R. S., Dowling, P. J., Smart, J. P. & Huber, V. (1992), *Human Resource Management in Australia,* 2nd edition, Figure 1.1 p. 9, Figure 8.1, p. 311, Figure 8.3, p. 321, Figure 8.4, p. 324, Figure 8.5, p. 327, Figure 8.6. p. 331, Figure 8.7, p. 334, Figure 8.8, p. 336, Figure 8.9, p. 343, Figure 9.1, p. 362, Figure 9.4, p. 369, Figure 9.5, pp. 370–71, Figure 9.6, p. 372, Figure 9.7, p. 373, Figure 9.8, p. 375, Table 10.1, p. 413, Table 10.2, p. 421, Figure 10.4, p. 430

Schuler, R. S. & Dowling, P. J. (1990), 'Human Resource Management', in R. Blanpain (ed.), *Comparative Labour Law and Industrial Relations in Industrialized Market Economies Volume 2,* Kluwer Law and Taxation, p. 61

Schuler, R. S. & Jackson, S. E. (1996), *Human Resource Management: Positioning for the 21st Century,* 6th edition, West Publishing, Table 5.1, p. 162, Figure 5.5, p. 179, pp. 181–82, Figure 5.6, p. 188

Schuler, R. S. & Walker, J. W. 'Human resources strategy: focusing on issues and actions', *Organizational Dynamics,* 1990, pp. 224–25

Schuler, R. S. (1988), 'Personnel and human resource management choices and organisational strategy', in R. S. Schuler, S. A. Youngblood & V. Huber (eds), *Readings in Personnel and Human Resource Management,* 3rd edition, West Publishing, Figure 1.2 p. 12

Schuler, R. S. (1992), 'Strategic human resource management: linking people with the strategy needs of the business', *Organizational Dynamics,* p. 59, Figure 2.4, p. 60

Schuler, R. S. (1995), *Managing Human Resources,* 5th edition, West Publishing, Figure 2.7, p. 69, p. 74, Figure 2.9, p. 75, Figure 11.2. p. 469, Figure 11.3, p. 482, Figure 6.3, p. 234, Figure 6.4, pp. 248–50, Figure 9.2, p. 365, Figure 9.11, pp. 393–94, Figure 9.12, pp. 394–95, Figure 9.13, p. 396, Figure 9.14, p. 397, Figure 9.15, p. 399, Figure 10.2, p. 414, Figure 11.1, p. 466

Schwartz, Adam/*Far Eastern Economic Review,* p. 524

Scott, Rebecca/*Sydney Morning Herald*, pp. 79–80

Shires, David/*Australian Financial Review*, pp. 160–61

Stace, D. A. pp. 550, 554, 562–63, 571, 577–82

Stewart, Cameron/*The Australian*, p. 506

Stickels, Georgi/*Business Review Weekly*, pp. 76–77

Storey, J. (1992), *Developments in the Management Of Human Resources*, Blackwell, Oxford, Figure 1.4, p. 20

The Hay Group Pty Ltd, p. 410, Table 10.3. p. 425

Thomas, Tony/*Business Review Weekly*, pp. 66–67

Tichy, N. M., Frombrun, C. J. & Devanna, M. A. (1984), *Strategic Human Resource Management*, John Wiley & Sons, p. 57

Toohey, J. 'Work stress', *Worksafe News*, p. 163, p. 179

Torbiorn, I./*International Studies of Management and Organization*, Table 13.4, p. 565

Treadgold, Tim/*Business Review Weekly*, p. 83

Tung, R. L. (1982), 'Selection and Training Procedures of US, European and Japanese Multinationals', *California Management Review*, Regents of the University of California, Table 13.1, p. 555

Walker, J. W. (1992), *Human Resource Strategy*, McGraw-Hill, Figure 2.5, p. 63, Figure 2.6, p. 65

Weiss, Julian/*HR Magazine*, reprinted with the permission of *HR Magazine* published by the Society for Human Resource Management USA, p. 144

Workcover News NSW, pp. 170–71, 176, 190–91, 200

Wyatt Company Pty Ltd, pp. 432–35

introduction

This book is intended to serve readers by fulfilling several specific purposes and by maintaining several themes throughout each of the chapters.

Purposes
The specific purposes are as follows:

- To increase your expertise in the functions and activities of human resource management
- To assist you in being an effective manager of human resources
- To present the complexities, challenges, and trade-offs involved in being an effective manager of human resources
- To assist you in being a more effective line manager.

Style of this book
The writing style employed in this book revolves around (1) applications and practical realities, and (2) theory and research. Each of these is integral in illustrating HRMs importance and in demonstrating how HR managers can help organisations effectively use their human resources.

Applications and practical realities. Examples from organisations and human resource managers are used throughout the book to illustrate the practical realities of the HR activities being examined. Each chapter begins with a recent excerpt from the business press called (HRM in the News). Cases are also included to provide you with a first-hand opportunity to deal with the challenges and practical realities of HRM.

Theory and research. Another major theme of this book is the most current and useful information related to human resource management. Thus, the book extensively uses current research and theory related to the effective use and management of human resources. You will receive not only an extensive description of all the current HRM functions and activities but also an understanding of why these functions and activities should work and how they actually do. With this knowledge, you can decide how to make these functions and activities work better.

For whom is this book written?
This book is written for those who are now working, or who will one day work, in organisations or for anyone interested in the subject. Knowledge of effective HRM

functions and activities is vital for anyone, particularly line managers and especially human resource staff (specialists or generalists) and managers. This is true whether the organisation is private or public, large or small, slow-growing or fast-growing. Although the type and size of the organisation may influence the size of the HR department, the functions and activities that are performed, and even the roles that are played, *there is an HR role in any organisation—and effective management of human resources is always necessary*. This is not to say, however, that human resources are managed in the same way in different types and sizes of organisations.

part 1

The HRM context

chapter 1
HRM—History, models, process and directions

chapter 2
Strategic human resource management

chapter 1

HRM—History, models, process and directions

Peter McGraw

learning objectives

After studying this chapter, you will be able to:

1. Understand the major functions and activities of HRM.
2. Describe the purpose of these activities in terms of organisational goals.
3. Outline the relationships influencing HRM functions and activities.
4. Analyse the growing importance of HRM in relation to the competitive pressures facing modern organisations.
5. Outline the historical growth and development of HRM.
6. Analyse the theoretical differences between HRM and personnel management.
7. Describe key trends in HRM.
8. Understand the role played by HR departments in organisations.

chapter 1

chapter outline

- The structure of this book — 6
- HRM functions and activities — 7
  - Planning for human resource needs — 7
  - Staffing the organisation's personnel needs — 7
  - Performance management and remuneration — 7
  - Improving employees and the work environment — 8
  - Establishing and maintaining effective working relationships — 8
- Objectives and purposes of HRM functions and activities — 9
  - Objectives of HRM — 10
  - Purposes of HRM — 10
- Relationships influencing HRM functions and activities — 11
  - Relationships with the internal environment — 11
  - Relationships with the external environment — 13
- The growing importance of HRM — 13
- An historical view of personnel management — 14
  - The growth of personnel in Australia — 17
- The difference between personnel and human resource management — 18
- Events influencing HRMs importance — 21
- Trends in HRM — 23
  - Managing new organisational forms — 23
  - Managing change — 24
  - Managing diversity — 26
  - Assessment of HRM — 28
  - Computer technology and HRIS — 30
  - Strategic involvement — 30
- Organising the HRM department — 32
  - Human resource roles — 32
  - HRM in the organisation — 34
  - Centralisation versus decentralisation — 34
  - Who is responsible for HRM? — 35
- Summary — 36
- Questions for discussion and review — 37
- Case study — 37
- Resources — 42
- References — 42

HRM IN THE NEWS

Cue for cultural change and workplace reform

BY PETER ROBERTS

Cultural change and workplace reform is emerging as a major competitive tool for business and a key method of squeezing maximum return from a given capital investment.

Thinking in industry in the past has been to clone high-performing factories and then chase increasing operational efficiencies.

Now there is a switch towards incorporating new forms of workplace organisation such as flat management, employee empowerment and cellular manufacturing when designing new plant.

According to a study by Professor Peter Robinson, deputy vice-chancellor of Wollongong University, advanced workplace organisation can reduce capital expenditure to a 'core' of equipment and facilities directly involved in production.

In his study of the automotive components industry, Robinson found capital costs of typical plants in the US and Australia to be roughly equal.

We know our plants are competitive because they are landing components ranging from aluminium road wheels to brake systems and engines in international markets at competitive prices.

But designing into new plants the elements of best practice already cropping up in our components sector has the potential to cut capital needs for a greenfields investment by 60 per cent.

Instead of a massive engineering department, for example, self-managing work teams are already responsible in the most advanced companies for collecting and analysing their own technical data.

Ordering and production scheduling is being performed by teams instead of centralised departments, and so on.

'There is a central productive capacity which you must maintain, however, you can drag all the ancillary overheads right down', says Robinson.

BHP steel's flat products works at Wollongong is one group increasing its return on capital by emphasising 'soft' issues such as employees involvement and Total Quality Management (TQM).

Paul Jeans, until yesterday the slab and plate division's group general manager, says capital invested by BHP in steel since the early 1980s had not shown its full return until a recent surge in productivity. This surge was driven by employee involvement.

The Wollongong plant produced 200 tonnes of steel per employee per annum in the early 1980s, rising to 500 tonnes by the end of the decade and further to 650 tonnes in the past three years. This puts the plant among the best 10 per cent of flat products steel plants worldwide.

BHP steel has embraced Japanese ideas that workplace organisation to involve shop floor people in continuous improvement can bring massive productivity gains through a series of small steps.

In one example, steel employees drove an improvement process to reduce the incidence of casting 'breakouts' in which manufacturing is interrupted when inner, molten steel breaks out through an outer solidified skin.

Shop floor people collected data, analysed steel casts and decision-making techniques and developed new standard operating procedures.

Employees now have the authority to change their own procedures.

The incidence of costly breakouts has fallen from five a month to less than one.

Says Jeans: 'This was a bottleneck department and it is now producing an extra million tonnes of steel a year'.

If workplace reorganisation at an existing plant can bring such improvements, just imagine the possibilities if it is explored at the plant design stage.

Source: *Financial Review*, 8 February 1996, p. 22.

HRM IN THE NEWS

Mobil's lab experiment pays off well

BY PETER ROBERTS

Mobil Oil's Yarraville plant, one of three lube oil blending sites, has undergone radical reform since a 'trip to the laboratory' in April 1993, when the company moved from two to one-shift operation.

All employees were called to the lab at the close of one shift and 20 fewer members of the national union of workers had their jobs the next day. The company selected employees to stay based on their adaptability, ability to work in teams and willingness to change—yet the NUW remained generally supportive.

Team working has become the central tenet of workplace organisation at Yarraville, with cross-functional teams given considerable autonomy over rosters and scheduling to meet production goals.

Workers' roles are being broadened—for instance from storeman to terminal operator to manufacturing technician—with training costing as much as 15 per cent of payroll in some years.

At the same time, the company has also switched to paying workers an annualised salary that includes payment for likely overtime—of the simplest but most effective ways of breaking down entrenched work practices.

Under the old overtime-driven system, there was an unstated incentive for workers to stretch out jobs and for equipment to break down and be repaired outside normal hours. Operators were working long hours and earning $80 000 to $90 000 a year.

But in 1992, Mobil lost $20 million in its core lubricants, with the Yarraville plant rated within the company as number 40 out of its 41 plants. Yarraville out-rated only Cameroon!

Since the site's first enterprise bargaining agreement in June 1993, Mobil has boosted production at Yarraville by 125 per cent without extra investment.

Customer service and quality measures have also risen with product deliveries made in full and on time rising from 20 per cent to more than 80 per cent.

At the same time, more than $8 million in costs has been removed from the plant, with Mobil's cost of producing lube oil falling from 20c a litre three years ago to 10.8c today.

The company believes Yarraville demonstrates leadership by managers in turning their backs on old-style 'directive' management, and leadership by union representatives and shop-floor workers.

It is true the NUW supported change to guard the viability of some of the best paid jobs in the old industry, but it is undeniable that its members traded high wages for better working conditions and more leisure

> time. Mr Lloyd Freeburn, an assistant state secretary of the NUW, says: 'Such successes almost always involve the trade union movement'.
>
> Here, then, is the real danger of any shift away from co-operation towards confrontation at the government and national union level. National co-operation has shifted the focus of industrial activity to the enterprise level with startling results.
>
> Confrontation at the peak level would threaten this focus, making the development of a constructive relationship with unions a key test of the Howard government.

Source: *Financial Review*, 11 March 1996, p. 23.

The 'HRM in the news' items reflect several significant points:

1 Organisations are now more concerned than ever about managing human resources effectively
2 Human resource management is critical to organisations because of the importance of productivity and the vital link between using human resources effectively and improving productivity
3 Successful HR management involves finding the appropriate balance between 'hard' issues such as maintaining productivity and 'soft' issues such as employee involvement and empowerment
4 A major trend in the human resources field is towards managing human resources in organisations which are flatter and more flexible than in the past
5 HR is moving away from being merely a departmental presence in organisations to becoming a broad corporate competency which includes all managers in partnership with HR specialists.

The success of the companies mentioned in the 'HRM in the news' illustrates that the effective management of human resources is a key ingredient in enhancing the competitiveness of Australian companies as they face the challenge of competing in an era of global competition.

The structure of this book

This book describes five functions and activities, which generally include all the functions and activities of human resource management within an organisation. The five functions are as follows:

1 Planning for human resource needs
2 Staffing the organisation's personnel needs
3 Performance management and remuneration
4 Improving employees and the work environment
5 Establishing and maintaining effective working relationships.

The chapters in the book broadly follow these five themes. In addition, the book contains a chapter on cross-cultural management which complements the chapter on international human resource management and also relates to the management of diverse workforces within Australia. Three themes of contemporary relevance are woven throughout each of the chapters in the book. These are: Future Organisational Forms, Managing Change and Managing Diversity. Each of these is introduced in more detail later in this chapter.

HRM functions and activities

As the 'HRM in the news' items illustrate, the role of HR within organisations is by no means uniform. In many organisations today, HRM is not an activity which is solely concerned with managing issues related to traditional employees but also concerns the management of people who work for the organisation but are not employees. Also, contemporary thinking on HRM tends to see it more as a broadly distributed organisational competence, including line managers, rather than just a group of specialists in an HR department. In this sense, the HR function is best thought of as the totality of people management systems in the organisation rather than just a narrow set of activities concentrated in the hands of HR specialists. Consequently, HR is evolving from a mainly administrative function towards one which is more strategically focused. This is dealt with at length later in this chapter. Notwithstanding these changes and the fact that the precise form of the HR activity will inevitably vary from organisation to organisation, the following basic activities are more or less common to the HR function in all organisations.

Planning for human resource needs

The function of planning for human resource needs involves two major activities: (1) planning and forecasting the organisation's short- and long-term human resource requirements, and (2) analysing the jobs in the organisation to determine their duties and purposes and the skills, knowledge, and abilities that are needed. These two activities are essential for effectively performing many other human resource management activities. For example, they help indicate the organisation's present and future needs regarding numbers and types of staff. They also help to determine how the employees will be obtained (e.g. from outside recruiting or by internal transfers and promotions) and what training needs the organisation will have. These two activities can be viewed as the major factors influencing the staffing and development functions of the entire organisation.

Staffing the organisation's personnel needs

Once the organisation's human resource needs have been determined, they have to be filled. Thus staffing activities become necessary. These include: (1) identifying job applicants (candidates), and (2) selecting from among the job applicants those most appropriate for the available jobs.

These staffing activities apply to external candidates (those not currently employed by the organisation) as well as to internal candidates (those currently employed by the organisation). After the candidates have been identified, they must be selected. Common selection procedures include obtaining completed application forms or résumés: initially interviewing the candidates; checking education, background, experience, and references; conducting various tests; and holding a final interview. These procedures must be related to the job and conform to equal employment opportunity (EEO) principles as well as laws and regulations. In other words, selection procedures must result in a match between a candidate's abilities and the skills that the job requires.

Performance management and remuneration

After employees or external staff are engaged, determining how well they are doing and rewarding them accordingly become necessary. If they are not doing well, the reasons must be determined. This determination may indicate that the reward structure needs to be changed or that training is necessary. To these ends, this function incorporates several activities associated with appraising and several associated with compensating. Activities associated with appraising include: (1) appraising and evaluating employee performance, and, (2) analysing and motivating employee behaviour. Although performance appraisal can be painful for both supervisor and employee, it is a critically important activity.

Employees are generally rewarded on the basis of their job's value as well as on their performance level. Which form of remuneration is most fair? Which form is most effective for the organisation? By what methods can jobs be evaluated fairly to determine their value? These concerns and others are part of the remunerating activity, which includes: (1) administering base pay on the basis of job evaluation, (2) providing performance-based pay, and (3) administering base pay benefits to employees in the organisation.

Improving employees and the work environment

In recent years, HRM interest has grown in three areas: (1) determining, designing, and implementing employee training and development programs to increase employee ability and performance, (2) improving the work environment, especially through quality of work life and productivity improvement programs, and (3) improving the physical work environment to maximise occupational safety and health. Training and development activities include training employees, developing management, and helping to develop careers. These activities are designed to increase employees' abilities in order to facilitate their performance, as well as benefit the employees themselves.

Establishing and maintaining effective working relationships

When the organisation has obtained the employees it needs, it must take care to induct them into the organisation, compensate them, and provide conditions that will make it attractive for them to stay. As a part of this, organisations must establish and maintain effective working relationships with the employees. Although doing this formally is required when the employees are covered by an industrial award or agreement which has been determined in conjunction with a trade union, it is also useful to establish and maintain effective relationships when they are not. Consequently, the three activities in this function are:

1. Recognising and respecting employee rights
2. Bargaining and settling grievances with employees and their representatives
3. Conducting research on HRM activities.

Increasingly, employees are gaining more rights. Consequently, employment decisions such as redundancy, retrenchment, and demotion must be made with great care, and on the basis of demonstrable evidence. It is important that managers of an organisation are aware of their employees' rights. The HR manager is in an excellent position to inform line managers of these rights.

When employees are protected by an agreement or industrial award, HR staff must become familiar with that agreement. When employees are unionised, HR staff also need to be familiar with the issues that relate to how employees organise themselves in dealing with the organisation and how the organisation bargains and negotiates with its organised employees. This is necessary because, on the one hand, the formal union–management relationship can effectively define the extent to which other HRM functions can be applied to the workforce and on the other, the union–management relationship can be instrumental in developing new HRM programs, e.g. those to improve productivity or compensation.

Objectives and purposes of HRM functions and activities

The five separate HRM functions and their related activities are important because they fulfil several organisational objectives and purposes. These are shown in Figure 1.1.

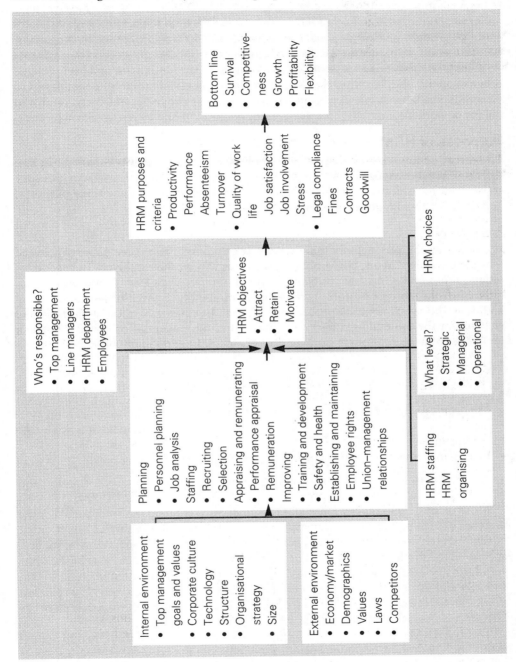

Figure 1.1 Objectives and purposes of HRM functions and activities

Source: Schuler et al. 1995, p. 19

Objectives of HRM

The three major objectives are to attract potentially qualified job applicants, retain desirable employees, and motivate employees. The growing importance of these functions in organisations is attributable to the recognition that effective HRM can and does have an impact on the 'bottom line' of the organisation. This term refers to the organisation's survival, growth, profitability, quality, flexibility, and competitiveness. In the case of non-profit and governmental organisations, the term refers to survival and the ability to do more with the same or fewer resources. Focusing on the bottom line and being results-oriented are key ways in which HRM can gain recognition and respect in organisations. Generally, the bottom line can be influenced through improved productivity, improved quality of work life, and legal compliance—the purposes of human resource management.

Purposes of HRM

The three purposes are to improve productivity, to improve quality of work life, and to ensure legal compliance. Although the several HRM functions and activities may serve the three objectives discussed above, each may also serve these three purposes, and thus the bottom line of the organisation.

Productivity

Without a doubt, productivity is an important goal of organisations. As we saw in the 'HRM in the news' items, HRM can do many things to improve it. The most productive organisations know this and treats their human resource departments in ways that are different from those of less productive organisations. US research has examined how highly productive American corporations are run. In comparing these with those less well run in the same industries, it was found that the leaders in productivity have a unique set of human resource management practices. In particular:

- They define the human resource role according to its level of participation in business decisions that implement business strategies
- They focus the current resources devoted to the human resource function on important problems before they add new programs or seek additional resources
- Their human resource staffs initiate programs and communication with line management
- Line management shares responsibility for human resource programs.

The corporate staffs share responsibility for human resource policy formation and program administration across organisational levels. (Piore & Sabel 1988)

More recently, research by Huselid, Jackson & Schuler (1995) has indicated that the presence of high performance strategically focused HR practices within an organisation have a positive and significant impact on corporate financial performance. Indeed, according to Huselid and his colleagues, 'on a per-employee, present value basis, a one standard deviation increase in HRM effectiveness was associated with $34 318, $19 189 and $11 663 higher sales, profits and market value, respectively, in 310 firms. Furthermore, HRM effectiveness was significantly influenced by the capabilities of the HR function's staff' (Huselid, Jackson & Schuler 1995, p. 2).

Today, HRM has a unique and timely opportunity to improve productivity. Increasingly, however, improving productivity does not mean just increasing output. It also means increasing output with higher quality. This new emphasis on quantity with quality is one of the many forces increasing the need for effective HRM. It is well known that in some areas Australian productivity rates are below those of our major trading partners. The current debate in Australia concerning global competitiveness, enterprise bargaining, and improvement in export performance has increased managerial and public awareness of the need to improve productivity and quality performance.

Quality of work life

The dissatisfying nature of industrial—or clerical—work is no longer disputed. Many of today's employees prefer a greater level of involvement in their jobs than was previously assumed. Many desire more self-control and a chance to make a greater contribution to the organisation. Apparently many employers are equally convinced of the importance of improved quality of work life, and particularly of the importance of greater worker involvement through employee participation in workplace decisions. Communicating with employees and encouraging them to communicate their ideas are critical roles for all those involved in managing human resources. These topics are dealt with in Part 2 of this book.

Legal compliance

In managing their employees, organisations must comply with many laws, guidelines, and court decisions. These laws and regulations affect almost all the functions and activities that HRM uses. Thus, HRMs constant concern is compliance with current laws, regulations, and court decisions. The main areas covered by legislation include occupational health and safety, freedom of information, equal employment opportunity, unfair dismissal and redundancy.

Relationships influencing HRM functions and activities

As shown in Figure 1.1, HRM functions and activities do not exist in a vacuum. Indeed, many aspects of the external and internal environment influence the five functions. Presented later in this chapter are discussions of those who are responsible for HRM and the levels at which it is practised. Relevant aspects of the internal and external environment are also considered in the remaining chapters. These discussions indicate the multitude of forces and events that help shape an organisation's HRM functions and activities. Although stating precise relationships among aspects of the environment and these activities is impossible, statements of general tendencies can be made. Familiarity with these is important in understanding how HRM is practised in organisations today and how it might be practised in the future. It is important to note that although each function and activity is discussed separately, each is highly related to the others: that is, the way in which one activity is done often influences the way in which another is done.

Relationships with the internal environment

Several features within organisations influence HRM, including top management, organisational strategy, technology, structure, culture, and size. Although these features are described separately here, they often influence each other. For example, top management's values help shape corporate culture, and strategy helps determine organisational structure. The key focus here, however, is how these features influence the HRM functions and activities.

Goals and values

Top management determines how critical human resource management will be in an organisation. If top management minimises the importance of people to the organisation's overall success, so will the line managers. In turn, those in the human resource department will perform only the most routine personnel activities. A likely consequence will be minimally effective HR management.

Strategy

As the 'HRM in the news' items illustrate, organisations are increasingly linking HRM to corporate strategy. Corporate strategy determines which general characteristics organisations need from employees. Figure 1.2 lists some of these characteristics.

Repetitive, predictable behaviour	—	Creative, innovative behaviour
Short-term focus	—	Long-term focus
Co-operative, interdependent behaviour	—	Independent, autonomous behaviour
Low concern for high quantity	—	High concern for high quantity
Low concern for quality	—	High concern for quality
Low risk orientation	—	High risk orientation
Concern for process	—	Concern for results
Preference to avoid responsibility	—	Preference to assume responsibility
Inflexible to change	—	Flexible to change
Low task orientation	—	High task orientation
Low organisational identification	—	High organisational identification
Focus on efficiency	—	Focus on effectiveness

Figure 1.2 General employee characteristics to complement an organisation's strategy
Source: Schuler 1988, p. 27

These characteristics contrast with the specific skills, knowledge, and abilities that employees need to perform their jobs—elements that are determined more by technology, organisational structure, and size than by strategy. Because HRM activities are capable of fostering such employee characteristics, once a strategy is selected, these activities are influenced. The nature of this is described later in this chapter, under Strategic Involvement and dealt with comprehensively in Chapter 2.

Culture

Organisational or corporate culture represents the sum of the organisation's value system. Strongly influenced by top management, corporate culture identifies the value of people to the organisation, the assumptions made about people, and the ways in which they are to be treated. Culture often comes to be reflected in the company's HR practices.

Technology and structure

Technology generally refers to the equipment and knowledge used to produce goods and services. For example, the technology that has been used to make automobiles is referred to as the assembly line. The use of assembly line technology has had a distinct impact on the way jobs have been designed and the types of individuals that have been hired. Similarly, in the last decade many jobs have been eliminated while others have either become de-skilled or up-skilled through the introduction of microprocessor technology.

Organisational structure describes the number of levels of employees in an organisation—both non-management and management levels. The trend has been for companies to restructure themselves to be most effective in terms of quality and cost. They have done this by reducing both the number and levels of employees and by decentralising the decision-making process.

Size

Organisational size is also an important factor in HRM activities. Although exceptions exist, generally the larger the organisation, the more developed its internal labour market and the less reliant it is on the external labour market. In contrast, the smaller the organisation, the less developed its internal labour market and the greater its reliance on the external.

As more reliance is placed on the internal labour market, the organisation relies more on itself in determining how to decide issues related to that market. For example, in deciding how much to pay people, job evaluation, job classification, and internal equity would be used. In contrast, as more reliance is placed on the external labour market, the rates that other organisations are paying and external equity would be used to decide how much to pay people.

Relationships with the external environment

Major components of the external environment influencing HRM functions and activities include the economy, demographics, social values, laws, and national and international competitors. Because the last four components are major factors contributing to the growing importance of HRM, they are described in the following section.

The national and state economies can have a significant impact. A strong economy tends to lower the unemployment rate, increase pressure for wage increases, make recruitment more necessary and more difficult, and increase the desirability of training current employees. By contrast, a weak economy tends to increase the unemployment rate, diminish wage increase demands, make recruitment less necessary and easier, and reduce the need for training and developing current employees. Although a weak economy may tend to diminish HRMs importance, other events in the external environment act to increase its importance. Recently, HRM has been significantly affected by the international economy, which has increased the level of competition and forced Australian enterprises to become more competitive, flexible, and oriented to the bottom line.

The growing importance of HRM

In a recent discussion of sustainable competitive advantage Jeffrey Pfeffer reviewed the top performing companies in the USA according to stock market performance over the period 1972–92 (Pfeffer 1995).

The five top performing stocks were in the airline industry (Southwest), retailing (Wal-Mart), food (Tyson Foods), electrical retailing (Circuit City), and Publishing (Plenum). Pfeffer then discussed these industries in the context of a analysis of the sources of competitive advantage advanced by Michael Porter in his influential framework of competitive advantage, that is, barriers to entry to the market of competitors, the availability of substitutable products, the bargaining power of buyers and suppliers and rivalry among existing competitors. Pfeffer concluded that, during the period under review, these industries were characterised by 'massive competition and horrendous losses, widespread bankruptcy, virtually no barriers to entry (for airlines after 1978), little unique or proprietary technology, and many substitute products or services' (Pfeffer 1995, p. 56). Pfeffer's point here is not that the traditional analysis of competitive strategy is inadequate but rather that the source of competitive advantage has shifted over time and that the firms in his study did not rely on technology or patents or strategic position for their competitiveness but rather looked for competitive advantage in the way that they managed their people.

There has been a growing recognition in the past decade as the traditional sources of competitive advantage have begun to erode, due to fiercer competition and the faster pace of diffusion of innovation, that a committed, skilled and flexible workforce is the key to sustained competitive advantage. The reason for this lies in the growing conviction among many strategists that the essence of competitive advantage lies in business processes and core competencies rather than specific products or technologies. Generating advantage from processes means better co-ordination and teamwork across different sections of the business and this inevitably involves HR initiatives to develop workforce competencies to enable streamlined processes. A cohesive and well-developed workforce is not easily replicated by a competitor and cannot be emulated in the short run. Pfeffer, in his discussion of the successful organisations, identified thirteen practices which characterised their approach to managing people. These are set out in Figure 1.3.

1 Employment security
2 Selectivity in recruiting
3 High wages
4 Incentive pay
5 Employee ownership
6 Information sharing
7 Participation and empowerment
8 Self-managed teams
9 Training and skill development
10 Cross utilisation and cross training
11 Symbolic egalitarianism
12 Wage compression
13 Promotion from within

Figure 1.3 Pfeffer's thirteen practices

Source: Pfeffer 1995, pp. 57–66

It is noteworthy that many of the practices identified by Pfeffer correspond closely to the practices identified in the case studies reported in 'HRM in the news' and those recommended in the normative HRM paradigm which will be discussed at the end of the next section. It is also worth noting that it is only in recent times that the potential contribution of effective HRM to the competitive position of the firm has been recognised. Before we specifically address the role of HRM in adding to the competitive position of the firm, it is important to consider how the role of HRM has evolved over time and the difference between older and more modern concepts of effective people management.

An historical view of personnel management

Personnel management has existed informally since people first started to come together to work for a common purpose. The first formal personnel practices emerged during the late Victorian period in England with the emergence of **Welfare Officers** in the factories of Victorian entrepreneurs such as Rowntree, Cadbury, Lever, Salt & Boot (Watson 1977). The first era of industrialisation had taken a large toll on the welfare of the new class of industrial wage labourers, and in response to some of the most obvious deprivations, these Victorian entrepreneurs employed welfare workers to administer programs such as sick pay schemes, medical centres and canteens (Legge 1995, p. 11). In describing the psychological make up of these early philanthropists Watson notes a combination of genuine concern for employees, fuelled in part by strong religious convictions (most of them belonged to strict Protestant sects), as well as the recognition that improving the welfare of their employees would also enhance their businesses. Cadbury explicitly made the connection between welfare and efficiency and described them as 'two sides of the same coin' in discussing his model factory at Bournville (Legge 1995, p. 11).

The second major influence was that of **Scientific Management** or Taylorism as it became known in recognition of its developer, F. W. Taylor. The essence of Taylorism was about eliminating inefficiency in the conduct of work which, according to Taylor, occurred largely as a result of deliberate underworking ('soldiering') by workers as they used their own 'rule of thumb' methods to determine the most appropriate way in which to complete a task. This in turn was facilitated by poor management control which allowed 'rule of thumb' working to flourish. According to Taylor, the way to overcome this was to apply the principles of scientific measurement to all aspects of work; the study of tasks to determine the 'best way'; task segmentation and job design based on this 'best way' (which separated the design of the job from its execution); the rigorous selection of the best person for the job; training in the job method; and re-design of the reward system so that all involved could share the benefit of the productivity arising from the scientifically redesigned job. Taylor also recommended that management should co-operate 'heartily' with workers to ensure that work was completed in line with scientific principles and that management should take over the work for which it was best suited. Clearly in outlining his principles Taylor laid the foundation for many of the components of personnel work from that time on; job analysis and design, recruitment and selection, training, and performance-based compensation.

The major problem with Taylorist work methods was the destruction of work group solidarity as jobs became prescriptive, isolated, individualised and outside the control of the worker. The ultimate expression of Tayloristic work design could be seen in production lines, the like of which were so comprehensively satirised in Charlie Chaplin's film 'Modern Times'. Nonetheless, the influence of Taylorism cannot be understated and production lines and other Taylorist work systems are still extensively used today. While initially designed to improve the productivity of manual workers, the general principles have since been used extensively in job and organisational design. Only in the last decade has there been any systematic re-evaluation of Taylorist job design principles (in the developed world at least) as the negative consequences of the method have become disadvantageous in an era when flexible work practices, teamwork and committed workers are the catchwords.

Parallelling the growth of scientific management was the growth of the **industrial psychology movement** from the First World War onwards. This movement developed out of a concern for productivity in munitions factories and was initially concerned with the effect of variables such as lighting, heating and ventilation on work performance. In time however the field broadened and, not surprisingly given the complementarity with Taylorism, eventually included areas such as psychological selection testing for which the field is probably better known today.

The next major theory to influence the development of the personnel management field was **human relations theory.** Human relations theory emerged from a series of experiments that were conducted from 1924–1952, by the Australian-born Harvard Professor Elton Mayo, at the Hawthorne plant of the Western Electric company situated just outside Chicago. Although the results of these experiments are controversial even today, they nonetheless paved the way for a school of thought which is still extremely influential. According to Huczynski (1993, p. 17) the six core propositions of human relations are:

1. A focus on people, rather than on mechanics or economics
2. People exist in an organisational environment rather than an unorganised social context
3. A key activity in human relations is motivating people
4. Motivation should be directed towards teamwork which requires both the co-ordination and the co-operation of the individuals involved
5. Human relations, through teamwork, seeks to fulfil both individual and organisational objectives simultaneously
6. Both individuals and organisations share a desire for efficiency, that is, they try to achieve maximum results with minimum inputs.

Human relations is often reported as springing up as a reaction to Taylorism. According to Huczynski, however, the message of human relations could supplement rather than supplant Taylorism (1993, p. 19). Mayo was all for retaining hierarchy and specialisation but he recommended not merely 'being nice to workers', which is how his message is often interpreted, but creating the concept of the 'family' within the workplace so that informal group dynamics could be fostered and made to work for the good or the organisation rather than against it (Huczynski 1993, p. 18). The significance of human relations as an influence is still obvious today and in fact many of the current trends seeking to elicit commitment and loyalty from the workforce are the very essence of human relations.

The **Neo-Human Relations** movement emerged in the late 1950s and is associated with the work of authors such as Maslow, Herzberg, McGregor, Likert, Schein & Argyris. The essence of this theoretical movement was that workers had an innate psychological need for expression in their work and that consequently one of the main reasons for employee demotivation, in all its manifestations, was poorly designed jobs which did not allow workers to express their natural creativity (in Maslow's terms to 'self-actualise'). Thus whereas Human Relations focused on the social nature of work and the importance of work groups on motivation, Neo-Human Relations focused on the individual and the need for individuals to derive intrinsic satisfaction from their work. Both movement recommended the redesign of jobs but in the case of Neo-Human Relations this was less about the social organisation of work and more concerned with the content of individual jobs. Hence, the typical prescriptions of the Human Relations theories were things such as job enrichment, job enlargement and the teaching, via organisational development initiatives, of better supervision styles for managers. Huczynski (1993, p. 19) has clearly summarised the common views held by writers in this area. They all:

1. Viewed 'conventional' formal organisation as a set of techniques embodying specific psychological assumptions
2. Asserted that the conventional formal type of organisation generated individual psychological distress and suggested that managers replaced these with more organic structures
3. Offered technical organisational prescriptions to improve matters

4 Held that managers should trust their subordinates to be more responsible for the performance of their jobs
5 Suggested that managers should permit their subordinates to be more responsible for the performance of their own jobs.

Clearly Neo-Human Relations theory was underpinned by a set of values about people and work. Margulies & Raia (cited in Huczynski 1993, p. 21) summarise these:

1 Providing an opportunity for people to function as human beings rather than as resources in the productive process
2 Providing opportunities for each organisational member, as well as for the organisation itself, to develop to their full potential
3 Seeking to increase the effectiveness of the organisation in terms of all of its goals
4 Attempting to create an environment in which it is possible to find exacting and challenging work
5 Providing opportunities for people in organisations to influence the way in which they relate to work, the organisation and the environment
6 Treating individual human beings as people with a complex set of needs, *all* of which are important to them in their work and life.

These values are central to the later development of human resource management theory (especially its soft variant), and as can readily be appreciated, are still central to the rhetoric of job and organisational redesign to this day.

We can see from the discussion above that personnel management has been influenced by a number of different theories as it has developed and that these theoretical influences have added new layers to the practice of personnel as it has developed throughout the century. Some other layers to the role have been added not by theoretical influences but by practical necessity. Two such roles that stand out are the **'industrial relations firefighter'** role, which came to prominence in the long postwar boom with the consequent increased pressure from unions and tight labour markets, and the **staff forecasting** role which emerged as a response to dealing with the complexities of staffing large and complex organisations during the same period.

The growth of personnel in Australia

There is not a great deal of research on the development of the personnel profession in Australia but what there is suggests that its growth parallels that in the UK and the US but with the initial stages coming at a later time. There is sporadic evidence of welfare schemes before the twentieth century but it seems that their spread began before the First World War and was greatly enhanced by the 'great strike' of 1917, after which employers started to introduce welfare schemes more widely in an attempt to diffuse militancy among the workforce (Gardner & Palmer 1992). It is also worth noting here that state promoted welfarism via the determination of substantive terms and conditions of employment was something that was in evidence in Australia from the first decade of the twentieth century. The reliance on state-mediated industrial conditions could very well have inhibited the growth of organisationally based welfare roles.

Scientific management was not systematically introduced into Australia before the Second World War but was used on a widespread basis during the long postwar boom (Gardner & Palmer 1992, p. 57). It is also after the Second World War during the period of rapid industrial expansion that modern style personnel departments started to emerge on a widespread basis. According to Kangan & Cook (cited in Gardner & Palmer 1992, p. 59) by the late 1940s, somewhere between 47 per cent and 65 per cent of firms had an organised personnel department. These were more common in firms with over 200 employees. The focus during this period was on welfare, recruitment, selection and training and on the introduction of scientific management and human relations-based initiatives. Another prominent role that emerged during this period was that of the industrial relations specialist who could deal with the complexities of federal and state industrial tribunals and awards. This role will be discussed in more detail in Chapter 3.

According to Dunphy (1987), the 1960s and 1970s saw the beginning of the organisational development, employee participation and job redesign initiatives associated with the Neo-Human Relations movement which was discussed earlier. It was during this period also that personnel moved beyond a series of ad hoc functions and evolved into a part of the organisation whose role was to implement corporate strategy in the people side of the business as well as to take responsibility for the remodelling of corporate structures (Dunphy 1987).

The final addition to the role—or as some would claim the metamorphosis of the role—came, in Australia and overseas, with the era of human resource management which began in the 1980s and has continued into the 1990s to such an extent that the term **human resource management** now defines the field.

The difference between personnel and human resource management

The term 'personnel management' is still used in many organisations in Australia to refer to the department that deals with activities such as recruitment, selection, compensation, and training, but 'human resource management' is now used to an increasing extent. This is in recognition of the vital role human resources play in an organisation, the challenges in *managing* such resources effectively, and the growing body of knowledge and professionalism surrounding HRM.

The conceptual differences between Personnel and Human Resource Management will now be discussed. It should be noted that in practice the distinctions are less clear and that a change in title does not necessarily represent a paradigm shift in organisational practice.

Conceptually, HRM is different from Personnel Management in that it is an explicit strategy to use the human resources of a firm to gain a competitive and comparative advantage (Guest 1987). Specifically, it is different from personnel in three critical ways.

1 HRM is strategic. The practice of HRM is about managing the human resource requirements of an organisation in line with the organisation's overall business strategy. There should be a good 'fit' between HR practice and business strategy and contradiction should be avoided.
2 HRM conceptualises the various elements of the organisation's approach to managing people as set of integrated activities. That is the system of recruitment, for example, should be complementary with that of compensation which in turn should be intimately connected with the performance appraisal system.
3 HRM involves a conceptual shift away from regarding employees as a cost to be managed towards and asset to be nurtured and developed. This difference can be illustrated by comparing sample definitions of personnel and HRM. The (then) Institute of Personnel Management—UK (now the Institute of Personnel and Development) previously defined personnel as:

... that part of management which is concerned with people at work and with their relationships within an enterprise. Personnel management aims to achieve both efficiency and justice neither of which can be pursued successfully without the other. It seeks to bring together and develop into an effective organisation the men and women who make up an enterprise, enabling each to make his own best contribution to its success both as an individual and as a member of a working group. It seeks to provide fair terms and conditions and satisfying work for those employed (IPM 1963).

Compare the above with the more recent definition of HRM provided by Beer & Spector:

> ... a set of basic assumptions can be identified that underlie the policies that we have observed to be part of the HRM transformation. The new assumptions are:
> - pro-active, system-wide interventions, with emphasis on fit, linking HRM with strategic planning and cultural change (c.f. old assumptions: reactive, piecemeal interventions in response to specific problems)
> - people are social capital capable of development (c.f. people as variable cost)
> - coincidence of interest between stakeholders can be developed (c.f. self interest dominates, conflict between stakeholders)
> - seeks power equalisation for trust and collaboration (c.f. seeks power advantages for bargaining and confrontation)
> - open channels of communication to build trust, commitment (c.f. control of information flow to enhance efficiency, power)
> - goal orientation (c.f. relationship orientation)
> - participation and informed choice (c.f. control from top) (Beer & Spector 1985).

The main areas of difference between HRM and traditional personnel, therefore, lie in the emphasis given to strategic fit and integration in HRM, and the emphasis on managing the culture of the organisation in line with the espoused values of 'developmental humanism'. (The importance of managing culture is implicit given the view that employee commitment, and thus performance, comes via consistency in communication, motivation and leadership.)

Other differences relate to the fact that HRM is aimed very much at managers as well as employees, whereas personnel was often seen as something that managers did to workers, and that, because of its centrality to strategy, HRM should be delivered wherever possible by line managers and should be part of the strategic decision-making apparatus of an organisation (Legge 1995). In this respect HRM should be regarded as functional competency broadly dispersed across the organisation rather than a functional presence represented by a large HR department. The result of this practice in some large organisations such as BHP has been somewhat paradoxical—HRM has become more influential in company decision making, yet has declined as a separate department within the organisation as HR tasks and decision have been devolved to line managers. Many leading edge HR practitioners now see themselves more in an internal consultancy capacity assisting line managers to devise and implement more sophisticated ways of managing people, rather than implementing and managing those systems themselves. Such HR managers would also claim to be working towards the eventual removal of their own positions within the organisation. Implicit in all this is the assumption that because of its importance, HRM strategy should be formulated and supported from the most senior levels of the organisation.

Storey (1992) has developed an ideal type description of what HRM might look like if the normative model could be fully implemented and contrasted it with a similarly abstracted version of the 'old' world of personnel/industrial relations. This is reproduced in Figure 1.4

DIMENSION	PERSONNEL AND IR	HRM
Beliefs and assumptions		
1 Contract	Careful delineation of written contracts	Aim to go 'beyond contract'
2 Rules	Importance of devising clear rules/mutuality	'Can-do' outlook; impatience with 'rule'
3 Guide to management action	Procedures	'Business-need'
4 Behaviour referent	Norms/custom and practice	Values/mission
5 Managerial task vis-à-vis labour	Monitoring	Nurturing
6 Nature of relations	Pluralist	Unitarist
7 Conflict	Institutionalised	De-emphasised
Strategic aspects		
8 Key relations	Labour-management	Customer
9 Initiatives	Piecemeal	Integrated
10 Corporate plan	Marginal to	Central to
11 Speed of decision	Slow	Fast
Line management		
12 Management role	Transactional	Transformational leadership
13 Key managers	Personnel/IR specialists	General/business/line managers
14 Communication	Indirect	Direct
15 Standardisation	High (e.g. 'parity' an issue)	Low (e.g. 'parity' not seen as relevant)
16 Prized management skills	Negotiation	Facilitation
Key levers		
17 Selection	Separate, marginal task	Integrated, key task
18 Pay	Job evaluation (fixed grades)	Performance-related
19 Conditions	Separately negotiated	Harmonisation
20 Labour-management	Collective bargaining contracts	Towards individual contracts
21 Thrust of relations with stewards (union delegates)	Regularised through facilities and training	Marginalized (with exception of some bargaining for change models)
22 Job categories and grades	Many	Few
23 Communication	Restricted flow	Increased flow
24 Job design	Division of labour	Teamwork
25 Conflict handling	Reach temporary truces	Manage climate and culture
26 Training and development	Controlled access to courses	Learning companies
27 Foci of attention for interventions	Personnel procedures	Wide ranging cultural, structural and personnel strategies.

Figure 1.4 Twenty-seven points of difference

Source: Storey 1992, p. 35

The above model is useful for illustrative purposes and for positing what many managers would consider an ideal state of affairs. It is not meant to represent the reality of what currently exists and, as already noted, in practice the difference between personnel and HRM is not nearly as clear cut. However, most managers and commentators agree that in the last ten years there has in fact been a considerable shift towards the right of the model in many cases. In reality, organisations do not evolve and change in line with normative models but in response to a complex series of pressures and the studies that have been done to determine the existence of HRM other than as a normative model confirm this (see Storey 1992 and Legge 1995 for a review).

This brings us to potential contradiction in HRM. How can HRM be universally development and strategic all the time? There are likely to be times when strategic need (e.g. organisational contraction) will fly directly in the face of a philosophy of paternal care for employees. This has led to the development of the so-called hard and soft versions of HRM. The hard version, associated with the Michigan University, stresses the link with the organisation's strategy whereas the soft version, also known as the Harvard Model, puts more emphasis on the ideology of development. One of the ways that many organisations have sought to overcome this contradiction is to segment their workforces into a core of permanent employees, who are nurtured, protected and developed and a more peripheral workforce of people on short-term contracts who are more or less disposable in relation to the state of the marketplace. Another response has been to sub-contract all non-core activities out of the organisation. Whether an organisation leans more towards the hard or soft version of HRM, or does not consider HRM to be relevant to its operation, depends very much on the values of the organisation which are discussed elsewhere in this chapter.

Events influencing HRMs importance

A recent survey counselling the views of approximately 3000 managers and consultants in twelve countries (Towers Perrin 1992) attempted to identify HRMs role in gaining a competitive advantage and the key priorities of decision makers in the HRM area. Looking towards the year 2000, the conclusions were that:

- Key factors influencing competitiveness were the globalisation of business, the reduced numbers of people entering the workplace, and the increasing diversity of the workforce
- High productivity, quality, customer satisfaction and linking HRM to the organisations business goals were seen as critical issues by both HR and line managers
- The biggest challenge facing HR managers was to shift the focus from current operations to strategies for the future
- HRM was seen to need to be responsive to the competitive marketplace
- HRM needed to focus on quality, customer service, productivity, employee participation, teamwork and the creation of a flexible workforce
- HRM practices should be jointly developed and implemented by HR and line managers.

Four issues are worthy of further comment here: (1) increased competition and therefore the need to be competitive, (2) the costs and benefits associated with human resource utilisation, (3) the increasing pace and complexity of social, cultural, legal, demographic, and educational changes, and (4) the symptoms of change in the workplace.

Increased competition

The impact of enhanced competition (both international and domestic) has influenced virtually every sector of the Australian economy. An increased awareness of the need to be competitive, reduce costs and improve quality has swept through the private sector and has also motivated government deregulation in a diverse range of areas such as finance, telecommunications, and transport. In some cases this has resulted in the privatisation or semi-privatisation of significant government business enterprises.

Human resource costs

The payroll costs of many organisations today are of such magnitude (30–80 per cent of total expenses) that senior managers must be concerned with human resources. This has given new emphasis to developing ways of determining the costs of employee behaviour and programs to reduce these costs (discussed later in this chapter). There is also a growing realisation that firms which compete in low value-added product markets solely on the basis of cost (generally subsidised by tariff protection) face a bleak future. In China and India, for example, total compensation per employee is estimated at less than one dollar per hour. The wage disparity between these countries and the advanced Western economies is likely to continue, given the fact that between now and the year 2000, 750 million more people will enter the labour force—90 per cent of them outside the industrialised countries. Australian firms will increasingly have to compete in differentiated product markets which are characterised by innovation and high-quality service and/or products. This will require more skilled employees who will expect a great deal more than a traditional authoritarian management style.

The pace and complexity of change

Several ongoing changes in the cultural and educational levels and the social order of Australia have contributed to the concerns of HRM. For example, because mid-life career changes are becoming more common, and most occupations require increased knowledge, training and development programs for all employees have developed rapidly.

The current workforce is generally becoming more knowledgeable and better informed. These high-quality human resources are potentially more productive. This opportunity, however, presents a real challenge to organisations: as societies become better informed, they also tend to become more critical, less accepting of authority, and more cynical. Younger workers appear to be particularly cynical about decisions made by supervisors and correspondingly more resistant to authority. Older workers, however, still tend to reflect the values of the society in which they grew up and are, therefore, more inclined to accept authority. Thus, the effective management of human resources requires not only knowing how to manage and channel the skills of the young workers but also knowing how to manage a workforce with a mixed set of values.

Symptoms of change in the workplace

Rapid social change has been accompanied by changes in the relationship between the worker and the job. Some of the terms used to describe what is happening in the workplace include worker alienation, anomie, boredom and job dissatisfaction. These symptoms are often associated with decreasing motivation and increasing counter-productive behaviour and worker demands on the workplace. Although these symptoms can certainly be found in most workplaces—whether they are factories or offices, public or private organisations—the extent to which they are reported to exist varies greatly. Where they do exist, however, it appears that they can be minimised through HRM programs designed to get employees more involved in decisions on the job.

Another symptom of change in the workplace is the desire for a more explicit statement of employee rights. Among these are the right to work, to know what the job requirements are, to participate in decisions, to be appraised fairly and with objective performance criteria, to be accountable, and to be able to take risks and make mistakes. All these issues are themes raised in the Karpin Report (Industry Task Force on Leadership and Management Skills 1995) on Australian Management and Management Education, which is referred to throughout this book.

Trends in HRM

Several major trends in HRM are: (1) managing new organisational forms, (2) managing the increasing pace of change in the workplace, (3) managing diversity in the workforce. These are major themes that are addressed in every chapter throughout the book. Other trends addressed in this section are: (4) assessment of HRM to determine its effectiveness, (5) use of computer technology and creation of human resource information systems, (6) strategic involvement of HRM in the organisation, and (7) customerisation.

Managing new organisational forms

One of the key challenges for managers as we move into the new century is to find ways of managing organisations which will be very different from any previously experienced. Factors shaping the new form of organisation are things such as the increasing intensity of competition on a global scale, the impact of new technology on organisations and careers, new patterns of competition and collaboration between firms, new forms of employment including the rapid growth in part time, casual and sub-contract labour, the emergence of 'network' and 'virtual' organisations, and major economic change resulting from the shift of economic power toward the Asia-Pacific area. It is a platitude to say that change is now constant. Peter Vaill (1989) has used the metaphor of 'permanent white water' in an attempt to capture this constant turbulence. Some of the challenges facing university business schools as a result of the development of 'virtual learning' opportunities are detailed in the 'New organisational forms' discussion below.

Kanter spelled out the implications of continuously turbulent environments for organisations where winning the new game requires:

> ... faster action, more creative manoeuvering, more flexibility, and closer partnership with employees and customers than was typical in the traditional corporate bureaucracy. It requires more agile, limber management that pursues opportunity without being bogged down by cumbersome structures or weighty procedures that impede action. Corporate giants, in short, must learn to dance (Kanter 1989, p. 20).

Issues related to how giants are coping with their dancing lessons and the implications for the employees of these organisations will be addressed in each chapter of this book.

Future organisational forms

The future of business schools

Cable operators, telecommunications companies, publishers and software houses will pose real competition for business schools, as the emerging infrastructure of information and communications technologies 'so fundamentally change the rule of supply and demand that a new economic order will result'.

Education increasingly will be dominated by virtual learning communities in which lifelong learning is driven by students rather than instructors, and in which the focus changes to 'just-in-time' education. Certification will be pushed aside by demonstrated skills of work products, and supplanted by non-university certification. There will be global disaggregation of learning resources, global collaboration of learners and faculty, open competition, a greater emphasis on such things as non-textual learning resources, computer simulations, university/business partnerships, and the merging of theory with real-world applications presented in hypertext learning environments. 'Surviving institutions will likely have the strongest brand names, be able to provide both scale and scope, and have the most flexible faculty ... the inflexibility of traditional universities suggests that nontraditional educational suppliers may be best positioned to exploit the lucrative market for business education in an electronic world'.

Source: Ives et al. 1996, p. 33.

Managing change

As the 'HRM in the news' cases and the 'Managing change' discussion illustrate, change management often propels HR to centre stage in organisations. This is due to the fact that managing change is often concerned with changing the way people behave in organisations in order to maximise process efficiency. Kotter (1995) has developed an eight step change model which is reproduced in Figure 1.5. It is evident from this model that HR plays a crucial role in change initiatives, with nearly all steps in the model involving elements of the HR function.

1 **Establishing a sense of urgency**
   Examining market and competitive realities, identifying and discussing crises, potential crises, or major opportunities.

2 **Forming a powerful guiding coalition**
   Assembling a group with enough power to lead the change effort. Encouraging the group to work together as a team.

3 **Creating a vision**
   Developing strategies for achieving that vision. Creating a vision to help direct the change effort.

4 **Communicating the vision**
   Using every vehicle possible to communicate the new vision and strategies. Teaching new behaviours by the example of the guiding coalition.

5 **Empowering others to act on the vision**
   Getting rid of obstacles to change. Changing systems or structures that seriously undermine the vision. Encouraging risk taking and nontraditional ideas, activities and actions.

6 **Planning for and creating short-term wins**
   Planning for visible performance improvements. Creating those improvements. Recognising and rewarding employees involved in the improvements.

7 **Consolidating improvements and producing**
   Using increased credibility to change systems, structures and policies that don't fit the vision. Hiring, promoting, and developing employees who can implement the vision. Reinvigorating the process with new projects, themes and change agents.

8 **Institutionalising new approaches**
   Articulating the connections between the new behaviours and corporate success. Developing the means to ensure leadership development and succession.

Figure 1.5 Eight steps to transforming your organisation

Source: Kotter 1995, p. 21

Buchanan & Boddy (1992) have defined an effective change agent as someone who can simultaneously manage three agendas which may often come into contradiction. First, is the content agenda; this is the substantive change that needs to be enacted, for example, a new production system. In relation to this area, the change agent must be competent in handling the technical side of change. Second, is the control agenda; this involves the traditional management agenda of planning, scheduling , budgeting, resourcing and mentoring. Third, is the process agenda; this is where the 'soft' HR skills are required. Here the change agent must be competent in communication, team building, negotiation skills, leadership skills and be able to overcome resistance to change.

Much of the early HR writing on change came primarily from the Neo-Human Relations and Organisation Development perspectives which were discussed earlier in this chapter. More recently as the pace of change has increased, a greater range of change strategies have been in evidence. This has led to the development of new change typologies and new theories of the links between change strategies and HR such as those outlined by Dunphy & Stace (1992; 1994) who argue that change programs are important intervening variables between business and HR strategy and usually involve attempts to move the organisation's HR policies back into 'fit' with its business policies. The Dunphy & Stace model is described more fully in Chapter 2 and examples of changed HR practices in support of broader organisational change are provided in each of the following chapters.

Managing change

Port Kembla a model of enterprise

BY PETER ROBERTS

Before the new Howard government embarks on its revamp of industrial relations, it needs to take a reality check on some of its views—especially the widely held one that there has been little positive coming from labor's enterprise bargaining system. In fact, as readers of this column will know, companies that bothered to take advantage of the system have negotiated changes to everything from hours of work and multi-skilling to basic employee relations.

One need look no further than the Port Kembla Steelworks to see the power of co-operative agreements forged under the system between business, employees and, yes, the dreaded unions.

After a decade of learning from best practice overseas, Port Kembla has become something of a magnet to leading steel companies, including the giant Posco company of Korea, wanting to study innovative employee/employer relationships.

They are visiting Wollongong to find out how a steelworks with a nameplate capacity of 3.9 million tonnes a year, but never capable of making more than about 3.6 tonnes, can crank up performance as BHP steel's flat products division has done.

In 1994–95, output at Port Kembla rose from 3.6 million tonnes of steel a year to 4.6 million tonnes. In the past three months, output has averaged 390 000 tonnes a month—nudging 4.8 million tonnes per year.

While BHP is spending $1 billion on a new blast furnace and other facilities at Port Kembla, Jerry Platt, a group general manager in charge of primary steelmaking, says the improvement is coming from fundamentally changed management/ employee relations.

Many, but certainly not all, employees contribute to improvement teams making a multitude of small improvements that add up to world-class performance. 'In the past, what we have done is spend money on the facilities and ignored the people', says Platt.

For example, teams of bricklayers, technologists and plant operators studied the heat-resistant refractory linings of the ladles and basic oxygen steel-making (box) vessels at the heart of the steel process.

By moving to different refractory materials, changing the way refractory bricks are laid and installing lids to prevent the bricks from rapid cooling, for a capital investment of $2.5 million, people effected savings of $10 million a year.

Other teams have even studied staffing levels and recommended smaller teams to operate the no. 4 and no. 6 blast furnaces. The story has been the same in non-monetary improvements such as environment protection.

With 50-plus improvement projects under way at any one time, the Port Kembla works is really humming. But not all is sweetness and light, of course, and the new relationships are fragile.

In any revamp of industrial relations, it is vital that we recognise there have been fundamental changes in workplaces in the past decade. To pretend that change has been limited, threatens the very real progress already made.

Source: *Financial Review*, 7 March 1996, p. 23.

Managing diversity

The 1990s are a decade of increased ethnic, cultural and social diversity in Australia. Reflecting this, many stereotypical assumptions about the nature of the workforce are being questioned and managers are being challenged with the task of using the talents of a diverse workforce to the most productive ends. Managing diversity is not just a moral issue, though. There are many ways in which accepting the need to be more pro-active in managing the needs of a diverse workforce can contribute to the organisation's ongoing survival. Diversity issues confronting Australian organisations include the obvious EEO and discrimination issues as well as such issues as: the tolerance of individual difference, communicating effectively with and motivating ethnically diverse workforces, literacy and numeracy issues, managing workers with varying child care and family responsibilities, conflict resolution among ethnically diverse groups, managing older workforces, managing diverse career paths and managing diverse teams. Figure 1.6 outlines the various ways in which managing cultural diversity can contribute to an organisation's competitive advantage.

1 **Cost argument**

   As organisations become more diverse, the cost of a poor job in integrating workers will increase. Those who handle this well will thus create cost advantages over those who don't.

2 **Resource acquisition argument**

   Companies develop good reputations as prospective employers for women and ethnic minorities. Those with the best reputations for managing diversity will win the competition for the best personnel. As the labour pool shrinks and changes composition, this edge will become increasingly important.

3 **Marketing argument**

   For multinational organisations, the insight and cultural sensitivity that members with roots in other countries bring to the marketing effort should improve these efforts in important ways. The same rationale applies to marketing to subpopulations within domestic operations.

4 **Creativity argument**
Diversity of perspectives and less emphasis on conformity to norms of the past (which characterise the modern approach to the management of diversity) should improve the level of creativity.
5 **Problem-solving argument**
Heterogeneity in decisions and problem-solving groups potentially produces better decisions through a wider range of perspectives and more thorough critical analysis of issues.
6 **System flexibility argument**
An implication of the multicultural model for managing diversity is that the system will become less determinant, less standardised, and therefore more fluid. The increased fluidity should create greater flexibility to react to environmental changes (i.e. reactions should be faster and at less cost).

Figure 1.6 Cultural diversity and competitive advantage

Source: Cox & Blake 1991, p. 47

Managing diversity within an organisation includes a range of activities such as: affirmative action strategies for women and disadvantaged minorities, creating a tolerant organisational culture, developing management systems that are discrimination free, and promoting the acceptance of cultural and ethnic diversity (and managing resistance to this). An example of the approach to managing diversity taken by Pitney Bowes is given in the 'Managing diversity' discussion below and the managing diversity theme is developed more fully in Chapter 2 and addressed in each subsequent chapter.

Managing diversity

The US multinational Pitney Bowes has now started to introduce its award-winning diversity strategy into Australia. The vision statement on diversity reads, 'Pitney Bowes will provide an open, flexible and supportive work environment that values the uniqueness of each of its employees. Through leadership, communication and training programs, Pitney Bowes will aggressively promote an understanding of individual difference, including (but not limited to) age, gender, race, religion, ethnicity, disability, sexual orientation and family circumstances'.

The five goals of the Pitney Bowes strategic plan on diversity and examples of the action the company has taken to achieve these are set out below.
- **Goal 1: Communications:** Our vision of diversity and its implications for the organisation will be clearly communicated to all of us'. Action:
  - Formed diversity councils throughout the company
  - Engaged in widespread promotional activity to promote the diversity agenda
  - Development of diversity marketing guidelines for Pitney Bowes products and services.
- **Goal 2: Education and training:** 'We will become sensitive to and demonstrate an understanding of the value of differences through education and training'. Action:
  - Provided multiple training opportunities for the stimulation of diversity awareness
  - Identified high profile minority customers to address employees on diversity issues.

- Goal 3: Career development: 'We will create a culture that enables and encourages the development and upward mobility of all of us'. Action:
  - Introduced new succession planning process based on 'assessing competencies for tomorrow'
  - Published career networking directory
  - Increased opportunities for rotational assignments and cross-training
  - Increased participation in employee mentoring program.
- Goal 4: Recruitment and hiring: 'We will further increase the diversity of our employees so that our organisation reflects the demographics changes in our labour force'. Action:
  - Developed new minority recruitment campaigns including new promotional material and specific recruitment from schools with diverse populations
  - Supported minority scholarships and intern programs
  - Increased funding support for external organisations promoting the diversity agenda
  - Tied management bonuses to diversity recruitment goals.
- Goal 5: Work/life balance: 'We will provide a flexible and supportive work environment for employees in achieving a balance of work/life issues'. Action:
  - Developed training to enhance flexible work environment for all employees
  - Expanded child care, elderly care and school referral programs
  - Supported emergency sick child care
  - Conducted employee surveys on work/life balance
  - Piloted telecommuting program.

In order to achieve the five goals of diversity, the business units at Pitney Bowes have tied the concept of diversity to management performance ratings. Part of the incentive compensation plan for the corporate management committee, for instance, includes a diversity component directly linked to the business unit's diversity action plan, and all managers are held accountable for diversity through the performance appraisal system.

Source: Pitney Bowes 1994–95.

Assessment of HRM

HRM is often considered not vital to organisations because it fails to demonstrate its effectiveness. That is, it sometimes fails to show how it relates to the three objectives and the three purposes shown in Figure 1.1. Recognising this, human resource managers are starting to demonstrate their effectiveness just as other managers do: by assessing the costs of their activities against the benefits resulting from those activities.

Benefit criteria

These are indicators against which comparisons can be made to demonstrate value or benefit to the organisation. Three indicators used as benefit criteria are the purposes of HRM. These indicators and their specific components (and indicated direction for demonstrating effectiveness) are as follows:

- Productivity
  - Increased performance
  - Reduced absenteeism
  - Reduced turnover.

- Quality of work life
  — Increased job involvement
  — Increased satisfaction
  — Reduced stress
  — Reduced accidents and illnesses
  — Legal compliance
  — Reduced or eliminated costs of fines
  — Reduced or eliminated costs of lost contracts
  — Enhanced community goodwill and general reputation.

In general, productivity represents the efficiency with which an organisation uses its workforce, capital, material, and energy resources to produce its product. Other things being equal, reducing the workforce but getting the same output improves productivity. Similarly, if each employee's performance (quality or quantity) increases, total output increases, and so does productivity. Reducing absenteeism is also a way to increase productivity, as is the reduction in turnover of good employees. Improving the quality of work life may result in increased performance and in reduced absenteeism and turnover, but the results can also be measured in other ways. For example, the more the organisation meets individuals' preferences and interests, the more likely the workers will be involved with their jobs, register higher satisfaction with them, their supervisors, and co-workers, suffer less from stress, and have fewer accidents and better health.

Organisations must comply with many laws and regulations. Failure to comply can result in significant costs. Other effects may include cancellation of future contracts with federal, state, and local governments. In addition, individual employees can sue their organisation for violations of some laws and regulations. Finally, goodwill with potential job applicants and the community can be significantly diminished if a company chooses not to comply with laws and regulations.

Cost criteria

These are indicators against which benefit criteria can be compared to determine HRM effectiveness. Whereas benefit criteria generally apply to all HRM activities, cost criteria are more specific to each activity. For example, cost criteria appropriate for the safety and health activity may be supervisory training, the addition of newer and safer equipment, the removal of hazards and waste materials, and job redesign. Cost criteria for recruitment may be advertising, training, and recruiters' payroll.

After determining the appropriate cost criteria (based on the specific personnel activity of interest) and the appropriate benefit criteria (not all benefit criteria are equally relevant to each HR activity), these costs and benefits are compared. This comparison is increasingly being made on the basis of dollars and cents. Thus, the dollars and cents values of both the cost and benefit criteria must be determined.

Once these values are established, the HR department can demonstrate that the values of the cost criteria are no greater, or perhaps are even less than, those in other organisations (similar or different). Second, it can enhance the value of these comparisons by including relevant information on benefit criteria.

Although it may be neither feasible to obtain nor valid to use a dollars and cents valuation of the turnover of other organisations, it may be useful to compare rates of turnover or absenteeism. Thus, the human resource department could show the organisation that the costs for managing its human resources are producing more benefits (using only a comparison of turnover rates) than are those of other organisations.

The department can also demonstrate its effectiveness by comparing changes in benefit criteria levels with specific personnel activities. The valuation of the benefit criteria changes can then be compared with the valuation of the cost criteria associated with the specific HR activities.

Computer technology and HRIS

HRM requires a great deal of information. Computer technology enables organisations to combine human resource information into a single database. A computer-oriented information system used in the management of human resources is referred to as a human resource information system (HRIS).

There are four key advantages to a HRIS. First, the computer enables the department to take a more active role in organisation planning. Forecasting techniques are feasible that would require a significant time investment without the use of computer technology. Second, the computer integrates and stores in a single database all personnel information previously filed in separate physical locations. Thus, the human resource department can take a global view of its human resource stock and interpret it in more meaningful ways. For example, data on career interests may be more easily matched with career advancement and training opportunities by creating a simple coding system that automatically identifies candidates. The position and personnel data in the HRIS can then be used to make more effective internal selection and placement decisions and career development ones that are beneficial for both the organisation and the individual. Third, the computer speeds the process of comparing costs and benefits in HRM assessment. Fourth, an HRIS and computer technology facilitate the storage of and access to the personnel records that are vital for organisations.

In addition to internal data management, human resource professionals may benefit from having direct access to external databases that contain information affecting their work (e.g. literature, demographic data, other company practices, legal requirements), reducing time-consuming steps.

Strategic involvement

As has been noted earlier in this chapter, HRM departments have traditionally had a relatively limited involvement in the total organisation's affairs and goals. Human resource managers were often concerned only with making staffing plans, providing specific job training programs, or running annual performance appraisal programs (the results of which were put in personnel files, never to be used). Consequently, these managers were concerned only with the short-term operational and managerial—perhaps day-to-day—human resource needs.

Now, because of the extensive relationships among HRM activities and the internal and external environment, these managers are becoming more involved in the total organisation—where it's going, where it should be going—and are helping it to get there. As a consequence, they and their departments are playing many more roles and utilising the HRM functions and activities on a long-term basis as well as the more typical medium- and short-term bases. In utilising such functions and activities in these three distinct time horizons, human resource practitioners are really operating at three organisational levels: strategic, managerial, and operational.

At the operational (short-term) level, these practitioners make staffing and recruitment plans, set up day-to-day monitoring systems, administer wage and salary programs, administer benefits packages, set up annual or less frequent appraisal systems, set up day-to-day control systems, provide for specific job skill training, provide on-the-job training, fit individuals to specific jobs, and plan career moves.

At the managerial (medium-term) level, these practitioners may do longitudinal validation of selection criteria, develop recruitment marketing plans and new recruiting markets, set up longer-term compensation plans for individuals, set up validated systems that relate current conditions and future potential, set up assessment centres for development, establish general management development programs, provide for organisational development, foster self-development, identify career paths, and provide career development services.

At the strategic (long-term) level, some HR practitioners are beginning to seek ways in which organisations can gain competitive advantage—that is, beat their competitors—and to link their practices (functions and activities) to their organisations' strategies. Because the use of HRM at the strategic level in organisations is such a recent development, it is described in some detail in Chapter 2.

Customerisation

Adding to the human resource department's ability to gain strategic involvement are its knowledge of the business, its creative insights into how the organisation can be more effective, and its increasing familiarity with and acceptance by top management. More and more, these qualities are being found in departments that practice 'customerisation'. This means viewing everybody, whether internal or external to the organisation, as a customer and then putting these customers first. For human resource departments, customers are typically other line and staff managers. Increasingly, customers include other organisations, and even non-managerial employees.

An essential underlying ingredient in this philosophy is the recognition and conceptualisation of the fact that all human resource departments produce and deliver products and have customers. Another essential ingredient is the realisation that the products they must have to satisfy the customer are determined only by the customer. Giving the customer what is desired results in added value.

Two ways of adding value are through quality enhancement and innovation. The latter means creating and doing different things (HRM practices); quality enhancement means doing things (HRM practices) better. When a human resource department adds value, it enables the customer (the rest of the organisation) to be more effective and competitive. It enables the rest of the organisation to pursue competitive strategies of innovation and/or quality enhancement. This has been happening in such organisations as Ford, McDonald's and IBM. And when it does, these organisations realise they need different HRM practices. Consequently, they change their practices and get the employee behaviours they need to implement an innovation or quality enhancement strategy.

In pursuit of its high-quality (dependable) customer service, McDonald's emphasises training. 'Outstanding customer service requires commitment to ongoing training that stresses workers' job-related skills, positive attitudes toward customers and co-workers, and overall company knowledge', according to Robert L. Desatnick, former vice-president of human resources at McDonald's. In his book, *Managing to Keep the Customer* (1987), Desatnick maintains that comprehensive training programs are the key to successful customer service at many leading firms.

There are four major phases in HRM customerisation programs: (1) gathering information, (2) developing action agendas, (3) implementing the action agendas, and (4) evaluating and revising the agendas. To do these successfully, the human resource department must learn more about the business, actively seek to develop and deliver new HRM products (e.g. a new performance appraisal system), and constantly seek feedback from customers. Typically, during customerisation the department becomes more effective: it becomes a strategic player, it becomes more responsive, and its staff becomes more committed to the organisation (Schuler & Jackson 1988).

Organising the HRM department

The discussion thus far indicates that organisations can benefit by allowing their human resource departments to become pro-active and open, to engage in the several functions and activities at each of the three levels (strategic, managerial, and operational), and to demonstrate their effectiveness. Organisations, however, can also benefit by allowing these departments to address several issues associated with organising the department:

- The number of roles that HRM plays
- The need for the HRM staff to be where the action is and to identify with the organisation
- The need for a fair and consistent application of HR policies, regardless of how small or large or diversified the organisation
- The need for the department's views to be an integral part of HR policy
- The need for the department to have sufficient power and authority to help ensure that HR policies will be implemented legally and without discrimination
- The need for the department not just to react to HR crises but also to be active and innovative.

These issues, which are the essence of the roles that human resource departments can play, affect the organisation of the department. For example, it can be organised so that it effectively plays a single role, or so that it plays two or more. The number of roles played often depends on the way top management views HR activities and on what it is willing to let the department do.

Human resource roles

The HR function can play several roles in an organisation. The more roles it does play, the more likely it will be effective in improving the organisation's productivity, enhancing the quality of work life in the organisation, and complying with all the necessary laws and regulations related to human resource utilisation.

The policy formulator role

One role the department can play is that of providing information for top management's use (at the strategic level). The specific types of information can include employee concerns, the external environment's impact, and how HRM activities can be used to gain competitive advantage.

The department staff can also advise in the process of policy formulation. The chief executive may still make policy statements, but these could be regarded as policy drafts. Formal adoption of a final policy can then take place after other executives, such as the line managers, have had a chance to comment. A broad consultation not only helps ensure extensive informational input into HR policies but also increases the likelihood of these inputs being accepted.

The provider and delegator role

In reality, HR programs succeed because line managers (at managerial and operational levels) make them succeed. The department's bread-and-butter job, therefore, is to enable line managers to make things happen. In the more traditional HR activities such as selecting, interviewing, training, evaluating, rewarding, counselling, promoting, and firing, the HR department is basically providing a service to line managers. In addition, the HR department administers direct and indirect compensation programs. Because the line managers are ultimately responsible for their employees, many of them see these services as useful. The HR department can also assist line managers by providing information about, and interpreting, equal employment opportunity legislation and safety and health standards.

The department's responsibilities are to provide the services that the line managers need on a day-to-day basis, to keep them informed of regulations and legislation regarding human resource management, and to provide an adequate supply of job candidates for the line managers to select from. To fulfil these responsibilities, however, the department must be accessible, or the human resource manager will lose touch with the line manager's needs. The HR staff should be as close as possible to where the people and the problems are. Because bringing the staff close to the action is important, this is discussed in the section on departmental organisation later in the chapter.

The auditor role

Although the HR department may delegate much of the implementation of HRM activities to line managers, it is still responsible for seeing that activities are implemented fairly and consistently. This is especially true today because of equal employment and unfair dismissal legislation. Responses to these regulations can best be made by a central group supplied with accurate information, the needed expertise, and the blessing of top management.

Expertise is also needed for implementing many HR activities, such as distributing employee benefits. Since having personnel experts is costly, organisations hire as few as possible and centralise them. Their expertise then filters to other areas of the organisation.

In organisations that have several locations and several divisions or units, tension often exists between the need for decentralisation and the need for having the expertise necessary to comply with complex regulations and advise on the best methods for HR activities.

The innovator role

An important and ever-expanding role for the human resource department is that of providing up-to-date application of current techniques and developing and exploring innovative approaches to HR problems and concerns. Today, the HR-related issues demanding innovative approaches and solutions centre on how to improve productivity and the quality of work life while complying with the law in an environment of high uncertainty, energy conservation, and intense international competition.

The adaptor role

It is increasingly necessary that organisations adopt new technologies, structuring processes, cultures, and procedures to meet the demands of enhanced competition. Their human resource departments are expected to have the skills to facilitate organisational change and to maintain organisational flexibility and adaptability.

Because these departments are facing the same demands as the organisations they work for, they are streamlining and automating their own operations and focusing services on critical tasks. In the flat, lean, and flexible organisation, the HRM function is a small, high-performing staff one. Management wants the staff to dismantle unnecessary institutional trappings—policies, systems, procedures—and the staff find it essential to reduce the time demands of routine activities in order to find time for initiatives.

The challenge to human resource staff is to perform necessary roles while minimising the administrative burden on managers and the cost to the organisation. Flexible companies seek to streamline, delegate, automate, or eliminate all possible tasks. Thus, the human resource management staff must review and improve its operations, reduce costs, reduce paperwork, eliminate activities, and contract out services, as appropriate. Not waiting for mandated cutbacks, the department must continually review and evaluate expenses and implement incremental changes to become and stay lean. Through flexible HRM functions, the department members should seek to be perceived as 'bureaucracy busters', setting an example for other staff functions and line organisations. How effective an organisation is in addressing these issues depends on how well it organises and staffs the HR department.

HRM in the organisation

The importance that an organisation assigns to human resource management is reflected in the department's status in the hierarchy. To fulfil the five HR roles effectively, the top manager of the department should be at the top of the organisational hierarchy, with line authority to the chief executive officer (CEO).

The top manager and staff of the HRM department are increasingly expected to be functional experts, capable administrators, business consultants, and problem solvers. In short, management expects human resource staff to 'have it all'. As in traditional organisations, administrative skills are essential for efficient human resource management. Specialised human resource expertise is also important, particularly now in combination with business knowledge and perspective. In flexible organisations, problem solving and consulting skills are vital in guiding and supporting adoption of new management practices.

Managers would like human resource staff to work closely with them to help solve their people-related problems as efficiently and promptly as possible, allowing them to give more attention to other concerns. Peter Drucker observed that HR staff will 'move into line work', making decisions and taking actions, not merely advising. While managers may best understand their own people, they increasingly seek help in handling people problems. As human resource staff become more capable and effective, managers seek to work with them as partners.

Being at the top and having business skills allows the human resource manager to play a part in HRM policy formulation and to have the power necessary to ensure its fair and consistent implementation. When the department has this much importance, it is likely to be performing effectively at the operational, managerial, and strategic levels of personnel activity.

Centralisation versus decentralisation

The organising concept of centralisation versus decentralisation relates to the balance between getting the HR function to where the action is and applying HR policies fairly and consistently. It also relates to the balance between the benefits of having HR generalists and specialists. **Centralisation** means that essential decision making and policy formulation are done at one location (at headquarters); **decentralisation** means that essential decision making and policy formulation are done at several locations (in the divisions or departments of the organisation). This is also referred to as **devolution**.

With the recent increases in regulatory requirements for the use of human resources and the increased expertise necessary to deal with complex HR functions, organisations are moving away from HR generalists and towards specialists. And at the same time, organisations—especially larger ones—are moving HR staff into their divisions. As a result, *the trend is to centralise non-routine aspects of human resources and to decentralise day-to-day activities.*

Thus, in a large, multidivisional organisation (which describes most of the largest industrial, retailing, and financial organisations), there is generally a corporate human resource department, staffed largely with specialists, and several divisional HR departments, staffed largely with generalists. The headquarters department, then, has two purposes: (1) to develop and co-ordinate HRM policy for the HR staff in all locations, including headquarters, and (2) to execute the HRM functions and activities for all the employees at headquarters. As the divisions grow, they often begin to hire their own specialists and to administer almost all their own HR functions and activities. This may result in several almost complete human resource departments, similar to those that would be found in most organisations without divisions.

Who is responsible for HRM?

Everyone should be responsible, and as organisations demonstrate more openness and mutuality in their human resources policies and practices, everyone is.

The managers

Human resource management is the primary task of individuals who have specialised in and are primarily responsible for this aspect of the organisation. But, with the increase in flat, lean organisations, line managers also are becoming more directly involved. As the ratio between human resource staff and line employees increases, more and more responsibility for human resource administration falls to the line manager. In fact, effective line managers spend at least one-fifth of their time dealing with human resource issues. Routine activities include motivating/reinforcing, disciplining/punishing, managing conflict, staffing and training, and developing staff. This is not meant to imply that the HR manager never implements functions and activities or that the line manager does not get involved in their development and administration. Indeed, these two managers are interdependent in the effective management of human resources. But such management cannot occur without management's support and direction. Top management influences the number and execution of HR functions and activities in an organisation. This influence is best shown by the roles that top management allows the HR manager and the line managers to play in the organisation.

The employees

Employees are increasingly playing a role in human resource management. For example, they may be asked to appraise their own performance or that of their colleagues. Employees may also help determine their own performance standards and goals. It is no longer uncommon for employees to write their own job descriptions. Perhaps most significantly, employees are playing a more active role in managing their own careers, assessing their own needs and values, and designing their own jobs. Nonetheless, the human resource department must help guide this process to ensure that individual plans are congruent with organisational plans.

HRM titles

Note that the terms 'personnel manager' (or executive), 'human resource manager', and 'HR manager' refer to the person heading the human resource department. In some organisations, this position may also be called the 'general manager—personnel', or the 'general manager—employee relations'.

The term 'human resource department' can be used interchangeably with 'personnel department' or just 'human resources'. Different names are used in different organisations. Nevertheless, all the functions and activities of human resource management relate to any of them. The term staff or HR staff refers to the employees in the HRM department, either generalists or specialists.

Line manager (or supervisor) refers to the person in charge of the employees who are working directly on the product that the organisation produces. Individual, person, worker, and workforce refer to anyone in the organisation.

Perhaps the most effective person to head the human resource department is an outstanding performer with HRM expertise who has had line management experience in finance, marketing, or production.

> In essence, to be a true professional in many areas of HR management, individuals virtually have to have an advanced degree in the subject and spend full time in that field. Areas like compensation have become incredibly complicated because of their close connection to strategic, legal, financial, and tax matters. [But] with the exception of technical specialists, HR managers need to spend a significant amount of time in line-management positions. It is not enough for senior HR managers to have worked in different areas of the HR function; they must have had some line business experience so that they have a first-hand familiarity with the business operations (Lawler 1988).

Line experience gives HR managers influence over and credibility with other line managers. To understand just how far some companies have gone in this area, consider IBMs policy of assigning line managers to work in the corporate HR department for two or three years as a part of their career development.

Conversely, the HR specialist who wants to reach the top may benefit greatly by rotating through a line job in order to increase his or her ability to understand and deal with the entire organisation.

Summary

This chapter has examined the growing importance of the functions and activities of human resource management, defined what HRM is, contrasted it with traditional personnel management, outlined its growth, and listed its purposes. Because of the increasing complexity of HRM, nearly all organisations have established a human resources department. Not all of these, however, perform all the HR functions and activities discussed in this chapter. A department's functions and activities, and the way it performs them, depend greatly on the roles that it plays in the organisation. A human resource department can play five roles. Organisations that are most concerned with effective human resource management allow their departments to play the policy formulator, provider, auditor, innovator and adaptor roles. When this occurs, the departments have most often demonstrated their value to their organisations by showing how the several HRM functions and activities influence productivity, quality of work life, and legal compliance—all purposes associated with the organisation's bottom-line criteria. In addition, these departments are likely to be operating at all three levels in the organisation: operational, managerial, and strategic. Furthermore, they are probably doing this in a pro-active manner rather than waiting for the organisation to tell them what to do. A human resources department should demonstrate its effectiveness and help the organisation to attain its goals.

questions for discussion and review

1 What are the major activities of HRM and how do they contribute to organisational functioning?
2 How is HRM influenced by the external and internal environments?
3 What trends and crises are presently influencing the importance of HRM in organisations?
4 Why is assessing HRM effectiveness important?
5 How can HRM managers become pro-active in demonstrating their effectiveness?
6 What is the 'bottom line' of an organisation and how can HRM have a significant impact on this?
7 What are some of the different roles HRM can play in an organisation?
8 What is your view of the debate about the use of the terms 'HRM' and 'personnel management'?
9 Who should be responsible for HRM in an organisation?
10 Does HRM represent merely the addition of another layer to the personnel role or a genuine paradigm shift?

case study

Bring your home to life with Dulux

In the three years to 1992, Dulux Clayton has achieved:
- An increase in goods delivered in full and on time from 60 per cent to 98 per cent
- A reduction of 49 per cent in labour per product batch from 79 to 40 hours
- A reduction of 88 per cent in products reworked from 4.5 per cent to 0.5 per cent
- A reduction in employee absenteeism from 5.1 per cent to 2.3 per cent.

BACKGROUND OF THE COMPANY

- Nature of the business
- Size
- Number of sites
- Age
- Ownership
- Management structure
- Types of employees
- Unions on site.

Dulux Australia is Australia's largest producer of surface coatings. It has eight sites, sales in excess of $450 million and 2300 employees Australia wide. Since 1987 Dulux Australia has been a division of ICI Australia operations. To achieve its goal of increasing export markets in South-East Asia and the pacific region, Dulux has focused on its major operation at Clayton, Victoria. This plant employs 300 people, 190 of whom are covered by the Australian Liquor Hospitality and Miscellaneous Workers Union (ALHMWU).

INDUSTRIAL RELATIONS & ENTERPRISE NEGOTIATIONS

- Progress in award restructuring
- Implementation of structural efficiency principle
- Development of a single bargaining unit
- Industrial disputes.

Enterprise-based site agreements were implemented at Dulux Clayton in 1991. Prior to this there were many demarcation issues, and only informal and infrequent consultation with the unions. In the past five years there have been two industrial disputes resulting in time lost for short durations (1989 and 1990). The most recent of these disputes related to the transfer of national union of workers members to the ALHMWU.

Following the resolution of this dispute the ALHMWU has been the main union on site, and all parties worked towards a site agreement which was implemented in February 1991. Since this time two additional agreements have been struck (April 1992 and August 1992). These agreements have covered changes in the areas of grievance procedures, career progression and skills structure, job design, consultative process and project team participation. Since the implementation of these agreements productivity has improved by 40 per cent, no demarcations exist, and many jobs previously carried out by maintenance fitters are now done by the production team.

CONSULTATION PROCEDURES

Development of:
- Single bargaining unit
- Joint training committee
- OHS committee
- Steering committee for the introduction of workplace changes.

Included in the site agreements is a site consultative committee which comprises six management representatives, twelve employee representatives (elected by their peers) and the assistant secretary of the ALHMWU. This committee meets monthly to address issues such as job rotation, grievances regarding pay/skills, policy issues regarding employee conditions, site performance, new developments and annual renewal of agreements. This committee has undergone three days joint training in consultative processes with TUTA (the Trade Union Training Authority).

Every six months the managing director holds a 'state of the nation' meeting with all employees where he addresses any major changes under way or planned at Dulux Clayton. Every quarter each department meet as a whole to discuss departmental goals and progress.

PRODUCTIVITY MEASUREMENT

- What performance indicators are measured?
- How and by whom are they measured?
- How are standards set, how are they used?
- What are the procedures for feedback?

Dulux Clayton has established performance indicators and international benchmarks in three areas:

1 **Customer satisfaction—DIFOT** 'delivered in full and on time' to the customer. Previously the indicator 'assembled in full and on time' (IFOT) was improved from an average of 43 per cent in 1988 to 95 per cent in 1991. The more challenging and realistic measure of DIFOT, established through international benchmarking is now being used. Dulux's goal is to achieve and average 95 per cent DIFOT by 1992; Dulux Clayton has already achieved 98 per cent. **Customer complaints** are monitored and evaluated to determine the effectiveness of corrective actions. **Best-by-test analysis** of domestic and international competitors' products against customer requirements.

Dulux has recognised that superior customer satisfaction relates more to manufacturing effectiveness than efficiency, and is seeking new process control benchmarks in the international arena.

While the establishment of performance criteria and benchmarks are necessarily customer and best practice driven, their ongoing monitoring and improvement is a challenge for the whole workforce. Process-specific measurements are collected and analysed at the 'coal face', while departmental performance is evaluated with the assistance of management information systems. Key performance data are shown on large displays throughout the site, and discussed at weekly work cell meetings.

2 **Process improvement measures**—productivity efficiency indicators, including cycle time per batch, labour hours per batch, rework, inventory stock turns and unplanned maintenance activity, were established in 1989 by international benchmarking. Performance has improved significantly from 1989 to 1992, and further improvements will be based on internal 1995 goals and best practice standards.

3 **Workplace environment measures—annual employee attitude surveys** monitor morale, impact of management style, and workplace culture. These are integrated with staff assessing manager evaluations. Resultant constructive criticisms are analysed and acted upon, with feedback provided to the employees.

Physical environment emissions of volatile organic compounds, lead, dust and noise are regularly measured. **Monthly employee absentee rates** (down from 5.1 per cent in 1989 to 2.3 per cent in 1992) are monitored and graphed. Active counselling is undertaken where trends indicate that assistance to employees may be necessary. **Employee turnover** is monitored, and exit interviews are conducted with people resigning from the site. Turnover rate has been less that 2 per cent per annum for five years, which is considered to be of best practice standard.

QUALITY PROCEDURES & WORK AND JOB REDESIGN

- How and by whom is quality measured?
- What process is used for continuous improvement?
- How have the work process and jobs been redesigned to ensure continuous improvement?

Work processes and jobs have been significantly changed at Dulux Clayton. Market-focused work cells have been developed, covering a broad range of production functions. They do their own product testing and daily maintenance. Services providers such as expert maintenance work directly with their own group of work cells. Dulux's training strategy stresses teamwork, innovation and continuous improvement of quality and service. Within twelve months, all employees (in mixed groups of managers, team leaders and operators) will have taken courses in systematic problem solving, and will compete for the 1993 Australian Quality Awards. Dulux regularly holds customer luncheons, attended by all levels of employees and a selection of customer representatives. These meetings are used to get constructive feedback on quality performance and complaints handling.

PARTICIPATIVE PRACTICES

- What communication processes exist?
- What process enables employees to contribute to decision making?
- Does team work (multi-skilling, cross training, team meetings) exist?

A waste management team was recently formed to address the issue of removal of dry cardboard. Dulux has been paying for the removal of this waste, as it was being disposed of with other rubbish. The team established a process to segregate the cardboard, compress it and sell it to a paper manufacturer, thereby making the company a profit of $20 000 per annum.

A team calling itself SOS (site operations safety) formed with the goal of reducing the number of injuries on site. They are progressively working with each department to identify potential safety risks and provide appropriate training. To date the savings in medical, salary and equipment costs are running at $1.5 million per annum.

Every production employee is a member of a work cell of between four and nine operators. These teams are market-focused, work on one product (or group of products), and service one customer (or group of customers). For example one team produces paints solely for the automotive industry. As such, each cell covers a broad range of production functions, and each operator is skilled, or in the process of being skilled, in all of these functions. The machines used by these teams may be geographically separated, but are identified by being painted in the team's colour.

Each cell has a team leader who works approximately 60 per cent on production duties and 40 per cent on supervisory duties. These duties involve scheduling, training rosters, and leave and overtime management, continuous improvement activities, performance monitoring and budgets. In addition, each cell has a chemist or engineer who acts as a 'mentor' to the team. Their role is to pass on skills to the team, particularly to drive the problem solving process, in order to facilitate their continuous improvement effort. It is planned that as the work team develops the mentors' involvement will diminish.

A number of project teams has been established for improvement activities in engineering and product development. Where appropriate, representatives from health and safety, manual handling, waste management, process control, operations, and training are involved voluntarily in these committees to ensure the success of hardware, systems and formula design changes.

Both work cells and project teams are called customer first teams and meet regularly to review the goals, objectives and performance of the team, department, and company. These meetings are held away from the immediate work area, in company time. If a member of a work cell is attending a project team meeting, or absent for any other reason, the cell must determine its own work allocation and schedule to cope with this.

EQUAL EMPLOYMENT OPPORTUNITY

- Does the company have an EEO policy?
- Is this policy integrated with corporate strategy?
- What mechanisms ensure EEO (recruitment process, performance

The organisational changes being undertaken by Dulux Clayton provide the foundation of equity of opportunity for all employees. Developments in the areas of work and job redesign consultative and participative processes, and competency based training and career paths provide access to responsibility and promotion based on merit, and reflect a broader shift in organisational values.

- appraisal, structured career paths, multi-skilling)?
- Are diverse groups (e.g. women, aboriginal people, people of non English speaking background and people with disabilities) represented in all areas and levels of the organisation?

In addition, a site EEO Committee oversees the development and implementation of EEO Policy and strategy. The EEO activities include:

- **Professional development and advancement for women**—a customer first team is addressing the issue of career pathing to provide more opportunities for senior positions for women in the organisation.
- **Literacy training**—numeracy and literacy training which is focused on migrant employees, ensures that all employees have access to skilling programs, and therefore to career path advancement.
- **Handling discrimination training**—several line managers and service personnel are attending a three day training course on how to identify discrimination and how to handle discrimination complaints.

SKILLS FORMATION & CAREER PATH DEVELOPMENT

- Does the company have a strategic training plan?
- Is there integration between formal and on the job training?
- Are employees multi-skilled?
- Is there a structured career path which is equally accessible to all?

Dulux's training and development philosophy and strategic intent underpins their goal of manufacturing surface coatings to the highest levels of consistency. Their training approach is to provide internal and external competency based and evaluated training. The program focuses on skills training (to achieve company objectives) and personal development (to facilitate career paths) for all employees, and is based on a 1987 'training for management' needs analysis, a 1990 skills audit and a 1991 training needs analysis.

Employees were involved in the development of training programs through DACUM (developing a curriculum) workshops. Both TAFE and on-site training is undertaken by employees on company time. On-site training is delivered almost exclusively by site managers and team leaders, who have previously attended train the trainer courses.

All training is delivered in the form of competency based and evaluated training modules. These modules are linked to structured career paths for all operators. Each module is graded according to difficulty (a, b or c), and a payment attached to it. Employees receive a base rate of pay plus increments for each module successfully completed. This pay structure is incorporated in the site agreement.

SPECIFIC ISSUES AND PROBLEMS ENCOUNTERED

- As a result of structural changes, such as those undertaken at Dulux Clayton, individual jobs will change and sometime disappear

It has been widely experienced that the middle layers of management in larger companies are most resistant to change, and most vulnerable to its consequences. At Dulux Clayton, work redesign led to the disappearance of the role of production supervisors. This situation was managed by:

altogether. Dulux experienced this with the flattening of the organisation and the subsequent displacement of some levels of management.

- Involving employees in decisions affecting them.
- Communicating the larger vision for the company and providing leadership towards this.
- Ensuring security of employment for these employees in the form of redeployment in areas such as training development, systems managements, and other line management roles. The key to success of this is provision of comprehensive training for new positions.
- Offering employees who choose not to be involved in the changes a comprehensive retrenchment package.

DISCUSSION QUESTIONS

- Policies
- Enterprise agreements
- Training
- Performance measurement

- Name three policies or procedures supporting the introduction of workplace change at Dulux Clayton.
- How has development of enterprise agreements assisted Dulux with implementation of workplace change?
- Discuss the type of training and method of delivery appropriate for a new consultative committee such as at Dulux Clayton. What would the training cover? What are the advantages and disadvantages of joint training?
- How does benchmarking differ from traditional performance measurement? How has Dulux used it to increase their international competitiveness?

Source: Australian Chamber of Commerce and Industry.

Resources

Boxall, P. & Dowling, P. J. (1990), 'Human Resource Management and the Industrial Relations Tradition', *Labour and Industry*, vol. 3, no. 2/3, pp. 195–214.

Guest, D. A. (1987), 'Human Resource Management and Industrial Relations', *Journal of Management Studies*, vol. 24, no. 5, pp. 503–21.

Legge, K. (1995), *Human Resource Management: Rhetorics and Realities*, Macmillan Business, London.

References

Australian Chamber of Commerce and Industry, 'Integrated Workplace Change' [series].

Beer, M. & Spector, B. (1985), 'Corporate wide transformations in human resource management', in R. E. Walton & P. R. Lawrence (eds), *Human Resource Management, Trends and Challenge*, Harvard Business School Press, Boston, pp. 219–53.

Buchanan, D. & Boddy, D. (1992), *The Expertise of the Change Agent: Public Performance and Backstage Activity*, Prentice-Hall, International Series.

Cox, T. H. & Blake, S. (1991), 'Managing Cultural Diversity: Implications for Organisational Competitiveness,' *Academy of Management Executive*, vol. 5, pp. 45–56.
Desatnik, R. L. (1987), *Managing To Keep The Customers*, Jossey-Bass, San Francisco, CA.
Dowling, P. J. & Fisher, C. (1996), *HR Snapshots: Today and Tomorrow*, Australian Human Resources Institute.
Dunphy, D. C. (1987), 'The Historical Development of Human Resource Management in Australia', *Human Resource Management Australia*, vol. 25, no. 2, pp. 40–47.
Gardner, M. & Palmer, J. (1992), *Employment Relations: Industrial Relations and Human Resource Management in Australia*, Macmillan, South Melbourne.
Huselid, M. A., Jackson, S. E. & Schuler, R. S. (1995), 'The Significance of Human Resource Management Effectiveness for Corporate Financial Performance', Paper presented at the Academy of Management Confernce, August 5–8, Vancouver, Canada.
Huczynski, A. A. (1993), *Management gurus, What makes them and how to become one*, London, Routledge.
Ives, Blake & Jarvenpaa, Sirrka (1996), 'Will the Internet Revolutionize Business Education And Research?, *Sloan Management Review*, Spring, p. 33.
Kanter, R. M. (1989), *When Giants Learn To Dance*, Simon and Schuster, New York.
Kotter, J. P. (1995), *Leading Change*, Harvard Business School Press.
Lawler, E. C. III (1988), 'Human Resource Management: Meeting The Challenge', *Personnel Management*, January, pp. 24–27.
Pfeffer, J. (1995), 'Producing sustainable competitve advantage through the effective management of people', *Academy of Management Executive*, vol. 9, no. 1, pp. 55–69.
Piore, M. & Sabel, C. F. (1988), 'The Productivity Paradox: Why the Payoff from Automation Is Still Elusive and What Corporate America Can Do About It', *Business Week*, 6 June, pp. 100–114.
Pitney Bowes (1994–95), *The Power of Diversity*, Issue 1, Fall–Winter.
Porter, M. E. (1985), *Competitive Advantage*, Free Press, New York.
Schuler, R. S. (1988), 'Personnel and Human Resource Management Choices and Organisational Strategy', in R. S. Schuler, S. A. Youngblood & V. Huber (eds), *Readings in Personnel and Human Resource Management*, 3rd edition, West Publishing, St. Paul, Minn.
Schuler, R. S. & Jackson, S. E. (1988), 'Customerizing The HR Department', *Personnel*, June, pp. 36–44.
Schuler, R. (1995), *Managing human resources*, 5th edition, West Publishing, St. Paul, Minn.
Storey, J. (1992), *Developments In The Management Of Human Resources*, Blackwell, Oxford.
Towers Perrin (1992), *Priorities for Competitive Advantage: An IBM Study, Conducted by Towers Perrin*.
Vaill, P. B. (1989) *Managing As A Performing Art*, Jossey Bass, San Francisco, CA.
Watson, T. J. (1977), *The Personnel Managers: A Study in the Sociology of Work and Industry*, Routledge & Kegan Paul, London.

chapter 2

Strategic human resource management

Robin Kramar

learning objectives

After studying this chapter, you will be able to:

1. Identify some of the concepts associated with strategic human resource management.
2. Identify a number of models which describe strategic human resource management.
3. Describe some of the techniques associated with strategic human resource management.
4. Identify some of the major issues which will influence the development of human resource management policies.
5. Discuss future developments in strategic human resource management.

chapter 2

chapter outline

- Improving business outcomes — 48
  - Strategy — 49
  - Stakeholder — 50
  - Culture — 51
  - Organisational fit — 52
  - Alignment — 53
- Models of strategic human resource management — 56
  - General models — 56
  - Models detailing relationships within organisations — 57
  - Specific relationships — 59
- Processes associated with strategic human resource management — 63
  - Environmental assessment — 64
  - Strategy development — 65
  - Implementation — 66
- Understanding developments in the external environment — 67
  - Domestic and international competition — 70
  - Emerging social structure — 70
- Future developments in strategic human resource management — 74
  - Managing diversity — 74
  - Work and family — 77
  - Learning organisation — 80
  - Management education and development — 81
- Summary — 81
- Questions for discussion and review — 82
- Case study — 83
- Resources — 84
- References — 84

HRM IN THE NEWS

Human resources: flavour of the '90s

There's no doubt that human resources is helping to give companies a winning edge. Its rise in the corporate hierarchy has been rapid. But at what cost, asks Louisa Hatfield. In delivering what business wants, will employees suffer?

The NRMA was losing staff in droves. It was taking on employees and training them, only to see them walk away after three to five years. The high turnover was costing the company up to $38 000 an employee.

Ten years ago such a problem would have been ignored. But the NRMA asked its human resources department to look at who was leaving and why. It discovered a large number of those resigning were women, who were unable to combine the job with family commitments.

The solution was to help organise childcare facilities, arrange more flexible working hours and improve parental leave. The employee turnover dropped dramatically.

This, the experts say, is a classic example of a new era in company attitude towards the workforce. Businesses in the 1990s have finally realised the best asset they have is the people who work for them and to keep them happy and productive they need a first-rate human resources department.

In the past decade—and particularly the last five years—there has been a dramatic rise in the importance of human resources.

Sandra Cormack, national professional development manager for the Australian Human Resources Institute, says the role first evolved out of a welfare background and her own organisation started off as the Institute of Welfare Officers.

In the 1950s and 1960s, the job basically meant organising wages, sickness pay, hiring staff and sacking them when necessary.

It was about keeping the companies out of trouble, keeping the unions happy and making sure all the necessary legislation was being obeyed. Cormack says: 'Human resources officers were basically compliance officers and personnel administrators'.

Now human resources departments are much more involved with the hierarchy of a business and its strategic planning. The human resources director/manager will have a close relationship with the chief executive and play a key role in running the business. Wages and sickness are often handled by the accounts department leaving human resources to concentrate more on recruitment, staff training and performance management.

As Cormack says: 'There has been quite a movement in the last ten years not only in terms of status and recognition, but in the way the service is delivered'.

'There certainly is the compliance factor by businesses, but it is now more about how human resources can add value to the business'.

'Companies in the 1980s faced technology changes and international competition. There were a lot of investigations about how they could do better. There was more diagnosis of what was required to make the business successful and human resources started to get more attention'.

This growth in importance is reflected in the organisation's membership. It now has 11 000 members and is rising by 1000 a year.

One of the great success stories in human resources, which proves its dramatic change of status, is the company Morgan and Banks.

It finished its first year as a listed company by posting a 40 per cent increase in after-tax profit from $4.05 million to $5.67 million for 1995.

The joint managing director, Andrew Banks, says 'For years during my corporate life, chief executives were telling me that people were really important and then I watched them act in the opposite way'.

'Now in the 1990s, however, it [human resources] is right on top of the agenda. Not because the bosses wanted to wake up, but because they had no choice. Unless they got their people strategy right they knew it was going to cost them'.

'Everybody has tight margins and if you have got half the people in the wrong jobs or not trained and the business has the wrong culture—for example condoning harassment—then you will not survive'.

Workforce the key resource

'Everyone can access capital and technology so the competitive edge comes from knowledge and customer service. If you have both then you have the winning edge—people are the difference', says Banks.

Cormack agrees: 'The workforce is the cutting edge for beating the business down the road. A lot of technology is widely available but it is the people who make the difference'.

The key is to become an employer of choice.

So how does the human resources department help a company to become the place where the best and most skilled people want to work?

According to Cormack it needs to concentrate on—whatever the environment—'the deliverables'. In other words, what will improve the business. '[the human resources team] must understand the business that they're in and how best to help it', she says.

'You have to look at what the business imperatives are for that company. If it is quality then the human resources has to look at everything in its department that will ensure that happens—for example making sure you don't recruit staff with a laissez-faire attitude'.

It is this element in the changing face of human resources which is the subject of big debate at the moment. 'The question is, if human resources are delivering what the business wants, then is that a conflict with what the workforce needs', poses Cormack.

'The worry is that because human resources has moved itself up into the hierarchy and the human resources manager now has the ear of the CEO, he/she is now very well positioned for delivering and helping the business, but has this been at the cost of individual employees?'

'It is very complex and the ideal is to be both, but there will be clashes'.

Indeed at the moment Telstra unions are angry because of the plans being used by the company to decide which 9000 employees will lose their jobs over the next 12 months.

The plan will inevitably involve the human resources department and requires supervisors to rate the performance of employees in five different areas. Those who fail will face redundancy.

But the communications division of Telstra's largest union, the Communications, Electrical and Plumbing Union, claims the system would reduce Telstra workers to the status of cattle.

Cormack says there is much more emphasis on performance managements systems with ongoing dialogue on how a person is getting on. 'It used to be the first performance feedback a person got was the sack', she said.

'Now an important part of human resources is communication with the employees—having an open door and regular discussions about where the individual is going in the organisation and what their needs are. Are they in the right job, do they have the necessary equipment to do the job, do they need a new computer or more training'.

While salary is obviously important, it is not the main motivator for most people.

As well as remuneration there is reward. 'Remuneration is the dollars and the reward is the non-money rewards—such as a newsletter or an employee of the month scheme. It is becoming more difficult to pay people more so companies are looking for other ways to reward people', says Cormack.

Banks agrees: '... you have to offer them something else instead—if you work for us you will be cleverer and more valuable than if you take another choice; we will train you and so on'.

Many human resources jobs are done by on-line managers with the human resources experts simply giving guidance.

Cormack says there are good and bad points to this. 'Saving dollars is why it started, but unless it is properly supported by the central human resources unit is can go astray. It can also be positive'. For example, when recruiting, the on-line managers are the ones who know what the job involves and they will be working with the people taken on, but says Cormack, 'It is important to make sure they are heavily supported by the human resources department'.

And those involved in human resources are becoming more and more educated. The AHRI polled 3000 of their members in 1995—34 per cent had a tertiary degree, 24 per cent had completed a postgraduate degree and 19 per cent had a diploma or certificate. Ten years ago the figures were half that.

More and more universities are making human resources a part of business, commerce and economic degrees. Andrew Smith, Associate Professor in Human Resources Management at Charles Sturt University, says most of the courses specialising in human resources have been set up in the past five to six years. None, however, are solely human resources.

'Just doing human resources wouldn't be particularly productive, it is not a discipline in itself, but part of the overall discipline of managing a business. It is not a stand alone profession', he says. 'A company will want someone who knows about the whole area of running a business, not just the human resources aspect'.

Banks says: 'I have told my teenage kids not to get a job but a customer—make themselves invaluable to a customer'.

'I believe that the changes we have been experiencing are going to continue to accelerate and be very far reaching. There are some companies who have a shocking reputation for human resources and they are doing very well, but the question is for how long?'

'I am not saying that if you have a great human relations department that you are always going to be profitable, but it is going to improve your chances'.

Source: *Sydney Morning Herald*, 3 August 1996, pp. 3–4.

Improving business outcomes

The article 'Human Resources Flavour of the 90s' discusses some of the ways human resource policies can be used to improve business outcomes. These techniques include performance management systems, remuneration systems, and careful selection and placement. The article raises the debate about whether meeting business needs involves a fundamental conflict with the needs of employees. It suggests effective human resource management involves matching employee and organisational needs, by planning and implementing human resource policies which focus on business needs.

Chapter 1 identified trends in the way people are being managed. A major change has been the shift from a personnel to a human resource management approach. One of the commonly stated characteristics of this latter approach is the integration of human resource management policies and practices with business strategy (Guest 1987; Boxall & Dowling 1990). Guest identifies three aspects of integration: the integration or fit of human resource policies with business strategy; the development of policies which complement each other and encourage employee behaviour which displays commitment, flexibility and quality; the internalisation of the importance of human resources by line managers.

This emphasis on integration is a central characteristic of a particular approach to human resource management known as **strategic human resource management**. The term strategic human resource management began to appear in American literature in the 1980s (Nininger 1980; Miller & Burack 1981; Kanter 1983; Lundy & Cowling 1996).

A variety of models have been developed to explain the features and relationships associated with the integration of human resource policies with business strategy. These models include general frameworks, organisational frameworks and normative models which indicate how particular human resource policies are required to create a fit with business strategies. Some of these models (Miles & Snow 1984; Dowling & Schuler 1991) argue for the matching of an organisation's strategic orientation and human resource policies.

Five concepts are critical for an understanding of these models. These concepts are strategy, stakeholders, culture, organisational fit and alignment.

Strategy

The word 'strategy' is derived from the Greek word *strategos* which refers to the role of a military commander and general. As Legge (1995, pp. 96–97) points out this suggests strategy is a senior management activity involving the direction of resources to the achievement of goals. This meaning is reflected in Chandler's definition of strategy:

> ... the determination of the basic long-term goals and objectives of an enterprise, and the adoption of courses of action and the allocation of resources necessary for carrying out the goals (Chandler 1962).

It follows from this definition that the development of strategy should involve analysing the organisation's relationship with its external and internal environments while a strategy should be a scheme of managing these relationships (Kay 1993, pp. 8–9). One way in which such a scheme could operate is that the strategy dealing with the long-term direction of the organisation and the scope of its activities should influence the structure of the organisation (Chandler 1962). The assumption is then that other functions, such as human resources, will develop strategies to support the achievement of the business strategy (Miller 1993, p. 9).

However, as Legge (1995, p. 96) points out these definitions represent a normative model of 'what strategy should be rather than a description of the behaviours that are enacted under the loose label of strategy'. The above description suggests strategy is formed through formal, rational decision-making processes. Mintzberg (1988) argues this approach describes how strategies are supposed to be made, rather than how they are actually made. He has identified a range of strategies and classified these into groups. These are described in Table 2.1.

This chapter examines some of the processes associated with a rational approach to strategic human resource management.

Table 2.1   Classification of strategies

> **VARIOUS KINDS OF STRATEGIES, FROM RATHER DELIBERATE TO MOSTLY EMERGENT**
>
> - **Planned strategy**: precise intentions are formulated and articulated by a central leadership, and backed up by formal controls to ensure their surprise-free implementation in an environment that is benign, controllable, or predictable (to ensure no distortion of intentions); these strategies are highly deliberate.
> - **Entrepreneurial strategy**: intentions exist as the personal, unarticulated vision of a single leader, and so are adaptable to new opportunities; the organisation is under the personal control of the leader and located in a protected niche in its environment; these strategies are relatively deliberate but can emerge too.
> - **Ideological strategy**: intentions exist as the collective vision of all the members of the organisation, controlled through strong shared norms; the organisation is often pro-active vis-á-vis its environment; these strategies are rather deliberate.
> - **Umbrella strategy**: a leadership in partial control of organisational actions defines strategic targets or boundaries within which others must act (e.g. that all new products be high priced and at the technological cutting edge; although what these actual products are to be is left emerge); as a result, strategies are partly deliberate (the boundaries) and partly emergent (the patterns within them); this strategy can also be called deliberately emergent, in that the leadership purposefully allows others the flexibility to manoeuvre and form patterns within the boundaries.
> - **Process strategy**: the leadership controls the process aspects of strategy (who gets hired and so gets a chance to influence strategy; what structures they work within, etc.), leaving the actual content of strategy to others; strategies are again partly deliberate (concerning process) and partly emergent (concerning content), and deliberately emergent.
> - **Disconnected strategy**: members or subunits loosely coupled to the rest of the organisation produce patterns in the streams of their own actions in the absence of, or in direct contradiction to the central or common intentions of the organisation at large: the strategies can be deliberate for those who make them.
> - **Consensus strategy**: through mutual adjustment, various members converge on patterns that pervade the organisation in the absence of central or common intentions: these strategies are rather emergent in nature.
> - **Imposed strategy**: the external environment dictates patterns in actions, either through direct imposition (say by an outside owner or by a strong customer) or through implicitly pre-empting or bounding organisational choice (as in a large airline that must fly jumbo jets to remain viable); these strategies are organisationally emergent, although they may be internalised and made deliberate.

Source: Mintzberg 1988

Stakeholder

A second critical concept is **stakeholder.** The term stakeholder refers to any group or individual who has a legitimate expectation of the organisation. Stakeholders can include owners, shareholders, employees and managers, customers, business partners such as suppliers and creditors, governments, local and general communities and special interest groups. When organisations are viewed as a network of stakeholders who need to be managed, the process of strategic human resource management could be broadened from the management of relationships with employees to include the management of the relationships with all the stakeholders.

Success for different stakeholders involves the achievement of a variety of outcomes. Figure 2.1 illustrates some of the outcomes with which the various stakeholders will be most concerned. Strategic management involves acknowledging these desired outcomes and developing policies and practices, including human resource policies and practices which meet these stakeholder requirements. Alternatively, it can involve 'modifying stakeholders' expectations so they more closely match the capabilities or long-term interests of the organisation' (Saul 1991, p. 9).

Figure 2.1 What does 'success' look like?

Source: Strategic Consulting Group

Success will depend not only on satisfying these requirements, but satisfying them better than competitors. For instance, in order to retain valued employees it might not be enough for an organisation just to provide career opportunities. In order to be effective the career opportunities will need to be better than those in an organisation competing for the same labour.

Culture

The third concept, **culture** is complex. Culture has no fixed meaning, however a commonly accepted meaning refers to the common values, attitudes and behaviours that members of a group or society share and which are expressed, reproduced and communicated partly in symbolic form. Culture is transmitted over time in a gradual, yet dynamic way.

An instrumental organisational culture is characterised by norms and values supportive of the behaviours necessary to achieve organisational goals and management objectives or tasks associated with these goals (Alvesson 1993, p. 28). Where cultures are not supportive of an organisation's strategy, cultural change programs are often implemented to try to close the gap between the existing and the desired culture. Human resource policies and practices are influential in signalling and encouraging behaviours which reflect certain values. Consequently, effective strategic human resource management would utilise a range of human resource policies which contribute to the building of a culture intended to assist in the achievement of organisational objectives and goals.

In order to do this, it is necessary to know the dimensions of the organisation's existing culture and the character of the culture that you want to move towards. One of the techniques which can be used in this process is a cultural analysis. Kabanoff (1993) has developed a technique for doing such an analysis. The technique defines eleven dimensions of an organisational culture and then uses this to identify four basic organisational cultures present among Australian organisations. These dimensions are authority orientation, leadership, teamwork, participation, commitment, performance, reward, equity, affiliation, change and normative control.

The four basic organisational types identified are:

1 **Elite culture**—high on authority figures, high on rewards for senior managers, low on teamwork and participation. Examples of organisations in this category are Westpac, CBA and QBE.
2 **Meritocratic culture**—high on equity, participation and rewards for performance. Organisations in this category are Advance Bank, Telstra, Caltex and Australia Post.
3 **Collegial culture**—high reliance on members' commitment, participation and adherence to norms of behaviour, low on control and reliance on rewards. Examples of organisations displaying this culture include State Bank (NSW), Legal and General, CML.
4 **Leader focused culture**—low on equality of power and rewards, but high on teamwork, especially among a cadre of loyal members. Among the organisations in this category are CRA, Leighton Industries, A.V. Jennings, Defiance Mills.

One of the values of a culture analysis is that it is possible to determine if the existing practices create a 'fit' between strategy and culture. Kabanoff's description and analysis of organisations in the banking sector indicated that the espoused cultures of the four big banks in Australia: the Commonwealth, the ANZ, the National Australia Bank and Westpac, were consistent with the elite cultures. However, although theoretically there was a fit between espoused culture and espoused strategy, the stated emphasis on one of the dimensions, performance, as part of the banks' cultures was not evident. This can be explained in terms of the 'value systems in which the performance and integration of front-line staff are not evident as one of the concerns of the "people at the top" ' Kabanoff (1993) explained this in terms of senior management's value systems which neglect to acknowledge the importance of the performance of front line staff for organisational success.

Organisational fit

The concept of **organisational fit** is an essential element of the strategic approach to human resource management. Miles & Snow (1984) found there was organisational fit between a number of organisational factors in successful organisations. They argued these organisations have structures, cultures, missions, objectives, human resource policies and practices and managerial behaviour which indicate to employees how they are expected to behave and what they are expected to contribute. It is argued a tight fit can only be established when senior managers share a clear understanding of where the organisation is going and how to get there. Therefore, one of the purposes of human resource management policies and practices is to influence individual and collective behaviour so it is directed towards the achievement of organisational objectives.

Collins (1994, p. 41) claims establishing fit occurs at three levels:

1 **External fit**—between the organisation's capabilities and opportunities and constraints
2 **Internal fit**—between the macro features of the organisation: its mission, strategy, structure, technology, products and services, culture, workforce characteristics
3 **Human resource management fit**—between the various components of the human resource management function e.g. recruitment and selection criteria, induction, training, appraisal, rewards so that they consistently influence behaviour so that they enable strategy to be implemented and achieved.

Alignment

The fifth concept, 'alignment' refers to the matching of the organisations strengths and internal capabilities with the opportunities available in the external market. The alignment of employees expectations with the organisation's strategy can be developed through effectively communicating the organisation's strategic direction, translating the strategy into performance goals and objectives for business units, teams and individuals, and by developing an organisational culture in which the behaviour of organisational members is consistent and supported by the organisation's policies.

The strategic direction of the organisation is expressed in the vision, mission and values statements and the business strategy. These need to be communicated to stakeholders so they know what it means in general terms for their behaviour. The establishment of performance objectives and measures provides a guide for behaviour in specific terms. The process of developing an organisational culture needs to acknowledge how stakeholders' feelings and values will influence how they behave. Building a supportive organisational culture is a complex and time-consuming process.

HRM IN THE NEWS

Better milk from contented cows

BY ROSS GITTINS

It's a funny thing that, in our preoccupation with Australia's economic performance, we give a lot of attention to the policies pursued by the government, but remarkably little attention to something that's probably more important: the policies pursued by business.

The Australian media are renowned for their obsession with economics but, even in their business sections, they rarely say much about the art or science of management.

The result is that there are trends in management thinking and practice which are well known to business-people—

particularly executives in big companies—but are almost unknown to the public.

Last week the economic planning advisory commission published a paper it had commissioned from Professor Russell Lansbury and Dr Jim Kitay of Sydney University on 'human resource management'.

Predictably, it got little media coverage. I thought I'd tell you about it, however, because changes in management practices are an important element in the way our world is changing. In any case, many of us work for outfits—privately owned or government owned—where these practices are taking hold and affecting our lives.

The story is that pressure from growing international competition and major changes in technology is causing firms in all the developed countries to change their relations with employees.

This change is commonly labelled 'human resource management'. The central idea behind the name is that employees should be seen not as a cost to be minimised, but as assets in which the firm should invest to get better results.

There's a lot more to it than that, of course. Drawing on a host of research, Kitay and Lansbury identify four distinctive features of human resource management (HRM).

The first is that a firm's management of its employees—its industrial relations and its personnel management—should be integrated with its overall strategy for competing in its markets.

The second is that firms should work to gain the 'commitment' of their employees to the organisation's goals. It's assumed that committed employees will be more satisfied, productive and adaptable.

Linked with commitment is the question of employee involvement. If employees have an input into or control over the firm's decisions, they're likely to be more committed to both the processes and the results.

In the jargon of HRM, employees should have feelings of 'ownership' of their work. If objectives and processes are simply imposed by senior management, it's unlikely that employees will feel ownership over what they're doing.

And if problems arise the likelihood is that employees will see it as management's problem rather than something they should be involved in solving.

The third distinctive feature of HRM is the desire to make enterprises more flexible and adaptable. The environment in which firms exist is continually changing and managers want to be able to respond to those changes more quickly and easily.

As it relates to workers, the push for flexibility can involve many things: the greater reliance on part-time and casual workers, the 'outsourcing' of peripheral activities formerly performed in-house, the ability to adjust the number of working hours and the timing of work through overtime, shift work and staggered leave, and greater freedom to change the deployment of workers to different activities (which is made possible by fewer demarcations and greater 'multi-skilling').

The final feature of HRM is a commitment to 'quality'—the provision of goods and services that not only are free from deficiencies but also meet customers' needs.

Quality can be achieved by rigorous supervision of employees, but the HRM approach involves passing the responsibility for quality to those who are actually producing the goods and services.

It's usually argued that high-quality goods and services require a high-quality workforce—which, in turn, means giving a lot of attention to the training of workers.

Now, I have to tell you that I'm excited by the ideals of human resource management and I'm a great believer in it. For a start, it's an important means to the end of more competitive, successful Australian firms—which means a better functioning economy.

Even better, it's an end in itself. Most of us have to work for a living. Most of us would like to earn a better living. But what a bonus it would be to get more enjoyment out of our work.

And that's the prospect HRM holds out. Bosses treat us as valuable assets to be nurtured, not costs to be controlled. We're given fewer orders, more autonomy and responsibility. Our skills are valued, we get a say in decisions that affect us plus more training to make us more valuable.

We're treated as adults rather than children. We work in an environment of mutual respect, trust and co-operation. We believe in our organisation's goals and when problems arise we play our part in solving them.

Suddenly, we not only enjoy picking up our cheque at the end of the week, we also enjoy going to work. Does that raise our quality of life, would you think?

That's the vision of human resource management and, as I say, I believe in it. But I also have to say that the vision and the reality are often far apart.

These days most big organisations profess to be following the precepts of HRM. Most have replaced their industrial relations departments or personnel departments (or both) with human resource departments. (Does that ring a bell with what's happening at your work?)

HRM is the fashion. But the actual commitment to it varies through the spectrum from full-on to lip-service.

Sometimes the motivation for adopting HRM is suspect. Some senior managers want to use professions of love and care as a substitute for money. That is, to con workers into contributing more without them getting their fair share of the proceeds of their extra effort.

Some managers want workers to be more co-operative without those managers giving up their prerogative to call the shots.

Sometimes, bosses' vision of better relations with their employees means being able to deal directly with workers without the involvement of unions. To them, 'industrial relations' means unions and is bad, whereas 'employee relations' means no unions and is good. Not surprisingly, some unions see HRM as an anti-union plot.

But enlightened bosses know they need to work through the relevant unions to achieve improved relations with their employees, and enlightened unions are co-operating with HRM because they know it will benefit their members.

Even when motives are genuine, however, there still can be problems. For instance, there is potential for conflict between the goal of greater flexibility—being able to turn labour on and off—and the view of employees as valuable assets to be husbanded.

Genuinely applied, it is an expensive strategy that stresses quality rather than price. You put money into developing and training your staff, and you don't part with them just because there's a temporary fall in the demand for your product.

What's more, the experts say that the payoff from it can take maybe seven to ten years—which doesn't sit easily with the short-term performance appraisal to which listed companies in English-speaking countries are subjected.

Consider the way many big companies resorted to cost-cutting and extensive redundancies during the recession, in an attempt to bolster their weak financial performance and sagging share prices.

I remain a believer in the value of human resource management. But, clearly, we have a lot to learn and a long way to go.

Source: *Sydney Morning Herald*, 7 June 1995, p. 17.

This process of alignment involves the management of organisational change so that the organisation is able to deal effectively with the environmental influences and pressures which are expected to occur. This involves developing policies and providing leadership which encourages the desired behaviour, values and combinations of stakeholders, appropriate organisational structures and strategy, and effective communication techniques. The process is likely to involve a transition from one culture to another.

The process of managing change can involve more than responding to changes in the environment or imitating the practices of successful competitors. Hamel & Prahalad

(1989, pp. 64–65) argue that successful companies have an 'obsession with winning at all levels of the organisation' and that they are able to maintain this obsession over a long-term period. Rather than restricting ambitions in response to limited resources, these companies based their strategy on leveraging resources to achieve an apparently unattainable position of leadership. This approach to change is called **strategic intent**.

The extract from the article 'Better milk from contented cows' highlights some of the benefits of human resource management policies for some of the stakeholders in the employment relationship. It also highlights some of the issues associated with its application, particularly with its implementation.

Models of strategic human resource management

A variety of models provide insights into the character of strategic human resource management based on a rational approach. Although these models all identify the relationship between the external and internal environments of the organisation and human resource management policies, there are differences in the extent to which the models describe and emphasise aspects of policies and practices within the organisation. They also differ in the extent to which they address the dynamic nature of strategic human resource management. Rather than identifying the 'one best model', a range of models are described.

These models can be categorised into three groups:

1 **General frameworks** which identify relationships between external and organisational factors
2 **Organisational frameworks** which identify relationships between factors within the organisation
3 **Frameworks** which identify specific human resource policies for particular organisational and external conditions.

The first group includes the Harvard model developed by Beer, Spector, Lawrence, Mills & Walton (1985), and the model described by Collins (1994). The second group includes the model of Devanna, Frombrun & Tichy (1984) which identifies specific relationships between strategy, structure and human resource policies and the model developed by Schuler and labelled 'The 5P model'. The third group includes models which detail the particular types of policies which are appropriate for certain situations. These include the Dowling & Schuler (1991) framework and the Dunphy & Stace (1992; 1994) frameworks.

General models

Harvard model

The first model of human resource management which became commonly known was the model developed at Harvard by Beer et al. (1985). This model was a watershed because it reconceptualised human resource policies in terms of four policy choices:

1 Employee influence
2 Human resource flow
3 Reward systems
4 Work systems.

It also identifies a variety of stakeholders who have interests in the practice and outcomes of human resource management policies. Figure 2.2 describes the relationships between stakeholder interests, situational factors, HRM policy choices, HR outcomes and Long-term consequences. However, this model does not provide insights into the processes of formulating and implementing HRM policy choices.

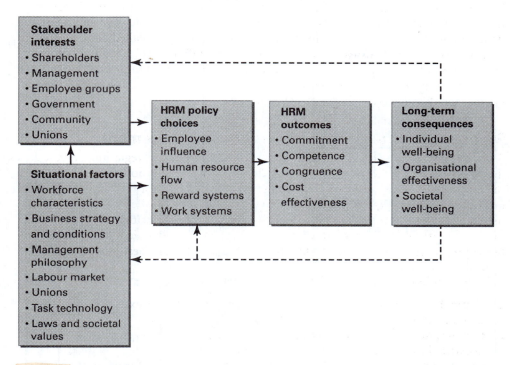

Figure 2.2 Map of the HRM territory
Source: Beer et al. 1985, p. 16

Collins model

Collins (1994) uses a systems framework to describe the relationships between the key factors involved in effective strategic human resource management. A modified form of this framework is described in Figure 2.3.

This model identifies some of the key issues associated with creating internal and external fit. These include mission, strategy, structure, culture, workforce characteristics and personnel or human resource policies. The outcomes of the effectiveness of the policies in creating 'fit' are identified as profitability, market share, product quality, corporate image, innovation, productivity, morale and turnover.

This model does not, however, provide insights into which particular human resource management strategies and policies are appropriate for particular organisational strategies and structures. Nor does it address the importance of creating a fit between the structures associated with the provisions of human resource management policies and other structures and strategies in the organisation.

Models detailing relationships within organisations

Frombrun, Tichy & Devanna

Frombrun, Tichy & Devanna (1984) developed specific details on the relationship between strategy, structure and human resource policies. They argue that just as organisations will face inefficiencies when they try to implement new strategies with outmoded structures so too will they face problems when they try and implement

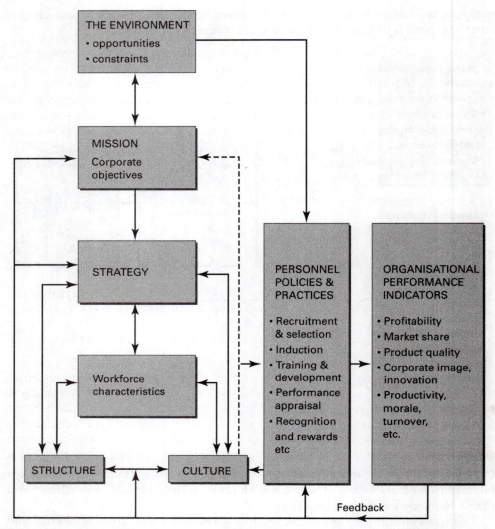

Figure 2.3 A framework depicting selected aspects of organisation design, with personnel function and organisational performance

Source: Collins 1994, p. 42

strategy with inappropriate human resource systems. They claim four human resource systems need to be considered. These are the systems of selection, appraisal, rewards and development.

They point out that HR departments are really functioning at three levels: the strategic, managerial and operational which involve three time frames. Their framework details the relationship between business functions and human resource functions at the day-to-day operational level, at the medium-term managerial level and at the longer-term strategic level. At the strategic level, these activities include policies designed to encourage 'fit' in the future; at the managerial level, these activities include those which ensure the acquisition, retention and development of people; while at the operational level the activities include daily support of business activities.

Schuler 5Ps

This model (Schuler 1992) is useful because it provides insight into the scope of human resource activities. The 5-P model develops the interrelationships between the strategic needs of an organisation and five human resource activities which have been labelled as the five Ps. By identifying these five activities this model identifies the complex interaction of human resource activities necessary to shape individual and group behaviour so that it achieves the strategic needs of the organisation. These strategic business needs are expressed in the mission or vision statements and then these are translated into strategic business objectives.

Figure 2.4 describes the five human resource activities which can be used to shape behaviour. These are:

1. **Human resources philosophy**—a statement of how an organisation regards its human resources
2. **Human resource policies**—expressed as shared values which serve as guidelines for action on people-related issues
3. **Human resources programs**—co-ordinated efforts to achieve strategic goals and expressed as human resource strategies
4. **Human resources practices**—identifying the behaviours needed to achieve the three roles of leadership, managerial and operational and developing HR practices to cue and reinforce these behaviours
5. **Human resources processes**—'how' all the above activities are identified, formulated and implemented.

Schuler (1992, pp. 30–31) suggests successful efforts at strategic HR management commence with the identification of strategic business needs and the systematic analysis of their impact on the five human resource management activities. The link between strategy and HR practices can be fostered by involving employees in the identification of their new roles. In addition, executives involved in the process of strategic human resource management require a systematic and analytical manner when identifying strategic needs and designing HR activities. The process of strategic human resource management also provides HR departments with an opportunity to be involved in the formulation of strategy.

These models however, don't identify when particular human resource policies are appropriate. The following two models identify the way particular human resource policies can be used to create organisational fit and align the organisation to its business strategy and environment.

Specific relationships

Dowling & Schuler

Dowling & Schuler (1990) have developed a model which identifies the types of human resource policies which are appropriate for encouraging the behaviour necessary for the achievement of particular competitive strategies. They identify three competitive strategies: quality enhancement, cost reduction and innovation strategies.

Dowling & Schuler (1990, pp. 144–46) argue that the appropriateness of competitive strategies is influenced by the life-cycle stage of the firm. They identify three stages:

1. The entrepreneurial/growth stage
2. The mature/decline stage
3. The turnaround stage.

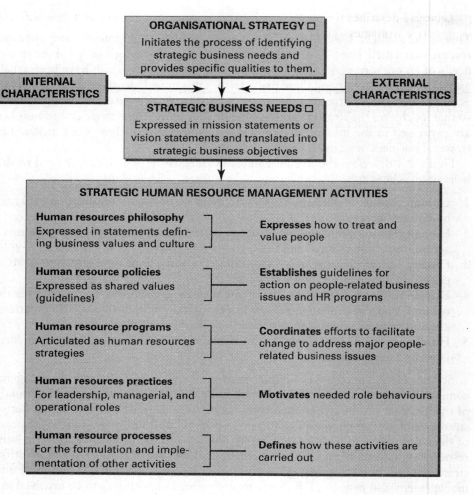

Figure 2.4 The 5-P model: linking strategic business needs and strategic HR management activities

Source: Schuler 1992, p. 20

During the entrepreneurial/growth stage, the strategy stresses innovation and new product development and is facilitated by employees who are innovative, co-operative, longer-term oriented, risk taking, and display willingness to assume responsibility. In comparison, during the mature/decline stage the emphasis on strategy is 'taking away as much as possible from the existing product ... emphasis is on increased production runs and cost cutting, the real HRM challenge is attracting and retaining capable employees' (Dowling & Schuler 1990, p. 146). The final stage is the turnaround stage during which organisational survival is stressed through cost cutting. This can occur by reducing the number of employees and by enhancing the number of the employees and enhancing the quality of products.

Table 2.2 describes the packages of HRM practices which are consistent with these competitive strategies and life cycles.

Table 2.2 Consistent packages of HRM practices and competitive strategies

INNOVATION STRATEGY AND KEY HUMAN RESOURCE MANAGEMENT PRACTICES	Mostly short-term criteria
	Same group criteria
	Some employment criteria
High participation	Some incentives
Implicit job analysis	Egalitarian pay
External sources	Extensive training
Broad career paths	Co-operative labour–management
Process and results criteria	relations
Long-term criteria	
Same group criteria	**COST-REDUCTION STRATEGY AND KEY**
Some employment security	**HUMAN RESOURCE MANAGEMENT**
Many incentives	**PRACTICES**
Egalitarian pay	Low participation
Extensive training	Explicit job analysis
Co-operative labour–management relations	Mostly internal sources
	Narrow career paths
	Results criteria
QUALITY-ENHANCEMENT STRATEGY AND KEY HUMAN RESOURCE MANAGEMENT PRACTICES	Short-term criteria
	Mostly individual criteria
	Little employment security
High participation	Few incentives
Explicit job analysis	Hierarchical pay
Some external sources	Little training
Narrow career paths	Traditional labour–management relations.
Mostly results criteria	

Source: Dowling & Schuler 1990, p. 137

Dunphy & Stace

Dunphy & Stace (1992; 1994) claim an organisation's change program which is designed to move the organisation back into strategic fit with its environment is a major determinant of the types of human resource strategies and policies which are most appropriate. They claim the organisation's change program is an important intervening variable between the broader business strategy and HRM strategy.

Their model identifies the types of leadership behaviour, communication strategies, human resource policies, organisational change and business strategies appropriate to particular environmental conditions. Their research identified four approaches to change which have been successfully used in Australian organisations to maintain or realign their organisations with the business environment. These four approaches are:

1   Developmental transitions
2   Task-focused transitions
3   Charismatic transformations
4   Turnarounds.

They found that in environments where markets are growing, a successful model of change is the developmental transitions model which requires leaders who are coaches and able to develop commitment to a shared vision. In environments where markets/products/services are undergoing major changes and where 'niche' exploratory strategies are widespread, a successful model of change is the task-focused transitions model and this requires leaders who are captains and able to obtain compliance with internally consistent redefinition of task performance systems. In circumstances when the business environment changes dramatically or a radical repositioning of the organisation is required, the charismatic transformation model was found to be successful. It required charismatic leaders who were able to secure voluntary commitment to a radically new vision. The fourth change model was found to be successful in environments where the organisation was not aligned with its environment and it was necessary for leaders to behave like commanders and obtain compliance to radically redefined behavioural goals, norms and performance standards.

It is possible to draw out the implications of these relationships for human resource policies. For instance, if a fit between the external conditions and internal conditions is to be achieved, there needs to be a fit with human resource policies such as the selection criteria, training arrangements and performance and reward policies will depend on the type of change strategy used.

Future organisational forms

How a strife-torn factory got back on the rails

The culture of a Melbourne transport engineering works has been transformed since its new owner involved the workers in decision-making.

BY DAVID FORMAN

Pat Rochford remembers the day Lars Brodin, the managing director of Asea Brown Boveri Transportation in Australia, came to address the workforce at the company's newly acquired train and tram factory in the Melbourne suburb of Dandenong.

Brodin's visit was the start of a process that is transforming the business from an industrial relations disaster into an organisation revitalised by a committed workforce. What has happened in the Dandenong workshops is an example of how ABB applies its international program of workplace culture reform. Although the model that is developing in Dandenong has similarities to programs ABB has in other factories, it has been allowed to evolve to suit local requirements; it has not been imposed from above. A once militant workforce has embraced the program, and Rochford—a former shop steward—is now second-in-charge of it.

ABB, a big Swedish–Swiss engineering group, has an international strategy to flatten its management structures and reduce the barriers between white-collar and blue-collar workers. The linchpin of the program is to increase the level and the extent of

> workforce skills, giving employees more control over the work that has to be done.
>
> The method of applying the strategy is consistent with what ABBs chief executive, Percy Barnevik, calls the three internal contradictions of the organisation: it is global and local, big and small, and decentralised but with central reporting and control. Barnevik says all businesses within the ABB global conglomerate operate as insiders within their home markets to maximise their own performance. At the same time, the core skills in each of the parts of the organisation can be brought together to bid for international work, providing advantages of scale and skill.

Source: *BRW*, 26 March 1993, pp. 68–70.

The article 'How a strife-torn factory got back on the rails' highlights some of the key issues of strategic HR:

1. The relationships between strategy, structure and an organisational change program which in this case has as its linchpin human resource policies focusing on work reorganisation and the empowering of employees.
2. The partnership between various stakeholders, such as the international and Australian managements, the employees and external consultants.
3. The interaction between human resource policies such as work organisation, industrial relations, human resource planning and training.
4. Employees are seen as more than just cogs in a production process and a cost, but as valuable sources of information and skills necessary for the design of the production process.
5. The need to develop and train employees so they are able to enhance their skills.

Processes associated with strategic human resource management

When a rational approach is adopted the process of strategic human resource management has two components. These components are first, strategy formulation which includes environmental assessment and strategy development and second, strategy implementation. The effective development and implementation of strategic human resource management requires an assessment of the impact of current and expected developments in the external and internal environments on the organisation and then an assessment of what this means for human resource management policies and practices. Figure 2.5 describes the three components and key elements of the strategic management process.

ENVIRONMENTAL ASSESSMENT	STRATEGY DEVELOPMENT	STRATEGY IMPLEMENTATION
Scan external and internal environment	Review/revise mission, vision	Align expectations, organisation, people, and performance management
	Set strategic objectives	
Assess strengths, weaknesses, opportunities, and treats (SWOTs)	Develop action plans/ programs	Apply systems and technology
Define core competence, competitive advantage	Allocate resources	Evaluate effectiveness
Define strategic issues		

Figure 2.5 The strategic management process
Source: Walker 1992, p. 68

Environmental assessment

A variety of aspects of the external environment will have a critical influence on the identification of human resource issues and the development of human resource management policies. These aspects include domestic and international competition, population and workforce demographics, legislation, technology, trade unions, business partners and government policy. These issues are considered briefly in the next section of the chapter. Similarly, some of the factors within the internal environment which will influence human resource issues are employees and managers, organisational structure, the culture, resources, organisational strategy.

An assessment of the organisation's internal and external environment involves collecting and examining data which will indicate future trends and changes in the organisation and in the external environment. Once a wide collection of information has been made, there are two fundamentally different ways to identify noteworthy changes in the environment. These two ways are:

1. Incremental change analysis
2. Futures analysis.

Incremental change analysis

Incremental change analysis involves identifying the changes which are expected to occur in the environments and the implications of these changes for human resource issues. This identification can involve collecting information from a variety of stakeholders through surveys, focus groups and interviews and from secondary sources such as newspapers, magazines, journals and government publications. Organisations then assess their human resource practices relative to those of competitor companies. The process of benchmarking practices against other organisations which are regarded as 'best practice' is one way of doing this assessment.

This incremental change analysis of the environment can be understood through a process which involves:

1. Gathering current data
2. Forecasting future conditions
3. Identifying and prioritising major issues that effect HR management
4. Developing plans that anticipate those issues
5. Preparing the organisation for successfully dealing with them.

Futures analysis

The second way of conducting an environmental assessment is to focus on the longer-term future using the process of visioning or 'futures analysis'. This process often requires stakeholders to go beyond the strategic planning period to say the year 2010. Futures analysis involves open thinking about future issues and options. The methods which can be used to help define future human resource management issues are brainstorming, visioning or modified Delphi analysis. Outside consultants can be useful facilitators and sources of information on demographic, technological and environmental futures (Walker 1992, pp. 30–31). The process of futures analysis examines discontinuities in the environment, while the incremental change analysis examines continuities (Drucker 1980).

Regardless of the type of environmental assessment process used, the process of identifying the gaps between the present and future positions involves assessing the strengths, weaknesses, opportunities and threats in the environment which will influence the achievement of the required human resource strategy. It also involves defining the core human resource competencies.

Strategy development

Once the environmental assessment is conducted, the process of strategy development takes place. This requires identifying the way human resource issues can be effectively managed to achieve the organisation's strategic mission and vision and to support the values of the organisation. This development can, like other organisational strategies, involve a two-way process of planning. It can involve a top-down process and a bottom-up process. The top-down process provides a long-term time horizon and a context for the development of action plans and performance plans. The bottom-up approach rather than breaking broad strategies down, involves the aggregation and synthesis of information about human resource issues and ways of dealing with them as identified by divisions, departments and human resource staff. These processes can involve the identification of human resource objectives.

Two other parts of the strategy formulation process involve the translation of the human resource issues into action plans and the identification of the resources required for the achievement of these action plans. These action plans deal with how the plans will be implemented by managers, the communication of changes, the implementation of training programs, the identification of performance objectives, incentive programs and measures used for the evaluation of the success of the human resource strategies.

A human resource strategy requires the use of resources, so action plans need to also specify the costs and resources required to achieve the plans. These costs can include employee salaries, office expenses, consultants fees, survey costs, development and relocation costs. Figure 2.6 describes the main aspects of the process of strategy formulation.

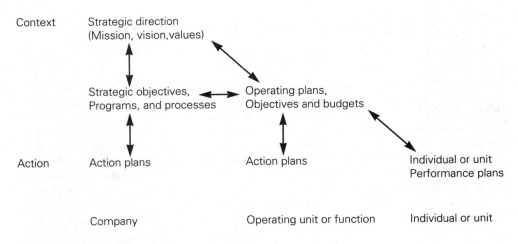

Figure 2.6 Elements of strategy formulation
Source: Walker 1992, p. 69

Implementation

An excellent strategy is unlikely to achieve the organisation's objectives unless it is effectively implemented. Effective implementation requires the alignment of employee expectations, organisation design, staffing and development capabilities, and performance management with strategy (Walker 1992, p. 82). It also requires the application of a variety of resources including people and skills, technology, systems and finance.

The process of implementation can best be achieved by anticipating which aspects of the organisation will support or impede the implementation of policies. The implementation plan needs to include multiple actions so the application of actions can change as conditions change and lessons are learnt about the process of implementation. An implementation plan contains explicit elements which are precisely expressed and also implicit elements which emerge informally.

Important elements of the implementation process are that of monitoring and evaluation. Monitoring involves having procedures in place which check that a change in policy is being implemented. This could take the form of an Action Sheet which identifies who is to co-ordinate the implementation, the time frame during which the policy will be implemented, the resources required and any anticipated problems.

The results of the human resource strategies can be evaluated using a variety of indicators such as turnover and absenteeism rates, performance assessments, customer satisfaction, wastage rates and accident rates. It is difficult drawing a clear line of causation between HR policies and organisational performance indicators, such as profitability and market share. However, expenditure on wages and salaries can influence costs and profitability, and particular employee behaviour, such as innovation and entrepreneurship can facilitate increases in market share.

HRM IN THE NEWS

Concretes' twin pillars of growth

BY TONY THOMAS

'Staying in profit in our business is a pretty wonderful thing', John Lewis, the chairman, says. Known in the trade as 'Concretes', it is one of three big private contractors in Australia; the others are Grollo and the Perth-based multiplex of John Robert.

Lewis is overseeing a big overhaul of his company by managing director Paul White, to match the hard times; about 45 staff out of 970 are being retrenched. The grand plan is for a push into Asia and for 40 per cent of turnover to be generated overseas by 1995.

The group has a dual strategy of building Asian operations to escape the local boom/bust cycle, and winning local work through an ability to guarantee on-time, on-budget performance, thanks to Concretes' harmonious workplace relations.

The Asian push is based on planning rather than ad hoc securing of overseas contracts. Managing director Paul White heads a team that tested the countries in search of political stability, seeking gaps the company could fill in the construction sector.

'For example, Hong Kong, Taiwan, Singapore and Korea have big projects but plenty of good foreign and local contractors. For us, it was really a matter of finding which countries consistently were unable to bring big projects in on time, quality and budget'.

In Australia, Concretes' goal is to lift its performance to enable it to meet any client demands for on-time, on-budget and on-quality guarantees. 'Otherwise, we would be back there with the pack', says White, who has been with Concretes for 30 years. 'Our strength is in the planning and investigation stage, where we can anticipate the problems'.

In the late 1980s, no amount of back-office planning could offset the problems created by sour industrial relations on site and lack of career progress for workers. 'For example, someone pushing a broom expected to be still pushing it 40 years later', White says.

The system had been negotiated centrally between the employer associations and the peak federal unions. Bill Stelmach, Concretes' human resources manager, says: 'Of course, no one at grass roots really understood it, and since they had never been consulted about it, they had no loyalty to it. Things stayed adversarial'.

The breakthrough began late in 1987, when managers were presented with about 20 demands by their six Sydney crane drivers for wage rises, Gucci sunglasses, deerskin boots and extra climbing-up-and-down time. The issues went to the 'lofty drivers' committee' which included some crane drivers from rival groups such as multiplex.

Concretes asked the committee if the company had a right to remain competitive, in other words, survive.

Source: *BRW*, 26 March 1993, pp. 64–67.

The extracts from the article 'Concretes' twin pillars of growth' identifies some of the processes associated with a strategic approach to human resource management. Note the use of environmental assessment to develop a business strategy and goals within particular countries. Also note the way particular human resource policies were identified as being important for the achievement of these goals.

Understanding developments in the external environment

Managing change

Universities confront the need for a new discipline

Australia's academics have languished in age-old practices for decades. However, the new era of education as a more social apparatus requires change.

BY DAVID JAMES

Ken Jarrott, director of enterprise training at the Royal Melbourne Institute of Technology, says that universities have been open to manipulation because they lacked a defined objective. 'Management has been more laissez-faire, even fairly anarchic, meaning that it has relied heavily on the quality of individuals', he says.

Jarrott says there is a long-term trend away from different sources of private funding. He believes there will be increasing competition among universities to attract funding from a variety of sources. 'The growth is not going to come from federally funded university places', Jarrott says. 'The universities are starting to move into multifaceted partnerships, which will require greater flexibility. It will also mean that universities will lose some autonomy. It will mean that some people in the university will be pursuing their individual interests, some will pursue the interests that match the corporate strategy, and some will pursue interests that reflect outside funding'.

The challenges facing academic management are similar to those facing many other organisations: adapting to change, serving their clients well (either when teaching or researching), moving to a more global perspective, developing multi-skilled teams, managing facilities more effectively, and eliciting participation through proper management and leadership. What is different is the sheer complexity of the task because of the variety of allegiances.

'Initially many of the academics asked, What are management skills, and why should we be concerned? but they realised that it is important to develop leadership and vision and management skills to lead us through this period of change'.

'Some of the Asian countries prefer education on their own shores, but with international support. Some universities are establishing partnerships overseas. There are open universities here and in Britain already'.

'Leaders must go to the group and ask what they would like to be, and what they would like the department to be like. That process gets people involved'.

If the management of people is improving in universities, the management of physical resources still lags. Most universities are empty for one-third of the year, suggesting that the over-crowding during the remaining two-thirds could be alleviated with some lateral thinking. However, there have been few attempts to rationalise physical resources more effectively, although many universities are running non-degree summer school courses.

Drucker argues that education will increasingly have to merge its traditional concerns with more practical technical and commercial considerations.

'The educated person will have to be prepared to live and work simultaneously in two cultures, that of the intellectual who focuses on words and ideas, and that of the manager who focuses on people and work. They relate to each other as poles, rather than contradictions. The intellectual's world, unless counterbalanced by the manager, becomes one in which everyone does his own thing but nobody does anything. The manager's world, unless counterbalanced by the intellectual becomes bureaucracy and the creative greyness of the organisation man. But if the two balance each other there can be creativity and order, fulfilment and mission'.

Source: *BRW*, 5 March 1993, pp. 80–83.

The article 'Universities confront the need for a new discipline' highlights some of the HR implications of changes in the environment on staff in Australian universities and on human resource management policies and practices. The reduction in government funding has increased competition between universities. There have also been other changes such as a fall in real wages, the development of a global perspective and a government decision to amalgamate tertiary institutions of education.

The article highlights the way the changes in the external environment have influenced human resource issues such as the organisational structures in universities, the development of more participative management processes, the way university work, particularly teaching and research, is done and the understanding of skills required of academics. It shows the importance of understanding the external environment and knowing what is going on out there. This means continually scanning the environment and determining what it means for human resource management.

Figure 2.7 describes an exercise which allows you to assess the future impact of developments in the environment on human resource issues. Study the Figure and answer the questions. Describe the implications of the discrepancies between your answers for today and the year 2000 for the impact on human resource management.

Many observers have predicted significant changes in the environment for the twenty-first century. Some of these changes are listed below. Please choose and rank the *five* changes that you think currently have the most impact on HR management, and the *five* that you think will have the most impact in the future: '1' indicates the highest impact, '2' indicates the next highest impact, etc.

Today		Environment	2000+
_____	a	Increased national/international competition	_____
_____	b	Increased governmental regulation	_____
_____	c	Globalisation of corporate business structure	_____
_____	d	Growth in nontraditional business structure (e.g. business alliances, joint ventures)	_____
_____	e	Globalisation of the economy/breakdown of trade barriers	_____
_____	f	Increased energy costs	_____
_____	g	Increased reliance on automation/technology to produce goods and services	_____
_____	h	More sophisticated information/communication technology	_____
_____	i	Changing attitudes of society towards business	_____
_____	j	Heightened concern about pollution and natural resources	_____
_____	k	Heightened focus on total quality/customer satisfaction	_____
_____	l	Changing employee values, goals, and expectations (e.g. less loyalty to current employer)	_____
_____	m	Fewer entrants into the workforce	_____
_____	n	Inadequate skills of entrants into the workforce	_____
_____	o	Cross-border application of employee rights	_____
_____	p	Changing composition of the workforce with respect to gender, age, and/or ethnicity	_____
_____	q	Greater concerns about the confidentiality of personal information	_____

Figure 2.7 Implications of changes in the environment

Source: Schuler 1995, p. 63, based on *Priorities for Competitive Advantage* (IBM, Towers Perrin, 1992)

Many aspects of the external environment have an impact on an organisation's human resource management policies. Legislation such as affirmative action and anti-discrimination, occupational health and safety and industrial relations legislation prescribe certain standards for human resource policies and stakeholder behaviour. The details of this legislation are examined later in the book.

Other aspects of the external environment will continue to change and these changes will have implications for human resource management. These changes include developments in domestic and international competition, the emerging nature of the workforce, including changes in its demographic characteristics, developments in industrial and economic structures and advances in technology.

Domestic and international competition

Domestic and international competition has increased in recent years as a consequence of a number of policy developments. Deregulation of many areas including the financial markets and telecommunications and the removal of protection from some industries such as the clothing, textile and footwear industries have increased competition from overseas organisations. The Commonwealth government has also allowed the exchange rate to float, thus forcing investments in Australia to compete with those from other countries. Trade within the Asia-Pacific region will open up in the future as a result of the Asia-Pacific Economic Co-ordination agreements.

Intense levels of domestic and international competition are forcing organisations to reform their business strategies and to be more productive using more efficient human resource management policies. Increasing levels of competition have also encouraged the reform of industrial relations practices with the introduction of principles which link wage and condition increases to improvements in productivity. Governments have supported these changes through a variety of measures including the establishment of programs supporting the implementation of workplace reform, the amendment of industrial legislation and the ratification of ILO Conventions.

Some of the trends resulting from these economic and legislative reforms which are expected to continue are the growth in Australian organisations doing business overseas, particularly in the Asian region, and an increase in exports of elaborately transformed manufactures and high value-adding services (Industry Task Force on Leadership and Management Skills 1995, pp. 55–61). The majority of manufacturing and service exporters are small to medium-sized enterprises and it is expected these will generate employment growth in the future. Greater numbers of Australian organisations will also face competition from overseas companies in the domestic market. Consequently, in an environment where the domestic market is not large enough to support the populations aspirations for a high standard of living, there will be a continuing need for Australian organisations to reform their employment practices.

Some of the implications of increased international competition and a larger export market will be the need for managers to develop a broader range of skills, and a capacity to learn their roles as managers. The skills managers will need to include the ability to manage customers from diverse cultural backgrounds, greater cross-cultural awareness, the development of leadership skills, including a long-term focus, people and entrepreneurial skills (Industry Task Force on Leadership and Management Skills 1995, p. 136).

The effective management of people has been identified as essential in these increasingly competitive circumstances. It has been claimed that organisations will need to compete on quality, innovation, R&D, and on people. Long-term success results from continuous improvement, new systems of work, flattened hierarchies, self managing work groups, simultaneous design in manufacturing, total quality systems and open communications. Long-term competitiveness is not seen to result through cutting benefits from its people (Schneider 1994).

Emerging social structure

Another expected development in the external environment which is influencing the development and implementation of human resource policies is the changing nature of the social structure. Three shifts in Australian social structure have been identified as being most significant for the management of organisations in the future (Carter,

Nicholson & Barlow 1995). These three shifts are:
1. Growth in flexible working arrangements
2. Group of women in management
3. Increasing levels of education in the workforce generally.

A further change will be the continuing increase in the representation of women in the workforce in general. Women, especially women with dependents, will increase their involvement in the labour market. This particular change is an integral part of the first two shifts, growth in flexible working arrangements and women in management, and is therefore considered first.

Women in the workforce

The composition of the workforce has become more diverse since the end of the Second World War. Women, particularly married women and women with children, have become a more important part of the workforce. The representation of women in the workforce increased from 25 per cent in 1947 to 42 per cent in 1993 (ABS Catalogue no. 4102.0, p. 100). Between 1954 and 1990, the proportion of married women in the workforce increased from 17 per cent to 53 per cent (ABS Catalogue no. 6224.0) and in 1990, 59 per cent of these women had dependent children.

Figure 2.8 describes the changing nature of the impact of having children on women. It shows that during the 1970s nearly 90 per cent of women resigned from their jobs following the birth of a child, while by the late 1980s, a higher number of women remained in the workforce. The representation of women is expected to increase. It is predicted that by the year 2000, 59 per cent of women will be in the workforce and that this will be driven by married women remaining in the workforce after the birth of their children (Carter, Nicholson & Barlow 1995, p. 1260).

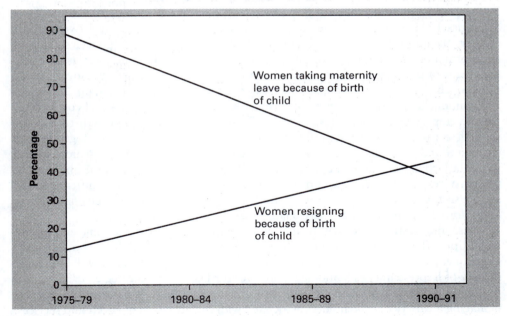

Figure 2.8 The impact of children on working women (%)
Source: Carter et al. 1995, p. 126

An increasing proportion of the workforce combine domestic, child care and employment responsibilities and it is expected that this will continue. Women continue to perform most of the domestic and child care activities in households (Bittman 1991) and the ABS studies demonstrate employees seeking to balance work and family life experience stress and difficulties (Wolcott 1991) and that for women these difficulties increase with the number of hours worked (ABS Catalogue no. 4418.0).

The structure of families are also changing with increases in divorce and single parent families (ABS Catalogue no. 4420.0). Single parent families with dependent children represented 15 per cent of all families in 1990 and of those households with children under 15 years of age, 47 per cent of single mothers and 69 per cent of single fathers were in the labour force (Vanden Heuval 1993, p. 8). Even in married-couple families with dependents present 58 per cent of families had both partners in the workforce (ABS Catalogue no. 6224.0).

Consequently, one of the issues human resource professionals will need to address in the future will be the implementation of policies which facilitate the combination of employment and the fulfilment of domestic responsibilities. The Australian government supports the development of these policies in a number of ways including through the Work and Family Unit which produces booklets to assist employers with the development of these policies and through assistance with the provision of child-care services. The Australian Industrial Relations Commission (AIRC) also supports the implementation of these policies through its decisions which provide for parental leave and the more flexible use of sick leave.

Flexible working arrangements

Flexible working arrangements in the form of part-time employment, casual work and the use of contractors have increased during the last ten years (ABS 1994 Australian Social Trends, p. 103; House of Representatives Standing Committee for Long Term Strategies 1995) and are expected to continue to increase during the next twenty years (Carter, Nicholson & Barlow 1995). The concept of employee is undergoing a significant transformation as some employees through their superannuation funds increasingly own the means of production. However, at the same time, they are legally employees: being hired, open to being fired and receiving a salary or wage (Drucker 1994, pp. 53–80).

Economic and industrial relations changes have resulted in substantial cost savings for the employment of part-time labour. These include the high growth rate of the services sector, particularly in the information and personal services areas, together with structural and workplace changes in many service occupations. These structural and workplace changes include the introduction of split or 12-hour shifts, the abolition of penalty rates and the relaxation of restrictions on trading hours. It is anticipated the service sector will continue to grow in areas such as tourism, health, personal services and information technology. These changes are detailed in Table 2.3.

These industrial changes will further enhance the demand for part-time employees. In addition the it is anticipated increasing amounts of work will be 'outsourced'. Consequently, a wide range of opportunities in the area of small business will be created (House of Representatives Standing Committee for Long Term Strategies 1995, p. 11).

One of the results of these changes is that managing human resources will involve managing a variety of stakeholders associated with the provision of goods and services. This will involve not only managing employees, but also consultants, subcontractors and joint venture partners. As demonstrated by the CRA dispute in 1995 involving a dispute about the relative pay rates of employees and contractors performing the same work. This will further complicate human resource management and require excellent communication, negotiation and strategic planning skills.

Table 2.3 Australian Industry 1800–2030

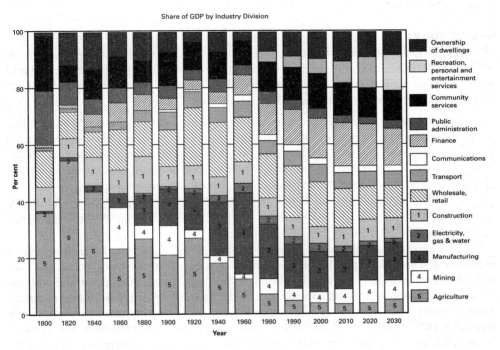

Source: House of Representatives Standing Committee 1995, p. 7

Women in management

Although women represented 42 per cent of the workforce in 1993, they represented only 26 per cent of the managerial workforce. However, their representation in senior managerial positions is even less than this, with women representing only 14 per cent of general managers and 22 per cent of specialist managers, while they represent 33 per cent of managing supervisors, sales and service managers and 11 per cent of other managing supervisors (Burton & Ryall 1995, p. 773). The progress of women into senior management has been slow and compared to other industrialised countries the representation of women in managerial positions is one of the lowest percentages (Still 1993, p. 26).

There are two conflicting views about the nature of women's representation in management in the future. One view which is widely held is that the **glass ceiling** is becoming thicker and even being lowered, so it will be even more difficult for women to enter senior management positions. The other view indicates that women will enter management positions in even greater numbers because of their increasing representation in the workforce, their high educational qualifications and general community expectations about the role of women in organisational structures (Report on the Industry Task Force on Leadership and Management Skills 1995, pp. 124–25).

Educational attainment

Another major shift will be the increasing education level of the workforce. In 1987, 46 per cent of the workforce held a tertiary qualification, and it is predicted that by the year 2001, nearly 60 per cent of the workforce will hold a tertiary qualification. This development will facilitate the greater involvement of employees in decision making, information digestion and increased autonomy in the workplace (Carter, Nicholson & Barlow 1995, pp. 1265–66).

Technology

Technology generally refers to the equipment and knowledge used to produce goods and services. There has been a virtual discarding of the technology used in the past and in their replacement with new technologies such as the 'lean' production systems of Eiji Toyoda of Toyota and his production genius, Taiichi Ohno:

> Just as the mass-production principles pioneered by Henry Ford and General Motors' Alfred Sloan swept away the age of craft production after the First World War, so the ideas of Toyoda and Ohno are today chipping away at the foundations of mass production. We call their system 'lean' production because it uses less of everything than a comparable mass-production operation: half the investment in tools, half the engineering hours to develop a new product. Lean production is built not simply on technical insight but on a precisely defined set of relationships that extends far beyond the factory floor to encompass designers, suppliers, and customers (Schuler 1995, p. 92).

In many organisations today, current employees skills are insufficient because of these technological changes. Employees need to not only learn new skills now, but they will need to continually retrain. Changing technology necessitates continual training program formulation and implementation, and employees who are willing to adapt, to be reassigned to different jobs, and to be retrained. By encouraging and supporting employees in these efforts, employers can assist with providing employment security.

In Australia, a number of approaches to this need have been developed. The Australian government is seeking to encourage employers to spend more on training and development. Changes in the industrial relations arena also attempt to do this through rewriting awards by changing job classifications, including training provisions and developing career paths. The concept of the **learning organisation** has also been developed to encourage an attitude to continual learning in the workplace. It is concerned with broader issues of changing the culture of organisations so they are able to achieve their vision.

Future developments in strategic human resource management

These developments have implications for the human resource issues and policies which will be formulated in the future. The changing nature of the workforce will require the expansion of the concept of EEO to that of **managing diversity** and it will also require that greater attention be given to **work and family programs**. Where these developments have been introduced they have been regarded as an important part of doing good business and when the policies are at their most advanced stage, they seek to promote organisational culture change.

Managing diversity

Managing diversity refers to valuing differences between stakeholders, and particularly employees, and developing and implementing policies to manage these differences.

Although, the concept is not commonly used in Australia, in the United States many organisations have taken diversity issues seriously. Human resource managers have typically focused on nine key areas when managing diversity.

1. **Recruitment**—conducting a concerted effort to find quality minority employees by improved college relations programs.
2. **Career development**—expose those minority employees with high potential to the same key developmental jobs that traditionally have led to senior positions for their white, male counterparts.
3. **Diversity training for managers**—address stereotypes and cultural differences that interfere with the full participation of all employees in the workplace.
4. **Upward mobility**—break the glass ceiling and increase the number of minorities in upper management through mentors and executive appointment.
5. **Diverse input and feedback**—ask minority employees themselves what they need versus asking managers what they think minorities need.
6. **Self-help**—encourage networking and support groups among minorities.
7. **Accountability**—hold managers accountable for developing their diverse workforces.
8. **Systems accommodation**—develop respect and support for cultural diversity through recognition of different cultural and religious holidays, diet restrictions, and so forth.
9. **Outreach**—support minority organisations and programs, thus developing a reputation as a 'diversity' leader.

Figure 2.9 describes the approach of Northern States Power (NSP) in Minneapolis to diversity. In the 'HR Advice and Application: Diversity is Valuing Differences at NSP', sees diversity along a number of characteristics identified in the figure. It sees the development of a diverse workforce as an opportunity and it has a number human resource programs that enable it to 'capitise on diversity'.

HR ADVICE AND APPLICATION

Diversity is valuing differences at NSP

Race	Age
Minnesotan	I.Q.
Non-Minnesotan	Smoking preference
Weight	Differently abled
Traditional thinker	Economic status
Nontraditional	Marital status
Thinker	Nationality
Non traditional job	Appearance
Education	White collar
Religion	Blue collar
Language	Single parent
Height	Affectional
Gender	Preference

Figure 2.9 HR advice and application
Source: Schuler 1995, p. 74

Other organisations have appointed managers responsible for managing diversity and/or implemented policies specifically designed. Digital Equipment Corporation has a manager with the title, Manager of Valuing Differences. Honeywell Inc. has a Director of Work Force Diversity and Avon Products Inc. has a Director of Multicultural Planning and Design. Hewlett-Packard conducts training sessions for managers to teach them about different cultures and races, and about their own gender biases and training needs.

One of the objectives of a Managing Diversity Program could be to break the glass ceiling. The **glass ceiling** refers to the invisible barrier which prevents women attaining senior positions in organisations and is discussed in more detail in Chapter 4. The glass ceiling seems very resilient in Australia, with the lowest percentage of women managers among the industrialised countries and the relatively slow increase in the numbers of women managers (Burton & Ryall 1995, p. 773).

Managing diversity

What must be changed to get women 'on the team'

More companies are making a real effort to get diversity in their pool of executive talent, but ultimately men must be persuaded to let it develop.

BY GEORGI STICKELS

Bob Slagle, managing director of Alcoa Australia, scoffs at those who still say that a factory in the bush or an aluminium smelter is no place for a woman. He believes both situations can be—if the woman is qualified and wants to be there. His outlook may not yet be the norm, but such attitudes suggest that executive equality has come a long way since the days just after the Second World War.

It is difficult to conclude that women are not interested, or not qualified. These days, more than half of all university graduates are women. Even in the traditionally male bastion of engineering, the proportion of female graduates has gone from 5 per cent to 15 per cent in the past 10 years.

A new study by Amanda Sinclair, Associate Professor at Melbourne University's Business School, concludes that the very nature of corporate Australia is preventing many women from reaching the top of their profession. 'It's clubbish, with a very Australian flavour; a combination of patriarchal elitism and locker-room larrikinism'.

Sinclair says this culture manifests itself in many ways, from the way men talk about women when they are not present, to sponsoring a box at traditionally male sports such as football and cricket.

Even the notion of 'team player' can conjure up masculine images, Sinclair says, and it traps men just as much as women. 'Lots of men don't like having to go to those boxes either, but it's part of getting along'. Sometimes, women are not invited simply because of their gender'.

Sinclair says double standards abound. 'In a man, the word "strong" describes fairly aggressive behaviour, but when a woman does that it's not admirable any more. In a woman it's her ability to withstand setbacks'. Sinclair says women who try to be too much like men are frowned upon. Women who succeed are typically seen as 'quiet achievers' and experts in their field.

However, Sagle says that corporations worldwide are starting to employ more women in executive roles as they gain better qualifications and experience. Directors

> realise they are only shooting themselves in the foot by not encouraging greater executive diversity.
>
> Slagle believes there are subtle advantages in being seen to be at the cutting edge in this respect, as well as the tangible benefits of choosing executives from a bigger pool of talent. 'We wouldn't dream of ignoring half our potential customers, so to ignore half your potential staff is unthinkable', he says.

Source: *BRW*, 19 December 1994, pp. 92–93.

The persistence of the glass ceiling seems to be the result of a number of factors including the non-application of the merit principle, the 'maleness' of management and organisational culture which has been found to be dysfunctional for women and organisations, and lack of CEO commitment to the involvement of women in senior management (Burton & Ryall 1995, pp. 775–76). The article by Stickels, 'What must be changed to get women "on the team"' describes these factors in a number of Australian organisations. The article also discusses the need to acknowledge the family responsibilities of both women and men as a way of breaking the glass ceiling.

Work and family

Changes in the participation rates of women in the workforce and the structure of families have encouraged employers to develop policies which facilitate employees balancing work and domestic responsibilities. The ratification of ILO Convention no. 156, 'Workers with Family Responsibilities', by the Australian government in 1990, together with the International Year of the Family in 1994 and an increasing awareness of employers of the need to retain skilled employees have also highlighted the important role of these policies.

Many Australian organisations already have some policies which facilitate this combination. The provision for unpaid parental leave for up to 52 weeks, provision to work part-time and the use of sick leave to care for sick dependents are common policies. A small number of organisations have become aware of the problems existing employment practices create for employees seeking to simultaneously maintain their employment and domestic responsibilities and the costs associated with not addressing these issues. To deal with these difficulties they have identified employees' needs and developed policies such as career break schemes, child-care assistance programs and home-based work. Most organisations develop individual policies to deal with particular issues, and they see these as an add-on to their human resource policies. A small number of organisations have developed **Work and family programs** or **Work and family strategies** which seek to systematically create a culture in which work and family issues become linked to strategic business planning.

Six steps provide the basis for developing a 'work and family' program. These steps are:

1 Get the issues onto the organisation's agenda.
2 Conduct a needs assessment of both the organisation and the workforce:
   a examine organisation's needs
   b staff survey.
3 Circulate a work and family statement, which describes the integrated set of policies dealing with the issues.
4 Systematic development of the program:
   a appointment of senior executive responsible for the program
   b planning

    c development of measures to implement the program
    d conduct a feasibility assessment of the program
    e conduct a cost–benefit analysis
    f determine the time frame for the introduction of the policies
    g calculate a budget
    h develop a mechanism for monitoring and evaluating the policies in the program
    i develop consultative mechanisms
    j examine legal and award provisions
    k examine the opportunity for including work and family initiatives in workplace bargaining.

5 Implementation:
    a put initiatives into action
    b run briefing sessions for manager/supervisors
    c develop a training policy and communication policy for work and family policies
    d produce regular newsletters.

6 Monitor, evaluate and review:
    a develop a variety of measurement tools which assess the interaction between employees family and work lives, e.g.
      ii absenteeism
      iii maternity turnover
      iv female/male resignation rates
      v morale, satisfaction of employees with policies (Department of Industrial Relations, 1994, p. 22).

Case studies of five organisations (Kramar 1995) which have developed work and family policies indicate a number of factors are critical for the successful formulation, development and implementation of work and family policies. The factors critical for the development of policies included the support of at least one senior manager or group of employees with effective organisational skills, the allocation of sufficient resources for processes such as conducting employee surveys, establishing a child-care centre or distributing information about the policies, access to expert advice from consultants and government departments and the integration of the policies into wider organisational policies. Other factors were also critical such as consultation with employees and trade unions, steering committees, the establishment of the need for a particular policy, effective communication of the policies and an understanding that the policies benefited everyone in the organisation, not just women.

NRMA has developed a Work and Family Program designed 'To assist all NRMA employees balance their work and family pressures'. This program was developed in response to the needs of employees identified through results of an employee attitude survey and focus groups. The major steps involved in the development of the Work and Family Program in NRMA involved establishing a communication strategy, assessing employees' needs through a survey and focus groups and establishing an implementation team. The policies developed under the Work and Family Program have been integrated into the Human Resources Business Plan as objectives to achieve the Key Strategy to 'create the framework for a keen, competitive, urgent culture'. The implementation of the Work and Family Program is expected to contribute to performance indicators such as a reduction in unavoidable turnover and legal compliance.

One of the issues associated with employees balancing between work and family concerns is flexibility about the place of work. Working from home, rather than an office for some of the working week has been seen as a way of accommodating employees domestic and employment needs and as a way of improving organisational efficiency. Efficiency can be improved by utilising office space more effectively (James 1993, pp. 62–63) and through the application of developments in technology. Advances in telecommunications and computing have facilitated white-collar and professional employees working from home or from 'hotel offices'. In the United States in Ernst & Young and Anderson Consulting the concept of 'hotel offices' is being adopted. It involves employees booking space in a set of offices and remaining there for only as long as they need to. The night before an employee's use of the room, their personal effects such as pictures and momentos are retrieved from private lockers and put in the office (Churbuck & Young 1993, pp. 66–68).

In Australia, **telecommuting** or **teleworking**, that is working from home, and being hooked to the office via a personal computer, telephone and/or modem has been slowly developing. There are about 300 000 teleworkers in Australia, with most being in the private sector. Many are self-employed or if they are an employee they work from home on an informal basis (Scott 1995, p. 25A). In the Commonwealth public sector an Agreement between the Commonwealth Public Service Union (CPSU) and the Public Service Commission was certified early in 1994 and it provides for workers to spend two days a week in the office and spend the rest of the time working at home. It has been estimated that telecommuting increases productivity by at least 20 per cent. The article ' "Tele-guerilla" armed with modem, laptop' describes the benefits of telecommuting for one Australian manager.

HRM IN THE NEWS

'Tele-guerilla' armed with modem, laptop

BY REBECCA SCOTT

Ken Thomas is the NSW manager for BMW Australia. But he doesn't have a company office. He is a telecommuter. He works from his home office, or as a 'tele-guerilla', roaming around the city jungle between dealerships, using his mobile phone, his laptop computer and fax and modem communications to stay in daily contact with head office in Melbourne.

When BMW Australia closed its Alexandria office last year and centralised its operations in Melbourne, the company set up its six remaining NSW sales staff as telecommuters. They work out of their cars, at the dealerships they visit or from their home offices. There is no BMW Australia office in Sydney.

According to Ken Thomas, the benefits flow more to the company than to the individual. He now works much longer hours, regularly going into his home office after dinner or at the weekend, instead of relaxing or watching television. He also does the work previously done by office support staff. He types his own letters, buys his own stationery, and posts and collects his own mail.

When he tells people he works from home, he says it is sometimes hard to convince them he is for real. 'They think when I say I'm an area manager for BMW Australia and I work from home that I'm telling them porkies. Or they think that I don't really work. There is this idea that you are not legitimate unless you have a proper company office'.

However, he likes telecommuting, and says he feels it has greatly improved his

> productivity. While he likes the increased flexibility, and believes life as a telecommuter is less stressful, he thinks his wife may sometimes hanker for the days when he left home early in the morning and spent his working life elsewhere. Now, he says, he shares the daily frustrations of his job with her, rather than with his company colleagues.
>
> He has a rule that his residence is primarily his home, and that its function as an office is secondary. So if one of his daughters is having a piano lesson, and he is on the phone to Munich in his adjoining office, the piano lesson takes precedence.
>
> 'Otherwise you get to the stage where the company takes over your home'.
>
> He is grateful that he no longer has to spend almost three hours a day commuting from the upper north shore to Alexandria, but thinks that the ideal situation would be to have two offices—not simply for convenience, but also to ward off any feeling of isolation from the business entity.
>
> 'You need a home office so you can remain productive but you probably need a company office as well, particularly in a business with an outward face—things that will remind you of the corporation that you work for'.

Source: *Sydney Morning Herald*, 1995.

Learning organisation

Continuous learning and the development and transfer of skills have been recognised as important processes in workplace reform and adaptation to environmental changes. The concept of the 'learning organisation' has been used as a way of organisations developing competitive advantage and as a way of empowering employees (Senge 1990). In Australia, a number of organisations have applied this concept in their approach to workplace reform and the development of their workforces. They have used the term 'learning enterprise'.

The Lend Lease Corporation, Westpac, ICI Botany and the Kent Brewery (Carlton United Brewery in Sydney) are four organisations which have adopted the concept of the learning enterprise. The concept involves the development of a shared learning relationship between the stakeholders so it will result in innovation and continuous improvement. The Enterprise Development Agreement signed between the Westpac Banking Corporation and the Finance Sector Union defines the 'learning enterprise' as 'one where individuals, teams and the enterprise itself are learning together and transferring skills and knowledge throughout the enterprise to create a dynamic competitive advantage through continuous improvement and innovation' (Enterprise Development Agreement). The learning enterprise seeks to change the bank's culture by integrating people, technical systems, processes and the workplace in a cohesive and co-ordinated way so Westpac achieves 'Best Bank' status.

At Lend Lease the training company has been renamed Lend Lease Learning. It seeks to develop Lend Lease into a learning organisation by multi-skilling the workforce, removing demarcation and providing career opportunities for employees (Lend Lease 1991–92, p. 3). One of the aims is to develop a strong corporate culture where employees develop a capacity to learn from other cultures, are able to search for, evaluate, and adapt alien concepts, use new concepts to challenge traditional mindsets and absorb and integrate new people, processes and experiences (Ford 1995, p. 24).

Management education and development

Developments in the Australian economy will require the nature of management and the role of managers to change. The Industry Task Force on Leadership and Management Skills (1995, pp. 22; 136–37) predicted that senior managers in the future would be leaders/enablers rather than autocrats or communicators. In order to compete successfully in the international market they would require improvements in their people skills, leadership skills, international orientation, entrepreneurship skills, better skills for building relationships between organisations, more effective handling of the transition from specialist to manager and the management of diversity.

The Industry Task Force (1995, pp. 142–51) highlighted the importance of 'achieving best practice management development'. They found there was a need for Australian organisations to change their approach to management development by increasing the levels of education and training undertaken, reduce the reliance on short courses, shift the emphasis from current to future skill requirements, link management development to strategic direction and evaluating the effectiveness of management development activities. They particularly stressed the need for organisations to introduce management development which is enterprise or business driven from strategic or corporate plans, rather than driven by the providers of development and training.

Summary

The most common view of strategic human resource management is that it is a systematic way of achieving the goals of the stakeholders in an organisation. It explicitly acknowledges that organisational outcomes will be influenced by the relationship between aspects of the external environment, the internal environment, organisational strategy, structure, culture, leadership and human resource policies. Strategic human resource management is unlike other approaches to the management of employees because it is a partnership of everyone in the organisation, involving business partners and all the stakeholders associated with the organisation. It is a systematic, dynamic, pro-active process requiring consideration of short-term, medium-term and long-term goals.

A number of models and frameworks have been developed to describe these relationships. These models can be divided into three categories:

1. General frameworks
2. Organisational frameworks
3. Frameworks identifying specific relationships between human resource policies and aspects of the environment.

The models and frameworks in these categories provide insights into the relationships between the external and internal environments, organisational characteristics, employment policies and organisational outcomes. All the models identify the way these relationships can be utilised to create a 'fit' between the various aspects of the organisation, the environments and human resource policies.

The process of strategic human resource management involves two components:

1. Strategy formulation
2. Strategy implementation.

Strategy formulation requires that the various aspects of the environment are examined and their impact on the organisation and the implications for human resource policies assessed. This process is known as **environmental assessment**. The second part of strategy formulation is strategy development, which can involve a variety of stakeholders, the formulation of action plans, communication strategies and evaluation measures.

Strategy implementation requires anticipating which aspects of the organisation will support or impede the implementation of policies and developing techniques which will be effective in overcoming the barriers. Another part of this process is the monitoring of the implementation process and the use of the evaluation procedures. However, it is important to remember that it is difficult drawing a clear line of causation between human resource policies and particular organisational outcomes.

Strategic human resource management involves building relationships which can meet current and future organisational goals. Consequently, the environmental assessment requires anticipating the changes in the environment which could affect the organisation, its workforce and the use of particular human resource policies. Changes such increasing international competition, developments in the demographics of the workforce, particularly the increasing representation of women in the labour market and possibly in management and the increasing educational attainment of the workforce, and advances in technology are expected to have an impact on the nature of human resource management practice. Increasing attention will probably be paid to flexibility in employment, such as flexible work schedules, telecommuting, career breaks, work and family policies and managing diversity issues.

questions for discussion and review

1. Identify the principles which facilitate the effective integration of human resource management policies and practices with business strategy.
2. Explain the benefits of using a strategic human resource management approach.
3. Identify some of the limitations of the rational approach to strategy development.
4. Identify the key factors of a strategic human resource management approach to management.
5. Identify the major components of the models which have been developed to provide some understanding of strategic human resource management.
6. Assess the value of these models.
7. Identify two methods which could be used to do an environmental assessment.
8. Identify some measures which could be used to evaluate the success of a human resource strategy and policies.
9. Discuss the impact of changes such as domestic and international competition, changes in the social structure and developments in technology on human resource strategy and polices.
10. Predict three future developments in the social, economic and/or technological arena, and assess their likely impact on the development of human resource management policies and practices.

case study

Born-again bank prepares for a new age of business

BY TIM TREADGOLD

Reinventing a bank that is almost 100 years old sounds like a difficult business. But that, in effect, is the job being done by a 60-member management team at the R&I Bank of Western Australia, a government-owned bank being prepared for a public float.

For most of its life the bank has worked comfortably and safely as a government agency, first as the agricultural bank of WA, later as the rural and industries bank and now as the R&I. Profits have been important but until recently, service—in a public service sense—came first.

Going public is changing everything at the R&I. The bank is now very much focused on true management principles. The staff (3100 full-time equivalent) have been told to prepare for a period of great change. Nothing is sacred: everything from the balance sheet and credit policy to the design of business forms and layout of branches is being scrutinised.

It is hoped that the radical restructuring of the R&I will produce a stream-lined business unit able to withstand two big tests and the pressure of rising competition. The first test will be the price realised by the state when it floats the bank. The second one, possibly of greater importance, will be the credit rating assigned to the bank's debt by international agencies such as Moody's investors service.

The corporate lending unit has been completely overhauled. The team of twenty now includes just one of the people who was working in corporate lending two years ago. In a recent speech, Warrack Kent (MD) noted that the R&I was not equipped to handle the competitive environment that resulted from deregulation of the financial markets in the mid-1980s. Many of the new faces have moved across Perth's main street, St George's Terrace, from Westpac, where Kent once had a senior role.

McGurk and his VIP team, assisted by consultants from PA Consulting group have set about their task of changing the bank from being a centralised office on the 23rd floor of the Tower in central Perth. Every function is being assessed with the aims of lower costs, higher revenues and new ideas to attract and hold more customers.

Our studies indicate that the VIP program should add tens of millions of dollars to the bank's profits over the next few years', Kent says. 'VIP will ensure that the bank is not only the biggest and most profitable bank based in WA, but also the bank with the best customer focus and best products'.

McGurk's VIP team has started with 16 projects looking at all bank functions in what is termed a 'whole of bank' approach.

Some changes are expected to flow quickly. Kent says the first six months are critical, but the maximum benefits will take several years. One likely discovery of the VIP work is that the is heavily overstaffed in a modern, technology-driven environment. A strong hint of this was contained in an early promise that any staff cuts would be by natural attrition and voluntary redundancy before compulsory cuts were made. It was the first softening-up from management for what will almost certainly come, just as it has at Westpac, the Commonwealth and other banks.

A mission statement from the bank's general manager of retail banking, David Taylor, highlighted the new look required by the bank. It reads: 'To secure our future we must be a strong, results-driven bank, dedicated to WA, with a deep commitment to deliver superior value through skilled staff working as a team'.

Source: *BRW*, 13 August 1993, pp. 58–60.

> **Questions**
> 1 Identify the changes in human resource policies which followed the changes in R&I's business strategy.
> 2 What is the VIP and what are its measures of success?
> 3 Identify some human resource issues which R&I will need to address in the future.
> 4 Assess the mission statement.
> 5 Identify the skills necessary to implement the changes in human resource policies in R&I.

Resources

Books and articles
Legge, K. (1995), *Human Resource Management: Rhetorics and Realities*, Macmillan Business, London.
Saul, P. (1991), *Strategic Team Leadership*, McGraw-Hill, Sydney.

Videos
BBC 'Benchmarking'.
BBC 'The Learning Organisation'.

References
ABS Catalogue no. 4102, *Australian Social Trends*.
ABS Catalogue no. 4418.0, *Australian Families—Selected Findings From the Survey of Families in Australia*.
ABS Catalogue no. 4420.0, *Focus of Families Demographic and Family Format*.
ABS Catalogue no. 6224.0, *Labour Force Status and Other Characteristics of Families*.
Alvesson, M. (1993), *Cultural Perspectives on Organisations*, Cambridge University Press, Cambridge.
Beer, M., Spector, B., Lawrence, P., Mills, D. & Walton, R. (1985), *Human Resources Management: A General Manager's Perspective*, Free Press, New York.
Bittman, M. (1991), *Juggling Time—How Australian Families Use Time*, Office of the Status of Women and the Department of the Prime Minister and Cabinet, Canberra.
Boxall, P. & Dowling, P. (1990), 'Human Resource Management and Industrial Relations Tradition', *Labour and Industry*, vol. 3, no. 2/3, pp. 195–214.
Boxall, P. F. (1992), 'Strategic human resource management: beginnings of a new theoretical sophistication?', *Human Resource Management Journal*, vol. 2, no. 3, pp. 60–79.
Burton, C. & Ryall, C. (1995), 'Managing for Diversity', in the *Report of the Industry Task Force on Leadership and Management Skills, Enterprising Nation*, Australian Government Publishing Service, Canberra.
Carter, C., Nicolson, J. & Barlow, M. (1995), 'The Australian Manager of the Twenty First Century', in the *Industry Task Force on Leadership and Management Skills, Enterprising Nation*, Australian Government Publishing Service, Canberra.
CCH Australia Ltd. (1995), *Australian Human Resources Management*, CCH Australia Ltd, North Ryde.
Chandler, A. D. (1962), *Strategy and Structure*, MIT Press, Cambridge, Mass.

Churbuck, D. & Young, J. (1993), 'Who Needs an Office in these Days of Miracles and Wonders?', *Business Review Weekly*, 14 May, pp. 66–67.

Collins, R. (1994), 'The strategic contributions of the personnel function', in A. R. Nankervis & R. L. Compton (eds), *Readings in Strategic Human Resource Management*, Thomas Nelson, Melbourne.

Department of Industrial Relations (1994), *The Workplace Guide to Work and family*, Work and Family Unit, Department of Industrial Relations, Australian Government Publishing Service, Canberra.

Department of Industrial Relations (1995), *Enterprise Bargaining in Australia, Annual Report*, Australian Government Publishing Service, Canberra.

Department of Industrial Relations and Australian Manufacturing Council (n.d.), *Best Practice Program Profile*, Canberra.

Dowling, P. & Schuler, R. (1990), 'Human Resource Management', in R. Blanpain (ed.), *Comparative Labour Law and Industrial Relations in Inustralised Market Economics*, vol. 2, Klumer Law and Taxation Publishers, Boston.

Drucker, P. (1980), *Managing in Turbulent Times*, Harper & Row, New York.

—— (1994), 'The Age of Social Transformation', *The Atlantic Monthly*, November, pp. 53–80.

Dunphy, D. & Stace, D. (1992), *Under New Management*, McGraw-Hill Book Company, Sydney.

Enterprising Nation: Renewing Australia's Managers to Meet the Challenges of the Asia Pacific Century, Australian Government Publishing Service, Canberra.

Ford, B. (1995), 'Integrating people, process and place—the workplace of the future', Australian Quality Council 8th National Quality Management Conference, Australian Quality Council, St. Leonards.

FSU and Westpac Enterprise Agreement (1995), Sydney.

Guest, D. (1987), 'Human resource management and industrial relations', *Journal of Management Studies*, vol. 24, no. 5, pp. 503–21.

Hamel, M. & Prahalad (1989), 'Strategic Intent', *Harvard Business Review*, May–June.

Hendry, C. & Pettigrew, A. (1990), 'Human resource management: an agenda for the 1990s', *International Journal Human Resource Management*, vol 1, no. 1, pp. 17–44.

—— (1992), 'Patterns of strategic change in the development of human resource management', *British Journal of Management*, vol. 3, no. 3, pp. 137–56.

House of Representatives Standing Committee for Long Term Strategies (1995), 'Report of the Inquiry into the Workforce of the Future', Australian Government Publishing Service, Canberra.

Hyman, R. (1987), 'Strategy or structure: capital, labour and control', *Work, Employment and Society*, vol. 1, no. 1, March, pp. 25–55.

Industry Task Force on Leadership and Management Skills (1995), Enterprising Australian, Australian Government Publishing Service, Canberra.

James, D. (1993), 'Making the Most of That Necessary Evil: the Office', *Business Review Weekly*, February, vol. 19, pp. 62–63.

Kabanoff, B. (1993), 'An exploration of espoused culture in Australian organisations', *Asia Pacific, Journal of Human Resources*, vol. 31, no. 3, pp. 1–29.

Kanter, R. M. (1983), 'Frontiers for strategic human resource management', *Human Resource Management*, vol. 22, nos. 1 & 2, pp. 9–21.

Kay, J. (1993), *Foundations of Corporate Success: How Business Strategies Add Value*, Oxford University Press, Oxford.

Kramar, R. (1995), 'The Processes and Outcomes of Family Friendly policies in Australian Organisations', Unpublished Report to the Work and Family Unit, Department of Industrial Relations, Canberra.

Legge, K. (1995), *Human Resource Management: Rhetorics and Realities*, Macmillan Business, London.

Lend Lease, *Annual Report 1991–92*, Sydney.

Liebfried, K. H. J. & McNain, C. J. (1992), *Benchmarking: A Tool for Continuous Improvement*, Harper Business, New York.

Lundy O. & Cowling, A. (1996), *Strategic Human Resource Management*, Routledge, London.

Miles, R. E. & Snow, C. C. (1984), 'Designing strategic human resources Systems', *Organisational Dynamics*, vol. 13, no. 1, pp. 36–52.

Miller, E. L. & Burack, E. W. (1981), 'A status report on human resource planning from the perspective of human resource planners', *Human Resource Planning*, vol. 4, no. 2, pp. 33–40.

Miller, S. (1993), 'The nature of strategic human resource management', in R. Harrison (ed.), *Human Resource Management, Issues and Strategies*, Addison-Wesley, Wokingham, pp. 3–33.

Mintzberg, H. (1988), 'Opening up the definition of strategy', in J. B. Quinn, H. Mintzberg & R. M. James (eds), *The Strategy Process*, Prentice-Hall, Englewood Cliffs, NJ.

Nininger, J. R. (1980), 'Human resources and strategic planning: a vital link', *Optimum*, vol. 11, no. 4, pp. 33–46.

Saul, P. (1991), *Strategic Team Leadership*, McGraw-Hill, Sydney.

Schneider, T. (1994), 'People the vital element of change', *Benchmark*, no. 8, July, p. 17.

Schuler, R. (1992), 'Strategic Human Resources Management: Linking the People with the Strategic Needs of Business, *Organisational Dynamics*, Summer.

Schuler. R. S. (1995), *Managing Human Resources*, 5th edition, West Publishing, St. Paul, Minn.

Schuler, R. S & Dowling, P. J. (1990), 'Human Resource Management', in R. Blanpain (ed.), *Comparative Labour Law and Industrial Relations in Industrialised Market Economies*, vol. 2, Kluwer Law and Taxation, Boston.

Scott, R. (1995), ' "Tele-guerilla" armed with modem, laptop', *Sydney Morning Herald*, 24 June, p. 25A.

Senge, P. M. (1990), *The Fifth Discipline*, Doubleday Currency, New York.

Stace, D. & Dunphy, D. (1994), *Beyond the Boundaries*, McGraw-Hill, Sydney.

Still, L. V. (1993), *Where to From Here? The Managerial Woman in Transition*, Business and Professional Publishing, Sydney.

Tichy, N. M., Fombrun, C. J. & Devanna, M. A. (1984), *Strategic Human Resource Management*, John Wiley and Sons, New York.

Vanden Heuval, A. (1993), *When Roles Overlap*, Australian Institute of Family Studies, Melbourne.

Walker, J. W. (1992), *Human Resource Strategy*, McGraw-Hill, New York.

Watson, G. H. (1993), *Strategic Benchmarking*, John Wiley and Sons Ltd, New York.

Westpac Banking Corporation, *Enterprise Development Agreement* (with Finance Sector Union).

Wolcott, I. (1991), *Work and Family: Employers' Views*, Monograph no. 11, Australian Institute of Family Studies, Melbourne.

Wittington, R. (1993), *What is strategy and what does it matter?*, Routledge, London.

part 2

The external environment

chapter 3
Industrial relations and enterprise bargaining

chapter 4
Equal Employment Opportunity

chapter 5
Occupational health and safety

chapter 3

Industrial relations and enterprise bargaining

Ed Davis

learning objectives

After studying this chapter, you will be able to:

1. Explain the nature and importance of industrial relations.
2. Discuss the interrelationship of industrial relations and HRM and their significance for performance.
3. Understand the extent to which broad economic, political and other developments influence industrial relations.
4. Analyse the role and experience of the major parties in industrial relations.
5. Explain the pattern and trends in industrial conflict.
6. Discuss the significance of enterprise bargaining and explain trends in recent developments.
7. Analyse the main features of recent proposals for industrial relations reform.

chapter 3

chapter outline

- HRM and industrial relations — 92
- The broader context — 92
  - Economic context — 93
  - Politics and industrial relations — 94
  - Technological change and industrial relations — 96
  - Social change — 97
  - Environment — 97
- The parties — 98
  - Unions — 98
  - Union membership — 99
  - Employers' associations — 100
  - Government — 102
  - Industrial tribunals — 103
- Conflict in industrial relations — 104
- Enterprise bargaining — 107
  - Hancock Committee of Inquiry — 107
  - National Wage Cases 1987–91 — 108
  - Equity and enterprise bargaining — 110
  - Workplace practice — 111
- Recent reforms in industrial relations — 114
  - Workplace Relations Act — 114
- Summary — 116
- Questions for discussion and review — 117
- Resources — 118
- References — 119

HRM IN THE NEWS

Joint statement

BY THE PRIME MINISTER, THE HON P. J. KEATING MP, AND THE ACTU, 22 JUNE 1995—ACCORD MARK VIII: 'SUSTAINING GROWTH, LOW INFLATION AND FAIRNESS'

The Government and the ACTU have today concluded a new Accord for a productive, fair and just Australia.

This new agreement, Accord Mark VIII, will provide a framework for another four years of low inflation, high productivity, high growth and sustained falls in unemployment.

It continues the tradition of underpinning industrial harmony and social justice with an ongoing process of industrial relations and workplace reform and the move to **decentralised** wage fixing based upon an effective **award** safety net.

The eighth Accord between the Government and the ACTU is proof that the relationship works and has resulted in the most successful social, economic and industrial relations partnership anywhere in the world.

The shared objectives to be pursued through this Accord are:

- sustainable economic growth and a substantial reduction in unemployment with a commitment to 5 per cent unemployment being within reach by the end of the decade
- a low underlying inflation rate of 2 per cent to 3 per cent on average over the cycle to ensure continued economic prosperity
- continued microeconomic and workplace reform
- greatly increased national savings to provide a better retirement income for all workers
- an adequate **social wage** to improve the living standards of all Australians, and
- maintenance and improvement of living standards through commitment to an equitable system of wage fixing and sustainable real wages growth.

To these ends, this Accord will further develop the arrangements agreed to under Accord VII and will operate until March 1999.

Source: ACTU 1995b, p. 1.

HRM IN THE NEWS

PRIME MINISTER JOHN HOWARD, ADDRESS TO THE BUSINESS COUNCIL OF AUSTRALIA, 26 MARCH 1996

Let me say very calmly, but in very deliberate terms, that if the word mandate means anything, if people vote for any policy, ever, at any election, then I would argue with all the strength I can muster, that the Australian people did vote on the 2nd of March, to change Australia's industrial relations system.

And I have a very strong commitment, a very strong personal commitment and my new government has a very strong collective commitment to changing Australia's industrial relations system.

Source: *Business Council Bulletin* 1996, p. 10.

HRM IN THE NEWS

Business Council of Australia on enterprise bargaining

The Australian economy is irrevocably being more fully exposed to international competition. It is also grappling with chronic balance of payments and external debt problems. In these circumstances, all aspects of our economic and industrial life need to be examined to ensure that we maximise our creativity and comparative advantage and that unnecessary impediments to international competitiveness are eliminated. As one contribution to these objectives, the Business Council of Australia has decided to undertake a review of Australia's industrial relations.

In seeking changes in our industrial relations system, the Council has set out its objectives in its policy statement, 'Towards an Enterprise Based Industrial Relations System' of March 1987. In brief, the Council's overriding objective is to create an industrial relations environment where people can work together most effectively and with greatest satisfaction; where the highest possible productivity becomes the common goal for all; and where healthy enterprise performance provides the best outcomes for employers and employees alike. The Council believes that these objectives will be best served by a fundamental reorientation of the system away from one largely focused outside the enterprise and adversarial in nature and towards one which is centred on the enterprise, develops a high degree of mutual trust and interest, and strengthens the direct relationships between employers and employees. Much of the responsibility for implementing this reform rests with company management.

Source: BCA 1989, p. ix.

These three statements point to the perceived importance of industrial relations in Australian society. Former Prime Minister Paul Keating, Leader of the Australian Labor Party (ALP), and Martin Ferguson, then President of the Australian Council of Trade Unions, welcomed the eighth Accord between their institutions. This Accord, following in the footsteps of its predecessors, focused on the contribution of industrial relations to economic performance and social welfare. The new Prime Minister, John Howard, also recognised the importance of industrial relations; indeed he identified it as the sphere in which he was most determined to achieve change, following the electoral victory of the Liberal–National Party Coalition in March 1996.

The Business Council of Australia, representing large enterprises in the private and public sectors indicated that it saw industrial relations as pivotal. In *Enterprise-based Bargaining Units: A Better Way of Working* (1989) it argued at length for changes in approach designed to lift the competitiveness of Australian enterprises. It saw such changes as critical to improve national economic fortunes.

The nature of relations between people at work, and particularly between managers and those they manage, influences the quantity and quality of work performed, customer satisfaction, competitiveness and profitability. It has therefore an important impact on the production of goods and services. Equally, industrial relations has significance for the consumption of goods and services since a focus of the relationship is the negotiation of wages and conditions. It is no longer just an issue of which group of employees receives what level of pay. Unions representing employees, and employer organisations representing their members, seek to negotiate with government over matters such as the level of pensions, superannuation and taxation.

A further element reflecting the importance of industrial relations is its contribution to the rights enjoyed by employees and unions. As the various Accords have demonstrated, unions have sought and often achieved increased rights for employees in the form of rights to information and to consultation over matters such as organisational and technological change, affirmative action and occupational health and safety. In this sense industrial relations plays an important part in shaping the character and style of democracy in Australia.

HRM and industrial relations

The Economic Planning Advisory Commission (EPAC) a tripartite think-tank established to advise the federal Labor government (1983–96), convened a meeting in 1995 which discussed the significance of HRM for workplace change (EPAC 1995). One of the matters discussed was the distinctiveness of HRM. Even fifteen years earlier there were marked stereotypes for HRM and industrial relations. HRM was perceived to deal with payroll and personnel matters and had a strong unitarist flavour. It concerned structures and processes to commit and motivate employees. It looked at matters such as training, occupational health and safety and EEO. The perceived concern of industrial relations, by contrast, was adversarial workplace relations. It focused on strikes, wages, unions, bargaining and the industrial relations tribunals. The teaching of industrial relations was firmly established in several Australian universities and boasted a major journal, the *Journal of Industrial Relations*. HRM then was a poor cousin.

In the mid-1990s the stereotypes are anachronistic. HRM is inevitably influenced by developments in the broader environment in which workplaces operate. The shift in balance from the highly **centralised** determination of pay and conditions to greater responsibility at the enterprise level has meant that more managers have had to play an increased role in the management of people. In large and medium-sized workplaces this has meant more attention to workplace issues. Bargaining has played an increasingly important part in HRM.

The industrial relations agenda too has undergone change. It has broadened to include a range of matters which used to be considered the preserve of HRM. Matters such as training, EEO and the management of occupational health and safety are up for negotiation. They are common fare in industrial awards and **enterprise agreements**. Both HRM and industrial relations are considered to be pivotal to the lifting of levels of performance and improving quality in Australian workplaces. The EPAC found few prepared to argue that there remain meaningful boundaries separating the two fields of study. Both HRM and industrial relations explore 'the behaviour and interaction of people at work' (Deery & Plowman 1991, p. 2).

The broader context

Experience in industrial relations is shaped by developments in several spheres. Among the main spheres are the economy, the political system, technology and the social system. An additional source of influence is the environment. Concern for the environment has led to changes in legislation with an impact on workplaces and environmental issues are finding their way onto the bargaining agenda.

A feature of industrial relations over the last decade has been the broad and rapid spread of change. This has not been confined to Australia. The International Labour Organisation established in 1919 to consider and recommend labour standards in those countries affiliated to it is now made up of approximately 170 member states. An ILO Bulletin in 1992 remarked:

> Rapid technological change, ever intensifying competition, large-scale reorganisation: in the turbulence at the end of this century, the world of work and employment is like a tossing ship caught in crossed winds. For the captains of industry as well as the bosses of small enterprises, the direction to follow is not always sure, the margins of manoeuvre confined (ILO 1992, p. 1).

Professor John Niland, a leading writer in Australian industrial relations, commented in similar fashion that, 'the changes currently running are more profound, and probably more permanent in their fundamental impact, than anything witnessed since industrial relations has become an identifiable academic discipline' (Niland 1994). There is then a profound sense of change and recognition of its importance for workplace relations.

Economic context

The American writer on industrial relations, John Dunlop, believed that there was a crucial interrelationship involving the economic and industrial relations sub-systems (Dunlop 1958). Put simply, the level and movement of key economic variables can be seen to have an impact on the parties to industrial relations. High levels of economic growth and employment will generally boost the bargaining power of employees and the unions that represent them. High levels of inflation will encourage unions to seek pay increases to match or exceed price increases. Conversely low growth and high unemployment will bolster employers' bargaining power and may emasculate unions.

A feature of economic experience over the past twenty years has been the rapidity of change. In contrast to the 1960s which witnessed steady economic growth, low levels of inflation and high employment, the 1970s, 1980s and 1990s have seen pronounced fluctuations in these variables. Table 3.1 looks at the movement of key variables since 1987/88.

Table 3.1 Selected economic variables: 1987/88–1994/95

	GDP (A) % CHANGE P.A.	UNEMPLOYMENT % CHANGE P.A.	CPI % CHANGE P.A.	CURRENT ACCOUNT DEFICIT % GDP
1987–88	5.4	7.8	7.3	–3.4
1988–89	4.4	6.6	6.6	–5.1
1989–90	3.3	6.2	6.7	–5.8
1990–91	–1.0	8.3	5.6	–4.0
1991–92	0.7	10.3	3.0	–3.0
1992–93	3.2	11.0	2.0	–3.7
1993–94	4.1	10.5	2.3	–3.9
1994–95	4.8	8.9	2.6	–6.0

1 Average Gross Domestic Product at 1989–90 prices
2 Consumer Price Index (excluding shelter)

Source: Based on ABS, Cat. no. 1350.0

The fluctuations in growth of Gross Domestic Product are substantial with the strong growth of the late 1980s collapsing in 1990–91. The economy then began a slow recovery, which saw the return of moderate then relatively strong growth. The proportion of the workforce unemployed has remained high in contrast to the very low levels of the 1950s and 1960s when it was usually below 2 per cent. Responding to the fluctuations in GDP, unemployment varied between 6.2 and 11.0 per cent in the period examined. Inflation measured by movements in the Consumer Price Index also underwent marked change, from 7.3 per cent to 2 per cent in the early 1990s.

The Current Account Deficit, as a proportion of GDP, is often considered an important influence on the movement of other key economic variables. For instance, if there is a judgement in domestic and international money markets that the deficit is too high, then the Australian dollar will be sold in preference for other currencies perceived to be more stable. The foreign exchange value of the Australian dollar will fall and this customarily leads to increased domestic inflation. As indicated in Table 3.1, the deficit has fluctuated between a low of 3 per cent and a peak of 6.0 per cent. It continues to be watched closely.

The connections between the economic and industrial relations spheres are many. A distinguishing feature of government policy in the 1980s to the mid 1990s has been the determination to shape industrial relations to aid pursuit of national economic goals. This was most obvious in the Accords agreed by the ALP and the ACTU. The first, in 1983, and subsequent Accords sought to provide an additional lever to influence economic change. The architects and supporters of the Accord argue that governments have usually been restricted to monetary and fiscal measures; for instance, the adjustment of interest rates and levels of government spending and taxation. The Accords had a broad agenda including prices, wages, non-wage incomes, social welfare payments and superannuation. This meant that the ALP in government was able to pursue faster economic growth and reduced unemployment on the understanding that unions would not take advantage of this increased demand for labour to secure higher pay. The danger of the push for higher pay was that it often proved inflationary and this in turn put a brake on pursuit of economic growth. The original Accord was deliberately fashioned to permit growth and the simultaneous reduction of inflation and unemployment.

Concern for the national or macroeconomy was a theme of all the Accords. They were also concerned with spurring improved performance in the workplace. Where the early Accords depended on the involvement of the industrial tribunals, more recent Accords have argued that managers, employees and their unions should assume increased responsibility at the workplace for the determination of pay and conditions. Enterprise bargaining was selected as the vehicle to lift workplace performance and improve pay and conditions. It will be discussed in more detail below.

Politics and industrial relations

HRM IN THE NEWS

Union support for the Labor party

Trade unions would be making a major contribution to the Labor Party's re-election efforts by campaigning in support of the Keating Government in next year's

> federal election, the ACTU president-elect, Ms Jennie George, said yesterday. Ms George said union leaders at yesterday's ACTU executive meeting had indicated they would match the financial and organisational contributions made by the union movement to Labor's last federal election campaign in 1993.
>
> 'The unions have indicated around the table that their level of commitment to the re-election of a Labor government will be on a par with what we did in 1993', she said. 'For the first couple of months of next year it will be a very full-on campaign by the union movement about industrial relations'.
>
> 'We will again do what we did last time—target marginal seats and put a lot of effort on the ground in terms of ensuring workers have a clear understanding of the differences between the Labor and Liberal parties in terms of their industrial relations policies'. Ms George said she and the outgoing ACTU president, Mr Martin Ferguson, would be campaigning personally for Labor in several marginal electorates. The ALP benefited substantially from union assistance in the last federal election campaign, with Australian Electoral Commission records showing unions donated $1.7 million and spent a further $830 000 on pro-Labor advertising. The ALP also relies on union volunteers to distribute election material in workplaces and marginal electorates.

Source: *Financial Review*, 15 December 1995, p. 3.

Discussion of the Accords has already identified the linkage of politics and industrial relations. Unions in the 1890s in most Australian colonies had formed Labor parties to represent union interests in parliament. The achievement of state and federal governments followed although unions soon found that Labor governments would not simply do their bidding. Relations between Labor's industrial and political wings were frequently tense (Martin 1980, p. 7). Many unions have remained affiliated to, and strong supporters of, the ALP. The support is demonstrated in several ways. Affiliation means the regular payment of dues to the Labor Party. Many unions will raise and pay additional amounts to support the ALP in election campaigns and will assist ALP candidates by door-knocking and other measures to promote ALP candidates. The links between unions and the ALP were also on show following the election of the ALP in the 1983 federal election. The then new Prime Minister, Bob Hawke, was a former president of the ACTU and the new Minister for Industrial Relations, Ralph Willis, had worked for the ACTU. Several other ministers also had strong links to unions. In 1989, the then ACTU President Simon Crean, announced that he would seek parliamentary preselection. On his arrival in Canberra in 1990, he was rewarded with a senior Ministerial post. In 1995 his ACTU successor, Martin Ferguson, followed suit, winning his parliamentary seat in 1996.

The linkage between employers, employer associations and conservative parties is not so obvious or straightforward. Direct affiliation has been rare, nonetheless employer associations have frequently leant support to non-Labor parties in elections and have acted as a recruiting ground for conservative members of parliament. David Plowman noted that twenty Coalition members in the first federal government led by Malcolm Fraser had been active in employer organisations before coming to parliament (Plowman 1987, p. 245). Nonetheless, many employers and employer associations take care not to appear aligned to either of the major political camps. The risk is that offence might be given and rebound to their disadvantage.

Technological change and industrial relations

The impact of technological change on industrial relations can be considerable. The chain of inspiration and innovation leading to the development of the motor car spawned a new and huge industry with accompanying demands for new resources, labour and skills. There were necessarily negative implications for many employees and managers in horse-drawn transport. The introduction of large containers onto the waterfront meant decreased dependence on manual labour; cranes lifted the containers off the docks and placed them in shipholds. More recently the development of microelectronic processors has meant major change to work organisation and performance in many enterprises. One example is the ability of journalists to key-in stories on their word processors. Their work is stored and edited. Newspaper and bulletin pages are created electronically without the need for printers.

In the 1970s there were widespread concerns that rapid technological change across industries was contributing to the steady rise of unemployment. It seemed self-evident that increased automation in manufacturing and services meant a reduction in the demand for labour. Prime Minister Malcolm Fraser in 1978 established a committee of inquiry, chaired by Rupert Myers, to investigate technological change in Australia (Committee of Inquiry into Technological Change in Australia 1980). The report defined technological change as 'change in processes, materials, machinery or equipment ...'. It recognised the potential for technological change to influence the level and type of employment in different markets, to challenge the direction of education and to have major repercussions for wages, workplace conditions and the control and supervision of work. The committee did not recommend resistance to technological change; indeed it saw such change as often playing a vital part in enterprise, industry and national competitiveness. Instead it advocated a series of measures to prepare employees and workplaces to maximise the benefits and minimise the costs (Lansbury & Davis 1984).

One important outcome of the Committee's report was the establishment of a **test case** on standards for job protection. The ACTU argued before the then Conciliation and Arbitration Commission that it should amend awards to provide for employee and union rights to information and consultation in the face of organisational and technological change. It also sought increased **redundancy** payments. The Hawke-led Labor government supported the ACTU in the hearings before the tribunal.

The President of the Commission, Sir John Moore, concluded in a statement at the end of the case:

> As to the introduction of major changes in production, program organisation, structure or technology which are likely to affect employees significantly we require that the employer notify the employees and their union or unions. We also require that the employer discuss with the employees affected and their union the effect of such changes. We require that the discussion shall commence as early as practicable after a firm decision has been made by the employer. We also require the employer to supply in writing to the employees concerned and their union relevant information about the changes including the nature of the changes proposed (Moore 1984, p. 2).

Nearly a decade later in 1993, the *Australian Industrial Relations Act 1988* was amended to reaffirm the importance of management consultation with employees and their unions. For instance, the Industrial Relations Commission will not certify enterprise agreements unless 'the agreement establishes a process for the parties to the agreement to consult each other about matters involving changes to the organisation or performance of work in any place of work to which the agreement relates ...' (*Australian Industrial Relations Act 1988, 1994*, S170MC (d) (I)). The amended Act also makes specific provision for management and union consultation over the termination of 15 or more employees (S.170GA).

There is therefore broad recognition of the potential impact of technological change on industrial relations. The rules and regulations governing employee and managerial behaviour in the workplace have been refashioned to reflect this.

Social change

There has been enormous change in the nature of society over the past several decades. One change with significant impact on industrial relations is the increase in the proportion of women in the workforce. This in turn is related to a range of economic and other factors which have encouraged greater numbers of women to seek paid employment. Fifty years ago just over 20 per cent of the workforce was female. In 1995, this has increased to 42 per cent (Davis & Harris 1995, p. 88) and the Australian Bureau of Statistics (ABS) has projected 46 per cent in 2005. Much of this growth can be linked to the strong growth in part-time work which has remained predominantly female. Table 3.2 indicates the growth of part-time work, 1970–94:

Table 3.2 Part-time workers 1970–94: per cent of total workers, Australia

	% MALE	% FEMALE	% TOTAL
1970	2.7	7.1	9.9
1980	3.3	13.1	16.4
1994	6.1	18.0	24.1

N.B. Part-time is defined as less than 35 hours per week
Source: Based on ABS, Cat. no. 6203.0

These are major changes in the composition of the workforce and they have meant increased attention to issues such as child care, equal employment opportunity, equal pay, maternity and paternity leave, and leave to care for children, other family and dependents. These matters were discussed in the ALP–ACTU Accords: several have been the subject of test cases before the industrial tribunals and they are matters for enterprise bargaining.

Environment

The ILO decided that it could not ignore the debate about environmental change and economic and industry developments. In 1990 it stated:

> Is not much of the damage to the environment created by our industrial society, by production, by labour? So although the International Labour Organisation is not involved with physical realities such as global warming, clean water or biological diversity, it has a clear duty to study the implications for the working world of measures taken to protect the environment. To be more precise, it must study their effects on employment and incomes, on the development of human resources and on the quality of conditions of work and life (ILO 1990, p. 1).

In 1994, the ILO reaffirmed the importance of developing policies designed to achieve safe and healthy working and living conditions, as well as the achievement of social justice and human dignity (ILO 1994).

The significance of the environment for industrial relations was raised in Australia in the early 1970s. A union leader in the building industry, Jack Mundey, supported a series of union bans on the proposed demolition of parks and reserves to make way for housing and industry development (Mundey 1981). These drew attention to the linkage of environmental and industrial issues and proved at least partially successful. In the late 1980s, reflecting increasing social concern about damage to the environment, the ACTU and employer organisations set about the determination of policy. There appeared to be a broad consensus that steps should be taken to curtail damage to the environment. On the other hand, neither unions nor employers favoured measures which would restrict economic and employment growth. The outcome was support for 'sustainable economic development' which was envisaged as marrying economic and environmental goals (ACTU 1989). In practice these objectives have often been difficult to reconcile. An example is the timber industry. Protection of trees, especially in old growth forests, has threatened the livelihood of timber workers.

The ACTUs advice to its affiliates is to seek to bargain with employers over a joint approach to raise levels of awareness in the workplace and to put in place appropriate measures. In many workplaces, environmental issues have been added to the work of occupational health and safety committees. The sorts of issues considered include: energy efficiency, waste minimisation and recycling, pollution and emission controls, workplace environment and compliance with statutory requirements (ACTU Congress Strategy Papers 1993).

To recap, the behaviour of people at work and the nature of their relationships are profoundly influenced by what happens in several spheres. Developments in the economy, in technology, in political fortunes and in the make-up of society often have a marked impact on industrial relations. The environment can be added to this list. It is difficult to make sense of industrial relations and human resource management without reference to the changes occurring in these spheres.

The parties
Unions

Unions are widely perceived to be influential organisations in Australian society. Indeed, they have been considered by many 'to have too much power' (Davis 1979, p. 387). The image of union power rested in the 1960s and 1970s on almost daily accounts of **strikes** and other industrial action bringing to a halt the railways, waterfront, mines and car industry. Strikes made for dramatic stories in the print and electronic media and embedded an impression of considerable union influence. The decline in strike action over the past dozen years, as detailed later in this chapter, has eroded this contribution to the image of union power. The Accords and close relationship of union and Labor government leaders filled the gap. Impressions of union power were fed not on images of striking workers but on the apparent evidence of union influence in government.

Before further discussion it is important to note that unions differ amongst themselves. They differ most obviously in size, historical experience, the industrial and occupational characteristics of members, geographic spread and the political leanings of activists and leaders. This makes generalisation hazardous. Nonetheless, unions operate in the same political–economic environment; they seek to improve members' wages and conditions, and with very few exceptions, they are affiliated to the ACTU.

Unions have undergone major change over the past twenty years. This can be seen in terms of strategy, structure and membership. Up to the mid 1970s unions could be described as focused on increasing the money wages of their members. In addition, they sought to protect and improve members' conditions at work. The major levers used were representation before the industrial tribunals and collective bargaining by those groups with bargaining power. By the end of the 1970s however the traditional strategy appeared flawed. Pursuit of increased money wages in an inflationary context had ratcheted up both wages and prices and resulted in side effects such as increased interest rates and the movement of wage earners into higher tax brackets. Taken together, little progress was made in advancing net real disposable income. Living standards were also adversely affected by cutbacks to social welfare services and the impact of increased unemployment.

From the end of the 1970s unions' strategy changed and broadened. Unions identified their target as the improvement of members' living standards rather than merely their money wages (Davis 1987). This meant union concern for government economic, industry and social policy. Since there appeared little hope of the then conservative government implementing the policies favoured by unions, it meant working with the ALP to secure its election to government and then pursuit of jointly agreed policy. The *Statement of Accord* was the outcome of ALP–ACTU discussions and played a crucial part in the electoral victory of the ALP in 1983. The Accord period, 1983 to early 1996, saw union–government consultation over a raft of economic, industrial and social issues and, without doubt, the policies determined by government reflected the considerable influence of union leaders.

The contribution of unions to national policy development was praised by both Labor Prime Ministers in this period:

> Throughout the life of the Government the trade union movement has been a vital contributor to our policy making, an active participant in the great challenges of our day, and, thus an essential component of the political and economic success of the government (Hawke 1987, p. 43).

and:

> The Accord has helped create the culture in which change can take place; in which the imperatives of competitiveness have been recognised; in which workers' **superannuation** is laying the foundations of a national savings program—and all of this in the context of real protections for those at risk of disadvantage from reform. Each employment target has been met, underlying inflation has been reduced dramatically, and at the same time Australia has been opened up to international trade and regional growth (Keating 1995, p. 5).

The change of federal government in 1996 brought with it an end to praise of this magnitude. Prime Ministerial rhetoric has been transformed with unions more frequently described as obstacles to economic growth and social progress.

Union membership

At the same time that unions and their leaders were being lauded by Labor governments, union membership as a proportion of the workforce (union density) was undergoing steady and significant decline. This is indicated in Table 3.3 which illustrates both the absolute number of union members and the proportion of the workforce unionised. The data are drawn from the household surveys, Trade Union Members, conducted by the Australian Bureau of Statistics since 1976.

Table 3.3 Trade union membership 1982–94

	1982			1994		
	UNION MEMBERS (000s)	EMPLOYEES (000s)	UNION DENSITY %	UNION MEMBERS (000s)	EMPLOYEES (000s)	UNION DENSITY %
Males	1706.9	3194.4	53	1375.8	3626.8	37.9
Females	860.7	1993.4	43	907.5	2899.0	31.3
Total	2567.6	5187.9	49	2283.4	6525.8	35.0

Source: ACTU 1995a, p. 30

Table 3.3 indicates a fall in the absolute number of male members, 1982–94, and a significant fall in density, from 53 per cent to 37.9 per cent. The absolute number of female union members increases; the fall in density is significant, although smaller than the decline in male density. Overall, density fell from 49 per cent to 35 per cent.

Many other comparable countries suffered similar declines suggesting that the explanation for the declines should not be confined to country-specific factors (OECD 1991, pp. 97–134). Factors regarded as influential have included change in the structure of industries, with a shrinking of employment in union strongholds such as mining, the waterfront, manufacturing and the public sector and the expansion of the traditionally lowly unionised services sector; the expansion of the proportion working part-time and the expansion of small businesses and workplaces. The decline in membership has left unions vulnerable to claims that they have lost the confidence of Australian employees and no longer have the right to represent their voice in government and other places. The improved recruitment and retention of members are, understandably, priorities for unions. Many are looking to enterprise bargaining as the vehicle to remind employees of the benefits of membership and, in this way, restore union relevance (Davis 1996).

Employers' associations

The early growth of trade unions in Australia encouraged the development of employers' associations and led them to place greater emphasis on industrial relations functions than their counterparts in some other countries. Numerous employers' associations have a direct role or interest in industrial relations (Plowman 1989). However, there is great variation in the size and complexity of employers' associations from small, single-industry bodies to large organisations which attempt to cover all employers within a particular state. In 1977, the Confederation of Australian Industry (CAI) was established as a single national employers' body, almost 50 years after the formation of the Australian Council of Trade Unions (ACTU). In 1983, a group of large employers set up the Business Council of Australia (BCA) partly as a result of their dissatisfaction with the ability of the CAI to service the needs of its large and diverse membership. Membership of the BCA comprises the chief executive officers of each member company, which has given it a high profile and significant authority when it makes pronouncements on matters such as industrial relations.

Since the mid-1980s there have been several important departures from the CAI. These included large affiliates such as the Metal Trades Industry Association (MTIA) in 1987 and the Australian Chamber of Manufacturers (ACM) in 1989. One repercussion has been employers airing their different viewpoints at events such as **National Wage**

Case hearings. In 1992 the CAI attempted to present a more united front and to attract back former affiliates by merging with the Australian Chamber of Commerce to form a new organisation, the Australian Chamber of Commerce and Industry (ACCI).

Employer associations have been hit by falling membership, mirroring the experience of unions. They too have had to regroup and reconsider the sorts of services that their members require. A number of employer associations have closed. Two examples of associations that have restructured their operations are the Metal Trades Industry Association and the former New South Wales Chamber of Manufacturers, now titled Australian Business Limited. The current emphasis of both organisations is the promotion of services available to members.

HRM IN THE NEWS

MTIA: The bottom line

MTIAs transition (which began many years ago) from being largely an 'industrial relations' oriented organisation to one which networks across most company operations and company managements, has never been more evident than it is now.

A very strongly held philosophy in today's MTIA is that the enhancement of each member's profitability must always be the main focal point of the Association's activities. This applies whether we are engaged in negotiating better enterprise agreements, working to reduce government charges and taxes, advising on product quality improvement, or helping to expand market opportunities for the industry. It's all about the bottom line.

International database

For example, a special MTIA linkup with the World Trade Centre, Sydney and its database communications system is being promoted which will, at reasonable cost, enable individual MTIA members equipped with a computer terminal, a modem, and a telephone to make their offices virtual international trading centres as well. They will be able to advertise their products to, or make inquiries of, many thousands of other firms in 750 cities around the world, communicating direct through the keyboard to a market of immense possibilities. The Global Village has indeed arrived.

Hong Kong—workshop shows how

Also this week MTIA is releasing a special report aimed at maximising the involvement of Australian manufacturers and suppliers in the huge ($22 billion) Hong Kong Airport Project. To help achieve this, MTIA is working within a closely integrated framework with Austrade and the Industrial Supplies Office (ISO).

The on-going service output

While initiatives like the above deserve and receive special attention, MTIA expertise operates in dozens of other ways as an effective extension on the MTIA member company's own management resources, in industrial relations and award matters, in education and training, in commercial, legal and economic services appropriate to the expansive range of industry sectors represented by the Association.

These are the services which are up-front, utilised continuously by company after company across all states.

The unseen underpinning

Underpinning the viability of companies is another MTIA supporting structure which is largely out of sight. MTIA represents its members on no less than 31 national and 61 state statutory and similar bodies which are instrumental in one way or another in influencing members' bottom line. Our representative role extends to the formative function of addressing the real political issues affecting members' businesses and growth: our stakeholder status means new policies and their administrative implementation by governments are usually structured with industry and commercial considerations at the forefront. MTIA constantly monitors developments for industry as a whole, identifying those that may be to our detriment, and, putting forward constructive suggestions designed to make regulations less onerous and compliance thereby less burdensome for business.'

Beyond one company's resources

Industry financial incentives, taxation administration, exports, imports, defence procurement, training and apprenticeship, TAFE, workers' compensation, energy costs, standards, government purchasing, trade practices, these are some of the subjects which come readily to mind in this regard. Add to this all the pre-budget and other submissions to governments throughout the year, and it is clear that no single company could hope to maintain a watching brief across all industry pressure points or argue persuasively for much needed change, using its own resources.

Stability in policymaking

The fact that MTIA services reflect so well the needs of its members is due in no small measure to the stability of its policymaking State Councils and National Executive Committee, whose members are either chief executives or owners of companies faced with the same kind of problems as those which the Association exists to address. Born in 1873, the Association is 'still going stronger' because it continues to focus on the things that make its members more viable in today's rapidly changing and demanding global marketplace.

Source: MTIA (orig.) 1993, pp. 1–3.

Australian Business Limited in 1995 described its services as including:

- business management advice and consulting
- industrial relations advice and advocacy
- representation on industry's needs to government
- education and training programs
- occupational health and safety
- international business and trade advice
- new business opportunities, advice and planning
- leading-edge information on environmental management issues
- interpretation of economic trends and statistics
- access to private investors for small companies in need of new capital (Australian Business Limited 1995, p. 1).

The challenge, therefore, for employer associations as for trade unions is to demonstrate their relevance. Unconvinced members will not pay their subscriptions.

Government

Government at federal and state levels also plays an important role. The federal government has been constrained by the Australian Constitution in its ability to influence industrial relations. The Constitution specifies that the federal Parliament has the power to make laws with respect to:

> **conciliation** and **arbitration** for the prevention and settlement of industrial disputes extending beyond the limits of any one state (S.51.35).

State parliaments are not so constrained. In the 1990s both Labor and Coalition federal governments have looked to other powers in the Constitution, such as the External Affairs (S.51.29) and Corporations' (S.51.20) powers as bases for amendments to industrial relations law, designed to extend the reach of government (Fox, Howard & Pittard 1995, p. 369).

Federal and state governments therefore exert a direct influence on industrial relations through the enactment of law. They also play an important role in their appearance at national and state wage case hearings and in other test cases before industrial tribunals. Alongside unions and employer organisations, they make submissions to the tribunals. Labor governments have generally supported the submissions of unions and Coalition governments, employer associations. When two of the three major parties have combined, this has often appeared to influence the thinking of tribunals but on occasion they have reminded all groups of their independence and their determination to judge the issues before them on their merit.

Governments influence industrial relations in other ways too. They directly influence the pay, conditions, and opportunities of those they employ. In 1994, the Australian Bureau of Statistics reported a total of 6.5 million employees, with approximately 4.9 million (75 per cent) in the private sector and 1.6 million (25 per cent) in the public sector (ABS, 1995). It therefore represents a significant proportion of the total workforce. Finally, government influences industrial relations indirectly by its policies and strategies in other spheres. This is most obvious with regard to economic policy where government measures may affect the rate of economic growth, the tightness of labour markets and bargaining power.

Industrial tribunals

These play an important part in federal industrial relations and most state systems. Their origins can be traced to the very disruptive strikes of the early 1890s which upset the pattern of trade and commerce. Colonial governments passed laws to establish courts which could hear and settle industrial disputes. In the realm of theory, strikes were rendered redundant. In practice, strikes continued but the tribunals were available to encourage conciliation and to arbitrate where necessary.

The *Commonwealth Conciliation and Arbitration Act 1904* was repealed by the Hawke Labor government and replaced by the *Australian Industrial Relations Act 1988* The objects of the Act, as described in 1989, were:

a to promote industrial harmony and co-operation among the parties involved in industrial relations in Australia
b to provide a framework for the prevention and settlement of industrial disputes by conciliation and arbitration in a manner that minimises the disruptive effects of industrial disputes on the community
c to ensure that, in the prevention and settlement of industrial disputes, proper regard is had to the interests of the parties immediately concerned and to the interests (including the economic interests) of the Australian community as a whole
d to facilitate the prevention and prompt settlement of industrial disputes in a fair manner, and with the minimum of legal form and technicality
e to provide for the observance and enforcement of agreements and awards made for the prevention or settlement of industrial disputes
f to encourage the organisation of representative bodies of employers and employees and their registration under this Act
g to encourage the democratic control of organisations, and the participation by their members in the affairs of organisations, and
h to encourage the efficient management of organisations (S.3, as at 1989).

The role of the federal Industrial Relations Commission has been to pursue these goals. To this end it has sought to assist unions and employers in disputes and has conducted National Wage and other hearings to provide and adjust the framework for harmonious industrial relations.

There has been increasing controversy over the role and place of the Commission. The Committee to review Australian Industrial Relations Law and Systems, chaired by Keith Hancock, endorsed the prominent part played by the Commission (Committee of Review 1985). The Business Council of Australia, however, argued that the role of third parties such as tribunals, unions and employer associations should be reduced and enterprises encouraged to work out their own relations (Business Council of Australia, 1989). The BCAs energetic lobbying resulted in a widespread reevaluation of the extent of the Commission's role in the early and mid 1990s. Labor government amendments in 1992 and 1993 to the *Industrial Relations Act 1988* and the Coalition's *Workplace Relations Act 1996* were designed to constrain the role of the Commission and facilitate the workplace or 'decentralised' determination of industrial relations (see below).

Conflict in industrial relations

The conflicting interests of unions and employers have, for many, been at the heart of the study of industrial relations. Employers, in search of greater profits, seek to bear down on the cost of staff wages and conditions; they strive to maintain and extend managerial prerogative. Unions, representing their members' interests, pursue improved wages and conditions and seek to expand their sphere of control within the workplace. The outcome has been a stream of claims met by resistance and counter claims.

Industrial conflict has been viewed from a variety of perspectives. Alan Fox described as 'unitarist' those who liken workplace organisations to 'teams' or a 'family' (Fox 1969). They assume that all employees within the organisation share the goals defined by senior management. Everyone will seek to 'pull their weight'. Conflict within the team or family will be an aberration or the product of disloyalty. It may be the work of stirrers or agitators. 'Pluralists', however, accept that organisations are complex, made of many parts and involve different stakeholders. Everyone will not share identical interests. Among stakeholders may be, for instance, shareholders, top management, supervisors, clerical workers, maintenance workers and process workers. Each group will have its own goals and these may overlap but also may differ from the goals of other groups. From this perspective, conflict is to be expected and even positive to the extent that it reflects legitimate pressures and tensions. The challenge for managers is to develop an effective system of communications to facilitate the expression and resolution of conflicting viewpoints without damaging organisational performance.

A third view of conflict, a radical-left perspective influenced by the writings of Karl Marx, focuses on the imbalance of power between employers and employees. This imbalance is believed to be so great that employees are impelled to overthrow their masters. In the words of Marx and Engels:

> The proletarians have nothing to lose but their chains. They have a world to win (Marx & Engels 1973, p. 96).

Workplace tensions and conflict are expressed in both collective and individual ways. The most obvious and frequently discussed collective expression is strike action. Other forms include bans, work-to-rule and go-slows. The distinguishing feature of these types of action is that they are the product of a collective decision. In the main they involve a union full-time official or union workplace representative, or both. Examples of individual expressions of workplace conflict include voluntary turnover (employees choosing to leave their jobs), absenteeism, sickness, and low morale and motivation. These are not the product of collective decision making and action but the response of the individual to tensions at work.

An indication of days lost through strikes and the pattern since 1980 is indicated in Table 3.4.

Table 3.4 Industrial disputes by incidence, employees involved and working days lost, 1980–95

YEAR	NUMBER OF DISPUTES (IN PROGRESS)	EMPLOYEES INVOLVED DIRECTLY AND INDIRECTLY (000s)	WORKING DAYS LOST PER 1000 EMPLOYEES
1980	2429	1172.8	650
1981	2915	1247.2	797
1982	2060	706.1	358
1983	1787	470.2	249
1984	1965	560.3	248
1985	1895	570.5	228
1986	1754	691.7	242
1987	1517	608.8	223
1988	1508	894.4	269
1989	1402	709.8	190
1990	1193	729.9	207
1991	1036	1181.6	248
1992	728	871.5	147
1993	610	489.6	100
1994	560	265.1	76
1995	642	344.0	79
1996	525	576.9	131

Source: Based on ABS, Cat. no. 6321.0

During the 1970s and 1980s a common presumption was that Australia was 'strike-prone' and that this had an adverse impact on the international competitiveness of Australian enterprises. For instance, other countries might prefer to buy their resources elsewhere where lines of supply were less liable to disruption. The Hancock Committee of Review suggested that too much might have been made of this. When Australia's strike propensity was compared to that of other advanced, industrial societies, Australia emerged somewhere in the middle. Taking the annual average of working days lost per 1000 workers, for the period 1962–81, Australia recorded 497. This was close to 386 for the United Kingdom and 474 for the United States. Countries such as Canada (765) and Italy (1347) had much higher strike propensities and countries such as Germany (47), Japan (113) and Sweden (91) were lower (Committee of Review, vol. 2, 1985, p. 133).

A feature of Table 3.4 is the significant fall in strike propensity since 1981. Indeed, working days lost per one thousand employees in 1995 are ten times lower than the rate in 1981. The continuing decline in strike propensity has been the subject of considerable discussion (Dabscheck 1991). The Accord partners have claimed the credit, arguing that government and unions stuck to their agreements. In particular, unions abided by the pledge that they would make 'no extra claims' in return for improvements to living standards. In addition, union leaders from the mid-1980s proclaimed the importance of working co-operatively with managers, to pursue improved performance and rewards for both managers and employees (Australian Manufacturing Council 1994).

There were other influential factors. The industry restructuring, expansion of small business and increase in part-time and casual work no doubt contributed. Indeed, the most strike prone sectors shrank as a proportion of the workforce. Further, the level of unemployment remained relatively high from 1982 and this may have dampened readiness to take strike action.

The Australian Workplace Industrial Survey (AWIRS) brought more insight to bear. Its analysis of 2353 workplaces with five or more employees found that there was a very uneven spread of industrial action with 88 per cent of all workplaces reporting no industrial action at all in the year reviewed (Callus 1991, p.63).

Table 3.5 Types of industrial action which occurred in the last year*, by sector

TYPE OF INDUSTRIAL ACTION	% OF WORKPLACES WITH INDUSTRIAL ACTION			% OF EMPLOYEES AT WORKPLACES WITH INDUSTRIAL ACTION		
	PRIVATE	PUBLIC	ALL	PRIVATE	PUBLIC	ALL
Strikes	4	20	6	15	38	22
Stop work meetings	4	29	8	21	53	32
Overtime bans	1	12	3	10	26	16
Go slow	0	2	1	3	8	5
Picketing	0	2	0	2	9	4
Work to rule	0	13	2	3	14	6
Other bans	1	10	2	4	21	10
No industrial action	93	57	88	75	34	62

Population: Australian workplaces with at least five employees. Figures are weighted and are based on responses from 2353 workplaces.
Note: Some workplaces had several types of action.
* the data were collected in 1989–90.
Source: R. Callus et al. 1991, p. 63

Table 3.5 indicates that the public sector and larger employers, whether private or public, have a greater experience of some form of industrial action. The reverse of this is that for small and medium-size enterprises, collective industrial action is rare.

The AWIRS also explored individual expressions of conflict. It found that voluntary annual **turnover** across Australian workplaces was 19 per cent (21 per cent in the private sector; 11 per cent in the public sector) and that 4.5 per cent of employees were absent from work in the average week (private sector, 4.2 per cent; public sector, 6.6 per cent) (Callus 1991, pp. 54–61). It can safely be concluded that the cost of high turnover rates and days lost through **absenteeism** dwarf the costs and time loss through strike action, yet strikes and industrial action have retained a much stronger hold on public interest and imagination. Indeed the preoccupation with industrial action and its resolution may have distracted attention away from pursuit of fair and effective HRM. The challenge for enterprises is not simply to stave off industrial action but to foster systems of HRM where there is high trust and high quality relations between managers and their employees. Levels of turnover and absenteeism and surveys of managers and employee opinions may play a useful part in reflecting the state of HRM and providing the basis for discussion of strategy to improve HRM.

Enterprise bargaining

The Australian emphasis on the centralised determination of industrial relations is relatively unusual. Only New Zealand has trodden a similar path (until 1991) although all comparable systems in practice involve centralised and decentralised elements. Notwithstanding the prominent role of state and federal industrial tribunals in Australia, many unions have engaged in bargaining at industry, enterprise and workplace levels. Much of the bargaining has taken place within the broad framework of conciliation and arbitration.

Hancock Committee of Inquiry

In the first Accord of the ACTU and the ALP, it was agreed that 'a centralised system of wage fixation is desirable for both equity and industrial relations reasons ...' (ALP/ACTU 1983, p. 5). Also agreed was the establishment of a major review of industrial relations. Arguably the major issue before the Committee of Review was the appropriate balance to be struck between bargaining and the central determination of pay and conditions.

The Committee received written submissions and held numerous public meetings. It reported that it had heard no convincing case for radical change. It had heard persuasive arguments, from governments, unions and employer organisations, that the centralised system should be endorsed and changes made to increase the effectiveness of the system (Committee of Review 1985, vol. 2).

The publication of the Committee's Report was not however to prove the finest hour for proponents of centralisation. Rather, it marked the beginning of a vigorous push for more bargaining by those opposed to the Committee's recommendations. Their campaign was aided by the relatively high levels of inflation and large current account deficits of 1985 and 1986. The federal government no longer supported the automatic indexation of wages based on price movements. It began to see bargaining as a viable alternative which would link pay increases not to prices but to improved performance.

The ACTU, confronted with alarming evidence on the state of the economy, was pressed to accept the major change of direction. In its report, *Australia Reconstructed*, the ACTU indicated its formal support for the maintenance of centralised wage fixing. It also recognised the need to encourage higher levels of performance (ACTU 1987, pp. 44–56). The solution it advocated was a two tier system of wage fixation with the Commission determining a first tier of pay increases for all workers at the same time. The interests of workers without bargaining power would be protected by such increases. A second tier of wage increases would result from bargaining at industry or enterprise level and would be linked to measures to improve performance. Conscious of the need to guard against inflationary pressure, the ACTU argued for a centrally determined limit on second tier pay increases. Nonetheless, such increases represented a significant break from the centrally determined and uniform system characteristic of the past decade of wage fixation.

National Wage Cases 1987–91

The National Wage Cases (NWC) of 1987–91 reshaped the process of wage determination. In the March 1987 NWC the Commission provided for a **flat-rate** increase of $10 to be paid to all employees on federal awards. There was provision for up to a further 4 per cent increase to be determined on the basis of industry or enterprise bargaining. In addition the bargaining should include changes to work and management practices and matters such as the elimination of work **demarcation** barriers and improvements in training and re-training. The pay increase was therefore to be offset by gains in organisational restructure and efficiency. The NWC decision was a major fillip to bargaining since it was now the sanctioned route to wage increases and to workplace reform. The 1988 and 1989 NWC decisions built on this structure. The bargained agreements were submitted to the Commission for approval or rejection.

One enterprise that was widely recognised for its effective bargaining was ICI Botany.

Managing change

ICI: new ways of working

ICI Botany is a large chemical plant with a history of high levels of industrial disputation resulting from poor relations between management and unions and employees. ICI has addressed this problem by making significant changes to work organisation and practices:

- almost all workers are now paid an annual salary which absorbs **overtime**
- the number of management layers has been cut from seven to four, and the site has been put under the control of one manager rather than three, and
- the production strategy has switched from maximising production and minimising costs to maximising quality. Workers now have the power to stop the manufacturing process to reduce product variability.

When things did not go smoothly, employees used to work longer hours and were paid overtime. The new system gives the 1000 workers a strong incentive to make things work first time, thus enabling them to cut their hours. The results have been impressive:

- sick leave is almost nil, and absenteeism is down from 12 to 2 days a year per worker
- shift teams are managing their own rosters and training schedules
- supervisors are doing diagnostic work, rather than allocating overtime and work
- plant technicians now have a vested interest in operating the production technology to its maximum efficiency rather than 'creating' overtime through plant **downtime**—they are now doing work which was traditionally done on overtime
- the technicians are actively involved in developing training manuals
- quality performance is at an all-time high, while production levels are constantly improving, and
- there has been no industrial disputation.

Source: EPAC 1991, p. 8.

In 1990 the Labor government and the ACTU presented submissions to the National Wage Case calling for additional measures to encourage bargaining. In the main, this meant a reduction in the tests for agreements' approval applied by the Commission.

The Commission, however, in its April 1991 NWC Decision doubted that a greater role for bargaining and reduced role for the Commission would improve economic performance. It therefore refused to endorse the government and ACTU submissions; its emphasis instead was to call for more attention to preparing the ground before moving to greater reliance on bargaining.

The government and the ACTU indicated their dismay at the April NWC decision. They pledged that they would continue to seek a greater role for bargaining and a diminished emphasis on the centralised determination of pay and conditions. ACTU Secretary Bill Kelty's support for more bargaining was indicated in papers to the 1991 ACTU Congress.

HRM IN THE NEWS

Bill Kelty on wages

While there have been undoubted benefits from national wage fixing, particularly during the economic transitionary period of the 80s, there are some undesirable effects of totally removing wage setting from the workplace.

It removes perhaps the main incentive in getting workers active, interested and involved in their workplace. It also reduces the influence of workers in their own workplace, and by implication, workers' self-worth.

The result of wages being totally controlled by people workers don't know, by people who have never visited their workplace, and through a process which workers do not understand or have direct input into, I believe, has reduced workers capacity, willingness and confidence to use their creativity and put forward innovative ideas.

The new wage bargaining strategy is a strategy designed to create more interesting and financially rewarding jobs, by stimulating greater worker involvement in all aspects of the way their industry and workplace operates, thereby driving enterprise reform and pushing up productivity levels.

A more decentralised wage fixing system will put the spotlight back on the only place where Australia's real economic battle will be won—in Australian workplaces.

Overall, I believe that the effects of this policy will be very positive for unions. Workers will be able to see for themselves how wages are improved, and see the benefits that unions deliver'.

Source: ACTU 1991, p. 1.

A second NWC in 1991 saw the Commission respond to the chorus of government, union and employer submissions. The October NWC introduced an Enterprise Bargaining Principle.

The tests for approval of agreements were eased but still required evidence that wage increases were based 'on the actual implementation of efficiency measures designed to effect real gains in productivity' (NWC October 1991). The agreements were also required to contain a broad agenda of items, to involve single bargaining units and to include union pledges to make 'no extra claims'. The Commission warned that many bargaining mechanisms remained inadequate and unlikely to lead to increases in performance. It noted the risk of increasing industrial disputes and the unleashing of a new round of inflationary pressures.

The Labor government, though it welcomed the October NWC decision, evidently considered that the Commission had not gone far enough. In 1992, it introduced a significant batch of amendments to the Industrial Relations Act 'to facilitate the making and certifying of agreements ...' (S.134A(1)). The Commission was now obliged by the amended Act to certify agreements if six tests were met:

- employees must not be disadvantaged by the agreement
- a disputes settlement procedure must be included
- a term of operation must be specified
- in a single enterprise agreement, at least one union with members at the workplace must be party to the agreement
- unions must consult their members about the terms of the agreement
- unions must report the outcomes to the Commission [S.134E(1)].

These changes were then consolidated in the further reworking of the *Industrial Relations Act 1993*. The new provisions, in operation from March 1994, encouraged both the making of collective agreements and enterprise flexibility agreements. The former required the involvement of unions; the latter were open to non-union members but involved some additional tests, including the Commission's view that such agreements were 'in the public interest'. Although, these agreements were designed to facilitate bargaining by non-unionists, the unions capable of covering the employees had the right to be heard at Commission hearings. This may well have proved a factor dissuading employers from seeking enterprise flexibility agreements, fearing that unions might recruit their previously non-unionised employees. Only a relatively small number of such agreements were ever signed.

Equity and enterprise bargaining

The conventional wisdom was that bargaining disadvantages those groups without bargaining power. For instance, the pay and conditions of women workers, workers from a non-English speaking background and young workers might be expected to fall behind those of male, English-speaking and mature workers. The reasons for this include the concentration of disadvantaged groups in occupations and industries characterised by low pay and conditions, the high proportion working part-time, lower unionisation rates and poor representation within bargaining units.

The ACTU and Labor government addressed the linkage of bargaining and inequity in their seventh Accord. It committed the partners to enterprise bargaining but also to a range of measures to counteract regressive forces. The amended Industrial Relations Act included among its objectives the prevention and elimination of discrimination, 'on the basis of race, colour, sex, sexual preference, age, physical or mental disability, marital status, family responsibilities, pregnancy, religion, political opinion, national extraction or social origin' [*Industrial Relations Act 1988, 1994*, S.3(g)]. An example of the application of this was that employers were forbidden to terminate employment on one or more of these grounds (S.170DF(1)(f)). The Act also stipulated that there should be 'equal remuneration for work of equal value' (S.170BA). The term 'remuneration' was preferred to 'pay' since it included bonus and other arrangements, which might apply unequally in the workforce. The Act also stated that Commissioners must refuse to certify bargained agreements if they saw evidence of discrimination (S.170MDS).

The extent to which these measures counteracted the assumed discriminatory impact of bargaining is uncertain. Labor government and ACTU leaders argued that the safeguards, the maintenance of award pay and conditions as a safety-net and agreed safety-net pay increases should have the combined effect of protecting those with little bargaining power while encouraging others to engage in workplace negotiations (George 1995 and Johns 1995). The Department of Industrial Relations' report, *Enterprise Bargaining in Australia* (1995), found little evidence that bargaining was associated significantly with unequal pay outcomes for men and women workers. Indeed women were more likely than men to state that bargaining had left them 'better off' (Department of Industrial Relations 1995, p. 253). The report suggested that the women employees engaged in bargaining fared as well as their male counterparts. But since a smaller proportion of women are union members and a greater proportion are concentrated in a small number of occupations characterised by low pay and conditions, the overall impact may be a widening of the gap between male and female earnings and opportunities. As nearly all commentators agree, it is too early to be definitive about the impact of the recent shift to bargaining on equity.

Workplace practice

By the middle of the 1990s, the laws of federal and state governments in Australia had been substantially amended to promote enterprise bargaining and decisions of the federal Industrial Relations Tribunal reflected its measured support for bargaining. On top of this union and employer peak councils and both sides of politics apparently agreed on the need for an enhanced role for bargaining. What, then, was the outcome? Did the rewriting of rules and diverse expressions of support produce a surge of workplace bargaining?

The picture is mixed. Table 3.6 reveals the recorded number of registered agreements and the approximate proportion of employees, by jurisdiction, covered by such agreements.

Table 3.6 Number of registered agreements and employees covered, September 1995

JURISDICTION	NUMBER OF AGREEMENTS*	% OF EMPLOYEES IN JURISDICTION COVERED**
Federal	5130	58
NSW	1570	29
Victoria	457	n.a.
Queensland	667	30
South Australia	255	22
Western Australia	583	15
Tasmania	705	5

Source: ACIRRT, ADAM 1995, p. 4.
*These are collective union and non-union agreements only.
**This figure represents the proportion of employees covered by agreements who are eligible to be covered by awards in each jurisdiction.

The table indicates over 5000 registered agreements covering federal award employees, nearly 60 per cent of this group. The numbers of agreements and proportions covered in the larger, state award sector are significantly smaller with the overall result that by the end of 1995 perhaps a quarter of Australian wage and salary earners were covered by registered agreements. Since bargaining had such apparently broad support and since it was also the route sanctioned for pay increases and workplace reform, this may appear disappointingly modest coverage. Proponents of bargaining have countered that the data may misrepresent the true state of bargaining. A Department of Industrial Relations survey in 1993 found that some 47 per cent of workplaces were covered by some type of agreement, but only 11 per cent of workplaces were covered by agreements ratified by an industrial tribunal. The majority of employees were covered by written unratified or verbal agreements (Department of Industrial Relations 1993, p. 4).

It is important also to explore the quality of bargained agreements, although this is difficult to do in the case of unregistered agreements. Even in the case of registered agreements, it must be remembered that the agreements are not necessarily a guide to what happens in practice in workplaces. Good intentions in agreements may fall by the wayside. An example are commitments to establish consultative bodies. These may never meet, may meet irregularly or may find their work restricted and not worth their while.

Several research findings are pertinent. A 1994 DIR survey of 1060 workplaces suggested that 50 per cent bargained over at least one condition but this might be pay rates. Table 3.7 indicates the extent to which bargaining occurred over a range of key issues:

Table 3.7 Proportion of workplaces involved in bargaining: by issue

Work organisation	27%
Management systems	24%
IR systems	21%
Employment patterns	17%
Working time	12%
Work and family	5%

Source: DIR 1995, p. 353

It is instructive that in a period of major and turbulent change, the great majority of organisations were not negotiating over the issues listed in the table.

The Australian Centre for Industrial Relations Research and Teaching (ACIRRT) has pointed to further limiting features of bargaining. Bargaining appears to be initiated by managers or union officials outside the workplace and it is these players who then comprise the key negotiators (ACIRRT, ADAM 1995, no. 7, p. 11). The rationale for workplace bargaining is to bring managers, employees and their union representatives together to discuss and resolve pertinent issues. The ambition is that the process will bring the participants closer together and the outcome will be improved performance, pay and conditions. If the process involves mainly those beyond, rather than within, the workplace then it is less likely that these gains will be captured. Indeed, the differences between the centralised determination of industrial issues and bargaining are minimised since both processes occur outside the workplace.

The points made by Dr Ray Marshall are relevant. The successful workplace of the future, in his view, will be characterised by high levels of employee involvement, major investment in training and concern for fairness. This formula will lay the foundation for high quality performance.

Future organisational forms

Workplace relations: Best Practice

BY DR RAY MARSHALL

There are only two choices: you can either compete with wages or improve productivity. There are no other options. Most people, if they consider it, will do as you have done in Australia—reject the low wage option. Why?

It implies lower and more unequal incomes, which is what we're getting in the US. It also implies something else very important: that is that the only way you can maintain and improve your position is to work harder, and there is a limit to how hard you can work.

The other option to improve productivity and quality puts you on a very steep earning and learning curve by substituting ideas, skills and knowledge for physical resources.

What must you do if you pursue the high-productivity option? I think best practice is what it is all about. Right now, it is obviously quality-driven. Why?

We are in a market-driven world and that means that you have to meet your customers' needs or your constituents' needs or your students' needs. We applied that bureaucratic system to governments and to schools and they were producer-driven. Henry Ford said that you could have whatever colour car you liked as long as it was black. Well nobody would say that these days: that's a producer-driven system.

There is monumental waste in mass production systems, and one of the easiest things is to go in and cut out the waste. Then, after you do that, you have to change the structure and produce more productivity and quality. You also need flexibility.

Another thing to be concerned about is equity and fairness. In the traditional economics there is a trade-off between equity and fairness—and what you recognise, and very few economists recognise, is that a fair system is an efficient system because, by definition, it is a system and equity is one of the most important driving forces.

You must worry about flexibility to ensure you don't shift all the costs of the system to the weak and marginalised in the system and call that flexibility. Some people are trying to do this—get flexibility by eliminating the safety nets. That is not a good way.

And then you've got to develop and use leading-edge technology. And you need a well-trained, well-educated workforce. One of the big mistakes that American companies made when the economy was opened and they had to compete is they decided not to pay any attention to the workers and their skills, but opted to leapfrog the Japanese by automating.

General Motors spent about $US77 billion on that theory and by the end they were worse off than when they started. Why? You have to do what the Japanese call giving wisdom to machines. The people make the machines work. The machines are relatively unimportant.

You don't go to unskilled workers and smart machines. That's a losing model. You go to smart workers and smart machines—that's what best practice is all about.

Two of the most important skills that our mass production schools didn't turn out are: you have to have the ability to impose order on information and you need the learning skills. Learning is one of the most important things in life.

A good hypothesis about best practice is that the very best companies will be those that are the best learning systems. They learn more from their customers, from each other and from other people by benchmarking.

Source: *Financial Review*, 2 March 1994, p. 15.

The major DIR report on enterprise bargaining in 1994 found some employees perceiving that they were left better off by bargaining but a similar proportion reporting that they were worse off. A yet larger group perceived 'no change':

Table 3.8 Enterprise bargaining: employee* views of changes over the previous 12 months (1994–95) (%)

	HIGHER %	NO CHANGE %	LOWER %
1 Ability to influence hours of work	16	70	13
2 Say in decisions	23	57	19
3 Information provided by management	23	53	24
4 Satisfaction with management	14	44	42

*11 296 employees were surveyed; this table gives the responses of those covered in Part VI B agreements
Source: DIR 1995b, p. 376

The 'no change' or lower levels of satisfaction with management might be linked either to the content or the process of bargained agreements. Many agreements involved the lengthening of normal working hours and many introduced measures to reduce the labour force. Many of the wage increases gained were relatively modest. Where these conditions prevailed, employee satisfaction was likely to be muted. But for many employees, as indicated, the process may also have lacked charm. It may have appeared limited and imposed rather than embracing the broad issues of concern to employees and jointly determined.

There are therefore several indicators that enterprise bargaining has failed to extend its coverage broadly across the workforce and that the quality of many negotiated agreements may be relatively poor. On the other hand, there have been some outstanding agreements which have achieved major improvements in performance and well rewarded both managers and employees. Many such cases are recorded in the Best Practice program publications and in the DIRs journal *Benchmark*. The broader concern is that these may have been 'islands of excellence', far from typical of the experience of bargaining of most Australian workplaces.

There are important implications for HRM. Bargaining has the potential to bring managers, their employees and where appropriate their representatives together to discuss the major issues facing the workplace and to determine agreed strategies. But it cannot be assumed that managers, employees and their representatives will arrive at the process with 'listening' and negotiation skills. The ground has to be prepared carefully, with consultation and training playing their part to assist those involved. There needs also to be recognition that the process is time-consuming and not necessarily smooth. The prize lies in the potential to improve broad HRM.

Recent reforms in industrial relations
Workplace Relations Act
The Howard-led Coalition announced a program of industrial relations reform in the run-up to the 1996 federal election. Though both Labor and the Coalition advocated

a major role for bargaining and an important role for the Industrial Relations Commission, they differed in the weight given to the Commission's role and in their view of unions. The Coalition indicated its wish to restrict the ambit of the Commission and to provide alternative vehicles to determine industrial relations. One reflection of this was the proposed creation of Australian Workplace Agreements (AWAs) which could involve managers and individuals or groups of employees. Such agreements need not be scrutinised by, or registered with, the Commission and need not involve unions. A new body, the Employment Advocate, was proposed to provide advice to employers and employees and to file AWAs (Coalition 1995).

The *Workplace Relations and Other Legislation Amendment Bill 1996* was introduced into the Parliament soon after the Coalition's electoral victory. Denied a majority in the Senate, the Bill went before a Senate Committee and was the subject of lengthy negotiations with the Australian Democrats and other minor parties and Independent Senators. The Bill was passed in late 1996. The objects of the Act reflect the Coalition's wish to entrench the workplace as the focus for industrial relations and to provide employers and employees with a choice over the form of agreement to rule in the workplace. A feature of the Act is the specification of 'allowable matters'. The Commission's powers in relation to arbitrating disputes and making awards are confined in the main to approximately twenty matters, including ordinary hours of work and rates of pay; annual, long service, parental and family leave; penalty rates; dispute settlement and other specified matters. Before, the Commission had the right to consider and determine a broad array of matters. Unions have complained that this represents an intolerable attack upon the Commission and will lead to the removal of important conditions and rights for employees. Some employer organisations have countered that the Commission retains sway over the most significant matters and that this limits the flexibility of employers and employees to make agreements of their choice.

Other features of the Act are the strengthening of sanctions in the face of industrial action and measures to encourage the formation of enterprise unions. The Act also provides assistance for those sections of unions which may wish to withdraw from amalgamations. These are bitter-sweet provisions for many employers. While they may wish to see smaller and weaker unions, few relish the prospect of unions competing aggressively for membership. One scenario is that unions would vie to outbid each other in claims of the pay increases they can deliver.

The government's defence of the changes enacted is that they will simplify the rules governing industrial relations, provide more choice and encourage compliance. The Act certainly represents a further step on the path to reform, begun in the mid-1980s. There will be a further shift to more decentralisation. From another angle, the impact might be more modest. Relatively little change will be visited upon the significant section of the workforce (65 per cent) that is non-unionised and it is probable that large employers, in the public and private sector, with high levels of union membership will continue to bargain as before over awards and agreements. The trend may well be mixed with some sectors seeing increased unionisation, while others may see a continuing decline and a raft of AWA or informal agreements covering pay and conditions. In many small workplaces there will continue to be no agreements at all.

A remaining concern of unions is that the Act will leave those with little bargaining power, and particularly women workers, worse off.

Managing diversity

Workplace Relations Bill: some union concerns

The Government is proposing to remove from awards a number of significant conditions, such as clauses dealing with:
- consultative arrangements
- EEO and workplace harassment
- procedures for dealing with termination of employment
- superannuation
- transport
- occupational health and safety
- comprehensive right of entry to workplaces for union officials.

The terms of the Workplace Relations Bill require that existing clauses covering these issues be removed from awards following eighteen months transition period. The Commission would be prohibited from inserting such award clauses after the commencement in awards and the Act would be prohibited from arbitrating in respect to any dispute involving these issues.

As these provisions will not be included in awards they will continue to apply only if employers agree to include them in agreements. It is unrealistic to expect that most women, particularly those employed in small business, will be able to negotiate these provisions with their employer. This is a terribly retrograde step for all of us who have sought to achieve understanding of equal employment opportunity and sexual harassment principles by employers and workers. And who have sought to have policies and procedures for dealing with these issues put in place at a workplace level.

All EEO practitioners understand how hard it is to get more than lip-service given to the principles involved in genuine equality of opportunity and the importance of having specific procedures put in place to ensure adherence of these principles.

In practice, notwithstanding overall company adoption of EEO principles it has often been at the middle or lower level management structures that problems arise.

Often there is inevitable conflict between a company's EEO objectives and their commercial imperatives.

Having award status brought EEO provisions into the mainstream of industrial relations practice and forced all involved—management at all levels and union members and delegates—to treat the issues seriously. So it is a tragedy that these clauses are to be removed from awards. In the unequal bargaining position of workers and management and the unequal status given to EEO and Sexual Harassment compared to other more immediate concerns of workers where there is some bargaining capacity, we do not expect EEO and Sexual Harassment procedures to be the subject of many outside award agreements.

Source: George 1996, pp. 12–14.

Summary

The 1980s to the mid-1990s have witnessed major changes in Australian industrial relations. These have been linked to the turbulent economic environment and to a broadly perceived need to improve industrial relations in the search for greater industry and enterprise performance. The long period of Labor government was also important as government forged agreement with union leaders on economic, industry and social policy. The Accords reflected the prominent role of unions; members and potential members may not have shared their leaders' satisfaction. Union membership fell steadily, to approximately a third of the workforce in the mid 1990s.

There has also been a significant shift in the balance between centralisation and decentralisation. During the late 1980s and early 1990s seemingly both Labor and the Coalition argued for a greater role for workplace bargaining and a diminished role for the Commission. The ACTU and employer organisations and councils similarly sought more bargaining. The apparent consensus was misleading since each group retained its own interpretation of bargaining and the appropriate framework for its operation.

One lesson from the previous decade has been the decreased relevance of efforts to distinguish industrial relations from HRM. Both are concerned with the relations of managers and their employees. Both highlight the importance of equity in the workplace and both focus on the links to be found between good industrial relations, high quality HRM and high levels of performance.

questions for discussion and review

1. Why and in what ways is industrial relations important?
2. What most influences developments in industrial relations? How important are changes in the economy?; changes in government?
3. Why has the proportion of workers in unions fallen so much over the past ten years?
4. Is Australia strike-prone? Does it have too many strikes?
5. What are the main features of enterprise bargaining in Australia?
6. Is it useful to talk about differences between industrial relations and HRM? In what ways are they similar and different?
7. Discuss the ways in which major changes impact on workplace relations. What does it mean for the workplace of the future? What will industrial relations look like?
8. Is there still a role for centralised industrial relations tribunals or should industrial relations be left to managers and their employees?
9. Has there been too much emphasis on conflict in industrial relations? Managers and employees share an interest in the prosperity of their organisation: should this be the core of industrial relations?
10. Has enterprise bargaining failed to deliver improved performance? What should be done to encourage fairness and high quality performance at work?

case study

HRM and enterprise bargaining

Only four months after Melbourne's Sheraton Towers Southgate opened for business in June 1992, the Industrial Relations Commission certified the new hotel's enterprise agreement.

In partnership with the Australian Council of Trade Unions and the Australian Liquor, Hospitality and Miscellaneous Workers Union, the senior management began negotiating an enterprise agreement 12 months before the hotel opened. All parties recognised that they had a unique opportunity to adopt a fresh approach to the hotel's resource planning and management. It was agreed that the agreement needed to incorporate the principles of empowerment, customer focus and continuous improvement.

A key feature of the enterprise agreement is the way in which it deals with penalty rates and flexible working hours, a major issue in the 24-hour, seven-day tourism and hospitality industry. Penalty rates were incorporated into a base-hourly rate only after a lengthy process of consultation with the union and employees within the context of the broader process of workplace reform, rather than as an isolated and negative cost-cutting exercise.

The system of remuneration reinforces the emphasis on multi-skilling. The broadbanded structure provides increased flexibility by reducing the need to hire additional staff or pay employees different rates for occasionally working in higher classifications. This new classification structure has led to a reduction in administrative costs and demarcation disputes, greater cross-task flexibility through multiskilling and greater flexibility in replacing employees who are absent for short periods of time.

Another central aspect of the enterprise agreement is the commitment to permanency of employment for employees and a much higher percentage of full-time employees than usual in international hotels in Australia. The agreement states that: 'Except in exceptional circumstances, there will be no positions offered to casual employees'.

The 384-room Sheraton Southgate has 400 employees at present, says Human Resources Director Gary Black, and 70 per cent are permanent, full-time staff. The remainder are permanent but working only part time. 'Normally around 60 per cent of staff in hotels are employed on a casual basis so it is quite a change', he says.

The result is greater job security for employees and, over time, significant savings to Sheraton from substantial reductions in training and administrative costs such as turnover and absenteeism. The agreement has already led to significantly improved turnover rates by comparison with other new hotels—currently averaging 37 per cent at Sheraton Southgate as against the 60–80 per cent experienced by other new hotels in the first two years of their operations—has substantially improved the skill base of the organisation and has made a major contribution to permanency in employment in an industry traditionally characterised by casual employment.

Source: DIR 1995b, pp. 22–23.

Questions
1. What did hotel management gain from the enterprise agreement?
2. What did employees gain from the agreement?
3. What were the links between the agreement and the broader process of workplace reform?
4. What is multiskilling? Does it mean more work and more stress for employees?
5. Why is employee turnover relatively high in the hotel industry?
6. Once agreements are made, what is required to translate the content of agreements into practice?

Resources

Callus, R. et al. (1991), *Industrial Relations at Work: the Australian Industrial Relations Workplace Survey*, Australian Government Publishing Service, Canberra.

Deery, S. & D. Plowman, (1991), *Australian Industrial Relations*, McGraw-Hill, Sydney.

Department of Industrial Relations (1996), *Enterprise Bargaining in Australia: Annual Report 1995*, Australian Government Publishing Service, Canberra.

Economic Planning Advisory Commission (EPAC) (1995), *Human Resource Management and Workplace Change*, Australian Government Publishing Service, Canberra.

Fox, C., Howard, W. & Pittard, M. (1995), *Industrial Relations in Australia*, Longman, Melbourne.

References

Australian Bureau of Statistics (ABS) *Australian Economic Indicators*, Cat. no. 1350.0.
—— *Industrial Disputes, Australia*, Cat. no. 6321.0
—— *The Labour Force*, Cat. no. 6203.0.
Australian Business Limited (ABL) 'An Introduction', ABL, Sydney.
Australian Centre for Industrial Relations Research and Teaching (ACIRRT) (1995), *Agreements Database and Monitor (ADAM)*, ACIRRT, Sydney.
Australian Council of Trade Unions (ACTU) (and Trade Development Council) (1987), *Australian Reconstructed*, Australian Government Publishing Service, Canberra.
—— (1989), *Report on the Environment to 1989 ACTU Congress*, ACTU D197, Melbourne.
—— (1991), *Together for Tomorrow*, Congress, ACTU, Melbourne.
—— (1995a), *The Future of Unions in Australia*, Report to 1995 Congress, Melbourne.
—— (1995b), *Accord Mark VIII, 1995–1999*, Melbourne, ACTU, D. no. 055, Melbourne, p. 95.
—— (1989), Resolution in Minutes, 1989 ACTU Congress, Melbourne.
Australian Industrial Relations Act 1988 (1994), CCH, Sydney.
Australian Labor Party (ALP) & ACTU (1983), *Statement of Accord*, ACTU, Melbourne.
Australian Manufacturing Council (AMC) (1994), *Discovering Best Practice: the Union Experience*, AMC, Melbourne.
Business Council of Australia (BCA) (1989), *Enterprise-based Bargaining Units: A Better Way of Working*, BCA, Melbourne.
—— (1996), *Business Council Bulletin*, no. 130, May 1996.
Callus, R. et al. (1991), *Industrial Relations at Work: the Australian Industrial Relations Workplace Survey*, Australian Government Publishing Service, Canberra.
Coalition (1995), *Better Pay for Better Work*, Andrew Robb, Melbourne.
Committee of Inquiry into Technological Change in Australia (1980), *Technological Change in Australia*, Australian Government Publishing Service, Canberra.
Committee of Review into Australian Industrial Relations Law and Systems (1985), *Report*, Australian Government Publishing Service, Canberra.
Dabscheck, B (1991), 'A Decade of Striking Figures', *Economic and Labour Relations Review*, vol. 2, no.1, pp. 172–96.
Davis, E. M. (1979), 'Community Attitudes Towards Trade Unions', *Journal of Industrial Relations*, vol. 21, no. 4, pp. 381–97.
—— (1987), 'Roles of Australian Unions in Industrial Relations', in G. Ford, J. Hearn & R. Lansbury (eds), *Australian Labour Relations*, 4th edition, McGraw-Hill, Melbourne, pp. 280–97.
—— (1996), 'The 1995 ACTU Congress: Recruitment and Retention', *Economic and Labour Relations Review*, vol. 7, no. 1, pp. 165–81.

Davis, E. M. & C. Harris, C. (eds) (1995) *Making the Link: Affirmative Action and Industrial Relations*, no. 6, Australian Government Publishing Service, Canberra.

Deery, S. & Plowman, D. (1991), *Australian Industrial Relations*, McGraw-Hill, Sydney.

Department of Industrial Relations (1993), *The Spread and Impact of Workplace Bargaining*, Australian Government Publishing Service, Canberra.

—— (1995a), *Enterprise Bargaining in Australia, Annual Report 1994*, Australian Government Publishing Service, Canberra.

—— (1995b), 'HRM and enterprise bargaining', *Benchmark*, May, pp. 22–23.

Dunlop, J. (1958), *Industrial Relations Systems*, Southern Illinois University Press.

Economic Planning Advisory Commission (EPAC) (1995), *Human Resource Management and Workplace Change*, Australian Government Publishing Service, Canberra.

Fox, A. (1969), 'Management Frame of Reference', in A. Flanders (ed.), *Collective Bargaining*, Penguin, Harmondsworth, pp. 390–409.

Fox, C., Howard, W. & Pittard, M. (1995), *Industrial Relations in Australia*, Longman, Melbourne.

George, J. (1995), 'Women and Enterprise Bargaining', in E. M. Davis & C. Harris, *Making the Link: Affirmative Action and Industrial Relations*, no. 6, pp. 5–7, Australian Government Publishing Service, Canberra.

—— (1996), 'Workplace Relations Bill: some union concerns', Extract from address to 8th Women, Management and Industrial Relations Conference, 24 July, Sydney.

Hawke, R. J. (1987), Address to ACTU Congress 1987, *Attachments*, ACTU, Melbourne, pp. 43–55.

Howard, W. A. (1977), 'Australian Trade Unions in the Context of Trade Union Theory', *Journal of Industrial Relations*, vol. 19, no. 3, pp. 255–73.

International Labour Organisation (ILO) (1990), *Environment and the World of Work*, ILO, Geneva.

—— (1992), *Information Bulletin*, August, ILO, Geneva.

Johns, G. (1995), 'Industrial Relations Reform and EEO', in E. M. Davis & C. Harris (eds), *Making the Link: Affirmative Action and Industrial Relations* no. 6, pp. 1–4, Australian Government Publishing Service, Canberra.

Keating, P. J. (1995), Address to ACTU Congress, *Minutes*, (Attachment B), ACTU, Melbourne, pp. 1–11.

Lansbury, R. D. & Davis, E. M. (1984), *Technology, Work and Industrial Relations*, Longman, Melbourne.

Martin, R. (1980), *Trade Unions in Australia*, Penguin, Harmondsworth.

Marx, K. & Engels, F. (1973), *The Manifesto of the Communist Party*, Progress, Moscow.

Metal Trades Industry Association (1993), Newsletter, vol. 10, no. 6, pp. 1–4.

Moore, Sir John (1984), 'Termination, Change and Redundancy Case', Statement, Melbourne, 2 August, Australian Conciliation and Arbitration Commission, Melbourne, p. 2.

Mundey, J. (1981), *Green Bans and Beyond*, Angus & Robertson, Sydney.

Niland, J. (1994), 'Change and the International Exchange of Ideas', in J. Niland, R. Lansbury & C. Verevis, *The Future of Industrial Relations*, Thousand Oaks, Sage, pp. 451–71.

Organisation for Economic Cooperation and Development (OECD) (1991), *Employment Outlook*, OECD, Paris.

Plowman, D. (1987), 'The Role of Employer Associations', in G. Ford, J. Hearn & R. Lansbury (eds), *Australian Labour Relations Readings*, 4th edition, Macmillan, Melbourne, pp. 229–48.

Chapter 4

Equal Employment Opportunity

Robin Kramar

learning objectives

After studying this chapter, you will be able to:

1. Explain the reasons Australian organisations are required to create EEO.
2. Identify and assess the implications of the legal requirements for EEO and anti-discrimination for human resource policies and practices.
3. Identify examples of best practice EEO initiatives.
4. Discuss future developments in EEO.

chapter 4

chapter outline

- Introducing Equal Employment Opportunity — 126
  - Discrimination — 126
  - Equal Employment Opportunity — 127
  - Affirmative Action — 127
  - Sexual harassment — 127
- Reasons for the development of Equal Employment Opportunity — 129
  - International standards — 129
  - Legislation — 129
- Australian developments — 130
  - Anti-discrimination — 130
  - Affirmative Action — 131
  - Effectiveness Review of the Affirmative Action Act — 132
  - Work and family — 133
- Equal Employment Opportunity legislation in Australia — 134
  - Discrimination legislation — 134
  - Affirmative Action and Equal Employment Opportunity legislation — 137
  - Industrial relations legislation — 143
- Implications for human resource policies and practices — 145
  - Potential wide-ranging implications — 145
  - Continued improvement in compliance — 145
  - A narrow interpretation of Equal Employment Opportunity — 146
- Examples of Best Practice EEO initiatives — 147
  - Air International — 149
  - National Roads and Motorists' Association — 150
  - Caltex — 150
- The future — 152
- Summary — 153
- Questions for discussion and review — 154
- Case study — 154
- Resources — 156
- References — 156

HRM IN THE NEWS

'Family-friendly' policies do not lead to equal opportunities

BY MAUREEN FASTENAU

Many organisations have developed family-friendly policies and practices to facilitate equal opportunity—and equal rewards—for women in the workforce. While these policies have undoubtedly made it easier for women to participate in or return to the workforce, they have not made the workforce a place of equal opportunities.

This is because organisational values and culture have not correspondingly changed; family-friendly policies have not altered the gender privilege of men. Although such policies are equally available to men and women, it is the rare male employee who uses them. These are often seen as policies and practices for women, and the women who use them are generally perceived as having their loyalty split between their families and the organisation and thus are suspect.

For example, *BRW* reported recently on a case before the Equal Opportunity Board in Melbourne in which a woman employee of a major oil company alleged that upon return from maternity leave she was expected to take a lesser position than the executive position she had previously held.

The federal human rights and equal opportunity commissioner, Sue Walpole, noted than this case was not an isolated example. There are increasing numbers of complaints from senior and middle women managers who report that they have encountered discrimination in employment when they are pregnant or return from maternity leave.

It appears that male managers and colleagues make negative assumptions about the capabilities and priorities of women with children.[1] Thus while organisational policies allow for maternity leave, organisational culture and values effectively penalise women who use it.

Several studies[2] of men in non-traditional careers (nursing, primary school teaching, social work, librarianship) highlight the difficulties of making the workforce a place where merit, rather than gender, is the measure for access to equal employment opportunities. One of the authors was inspired to describe men's experience in female-dominated occupations as the 'glass escalator' to contrast with the 'glass ceiling' encountered by women.

Women seeking to enter traditionally male-dominated occupations or levels of employment encounter discrimination—subtle and not-so-subtle—that hinders their employment or advancement. Men seeking to enter gender-atypical occupations will also encounter discrimination—but it will most usually be favourable to them.

The first discrimination women encounter is when seeking initial employment. While overt discrimination is now relatively rare, it still occurs: witness the recent case where two women seeking employment as race stewards were asked questions about their relationships, their intentions to start a family, and their dress.

The absence of overt discrimination does not mean, however, that women do not still face direct, indirect, and systematic discrimination. Hostile questioning, the presence of only one woman on the selection panel (often clearly junior to the men), and measures of merit based on male presentation can all work to undermine women's ability to present themselves well or to be perceived favourably.

Men seeking to enter female-dominated occupations—except in relatively few areas such as kindergarten teaching or midwifery—are welcomed and often preferred to women applicants. And, while male applicants may be 'tracked' out of or away from the most female-identified specialty areas of female-dominated occupations, they are generally 'tracked' into those areas that provide access to greater power, status, and financial rewards.

If they are hired, women who enter male-dominated occupations or employment levels often report encountering 'poisoned work environments' where they feel unwanted, isolated, and unsupported. Many report being sexually harassed, making their work environment uncomfortable or threatening.

Men in female-dominated occupations or workplaces do not suffer similarly hostile environments. First, men in female-dominated occupations are more likely to be supervised by men than women in male-dominated occupations are to be supervised by women. Thus even in female-dominated occupations and workplaces, men are provided with support and mentoring that enhances their opportunities for success and acceptance.

Men in gender-atypical occupations are more likely to have their gender 'construed as positive difference ... they have an incentive to bond together and emphasise their distinctiveness from the female majority' (Williams 1992, p. 259).

Women, on the other hand, because they do not feel accepted by their male colleagues and by male managers—because women's gender is likely to be construed as negative difference—seek to avoid situations that call attention to their gender by, for example, associating frequently and closely with their female colleagues. Men employed in female-dominated occupations do not report hostility from their female colleagues or experience a sense of isolation. None of the men in the studies reported being sexually harassed. While men were often required—or requested—to undertake what might be regarded as gender-specific tasks or functions (e.g. catheterising male patients, handling boys with discipline problems), this was more likely to be regarded by them and their female colleagues and managers as 'being appreciated for the special traits and abilities [men] could contribute to their professions'.

Most of the men involved in the studies indicated that they were invited to participate in the informal social activities organised by their female colleagues. Men in female-dominated workplaces and occupations were thus more likely than women in gender-atypical work situations to find their work environment comfortable, congenial, and supportive.

Men in female-dominated occupations—like their counterparts in male-dominated occupations—are less likely than women to require organisational flexibility with regard to combining work with family responsibilities. Even in female-dominated occupations and workplaces, there is little tolerance for women's 'divided loyalties' or appreciation of the skills developed through responding to and meeting family and community responsibilities.

Men are more likely to have uninterrupted careers and to be able to adjust their lives around work requirements. Even in female-dominated occupations and workplaces, these demonstrations of men's organisational commitment—often based on their female partner's willingness and ability to shoulder family commitments—will be rewarded without questioning the gender assumptions on which it is based.

Williams (p. 264) concludes her study of men in female-dominated occupations with the observation:

'The stereotypes that differentiate masculinity and femininity, and degrade that which is deemed as feminine, are deeply entrenched in culture, social structure, and personality. Nothing short of a revolution in cultural definitions of masculinity [and femininity] will effect the broad scale social transformation needed to achieve the complete occupational integration of men and women'.

Organisations are to be commended for establishing family-friendly policies and practices. If, however, they are committed to enabling women to have equal employment opportunities, they must ensure that there are corresponding changes to the organisation's culture and values that recognise employment is not the secular equivalent of religious vows. Work is a part of life, not life itself; organisations that offer women real opportunities for careers have cultures and values that recognise this fact.

References

1. Amanda Gome, 'Career Risks Of Getting Pregnant', *Business Review Weekly*, 6 May 1996, pp. 22–25.
2. See Christine Williams, (1992), 'The Glass Escalator: Hidden Advantages For Men In The 'Female' Professions', *Social Problems*, vol. 39, no. 3, pp. 253–67. E. Joel Heikes, (1991), 'When Men Are The Minority: The Case Of Men In Nursing', *The Sociological Quarterly*, vol. 32, no. 3, pp. 389–401.
See also Janice D. Yoder, (1991), 'Rethinking Tokenism: Looking Beyond Numbers', *Gender and Society*, vol. 5, no. 1, pp. 178–92; and Joan Acker, (1990) 'Hierarchies, Jobs, Bodies: A Theory Of Gendered Organisations', *Gender and Society*, vol. 4, no. 2, June: pp. 139–58.

Source: *HRMonthly*, July 1996, pp. 28–29.

Introducing Equal Employment Opportunity

This article highlights that the creation of Equal Employment Opportunity (EEO) in Australia is a slow process. EEO refers to an employment situation in which every individual has access to employment and its benefits. It is an issue which all employers, managers, employees, trade unions, industrial tribunals and policy makers must take into account when developing and implementing human resource policies and when dealing with employees. Federal and state legislation requires that employment policies and practices do not discriminate. Although legislation designed to create equity in the workplace has existed for more than ten years, EEO is still widely misunderstood and emotive.

Discrimination

Employment policies which discriminate can take two forms, either direct discrimination or indirect discrimination. Direct discrimination refers to the exclusion of an individual or a group from an employment opportunity or benefit because of a personal characteristic which is irrelevant to the performance of the tasks. Policies, practices and behaviour which directly discriminate are readily identifiable and the result of conscious intent. In comparison, indirect discrimination is not as easy to identify. It refers to the exclusion of an individual or group from an employment opportunity or benefit because of the application of conditions or requirements, which although apparently neutral, discriminates because they incorporate attitudes or assumptions which disadvantage individuals in some groups more than others. For instance, the use of height as a selection criteria when height is not a requirement for effectively performing the job would be regarded as a form of indirect discrimination.

One way of removing direct and indirect discrimination is to ensure human resource management policies do not discriminate between individuals on the basis of stereotypes or prejudice. Discrimination and affirmative action legislation is a means of limiting these forms of discrimination.

A more encompassing form of discrimination is structural or systemic discrimination. Structural or systemic discrimination refers to the pattern of institutional and social arrangements embedded in society. The custom of a continuous working life, or low priority being given to funding of quality child care or paid parental leave are examples of structural or systemic discrimination.

Another form of discrimination involves an action which seeks to overcome or modify the effects of past discrimination and is known as positive or reverse discrimination. In the United States, setting quotas which require that a certain number of women or African–Americans are hired to correct under-utilisation or past discrimination, may result in the violation of the Fourteenth Amendment and against Title VII protection against all discrimination. However, the courts have generally held in favour of goals as the only way to reverse previous practices of discrimination (Detroit Police Officer's Association v. Coleman Young 1979; Charles L. Maehren v. City of Seattle 1979; City of St Louis v. USA 1980).

In Australia, organisations are not required to set quotas for any particular group. The legislation designed to prevent discrimination does not require employers to implement employment policies which acknowledge that employees have been discriminated in the past. Instead, employers are required to develop and implement policies which ensure 'merit' is the basis of employment decisions.

However, merit is not a value-neutral term. The implementation of human resource policies requires reference not only to skill and knowledge, but also to 'organisational and institutional interests' (Cohen & Pfeffer 1986, p. 2). Burton (1991, p. 25) argues that subjective assessments of relative suitability are made when policies are formulated and implemented.

Equal Employment Opportunity

Equal Employment Opportunity (EEO) refers to an employment situation in which every individual has access to employment and its benefits. EEO refers to the outcomes of human resource management policies and practices and employee and management behaviour. The creation of EEO has both a long-term and a short-term agenda. The long-term agenda involves a transformation of organisations and a review of the processes associated with the creation and use of power by some groups. The short-term agenda involves the implementation of new measures and policies which attempt to remove bias from procedures such as recruitment and promotion (Cockburn 1989, p. 218).

Affirmative Action

The term Affirmative Action refers to the techniques and methods used to create EEO. Affirmative Action concerns the processes used to achieve an equitable workplace. In Australia, the *Affirmative Action (Equal Employment Opportunity for Women) Act 1986*, requires removal of direct and indirect discrimination through the application of the merit principle in employment policies.

Sexual harassment

Sexual harassment refers to unlawful behaviour by a co-worker or a superior/supervisor towards an employee. The Commonwealth Sex Discrimination Act was amended in 1993 to broaden the definition of sexual harassment so that the harassed person no longer had to show that he or she had been disadvantaged. Equal opportunity legislation in Victoria, South Australia, Queensland, Western Australia and the Australian Capital Territory and the *Commonwealth Sex Discrimination Act 1984* make sexual harassment unlawful. Although New South Wales legislation does not make sexual harassment unlawful, case law has held such behaviour to be unlawful.

The Commonwealth Sex Discrimination Act states that a person harasses another person if the person:

1 'makes an unwelcome sexual advance, or an unwelcome request for sexual favours, to the person harassed, or
2 engages in other unwelcome conduct of a sexual nature in relation to the person harassed,

In circumstances in which a reasonable person, having regard to all the circumstances, would have anticipated that the person harassed would be offended, humiliated or intimidated'.

The types of conduct which might be included within this definition include:

- attempts at sexual intercourse or some other overt sexual connection such as kissing touching or pinching
- gender-based insults or taunting
- statements of a sexual nature, either verbal or written and made either to a person or in their presence
- suggestions or innuendo
- intrusive questions asked at pre-employment interviews.

An isolated incident could amount to harassment. However, it usually requires a series of incidents or persistent or unwelcome conduct (CCH Australia Ltd 1995).

Managing change

Disabilities no bar to useful work

BY NARELLE HOOPER & GEORGI STICKELS

We have to ask ourselves the question, What is a disability? All of us bring to our employers a collection of talents and disabilities ... a disability is irrelevant in the workplace if we find a person with the right set of motivations and abilities to do the job.

The Canberra Centre carpark, run by Burnett Colliers Jardine and employing 12 people, over the past two years has been involved in the Commonwealth Rehabilitation Scheme (CRS) providing training for people with schizophrenia who have their condition under control and are trying to rejoin the workforce. The company has trained four people as maintenance assistants on a three-month full subsidy and 18 months ago took a full-time cashier, Gary Patterson. The CRS paid Patterson's wages during the trial period. Now, says Swieringa, Patterson performs as useful a role as any employee.

Swieringa says that people with a disability tend to have low levels of absenteeism and staff turnover, which makes them valuable employees. 'All people who have been unemployed for a long time are so appreciative', he says. 'Once they settle down, they really treasure their job, so it makes good commercial sense to have those people in your workplace'.

Barbara Moxham, human resources manager of CCH, says her company is reaping the benefits of considerable savings in recruitment and training costs as a result of employing people with disabilities. CCH employs five people with intellectual disabilities in a range of clerical positions at its office in North Ryde in Sydney. Moxham says these positions would normally be filled by a disinterested junior.

Source: *BRW*, 31 October 1994, pp. 63, 65.

Reasons for the development of Equal Employment Opportunity

The development and acknowledgment of EEO as an important human resource issue has been a gradual process in Australia. It was stimulated by international standards regarding appropriate policy and behaviour in the workplace, government action, trade union policy and the increasing participation of women in the workforce. Federal and state governments have supported EEO and the removal of discrimination from the workplace through a variety of actions, most particularly through legislation.

International standards

ILO conventions

The International Labour Organisation (ILO) has advocated the principle of equality of opportunity and equality of treatment since its establishment in 1919. The principle was regarded as being of 'special and urgent importance'. The desire to promote women's rights as workers was reaffirmed in 1944 with the Declaration of Philadelphia which proclaimed all human beings have the right to pursue their material well-being and spiritual development in conditions of economic security, freedom and dignity and equal opportunities (ILO 1987, p. 2).

A number of ILO conventions and recommendations, known collectively as the International Labour Code, specifically address issues associated with the achievement of equal opportunities and equal remuneration for women workers. These include:

- Equal Remuneration Convention 1951 (no. 100)
- Discrimination (Employment and Occupation) Convention 1958 (no. 111)
- Equal Treatment for Men and Women Workers: Workers and Family Responsibilities Convention 1981 (no. 156).

The ILO seeks to ensure member states promote EEO irrespective of their rate of economic growth and conditions operating in the labour market. Member states that ratify the ILO conventions have a responsibility to undertake legislative and policy measures promoting principles embodied in these conventions. Therefore, within member states, these conventions should influence the behaviour of employers, trade unions, tribunals and employees and employment decisions about selection, training, working conditions and pay.

Legislation

Countries have adopted a variety of legislative and policy measures to promote the principle of equality of opportunity and treatment between male and female workers. Equal opportunity and anti-discrimination legislation has been enacted in a number of countries to promote this principle. Anti-discrimination legislation seeks to prohibit discriminatory behaviour, while equal opportunity legislation seeks to systematically remove discrimination from the labour market by requiring employers to take positive action to ensure their employment policies do not discriminate against women. The provisions of anti-discrimination and EEO legislation vary between countries, so that differences are created in the practical scope and potential effect of the legislation. Legislation varies according to the breadth of the definition of discrimination, the scope of affirmative action and the availability of taking class actions.

Legislation was enacted in the United States in 1964 and 1969 with the passing of the Civil Rights Act, and the Equal Employment Opportunity Act in 1972. Title VII of the Civil Rights Act prohibits discrimination against individuals on the basis of race, colour, religion, sex or national extraction. The European Community (EC) has shown a commitment to equal opportunities and issued legislative directives regarding equal pay and equal treatment for women. Consequently, Britain developed or amended its existing legislation, the *Equal Pay Act 1970* and the *Sex Discrimination Act 1975*.

Broad definitions of discrimination, including the principle of indirect discrimination, are incorporated into both the American and British legislation. The legislation in the United States provides a broader scope for affirmative action and class actions. It requires private employers with more than fifteen employees, federal government contractors, state and local governments and labour organisations with fifteen or more employees or members, to voluntarily develop affirmative action policies and programs. The legislation provides for the legitimacy of these plans to be tested in court cases and provides the opportunity for class actions to establish the existence of discrimination. These actions can result in employers incurring financial costs for discrimination.

Legislation in the United Kingdom takes the form of anti-discrimination legislation and only provides for individuals to bring complaints of discrimination. As there is no affirmative action legislation, employers are under no obligation to be pro-active in promoting EEO. However, they can provide special training and work experience where it can be shown that certain groups are under-represented in a certain area of work (Harris 1990; Dex & Walters 1989; De Cenzo & Robbins 1988).

A small number of employers in the United Kingdom have taken initiatives such as enhanced maternity leave provisions, career break schemes, flexible working patterns, workplace nurseries and other child-care provisions in an attempt to recruit and retain valued employees (Dickens 1992). EEO has been promoted in the United Kingdom through the Opportunity 2000 initiative. This initiative was developed by a group, Business in the Community, consisting of about 200 organisations in the public and private sector who have pledged to achieve a better balanced workforce. Although Opportunity 2000 is a business initiative, it is supported by the government.

A variety of projects has been undertaken as part of Opportunity 2000. A guide to the development of a cost–benefit approach to the implementation of policies supporting employees has been produced. Other projects involve the provision of out-of school care services with demonstration projects and the 'Employers for Child-care' project. This project involves a powerful group of CEOs lobbying governments to enter into partnership with business to provide a number of child-care services (Foster 1994, p. 41; Business in the Community/Institute of Personnel Management 1993).

Australian developments
Anti-discrimination
Federal and state governments have undertaken a variety of measures in their attempts to create EEO. Early government action involved formal endorsement of international standards. Ratification of ILO Convention 111 stimulated the establishment of national and state committees which were set up to investigate complaints of discrimination. Ratification also stimulated the enactment of anti-discrimination legislation in three states soon after. Eventually, the other states and the federal government enacted anti-discrimination legislation and the federal government enacted affirmative action legislation in 1986.

The first three states to pass anti-discrimination legislation were the South Australian, New South Wales and Victorian governments between 1975 and 1977. These pieces of legislation were 'complaint-based' pieces of legislation which enabled individuals to bring grievances before a special board or tribunal. The federal government enacted the Sex Discrimination Act in 1984. The objectives of the Act were:

- To give effect to certain provisions of the United Nations Convention on the Elimination of all Forms of Discrimination Against Women, which had been ratified in 1983.
- To eliminate discrimination on the grounds of sex, marital status or pregnancy in the areas of employment, education, accommodation, the provision of goods, facilities and services, disposal of land, the activities of clubs and the administration of Commonwealth laws and programs, and discrimination involving sexual harassment in the workplace and in educational institutions.
- To promote recognition and acceptance within the community of the principle of the equality of women.

Any reference to affirmative action had been removed from the *Sex Discrimination Act 1984*. An earlier Sex Discrimination Bill introduced in 1981 as a private members Bill, sought to promote affirmative action for women, but provisions relating to this were removed following reservations of the ACTU and lack of support by the Fraser government and employers. All these groups expressed a desire for the encouragement of affirmative action through voluntary means, rather than compulsory means.

Affirmative Action

Although these provisions were removed from the *Sex Discrimination Act 1984*, the federal Labor government, elected in 1983, was keen to explore the introduction of other measures to remove discrimination from the labour market. In May 1984, it released a two volume Green Paper, *Affirmative Action for Women* (Department of Prime Minister and Cabinet 1984). This Green Paper discussed the concept of affirmative action, outlined the government's proposals with regard to affirmative action, included a statistical analysis of the position of women in the labour market and announced the implementation of a voluntary pilot program.

The voluntary pilot program involved 28 private sector organisations and three tertiary educational institutions. These organisations were to set up affirmative action programs for their female employees with the assistance of a special affirmative action resource unit located in the Office of the Status of Women in the Department of the Prime Minister and Cabinet. The pilot program was reviewed by a working party which found that despite the good intentions of the participants, affirmative action was afforded a low priority and ill conceived. Two-thirds of the organisations appointed part-time affirmative action managers and developed plans for a small number of employees. The working party recommended that legislation be passed to require organisations to establish affirmative action programs for women. It also recommended that a range of supportive measures be undertaken in the areas of education, child care and legislative restrictions to women's employment.

These recommendations were accepted by the government in 1985. Consequently, the Affirmative Action (Equal Employment Opportunity for Women) Bill was introduced into Parliament on 19 February 1986 and the Australian Women's Employment Strategy was implemented by the Department of Employment, Education and Training. The federal government recognised employers concern about interference with managements right to manage, and allowed for affirmative action programs to be tailored to a particular organisational and industrial culture.

The Affirmative Action (Equal Employment Opportunity for Women) Act was proclaimed to commence from 1 October 1986. It was progressively implemented according to the timetable in Table 4.1. Group Training companies, and non-government schools were covered by the Act in 1992 and reported to the Affirmative Action Agency for the first time in 1994. Trade unions reported to the Agency for the first time in 1988.

Table 4.1 Timetable for the Affirmative Action (Equal Employment Opportunity for Women) Act 1996

ORGANISATION	PROGRAM COMMENCEMENT DATE	FIRST REPORT DATE
Higher education institutions	1 October 1986	1 October 1987
Companies with 1000 or more employees (Band 1)	1 February 1987	1 February 1988
500–999 employees (Band 2)	1 February 1988	1 February 1989
100–499 employees (Band 3)	1 February 1989	1 February 1990

Source: Schuler et al. 1992, p. 136

Effectiveness Review of the Affirmative Action Act

An Effectiveness Review of the Affirmative Action Act was conducted five years after the Act was enacted. The terms of reference of the Review required the Director of the Affirmative Action Agency to 'review the effectiveness of (the) Act in achieving its purposes'. The Review assessed:

- the awareness of relevant employers of their responsibilities under the Act
- the extent to which relevant employers have developed the affirmative action programs required by the Act
- the general quality of the programs
- the extent to which the programs have been implemented, and
- the effectiveness of the programs in promoting equal employment opportunity for women.

In the light of these assessments the review:

- made recommendations about what, if any, amendments might be needed to the *Affirmative Action (Equal Employment Opportunity for Women) Act 1986*, and
- reported on the implications any amendments to the Act might have for the operation of the Affirmative Action Agency.

The Review was conducted in 1991–92. A principal consultant managed the Review in consultation with the Director and an internal steering committee. Staff at the Agency prepared discussion papers on coverage and sanctions, conducted research on employers' programs and reporting. External consultants and academic researchers reviewed the Agency's internal operations, examined workplace attitudes, women's employment data, employers' views on compliance and the process of affirmative action implementation. The results of the investigations formed the basis for the development and refinement of recommendations.

Among the findings of the Review were that:

- women had still not attained economic and social equality.
- the Act had been successfully implemented across the full range of its coverage, with more than 95 per cent of those required to report doing so.
- the Act enjoyed sufficient community support to ensure organisations preferred to comply rather than attract the sanction of naming in federal parliament.
- there was a strong values base for affirmative action but that it was not effectively supported by knowledge about affirmative action requirements and programs.
- reporting facilitates program development and that many organisations would abandon programs if reporting was not compulsory. Most difficulties were experienced in consulting unions and employees, analysing the workforce profile, monitoring and evaluating programs and setting forward estimates.
- the rate of affirmative action progress was uneven, with some organisations being untouched by EEO.
- EEO needed to be managed better by integrating affirmative action with organisational strategy, the appointment of more skilled, specialised EEO officers and the provision of more accurate and comprehensive measurement of affirmative action program performance.
- organisations were prepared to share information and learn from each other.
- few organisations have effective mechanisms in place for involving employees and consultation with unions was viewed as ineffective by both unions and employers.

As a consequence of the Review it was recommended that:

- there should be a focus on the outcomes of program development rather than extending coverage.
- voluntary bodies should be covered by the Act.
- reporting should be more flexible, with employees and unions receiving reports one month prior to submission and affirmative action should be included in the annual reports of public companies. It was also suggested that there should be increased flexibility in the content of reports submitted to the Agency, while retaining the annual reporting cycle.
- Commonwealth contract compliance should be introduced whereby compliance with the Affirmative Action Act is a prerequisite for obtaining Commonwealth government contracts.
- more attention should be given to encouraging quality program development.
- A tripartite advisory committee should be established with employer, union and Agency representation to develop program performance standards, codes of practice and guidelines (Affirmative Action Agency 1992).

Work and family

The previous federal Labor government also promoted the creation of EEO by seeking to remove discrimination against workers with family responsibilities. It did this in a variety of ways including the ratification of ILO Convention no. 156 on Workers with

Family Responsibilities in 1990, establishing a Work and Family Unit in the Department of Industrial Relations, developing a Strategy for Implementing International Labour Organisation Convention 156 across Commonwealth policies and programs (Strategy), amending the *Sex Discrimination Act 1984* and passing the *Industrial Relations Reform Act 1993* so they prohibit discrimination on the basis of family responsibilities in employment.

The *Workplace Relations Act 1996* seeks to facilitate the determination of employment conditions which prevent discrimination on the basis of family responsibilities. Unpaid parental and adoption leave remain a minimum entitlement under this Act. The Act also seeks to encourage regular part-time employment.

Many Australian organisations have in place policies which facilitate employees accommodating employment and domestic responsibilities. Awards often make provision for maternity and paternity leave, flexible working arrangements, part-time work and parental leave to care for sick children. Other organisations have introduced assistance with child care, career break schemes and assistance with relocation of families.

Equal Employment Opportunity legislation in Australia

Legislation in a number of areas establishes standards for employment policy and workplace behaviour in both the private sector and public sectors. This legislation includes discrimination, affirmative action and equal employment opportunity and industrial relations legislation. There are differences between the provisions of the various Acts in each jurisdiction, particularly with regard to the grounds for unlawful discrimination.

Discrimination legislation

Coverage of the legislation

Discrimination or anti-discrimination legislation attempts to prohibit behaviour which discriminates against individuals on the basis of specified grounds such as sex, marital status or race in a number of contexts, including employment. Anti-discrimination legislation has been enacted in most Australian states and in the federal jurisdiction. Legislation exists in New South Wales, Victoria, Queensland, Western Australia, South Australia, Tasmania and the ACT. Although the grounds and contexts specified in different jurisdictions vary, the primary objective of all the legislation is to ensure every person has equal access to employment and its benefits.

The grounds for discrimination in the legislation include sex, marital status, religion, physical impairment, sexuality, race, family responsibilities, intellectual impairment, age and medical record. The types of employment situations commonly covered by the legislation include contents of application forms, access to interviews, terms and conditions of employment, access to promotion, training and transfer opportunities, preparation of job descriptions and specifications and retrenchments. These grounds and employment situations provide some indication of the nature of the coverage of the legislation, however, the relevant Act in each state should be checked separately to determine the nature of the coverage.

Although there is no legislation in Tasmania and the Northern Territory, employers are bound by the provisions of the federal legislation. People in the other states and the ACT have a choice of lodging complaints either under their State legislation or the federal legislation.

Procedures

The legislation also provides procedures for lodging and resolving complaints of alleged discrimination. These steps usually provide for processes of conciliation regarding a complaint and if these are unsuccessful, provision for a tribunal to hear and determine the complaint. The complaint resolution process is similar under each jurisdiction. Figure 4.1 illustrates the complaint resolution process in New South Wales which is typical, but not identical to the steps in other jurisdictions.

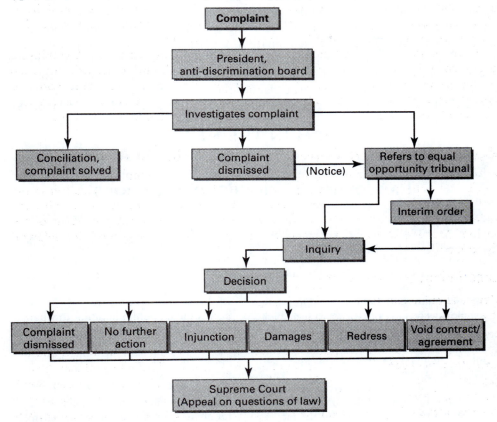

Figure 4.1 Resolution of a complaint—New South Wales

Source: CCH Australia 1995, p. 10–620

Discrimination legislation is 'complaint based'. The onus of proof in a complaint rests with the complainant. The complainant must prove on the balance of probabilities that the ground of alleged discrimination contributed to the act which resulted in the alleged discrimination. The complainant does not have to prove that the act was intentional.

Each Act provides for remedies in the event of a complaint of discrimination being substantiated. These remedies include:

- an injunction prohibiting the respondent from continuing or repeating the act or conduct complained of
- an order for the respondent to pay the complainant damages to compensate for financial or non-financial detriment suffered

- an order that the respondent redress the loss or damage suffered by the complainant, for example through reinstatement, backdating of promotion, offering an equivalent alternative benefit and/or
- cancellation or variation of a contract or agreement which contravenes the Act.

The extracts from the article 'Landmark discrimination decisions' detail some of the most significant decisions in the federal and state jurisdictions. It provides examples of decisions which found discrimination occurred in the workplace on the basis of either sex, disability or race and describes the damages which had been awarded. To date, there have not been many successful indirect discrimination claims. However, proposed changes to the Sex Discrimination Act will shift the onus of proof to the respondent. The respondent will have to prove that the action was reasonable. One of the most successful indirect sex discrimination cases involved BHP Australian Iron and Steel and more than 700 women, who claimed the 'last on, first off' principle indirectly discriminated against them because they tended to be the 'last on' (Manns 1995, p. 18).

HRM IN THE NEWS

Landmark discrimination decisions

Sex
- Sex discrimination by Qantas against women flight attendants.
  Each awarded maximum damages available ($40 000) if they had been compulsorily retired, plus agreed unspecified damages and reinstatement to appropriate employment conditions for 29 women, plus all their legal costs (still being mediated). Total damages not disclosed, well in excess of $1.2 million in damages alone, plus legal fees not yet finalised—*October 27, 1994.*
- Sexual harassment, and victimisation of complainant (employer pressured complainant to settle). $50 000 damages apportioned between supervisor and director of company—*September 15, 1994.*

Disability
- Since July 1994, 41 'interim determinations' have been made by the human rights and equal opportunity commission under the Disability Discrimination Act.
- TransAdelaide transport restrained from proceeding to call tenders for an inaccessible bus fleet—*September 13, 1994 (settled October 1994).*
- A similar complaint by people with disabilities (NSW) against the state transit authority of NSW—*settled July 14, 1995.*
- State transit (NSW) agreed to make all its buses accessible to people with disabilities over next 10 years; estimated cost in excess of $20 million.
- Mobility-impaired people unable to access major public building through front door. 'Mainstream' principle established for first time. Estimated cost of appropriate lift $298 000. Queensland government ordered to pay all the legal costs as well—*September 2 & 21, 1994.*
- Man with paranoid schizophrenia sacked for pre-hospitalisation performance deficiencies caused by symptoms of disease. Burden of proving incapacity to do particular job with or without special services on the employer. $20 000 damages—*July 8, 1994.*
- Indirect disability discrimination: Telstra not entitled to refuse outright to provide deaf man with TTY (text transmission machine) or other effective access to telecommunications system. Required to provide TTY to complainant and 21 000 other deaf Australians at an estimated cost of $4 million to $12 million. Decision is on appeal.

Race
- Indirect race discrimination as a result of closing a school with a spectacular success rate for aboriginal students.
  Discontinuing a special program, which results in aboriginal students being unable to access public education, may be indirectly discriminatory; individual human rights consideration may be given priority over state government economic policies, and existing special programs may effectively become 'minimum standards'. No damages sought, school ordered reopened (cost more than $2 million): state's legal fees exceed $690 000—*a series of decisions between 1992 and 1995).*
- Race discrimination: refusal to hire caravan to Aborigines. Record damages of $20 700, plus two public apologies in local newspapers for wilful and deliberate race discrimination—*July 19, 1993.*
- Race discrimination: overseas-trained doctor required to recontest eligibility for permanent registration to meet quota each year. Damages on torts principles and intended to contribute to legal costs of $50 000 (Commonwealth government has appealed to the federal court)—*August 1995).*

Source: *Financial Review*, 2 August 1995, p. 18.

Affirmative Action and Equal Employment Opportunity legislation

Coverage of the legislation

In comparison to discrimination legislation, affirmative action or equal employment opportunity legislation attempts to provide for the systematic removal of direct and indirect discrimination from employment policies and practices. Provisions within state discrimination and equal employment opportunity legislation provide for affirmative action for employees in the public sector (Table 4.1 identified this legislation).

Commonwealth legislation covers employees in the public sector and the private sector. The *Affirmative Action (Equal Employment Opportunity for Women) Act 1986* requires private sector organisations with more than one hundred employees to develop affirmative action programs. The legislation covers five types of employers:

1. Private employers
2. Trade unions
3. Higher education institutions
4. Community organisations
5. Non-government schools.

These organisations are required to demonstrate that they have followed eight steps when developing their affirmative action program and that these eight steps are the basis of a cycle of continuous improvement. Section 3 of the Act defines an affirmative action program as:

'a program designed to ensure that:

a appropriate action is taken to eliminate discrimination by the relevant employer against women in relation to employment matters, and
b measures are taken by the relevant employer to promote equal opportunity for women in relation to employment matters'.

The eight steps involved in the development of a program are:

1. To issue a policy statement
2. Appoint a senior member of staff with responsibility for the development and implementation of affirmative action program
3. To consult with trade unions represented in the workplace
4. To consult with employees, particularly women
5. To establish and analyse the employment profile of the organisation
6. To review and analyse personnel policies and practices
7. To set objectives and forward estimates for the program
8. To monitor and evaluate the program.

The Act is not prescriptive about the particular policies developed within this framework. However, it does require employers in most circumstances to submit two reports to the Affirmative Action Agency each year. These reports require employers to describe the steps taken to introduce an affirmative action program. The shorter of these two reports is for public scrutiny, while the more detailed, confidential report is for evaluation by Affirmative Action Agency staff. Reports must be lodged within three months of the reporting date unless an extension of up to six months has been granted by the Director of Affirmative Action.

Reporting form

As a consequence of the Effectiveness Review of the Affirmative Action Act, the Affirmative Action Agency in 1995 released a new reporting form which was designed:

- to assist employers to comply with the Act, and
- to provide a strategic planning model to link affirmative action to organisational goals and objectives.

The introduction of this revised reporting form is part of the Agency's move to a quality focus and the introduction of performance standards for employers. The form is designed to allow organisations with high quality programs to show progress from year to year and to encourage programs to focus on results rather than processes (*Affirmative Action Agency 1995*). These performance standards are designed to:

- provide employers with a clear guide on the goals they should be aiming for
- assist employers to measure their own progress, and
- enable the Agency to map the connection between high quality programs and positive affirmative action outcomes.

Unlike the previous report forms, the report form introduced in 1995 is based on a strategic planning model which aims to develop an integrated, consultative approach to affirmative action. It seeks to achieve this by requiring employers to demonstrate:

- a strong link between affirmative action and organisational goals and objectives
- the integration of the program into all aspects of operation and decision making
- consultation with and participation of all stakeholders, and
- a continuous process of analysis, strategy development, implementation, monitoring, evaluation and reporting (Affirmative Action Agency 1995).

The report form is structured in such a way that it allows employers to highlight the systems organisations have in place to underpin their affirmative action program. It also enables them to provide a snapshot of the current EEO situation in their organisation and a means of evaluating their progress and achievements.

Strategic Planning Model

The model is depicted in Figure 4.2. It has three interrelated stages. These stages each include a number of the eight steps specified in the Act. These three stages are identified as:

1. Establishing support systems for an affirmative action program
2. Establishing equity in key performance areas
3. The development of an affirmative action program.

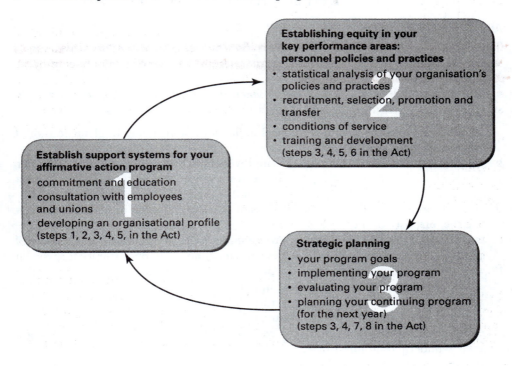

Figure 4.2 Affirmative action strategic planning and affirmative action program

Source: Affirmative Action Agency 1995, p. 5

A Practical Guide to Affirmative Action (Affirmative Action Agency 1995) describes these stages. It indicates the purposes of each stage and suggests actions which could be taken at each stage.

Quotas, targets, objectives and estimates

Although the *Affirmative Action (Equal Employment Opportunity for Women) Act 1986* does require employers to establish objectives and estimates, it does not require employers to fill quotas (i.e. establish a fixed percentage of women employees that must be attained regardless of the number of qualified applicants available). A quota system is regarded as inconsistent with the essential principle of employment practices based on merit.

Chapter 4 Equal Employment Opportunity **139**

In comparison, an estimate or a target is the number of women the organisation is aiming to reach by setting more specific objectives and strategies to achieve them. Estimates or targets need to take into account what is achievable within a given time frame. For instance, one of the goals of an affirmative action program could be to increase the percentage of women in non-traditional jobs. Consequently, one of the specific objectives associated with this could be to expand the pool of applicants to entry level technicians jobs. In order to determine a realistic estimate or target, factors such as the percentage of women graduating as technicians need to be considered. If women represent ten per cent of graduate technicians, then it would be realistic to establish an estimate or target of base level women recruits at 10 per cent.

Affirmative Action Agency

The administering body for affirmative action programs is the Affirmative Action Agency headed by the Director of Affirmative Action. The Agency operates within the Department of Industrial Relations.

The *Affirmative Action (Equal Employment Opportunity for Women) Act 1986* states that the Agency's fundamental role is:

a to advise and assist relevant employers in the development and implementation of affirmative action programs
b to issue guidelines to assist relevant employers to achieve the purposes of this Act
c to monitor the lodging of reports by relevant employers as required by this Act and to review those reports and deal with them in accordance with this Act
d to monitor and evaluate the effectiveness of affirmative action programs in achieving the purposes of the Act
e to undertake research, educational programs and other programs for the purpose of promoting affirmative action to achieve equal employment opportunity for women
f to promote understanding and acceptance, and public discussion, of affirmative action to achieve equal employment opportunity for women
g to review the effectiveness of this Act in achieving its purposes
h to report to the Minister on such matters in relation to affirmative action to achieve equal employment opportunity for women as the Agency thinks fit (including a review under paragraph (g)).

Assessment framework

The Affirmative Action Agency has prepared a framework to assess reports. This assessment is used:

- to provide feedback to organisations about their programs
- to facilitate the development of benchmarks on an industry basis
- to identify examples of best practice which can be used as models for improvement.

Table 4.2 outlines the framework used to assess reports. It reflects the format and approach of the recently introduced report form. Five broad levels relating to standards are identified in terms of a general, broad description and in terms of indicators. These levels range from below minimum standards to best practice. In order to satisfy the standard required for minimum compliance, an organisation must report and show they have an affirmative action program in place. The assessment framework requires an organisation to describe in its report the structure/framework of its affirmative action program, the strategies implemented as part of this framework and the employment profile of its workforce.

Table 4.2 Assessment model for affirmative action reports

LEVEL	STANDARD	DESCRIPTION	INDICATORS
5	Outstanding level of progress in developing and implementing an affirmative action program.	Demonstrated implementation of a program: • covering a range of areas based on strategic planning • integrated with the organisation's human resource management and industrial relations practices • linked to the business objectives of the organisation.	Report provides evidence of a comprehensive affirmative action strategic plan including: • support systems including formal mechanisms for consultation • analysis of employment profile • review of personnel policies and practices • analysis and review is linked to the program goals etc. • goal(s), objectives, strategies in place • action plan in place • monitoring mechanisms in place and results outlined • evaluation of the program • evidence of further development, connections made to following year's program • evidence of integration with HRM/IR practices in the organisation • evidence of link between AA program and business objectives.
4	High level of progress in developing and implementing an affirmative action program.	Demonstrated implementation of a strategically planned program.	Report provides evidence of an affirmative action strategic plan in place including: • support systems including formal mechanisms for consultation • analysis of employment profile • review of personnel policies and practices • analysis and review is linked to the program goals etc • goal(s), objectives, strategies in place • action plan in place.

LEVEL	STANDARD	DESCRIPTION	INDICATORS
3	Medium level of progress in developing and implementing an affirmative action program.	Demonstrated implementation of a program with connection made between analysis/review and initiative undertaken.	• monitoring mechanisms in place and results outlined • evaluation of the program. Report provides evidence of an affirmative strategic plan including: • support systems in place • analysis/review undertaken • goal(s)/objectives and strategies in place • outline of results achieved.
2	Minimum level of progress in developing and implementing an affirmative action program.	Implementation of a program.	Report provides an outline of the program and evidence of activity: • a description of the structure/framework of the program • a description of strategies to demonstrate that an affirmative action program is in place.
1	Below the minimum requirements of the *Affirmative Action (Equal Employment Opportunity for Women) Act 1986*.	Report does not provide one or more of the following: • employment profile • outline of the program • detailed analysis of program activity.	Report does *not* provide • a description of the structure/framework for the program, AND • evidence of activity to further develop and implement the program.

Source: Affirmative Action Agency 1995

There are two major sanctions applying to organisations that do not comply with the Act. First, these organisations may be named in federal parliament in a report submitted by the Director of Affirmative Action. Organisations are deemed not to have complied with the Act if they either fail to submit reports or fail to provide further information upon request, without reasonable excuse. The second sanction involves the ineligibility of organisations who have not complied, to secure government contracts and specified forms of industry assistance. Organisations which demonstrate outstanding progress now only need to report once every three years to the Affirmative Action Agency.

Industrial relations legislation

The *Workplace Relations Act 1996* and the *Workplace Relations and Other Legislation Amendments Act 1996* also seek to remove discrimination from the workplace. The Australian Industrial Relations Commission is required in its award-making role to prevent and eliminate discrimination from the minimum conditions and wages contained in awards. Among the matters which may be included in awards are parental leave and personal/carer's leave.

Managing diversity

Report calls for a more fair workplace

BY MATTHEW RUSSELL

Australian workplaces may be radically transformed by a proposal to outlaw all forms of discrimination now being considered by the Australian Industrial Relations Commission (AIRC).

A confidential AIRC discussion paper, obtained by the *Herald*, outlines plans to allow workers who are not Christians to take time off during their religious holidays.

It will also look at other areas of hidden discrimination which may be banned, including:

- Less favourable conditions applying to part-time work compared with full-time work because more women work part-time
- Allowances or benefits awarded to workers based on continuous service considered discriminatory because more women may interrupt their careers to take time off to rear children
- Specifying certain qualifications which may also be indirectly discriminatory on the grounds of race and sex.

And NSW awards covering more than two-thirds of the state's workforce could soon follow.

Some companies already have adopted some of the provisions in enterprise agreements. Ford Australia, for instance, just a week ago signed an enterprise agreement with its workforce, which besides giving workers an 11.5 per cent pay rise over two years, also gave all its workforce holidays for religious festivals such as at the end of Ramadan, Greek New Year and Chinese New Year.

Source: *Sydney Morning Herald*, 11 June 1995, p. 7.

The extract from the article 'Report calls for a more fair workplace' identifies other ways the Australian Industrial Relations Commission could be involved in the future in promoting EEO in workplaces. It highlights that an EEO environment requires the acknowledgment of differences between employees and the use of employment practices which acknowledge and accommodate these differences.

Future organisational forms

Telecommuting boosts employee output

Several companies experience productivity gains, better morale and lower business costs through telecommuting.

BY JULIAN M. WEISS

For some companies, telecommuting is a performance-enhancement tool with employees responding favourably to the freedom that comes with the responsibility. But in the past, fear of losing control over workers prevented line supervisors from exploring telecommuting.

'We learned to look at employee effectiveness', says Bell Atlantic's telecommuting manager, Ed Kirk.

Today, some three to six million white-collar workers telecommute two to five days a week and the numbers are growing. And proponents estimate that in most companies, 5 per cent to 40 per cent of the workforce are able to join the work-at-home set.

The right candidate plus proper training equal higher output and lower costs for companies, important concerns in this era of downsizing. Studies show that employees generally produce 20 per cent to 30 per cent more in quantifiable results when they telecommunicate.

Pacific Bell allows its sales force of more than 400 to avoid the conventional office setting by telecommuting. The company discovered its $1.5 million investment in state-of-the-art equipment was quickly returned by enormous productivity gains, on top of $400 000 in office space savings.

Storage Tek in Boulder, Colorado, USA, Reported a 144 per cent increase in productivity among engineers and other employees.

Bell Atlantic, the east coast telecommunications firm, conducted a pair of pilot programs in 1990. It concluded that 27 per cent of 100 managers in one pilot had higher work ratings than before, and several were promoted at a time when promotions were not that common. Many recorded 200 per cent increases in output, with others showing a 20 per cent time reduction completing assignments. Formal telecommuting options will expand, and bell atlantic executives say a tenth of the population will become telecommuters.

Far fewer sick days are reported from telecommuters, say sources at J. C. Penney, Hewlett-Packard, Citicorp and American Express. James Kalach, a spokesman for Travelers Insurance Co., found absenteeism from sickness 'drops way down'. Many workers don't 'peak' until late afternoon, so the standard 9 to 5 routine sacrifices considerable energy. Reduced turnover is another gain. Ann Heyden, a vice president at Metropolitan Life Insurance Co., calls telecommuting 'a strategic staffing asset'. Other companies have found that job satisfaction increases markedly.

State governments have had positive results from pilot programs. In the quest for greater productivity, the general services administration joined the Office of Personnel Management (OPM) in 1992 to put 1000 workers nationwide on telecommuter status. Job responsibilities varied, and participants included senior managers from several agencies. 'among even the minority of managers who weren't converted', says Wendell Joice at OPM, 'most felt it could work well with a few changes'.

Source: *HR Magazine*, February 1994, pp. 51–53.

Implications for human resource policies and practices

Potential wide-ranging implications

The development of EEO in an organisation through the implementation of an affirmative action program can have major implications for the development and implementation of human resource policies, the participation of certain groups in decision making, the methods of communication, the determination of organisational priorities and the allocation of resources. Affirmative action programs which are integrated with organisational objectives and strategic plans require an analysis of the organisation's employment profile and employment policies. The affirmative action program also needs to be sold to all members of the organisation. This process requires the time and skills of an employee with a good understanding of strategic planning and management systems, knowledge of human resource and industrial relations issues, high level facilitation, training, negotiation, data analysis and planning skills, an ability to foster commitment from managers, employees and unions and an ability to work with others and a commitment to the principles of equal employment opportunity (Affirmative Action Agency 1995, p. 10).

A culture based on EEO principles can increase productivity by improving the retention of employees and consequently reducing costs. Following the introduction of a number of policies including flexible working arrangements, dependent care provisions and encouraging employees to return from maternity leave, NRMA reported turnover rates and return from maternity leave improved. The percentage of staff leaving NRMA for family reasons declined from 25.4 per cent to 21.9 per cent, while the number of women returning from maternity increased from 34 per cent to 61 per cent (O'Connor 1994). The savings in human resource management costs were significant. NRMA had estimated that it costs $48 000 to replace managers, $29 000 to replace senior specialists, $21 000 to replace specialists and $12 000 to replace other staff.

EEO can also improve business outcomes. Research in the United States found that firms that win US Department of Labour Awards for their success in implementing affirmative action awards experienced an increase in share price within ten days of the announcement. In comparison, firms that discriminate against women or minorities experience a fall in share prices (Wright et al. 1995, pp. 272–87).

Continued improvement in compliance

Since the Effectiveness Review, the majority of organisations have continued to formally comply with the Affirmative Action legislation and compliance on most steps has improved. In 1994, 82 employers which represented 3 per cent of organisations covered by the Act failed to meet the requirements of the Act, by either not providing a report to the Affirmative Action Agency or by providing reports which did not meet the minimum requirements of the Act (Affirmative Action Agency 1994a, pp. 8–9). However, there were small increases in the overall reported level of activities undertaken in private sector organisations, with the Agency reporting that:

> While the increases are only small it is significant that companies are continuing to improve their performance in relation to steps of an affirmative action program (Affirmative Action Agency 1993, p. 15).

Two steps continue to be poorly undertaken by employers. Only 51 per cent of private employers consulted trade unions about the development of an affirmative action program and less than 42 per cent set forward estimates (Affirmative Action Agency 1994a, pp. 13–14). The Effectiveness Review of the Act found that organisations were reluctant to set objectives and estimates because they were unsure about what was expected of them and they were uncertain about what it meant not to meet the objectives and estimates (Affirmative Action Agency 1992, p. 22).

A narrow interpretation of Equal Employment Opportunity

Most Australian organisations have taken a narrow view of EEO and the role of affirmative action programs in promoting culture change. Studies in Australia indicate the basic conditions necessary for the creation of EEO are lacking. It is claimed:

> EEO is most likely to thrive where there is a supportive values base, people are knowledgeable about EEO programs, affirmative action officers are well informed about issues and strategies, managers and supervisors understand and support the program and senior managers commitment is reflected in allocation of necessary resources and support. Under these circumstances the organisational culture will reflect EEO through integration of it with all planning, managing and accountability processes (Affirmative Action Agency 1992, p. 59).

The most important success factors for the implementation of EEO in a study of public sector organisations in the USA were adequate communication to implementers about what is expected of them, appropriate resources such as staff, expertise, authority, facilities and equipment, number of EEO personnel, moves to a representative bureaucracy, organisation size, commitment to affirmative action and overall increases in the level of education.

However, in many Australian organisations these factors are not present. There is poor understanding about EEO among the workforce, consultation is not systematic, EEO is accorded low priority, is inadequately resourced and developed in a superficial way. Knowledge of EEO is frequently poor among managers, supervisors and particularly among employees (Affirmative Action Agency 1992, p. 17). A study of almost 4000 people from 76 companies covered by the Act found only 30 per cent of respondents reported their company had an affirmative action program compared to 58 per cent of respondents who were aware of the organisation's occupational health and safety program. Table 4.3 indicates that knowledge of the program is better among managers than employees. Not only were respondents unaware of the existence of programs, but many respondents misunderstood the nature of affirmative action. Three quarters of respondents thought affirmative action involved the use of quotas to employ and promote women.

Table 4.3   Awareness of Affirmative Action by employee level

LEVEL	PERCENTAGE REPORTING THAT THEIR COMPANY HAD AN AFFIRMATIVE ACTION PROGRAM
Senior management	55%
Middle management	43%
Line management	39%
Employees	28%

Source: Affirmative Action Agency 1995, p. 17

Even when consultation does occur with employees, it appears to be informal, rather than formal or based on existing consultative structures. It also appears to involve a flow of information between management and employees, rather than a process of joint decision making. It was found informal consultation could work well with highly skilled managers and where levels of conflict were low (Affirmative Action Agency 1992, p. 22).

Another study of EEO contacts and Chief Executive Officers in 153 companies found 'EEO was generally a low priority for management and debate about it rare at management level' (Affirmative Action Agency 1992, p. 27). This study also found many women and unions were not interested in the issue of EEO. However, most of these respondents believed the affirmative action legislation was reasonable and that the government had the right to pass it.

One of the consequences of the low level priority accorded to EEO by management is that resources are not allocated to the development of EEO. This lack of resources is reflected in poor staffing of EEO positions and the limited time accorded to EEO activities. Only a quarter of workplaces with more than 20 employees had an affirmative action/EEO co-ordinator and only 9 per cent of them spent most of their time on affirmative action/EEO (Department of Industrial Relations 1991). Table 4.4 indicates that in organisations with 100 or more employees, 77 per cent had an affirmative action/EEO officer and only 35 per cent of them spent most of their time on affirmative action/EEO.

Another consequence is that most senior managers followed EEO mechanically and superficially. This approach was reflected in the selection criteria which they used. These criteria provided considerable potential for discrimination. For instance, high priority was given to formal qualifications (63 per cent), relevant skills (79 per cent), experience (63 per cent), potential (77 per cent), personality (73 per cent), good looks (30 per cent) and age (34 per cent) (Affirmative Action Agency 1992, pp. 58–59).

This mechanical and superficial approach is also reflected in the approaches to management and reporting on affirmative action.

> The concepts that most companies work with are fairly hostile to affirmative action ... most companies put more energy into getting around the legislation than they do in complying with its spirit (Bagnall 1994, p. 37).

Although most organisations comply with the *Affirmative Action (Equal Employment Opportunity for Women) Act 1986* there are a number of limitations regarding the way it has been developed and implemented. The Director of the Affirmative Action Agency claims 'affirmative action has failed because it has not sold itself commercially ... She wants to speed up the profit driven reasons for organisations to recruit and promote women' (Bagnall 1994, p. 37).

Examples of Best Practice EEO initiatives

Despite these general shortcomings, a number of initiatives have been undertaken in Australian organisations which seek to enable women to participate equally in the workforce. Examples of organisations which have sought to integrate affirmative action initiatives into broader human resource planning have been recognised in the *Business Review Weekly* (BRW) Affirmative Action Awards. A feature of some of these initiatives has been the acknowledgment of employee needs in the formulation and development of policies.

Table 4.4 Equal Employment Opportunity and Affirmative Action in Australian workplaces

	WRITTEN POLICY PRESENT %	EEO/AA OFFICER PRESENT %	MAJORITY OF TIME SPENT ON EEO/AA ACTIVITIES %
No. of employees			
20–49	49	20	5
50–99	54	22	6
100–199	72	39	8
200–499	84	47	16
500+	87	63	35
All (20+)	58	26	9
Sector			
Public	88	41	13
Private	45	20	6
Industry			
Mining	63	32	0
Manufacturing	41	25	3
Electricity, gas and water	71	23	14
Construction	46	15	7
Wholesale and retail trade	60	24	8
Transport and storage	60	25	15
Communication	99	55	2
Finance, property and business services	63	21	7
Public administration	73	46	28
Community services	72	32	10
Recreation, personal and other services	34	16	13
Organisational Status			
Multi	68	30	9
Single	16	13	12
All classified workplaces	54	26	9

Source: Based on Callus et al. 1991, p. 316

HRM IN THE NEWS

A large bank with close to 30 000 employees reached a *level 5* on the assessment scale. The bank's report stood out primarily because its extensive program was well integrated with its human resource management and industrial relations processes and was clearly linked to its business objectives.

The bank was able to demonstrate high level consultative processes and real achievements including a 13 per cent increase of women in management.

The bank's top priorities were to address the under-representation of women in senior management positions and the need for more flexible working conditions. The bank also indicated that it wanted to review its base level recruitment processes to ensure that they were equitable.

Their enterprise bargaining EEO subcommittee developed proposals that were then negotiated and made part of the enterprise development agreement. Its next task is to publicise the new arrangements through the production of a kit for distribution to all staff.

The representation of women is subject to top level scrutiny with quarterly reports to the senior management team. In this way the strategies are carefully monitored to ensure that objectives are met. Mentoring, training and other strategies have contributed to their success in improving women's representation.

Their selection processes at the base level were completely revised to ensure that recruitment is based on demonstrated skills rather than formal qualifications only or years of experience.

The bank sees the retention of women and their representation at all levels as a major business issue. It is able to quantify the cost of turnover to the company in lost skills and experience and is aware of the need for the bank to be in tune with its changing customer base.

Source: Affirmative Action Agency *Annual Report* 1994–95.

Air International

The 1994 Overall Winner of the BRW Affirmative Action Awards, Air International—encouraged by its involvement in the Australian Best Practice Demonstration Program—reviewed its human resource management policies and as part of this review sought to create EEO. It did this by seeking to improve the calibre of the people employed, the structure of the work practices and the upskilling of existing employees through training. Air International is an Australian manufacturer of automotive air-conditioning, heating, ventilation systems and steering columns. It employs about 370 employees, most of which are from non-English speaking backgrounds and about 22 per cent of the workforce are women.

As part of the Best Practice Program, Air International introduced lean manufacturing principles, continued development of a competency-based skills structure, expansion of literacy and numeracy education, benchmarking against 'best in class' automotive component companies and the development of appropriate performance measures. The affirmative action initiatives included establishing recruitment and selection criteria which relate only to the effective performance of the job or task. Continuing training is provided so employees may be prepared for promotional opportunities. In addition, all job titles are now gender-free titles and production classifications emphasise level of skills rather than gender. Training programs addressed affirmative action issues such as sexual harassment and its implications for managers and team leaders. While the introduction of basic air-conditioning principles and assertiveness training enabled secretarial staff to liaise with customers. In addition, staff are able to use various conditions in a flexible way in order to balance work and family (Affirmative Action Agency 1994, pp. 9, 2–3).

Other organisations have also explicitly taken into account the needs of employees as part of their approach to employee management. These organisations have explicitly acknowledged the interaction between work and non-work responsibilities and have sought to manage this interaction in order to improve employee performance. A number of organisations have surveyed their employees to formally find out how employment policies could be changed to facilitate the management of domestic responsibilities and employment. These organisations include the National Roads and Motorists' Association (NRMA) and Caltex.

National Roads and Motorists' Association

In NRMA the Employment Relations Manager and Employee Relations Officer included an objective in the 1991 Affirmative Action Report which eventually stimulated the development of a Work and Family Policy. The objective 'to target issues for the development of EEO in NRMA as defined by the staff' resulted in a survey of staff which enabled the identification of major concerns among employees regarding the creation of EEO. The identification of these concerns provided the basis for the development of a variety of policies including family sick leave, flexible working hours, work teams organising their own rosters/time off, reservation of child care places, extended parental leave, job sharing and a trial of working from home (Kramar 1996).

Caltex

Caltex also conducted a comprehensive survey of employees with a view to establishing a 'family-friendly' culture. In 1990, workshops identified that women had difficulties developing a career in Caltex because of inadequate employment policies and the organisation's culture. As a consequence, in 1992, a survey and workshops were conducted. In order to meet the needs of the employees which were identified in this process, existing policies such as maternity leave, personal leave, extended leave and relocation policies were enhanced. Caltex also implemented a child-care information and referral service, introduced Family Days in some locations and began a major project to develop policies for flexible hours, part-time work, job share and work-from-home. A commitment to the development of EEO was demonstrated by the allocation of resources with the appointment of a full-time EEO co-ordinator (Affirmative Action Agency 1994, pp. 10–11).

 Managing change

Affirmative amalgamation

Action
The Australian Services Union (ASU) developed a systematic process of reviewing and rebuilding the union's women's structures.

Aim
To ensure women's concerns were taken into consideration during the amalgamation of the ASU.

Background
The ASU is one of Australia's largest unions with a membership of over 20 000 employees in a diverse range of industries. ASU members are employed in such industries as local government, transport, airlines, shipping, travel, community services and information technology. The union was formed in July 1993 from an amalgamation of the Federated Clerk's Union, the Municipal Employees' Union and the former Australian Services Union. Women constitute about 42 per cent of the new union although this figure varies across ASU divisions and the work areas they cover. Of the 400 ASU staff, 49 per cent are women and it is estimated 30 per cent of workplace union representatives are women.

In short
The ASU developed a strategy to ensure women's interests would not be overlooked during its amalgamation. The policy included the development of a consultancy committee which plans to conduct a national women's conference for women delegates. The ASU also plans to conduct a publicity campaign to address the needs of women in specific occupations, locations and industries. The ASU has also identified positions for women on the union's executive.

In detail
It was recognised that women members may be overlooked in the amalgamation process unless a commitment was made by

all parties to take into consideration women's role in the new union.

To address this concern, a memorandum of understanding of national women's policies was drawn up. It was agreed that a national women's consultative committee would be established to make recommendations to the national executive about the formulation and implementation of women's policies.

The ASU plans to conduct a national publicity strategy to address the needs of women in specific occupations, locations and industries.

The union plans to develop policies on issues of concern to women such as outwork, child care, workplace harassment and discrimination, in accordance with the ACTU working women's charter.

A full-time national women's officer will be appointed to conduct research and implement policies for women in the union.

The ASU has guaranteed positions for women on the union's executive. This has paved the way for other unions to take steps to improve female representation as part of the amalgamation process.

Audit

The ASU conducted an audit to determine the impact of the amalgamation on its three divisions, twenty-two branches and two national offices. One of the first stages of the project was to conduct an audit of women's policies and approaches to affirmative action in the branches.

Source: Affirmative Action Agency 1994a, pp. 22–23.

The extract from the article 'Affirmative amalgamation' describes the way one organisation took into account EEO issues when it was being restructured. The organisation, the Australian Services Union (ASU) was concerned women's needs in the new trade union organisation resulting from the amalgamation of the Federated Clerks' Union, the Municipal Employees' Union and the former Australian Services Union would be neglected. The ASU was concerned to ensure women's interests were taken into account in both the management structures, representation in the workplace and in the policies it pursued.

HRM IN THE NEWS

Push is on for flexible working hours

BY MATTHEW RUSSELL & LEONIE LAMONT

Enterprise agreements and awards are putting family duties squarely on the negotiating table as dual income families juggle their work and family lives.

Today, the Reserve Bank Officers' Agreement is expected to be registered in the Industrial Relations Commission, and joins a growing list of enterprise agreements with provisions for flexible working hours.

Last year, the ACTU launched its family leave test case in an effort to add an extra five days to holidays and, although it was defeated, the concept of family leave was recognised.

The new work arrangements are posing a challenge within the workplace and the family. A growing number of men, especially those with working partners, are now expected to do duties such as picking up children from after-school care or day care. While the flexibility is there, men who take it up can be penalised financially, or more subtly are viewed by colleagues and managers as not being committed to their jobs.

Some companies are at the cutting edge. The computer software outfit UNISYS has such flexible working hours that it doesn't have set days per week or hours of work, just a demand that the job gets done on time.

The active work and family programs at Esso and the NRMA have demonstrated that the policy helps the bottom line. Esso has found the combination of work-based child care with flexible working arrangements has resulted in a 100 per cent retention rate of professional women returning from maternity leave. The NRMA has estimated at least $650 000 in annual savings.

But according to the Australian Centre for Industrial Relations Research and Training at the University of Sydney which has a comprehensive database of enterprise agreements, such clauses are still not widespread—and can be limited to certain industries.

Companies in the financial services sector already have these provisions written into agreements—Commercial Union, FAI insurance, Lend Lease, ANZ, Westpac, National Australia Bank and West-Australian-based Challenge Bank.

Many agreements already allow workers, most of them white-collar, to restructure their day to accommodate family needs. But staff are demanding less rigid working times from management.

Dr Kerri Spooner, a lecturer in industrial relations at the University of Technology, can see troubles ahead.

She said that when bosses talk about flexibility they want staggered starting times set well in advance, but when workers talk about flexibility they want to be able to meet unforeseen crises on a daily basis.

Source: *Sydney Morning Herald*, 19 June 1995, p. 3.

The future

The desire to provide flexible working arrangements can be assisted by developments in technology. The extracts from the article 'Push is on for flexible working hours' indicate how enterprise agreements can provide for flexible working arrangements. It also demonstrates some of the benefits and challenges associated with these arrangements.

The development of EEO in the future will involve management dealing with EEO as an integral part of business activity and success. This will require the reconceptualisation and understanding of EEO as a means of improving organisational performance through the creation of a flexible, co-operative, diverse workforce. Two developments will encourage this. The Affirmative Action reporting form introduced in 1995 encourages the integration of affirmative action plans into the strategic planning process. The Industry Task Force on Leadership and Management Skills Report (the Karpin Report 1995) claims there is an urgent need to develop diversity in employment, particularly women in senior management.

The Karpin Report (1995) claimed the effective management of a diverse workforce is a source of competitive advantage through improved efficiency, the expansion of creative ideas, enhanced marketing opportunities, a more open and ideas-oriented organisational culture. 'Encouraging effective management for diversity is an important "missing link" in improving the competitiveness of Australia's industry and upgrading the management performance of individual enterprises across the board'. The Report claimed there was an immediate challenge to utilise and capitalise on the talents of the multicultural workforce and women. The need to ensure women attain senior management positions was identified as an area in need of the 'most urgent strategies' (Report of the Industry Task Force on Leadership and Management Skills 1995, p. 30).

The concept of affirmative action will broaden to that of 'managing diversity'. This concept is already being used in some organisations in the United States. 'Managing diversity' seeks to achieve a workforce with a mix of talents, religious beliefs, political views and values and at the same time values and promotes different points of view in the decision-making process. Such an approach to employee management and organisational culture is claimed to improve business, decision making, quality of life in the workplace and relations with stakeholders (Shipper & Shipper 1987). Human resource managers in the United States typically need to focus on nine key areas when managing diversity. These include recruitment, career development, diversity training for managers, enhancing career development of employees with a variety of personal characteristics, communication channels allowing input and feedback from diverse groups, encouragement of networking and support groups, developing accountabilities so managers are responsible for developing their diverse workforces, develop support for cultural diversity through recognition of different cultural and religious holidays, diets, etc. and by supporting minority organisations and programs (Schuler 1995, pp. 73–75).

An additional area which will develop in the future is the area of work and family. A number of Australian organisations have developed policies to assist employers in accommodating employees' work and family needs. These include leave policies such as parental leave, family leave, flexible work arrangements such as part-time employment, telecommuting and the provision of dependent care services such as child care and elder-care services. The provision of elder-care services will become increasingly important as the population ages.

A work and family program seeks to build a culture which is based on equity and diversity and which acknowledges explicitly the relationship between an employee's work and non-work life. The Australian Industrial Relations Commission and the ACTU have developed principles and strategies which facilitate employers and employees performing well at work and managing their non-work responsibilities.

A further area which will develop in the future is employers' desire to conduct evaluations of EEO policies through the costing, surveying and benchmarking of policies. These evaluations will be encouraged by the development of the integration of human resource strategy and affirmative action with strategic planning, a process which explicitly links the contribution of human resource policies to the achievement of organisational objectives. Organisations are only starting to conduct such analyses, however, there is increasing recognition that human resource initiatives, including affirmative action policies, will be more readily implemented if it can be demonstrated that they contribute to improvement in organisational performance. Techniques are being developed to cost the outcomes of human resource policies, such as turnover, absenteeism and training (Cascio 1991). Similarly, the conduct of cultural and attitude surveys provides a guide to the impact of policies on employee morale and behaviour. The process of benchmarking human resource policies and outcomes against those of other organisations also provides a means of benchmarking policies against competitors and other 'best practice' organisations.

Summary

International labour standards support the removal of discrimination from the labour market and the creation of EEO. Australian governments have sought to create EEO through a variety of policies, most importantly through affirmative action and anti-discrimination legislation. The legislation sets standards for behaviour in the workplace.

Although almost all organisations covered by the affirmative action legislation have formally complied with the legislation, they have been slow to make changes which demonstrate that EEO is an integral part of good management practice. However, the reporting form introduced in 1995 should encourage the development of human resource policies which create EEO and which are a part of the strategic planning process. This integration will be further encouraged by the realisation that EEO can contribute to organisational efficiency and the building of an organisational culture. The Karpin Report indicated the importance of building a management team which reflected the diversity of the workforce and the population.

It is also likely that the approach to EEO will broaden as concepts associated with managing diversity and work and family become part of a human resource management strategy. Such a human resource strategy will increasing provide flexibility in employment and conditions which take into account the impact of non-work responsibilities, such as care of dependents.

questions for discussion and review

1. What are organisations in Australia required to do to comply with the *Affirmative Action (Equal Employment Opportunity for Women) Act 1986* legislation?
2. Identify the differences between affirmative action and equal employment opportunity.
3. Discuss the ways affirmative action can improve organisational performance.
4. Discuss three initiatives which have been recently introduced in Australian organisations to promote EEO.
5. Identify some of the barriers confronting the implementation of equal employment opportunity and affirmative action.
6. Discuss the implications of the Karpin Report (1995) for EEO initiatives in Australian organisations.
7. Suggest policies which could be developed in an organisation with which you are familiar to promote EEO.
8. Explain how objectives and estimates differ from quotas.
9. Explain how the assessment framework can assist in the improvement of affirmative action plans.
10. Identify ways the glass ceiling could be shattered.

case study

Aged care and the workplace

BY SHERYLE BAGWELL

Last week I found myself in the sort of crisis being faced by a growing number of people with extended family responsibilities. I had to drop what I was doing at work and rush my elderly grandmother to hospital where she underwent a major operation. From now on my grandmother, an independent woman who had lived alone and enjoyed good health, will probably require more assistance in her daily tasks. Due to the circumstances of my family, I expect a large share of that responsibility will fall on my shoulders.

The demographics tell me I am not alone. Australia, like most countries, is growing old. An economic planning and advisory commission (EPAC) paper last year estimated nearly a quarter of the population will be aged over 65 by the middle of the next century, while the numbers of those over 80 will rise six-fold. That means nearly all of us will experience the aging of a parent or relative at some point, while the same can't be said of child rearing these days (or, more likely, we will experience both). Indeed, according to an Australian Institute of Family Studies report called *When Roles Overlap*, more employees will have dependent elders in the 21st century than dependent children.

What does that mean? It means a lot considering we have less time to care for elders than ever before. The increase in the numbers of women working and the fact that most of us are working longer hours anyway means that elder care will be a potentially stressful issue for workers—one they will have no choice but to bring them to work with them, whether employers like it or not.

Yet at present elder care and its impact on the workplace is still a relatively 'hidden issue' compared with child care related concerns, despite the fact that 15–33 per cent of workers say in surveys they have responsibility for dependent elders. 'Telling your boss you have to leave work early to take granny for a check-up may not get the same response as saying you have to take your child for an inoculation, yet the demands on the worker are the same', says Barbara Holmes, of the consultancy Managing Work and Family. 'The issue is just not on the agenda yet'. (Holmes says the stress is even greater for workers with parents overseas.)

But others like Libby Brooks, an elder care consultant who has just completed a report for the federal Department of Industrial Relations, says there are signs employers are becoming aware of the ramifications of the issue as they, too, begin to personally experience the stress of caring for aged parents. 'I'm seeing CEOs starting to take the issue on board—even more than child care in some cases—because the issue has more personal relevance to them', says Brooks. It is also an issue that crosses gender lines, although women probably traditionally take more of the caring burden than men.

Brooks has won a Fulbright award to study elder care in the US, where the private sector has gone so far as to fund elder care centres. With government so heavily involved in aged care in Australia, it may take some time before employers see a similar role for themselves. But Brooks says offering employees flexibility in their hours—even providing 'windows' in the middle of the day to allow a worker to care for an aged parent—is a good start.

In the end it will all help relieve the increasingly harried worker, allowing them to concentrate better at work. And that, in the long-term, benefits the company.

Source: *Financial Review*, 2 August 1995, p. 15.

Questions

1. Explain why employer policies facilitating 'elder care' constitute an EEO issue.
2. Suggest some policies which could be implemented as part of an affirmative action program to assist employees with their elder care responsibilities.
3. In what ways do you think the issue of elder care will be an issue in an organisation or industry with which you are familiar?
4. Identify some of the problems which could be confronted in implementing elder care policies.
5. Develop a strategy for implementing these policies.

Resources
Articles and books
Affirmative Action Agency (1995), 'A practical guide to affirmative action: Towards a better workplace', Australian Government Publishing Service, Canberra.
—— (n.d.), Workshift Information Series: no. 1, *Women and Training in the 90s*; no. 2, *Affirmative Action and Skills Audits*; no. 3, *Integration of Permanent Part-time Workers*; no. 4, *Job Sharing*; no. 5, *Linking Workplace Bargaining and Affirmative Action*.
—— (1996), *Best Employers in Affirmative Action*, Affirmative Action Agency, Sydney.
Burton C. (1991), *The Promise and the Price: The Struggle for Equal Opportunity in Women's Employment*, Allen & Unwin, Sydney.
—— (1995), *Redesigning Women's Work: A case study in the community sector*, Affirmative Action Agency, Sydney.
Poiner, G. & Wills, Sue (1991), *The Gifthorse—A Critical Look at Equal Employment Opportunity in Australia*, Allen & Unwin, Sydney.

Videos
Work and Family Unit (1995), 'Some family ... Family-friendly Solutions at work', Department of Industrial Relations, Australian Government Publishing Service, Canberra.

References
Affirmative Action Agency (1992), *Quality and Commitment: The Next Steps, The Final Report of the Effectiveness Review of the Affirmative Action (Equal Employment Opportunity for Women) Act 1996*, Australian Government Publishing Service, Canberra.
—— (1994a), *Affirmative Action Annual Report, 1993–1994*, Australian Government Publishing Service, Canberra.
—— (1994b), *Triple A List*, Australian Government Publishing Service, Canberra.
—— (1995), *A Practical Guide to Affirmative Action: Towards a Better Workforce*, Australian Government Publishing Service, Canberra.
Bagnall, D. (1994), 'He's (still) the boss', *Financial Review*, October, p. 37.
Business in the Community/Institute of Personnel Management (1993), *Corporate culture and caring: the business case for family friendly provision*, Business in the Community/Institute of Personnel Management, London.
Callus, R., Morehead, A., Cully, M. & Buchanan, J. (1991), *The Australian Workplace Industrial Relations Survey*, Australian Government Publishing Service, Canberra.
Cascio, W. (1991), *Costing Human Resources: The Financial Impact of Behaviour in Organisations*, PWS-Kent, Boston.
CCH Australia Ltd. (1995), *Human Resources Management*, CCH Australia Ltd, Sydney.
Cockburn C. (1989), 'Equal opportunities: The short and long agenda', *Industrial Relations Journal*, vol. 20, no. 3, pp. 213–25.
Cohen, Y. & Pfeffer, J. (1986), 'Organisational Hiring Standards', *Administrative Science Quarterly*, vol. 32, pp. 1–24.
De Cenzo, D. A. & Robbins, S. P. (1988), *Personnel/Human Resource Management*, Prentice-Hall, Englewood Cliffs, NJ.
Department of Industrial Relations (1991), 'Industrial Relations at Work: The Australian Workplace Industrial Relations Survey', (by R. Callus, A. Morehead, M. Cully & J. Buchanan), Australian Government Publishing Service, Canberra.

Department of the Prime Minister and Cabinet (1984), *Affirmative Action for Women*, vols. 1 & 2, Australian Government Publishing Service, Canberra.

Dex, S. & Walters, P. (1989), 'Women's occupational status in Britain, France and the USA: Explaining the difference', *Industrial Relations Journal*, vol. 20, no. 3, pp. 203–12.

Dickens, L. (1991–92), 'Road blocks on the route to equality: The failure of sex discrimination legislation in Britain', *Melbourne University Law Review*, vol. 18, pp. 277–97.

Fastenau, M. (1996), 'Family-friendly policies do not lead to equal opportunities', *HRMonthly*, July, pp. 28–29.

Foster, J. (1994), 'Equal Opportunities in the European Commission', in E. M. Davis & V. Pratt (eds), *Making the Link, no. 5*, Affirmative Action Agency and Labour Management Studies Foundation, Sydney.

Gillespie, J. (1995), 'How to be Heard by Business—A Customer Centred and Cost Benefit Approach to Diversity Policies', *Recruiting, Developing and Retaining the Corporate Woman*, IBC Conference, 30–31 October, Sydney.

Harris, H. (1990), 'Aussie rules—A fair go for all', Unpublished report, October, Sydney.

Industry Task Force on Leadership and Management Skills (1995), *Enterprising Nation, Renewing Australia's Managers to Meet the Challenges of the Asian Pacific Century*, Australian Government Publishing Service, Canberra.

International Labour Office (1987), *Women at Work, no. 2, Equal Opportunity: Trends and Perspectives*, International Labour Office, Geneva.

Johnston, R. (1995), 'Creating the Cultural Starting Point', *Recruiting, Developing and Retaining the Corporate Woman*, IBC Conference, 30–31 Oct., Sydney.

Kramar, R. (1996), 'Work and family policies in Australia: critical processes', *Equal Opportunities International*, vol. 15, no. 8, pp. 19–35.

Krautil, F. (1995), 'Setting Goals For Recruitment and Retention of the Corporate Woman and Measuring Success', *Recruiting, Developing and Retaining the Corporate Woman*, IBC Conference, 30–31 October, Sydney.

Lambert, S. et al. (1993), *Added Benefits*, University of Chicago Press, Chicago.

Manns, R-A. (1995), 'Indirect discrimination: The Big Sleeper', *Financial Review*, 2 November, p. 18.

Miller, J. (1995), 'The Glass Ceiling: American Experience', in E. Davis & C. Harris (eds), *Making the Link, no.6*, Affirmative Action Agency and the Labour Management Studies Foundation, Sydney.

O'Connor, D. (1995), 'Equity in the Workplace', in E. Davis & C. Harris (eds), *Making the Link, no. 6*, Affirmative Action Agency and the Labour Management Studies Foundation, Sydney.

O'Connor, M. (1995), 'Work and Family at NRMA: A Business Imperative', in E. Davis & C. Harris (eds), *Making the Link, No. 6*, Affirmative Action Agency and the Labour Management Studies Foundation, Sydney.

Russell, M. (1995), 'Report calls for a more fair workplace', *Sydney Morning Herald*, 11 July, p. 7.

Schuler, R. (1995), *Managing Human Resources*, West Publishing, St. Paul, Minn.

Shipper, F. C. & Shipper, F. M. (1987), 'Beyond EEO: towards pluralism—moving toward a pluralistic work force', *Business Horizons*, vol. 30, May–June, pp. 53–61.

Wright, P., Ferris, S. P., Hiller, J. S. & Kroll, M. (1995), 'Competitiveness Through Management of Diversity: Effects on Stock Price Valuations', *Academy of Management Journal*, vol. 38, no. 1.

chapter 5

Occupational health and safety

Lindsay Nelson

learning objectives

After studying this chapter, you will be able to:

1. Explain why it is important for businesses to improve occupational health and safety.
2. Explain the model of occupational health and safety.
3. Describe the legal environment of occupational health and safety in Australia.
4. Relate hazards to occupational accidents and diseases.
5. Describe and explain strategies for improving the standard of occupational health and safety.

chapter 5

chapter outline

- Occupational health and safety — 161
- Why is it important to improve occupational health and safety? — 162
  - The benefits of a safe and healthy work environment — 163
  - The costs of an unsafe and unhealthy work environment — 163
- Legal considerations — 168
  - Statute law — 168
  - Workers' compensation — 176
  - Common law — 178
- A model of occupational health and safety — 179
- Hazards in occupational health and safety — 179
  - Occupational accidents — 180
  - The unsafe employee? — 180
  - The violent employee? — 181
- Occupational diseases — 183
  - Categories of occupational diseases — 184
  - Occupational groups at risk — 184
  - When the quality of working life is low — 185
  - Organisational stress — 185
- Strategies for improvement of OH&S and preventing accidents — 187
  - Health and safety performance indicators — 188
  - Accident control — 189
  - Ergonomics — 191
  - Safety committees — 192
  - Behaviour modification — 192
  - Management by Objectives programs — 193
  - Reducing occupational diseases — 193
  - Employee assistance programs — 194
  - Total Quality Management — 195
  - Role of HRM — 195
  - Work environment — 197
- International safety and health issues — 198
  - Closer monitoring of foreign firms — 198
- Current trends — 199
  - Occupational health policies — 199
  - Wellness programs — 200
  - Ethics in shaping behaviour — 201
- Summary — 201
- Questions for discussion and review — 202
- Case study — 202
- References — 205

HRM IN THE NEWS

Business push for penalties to cut $20bn safety cost

BY DAVID SHIRES

Stiff fines for business and tougher but simpler laws are needed to cut the $20 billion annual cost to Australia of work-related accidents and sickness, the Industry Commission has warned.

In a controversial report, the commission has also called for more prosecutions of employers and for uniform occupational health and safety laws throughout the country.

The presiding commissioner, Mr Jeffrey Rae, said that while breaches of the Trade Practices Act attracted fines of up to $10 million, the maximum fine in some states for OH&S breaches was as low as $50 000.

'Ripping off your customers is apparently far worse than killing one of your employees through negligence', he said. 'I think responsible business recognises that significant breaches of the law require significant penalties'.

The report, *Work, Health and Safety*, found that each year up to 2700 Australian workers die of work-related health problems—most from exposure to hazardous materials—and 650 000 suffer injuries and illness from work.

But industry groups expressed disappointment last night with the report's emphasis on enforcement.

The $20 billion cost of work-related accidents and sickness comprises:
- $6 billion borne by injured workers
- $7 billion to employers—$5 billion in workers' compensation premiums, and $2 billion in lost productivity and extra overtime
- $7 billion to taxpayers, in social security and subsidised medical services.

'Hence, health and safety at work is a major issue in microeconomic reform', the report says.

The chief executive of the Chamber of Commerce and Industry, Mr Ian Spicer, said last night that the report should have emphasised improved funding for cultural change in the workplace.

'Instead, the commission has focused unduly on enforcement and penalty measures, which have in the past proven to be less than effective, and which have the effect of drawing resources away from the major new initiatives required in changing the safety ethic within workplaces'.

The report found that, at any time, up to 115 000 workers are unable to work at full capacity, and about 200 000 have to permanently reduce their working hours. Another 200 000 are prevented from working at all—the 'vast majority' of those for more than a year, according to the report.

But it was governments that bore the brunt of responsibility for reform.

The report found that state and territory governments had intervened in areas and ways that could not be justified on grounds of economic efficiency or equity. There was too much legislation governing OH&S regulations, and codes of practice were of little practical use.

Enforcement was identified as a large part of the problem. Although OH&S agencies spent 60 per cent of their time on enforcement, penalties were issued in less than 10 per cent of cases in most jurisdictions. Maximum penalties varied enormously between States.

Courts were also unwilling to impose strong penalties:

'Even in cases where workers have been killed or seriously injured, courts impose low fines on culpable employers'.

'Although the courts convict roughly 75 per cent of all prosecuted offences, the average fine is $ 2683'.

Enforcement should be deterrence-orientated, and 'focus on ensuring compliance with the duty of care'.

> The report also says there is too much regulation: each state or territory has an OH&S act, as well as other related legislation.
>
> 'Small employers, in particular, are faced with an impossible burden'.
>
> All legislation relating to workplace health and safety that pre-dated the passage of principal OH&S sets should be reviewed and, if possible, repealed. As well, template legislation should be introduced to achieve a nationally consistent OH&S regime.
>
> A new regulatory regime should be introduced under a Commonwealth/state ministerial council that would preside over a recognised five-member National Health and Safety Commission. The latter would preside over a reorganised Worksafe Australia.

Source: *Financial Review*, 13 April 1995, pp. 1, 10.

This news item illustrates some crucial issues about occupational health and safety (OHS). One is the enormous cost penalty of not having effective management of health and safety at work. Organisations therefore need to have greater emphasis on safety programs. Another is the benefit associated with workplace safety: a safe working environment keeps employees healthy and productive, and reduces workers' compensation costs that firms pay as insurance premiums. A third issue is the importance of making line managers responsible for safety through policies, goals, performance appraisal and compensation. The central role of HR managers in these tasks should be noted. While not in a line role themselves, they can still do much to assist line managers in making conditions safer and healthier. Of course, to do this effectively, HR managers need to know a lot about health and safety, and this chapter is an introduction into the issues of occupational health and safety in organisations, which can be seen as a partnership between line managers, HR professionals and employees (Table 5.1). Workplace hazards are divided into: (1) the accidents and diseases that produce physiological and physical conditions, and (2) the stress and low quality of working life that result when psychological conditions are not optimal. We will briefly examine the role of government at federal and state levels in establishing and enforcing safety standards. Then we will look at strategies to improve employee health and safety, including such measures as improved record keeping, job redesign, ergonomics, and educational programs (Johnson 1994).

Occupational health and safety

Occupational health and safety concerns the physiological/physical and psychological conditions of an organisation's workforce that results from the work environment provided by the organisation. It refers to the promotion and maintenance of physical and psychological well-being of workers and the prevention of any departure from this goal. It thus seeks to prevent accidents and diseases by ensuring workplaces are free from hazardous conditions.

If an organisation takes effective health and safety measures, fewer of its employees have short- or long-term ill effects as a result of being employed at that organisation. Adverse physiological/physical conditions include occupational diseases and accidents such as loss of life or limb; cardiovascular diseases; various forms of cancer such as lung cancer and leukemia; emphysema; and arthritis. Other conditions that are known to result from an unhealthy work environment include white lung disease, brown lung disease, black lung disease, sterility, central nervous system damage, and chronic bronchitis.

Psychological conditions refer to organisational stress and low quality of working life. These encompass dissatisfaction, apathy, withdrawal, projection, tunnel vision, forgetfulness, confusion about roles and duties, mistrust of others, vacillation in decision making, inattentiveness, irritability, procrastination, and a tendency to become distraught over trifling matters.

Throughout this chapter the responsibilities for OHS should be seen as a partnership between line managers, HR professionals and employees.

Table 5.1 Partnership in safety and health

LINE MANAGERS	HUMAN RESOURCE	EMPLOYEES
Make safety and health a major objective of the firm.	Work with other professionals such as medical doctors and industrial engineers to develop new programs.	Participate in the development and administration of safety and health programs.
Support the HR professionals' efforts to train all employees in safety and health.	Create HR programs that train employees for safe and healthy behaviours and reward them for their success.	Perform in accordance with established safety and health guidelines.
Allow for employees to have more participation in decision making.	Design and deliver stress management programs.	Accurately report work-related illnesses and injuries.

Source: Schuler & Jackson 1996, p. 539

The HR role is to develop policies and programs with other professionals based on identified needs and after consultation with the other 'partners'. Line managers have a large responsibility in ensuring that program interventions are implemented, demonstrating to workers that OHS objectives are supported at all levels. Employees should have the opportunity to participate in developing programs because they will be required to operate according to espoused program details.

Why is it important to improve occupational health and safety?

Benefits of a safer and healthier work environment are increased productivity, lower workers' compensation costs and less down-time at work.

Improving health and safety conditions can reduce the symptoms and costs of poor health and safety. Certain groups of employees appear to be more affected than others and perhaps should be targeted for more intensive efforts. Labourers and related workers have the highest number and also the greatest incidence of workers' compensation cases, (Worksafe Australia 1995a) suggesting that blue-collar workers are at great risk. Industries associated with this risk are in mining, followed by agriculture, forestry, fishing & hunting, then transport & storage, and construction.

Fishing, in particular, appears to have a heavy death toll:

> New Worksafe research, based on its work-related fatalities study, shows that fishing has a fatality incidence of 143 people for every 100 000—18 times higher than the total workforce.

It is also considerably higher than for the mining and agricultural industries, both identified by the Worksafe work-related fatality study as high risk. Sixty-eight per cent of the deaths were caused by drowning, following boats capsizing or sinking, and 13 per cent from physical trauma. Rough weather, non sea-worthy vessels, inadequate use of personal flotation devices and inexperience were associated with most of the fatal accidents (Worksafe Australia 1994, p. 22).

Blue-collar workers are not the only ones to suffer from workplace hazards. White-collar workers, including managers, also encounter workplace hazards. According to one report:

> Stress at work has recently been recognised as a factor in the management of human resource losses associated with absenteeism, illness and workers' compensation ... stressors include work overload, and underload, shiftwork, perceived danger, heavy work and physical environmental factors (Toohey 1994, p. 15).

Toohey goes on to point out that in a Comcare study stress accounted for 4.6 per cent of all claims but a massive 18 per cent of costs, at $30 000 each.

Although the traditional ill effects on the white-collar workforce have been those related to psychological conditions, there is growing concern today over physical conditions relating to a number of factors. These include unforeseen effects of the computer terminal (eyestrain, miscarriages, carpal tunnel syndrome) and closed office buildings, where chemical components from sources such as carpeting and building construction build up and are circulated through the ventilation system. They have become known as 'sick building syndrome'.

The benefits of a safe and healthy work environment

If organisations can reduce the rates and severity of their occupational accidents, diseases, and work-related stress levels and improve the quality of work life for their employees, they can become more effective. Such an improvement can result in:

1. more productivity due to fewer lost workdays
2. increased efficiency from a more committed work force
3. reduced medical and insurance costs
4. lower workers' compensation rates and direct payments because fewer claims are filed
5. greater flexibility and adaptability in the work force as a result of increased participation and an increased sense of ownership, and
6. better selection ratios because of the enhanced image of the organisation (Matthes 1992).

Companies can thus increase their profits or levels of service substantially.

The costs of an unsafe and unhealthy work environment

> Workplace health and safety record a national disgrace, says Dr Emmett. Australia's poor occupational health and safety record is a national burden and a national shame, the chief executive of Worksafe Australia, Dr Ted Emmett, has said.

> 'Workplace injury and disease shows no sign of being easily eliminated—and needs urgent and continued attention, ... Part of the problem was an unhealthy and unsafe complacency'.

> 'Some unions, employers, bureaucrats and individuals have shared this complacency', he said (Worksafe Australia 1995 p. 8).

These seem strong words indeed, in view of the fact that many people take for granted a healthy work environment. However, with well in excess of half a million workers each year suffering work-related injuries and illnesses, at an estimated cost of $20 billion, we have a situation which is very difficult to ignore. The costs of an unsafe and unhealthy work environment can be viewed in three ways: as direct costs by way of workers' compensation, as indirect costs in terms of lost productivity and the wider community at large, and also in terms of human pain and suffering. The following Table gives more detail.

Table 5.2   A tally of injury and disease from work

Workplace injury and disease has a far greater impact than many appreciate:
- up to 2700 workers die each year due to work-related health problems—the majority from hazardous materials
- each year, up to 650 000 workers suffer injuries and illnesses from work—one in twelve workers—and almost two-thirds will have to take time off work

At any time, work-related injury and ill health means that:
- up to 115 000 workers cannot work at full capacity
- about 200 000 workers have had to reduce permanently their hours at work, or change their jobs, and
- almost 200 000 persons are prevented from working at all—disturbingly, the vast majority of these have not worked for over a year.

Work-related health problems also affect persons in their retirement—up to 285 000 persons over the age of 65 are estimated to be suffering from work-related health problems.

Source: Industry Commission 1995, p. x

These figures are derived from data gathered by the Industry Commission in compiling a recent report and translate to between 125 000 and 170 000 workers in any fortnight requiring at least one day off work. Expressed a different way, between 20.2 million and 22.5 million working days lost, compared with 500 000 days lost due to strikes (Industry Commission 1995 pp. 319–20). These figures are alarming from the point of view that they far exceed those obtained from workers' compensation claims.

Workers' compensation data under-estimate the true picture of workplace injury and illness for a number of reasons. In the first place relevant legislation varies from state to state, resulting in different data being recorded and it is therefore difficult to make comparisons or even to arrive at reliable national figures. Secondly, many incidents go unreported for various reasons such as workers being self-employed, believing the injury was only minor, fear of retrenchment and workers who thought they were ineligible to claim compensation (Industry Commission 1995 p. 318). Thirdly, only incidents which resulted in an absence of five days or more appear in workers' compensation data. This means that workplace injuries and illnesses which incur an absence of under five days are disregarded for recording purposes. The Industry Commission report makes these issues abundantly clear:

> It is generally recognised that workers' compensation data cannot measure the real level of injury and disease occurring at the workplace with any accuracy ...

Workers' compensation data does not show the full extent of work-related injury and disease for a number of reasons:

- the self-employed and volunteer workers are excluded
- injuries or diseases which do not result in successful claims are excluded
- occupational accidents or diseases where no compensation claim is made are not included, and
- occupational disease, particularly those with a long latency period, will be poorly covered (Industry Commission 1995, pp. 809–10).

Attempts have been made to provide a national set of statistics as part of the role of the National Occupational Health and Safety Commission, which is perhaps better known under its corporate name of Worksafe Australia. These attempts have given birth to the National Data Set for Compensation-based Statistics, or NSD. However this is conceded as being an inadequate source of information due to an incomplete data-set and, among other things, absences less than five days (ten in Victoria) are not recorded (Industry Commission 1995 p. 813).

It is extremely difficult, therefore, to get an accurate picture of the real number of work-related deaths, injuries and illnesses. This needs to be remembered when costs and statistics associated with workers' compensation are examined. Table 5.3 shows the number of claims made in each state in 1991–92 for a national total of 164 500.

Table 5.3 Workers' compensation claims, by jurisdiction, 1991–92

JURISDICTION	MALES ('000)	FEMALES ('000)	NUMBER OF CLAIMS PERSONS ('000)
New South Wales	39.2	9.7	48.9
Victoria	32.9	10.9	43.8
Queensland	20.8	5.6	26.4
Western Australia	14.4	4.5	18.9
South Australia	8.6	4.0	12.7
Tasmania	2.8	0.9	3.7
ACT	na	na	na
NT	1.0	0.4	1.4
Commonwealth Sector	5.9	2.9	8.7
All	125.7	38.8	164.5

na: Not available
Note: Includes fatality claims
Source: Industry Commission 1995, p. 317

There is, as already pointed out, a considerable gap between claims for compensation and the actual number of workers who suffer injuries and illnesses from their work. Looking at financial costs we see a continuation of the duality in data, with workers' compensation being but part of a larger picture. Figure 5.1 reveals the cost of workers' compensation claims in Australia from 1977. Costs rose rapidly in the early 1980s, reached a peak in 1986–87 of over $5 billion but since then have slightly reduced, to stand at $4.8 billion for 1992–93.

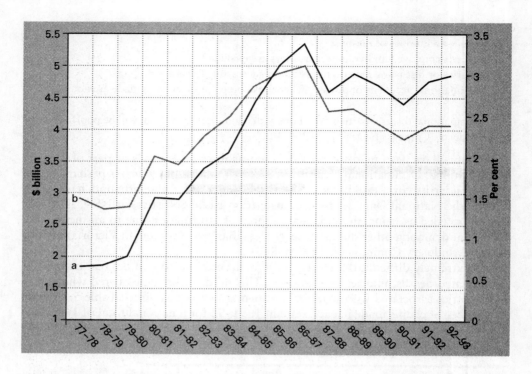

Figure 5.1 Workers' compensation claims: constant prices and as a percentage of non-farm wages, salaries and supplements, 1977–78 to 1992–93

Source: Worksafe Australia c.1993, pp. 19–20

Figure 5.2, however, shows that when we add these direct costs to indirect costs the actual amount is $20 billion. Indirect costs are those which are not covered by workers' compensation but are none the less real and a burden on organisations and the wider community.

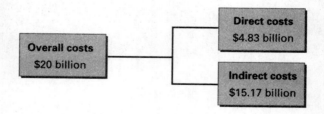

Figure 5.2 Relationship between direct and indirect costs

Source: Industry Commission 1995, p. 388

Another way of expressing this is to consider direct costs as those which may be insured and therefore may be shown separately from indirect or uninsured costs. Table 5.4 lists both insured and uninsured costs.

Table 5.4 The auditing of accident cost

INSURED COSTS

Injuries
- Compensation for lost earnings
- Medical and hospital costs
- Awards for permanent disabilities
- Rehabilitation costs
- Funeral charges
- Pensions for dependants.

Property damage
Insurance premiums or charges for
- Fire
- Loss and damage
- Use and occupancy
- Public and liability.

UNINSURED COSTS

Injuries
- First aid expenses
- Transportation costs
- Cost of investigations
- Cost of processing reports.

Wage losses
- Idle time of workers whose work is interrupted
- Hours spent in cleaning up accident area
- Time spent repairing damaged equipment
- Time lost by workers receiving first aid.

Production losses
- Product spoiled by accident
- Loss of skill and experience
- Lowered production of worker replacement
- Idle machine time.

Associated costs
- Difference between losses and amount recovered
- Rental of equipment to replace damaged equipment
- Surplus workers for replacement of injured employees
- Wages or other benefits paid to disabled worker
- Overhead costs while production is stopped
- Loss of bonus or payment of forfeiture for delays.

Off-the-job accidents
- Cost of medical services
- Time spent on injured workers' welfare
- Loss of skill and experience
- Training replacement worker
- Decreased production of replacement
- Benefits paid to injured worker or dependants.

Intangibles
- Lowered employee morale
- Increased labour conflict
- Unfavourable public relations
- Loss of goodwill.

Source: CCH 1987, p. 7

It is possible that many organisations only perceive workplace injuries and illnesses in terms of direct or insured costs, which is a rather superficial analysis of the issue, bearing in mind that the ratio of indirect to direct costs is over 3:1. The overall cost of $20 billion may also be viewed at the individual level and expressed as an average cost for each incident.

The Commission estimates the average cost of a work-related injury or disease at between $27 000 and $28 000. The distribution of the burden of this cost varies between employers, individuals and the community:

- employers bear about 40 per cent—costs include workers' compensation, loss of productivity, and overtime
- individuals bear about 30 per cent—costs include lost income, pain and suffering, loss of future earnings, medical costs and travel costs, and
- the community bears about 30 per cent—costs include social welfare payments, medical and health costs, and loss of human capital.

The cost of a workplace injury or disease depends upon its severity. For those involving less than five days off work the cost is $1000 whereas the cost of an incident causing permanent incapacitation is almost $600 000 (Industry Commission 1995, p. 17).

Although human pain and suffering are mentioned in the passage above, these intangibles are difficult to measure. In a number of cases they may persist long after the compensation files are closed. They are never the less a compelling reason for organisations and the community to express concern because they have an impact on people as both employees and family members.

Legal considerations

There are three major categories into which the legal framework for occupational health and safety can be divided: statute law, workers' compensation, and common law. Statute law is aimed at providing a safer and healthier workplace. Should an accident occur, however, workers' compensation is designed to meet associated medical expenses and weekly payments to the injured person together with rehabilitation. Common law provides a mechanism for injured workers to seek redress for the employer's negligence.

Responsibility for OHS is shared between employers and employees. It is made clear under statute law, workers' compensation and common law that there are obligations for all employers to provide a safe and healthy workplace. Equally, however, employees are obliged to obey OHS policies and rules designed for their safety. At the workplace, front-line managers and HR managers share a joint responsibility to ensure that both employees and the employer act within the letter and spirit of relevant OHS rules.

The applicability of these laws depends upon whether workers are regarded as employees or independent contractors. In a recent case involving courier firms in NSW reported by Long (1996), the court decided that courier workers were in fact independent contractors and therefore not subject to the employee–employer relationship that lies at the centre of the legal obligations outlined above. This decision was consistent with the 1986 High Court decision on Stevens v. Brodribb. The question now arising is whether more companies will seek to classify workers as independent contractors, thereby avoiding the legal obligations of employers.

Statute law

Laws have been enacted at both federal and state levels in Australia. The most significant piece of federal legislation is the *National Occupational Health and Safety Commission Act 1985*, which established the National Occupational Health and Safety Commission (NOHSC) in order to raise awareness, give focus, and facilitate a national approach to occupational health and safety. The Commission is probably better known as Worksafe Australia. Figure 5.3 shows the structural relationships between various OHS entities at federal and state levels in Australia.

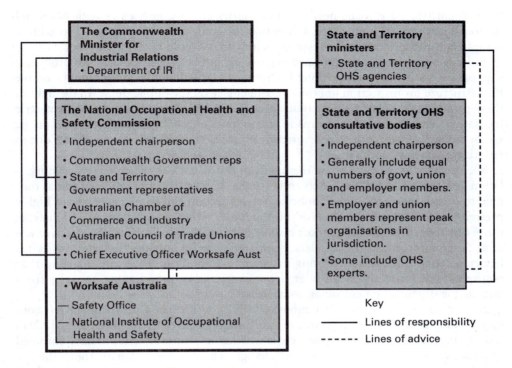

Figure 5.3 Current national institutional arrangements
Source: Industry Commission 1995, p. 163

The Commission, through Worksafe Australia, is vested with a role which although aimed at achieving a safe and healthy workplace, has no power of enforcement, this being in the hands of the states. In recent years a major task has been to facilitate and co-ordinate national standards in OHS. Given what could be seen as only having limited powers, Worksafe has done much to raise awareness of OHS in Australia; however, this has not been without some criticism. At a recent enquiry into workplace health and safety some concerns were registered about its structure and performance, particularly with regard to a membership which could have a more representative base, mixed loyalties of members and a lack of support by state and territory governments (Industry Commission 1995 pp. 165–66).

Approaches to enforcement in Australia have been influenced by the Robens (1972) report in Great Britain, which led to the 1974 Health and Safety at Work Act in that country. The Robens report argued for a tripartite responsibility for OHS, between employers, employees and trade unions but eschewed a proliferation of regulations and recommended a self-regulating system. This report recommended that the plethora of regulations be replaced by a voluntary set of codes wherever possible. Since then a number of critics have pointed to the shortcomings of relying too much on a de-regulated system (see, for example, Brooks 1994). In particular, it is argued that industry is unlikely to comply with self-regulation when it is unwilling to comply with laws supported by criminal penalties; moreover a plethora of rules and apathy is a reason for rationalisation, not elimination, of rules. In other words, overcoming the faults identified by Robens need not necessarily entail doing away with rules and demolishing the legal framework. Given that the goal of OHS legislation is to achieve compliance, the question to be resolved is how that should best be achieved.

Enforcement by a system of inspectors, usually public officials, raises two problems: support for good OHS from within the company may still not be forthcoming, and the infrastructure for inspection imposes a cost penalty on the public purse. In the light of these problems it is little wonder that states in Australia have embraced Robens-style legislation. The point needs to be made that in times of economic stringency and public sector cutbacks, inspections are less frequent, probably with deleterious effects due to enforcement being less likely.

Such powers as do exist are in the hands of states, each of which has its own legislation (see Table 5.5). All these Acts embrace the spirit of Robens (1972) insofar as they tend to encourage a streamlined approach to legislation and move away from a highly prescriptive form to a focus on desirable outcomes rather than the means of achieving those outcomes. The Robens report also saw that there are limits to the effectiveness of negative enforcement by outsiders, compared to self-regulation. In other words it is better to encourage organisations to become actively involved in ensuring that workplaces are safe and healthy environments, rather than having agencies from outside the organisation enforcing compliance.

According to Braithwaite & Grabosky (1985), writing in a post-Robens environment, education and persuasion are more important than enforcement of OHS legislation by authorities. The issue here is whether it is more effective to have enforced compliance or persuasion as a tool of change. There is some debate about this: in addition to Brooks (1988, 1994), Creighton (1982; 1984), Gun (1992), Gunningham (1985) and Merrit (1983) have all expressed concern over the wisdom of deregulation. In Australia the approach is to combine persuasion with provision for strong penalties and as the study box below illustrates, fines may be substantial.

It can be seen from Table 5.5 that the provision of OHS committees and representatives is not automatic; establishing them is contingent upon certain conditions being fulfilled such as a request from employees and, in most cases, workplaces meeting a required minimum number of employees. Even in instances where there is a health and safety representative the Table reveals that their powers are limited, although there is variation from one state to another. There is also considerable difference in the range of fines operating between the states.

HRM IN THE NEWS

Inspector Gordon v. Shortland Electricity

- 5 May 1995
- Prosecution under s.16(1) of the
- *Occupational Health and Safety Act 1983*
- Plea of guilty
- Heard in the Industrial Court
- Fined: $85 000

The charge arose from the deaths of two employees of Shortland Electricity (now known as Orion Energy) while carrying out linesmen's routine maintenance duties from an elevated work platform (EWP) in Mayfield, Newcastle, on 26 November 1992.

The men received fatal burns when the hydraulic power tool they were using contacted unprotected low-voltage conductors. The oil line to the hydraulic tool ruptured, the oil was ignited, and the clothing of both workers caught fire. One worker jumped from the EWP to the footpath below. His workmate fell from the EWP shortly afterwards. One man died at the scene of the accident. The other died in hospital a few weeks later.

Pointing out that the maximum fine for a breach of s.15 of the Act is a fine of $250 000, Justice Marks noted that '... although there was clearly a lack of foresight and perhaps to some extent vigilance, this is not a case of blatant, wilful or reckless disregard of obligations under the Act which, if present, would attract the maximum permissible penalty'.

WorkCover has lodged an appeal on the basis that the penalty was inadequate in the circumstances.

HRM IN THE NEWS

Hotel corporation fined over fall

An international hotel corporation was recently fined $12 000 for its failure to provide safe working equipment for a trapeze artist contracted to perform at the hotel.

Conrad International Hotel Corporation, in Queensland, was charged with failing to register a hoist and ensuring it met the appropriate safety standards. As a result, the 27-year-old trapeze artist, Heather Tetu, fell nine metres, smashing both her ankles and injuring her back when a cable broke during the performance. She spent nine months in a wheelchair.

The Queensland Workplace Health and Safety Division prosecutor said the Corporation had tried to avoid its legal responsibilities for ensuring a safe work environment by blaming the production company which designed the trapeze for the performance and for failing to register the design.

Source: *WorkCover News* no. 24, 1995, p. 20.

The fact that penalties are contained within the legislative framework should not be seen as turning away from persuasion. Approaches to improving OHS in fact involve both deterrence through enforcement and compliance through persuasion. As Gunningham (1994) argues, it is not so much a question of choosing between deterrence or compliance as achieving a good mix of both. The situation in Australia, then, appears to be that although a scale of fines exists by way of statute, the general approach has been to encourage self-regulation and persuasion. Within the framework of enforcement there are stages of persuasion which precede litigation as can be seen in Figure 5.4.

Table 5.5 Occupational health and safety legislation in Australia

	VICTORIA	NSW	SOUTH AUSTRALIA	WESTERN AUSTRALIA	TASMANIA	NORTHERN TERRITORY	QUEENSLAND
Legislation	Occupational Health and Safety Act 1985.	Occupational Health and Safety Act 1983.	Occupational Health Safety and Welfare Act 1986.	Occupational Health Safety and Welfare Act 1984	Workplace Health and Safety Act 1995	Work Health Act 1992	Workplace Health and Safety Act 1989
Duty of employer	To provide and maintain so far as is practicable for employees a working environment that is safe and without risks	To ensure the health safety and welfare at work of all his employees.	To ensure, so far as is reasonably practicable, that the employee is, while ar work, safe, from injury and risks to health.	So far as practicable, to provide and maintain a safe working environment in which his employees are not exposed to hazards.	So far as is practicable, to provide and maintain a safe working environment, safe system of work and plant, and substances in a safe condition.	To provide and maintain, so far as practicable, a working environment that is safe and without risks.	So far as it is practicable, ensure the health and safety at work of their employees.
Duty of employee	To take reasonable care for his or her own health and safety and that of others, to co-operate with employer's.	To take reasonable care for the health and safety of others, to co-operate with employers to comply with OH&S requirements.	To protect his/her own safety and to avoid adversely affecting the health and safety of and other person and to co-operate with the employer.	To ensure his own health and safety at work to avoid adversely affecting health or safety of any other person through any act or omission at work.	To take reasonable care for own health and safety, and for health and safety of other persons. Penalty: 100 units.	To take appropriate care for his own health and safety and for others who may be affected by his acts in the workplace.	Not to wilfully act in a manner that endangers the health and safety or himself or any other person so as to comply so far as practicable with his employer for safety or persons at work.
Penalties serious offences	Corporations: 400 penalty units Individuals: 100 penalty units. Note: Each unit is currently worth $100.	Corporations: 2500 penalty units Any other case: 250 penalty units. Note: Each unit is currently worth $100.	Corporations: max. $50 000 (first offence) max $100 000 subsequent offences Individuals: max. $5000.	Corporations: max $50 000 individuals: max. $5000.	Breach of employer's duty; Body corporate 1500 penalty units, natural person 500 penalty units. Note: Each unit is currently $100.	Corporations: max $5000 Individuals: max $1000 or 6 months imprisonment.	Corporations: max $120 000 Individuals: max $30 000

Health and safety representatives	Any union, a member or members of which work as employees in a designated work group, may conduct an election for a health and safety representative.	No provision	Designated work groups are to be identified. Every member of the DWG is entitled to vote to elect their own safety representative.	An employee may give notice requiring the election of a health and safety representative. Consultation must follow to determine number, training & election procedures.	Where 10 or more employees employed at the workplace, an election may be held for a safety representative. The employer must confer with the employee's representative. Penalty exists for breach.	Not less than 1/2 of the members of the health and safety committee shall be workers elected by other workers.	Employees may elect a health and safety representative(s) where agreement has been obtained from the employer.
Safety Committees	A health and safety representative has the right to establish a joint health and safety committee	Shall be established at a place at work where there are 20 or more persons employed and majority of employed requests such committee of it the council directs establishment of such a committee.	An employer must set up an OH&S committee at the request of a health and safety representative, a majority of employees at the workplace or a 'prescribed number of employees at a workplace' not applicable.	The health and safety representative may request the employer to establish health and safety committee if there are more than 10 employees.	Where 20 or more persons employed, if requested by a majority, the employer must establish a health and safety committee. Penalty exists for failure to do so.	Employer who employs more than 20 workers at a workplace shall, if requested by a majority establish a health and safety committee.	May be established in any workplace on the employer's initiative, when a request is received from the health and safety representative or at the direction of the director.
Health and Safety Officers	No provision	No provision	No provision	No provision	A responsible officer must perform the duties of his or her employer at the workplace for which he or she if the responsible officer. Penalty: 250 penalty units.	The authority may appoint such persons as it thinks fit to be work health officers.	A workplace health and safety officer must be nominated by the employer where 30 or more persons are employed or where the authority or director determines.

Right of employees to cease work	Safety representatives may direct the cessation of dangerous work.	No provision	Safety representative may direct the cessation of dangerous work.	Where an employee has reasonable grounds to believe that as a result of work being carried on at the workplace, there is risk of imminent or serious injury or harm to health, an employee may refuse to work.	No provision	No provision
Work Inspectors	An inspector may enter, inspect and examine the workplace.	Inspectors may inspect the workplace.	Inspectors may enter and inspect the workplace and investigate and seize evidence.	May enter, inspect and examine the workplace.	Authorised officers are empowered to enter, inspect and examine the workplace.	Work health officers can access the workplace and carry out investigations.	Inspectors may inspect, audit occupational and investigate accidents.
Pin notices and prohibition posters	Inspectors have the power to issue improvement and prohibition notices. Safety representative may issue pin notices.	Improvement and prohibition notices can be issued under the Factories, Shops and Industries Act (NSW)	Inspectors may issue improvement and prohibition notices. Safety representatives may issue default notices.	Inspectors may issue improvement and prohibition notices.	Inspector may issue notice prohibiting carrying on of activity if activity involves risk of serious or imminent injury.	An authorised officer may serve a notice where he believes a situation endangering health and safety exist.	The authority may issue improvement or prohibition notices or may delegate the power to work health officers.

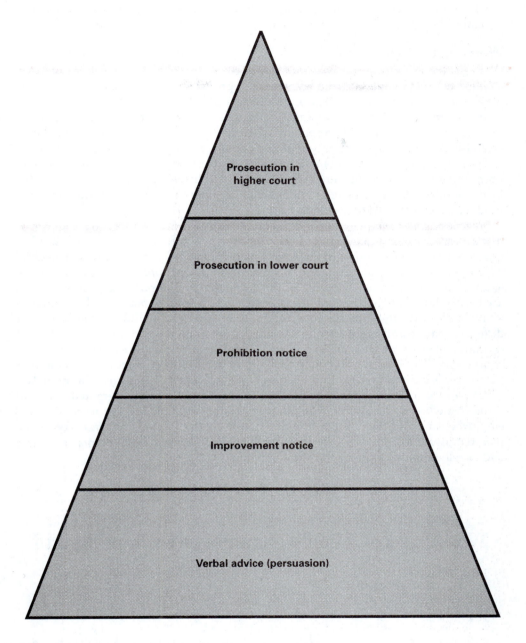

Figure 5.4 OHS enforcement pyramid
Source: Ayres & Braithwaite 1992, p. 35

It should be clearly understood that this is an integrated approach in which both strategies cohabit in a single hierarchy. Where verbal advice fails or should the incident be adjudged a serious breach of OHS rules then higher level action may be taken. An important feature of conceptualising the process as a hierarchy is that inspectors show a willingness to advance to the next higher level in the hierarchy, should the problem remain unresolved.

Workers' compensation

Workers' compensation is a system of giving employees insurance cover should they be injured or fall ill due to their employment. It provides for regular income during the period of incapacity and payment of necessary medical expenses.

In Australia, workers' compensation is legislated for on a state-by-state basis and arises because the alternative remedy of common law depends upon fault being established and attributed to the employer or some third party. Its origins, however, go back one hundred years or more to Bismark's Germany and to British legislation. From there it flowed to Australia where each state passed legislation based upon the British model. Although there are differences in important detail from state to state, fundamentally they all share certain features.

In general terms, employees are not required to prove that the workplace injury or disease was due to the negligence of the employer. It is sufficient that the incident has arisen out of or in the course of the employment. Some jurisdictions however, such as Tasmania, specify that the incident must arise out of *and* in the course of the employment but for practical purposes the distinction is unimportant. Thus employers are held to be legally liable, even in cases where the employee may have been careless or not followed safety instructions to the letter. Cases of wilful misconduct are a different matter and are normally excluded from compensation. Occasionally the definition of an employee is unclear, in an age when many people are engaged as private contractors. The question of employer liability in these case hinges on whether the contractor is an employee for the purposes of the relevant workers' compensation Act.

Employers are required to take out compulsory insurance unless granted approval to be treated as a self insurer. The effect of this provision is make it impossible for employers to avoid their responsibilities simply on the grounds of not carrying the required insurance. An employer thus is still held liable; the state appoints an insurer and usually imposes a penalty on the company.

HRM IN THE NEWS

WorkCover v. Thanh Thanh Ngo Fashion Pty Ltd

- 30 May 1995
- Prosecution under s.161(3) of the *workers' compensation Act 1987*. (Failure to produce for inspection a workers' compensation insurance policy in force between dates.)
- Maximum penalty $2000
- Heard in the Chief Industrial Magistrate's Court
- Fined $2000

The defendant failed to respond to a Notice requiring him to produce a workers' compensation insurance policy. The defendant further was deliberately obstructive, hindering WorkCover investigations, and failed to appear in Court. The Chief Industrial Magistrate recorded a criminal conviction and fined the company $2000 with costs in favour of WorkCover.

Source: *WorkCover News* no. 25 1995, p. 21.

Self-insurance is an arrangement where certain large employers are granted permission to take full responsibility for their own employees' workers' compensation and are therefore exempt from paying premiums to an insurer. However not all jurisdictions allow for self-insurance; Queensland is one such instance. In addition, some states control premiums by regulation while others such as Tasmania, Northern Territory and the ACT are unregulated. In an unregulated environment it is difficult to obtain reliable figures to compare with other jurisdictions. Premium rates vary according to the industry and number of claims, which means that organisations with few accidents and a small number of claims will have low premiums compared with an organisation in a relatively dangerous industry and a higher accident rate. Since insurance premiums increase or decrease according to the claim rate there is a tangible incentive for organisations to observe good OHS practices: fewer accidents and claims mean lower insurance premiums. In an effort to reduce the cost of workers' compensation, some jurisdictions have altered the conditions under which compensation is payable, for example, excluding injuries when travelling to and from work and making organisations pay for the first five days. It could be argued that this in itself does not necessarily reduce the number of injuries, merely shifts the burden of covering the cost from the insurer to the individual or the company. In the case of the five day rule, however, organisations have a yet stronger incentive to strive for a healthy and safe workplace.

Compensation benefits provide for weekly payments of money during the period of incapacity. The basis of determining the rate of pay varies from jurisdiction to jurisdiction. In some cases the weekly payments are capped, limited by a maximum amount beyond which no further payments are made. In addition to weekly payments, medical expenses such as hospital and doctors' charges and other costs incurred in treating the illness or injury are met. Lump sums are made in certain cases such as death or to redeem weekly payments. Upon recovery and return to work or perhaps on being awarded a lump sum settlement, the payments of compensation cease.

A feature of legislative changes to compensation commonly found across Australia today is rehabilitation, sometimes also called a return to work program. Rehabilitation is seen as the means by which employees successfully return to work earlier than would otherwise be the case. It is thus a way of reducing compensation costs and assisting injured persons to fully recover. Within the Commonwealth employment sector Comcare Australia appoints a case manager to co-ordinate a number of functions, including assigning a rehabilitation provider, consulting the worker and negotiating suitable duties with line managers.

> The experience of Australian Government employees clearly shows that the earlier the intervention the faster the employee returns to work ... the average cost of a stress claim will double if not assessed for rehabilitation within four weeks and triple if not assessed within 12 weeks (Comcare 1994, p. 1).

The pattern of rehabilitation is for this function to be organisationally separated from both employer and insurer. Organisations engaged in rehabilitation commonly go through a form of accreditation, for example companies in NSW providing rehabilitation services to injured workers are obliged to undergo a review process to determine whether they are able to meet the accreditation standards. Minimum standards of professional qualifications and experience; responsibilities to workers, employers and insurers; administrative procedures between providers, employers and insurers; and quality assurance systems must be in place before accreditation can be obtained (Casey

1995, p. 5). Rehabilitation has therefore emerged as a major strategy in returning people to work faster and in restraining the overall cost of workers' compensation. Significantly, it makes full use of specialist organisations as a third party to the employer and insurer. Some employers, however, prefer an in-house approach to rehabilitation. Hollingworth & MacRae (1995), for example, report the experience of a bank in providing in-house rehabilitation as part of its human resource management practices. They specifically examine the advantages and disadvantages of in-house approaches to rehabilitation.

Concern over workers' compensation costs has recently led to moves by some organisations to clamp down on claims by invoking techniques such as placing employees under surveillance. Employers are also attempting to rehabilitate workers earlier, thus saving direct and indirect costs.

Common law

In contrast to the specific legislation of OHS and workers' compensation throughout Australia, common law is based upon court decisions which have built up over time. This process is sometimes also referred to as civil action.

Although the right to take common law action is always a possibility, in many cases that action may be restricted by statute law, such as workers' compensation legislation. Unlike workers' compensation however, common law considers the aspect of negligence on the part of the employer. Negligence may be in the form of employers failing to observe their duty to provide:

- reasonably competent staff
- a sufficient number of workers to carry out the work safely
- a reasonably safe place to work
- proper plant and equipment, and
- a reasonably safe system or method of work (CCH 1991, p. 35).

In deciding whether there has been a breach of these duties, courts have regard to such matters as:

- foreseeability of risk of injury
- whether there was a practical means of avoiding of lessening the risk
- whether the fault involved 'caused' the injury, and
- whether failure to eliminate the risk amounted to a lack of care for the safety of the person injured (Lilley 1995, p. 54).

Implied in these matters are concepts of 'reasonable care' and whether measures to avoid injuries are practicable. At the same time, as safety measures improve over time and become more readily available, then the court's expectation of what is reasonable on the part of employers also changes. Thus actions brought against employers attempt to prove that there was negligence; employers for their part need to show that they acted with reasonable care according to existing good safety practices. As with any other common law claim of negligence, it is usual for the other party to mount a claim of contributory negligence.

In some states in Australia the right to take action under common law is restricted but even where this is not the case, settlements received under one avenue affect the other. For example, a settlement under common law would be reduced by the amount paid by way of workers' compensation. This prevents persons obtaining financial gain twice in respect of the one injury or illness.

A model of occupational health and safety

The sources of safety and health conditions in organisations can be labelled as workplace environment hazards; these are comprised of two components: the physical work environment and the socio-psychological work environment. Together, these sources, the physical / physiological and psychological conditions, and their outcomes constitute a model of occupational health and safety in organisations (Figure 5.5). This model is useful in analysing hazards in occupational health and safety

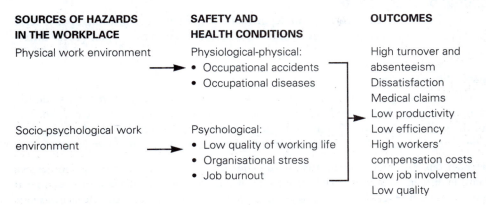

Figure 5.5 Model of occupational health and safety in organisations
Source: Schuler & Jackson 1996, p. 543

Hazards in occupational health and safety

Hazards stem from a variety of organisational aspects such as the type of occupation and industry. They include work-related diseases, low quality of worklife and stress. Many organisations today have the potential for catastrophic consequences, the nuclear industry is but one example. Perrow (1984) points out the dangers associated with risky enterprises and technologies in which there is a need to better understand the interactive complexity of such high-technology systems. He argues that cultures have developed which are accepting of high risks in which the focus is on dollars rather than social criteria. Although Perrow (1984) formulates his arguments against a background of high-technology systems the same reasoning may be applied to the current emphasis on productivity. The question needs to be asked whether, in a climate demanding greater output and productivity, this places excessive pressure on workers to the extent that safety is ignored.

As Figure 5.5 shows, both the physical and the socio-psychological aspects of the workplace environment are important components of occupational safety and health. Each aspect impacts on health and safety. Traditionally, hazards in the physical environment have received greater attention. Increasingly, however, it is being realised that socio-psychological conditions greatly impact on health and safety. An example of this is the need to combat stress and the role of management in ameliorating the symptoms.

> Managers should therefore recognise their role in assessing HRM interventions before the introduction of clinical medical interventions. These would include attention to workload; decision-making latitude; organisational support; and knowledge of job requirements. In addition, effective communication between managers and supervisors and employees should

be accepted as a priority for improving the quality of working life reducing stress-related problems (Toohey 1994, p. 18).

Today efforts to improve occupational safety and health are not complete without a strategy for reducing psychological work-related stress. Developing effective strategies begins with an understanding of the factors in the workplace environment that affect these two aspects of safety and health.

Occupational accidents

Certain industries, organisations, and departments within an organisation, always have higher occupational accident rates than others. Several factors can explain these differences.

Organisational qualities

Accident rates vary substantially by industry. For example, firms in the construction and manufacturing industries have higher incidence rates than firms in services, finance, insurance, and real estate. When employees believe this, they tend to think things cannot be changed and it is up to management to show that safety can in fact be improved:

> Hendersons Automotive (SA), Australia's major manufacturer of car seating components outside the car companies, faced some big problems back in 1985. They were operating at 60 per cent efficiency. On average, one worker in three was injured a year. Morale was low, absenteeism was high and labour turnover even higher. Management style was authoritarian—workforce participation and consultation just didn't exist ...

> Until 1986 management had very little to do with workers' health and safety. That changed when the new Divisional Manager arrived and took ultimate responsibility for all OHS matters. Hendersons' formal OHS program was put in place. An OHS Committee was established. Significantly, a Health and Safety Representative, elected by the workers, was appointed chairperson. Employee representatives outnumbered managers on the OHS Committee, further confirming management's willingness to involve workers in decision making. The OHS Committee began to deal with urgent issues that had been outstanding for too long. As improvements were made on the factory floor, the OHS Committee gained credibility. Next came the OHS Committee's development of an OHS policy, endorsed by management and unions. It was backed up by written procedures detailing how health and safety fitted into everyday work practices at Hendersons (Worksafe Australia c.1993).

Interestingly, small and large organisations (those with fewer than a hundred employees or more than a thousand) have lower incidence rates than medium-sized organisations. This may be because supervisors in small organisations are better able to detect safety hazards and prevent accidents than those of medium size and larger organisations have more resources to hire staff specialists who can devote all their efforts to safety and accident prevention.

In general, however, it is the working conditions (outdoors versus indoors), and the tools and technology available to do the job (e.g. heavy machinery versus personal computers) that most impact on **occupational accidents**. Next in line are the workers themselves.

The unsafe employee?

Although organisational factors certainly play an important role in occupational safety, some experts point to the employee as the pivotal cause of accidents. Accidents depend on the behaviour of the person, the degree of hazard in the work environment, and pure chance. The degree to which the person contributes to the accident can be an indication of an individual's proneness to accidents. Accident proneness cannot be considered a stable set of traits that always contribute to accidents. Nevertheless, certain psychological characteristics seem to make some people more susceptible to accidents than others.

For example, employees who are emotionally 'low' have more accidents than those who are emotionally 'high', while employees who have had fewer accidents have been found to be more optimistic, trusting, and concerned for others, than those who have had more accidents. Employees under greater stress are likely to have more accidents than those with poorer vision. Older workers are likely to be hurt less than younger workers. People who are quicker at recognising visual patterns than at making muscular manipulations are less likely to have accidents than those who are just the opposite. Many psychological conditions probably relate to accident proneness—for instance, hostility and emotional immaturity—may be temporary states. Thus they are difficult to detect until at least one accident has occurred. Because none of these characteristics is related to accidents in all work environments and because they are not always present in employees, selecting and screening job applicants on the basis of accident proneness is difficult.

It is possible for practical jokes to have serious consequences, resulting in injury to other employees. Where the employer is aware that an employee has a reputation for playing practical jokes, that employer can be held liable for any injuries sustained to other employees (see Wallace-Bruce 1994, pp. 127–29).

The violent employee?

Workplace violence is growing rapidly and employers are being held responsible. The key aspect is that if an employee is known to be violent, the employer may well be held liable. In the USA, for example, an employee in a car rental company who was known to be violent assaulted a customer with a blow to the head, kicked him while on the floor and pummelled him with 'judo chops'. A jury awarded the customer $350 000 in compensatory damages and $400 000 in punitive damages ('Workplace Torts' 1992). Also in the USA, death by homicide is the biggest cause of death in the workplace today (Filipczak 1993). While it may be difficult to identify the violent employee before the fact, there are some common signs that employers are urged to look out for. These are described in the following article.

HRM IN THE NEWS

The violent employee: warning signs

If any of the following warning signs are present, employers should consult resource specialists to determine whether monitoring is sufficient or whether immediate action is warranted. Possible resources include a company physician, an employee assistance provider, law enforcement officials, an attorney, or a violence-assessment specialist.

- **Verbal threats:** Individuals often talk about what they may do. An employee might say, 'Bad things are going to happen to so-and-so', or 'That propane tank in the back could blow up easily'.
- **Physical actions:** Troubled employees may try to intimidate others, gain access to places they do not belong, or flash a

concealed weapon in the workplace to test reactions.
- **Frustration:** Most cases of workplace violence do not involve a panicked individual who perceives the world as falling apart. A more likely scenario involves an employee who has a frustrated sense of entitlement to a promotion, for example.
- **Obsession:** An employee may hold a grudge against a co-worker or supervisor, which, in some cases can stem from a romantic interest.

Source: Schuler & Jackson 1996, p. 543.

As the next article shows, violence is an increasing safety issue facing organisations.

HRM IN THE NEWS

Violence action plan

People who work with the public may be exposed to violent attacks from clients or persons with criminal intent. The employees of banks and retail outlets, because they handle cash, are obviously vulnerable to such attacks.

However, employees of service organisations such as health care institutions, public transport and emergency services may also be exposed to various forms of violence at work.

For the employer, violence at work can lead to low morale and a poor image for the organisation, making it difficult to recruit or retrain staff.

For the employee, violence at work can cause pain, suffering and even disability or death.

Physical attacks are obviously dangerous but serious or persistent verbal abuse or threats can also damage employee's health and safety through anxiety or stress.

Solution

Under the *Victorian Occupational Health and Safety Act 1985*, employers have a general duty to provide a workplace that is safe and without risk to the health of employees.

Bearing this point in mind, employers must take the steps necessary to manage violence at work.

The action plan in outlined below has been prepared by the Occupational Health and Safety Authority of Victoria. It shows one way of dealing with violence at work. The plan enables the employer and employees to work together to decide on the most effective way to manage the problem of violence at work.

Benefits

Each workplace should introduce its own procedure, which specifically addresses local issues when dealing with potential violence to staff.

This plan provides a possible formula and some ideas for workplace safety practices.

Action plan for violence to staff

Step 1: Find out if there is a problem

The easiest way to find out is to ask your staff.

This can be done informally by managers, supervisors, safety representatives or trade union representatives, or through a short questionnaire.

The idea is to find out whether your employees ever feel threatened or under great stress.

You should tell your staff the results of your survey, so that if there is a problem they will realise you recognise it; if there isn't a problem, fears will be put to rest.

Step 2: Record all incidents

By keeping a detailed record of all incidents you can build up a picture of the problem.

A simple report form can be used to get the details of what happened, where, when, who was involved, and any possible causes.

Step 3: Classify all incidents

You will want to know what kinds of incidents are happening.

This means classifying them under various headings—place, time, type of incident, who was involved and the possible causes, lessons for late night opening of stores and shops.

Step 4: Search for preventative measures

The way jobs are designed can reduce the risk of violence.

There are no ready-made remedies; you will have to find measures that are right for your workplace. Here are some examples of measures that have worked for some organisation.

- Changing the job to give less face-to-face contact with the public
- Using credit cards or tokens instead of cash to make robbery less attractive
- Checking the credentials of clients
- Making sure that staff can get home safely
- Training your employees, either to give them more knowledge and confidence in their particular jobs.
- Changing the layout of public waiting areas
- Using wider counters, and raising the height of the floor on the staff side of the counter to give staff more protection
- Installing video cameras or alarm buttons
- Putting protective screens around the staff areas
- Using 'coded' security locks on doors to keep the public out of staff areas.

Step 5: Decide what to do

Employees are more likely to be committed to violence control measures if they help to design them and put them into practice.

In particular, many trade unions and safety representatives are experienced in the different measures that can be taken, and can make a valuable contribution.

Step 6: Put measures into practice

Whatever measures are decided on, you should include them in your policy for dealing with violence in your safety policy statement, so that all employees are aware of it.

This will help your employees to co-operate with you, follow procedures properly, and report any further incidents.

Step 7: Check that measures work

Once you have taken steps to reduce violence, check how well they are working. Many organisations have set up joint management and trade union committees to do this.

If the measures work well, keep them up. If violence is still a problem, try something else.

Go back through Steps 2 and 3 and identify other preventative measures that could work.

Source: *Australian Safety News* 1994, pp. 39–40.

Occupational diseases

Potential sources of work-related diseases are as distressingly varied as their symptoms. Several federal agencies in the USA have systematically studied the workplace environment, and they have identified the following hazards: arsenic, asbestos, benzene, bichloromethylether, coal dust, coke-oven emissions, cotton dust, lead, radiation, and vinyl chloride. Workers likely to be exposed to those hazards include chemical and oil refinery workers, miners, textile workers, steelworkers, lead-smelters, medical technicians, painters, shoemakers, and plastics industry workers.

The long-term consequences of these hazards have been linked to thyroid, liver, lung, brain, and kidney cancer; white, brown and black lung disease; leukemia; bronchitis; emphysema; lymphoma; aplastic anemia; central nervous system damage; and reproductive disorders (e.g. sterility, genetic damage, abortions, and birth defects). Continued research will no doubt uncover additional hazards that firms will want to diagnose and remedy for the future well-being of their work forces (Weaver 1989), thereby saving litigation costs.

Categories of occupational diseases

A major category of occupational disease involves illnesses of the respiratory system. Chronic bronchitis and emphysema are among the fastest growing diseases in the country, doubling every five years since the Second World War; they account for the second highest number of disabilities under Social Security (Weaver 1989). Cancer, however, tends to receive the most attention, since it is a leading cause of death in Australia (second after heart disease). Many of the known causes of cancer are physical and chemical agents in the environment. And because these agents are theoretically more controllable than human behaviour, the emphasis is on eliminating them from the workplace.

The emphasis on health is not aimed solely at eliminating cancer and respiratory diseases, however. Good OHS is also concerned with the following categories of occupational diseases and illnesses:

1. occupation-related skin diseases and disorders
2. dust diseases of the lungs
3. respiratory conditions due to toxic agents
4. poisoning (systematic effects of toxic materials)
5. disorders due to physical agents
6. disorders associated with repeated trauma
7. all other occupational illnesses (Wang 1979).

Employers should keep records on all these diseases.

Occupational groups at risk

Miners, construction and transportation workers, and blue-collar and lower-level supervisory personnel in manufacturing industries experience the bulk of both occupational disease and injury. The least safe occupations are mining, agriculture, and construction. In addition, large numbers of petrochemical and oil refinery workers, dye workers, dye users, textile workers, plastic-industry workers, painters, and industrial chemical workers are also particularly susceptible to some of the most dangerous health hazards. Interestingly, skin diseases are the most common reported occupational diseases, with leather workers being the group most affected.

Of course, occupational diseases are not exclusive to the blue-collar workers and manufacturing industries. The 'cushy office job' has evolved into a veritable nightmare of physical and psychological ills for white-collar workers in the expanding service industries. Among the common ailments are varicose veins, bad backs, deteriorating eyesight, migraine headaches, hypertension, coronary heart disorders, repetition strain injury and respiratory and digestive problems. The causes of these in an office environment include the following:

- too much noise
- interior air pollutants such as cigarette smoke and chemical fumes—for example, from the copy machine
- uncomfortable chairs
- poor office design
- new office technology such as video display terminals (Pelletier 1985, Hyatt 1985, Weis 1984).

In addition, dentists are routinely exposed to radiation, mercury, and anaesthetics, and cosmetologists suffer from high rates of cancer and respiratory and cardiac diseases connected with their frequent use of chemicals.

When the quality of working life is low

For many workers, a low quality of working life is associated with workplace conditions that fail to satisfy important preferences and interests such as sense of responsibility, challenge, meaningfulness, self-control, recognition, achievement, fairness or justice, security, and certainty (Schuler 1980; 1982).

Organisational structures that contribute to a low quality of working life include the following:

- Jobs with low task significance, variety, autonomy, feedback, and qualitative underload
- Minimal involvement of employees in decision making and a great deal of one-way communication with employees
- Pay systems not based on performance or based on performance not objectively measured or under employee control
- Supervisors, job descriptions, and organisational policies that fail to convey to the employee what is expected and what is rewarded
- Human resource policies and practices that are discriminatory and of low validity
- Temporary employment conditions where employees are dismissed at will (employee rights do not exist).

Many conditions in organisations are associated with a low quality of working life. The same is true of organisational stress. Remember, however, that a condition causing stress or low quality of working life for one individual may not cause it in another individual because of differences in preferences, interests, adjustment and perceptions of uncertainty in the environment.

Organisational stress

There is growing concern about the number of stress-related workers' compensation claims in Australia and Hooper (1995, p. 38) speaks of it as the 'modern madness' pointing to a recent study by Comcare which reveals that since 1989–90 claims have increased from 800 to 1772 in the public sector.

While some see this as a public sector 'rort', Hooper (1995) admits that in the private sector it is a growing problem that few companies are willing to talk about and that the true extent is probably hidden through other absences and lower productivity.

Prevalent forms of organisational stress include the four S's described below. Other major factors include change, work pace, the physical environment, and job burnout.

The four S's

Common stressors for many employees include the following:

1 Supervisor
2 Salary
3 Security
4 Safety (Shostak 1980).

Petty work rules and relentless pressure for more production are the major stresses that employees associate with supervisors. Both deny worker needs to control the work situation and to be recognised and accepted.

Salary is a stressor when it is perceived as being distributed unfairly. Many blue-collar workers feel they are underpaid relative to their white-collar counterparts in the office. Teachers think they are underpaid relative to people with similar education who work in private industry.

Employees experience stress when they are not sure whether they will have their jobs next month, next week, or even the next day. For many employees, lack of job security is even more stressful than holding jobs that are generally unsafe. At least the employees know the job risks, whereas the lack of job security creates a continued state of uncertainty.

Fear of workplace accidents and the resulting injuries or death can be stressful for many workers. When pressure for production is increased, this fear over workplace safety can increase to a point that production may decrease rather than increase. This result, in turn, may lead to a vicious cycle that is counter-productive for the workers and the organisation.

Organisational change

Changes made by organisations are often stressful, because they usually involve something important and are accompanied by uncertainty. Many changes are made without advance warning. Although rumours often circulate that a change is coming, the exact nature of the change is often left to speculation. People become concerned about whether the change will affect them, perhaps by displacing them or by causing them to be transferred. The result is that the uncertainty surrounding a change yet to come causes many employees to suffer stress symptoms.

Work pacing

Work pacing, particularly who or what controls the pace of the work, is an important potential stressor in organisations. **Machine pacing** gives control over the speed of the operation and the work output to something other than the individual. **Employee pacing** gives the individual control of the operations. The effects of machine pacing are severe, because the individual is unable to satisfy a crucial need for control of the situation. It has been reported that workers on machine-paced jobs feel exhausted at the end of the shift and are unable to relax soon after work because of increased adrenalin secretion on the job. In a study of 23 white- and blue-collar occupations, assembly workers reported the highest level of severe stress symptoms (Schuler & Jackson 1996, p. 547).

Physical environment

Although office automation is a way to improve productivity, it has stress-related drawbacks. One aspect of office automation with a specific stress-related drawback is the video display terminal (VDT). Currently, the findings are not complete on just how serious an effect VDT screens have on workers, although countries such as Sweden and Norway have taken more steps to deal with VDTs than the United States and Australia. Nevertheless, Worksafe Australia is gathering data on VDTs. Other aspects of the work environment associated with stress are crowding, lack of privacy, and lack of control over aspects of the environment that the employee would like to change (e.g. moving a desk or chairs or even hanging pictures in a work area in an effort to personalise it).

The stress-prone employee?

There are individual differences in how people respond to the conditions just described. A classic difference used in research into stress is referred to as Type A or Type B behaviour. Type A people like to do things their way and are willing to exert a lot of effort to ensure that even trivial tasks are performed in the manner they prefer. They often fail to distinguish between important and unimportant situations. They are upset, for instance, when they have to wait fifteen minutes to be seated in a restaurant, since this is not in compliance with their idea of responsive service. In short, the Type A person spends much of his or her time directing energy towards the noncompliances in the environment. Still, Type A people are 'movers and shakers'. They enjoy acting on their environment and enjoy modifying the behaviour of other people. They are primarily rewarded by compliance and punished by noncompliance. Type B people are generally much more tolerant. They are not easily frustrated, easily angered, nor do they expend a lot of energy in response to noncompliance. Type B people may be excellent supervisors to work for— that is, until you need them to push upward in the organisation on your behalf. They probably would permit you and other subordinates a lot of freedom but also might not provide the types of upward support necessary for leadership (Friedman & Roseman 1974). Type As and Bs, then, respond differently to stress, but also they may create stress or reduce stress for different employees. It should be remembered, however, that these are extreme types on a continuum, most people are a mix of Types A and B.

Job burnout

A special type of organisational stress is called job burnout. This condition happens when people work in situations in which they have little control over the quality of their performance but feel personally responsible for their lack of it. People most susceptible to burnout include police officers, nurses, social workers, and teachers. When people begin to show burnout, they reveal three symptoms:

1. emotional exhaustion
2. depersonalisation
3. a sense of low personal accomplishment.

Since this condition benefits neither the individual nor the organisation, many programs have been designed to help people deal with burnout.

Strategies for improvement of OH&S and preventing accidents

Managers firstly need to be able to assess the extent of workplace hazards and, secondly, develop strategies to remove or neutralise conditions hazardous to employees. These strategies are aimed at preventing accidents and diseases at work, and are therefore pro-active. Implementation of programs may be difficult in organisations where management sees good OHS as a cost rather than an investment. This is due to the fact that OHS programs must be financed before the benefits can be achieved. Of course, successful programs in hindsight can always be seen as justified, but management needs to be convinced beforehand that financing such interventions is an investment, not a cost. One way to do this is to make management aware that the eventual cost of poor OHS is much greater than the initial investment.

Once the causes of hazards are identified, strategies can be developed for eliminating or reducing them (see Figure 5.6). To determine whether a particular strategy is effective, organisations can compare the incidence, severity, and frequency of illness and accidents before and after the intervention. There are Worksafe Australia-approved methods for establishing safety and health rates; we will describe these first, and then present strategies for accident control and for reducing occupational disease and improving the sociopsychological work environment.

SOURCE	STRATEGY
Physical work environment	
Occupational accidents	Record the accident
	Redesign the work environment
	Set goals and objectives
	Establish safety committees
	Provide training and financial incentives
Occupational diseases	Record the disease
	Measure and work environment
	Communicate information
	Set goals and objectives
Socio-psychological work environment	
Stress and burnout	Establish organizational stress programs
	Increase employees' participation in decision making
	Establish individual stress programs
	Ensure adequate staffing
	Provide adequate leave and vacation benefits
	Encourage employees to adopt healthy lifestyles

Figure 5.6 Sources and strategies for improving occupational safety and health
Source: Schuler & Jackson 1996, p. 550

Health and safety performance indicators

OHS legislation requires organisations to maintain records of the incidence of injuries and illnesses. Basic performance indicators include the number of lost-time accidents and person-days lost to accidents. These are somewhat crude measures, however, which need to be seen in relation to the total number of employee hours worked. A more appropriate method is for organisations to record the incidence, frequency and severity of each.

Incidence rate

The most explicit index of industrial safety is the incidence rate. It is calculated by the following formula:

$$\text{Incidence rate} = \frac{\text{Number of injuries and illnesses} \times 200\,000}{\text{Number of employee hours worked}}$$

200 000 is the base for 100 full-time workers (40 hours per week, 50 weeks). Suppose an organisation had ten recorded injuries and illnesses and 500 employees. To calculate the number of yearly hours worked, multiply the number of employees by 40 hours and by 50 work weeks :

$$500 \times 40 \times 50 = 1 \text{ million}$$

The incidence rate thus would be 2 per 100 workers per year.

Severity rate

The severity rate reflects the hours actually lost due to injury or illness. It recognises that not all injuries and illnesses are equal. Four categories of injuries and illnesses have been established: deaths, permanent total disabilities, permanent partial disabilities, and temporary total disabilities. An organisation with the same number of injuries and illnesses as another but with more deaths would have a higher severity rate. The severity rate is calculated by this formula:

$$\text{Severity rate} = \frac{\text{Total hours charged} \times 1 \text{ million (hours)}}{\text{Number of employee hours worked}}$$

Frequency rate

The frequency rate reflects the number of injuries and illnesses per million hours worked rather than per year as in the incidence rate. It is calculated thus :

$$\text{Frequency rate} = \frac{\text{Number of injuries and illnesses} \times 1 \text{ million (hours)}}{\text{Number of employees' hours worked}}$$

Organisations need to bear in mind that setting such performance indicators and linking them to incentives and rewards may have dysfunctional consequences because there could be a temptation to not report hazards or even accidents.

Accident control

Designing the work environment to make accidents unlikely is perhaps the best way to prevent accidents and increase safety. Among the safety features that can be designed into the physical environment are guards on machines, handrails in stairways, safety goggles and helmets, warning lights. self-correcting mechanisms, and automatic shutoffs. The extent to which these features will actually reduce accidents depends on employee acceptance and use, together with monitoring by supervisors. For example, eye injuries will be reduced by the availability of safety goggles only if employees wear the goggles correctly.

If employees are involved in the decision to make some physical change to improve safety, they are more likely to accept the decision than if they are not part of the decision-making process. Thus the safety programs most likely to succeed are those that have the greatest support of all the employees. These programs are the ones likely to be the most thorough.

An example of such a program is described in the feature 'OHS Program helps Printing Authority of Tasmania'.

This article relates the case of how an OHS program revitalised one organisation and led to an improved financial position as well as better OHS. It demonstrates that good OHS goes hand-in-hand with management quality, a feature of which is problem solving at the shop floor level and participation by employees.

Managing change

OHS Program helps Printing Authority of Tasmania's over-all revitalisation

The Printing Authority of Tasmania's financial position is now greatly improved, due in part to introduction of a systematic program—and it is much better placed to face the challenges of the nineties and beyond.

In 1992 consultants recommended that PAT should be retained as a government-owned business, but substantially restructured to cut costs and return to profitability.

The government accepted the restructuring recommendation but the precise operating future of the company had still to be finalised.

An employee/management committee was set up to oversee a voluntary redundancy scheme and a change manager was appointed for six months in 1993 to facilitate the restructuring. More than 40 staff took advantage of the scheme and numbers have now fallen from 127 to 78.

Changes following the review caused considerable disruption, undermining morale and commitment. And frequent illness among staff began to focus attention on the work environment, with the need for change becoming crystallised when medical evidence showed a press room worker had suffered permanent liver damage from chemical exposure.

By 1991, sick leave for press room workers was running at 20 days a year while the lost-time injury frequency rate was 54. Manual handling was responsible for six out of ten injuries.

In the same years, the company employed its first OHS officer who quickly moved to implement an OHS management system. A new press room manager was appointed, too. He saw the link between efficiency, quality and the work environment. Management and workers and the OHS officer co-operated to improve the environment and introduced a chemicals management system.

Steps to create a comprehensive OHS management system began in late 1991 with development of general and specific policies and emergency procedures. In addition, managers, supervisors and workers were trained, OHS representatives elected on to a new committee, and OHS information was circulated.

Underlying philosophy

The philosophy underlying the new approach to health and safety—and subsequently enshrined in the 1993 OHS management plan—was that all safety problems must be solved, where practical, at the immediate and shop floor level.

The press room was one of the first areas to receive attention: MSDS were requested from suppliers and all chemicals were assessed for their health effects. A controlled chemical, buying policy was also introduced.

The program scored a major success by reducing chemical, products to just three, two of them water-based, compared to the 15 solvents originally used. Staff were trained in handling chemicals and work practices to conserve usage, prevent evaporation and reduce vapour, instigated.

Next problems to receive attention were housekeeping, manual handling and noise.

In a wider range of other improvements, all paper waste is now recycled. Some production areas have been moved to rationalise work flow and avoid unnecessary movement of materials between floors. Instances of backstrain have been dramatically reduced with increased use of hydraulic hoists and back care training programs. Wearing of hearing protection became mandatory.

Generally, an extensive program of OHS training and education was launched. Managers and supervisors were first in line.

PAT has been encouraging multi-skilling of staff in recent years, giving it flexibility to introduce a nine and a half hour day and four-day working week. Staff rotation keeps the company working five days a week but gives staff a three-day weekend, a very popular arrangement.

A standard OHS injury recording system, based on the Worksafe Australia standard, has been introduced.

Exemplary standards

PAT now enjoys OHS standards considered exemplary for the industry, notably in chemicals management.

Cost savings have been made and both quality and efficiency enhanced.

Customers who were taking their work elsewhere are turning to PAT. In the first nine months of 1993–94, the company showed an operating profit for the first time in three years.

The company says it is still early days for the process of change and much remains to be achieved to ensure its survival. However, staff agree that the OHS program has presented greater opportunities for communication; improved the work environment; and contributed to increased productivity.

Management says the solving OHS problems helped promote a sense of being cared for among employees at a time when PAT was under attack because of rising costs and people feeling threatened by redundancies. At times, it seemed the one cohesive element in an organisation which was severely distressed.

The program helped open a closed organisation to new ideas. People began to look at ways to make their jobs more interesting, their work environment safer and more comfortable—and guarantee their organisation was more efficient and responsive to customer needs. They are now trying to ensure that they and PAT have a future together.

Source: *Worksafe News*, May 1995, pp. 16–17.

Ergonomics

Another way to improve safety is to make the job itself more comfortable and less fatiguing through ergonomics. Ergonomics considers changes in the job environment in conjunction with the physical and physiological capabilities and limitations of employees. See for example, Commonwealth Department of Science and Technology (1982) for a guide to office design and layout.

In an effort to reduce the number of back injuries, the Ford Motor Company redesigns work stations and tasks that may be causing musculoskeletal problems for workers. For instance, lifting devices are being introduced on the assembly line to reduce back strain, and walking and working surfaces are being studied to see if floor mats can reduce body fatigue. Videotapes that feature Ford employees performing their jobs both before and after ergonomic redesign are used in training (Bulletin to Management 1988).

With the objective of cutting manual handling injuries in the health industry, a project undertaken at hospitals in Sydney found that poor ergonomic design of trolleys can result in serious back injuries. The study investigated trolley design, users' needs, tasks and the workplace environment. It was found that although ergonomic guidelines had been developed for a variety of products such as powered handtools and office equipment, trolleys had none. Many had been designed with scant regard for the needs of users and, in fact, some of the newer trolleys had the most design faults. Under new guidelines, attention to trolley design, selection and use based on ergonomic principles will help reduce the number and severity of injuries (Worksafe Australia 1994, pp. 30–31).

Safety committees

Another strategy for accident prevention is the use of safety committees. It can be seen from Table 5.5, discussed earlier in connection with Statute Law, that there is legislative provision in Australia for safety committees and safety representatives.

The HR department can serve as the co-ordinator of a committee composed of several employee representatives. Where unions exist, the committees should have union representation as well. Often organisations have several safety committees at the department level for implementation and administration purposes and one larger committee at the organisational level for policy formulation.

The HR department can be instrumental in accident prevention by assisting supervisors in their training efforts and by implementing safety motivation programs such as contests and in-house communications. Many organisations display signs indicating the number of days or hours worked without an accident. Many organisations also display posters saying 'Safety First.' In safety contests, prizes or awards are given to individuals or departments with the best safety record. These programs seem to work best when employees are already safety conscious and when physical conditions of the work environment pose no extreme hazards.

Behaviour modification

Reinforcing behaviours that reduce the likelihood of accidents can be highly successful. Reinforcers can range from nonmonetary reinforcers, such as feedback, to activity reinforcers, such as time off, to material reinforcers, such as company-purchased doughnuts during the coffee break, to financial rewards for attaining levels of safety.

The behavioural approach relies on measuring performance before and after the intervention, specifying and communicating the desired performance to employees, monitoring performance at unannounced intervals several times a week, and reinforcing desired behaviour several times a week with performance feedback.

A good example of an effective behaviour modification program was conducted in two food processing plants. Behaviour was monitored for 25 weeks—before, during and after a safety training program. Slides were used to illustrate safe and unsafe behaviour. Employees were also given data on the percentage of safe behaviours in their departments. A goal of 90 per cent safe behaviours was established. Supervisors were trained to give positive reinforcement when they observed safe behaviour. Following the intervention, the incidence of safe behaviour increased substantially—from an average of 70 per cent to more than 95 per cent in the wrapping department and from 78 per cent to more than 95 per cent in the make-up department. One year after the program, the incidence of lost-time injuries per million hours worked was fewer than 10, a substantial decline from the preceding year's rate of 53.8 (Komaki, Barwick & Scott 1978).

Management by Objectives programs

Behaviour modification programs are often linked successfully to management by objectives programs that deal with occupational health and safety. The seven basic steps of these programs are as follows:

1. Identify hazards and obtain information about the frequency of accidents
2. Based on this information, evaluate the severity and risk of the hazards
3. Formulate and implement programs to control, prevent, or reduce the possibility of accidents
4. Set specific, difficult, but attainable goals regarding the reduction of accidents or safety problems
5. Consistently monitor results
6. Provide positive feedback for correct safety procedures
7. Monitor and evaluate the program against the goals (Taylor 1980).

Reducing occupational diseases

By far occupational diseases are more costly and harmful overall to organisations and employees than occupational accidents. Because the causal relationship between the physical environment and occupational diseases is often subtle, developing strategies to reduce their incidence is generally difficult.

Record keeping

Organisations should measure the chemicals and other hazards in the workplace, and keep records of these measurements. Their records should also include precise information about ailments and exposures. Such information should be kept for as long a period as is associated with the incubation period of the specific disease—even as long as 40 years. Within Australia, requirements vary from state to state, however, most provide for record keeping in certain circumstances. Organisations are in any event required under state OHS laws to notify authorities of workplace injuries and illnesses, which involves keeping records. It is therefore in the interests of organisations to keep accurate records of hazards which need to be controlled regardless of whether an incident has occurred.

Communicating health and safety information

A second strategy for reducing workplace disease is to set up ways of communicating with employees. This should begin with information being freely available on hazardous substances including chemicals. Statistics and other recorded data are a means of providing this information to staff on the current status on toxic and harmful substances. Material safety data sheets contain safety information on a substance and should be widely communicated to employees at the worksite. In addition, workers need to know about the health effects of these substances, including routes of entry to the body and the means by which the company monitors dosage levels to ensure threshold levels are not exceeded. Means of communication include posters, printed matter, TV/films and appropriate training.

Monitoring exposure

While the obvious approach to controlling occupational illnesses is to rid the workplace of chemical agents or toxins, an alternative approach is to monitor and limit exposure to hazardous substances. For example, the US nuclear industry recruits hundreds of 'jumpers' who fix the ageing innards of the nation's nuclear generating stations. The atmosphere is so radioactive that jumpers can stay only about ten minutes before they 'burn out'. Their exposure has to be closely monitored to ensure that it does not exceed more than 5000 millirems (roughly 250 chest X-rays) annually.

Unfortunately, jumpers get rewarded for absorbing the maximum rather than a safe limit of radiation on any given job. Rather than twelve hours pay for their ten minutes of work, jumpers get a bonus of several hundred dollars each time they 'burn out' between jobs. Even with monitoring, it is estimated that 3–8 out of every 10 000 jumpers will eventually die as a result of exposure (Williams 1983).

In addition to monitoring for radioactivity, some organisations now monitor genetic changes due to exposure to carcinogens (e.g. benzene, arsenic, ether, and vinyl chloride). Samples of blood are obtained from employees at fixed intervals to determine whether the employee's chromosomes have been damaged. If damage has occurred, the employee is placed into a different job.

Genetic screening

Genetic screening is the most extreme, and consequently the most controversial, approach to controlling occupational disease. The genetic makeup of individuals may make them more or less predisposed to specific occupational diseases. By genetically screening out individuals who are susceptible to certain ailments, organisations lower their vulnerability to workers' compensation claims and problems. Opponents of genetic screening contend that genetic screening measures ones predisposition to disease, not the actual presence of disease; therefore, such testing violates an individual's rights (Olian 1988) and raises issues of discrimination.

Employee assistance programs

Employee assistance programs (EAPs) are a form of counselling which spread from the USA to Australia during the 1970s. They stemmed from concern about the affect on productivity of drug and alcohol abuse by employees. EAPs, however, have extended the range of counselling services to include help for employees experiencing problems associated with family matters, finance, bereavement, stress management, mental health or, in fact, any issue which impairs work performance.

A number of large organisations in Australia have established EAPs, they include BHP, James Hardie and Qantas. These programs provide professional counselling for employees aimed at restoring performance. While EAPs extend to a number of areas other than drugs and alcohol, these two issues are of concern because they have the potential to contribute to violence and accidents involving other employees, customers and the general public. Moreover, the problem is widespread; according to the International Labour Office, 15 per cent to 30 per cent of all work fatalities are alcohol or drug related while workers with alcohol or drug problems have 200 per cent to 300 per cent more absenteeism than other employees (CCH 1991, p. 185).

EAPs operate in all states under various names:

- NSW Industrial Programs Service
- Vic   Occupational Assistance Service
- Qld   Interlock Employee Assistance Programs
- SA   Occupational Consultancy Assessment and Referral Services
- WA   Indrad Services Inc
- Tas   Occupational Assistance Service
- ACT   Industrial Program Service
- NT   Employee Assistance Service Inc NT.

Total Quality Management

The philosophy of Total Quality Management (TQM) developed by Deming (1986) has a focus on continuous improvement and has clear implications for OHS. Production down-time due to accidents affects product quality, competitiveness and efficiency. In addition, it should be kept in mind that insurance only covers a relatively small proportion of the overall costs of accidents, as pointed out earlier in this chapter. A key ingredient of TQM is the diffusion of its principles throughout the organisation in such a way as to empower employees. Clearly, this fits with having safety advisory committees so that employees are equally involved with management in seeking continuous improvement to OHS.

Role of HRM

Earlier in this chapter the role of HR was depicted as one of being in partnership with line managers and employees (see Table 5.1). Although this is an accurate portrayal, HR holds the key to successful OHS interventions with respect to staffing and co-ordination. Staffing the OHS function may involve employing a number of professionals such as occupational hygienists, safety officers and nurses, or providing links to external consultants in these areas. Depending upon organisational need and the views of higher level management, the HR department has a role in providing access to OHS staff.

Whatever strategies are put in place, co-ordination is usually assigned to HRM. This could include a range of activities such as safety campaigns, accident investigations, monitoring of programs, and safety audits all of which fall within the normal role of HRM. In addition, any training aimed at accident prevention or general improvement in OHS would also be co-ordinated by HRM.

Another important activity for HRM concerns facilitating input from employee organisations. While it is recognised that the level of unionism has fallen dramatically in recent years, there is still a strong push among unions and employees for a safer and healthier workplace. It remains to be seen whether, in the light of a weaker union movement, management retains its enthusiasm for OHS. At a different level and on a more positive note, there are early signs of including OHS matters within the terms of enterprise agreements, as the following discussion shows.

Future organisational forms

Use enterprise agreements to improve OHS standards

Including OHS enhancements in enterprise bargaining may well result in real improvements to productivity, staff morale, and the company safety record.

BY NEVILLE BETTS

Today's emphasis on enterprise bargaining should be seen as an opportunity for HR and IR practitioners to further develop occupational health and safety standards, particularly at the shop floor level.

An examination of enterprise agreements certified to date shows that many have included segments on OHS, such as:
- Rehabilitation activities
- A new emphasis for workplace OHS committees

- Formalising procedures related to hazard identification and control
- The use of personal protective clothing
- Occupational hygiene and health monitoring issues.

For example Diane Lally, personnel manager at CIG-Gases, reported that the enterprise agreement reached between CIG-Gases and unions included clauses that committed employees to attending 10 safety meetings and two workplace inspections each year in order to receive a pay rise.[1]

OHS professionals support such activities, even though it is difficult to cost them as required by the Australian Industrial Relations Commission. Unfortunately, most employers are yet to introduce OHS monitoring systems that are capable of costing losses, let alone savings, that may flow from enterprise agreement safety initiatives.

These difficulties should not stand in the way of employers, employees or unions including OHS as part of their enterprise agreement. Their inclusion may well result in real improvements to productivity, staff morale, and the enterprise's safety record.

A word of warning, however: such initiatives must not in any way intrude upon or reduce the standards of OHS required by present legislation, regulations or codes of practice. All enterprise agreement activities must seek to improve upon these standards and not introduce greater risk exposures into the workplace.

Given that these values can be agreed upon, then both management and the unions will have several specific OHS issues that they can bring to the negotiating table.

What is required?

Most enterprises have occupational risk exposures. However, much of the existing research into OHS in this country is of a general nature. What is required is for enterprises to make their engineering and/or process controls associated with providing a safe and healthy workplace open to review. This will involve staff in developing improved OHS standards.

Occupational health and safety is not, and never has been, a managerial prerogative. While many enterprises have paid scant regard to other than the legislative requirements of health and safety, it has been those enterprises that have made these disciplines a priority that have succeeded.

Any enterprise agreement that attempts to move OHS standards towards some form of 'self-regulation', by virtue of it being included in a joint company/union enterprise agreement, must be viewed with suspicion.

After 30 years of being involved in OHS in the areas of administration, setting standards at the national, industry and enterprise levels, and as a practitioner, I have yet to find a joint management/union group that has developed a safe and healthy workplace that exceeds legislative requirements.

The existence of these legislative requirements, which includes the threat of prosecution should an enterprise fail to comply, ought to operate as a minimum standard for those negotiating enterprise agreements.

It should be remembered that employers are adversely affected by accidents and health exposures at the enterprise level. They suffer productivity losses and have to pay, either directly or indirectly, compensation and rehabilitation expenses.

Some state regulations require a level of expenditure be included in an enterprise's annual budget for OHS. In the same way, a lack of such expenditure is often used to prove negligence, to be held against an employer, whenever an injury has resulted from an industrial accident.

It would be in everyone's interest to have the annual budget, or minimum level of OHS expenditure, included as part of a negotiated enterprise agreement. As a percentage of payroll, perhaps?

Reference

1 *Occupational Health Newsletter*, Issue No. 290, 5 January 1993, p. 5

Source: *HRMonthy*, September 1994, p. 16.

Work environment

Increasingly, organisations are realising that managing the work environment, rather than medical solutions, hold the key to coping with stress. Medical models which rely solely on behaviour to define the problem and industrial models relying solely on job redesign are only of limited assistance, according to Toohey (1994). He points out that attention must be given to a wide range of organisational issues such as:

- coping with organisational change
- management downsizing
- redeployment
- redundancy
- devolution of responsibility
- financial accountability
- performance appraisal
- aggression, conflict and harassment
- technological change.

The causes of work-related stress may stem from any of a number of issues and for this reason stressors are often grouped in broad categories such as the four s S's already mentioned: supervisor, salary, security and safety.

In coping with stress it appears that home life plays a key role; in a study by Sloan & Cooper (1986) it was reported by airline pilots that the most important factor in dealing with stress was the stability of their home life and support from spouses and friends. The point to be made is that we should not think of stress in terms of only work, isolated from non-work aspects of life. Rather, a holistic viewpoint should be adopted, because the evidence seems clear that aspects of both work and home play significant roles.

Organisations can offer many activities or programs, one such approach is described in the following box. Selecting the most appropriate activity should be based on a thorough analysis of existing safety and health hazards. It also depends on an assessment of past activities and strategies used by other organisations.

HRM IN THE NEWS

Flight or fight? It's all a matter of 'reactivity'

BY NARELLE HOOPER

The Centre for Stress Research and Management at Monash University has conducted world-leading research on the causes and effects of stress, particularly in the workplace. It's director, Professor Chris Sharpley, says: 'It is important to understand that when people say they are stressed they are talking of their reactivity'.

Stress really has become a catch-all tag for a range of reactions people go through when physical or psychological demands are placed on them. Individuals respond in different ways and to a different extent. Under pressure the 'flight or fight' response is activated. The adrenal glands release cortisal, which prompts a higher heart rate, shaking and tremors, churning of the stomach, and sweat glands working overtime. It can all lead to a loss of ability to concentrate and solve problems.

Some personality types are more prone to reactivity, others have a greater capacity to tolerate stress. However, Sharpley says it is possible to reduce reactivity substantially.

The centre studied 80 people over three years, using biofeedback monitoring of pulse and blood pressure in their normal working environment to established individual reaction patterns.

Based on that information, people were trained in various techniques to reduce reactivity, including breathing and relaxation techniques to reduce the heart rate during times of unexpected pressure, and lifestyle changes. Sharpley says the study group showed a 93 per cent reduction in their reactivity, and the group worked more effectively. Most importantly, the techniques have been proved over time. Sharpley says the centre contacted the group more than two years later and 95 per cent were still using the techniques. They reported substantial improvements in personal relationships and lifestyle.

Sharpley believes that workshops on stress management are of little help if they don't have a long-term perspective. 'You get a bunch of people in a room and tell them to relax, but as soon as they go back into the workplace they forget how to do it'. Even stopping to think about how stressed you are can make you feel stressed. The centre has found that when people start complaining about how much pressure they are under, their heart rate rises.

Although there is a lot that management can do through better communications, techniques and processes, responsibility for dealing with reactivity to stress lies with the individual.

Sharpley says: 'It is a mistake to say that managers have to keep reconstructing the workplace'. Bruce Parry of the Industrial Program Service agrees. 'Often people say, "I'm overwhelmed, therefore it is work's fault", whereas it is rarely just work. It is the sum total of a person's life. Unfortunately, it is not always taken into account and it is a case of having someone or something to blame. The system is assisting that'.

Source: *BRW*, April 17 1995, p. 42.

Individual stress management strategies

Time management can be an effective individual strategy to deal with organisational stress. It is based in large part on an initial identification of an individual's personal goals. Other strategies that should be part of individual stress management include good diets, regular exercise, monitoring physical health, and building social support groups. Many large organisations such as Xerox encourage employees to enrol in regular exercise programs where their fitness and health are carefully monitored (O'Boyle 1990).

International safety and health issues

As consciousness of health and well-being has risen world-wide, pressures to improve health care in work environments have increased in some countries. In other countries, however, health hazards are still ignored; by having lax safety standards, developing countries can lure large multinational firms to their shores.

Closer monitoring of foreign firms

In 1996, following the leakage of lethal methyl isocyanate gas at Union Carbide's pesticide plant in Bhopal, India which killed more than 2000 people, India formed committees in every state to identify potential hazards in factories. While foreign investments and technology are still welcome, the government now insists on knowing more about potential risks as well as identified existing risks. New regulations in India require environmental impact studies for all new plants (Balgopal, Ramanathan & Patcher 1987 and *The Wall Street Journal* 1986).

The response to health hazards has been quite different in Mexico. A disaster that killed more than 500 people and wounded thousands at Pemex, a state-owned gas monopoly in Mexico, has had no noticeable effect on regulations. This is a common situation in developing countries. These countries are often so in need of economic development that they may accept any industry—even those that have the potential for significant harm. This, of course, presents serious ethical questions for firms operating in the developing nations.

Current trends

Companies are striving to be more competitive and at the same time achieve Best Practice standards under government encouragement. However, unless company OHS policies are carefully developed, there is a danger that undesirable consequences could follow.

Occupational health policies

Policies should be designed to keep pace with a range of changes sweeping through society and organisations. These changes influence HRM and impinge on OHS in a number of ways.

The use of enterprise agreements to achieve better OHS was pointed out previously in the 'Future organisational forms' discussion. In an industrial climate which fosters radical change in working arrangements, Australia is witnessing innovations which would not have been considered previously. Employers and workers are negotiating deals which in many ways are only limited by the imagination of both parties. But in striving for higher levels of productivity, care needs to be taken that new agreements do not have an adverse effect upon OHS. One such issue relates to shift work. In agreeing to extended shifts, sometimes for as long as 12 hours at a stretch, the question of fatigue and lack of sleep should be factored in. Vigilance decrement is known to be linked to fatigue (see, for example, Wickens 1992, pp. 40–49) and with workers already under pressure to increase output, managers could unintentionally be creating hazardous work situations. We have already seen from 'HRM in the news', problems associated with the body clock and work scheduling.

Workforce diversity creates wide-ranging issues for consideration. People with physical and mental disabilities, a multicultural workforce in which English is likely to be a second language, more equal gender mix in areas previously dominated by men or women, and other factors such as gender preference, ethnicity, age and religion, all indicate the need for care and sensitivity in the workplace. These translate into differences in values, attitudes and needs; organisationally, they impact on work routines, hours, communication, management style and the design of work. In rethinking work to accommodate diversity the requirement for a safe and healthy working environment should not be overlooked. As noted by Sauers (1993), one of the biggest challenges facing business managers is how to deal with an increasingly diverse workforce which can be a major strength or weakness.

Managing diversity

Funding for self-paced learning

Two major unions have received a Worksafe development grant for a so-called self-paced, multi-lingual OHS project.

The AFMEU and National Union of Workers have been granted nearly $70 000 for a joint seven-month initiative, recently approved by Worksafe.

The unions will produce and distribute about 40 000 audio cassettes and plain English booklets in 10 community languages covering general OHS problems and workplace hazards.

The project is aimed at workers from a non English-speaking background, particularly in the food, vehicle and metals manufacturing industry can apply health and safety principles in the workplace.

Health and safety information divided into three sections:
- a generic approach to all hazards
- noise hazards
- hazardous substances.

Worksafe's industry development branch officers say that NESB workers and women in these industries are concentrated in lower-paid classifications where availability of training and, therefore, career progression is limited.

They believe this is especially valid for women who often have families and may not be able to attend knowledge sessions outside work hours.

The development grant scheme was established to help meet Worksafe's strategic priorities.

Source: *Worksafe News*, October 1995, p. 23.

Another health issue currently being debated is the question of whether there should be mandatory testing for HIV in the health care system. It is argued that workers in health care are at risk and compulsory testing should be a matter of course. This raises some interesting issues such as the costs and infrastructure necessary for testing large numbers, whether it is practical, and the ethics of enforced testing. According to Kelly (1994), these arguments miss the point and will not solve the problem of inadequate workplace practices. The real issue is how to prevent a high level of needle-stick injuries in the first place. Having a code of practice giving sound advice on minimising injuries through better workplace design, and the use of infection control procedures which assume that all blood and body substances are infectious, is really the main issue.

Wellness programs

Corporations are increasingly focusing on keeping employees healthy rather than helping them get well. They are investing in wellness programs at record rates, and such programs appear to be paying off. A four year study of 15 000 Control Data employees showed that employees who participate in only limited exercise spend 114 per cent more on health insurance claims than co-workers who exercise more. Smokers and obese workers also had higher medical claims. Control Data, which has had its 'Stay Well' program in place since the early 1980s, now markets it program to other firms such as the National Basketball Association (James 1987).

Ethics in shaping behaviour

Employers have known for a long time that a small percentage of their workforce is responsible for the bulk of the health insurance claims. Originally, they tried to encourage their employees to be healthy by offering to subsidise health club memberships and building exercise facilities and jogging trails, but the results were disappointing. Now it appears that many companies are implementing incentive-based health-care programs.

While no one denies that health care costs are spiralling, some question just how far companies should be allowed to go in 'encouraging' their employees to shape up. How much should employers be allowed to know what employees do in their spare time? This is obviously the same question we asked in an earlier chapter on employee rights. Is it possible that company policies and practices will become so financially attractive to employees that they will do the things that they would not otherwise have done?

The potential for creating situations involving ethical or unethical behaviour needs to be watched closely. It is too early to tell just how the situation will unfold. Doubtless, employers and employees are concerned about costs and health; perhaps creative solutions will save the day. Such solutions will also have an impact not only on occupational safety and health, but also on employee rights and indirect compensation.

Summary

Employees' health will become increasingly important in the years ahead. Employers are becoming more aware of the cost of ill health and the benefits of having a healthy workforce. Federal and state governments, through OHS legislation, are also making it more necessary for employers to be concerned with employee health. The current concern is primarily with employee health as related to occupational accidents and diseases, both aspects of the physical environment. However, organisations can choose to become involved in programs dealing with employee health and the workers' socio-psychological environment as well. If organisations choose not to become involved with improving the socio-psychological environment, governments may prescribe mandatory regulations. Thus it pays for organisations to be concerned with both aspects of the work environment now. Effective programs for both environments can significantly improve both employee health and the effectiveness of an organisation.

When the adoption of improvement programs is being considered, employee involvement is crucial. As with many quality of working life programs, employee involvement in improving safety and health is not only a good idea, but also one likely to be desired by employees. Many things can be done to make work environments better, but it is important to distinguish two types of environments: the physical and the sociopsychological. Each is different and has its own unique components. Although some improvement strategies may work well for one component of the work environment, they will not work for others. Again, a careful diagnosis is required before programs are selected and implemented.

Assuming that a careful diagnosis indicates the need for a stress management or some other program, the challenge is in deciding which program or strategy to select from the many organisational and individual management strategies currently available. Programs such as time management or physical exercise could be set up so employees could help themselves cope, or the organisation could alter the conditions within the organisation that are associated with the stress. The latter requires a diagnosis of what is happening, where, and to whom before deciding how to proceed. Because so many possible sources of stress exist, and because not all people react the same way to them, implementing individual stress management strategies may be more efficient. However, if many people are suffering similar symptoms in a specific part of the organisation, an organisational strategy is more appropriate.

Information regarding many aspects of safety and health is insufficient—either because it does not exist (e.g. knowledge of causes and effect) or because organisations are unwilling to gather or provide it. From a legal as well as a humane viewpoint, it is in the best interests of organisations to seek and provide more information so that more effective strategies for improving safety and health can be developed and implemented. Failure to do so may result in costly legal settlements against organisations or further governmental regulation of workplace safety and health.

questions for discussion and review

1. How are physical hazards distinct from socio-psychological hazards? What implications does this distinction have for programs to deal with these hazards?
2. Is there such a thing as an unsafe worker? Assuming that accident prone workers exist, how can HR managers address this problem?
3. Who is responsible for workplace safety and health? The employer? The employee? The federal government? Judges and juries?
4. What requirements does statute law impose on the employer for promoting workplace safety?
5. Identify four sources of work stress. Why are claims relating to worker stress on the rise? How can organisations manage work stress?
6. What can employees do for themselves to manage work stress?
7. How might a company's strategy to prevent occupational accidents differ from a program to prevent occupational disease? In what ways might the programs be similar?
8. In an economy which is becoming increasingly deregulated, especially in OHS since the Robens report, what are the arguments for returning to more regulatory powers and monitoring?
9. In what ways can an organisation prevent occupational accidents?
10. What are some ethical issues in safety and health?

case study

Danum engineering: a healthier, safer future

Danum Engineering set up as a toolmaking operation at North Shore, Geelong, in 1957. Still at the same place, the company has expanded into fabrication and erection, plant installation and maintenance, shutdown and maintenance labour, mechanical contracting, hire labour and machining work.

Danum now has two other permanent work sites, the Corio Shell Refinery and

Point Henry Alcoa plant, as well as temporary locations. Of its 66 employees, 11 are administration and all tradespersons are male. Danum's workers are covered by the Metals and Engineering Workers' Union and the Federation of Industrial, Manufacturing and Engineering Employees.

Taking Control ten years ago Danum Engineering was facing a depressed market and high Workcare premiums. Today the market is just as tight—but not Danum's profits. The mechanical contracting company from Victoria drastically reformed its occupational health and safety (OHS) practices and now it's a better place to work, is more competitive and more profitable.

'If we were still paying the levels of premium for workers' compensation that we were 10 years ago we may not be in business'—Company Director.

It took Danum, a family-owned company with 66 staff, 10 years of commitment to get it right. Danum's Company Director, managers and workers designed an OHS plan that built safety into the company's priorities.

'The whole process (OHS reform) has helped in all areas, it hasn't just helped in safety. It's helped in understanding each other better; in industrial relations'—Company Director

They haven't had a serious lost time injury for more than 16 months, while the average for similar companies is five per year. But it wasn't always like that ...

THEN—There was division between 'them' and 'us': 'Every time there might have been an incident or an accident or whatever, it was either management blaming the guy—it's his fault that he's done it—or guys on the floor blaming management because they contributed to it'—Site Manager

NOW—Health and safety belongs to everyone:
- Safety committee—consists mainly of employees. They oversee safety policy and practices throughout the company. If something can be done more safely the Safety Committee will see that it happens.
- Safety Effort Recognition Scheme—teams made up of tradespeople, supervisors and office staff work together in the scheme. The team with no accidents after six months wins a trophy for their favourite charity.

Final straw

In 1986 there was one serious accident for every five shop floor workers at Danum. Because of the company's poor OHS performance, Workcare premiums were skyrocketing, morale was low and lost time was affecting production.

OHS was one of the buzz words in the 1980s. New legislation was in the wind. People were starting to take safety seriously.

A worker at a nearby site was killed on the job. Soon after, one of Danum's cherry pickers hit overhead power lines. It was pure luck the driver wasn't killed or seriously injured, but he could have been.

And that's when Danum started taking safety more seriously.

'... we felt we couldn't keep going the way we were going'—Company Director.

THEN—If '... someone had an accident, oh well, bad luck. Patch it up and get on with the work'—Company Director.

Their reaction was 'Say a little prayer and thank God no one died'—Shop Steward.

NOW—It's OHS practices that prevent accidents and health problems:
- Safety Action Plan—drawn up each year, it maintains existing effective strategies and outlines new ideas, training courses and ways of measuring Danum's OHS performance
- Job start—every working day begins with a meeting. Hazards, risks and precautions are discussed before anyone opens their tool box.
- Job task analysis—safety in doing large or unusual jobs is not left to

chance. Everyone involved sits down to talk through the risks. This way they are identified and controlled.
- Training and safety days—increase OHS knowledge and skills for tradespeople, administrative staff and management.

Long road ahead

The time for change had come. However, Danum realised that management and staff had to be both involved and committed if it were ever going to happen.

They brought everyone together to talk about safer work practices.

'Give your employees plenty of scope ... give them the chance to put plenty of input and they'll get right behind it'—Shop Steward.

The company invested time, effort and money in the changes. A Safety Committee was set up, safety gear bought, new ways of doing things were tested and a Safety Management Plan developed.

It's now the blueprint for all work practices at Danum's sites. Ten years down the track new employees, old hands, managers and workers are committed to following comprehensive OHS practices.

'The objective is to talk about safety at 7:30 in the morning, before you open your tool box ... the same [as putting] on their safety boots or overalls'—Site Manager.

Safety is a part of every manager's, supervisor's and employee's routine.

THEN—No-one kept statistics on injuries. So nobody had any idea how poor safety standards were affecting the company.

NOW—Consultation and communication happens at every level:
- Injury statistics—these are converted into graphs and displayed on noticeboards and discussed. This way it's easy to see safety trends over time.
- Safety news flash—bulletins to alert workers to on-site risks, and notify of accidents at other sites, are posted on noticeboards.
- Monthly newsletter—this goes out in pay packets. Everyone is assured of being able to keep up with safety achievements and problems.

Trying times

But there's no gain without pain. At first there was suspicion between workers and management. Neither side trusted the other's motives.

'Anything like that, in the early stages there's always a bit of mistrust—what are they after and are they fair dinkum about it ? We've found once things got rolling and issues came up and they were rectified and improved, that the sincerity was there'—Company Director.

Initially, Danum's new work practices cost them business. They couldn't compete with companies who were taking shortcuts with OHS, but they held their ground.

Over time, Danum's high standards have become a competitive advantage.

'It makes us a lot more competitive, a lot more viable and a lot more attractive to our clients. Clients want to deal with companies that have a good safety record and good performance ... we're a lot more marketable'—Company Director. THEN—Production was all that mattered: 'Getting the job done, getting it done when the client wanted it done, and safety wasn't considered'—Company Director.

NOW—Production and safety go hand in hand :
- Safety Management Plan—this is the company's code of practice. The plan is implemented on a day-to-day basis by everyone.
- Safety Manual—everyone has one, written by, and for, Danum employees.

Secrets of success

Danum wouldn't be where it is today if management and staff hadn't worked together. Everyone has to be committed to making their workplace safer.

'We've created a culture where people aren't scared to tell the boss they've slipped over and hurt their back, because they know that it'll be investigated and possibly it'll prevent one of their mates from slipping over and hurting their back'—Company Director.

Changes weren't made without consultation. There was no need to rush into things. They realised it was a learning process for everyone—and that it takes time.

From the beginning everyone talked about OHS. It was a real issue, not just a bulletin on a noticeboard. Danum continuously improves its OHS performance with a range of strategies. This keeps everyone interested and involved in the program.

There is no magic way to change poor OHS practices, but the 'pot of gold' at the end of the road makes it worthwhile.

'It can make work a lot more enjoyable and make work easier'—Site Manager.

'Wake up. The world's a nice place if you're fit and healthy'—Health and Safety Representative.

Source: Worksafe Australia 1993–94.

Questions

1. How can good OHS contribute to the financial 'bottom line' of companies?
2. Why should management listen to the views of workers about safe work practices when it is management's responsibility to ensure a safe working environment?
3. How may management overcome problems associated with a lack of trust between workers and management?

References

Ayres, I. & Braithwaite, J. (1992), *Responsive Regulation, Transcending the Deregulation Debate*, Oxford University Press, New York.

Balgopal, P. R., Ramanathan, C. & Patcher, M. (1987), 'Employee Assistance Programs: A Cross-Cultural Perspective,' Paper presented at the Conference on International Personnel and Human Resource Management, December, Singapore.

Braithwaite, J. & Grabosky, P. (1985), *Occupational Health and Safety Enforcement in Australia, A Report to the National Occupational Health and Safety Commission*, Australian Institute of Criminology, Canberra.

Brooks, A. (1994), *Occupational Health and Safety Law in Australia*, 4th edition, CCH Australia Ltd, North Ryde, NSW.

—— (1988), 'Rethinking occupational health and safety legislation', *Journal of Industrial Relations*, vol. 30, no. 3, pp. 347–62.

Bulletin to Management (1988), 'National ASPA Conference Highlights', 28 July, p. 239.

Casey, A. (1995), 'Rehabilitation programs: handling with care,' *WorkCover News*, no. 25 Sept.–Nov., Sydney.

CCH (1991), *Planning Occupational Safety and Health*, 3rd edition, CCH Australia, Ltd, North Ryde, NSW.

Comcare Australia (1994), *Return to Work Policy and Guidelines*, Commonwealth Government, Canberra.

Commonwealth Department of Science and Technology (1982), *Office Design at Work: A general guide*, Australian Government Publishing Service, Canberra.

Creighton, W. B. (1982), 'Statutory safety representatives and safety committees: legal and industrial relations implications,' *Journal of Industrial Relations,* vol. 24, pp. 337–64.

—— (1982), 'Occupational health and safety and industrial democracy: some legal and practical considerations', *Work and People,* vol. 10, no. 2, pp. 3–9.

Deming, W. E. (1986), *Out of the Crisis,* MIT Center for Advanced Engineering Study, Cambridge, Mass.

Filipczak, B. (1993), 'Armed and Dangerous at Work,' *Training,* July, pp. 39–43.

Friedman, M. & Roseman, R. (1974), *Type A Behavior and Your Heart,* Alfred A. Knopf, New York.

Gun, R. (1992), 'Regulation or self-regulation: is Robens-style legislation a formula for success?', *Journal of Occupational Health and Safety—Australia/New Zealand,* vol. 8, no. 5, pp. 383–88.

Gunningham, N. (1985), 'Workplace safety and the law: statutory regulation: the traditional system', in B. Creighton & N. Gunningham (eds), *The Industrial Relations of Occupational Health and Safety,* Croom Helm, Sydney.

Gunningham, N. (1994), *Consultancy into the Legal, Institutional and Industrial Relations Environment Governing OHS in Other countries,* Industry Commission.

Hollingworth, S. & MacRae, J. (1995), 'Managing Human Resource Costs through Employer-based Occupational Rehabilitation,' *Asia Pacific Journal of Human Resources,* vol. 33, no. 1, pp. 104–12.

Hooper, N. (1995), 'Coping with the modern "madness" ', *Business Review Weekly,* April 17.

Hyatt, J. (1985), 'Hazardous Effects of VDT Legislation,' Inc, March, p. 27.

Industry Commission (1995), *Work, Health and Safety,* Draft Report, An Inquiry into Occupational Health and Safety.

Industry Commission, *Work Health & Safety: Inquiry into Occupational Health & Safety,* vol. 2, Appendices.

James, F. B. (1987), 'Study Lays Groundwork for Tying Health Costs to Workers Behavior,' *The Wall Street Journal,* April 14, p. 37.

Johnson, L. (1994), 'Preventing injuries: the big pay-off', *Personnel Journal,* April, pp. 61–64.

Komaki, J. Barwick, K. D. & Scott, L. 1978, 'Pinpointing and Reinforcing Safe Performance in a Food Manufacturing Plant,' *Journal of Applied Psychology,* vol. 63, pp. 434–45.

Kelly, C. (1994), 'Doctor's demand for HIV tests not the real issue,' *Worksafe News,* July, pp. 4–5.

Lilley, B. (1995), 'Safety Law: Who's liable?' *Australian Safety News,* February, National Safety Council of Australia Ltd, Malvern, Victoria.

Long, S. (1996), 'Super clearance for courier firms,' *Australian Financial Review* September 10, p. 5.

Matthes, K. (1992), 'A Prescription for Healthier Offices', *HR Focus,* April, 4–5, Indoor Air Issues Confront Employers, *Bulletin to Management,* October, p. 329.

Merrit, A. 1983, 'Australian law on occupational health and safety: an up-to-the-minute report about what's not really happening', *Social Alternatives,* Sept.–Oct., pp. 33–36.

O'Boyle, T. F. (1990), 'Fear and Stress in the Office Take Toll,' *The Wall Street Journal* Nov. 6, B1, B2.

Olian, J. (1988), 'New Approaches to Employment Screening', in R. S. Schuler & S. A. Youngblood (eds), *Readings in Personnel and Human Resource Management*, West Publishing, St. Paul, Minn.
Pelletier, K. R. (1985), 'The Hidden Hazards of the Modern Office', *The New York Times*, Sept. 8, F3.
Perrow, C. (1984), *Normal Accidents: Living with High-Risk Technologies*, Basic Books, New York.
Robens, Lord (1972), *Report of the Committee 1971–72, Chairman Lord Robens, Safety and Health at Work*, HMSO, London.
Rowland, M. (1992), 'Matching Life-Styles to Benefits,' *The New York Times*, March 1.
Sauers, D. A. 1993, 'Managing Workforce Diversity: A Challenge for New Zealand Business in the 1990's', *Asia Pacific Journal of Human Resources*, vol. 31, no. 3, pp. 44–51.
Schuler, R. S. 1980, 'Definition and Conceptualization of Stress in Organisations', *Organizational Behavior and Human Performance*, vol. 23, pp. 184–215.
Schuler, R. S. (1982), 'An Integrative Transactional Process Model of Stress in Organisations,' *Journal of Occupational Behavior*, vol. 3, pp. 3–9.
Schuler, R. S. (1984), 'Occupational Health in Organisations: A Measure of Personnel Effectiveness', in R. S. Schuler & S. A. Youngblood (eds), *Readings in Personnel and Human Resource Management*, 2nd edition, West Publishing Company, St. Paul, Minn.
Schuler, R. S. & Jackson, S. E. (1996), *Human Resource Management: Positioning for the 21st Century*, 6th edition, West Publishing, St Paul, Minn.
Shostak, A. B. (1980), *Blue-Collar Stress*, Addison-Wesley, Reading, Mass.
Sloane, M. & Deves, L. (1995), 'Managing diversity: More issues than answers?', in L. Pullin & M. Fastenau (eds), *Employment Relations Theory and Practice: Current Research*, Gippsland School of Business, Monash University, Churchill, Victoria, pp. 449–64.
Sloan, S. J. & Cooper, C. L. (1986), 'Stress coping strategies in commercial airline pilots', *Journal of Occupational Medicine*, vol. 28, no. 1, pp. 49–52.
Taylor, H. M. (1980), 'Occupational Health Management-by-objectives,' *Personnel*, Jan–Feb, pp. 58–64.
The Wall Street Journal (1986), 'Foreign Firms Feel the Impact Most,' November 26, p. 24.
Toohey, J. (1994), 'Work Stress', *Worksafe News*, vol. 9, no. 4, October.
Wallace-Bruce, N. L. (1994), *Outline of Employment Law*, Butterworths, Sydney.
Wang, C. L. (1979), 'Occupational Skin Disease Continues to Plague Industry', *Monthly Labor Review*, February, pp. 17–22.
Weaver, C. S. (1989), 'Understanding Occupational Disease', *Personnel Journal*, June, pp. 86–94.
Weis, W. L. (1984), 'No Smoking', *Personnel Journal*, September, pp. 53–58.
Wickens, C. D. (1992), *Engineering Psychology and Human Performance*, 2nd edition, Harper Collins, New York.
Williams, M. (1983), 'Ten Minutes Work for 12 Hours Pay? What's the Catch?' *The Wall Street Journal*, October 12, p. 19.
WorkCover (1995), *WorkCover News*, no. 25 Sept.–Nov., Sydney.

'Workplace Torts', *Bulletin to Management*, October 1, 1992, p. 312.

Worksafe Australia (c1993–94), 'Hendersons Automotive (SA): An OHS led recovery,' *OHS building BEST PRACTICE*, Series of case studies produced by the National Occupational Health and Safety Commission, Sydney.

—— (1994), *Compendium of workers' compensation statistics 1991–92*, May, Australian Government Publishing Service, Canberra.

—— (1995a), *Estimates of National Occupational Health and Safety Statistics, Australia*, Australian Government Publishing Service, Canberra.

—— (1995), *Worksafe News,* vol. 10, no. 3, August.

—— (1994), *Worksafe News,* vol. 9, no. 4, October.

part 3

The internal environment

chapter 6
Human resource planning and career development

chapter 7
Job analysis and design

chapter 8
Recruitment, selection and placement

chapter 9
Performance management

chapter 10
Reward management

chapter 11
Training and development

chapter 6

Human resource planning and career development

Robert L. Kane

learning objectives

After studying this chapter, you will be able to:

1. Explain why human resource planning is important and how it has evolved.
2. Describe the phases involved in the human resource planning process.
3. Discuss the effects that a rapidly changing external environment have had on human resource planning.
4. Identify common barriers to human resource planning and suggest how these can be overcome.
5. Explain why organisations offer career planning and career management programs.
6. Describe how views on career choice and career development have evolved.
7. Give examples of the types of career management programs offered by organisations for employees at various career stages.
8. Explain what changes in career patterns and types are likely to be found in the future.
9. Discuss the new types of career management programs likely to be needed in the future.
10. Begin to plan your own career.

chapter 6

chapter outline

- Human resource planning and career development — 215
- Why is human resource planning important? — 216
- The evolution of the field of human resource planning — 216
- The human resource planning process — 218
- The four phases of human resource planning — 219
  - Phase 1: Gathering, analysing and forecasting supply and demand data — 219
  - Phase 2: Establishing objectives — 233
  - Phase 3: Programming — 223
  - Phase 4: Control and evaluation — 223
- Human resource planning in a changing environment — 224
- Barriers to human resource planning — 226
- Why is career planning and management important? — 227
- The evolution of the field of career development — 228
  - The trait-factor approach to career choice — 228
  - Individually-oriented models of career development — 229
  - Systems approaches to career management — 229
- Career management programs in the organisation — 232
  - Organisational entry programs — 232
  - Early career programs — 233
  - Mid career programs — 235
  - Late career programs — 236
  - Career counselling — 236
  - Career management in Australian organisations — 237
- Careers in the future — 237
  - Types of jobs — 238
  - Career flexibility — 238
  - Anarchic careers — 240
  - Career concepts — 240
- Emerging career management programs — 242
  - Managing career concepts — 242
  - Work–family interface programs — 245
  - Expatriate careers — 246
  - Outplacement counselling — 247
- Sharing the responsibility: launching your career — 248
  - Conducting a personal appraisal — 248
  - Identifying types of jobs, organisations and industries — 250
  - Preparing for organisational life — 251
- Summary — 252
- Questions for discussion and review — 253
- Case study — 254
- Resources — 255
- References — 256

HRM IN THE NEWS

Human resources planning at Woolworths

When Woolworths' profits slumped in 1987 from $100 million a year to almost zero, most in the industry assumed that the incoming chairman, Paul Simons, would take the axe to his workforce.

The company had 60 000 staff and was in big trouble. More than half of its NSW store managers had resigned in the space of a year. The retailer was on very shaky ground. Retrenchments would have cut costs in one fell swoop.

But Mr Simons took heed of the complaints of the company's resigning managers—that the shops were simply not competitive—and set out a plan aimed at revitalising the stores and restoring Woolworths' profitability.

It involved decentralising the operation, and giving general managers and their staff 'ownership' of their part of the business. He also figured that if the plan worked, then Woolworths would need all its existing staff members, plus more.

'We thought that if our strategy was successful, it wouldn't be long before we needed experienced and skilled staff', he said.

'We would be out in the market in 12 months' time, looking to rehire. If we reduced staff, we would have lost experience and it would have cost us money to retrain new people'.

It was a people-management decision which paid off. Woolworths now has 79 000 staff and is Australia's most successful retailing empire. It was a strategic approach to the workforce which benefited both the employees and, ultimately, the company.

Source: *Sydney Morning Herald*, 26 November 1994, p. 27A.

HRM IN THE NEWS

The rise and rise of Linda

BY BRONWEN GORA

Linda Volker did not choose her career. It chose her. And, along the way, the computer industry has not let her down.

Ms Volker has risen from the most junior of positions to the top of her field.

'I'll never move out of this industry', said Ms Volker, whose teenage ambition was to be a kindergarten teacher.

'It's too much fun. I like the people I work with, developing relationships with the customers and the dynamic nature of the computer industry'.

Towards the end of Year 12 at Pittwater High School, Ms Volker realised she wanted to travel a path that would lead to running her own business.

Uncertain as to how to go about it, she took up a secretarial course at a local TAFE college.

A year later, the 19-year-old found her first job as a receptionist in the city office of a computer sales company.

The nature of the business meant that, while her boss was out of the office, Ms Volker was left to demonstrate products such as the latest telex interfaces to customers.

'It did phase me at first but it was just something you had to learn', Ms Volker said.

'The boss I had at the time was willing to give me a go and allow me to learn and develop rather than simply staying a secretary'.

After two years, Ms Volker needed a change. She had moved from secretary, to personal assistant to performing demonstrations and felt she wanted to branch out.

A personnel consultancy had a job going for a legal secretary at Esso and, while Ms Volker had no experience in the legal field, she talked her way in.

But within the year, her former boss approached her to see if she would return.

This time it was not as a secretary but as a pre-sales staff member who would be assisting and training the sales team.

She was enjoying her job, had just met the man who would become her husband and anguished over the decision.

It was not until a director of the company asked her if she wanted to be a secretary all her life that she said yes.

'I thought this is probably the moment in my life to move on', Ms Volker said.

So, she packed up and returned to the company, Systems Solutions.

Her job involved visiting potential customers and demonstrating what then were the latest products in communications technology.

At the time, modems, word processing software and sending faxes by computer were all new to the market.

Trade shows were flourishing, business was booming and the company expanded rapidly.

'I really developed a love of the industry', Ms Volker said.

'It was a fun and dynamic time in the '80s. You met some very interesting people along the way'.

Ms Volker said she found she had a natural aptitude for learning the technical side of the business and was not deterred by the male-dominated industry.

'A lot of people talk about sexism but I have never even had to consider it', Ms Volker said.

Two years into System Solutions, Ms Volker was promoted from someone who simply stood alongside the salesman helping to give demonstrations to the ranks of the sales team.

'It was extremely challenging', Ms Volker said.

'I had to meet budgets and create territories'.

'I'd be selling into Melbourne, Sydney and Canberra by the telephone and then encouraging customers to fly to Sydney for a demonstration. It wasn't easy'.

'There was lots of cold calling and not being afraid to pick up the telephone and say "Here I am"'.

Tenacity paid off. Within the first six months, Ms Volker exceeded her targets and set the solid pattern for her continued success.

Over the ensuing months, her track record did not go unnoticed.

Through word of mouth she heard that another computer company was looking for sales people and nabbed a new job.

Her established customer base remained loyal to her, she moved into working with more advanced products and her selling skills developed even further.

Two years later it was again time to move on, and Ms Volker contacted the personnel agency Crowe and Associates.

But just as she was about to accept another sales position she was offered the chance to start an IT division within Crowe.

With her extensive contacts gained during almost 10 years in the industry, Ms Volker was a perfect choice.

'Once again it was a full-on sales role', she said.

'But when you're selling people it's so entirely different because you're selling their emotions and their careers'.

Ms Volker developed a strong client base for the company before being headhunted after several months.

The company, an American hub manufacturer, offered her a chance to develop a reseller and distributor base for its latest computer networking technology.

> Ms Volker accepted the job and became the company's major accounts manager for Australia and New Zealand.
>
> After a year another opportunity reared its head with a computer company in Sydney's south.
>
> The position was originally general manger but was later changed to sales director.
>
> After three-and-a-half years, Ms Volker, 34, is about to take her next step with a new job working for a major US company.
>
> Making moves that advance her career path and taking risks along the way have worked in her favour.
>
> 'I am lucky', Ms Volker said.
>
> 'I've worked for some extremely talented people who've allowed me to grow'.

Source: *Sunday Telegraph*, 28 January 1996, p. 81.

These news items raise some essential questions that both organisations and individuals need to face. These include:

1. What kind of workforce will be needed in the future, both in terms of numbers of employees and their attitudes and skills?
2. How can these needs be determined ahead of time, so that costly errors such as unnecessary redundancies can be avoided?
3. What are the implications for organisations of social changes such as more mobile employees and the increased role of women in the workforce?
4. How can an individual best manage his or her own career in a constantly changing environment so as to maintain both job satisfaction and adequate financial rewards over their working life?

As discussed throughout this book, in recent years major changes have been affecting many organisations and their employees around the world. Some of these changes, including the development of 'network' organisations, massive downsizings, delayering and recognition of the need to more effectively manage an increasingly diverse workforce, have perhaps impacted more dramatically upon the areas of human resource planning and career development than upon any other areas of human resource management. In response, innovative executives have developed new ways of organising and managing their employees, and writers in the field of human resource management have developed new perspectives and models to assist practitioners to cope with and even anticipate these changes. Thus the linear approaches to human resource planning and career development that were accepted as best practice ten or twenty years ago have now been supplemented by a range of alternative approaches, many of which have a greater focus on flexibility than on certainty.

This chapter defines some of the key terms in the two related areas of human resource planning and career development before considering why human resource planning is important in today's environment. The evolution of the field of human resource planning is then outlined, followed by the details of the processes involved. In the light of the changing environment facing many organisations, modifications to the basic approach to human resource planning have recently been suggested, and these are then explained, along with the kinds of barriers that have been found to exist. Career development is next considered, with the various approaches that have been developed being outlined. Finally, the issue of careers in the future is explored and a number of the implications for both organisations and individuals are described.

Human resource planning and career development

Human resource planning is an activity organisations carry out in an attempt to ensure a match between the knowledge, skills and abilities the organisation will need in the future and those it will have available. It involves a forecast of what human resources will be needed to achieve the organisation's strategic plans and objectives over some future time period, a comparison of the results of this forecast with the human resources that are likely to be available within the organisation in the future, and the development of a set of action plans to remedy anticipated over or under supply in any area.

Organisations vary greatly in terms of size, structure and the environments they face, and their strategic planning processes vary from informal through formal and detailed. Thus the amount and type of human resource planning carried out can vary enormously from organisation to organisation. Where a major new facility such as a factory or a mine is to be opened, human resource planning is often formal and detailed, because a major increase in staffing is likely to be needed at a particular time in the future (Dunphy & Mills 1982). At a less formal level, a type of human resource planning occurs when a sales manager decides not to immediately fill a vacant position because of a recent slump in sales.

Although human resource planning is carried out from an organisational viewpoint, an effective human resource planning process can benefit individual employees by making career paths more evident and by clarifying the knowledge, skills and abilities that will be needed in particular positions in the future. From an employee perspective, however, the development of their own individual career, which may well go beyond the confines of a single organisation, is likely to be the paramount concern.

A **career** is typically defined as the evolving sequence of a person's work experiences over time (Arthur, Hall & Lawrence 1989, p. 8). The term **career development**, on the other hand, carries with it the connotation of growth in the individual's knowledge, skills, abilities and potential to contribute to the organisation. Thus a particular career may or may not involve increases in pay and status and may range across a number of occupations and work settings. The term **career path** is often used to describe a logical sequence of positions which typically involves increases in skill and/or responsibility. Careers may be planned ahead of time or feature a large element of chance and expediency. **Career planning** is the process of identifying career goals and establishing activities that must be accomplished to attain those goals, with the term **career management** being used to refer to the assistance provided by an organisation to aid its employees in their careers. The career of Linda Volker, as described in our 'HRM in the news' section, for example, involves a change in occupation, several changes in work settings and major increases in salary and status. Although her career shows little sign of long-term planning or career management, significant career development has clearly occurred.

A human resource plan is unlikely to be successful if the organisation is unable to attract and retain suitable staff to fill anticipated positions, and individual career plans are unlikely to be actionable if there is no market for the knowledge, skills and abilities that the individual develops. Therefore, human resource planning and career management can be seen as complementary processes. Organisational level strategic planning and individual level career planning need to be closely related for the maximum outcome to be obtained by both parties.

Why is human resource planning important?

Human resource planning can serve many purposes. It can allow an organisation to use its people more effectively to achieve its longer-term strategies and goals. It can thus serve the interests of both the individual employee and the organisation. Human resource planning can help an organisation reduce costs by anticipating and correcting labour shortages and surpluses before they become unmanageable and expensive. For example, massive redundancies may be averted or at least reduced in scope and scheduled over a longer time period. The 'HRM in the news' section on 'Human Resource Planning at Woolworths' illustrates how the leader of one Australian organisation was able to anticipate its increased needs for staff in the future and avoid a costly round of retrenchments followed by re-hiring. Human resource planning also allows the organisation to make optimum use of employee aptitudes and skills, including capitalising on the diverse talents of women, members of minority groups, and disabled individuals.

Computer technology now allows extensive job-related records to be maintained on each employee by creating a **human resource information system** (HRIS). A human resource information system (HRIS) is a logical and systematic record of human resource information. These records can include information on positions, occupancy and vacancies, staff movements, training and development programs, employee job preferences, work experiences, and performance evaluations and a skills and competencies database (Brush & Nardoni 1992; Salmon 1995). They allow a job history to be kept on each employee, and they can provide a complete set of information on the jobs and positions within the organisation.

The changing external and internal environments facing many organisations have made implementing an appropriate approach to human resource planning more challenging than ever before. Factors cited by writers such as Schuler (1990) and Walker (1990) that impinge upon human resource planning include the rapid rate of change and accompanying higher levels of uncertainty; increasing competition, including international competitors which place pressures on both revenues and costs; rapid technological change and related needs for new skills; organisations that are more complex in terms of products, technologies and markets but are at the same time becoming flatter, leaner and more flexible; and the growingly diverse nature of the workforce in most industrialised countries.

A number of issues for human resource planning have arisen as a result of these ongoing changes in the environment. For example, the need to provide outplacement services for middle managers, a by-product of heightened global competitiveness and the need to downsize and reduce costs, is a recent addition to the growing list of HRM activities (Stratford 1994, 1996). The increasing potential for both technical and managerial obsolescence is another critical issue. Rapid changes in knowledge make it difficult for professionals, engineers, and managers to remain adept at their jobs. Social changes such as dual-career couples and single parents means an organisation can no longer assume that its employees can be moved anywhere and anytime. Careful planning is essential to address these issues.

Changes such as these increase the importance of HRM and the need for organisations to adopt a suitable human resource planning process.

The evolution of the field of human resource planning

Throughout most of the 20th century, the trend was for organisations to grow in size and complexity while the environment surrounding them also became more complex and changing. Organisations originally run by one person or a family tended to develop functional structures as they grew in size, with typical functional departments including sales and marketing, finance and accounting, operations or customer service and personnel. Simple 'family business' structures rarely needed human resource planning. In functional structures, a kind of seniority-based career pattern, where the junior accountant eventually became the senior accountant, was common. Where there was no one suitable within the organisation to fill a particular position, the situation was often easily resolved by an advertisement in the newspaper.

During the 1960s and 1970s, however, the situation became more complex. Larger organisations adopted divisional or matrix structures wherein career paths were less clear, and new types of jobs emerged along with a more varied workforce. The old approach of simply hiring staff when the need for them became obvious began to be seen as no longer sufficient for larger and more complex organisations. In the USA, where the concepts and techniques of human resource planning were developed, Nkomo (1980) observed that during the 1960s what was then called 'manpower planning' became an important task for many personnel executives. Miller & Burack (1981) suggested that during the early part of this period, the focus was still upon relatively short-range planning, and it was not until the 1970 to 1975 period that significant interest developed in longer-term, more comprehensive 'manpower planning'. Many of the human resource planning techniques currently used were developed during this period, such as staffing tables, skills inventories, statistical forecasting techniques and computer simulations (Nkomo 1980). By the early 1980s, a number of writers were criticising this 'top-down' approach for overlooking the complexity of the external environment, for the lack of a clear link to organisational strategy and for the lack of consideration of the needs and aspirations of the work force (Mackey 1981; Miller & Burack 1981; Nkomo 1980).

By the mid-1980s, there was considerable agreement amongst writers in the USA about the need for a more strategic, detailed and long-range human resource planning approach which was closely integrated with both organisational level strategy and individual career development needs. Surveys of human resource planning activity, however, revealed that many companies had not yet adopted this approach. Buller (1988) studied eight companies that had recently been recognised in some way for excellent management and found that only two had fully integrated business and human resource planning. In a broader survey, Nkomo (1988) found that 46 per cent of responding companies had no formal human resource planning, 39 per cent had some such planning and only 15 per cent were using a fully integrated approach.

The development of the theory and practice of human resource planning in Australia seems to have followed a similar pattern. In an early study, Lang (1976) found that labour demand forecasting was common on an annual basis and that a number of organisations monitored internal labour supply, although little monitoring of external labour supply seemed to be occurring. Around the same time, Bowey, Jefferies, Porter & Green (1977) suggested that the top-down approach to human resource planning typically being used in Australia was unlikely to be effective. As with the American writers of the period, they called for an integrated approach to corporate and human resource planning that included consideration of employee attitudes and career aspirations.

As is the case in the USA, a number of Australian surveys since that time have shown many organisations involved in human resource planning with expectations of increasing activity in the future. Stanton (1986) found that 62 per cent of a sample of Australian human resource managers expected their organisation to have a greater or much greater future interest in human resource planning, although only 17 per cent reported that the current extent of use was very great and only 14 per cent reported a very great extent of integration with the corporate plan. Midgley (1990) questioned Australian human resource managers regarding increases or decreases over the past three years in the emphasis upon a variety of HRM practices and found that workforce/HR planning had the highest average increase. Kane, Abraham & Crawford (1990) found that 53 per cent of organisations in their sample had a formal human resource plan, with 36 per cent of those with such a plan reporting a great deal of two way interaction between it and the corporate plan.

The human resource planning process

Based on the work of the 1970s and 1980s, a comprehensive overall model of long-range, integrated human resource planning can be presented, as shown in Figure 6.1. In the light of the organisation's purpose and mission, an analysis of the relevant aspects of both its external and internal environments needs to be undertaken. This is frequently referred to as a **strengths, weaknesses, opportunities** and **threats** (**SWOT**) **analysis**. To avoid the criticisms levelled at top-down only approaches, it is important that the knowledge, skills, abilities and career aspirations of current employees are taken into consideration. Some recent writers, such as Wright, McMahan & McWilliams (1994) and Lado & Wilson (1994) have gone so far as to suggest that it is actually an organisation's human resources that are most likely to form the basis for sustained competitive advantage. Perhaps more than any other resource, human resources can add value to the organisation, they are likely to be unique or rare amongst competitors and they are difficult to imitate or be substituted for by a different type of resource.

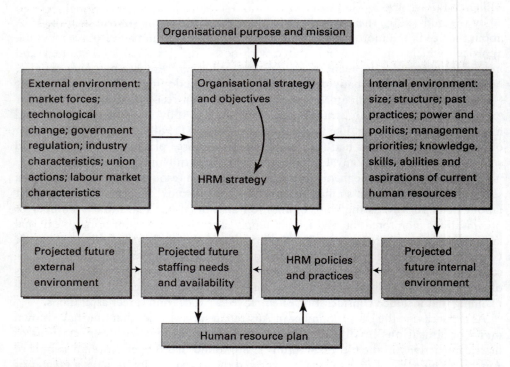

Figure 6.1 The process of human resource planning

Drawing on this SWOT analysis, organisational or corporate level strategy and objectives can be formulated. It is suggested that a human resource management strategy should be an integral part of corporate level strategy, as are other aspects such as production strategy and marketing strategy. Human resource planning, however, requires further steps, in particular **demand forecasting**, which is the projection of future staffing needs and **supply forecasting**, which estimates the likely availability of staff suitable to meet these needs. This can be achieved by projecting what the internal environment of the organisation will be like if current trends, policies and practices continue and what the external environment will be like, given reasonable projections of current and expected future trends. Future staffing demand and supply can then be assessed in the light of the human resource management strategy, based on the demands of the external environment, the likely availability of employees from the external labour market and the resources expected to be available from within the organisation. Where a gap between demand and supply is anticipated, a human resource plan can be developed which may call for some modification to HRM policies and practices to ensure that the gap is filled.

As a simple example, a business firm may have a strategy of retaining market share for a particular type of product or service. Considering the external environment, it may observe a trend towards a greater demand for customer service. On the other hand, it may find that current staff are mainly product rather than customer oriented. Current selection, appraisal, reward and training policies may support a product orientation and most career paths may be orientated around production expertise. In this instance, a human resource plan will need to focus on changing the HRM policies and practices to emphasise a greater customer orientation.

Of course the human resource planning process takes place in a dynamic environment, so all of the variables shown in Figure 6.1 are likely to change over time. The human resource plan should maintain a close relationship to organisational strategic planning and refocus as needed in the light of changing organisational objectives.

The four phases of human resource planning

Although the need for flexibility has been emphasised, the overall process of human resource planning generally occurs in four closely related phases (Mackey 1981):

1 Assessing supply and demand
2 Developing objectives
3 Designing and implementing programs
4 Evaluating outcomes.

The essential theme of linking back to the organisation's strategy and objectives remains, and these phases therefore need to occur in a consistent manner. Determining an organisation's needs for human resources lies at the base of human resource planning. The two major components of this determination are identifying the supply of workers and the demand for workers, which is the first phase in human resource planning.

Phase 1: Gathering, analysing and forecasting supply and demand data

A considerable amount of data should be gathered in this first phase. As noted earlier, this data can be useful in formulating corporate strategy and objectives as well as human resource objectives and policies. Information can be retrieved from the past, observed in the present, and forecast for the future. Obtaining data from the past can be difficult because of inadequate or nonexistent records, and forecasting data with reliability and accuracy involves uncertainty, the more so the farther out the forecast goes. Nevertheless, this data should be developed, however tentatively. The more tentative the data, the more flexible and subject to revision it should be. Contingencies causing uncertainties in the forecasts should be incorporated, perhaps in the form of estimated ranges. Organisations in unstable, complex environments are faced with many more contingencies than are organisations in relatively stable, simple environments. This first phase can be broken down into four steps.

Step 1: Analysis

The first aspect of a human resource analysis is the inventory of the current workforce and the current jobs in the organisation. Both tasks must occur if a careful determination of the organisation's capability to meet current and future needs is to be made.

Computers make compiling inventories much more efficient, and they enable a program to be dynamic and integrated. Through use of a computerised HRIS, employees and managers in separate divisions and in different geographical areas can find it easier to participate in the organisation's network for matching jobs and employees.

A second aspect of this analysis is determining the probable future composition of the relevant sections of the external work force. This determination is often based on wage, occupational, and industrial groups. Historical data on workforce composition, along with current demographic and economic data, can be used to make employment projections. These projections are not usually specific to any single organisation, but they can provide an organisation with useful information for its human resource plan, particularly for the long term.

A third aspect is assessing current and future productivity. Organisations can use their HRIS to evaluate the productivity of specific programs, offices, or positions. The HRIS is invaluable in projecting employee turnover and absenteeism, which influence an organisation's productivity and its future human resource needs. These projections might also indicate that the reasons for turnover and absenteeism need to be analysed. Strategies for dealing with this problem can then be formed. Note, however, that at some times and for some employees, increased turnover is desirable. For example, if an organisation finds itself with too many employees in a given area, increased turnover might be welcomed.

Finally, a fourth aspect, the organisational structure, must be examined. The probable size of the top, middle, and lower levels of an organisation needs to be determined. Any plans to reduce the number of layers of management, known as delayering, should be included. This exercise provides information about changes in the organisation's needs and about specific activities or functional areas that can be expected to experience particularly severe growth or contraction in the light of organisational strategy and objectives. As organisations become more technologically complex and face more complex and dynamic environments, their structures are likely to become both more complex and more fluid (Byrne, Brandt & Port 1993).

Step 2: Forecasting human resource demands

In the next step, organisational strategy and objectives should be used to forecast its future demands for employees across its various levels and functions. A variety of forecasting methods—some simple, some complex—can be used in this task. Which type will be used depends on the time frame and the type of organisation, its size and dispersion, and the accuracy and certainty of available information. The time frame used here frequently parallels that used in forecasting the potential supply of human resources and the needs of the organisation. Comparing the demand and supply forecasts then determines the organisation's short-, intermediate-, and long-term needs.

Forecasting results in approximations—not absolutes or certainties. The forecast quality depends on the accuracy of information and the predictability of events. The shorter the time horizon and the clearer the organisation's strategy and objectives, the more predictable the events and the more accurate the information. For example, organisations are generally able to predict how many graduates they may need for the coming year, but they are less able to predict their needs for the next five years.

Two classes of forecasting techniques are frequently used to determine projected demand for human resources. These are judgemental forecasts and conventional statistical projections.

Judgemental forecasting employs experts who 'judge' or estimate what the demand will be. The most common group used in this method is managers. Managerial estimates can be made by top managers (top-down). Alternatively, the review process can begin at lower levels (bottom-up) with the results sent to higher levels for refinement. The success of these estimates depends on the quality of the information available to the experts. Useful information can include data on current and projected productivity levels, market demand and sales forecasts, as well as current staffing levels and mobility information.

A more structured way to make demand judgements is the **Delphi technique** (Frantzreb 1981; Greer & Armstrong 1980). At a Delphi meeting, experts take turns at presenting their forecasts and assumptions to the others, who then make revisions in their own forecasts. This combination process continues until a viable composite forecast emerges. The composite may represent specific projections or a range of projections, depending on the experts' positions.

Another structured approach is the **nominal group technique** (Anderson & Ford 1994). Several people sit at a conference table and independently list their ideas. The ideas listed are recorded publicly, discussed and clarified, and any additional ones are added. Individuals then rank the ideas, with the highest ranking ideas overall being accepted as most important. This procedure has a number of advantages over more open group discussion, such as its greater task focus and likelihood of a balanced contribution from all members, regardless of their status (Anderson & Ford 1994, p. 66).

A number of statistical techniques have been used to assist in human resource forecasting (Dyer 1982: Greer & Armstrong 1980). Perhaps the most common statistical projections are simple and multiple linear regression analyses. In **simple linear regression analysis**, the projection of future demand is based on a past relationship between the organisation's employment level and a variable related to employment such as sales. If a relationship can be established between the level of sales and the level of employment, predictions of future sales can be used to predict future employment.

Multiple linear regression analysis is an extension of simple linear regression. Instead of relating employment to one variable, several variables are used. For example, instead of using only sales to predict employment demand, productivity data and turnover rates may also be used. Because it incorporates several variables related to employment, multiple regression analysis can produce more accurate demand forecasts.

Judgemental forecasts are less complex and rely on less data than those based on statistical methods such as those discussed above. Perhaps for this reason, they tend to dominate in practice. Stanton (1986), for example, found that 76 per cent of her sample of Australian organisations used quantitative human resource planning techniques either not at all or to a limited extent. Huselid (1993) sampled almost 1000 firms in the USA and found less than 10 per cent used any of a variety of statistical techniques, with the most common forecasting technique being supervisor estimates (51 per cent).

Step 3: Reconciling the budget

The third step puts the whole activity into an economic perspective. The forecast must be expressed in terms of dollars, including the costs of establishing a certain staffing profile (recruitment and training costs, etc.) and the annual salary costs of the profile once established. Obviously, this figure must be compatible with the organisation's profit objectives and budget limitations. While some aspects of a human resource plan may include difficult to quantify objectives such as employee commitment, where possible the costs of an activity should be compared with an estimate of its benefits, to justify the resources to be used. In some cases, the reconciliation process may indicate that the budget needs to be adjusted to accommodate the human resource plan if certain objectives are indeed to be achieved. The budget reconciliation is another opportunity to ensure that the objectives and policies of the HRM department are aligned with the strategy and objectives of the organisation.

Step 4: Forecasting human resource supply

Although supply forecasts can be derived from both internal and external sources of information, internal information is generally most crucial and more readily available. As in demand forecasting, two kinds of techniques—judgemental and statistical—are used to forecast the internal labour supply. Once made, the supply and demand forecasts can be compared to determine what actions need to be taken to identify talent and balance supply and demand.

Two judgemental techniques used by organisations to forecast supply are replacement and succession planning (Greer & Armstrong 1980). In **replacement planning**, charts are developed that list the current and potential occupants of positions in the organisation. Potential promotions and developmental needs are indicated by the performance levels of employees. Incumbents are listed directly under the job title. Those individuals likely to fill potential vacancies are listed next.

Succession planning is similar to replacement planning except that it is usually longer term and more developmental. Thus rather than focusing on a limited number of individuals who are likely to move into particular positions within the near future, succession planning typically targets a larger group of potential candidates for a broader range of positions. Extensive individual development plans are typically formulated for these candidates, which may include a variety of job assignments and the provision of extensive feedback on performance (Walker 1980).

In addition to succession planning and replacement planning, organisations can examine the supply of human resources with statistical models. One common component of these models is a **transition matrix** which traces the flow of human resources—that is, the movement of people in and out of the organisation and from one job to another (Manzini 1985). For example, suppose an organisation had 40 regional managers at the beginning of last year. A transition matrix may show that during the year, two retired, eight resigned, three were promoted and two transferred to other parts of the organisation. In terms of replacements, three transferred in from other parts of the organisation, four were promoted from area managers and eight were hired externally.

Such an analysis raises a number of human resource planning issues. For example, why were so few area managers promoted? It may be that an enhanced development program is needed for area managers, unless the organisation is consciously attempting to inject new ideas by hiring externally in this area. Is it appropriate to lose over one-third of what may be a key group of managers in a single year? If not, perhaps the reasons the eight regional managers resigned should be investigated and policies put in place to increase retention. It is also evident that, should the organisation be forecasting growth which would mean an increase in the number of regions, it will need to aim to acquire more new regional managers than the number of new regions, to cater for predictable resignations.

Phase 2: Establishing objectives

Human resource objectives are developed in Phase 2. They are (or should be, if the planning process is effective) a natural outcome of the established corporate strategy and goals. The objectives set will also depend upon the needs identified in Phase 1. Objectives may be set to modify or retain staffing numbers through targets in terms of recruitment, retention and staff redeployments or redundancies. They may also focus on the mix of knowledge, skills and abilities available and set targets in areas such as training and performance appraisal outcomes.

Increasingly, with greater attention being paid to issues such as organisational culture and employee attitudes such as commitment and customer focus, objectives may be set in terms of these less specific but crucial areas. For example, an objective could be to reduce the incidence of customer complaints about service staff by a certain amount, or to increase the organisation's ratings in particular areas by its employees in an annual survey of attitudes towards the company.

Phase 3: Programming

The third phase in human resource planning—programming—is an extremely important extension of the previous activities. After an organisation's needs are assessed, action programming must be developed to serve those needs. Action programs can be designed to increase the supply of certain categories of employees in the organisation (e.g. if the forecasts in Phase 1 showed that demand was likely to exceed supply) or to decrease the number of current employees (if the forecasts showed that supply could be expected to exceed demand). When done effectively, this may reduce the possibilities of the need for unplanned, large-scale redundancies in the future. Organisations can use many programs to address these purposes: diversity programs to make organisations more attractive to a broader array of applicants; programs to improve the organisation's socialisation efforts so that good employees want to remain with the organisation; and programs to downsize or 'rightsize' the organisation such as early retirement incentives and generous severance packages to complement the normal attrition process.

Regardless of which programs are implemented, they must be monitored and evaluated. This allows for controlling how well the programs are being implemented and allows them to be revised if necessary. Thus, control and evaluation comprise the necessary fourth phase in human resource planning.

Phase 4: Control and evaluation

Control and evaluation of HRM programs are essential to manage people effectively. Efforts in this area are often aimed at quantifying the value of human resources. These efforts recognise that people are the main asset an organisation has. An HRIS facilitates rapid and frequent collection of data. Data collection is important not only as a means of control, but also as a method for evaluating programs and making adjustments.

Evaluation is an important process not only for determining the effectiveness of human resource plans, but also for demonstrating the significance of planning and therefore of the HRM department itself to the organisation as a whole.

Dyer suggested a number of possible objective criteria for evaluating human resource planning include comparing:

- programs implemented against action plans
- actual staffing levels against established staffing requirements
- actual personnel flow rates against desired rates
- productivity levels against established goals
- program results against expected outcomes (improved applicant flows, reduced quit rates, improved replacement ratios)
- labour and program costs against budgets
- ratios of program results (benefits) to program costs (Dyer 1982, p. 72).

Other writers such as Bowen & Greiner (1986) have emphasised the need to evaluate the extent to which any HRM program meets user-needs rather than focusing exclusively on the achievement of set goals. Thus additional criteria might include the extent to which the human resource planning process and outcomes are seen as useful and accessible by managers and employees and the extent to which section heads are satisfied with their resulting staffing profiles.

Human resource planning in a changing environment

The human resource planning process discussed above is obviously a complex and time consuming one. Thus it is perhaps not surprising that, as noted earlier, most surveys, whether in the USA or in Australia, have shown that while the majority of organisations engage in some human resource planning activity, many do not adopt all aspects of the long-range, detailed approach described above.

Kane & Stanton (1994) have recently suggested that human resource planning should itself be viewed in a more strategic and contingent way. They identified three alternatives to the long-range, detailed human resource planning approach outlined above. One of these is continuing use of the older **Staff Replacement Approach,** wherein staff are recruited or promoted when a vacancy occurs, unless there are obvious reasons for not doing so, with little if any attempt at long-term or formal human resource planning. While the environment facing most organisations has been changing rapidly, some organisations still operate in a relatively stable environment and these organisations as well as very small organisations may have little trouble in recruiting any needed extra staff. Other organisations, such as some government departments and organisations composed of highly mobile professionally qualified staff, may have relatively little control over staff movements so that realistic projections of future staffing are essentially impossible.

A second option is what Kane & Stanton (1994) refer to as **Short-term Human Resource Strategy**. In this option, HR-related issues are seen as vital, but the future is too uncertain to place much faith in detailed long-range human resource planning. Speed of response and flexibility are emphasised and HRM issues are identified in reaction to rapidly evolving threats and opportunities. Schuler & Walker have described this approach as follows:

> In the past, HR planning might typically have begun with 20 'What if' questions focused on the longer term and based on the assumption that the future is extrapolated from the past. Now, HR strategy activities are being developed as HR and line managers together identify the key issues. A 'key issues' orientation helps companies (1) deal with the need to keep their planning systems flexible under conditions of high volatility, yet (2) at the same time address

more HR concerns that might ordinarily get pushed aside in such an environment because of the longer time frame generally required for HR issues (Schuler & Walker 1990, p. 8).

The third option is use of a **Vision-driven Human Resource Development** approach. Kane & Stanton (1994) suggest that use of this approach is often the result of an apparent need for relatively major shifts in employee attitudes, skills and behaviours along with changes in the culture which pervades the organisation. Although also long term in its orientation, it is driven by vision or a sense of mission and lacks the detail and specific targets characteristic of the kind of detailed human resource planning described earlier.

This change is a part of a general disillusionment with long-term, detailed business planning in rapidly evolving, uncertain environments (Mintzberg 1993; Peters 1990). Peters (1990, p. 79), for example, submits that the waves of change currently sweeping many organisations will redefine every career. He suggests: 'A new, highly automated facility belonging to the huge drug distributor, Bergen Brunswig, is illustrative: most manual work is done by machine, work teams that dot the facility are not so much in the business of "doing" (by old standards), but in the business of improving the system'. Boynton & Victor (1991, p. 62) give the example of Corning's 'treasury of process knowledge' which it views as a strategic resource and invests in continuously. They note: 'We found that Corning has invested a great deal in cross-functional and product innovation processes, training managers at all levels throughout the organisation to work in teams that are responsible for nurturing product ideas from inception through introduction'. Ulrich (1992) discussed the linking of human resource planning with a customer service orientation. He noted the importance of a focus on developing a shared mindset between employees and customers and suggested that the way managers are seen to spend time and energy ('social architecture') is a key aspect.

Thus organisational visions may differ. The above three articles, for example, discussed visions of continuous improvement (Peters 1990), product innovation (Boynton & Victor 1991) and customer service (Ulrich 1992). What they have in common from a human resource planning perspective is a focus on creating a new organisational culture and on the values, attitudes and skills all employees will need to have in order to ensure progress towards fulfilling the overall vision of the organisation.

The above examples are also related to what writers such as Senge (1990) have referred to as 'learning organisations'. Sharratt & Field (1993) suggest that the learning organisation has a number of differences from more traditional organisations, including: learning takes place at all levels within the organisation, with an important issue being the organisation's capacity to process and exploit this learning without becoming overwhelmed; learning how to learn is a key issue; there is a greater emphasis upon holistic thinking; and structures tend to be more fluid and interlacing. In relation to planning, Sharratt & Field (1993) suggest that it is valued as an opportunity to learn, through the opportunity to explore different scenarios in a non-judgemental manner.

In determining when each of the four approaches to human resource planning are likely to be appropriate, Kane & Stanton (1994) suggest that the three most important variables to consider are: the extent to which changes in workforce knowledge and skills are likely to be needed; the length of the desirable and feasible time span for planning; and the level of certainty with which the organisation's future environment can be predicted.

The relationship between these three variables and the four approaches to human resource planning are shown in Figure 6.2

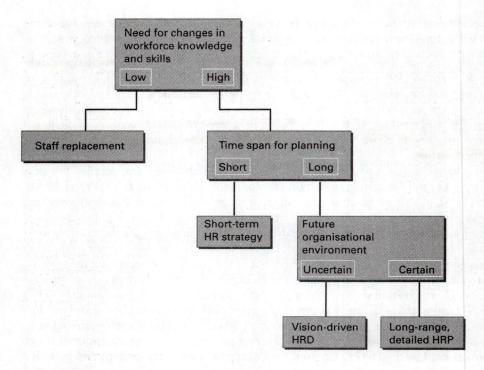

Figure 6.2 Choosing an approach to human resource planning

Source: Kane & Stanton 1994, p. 227

Where few changes are likely to be needed in employee knowledge, skills and abilities, the Staff Replacement Approach to human resource planning will be the most cost-effective. Where there is anticipated to be a moderate to high need for such changes, short-term human resource strategy will be the most appropriate approach where the planning horizon is relatively short. Where the planning horizon is longer, long-range, detailed human resource planning will tend to be most suitable when future needs can be forecast with a reasonable degree of accuracy. Where this is not the case, and future uncertainty calls for greater flexibility, the Vision Driven Human Resource Development approach is probably the most suitable choice.

Barriers to human resource planning

Even when the most suitable approach to human resource planning has been identified, adoption of and implementation of this approach may prove difficult. Kane & Stanton (1994) identified a number of possible barriers to the implementation of human resource planning. These include general resistance both to centralised planning and to changing what seems to have worked in the past, top managers giving HRM issues and staff relatively low priority, resources including knowledgable staff and suitable data/methods for forecasting not being available, and the impact of human resource planning programs being difficult to quantify. It is also not always clear how the various HRM functions can be integrated and used to achieve the objectives of a human resource plan, once such a plan is developed.

Thus in developing a human resource planning program, it is essential to gain top management support, perhaps through small pilot or demonstration programs in an area that is of concern to management. Failure to include line management in the design, development, and implementation of a human resource plan is a common oversight for first-time planners. Often tempted to develop or adopt highly quantitative approaches to planning, HRM professionals can find themselves with a final product that has little pragmatic value to line managers (Frantzreb 1981). A plan must be useful, and that means the needs of line managers must be met. An HRIS needs to be in place to gather and analyse relevant information and to project future states given particular policies. As Salmon (1995) points out, all too often HRIS lack the capacity to carry out strategic functions. He adds that even relatively limited HRIS '… are rarely finished, are poorly supported and usually have bugs in the software' (Salmon 1995, p. 307).

A lack of attention to issues of career planning and career management is another potential barrier. To be successful, human resource planning requires that both the company and the individual make the right choices. The company's path set out via its objectives is important, and individuals can better fit into this path—and even enable it—if they have an idea of where they as individuals are going. Employee empowerment and self-management are helping organisations and individuals figure this out. The following section will therefore focus on the individual dimension of human resource planning through a consideration of career development and career management.

Why is career planning and management important?

It is costly and time consuming for organisations to offer career management programs and for individuals to expend effort in attempting to plan their careers. The investments of money and time, however, can be worthwhile because career management fulfils many important purposes for both employer and employee. Individuals feel pressure to engage in career management because the current work environment is highly competitive. Indeed, many employees today are more willing than ever to assert themselves to achieve control over work and non-work pursuits. In addition, the meaning of success has been broadened to encompass not only salary and status, but also personal contribution and the realisation of one's potential. Employees today often feel that they are entitled to such things as enriched tasks, participation in decision making, flexible working hours, job security, and equitable treatment. Finally, many employees are increasingly concerned with balancing the demands of work, family, and leisure activities.

Effective career management means effective utilisation of human resources and equal employment opportunity, both of which are important to an organisation. If people are an organisation's most important asset, then employees whose skills are poorly utilised and who become disillusioned and dissatisfied are wasted assets. Since the image of the 'organisation man' has eroded, companies can no longer assume blind loyalty and automatic acceptance of promotions and relocations. Thus active involvement in the career management process is in the best interest of the organisation.

Equal employment opportunity concerns initially focused on recruitment and selection. Recently, however, equal employment emphasis has also been placed on individuals who are already employed by the organisation. Providing career opportunities for women and ethnic minorities is particularly important. Various groups (e.g. women, ethnic minorities, disabled workers, older workers) can benefit from assistance in career development.

The evolution of the field of career development

Prior to the period in history known as the Industrial Revolution which began in the late 18th century with the introduction of power driven machines, the choice of an occupation seems to have been generally straightforward. Men usually followed their father's occupation, whether this be as a serf, craftsman, merchant, or noble. Women tended to be absorbed into roles as wives, mothers, or domestics.

The spread of factory production processes during the late 18th and early 19th centuries, however, gradually created great changes in this stable pattern. Society at the time was generally characterised by rigid hierarchies and authoritarianism, and management beliefs in the early 20th century were summarised by McGregor as follows:

1 The average human being has an inherent dislike of work and will avoid it if possible
2 Because of this human characteristic of dislike of work, most people must be coerced, controlled, directed, threatened with punishment to get them to put forth adequate effort toward the achievement of organisational objectives
3 The average human being prefers to be directed, wishes to avoid responsibility, has little ambition, wants security above all (McGregor 1960, pp. 33–34).

Thus it is not surprising that various models and techniques were developed to help regain the sense of control and direction that had been disrupted by the Industrial Revolution. Nor is it surprising that most of these developments sought to reinforce management's authoritarian position and tended to draw upon the engineering concepts that had so successfully mechanised production processes.

The trait-factor approach to career choice

The view of careers that emerged in this early period can best be described as a career choice model, where individuals at the end of their schooling made a one-off choice of the occupation that they wished to enter. Given the supposedly permanent nature of this choice, it was seen as important, both for the individual and for the employing organisation, that this choice be the best one possible.

Thus early theorising in the **career development field focused on which worker traits were most usefully measured, which factors in jobs were most relevant, and on what kind of matching processes (tests, interviews, etc.) resulted in the best person–job match.** The use of these approaches was often known as the **trait-factor approach**, and the aim was to aid with what was seen as a one-off career choice (Betz, Fitzgerald & Hill 1989).

Although the conditions and assumptions that fostered the development of the trait-factor approach may seem very dated, some of its outcomes are still relevant today. Industrial psychologists have continued to search for more effective ways of defining and measuring the factors involved in successful job performance (job analysis). The search for more reliable and valid means of measuring applicant traits and skills and for better ways of matching people to jobs increased in pace with the introduction of legislation in the areas of equal opportunity and affirmative action in the USA and in Australia (Kramar 1986). As noted by Pithers, Athanasou & Cornford (1995), the original trait-factor approach has been broadened to include a range of individual differences such as abilities, competencies, temperament, education and experience, although the focus is still upon person–job matching. Pithers, Athanasou & Cornford (1995) describe recent work to develop a set of Australian occupational descriptors so that all of Australia's 1079 occupations can be described in comparable terms.

Thus modern versions of the trait-factor approach and the various measures of individuals and jobs that have been developed from this approach are still of use in job analysis, job evaluation, training needs analysis and employee selection, or, indeed, in any situation where job requirements are expected to remain relatively stable for a reasonable period of time. In a similar manner, a number of instruments, such as interest inventories and tests of aptitude, have been developed that can be of help to the individual when considering what occupation to train for or seek to enter.

Individually-oriented models of career development

If the period from the beginning of the 20th century to the advent of the Second World War can be seen as authoritarian and pre-occupied with control, the period from the end of the Second World War through to the early 1970s can be described as permissive and pre-occupied with growth. Aubrey (1977) attributed this change to factors such as:

- an increased desire by individuals for freedom and autonomy
- a newly found affluence
- a full employment market
- a general extension of education to hitherto denied groups.

At the same time as people's expectations were changing, there began to emerge some new approaches to management that focused more on the employee as a person, rather than as a 'round peg for a round hole'. Motivation theorists such as Maslow (1943) and McGregor (1960) put forth the argument that workers could be motivated to perform through attention to satisfying their needs, values, and aspirations.

Perhaps the major contribution of these writers was the concept of 'higher order needs' such as needs for challenge, achievement and responsibility. Maslow (1943), for example, maintained that all people had a need to develop to their full capacity as a person, a drive which he called **self-actualisation**.

Just as the trait-factor approach was consistent with the beliefs of society and with the management theory of its time, a new view of career development began to emerge that was consistent with the changed assumptions of the post-war period. In this new approach, counsellors supplanted vocational guidance officers, motivation theory became the new inspiration for organisations, and the concept of career development replaced the more limited one-off career choice. Super (1942), for example, proposed a model of career development that accepted earlier views of career choice, but added the following major stages:

- Trial (21 to 30 years of age)
- Advancement (30 to 45 years of age)
- Maintenance (45 to 65 years of age)
- Deceleration (65 to 70 years of age).

The work of the motivation theorists such as Maslow and McGregor can be seen as having legitimised concern with individual growth and development and with feelings and intuitions. These concerns are still relevant to understanding careers, and Super's career development model seems to accurately describe some of the career patterns found today (Michelson 1994).

Systems approaches to career management

Although the individually oriented approach expanded the field from one of career choice to one of career development and added several important concerns, in time it has become seen as limited in its own way. In part, this is because further research and newer theories pointed to additional factors. The environment within which many work organisations operate and the nature of the workforce have also changed, however, which may have led to these newer findings being more readily accepted.

The period from the end of the Second World War until the mid-1960s was generally one of stability, prosperity and growth in most industrialised countries. Promotions were easy to obtain in many occupations, and in this climate an emphasis upon self-development seemed to make sense. Energy crises in the 1970s, the discovery of stagflation, and rapid social, economic and technological changes served to dampen this sense of optimism. In addition, the workforce in most industrialised countries became less homogenous. For example, many more women with child-care responsibilities remained in or re-entered the workforce, reducing the number of careers that proceeded in simple stages such as those outlined earlier (Fitzgerald 1986).

Most of the new views of career development made use what could be called a **systems approach to career management**. This approach views the organisation, its environment and the people within the organisation as a complex open system. All parts of the system are seen as constantly changing and responding to change in other parts of the system. The problem then becomes one of managing this potentially chaotic system. Thus systems approaches to career development are much more compatible with human resource planning. Although there are a number of variants of the systems approach, most allow for trait-factor approaches to be used in areas such as selection, and for individually oriented career development counselling to occur at various points in the system. Probably the major potential advantages of a systems approach to career development are:

- the realisation that the organisation, the people in it, and the greater environment (social, political and economic forces) must all be assessed
- a greater appreciation of change in all parts of the system, and thus of the need for planning
- acceptance that the desires of individuals for satisfying jobs need to be related to the organisation's requirements for effectiveness and productivity.

One of the earlier and better-known systems approaches was developed by Schein (1978). Schein referred to his model as a human resource planning and development system, and outlined a series of organisational issues and activities, a parallel series of individual issues and activities, and a number of matching processes that need to occur to synchronise individual and organisational change. On the organisation's side, the environment needs to be constantly monitored and assessed, so that corporate plans and related human resource plans can be kept up to date. More specific plans then need to be made for staffing and replacement, and for the training and development of employees to suit current and anticipated needs. The individual is confronted with issues such as initial choice of occupation, establishment, advancement, change and disengagement.

The matching processes that should take place include a range of HRM activities such as recruitment, selection, appraisal, training and development activities and periodic career counselling. Schein (1978) emphasised the continuing need for dialogue and joint negotiation if both individual and organisational needs are to be met.

Another of Schein's (1978) contributions that went beyond the confines of earlier 'stage' models of careers was the concept of the **career anchor**. Schein (1978) suggested that as a result of their early career experiences, a person's perceptions about his or her own talents, motives and values tended to evolve into a relatively stable and enduring pattern. Through his research, Schein (1978) identified five basic types of career anchors:

- **Technical/functional competence**—where job moves are made to maximise a person's opportunities to remain challenged by the technical aspects of their field
- **Managerial competence**—where challenge is sought through obtaining higher level, more generalist managerial positions
- **Security and stability**—where long-run career stability, a good program of benefits and job security are the underlying concerns
- **Creativity**—where the ongoing need is to be an entrepreneur, to build or create something that is entirely one's own product.

Schein (1978, p. 127) suggested that 'The career anchor functions in the person's work life as a way of organising experience, identifying one's area of contribution in the long run, generating criteria for kinds of work settings in which one wants to function, and identifying patterns of ambition and criteria for success by which one will measure oneself'.

Organisational strategy and career development

While Schein (1978) presented a useful overall model, some writers have gone further to link career development more specifically with corporate level strategy, making use of the widely cited classification of organisational strategies developed by Miles & Snow (1978, 1984). Miles & Snow (1978, 1984) identified four basic organisational strategies: **Defenders,** who seek to defend a relatively narrow product/market position through stability and efficiency; **Prospectors,** who focus on product/service innovation and the creation of new markets; **Analysers,** who maintain some stable lines while searching for related new opportunities in emerging markets; and **Reactors,** who struggle to survive in a reactive manner rather than by trying to anticipate changes.

In one example, Fandt (1988) focused particularly on contrasting the career development profiles of Defenders and Prospectors. Defenders are more likely to focus on building internal resources and adopt formal and long-term procedures in areas such as career counselling, mentoring and training and development, with a focus on meeting organisational needs. Prospectors focus more on acquiring staff, with most career-related procedures informal and customised to meet the needs of the individual.

In a more in-depth analysis, Sonnenfeld & Peiperl (1988) identified four types of career systems. Two of these, which they refer to as the Academy and the Club, focus on the internal development of staff, who enter the organisation early in their careers. The Academy focuses on individual contributions and establishes elaborate career paths, particularly for high potential employees. The Club, on the other hand, has a greater emphasis on team or group contribution, reliability and commitment along with slower career paths. Of the two career systems which focus on external labour supply, the Baseball Team attempts to recruit high performing specialists at all career stages, provides little training or succession planning and has high turnover. The Fortress carries out little recruitment or training, values flexibility and generalist staff, and layoffs are frequent.

Sonnelfeld & Peiperl (1988) then suggested that Clubs are most likely to have adopted a Defender strategy; Baseball teams a Prospector strategy; Academies an Analyser strategy; whilst Fortresses are most likely to be Reactors.

The overall systems approach is summarised and contrasted with the two earlier approaches in Table 6.1.

Table 6.1 Approaches to career development compared

APPROACH	TRAIT-FACTOR APPROACH TO CAREER CHOICE	INDIVIDUALLY ORIENTED APPROACH TO CAREER DEVELOPMENT	SYSTEMS APPROACHES TO CAREER MANAGEMENT
Methods	Rational matching	Intuitive, emotional, personal experiencing	Rational contingency planning
Assumptions	Organisation and job given, person static	Organisation and job given, but person develops	Organisation, job and person interaction and change
Loyalty	Management oriented	Worker oriented	Systems interaction oriented
Time perspective usage	Past Selection, appraisal, career choice	Present All interviewing and counselling, motivation and morale	Future Career/staff development, job design, organisational design/change

Career management programs in the organisation

Organisations adopting the systems approach can offer a wide range of career management programs to assist employees in career planning and management and to ensure that the organisation's staffing needs are met. A number of programs will be examined here to illustrate the diversity of needs filled by these programs and the wide range of concerns that organisations consider important in career management. An understanding of typical career stages can help organisations understand the kind of issues and events likely to occur across a life span and thus to plan appropriate career management programs. We will examine four broad stages, some of the issues likely to be involved in each, and some of the types of career management programs that are likely to be relevant. The four stages are: (1) organisational entry, (2) early career, (3) midcareer, and (4) late career.

Organisational entry programs

Selecting a job and an organisation are the major focus here. An important issue for many during this stage is reality shock. Individuals sometimes have unrealistically high expectations and find that many entry-level jobs are not particularly challenging, at least initially. This stage usually occurs during the late teens and early twenties.

Although organisational entry always involves moving inside an organisation from outside, it also frequently entails moving from an educational environment to an organisational environment. Newcomers (especially those coming from tertiary education institutions) generally have inflated expectations even if they have engaged in self-assessment activities aimed at awareness of self and work environment. Inflated expectations may lead to disappointments (reality shock).

Organisations can use **realistic job previews** to counteract the effects of reality shock (Meglino, Denisi & Ravlin 1993). Unrealistically high expectations can stem from the educational process, the recruitment process, and organisational stereotypes. Realistic previews attempt to present both the positive and negative aspects of the job and organisation. Some organisations have also been experimenting recently with realistic orientation programs. These orientation programs provide the usual basic information about the organisation and employee duties and rights, and also warn of potential negative job experiences and provide suggestions as to how to cope with such experiences (Waung 1995).

Early career programs

The essential task at this stage is establishing oneself in a career and organisation. Two periods are encompassed by this stage: fitting into the world of work and struggling for achievement in one's chosen field. These concerns usually occupy an individual between the early twenties and age forty.

Many organisational career development programs are targeted at employees in this age group. These programs can include: establishing clear career paths, providing career planning services and provision of mentoring programs. These initiatives are described below.

Identification of specific career paths

Providing **career paths** involves several decisions on the part of an organisation. First, should there be an active policy of development and/or promotion from within? Second, should there be a training and development program to provide sufficient candidates for internal movements? If the answers to these questions are yes, then the organisation must identify career paths consistent with organisational and job requirements and employee skills and preferences. This may result in wide career paths where employees can move across many areas and functions within the company, or it may result in narrower **career ladders** where employees only move within a few areas and functions with a primary aim being preparation for promotion.

The movement to define the competencies required across positions at all levels may also make appropriate career paths and ladders easier for both the organisation and its employees to identify (Hearn, Close, Smith & Southey 1996; Wallace & Hunt 1996). Organisations with clearly defined career paths and ladders based upon identified competencies may also have an easier time attracting and recruiting qualified job applicants and a better chance of keeping them.

Career planning programs

Career planning activity aids an individual in his or her personal appraisal or self-assessment. When an organisation provides this service, it is likely to be related as much to the organisation's needs as to the individual's. An individual's personal appraisal, however, need not be related to a specific organisation. An example of a career planning guide from a large organisation appears in Figure 6.3.

Mentoring programs

Another type of program aimed to expand career opportunities for those who do not fall within an organisation's typical networks is the provision of formal **mentoring programs**. As Wilson & Elman (1990) note, informal mentoring occurs naturally in most organisations, but most typically involves people mentoring those that they perceive as most similar to themselves. Without this being supplemented by more formal programs, Wilson & Elman (1990, p. 90) suggest 'the danger is that quality mentoring

1 My job satisfaction on my present job is (circle) ....
  Very   Very
  Low   Low   Average   High   High
2 I would like to progress in my work by   Yes   No
  A Developing improved performances and results on my present job
  B Qualifying for the next logical higher position above my present one
  C Qualifying for a different type of work within another department
  D Qualifying for several positions above my present one
3 I consider myself best suited to
  A Supervision
  B Supporting staff work
  C Production of operation management
4 Goals
  A suitable job goal for me is _____
  _____
5 Qualifications
  Evaluate your own qualifications based on current standing and what is needed for your job goal.*
6 My development balance sheet
  A My strong points are
  B I like to do work that is
  C My limiting factors are
  D I dislike work that is
7 Development
  If I want to develop either on my present job or to qualify for a different job, I need the following:
  A More job knowledge in
  B I like to do work that is
  C A better attitude or outlook concerning
8 Taking action to reach your job goal
  List how you can develop greater knowledge, job skills, or personal abilities that will help you reach your career goals.
  A Formal study of a subject (list seminars, night school, company training program, or correspondence courses that will increase your knowledge of a subject):
  _____
  _____
  _____
  _____

* When this form is used within the company, space is provided so an individual is able to write a lengthy response. This is true for items 5–8.

Figure 6.3 Organisational career planning guide
Source: Schuler 1995, p. 130

may only be available to white males from dominant ethnic or religious groups rather than to the full range of people represented in the contemporary organisation'.

Kram (1983) reported that mentors tend to have two types of functions. Directly career-related functions may include sponsoring the mentoree for other programs and opportunities, enhancing the mentoree's visibility within the organisation, coaching in the handling of difficult situations and assigning challenging projects to the mentoree. Personal support functions include acting as a role model and providing acceptance and friendship. Kram (1983) also suggested that the career-related functions tended to emerge first in a mentoring relationship whilst the personal support functions became more prominent in later stages of the relationship.

Wilson & Elman (1990) observed that mentoring programs frequently take a 'sponsored but voluntary' approach, and may include a period where a group of potential mentors and mentorees mix informally so that both parties can meet and assess each other. In addition to the value to mentorees, Wilson & Elman (1990) suggest that the organisation benefits through enhanced motivation, job performance and retention rates, and that it can use mentoring as a mechanism for strengthening and assuring the continuity of organisational culture. Some studies of formal mentoring systems have supported their benefits. Chao, Walz & Gardner (1992), for example, reported that clear differences in outcome were found in their study between mentored and non-mentored individuals in areas such as organisational socialisation, satisfaction, and the salary levels attained.

Mid career programs

While some employees during the mid career stage (age 40–55) continue along the career path they have chosen, many experience a crisis at some point during this period (Hunt & Collins 1983; O'Connor 1981). This crisis, which has been called the **midlife transition**, entails a re-examination of one's accomplishments relative to one's initial career goals. Feelings of restlessness and insecurity are common. Individuals in this transition become aware of the signs of aging, and may experience a growing sense of obsolescence and changes in family relationships. All of these factors can create stress.

Organisations can help employees cope with this crisis by encouraging them to develop new skills and to serve as mentors for younger employees. Individuals can also engage in self-assessment activities. Self-assessment during the midlife transition should focus on the individual's feelings about middle age and determining the relative priority of work, family, leisure, and self-development.

At some point, nearly every employee reaches a **career plateau**, a situation in which the career slows and the prospects for promotion dramatically decrease (Bardwick 1986). Plateaus can be personal or organisational. Personal plateauing means that the employee has decided not to accept additional promotions in the organisation. Organisational plateauing occurs when the employee desires advancement but no opportunities exist, or the organisation does not consider the employee promotable. Since fewer opportunities exist at each higher level in companies, plateauing is natural and not indicative of success or failure. Employees, however, may need help in dealing with plateauing because our culture has tended to view advancement as a yardstick of success, and many employees feel like failures when they are no longer promotable.

Managers can take a number of steps to help employees cope with career plateauing. These steps include making the facts visible, being realistic about strengths and weaknesses of others, counselling people, eliminating skill obsolescence, letting people know they are appreciated, creating new rewards, encouraging initiative, discouraging employees from leading a 'workaholic' life, giving honest appraisals, and managing by 'walking around' and being available when needed (Bardwick 1986; Leibowitz, Kaye & Farren 1990).

Late career programs

The final career stage, the late career, involves continued productivity and eventual preparation for disengagement from work life. Although relatively little research has been directed toward the late career, a negative bias against older workers may exist (Patrickson & Hartmann 1992; Rosen & Jerdee 1985). In addition, successfully disengaging from the work role is a major challenge, and some organisations are attempting to assist older workers with this life transition.

Late-career individuals should actively manage their careers just as employees should at earlier career stages. Successful late-career management may help to dispel some myths and stereotypes about older workers. Late-career employees can also help themselves by actively planning for their retirement, whether the organisation provides retirement programs or not. The retirement transition can raise many fears, but it also contains many opportunities to pursue activities that could not be enjoyed during employment.

Retirement programs

The provision of retirement programs can help to ensure that these opportunities are seen and accessed. Typically, in these programs organisations offer seminars that provide information on finances, housing or relocation, family relations, and legal affairs. Since retirees may also face social and psychological adjustments, many retirement planning programs include additional components that allow for the sharing of emotional and developmental issues (Caro 1983). Caro (1983) reported that a study carried out in the USA in 1980 found that 56 per cent of respondents offered some form of retirement planning program. Patrickson & Hartman (1992) reported that 30 per cent of their sample of older Australian male employees had attended retirement seminars.

Both retiring employees and organisations can benefit from retirement planning options and seminars. By encouraging more senior employees to retire, companies open up jobs and promotion opportunities for less senior employees. Organisations must also consider the legal issues that affect the treatment of older workers, since age discrimination has been legislated against in some areas. Thus treating older workers fairly makes good business sense and also helps to avoid costly litigation. Because of these mutual benefits, it is likely that companies will increasingly offer retirement planning programs.

Career counselling

Career counselling typically involves a discussion of an individual's work values, career goals, current job activities and performance, and action plans. Thus career counselling may be a useful option at any of the above stages in an individual's career.

Counselling can be formal or informal in nature. Formal career counselling is usually conducted by career counsellors and vocational psychologists in individual sessions. On an informal level, discussions with supervisors are very important. Supervisors can be a primary source of career information and can do a number of things to facilitate the career counselling process. In order to function most effectively in a career counselling role, supervisors need: an understanding of career stages, types and issues; an understanding of any career relevant programs and career paths within their organisation; along with good listening and questioning skills.

Caro (1983, p. 9) reported that a 1980 survey in the USA found that approximately 30 per cent of respondents offered counselling to facilitate career exploration and planning. Another study focused on Lawrence Livermore Laboratories, which offered employees a combination of career development workshops, manuals and professional counselling. Positive results in terms of increased awareness of choices in career decisions and acceptance of responsibility for managing one's own career were reported following the workshop. In a six month followup, many participants were found to have enrolled in courses, workshops or self-development programs and to be rated higher by their supervisors in terms of the quality and quantity of their work and their morale (Caro 1983, pp. 10–11).

Career management in Australian organisations

In a recent Australian study, Kane (1994) reported on the approach adopted to career development by Australian organisations. The 541 respondents ranged from Chief Executive Officers through to non-managerial staff and came from a wide variety of industry sectors. The percentage results for the question regarding attitude towards career development in the organisation were:

- Career development is the responsibility of the individual (23.1 per cent)
- The individual's supervisor should encourage the career development of the individual in an informal way (12.9 per cent)
- The career development of their staff should be a major concern of every supervisor (13.3 per cent)
- The organisation has the responsibility to ensure that career development of employees is in line with future organisation needs (49.7 per cent) (Kane 1994, p. 168).

Thus almost half of the organisations surveyed appeared to adopt an approach to career development that is compatible with a systems, or human resource planning orientation. Combining the third and the final approaches would indicate that almost two-thirds of responding organisations consider career development an important issue. In terms of differences in responses, Kane (1994) reported a tendency for more senior level respondents, such as CEOs, to indicate that their organisation adopted the latter two, longer range approaches to career development.

Kane (1994) also found that reported career development approach was related to the level of support provided by the organisation for employees to engage in various types of training and staff development activities. For all types of training, the likelihood of support was lowest where the organisation left career development to the individual. Informal encouragement for career development by the supervisor was second lowest in terms of expected support for all types of training activity other than on-the-job training and in-house training by the organisation's own employees. Highest levels of expected support for all types of training was associated with career development to meet future needs, while the second highest level of support was associated with career development being a major concern of every supervisor. This would indicate that the majority of organisations which see career development as an important issue also are providing the training likely to be needed to support a career development strategy.

Careers in the future

Members of the general public as well as those concerned with career development have been bombarded with warnings and predictions about the future for at least the past 25 years. In Australia, for example, Barry Jones' (1982) *Sleepers, Wake* was widely discussed. Most of these writers saw the world as going through a rapid series of social, political, economic and technological changes, sometimes referred to as reflecting a 'post-industrial revolution' (Jones 1982). Lansbury (1992, p. 20) referred to this as 'an age of turbulence'. Perhaps the only universal among the predictions that have been made, then and now, about work in the future is that extensive changes will occur. It is useful, however, to identify what appear to be some major common strands.

Types of jobs

Existing data show that the number employed in areas such as agriculture and manufacturing has been in decline for many years, coupled with growth in service-based industries. Karpin (1995, p. 89), for example, noted that during the 1961 to 1991 period, Australia lost over half its manufacturing jobs as a percentage of its total labour force, registering one of the biggest losses in this area amongst the OECD. While service-oriented jobs grew during the same period, Karpin (1995, p. 90) warns that in the future, greater use of information technology may well affect this sector as well. Some years earlier, Jones (1982, p. 6) went so far as to predict that the impact of technology will ultimately usher in a post-service society where leisure-based activities will be the only employment growth area.

A ten-year projection of Australia's labour force supply and demand carried out by the Department of Employment, Education and Training (1991) covered 120 different occupations. Attempts were made to take into consideration likely expansion and contractions in particular types of industry, changes in productivity and the effects of changes in demand for particular occupations within industries. Productivity increases, for example, may generate increased output without any increase in employment. Overall, the study found that professional occupations such as the health professions were expected to grow at the highest rate and sales workers, tradespersons and para-professional groups were also expected to grow at above average rates. Clerical occupations were expected to grow at an average rate, while managers, machine operators and labourers were expected to grow at a low rate (Department of Employment, Education and Training 1991, pp. 4–7).

Career flexibility

A common projection is that because of the likelihood of continuing change, careers will need to be more flexible in the future, and people will need broad initial training covering a variety of knowledge and skills and will need frequent retraining. Andrewartha (1994, p. 23), for example, asserts that there are a number of significant changes increasingly impacting upon the career prospects of the Australian workforce, including:

- no career path can be seen as certain in the future
- long-term employment with one organisation is becoming a thing of the past
- there will be a greater focus on negotiated career transitions every few years
- part time, contract and transitory employment will become much more common
- ongoing education and training are becoming essential to maintain employability
- obtaining suitable employment will be increasingly dependent on the individual's ability to market his or her skills.

Critchley noted similar trends, and contrasted old and new views on the world of work:

Table 6.2   Old and new views on the world of work

OLD VIEW	NEW VIEW
Job	Work
Employee	Vendor
False sense of security	Sense of personal control
Employment	Employability
Job titles	Skill sets
Career ladder	Career lattice
One career	Portfolio career

Source: Critchley 1996, p. 22

One factor which is likely to emphasise the trends suggested by Critchley (1996) is the relative decline of older, bureaucratically structured organisations and the growth in network organisations, as discussed in the section 'Future organisational forms' below.

Future organisational forms

While any change in organisational structure or form affects the possible career paths for employees, one recent trend which has even greater potential to affect careers is the tendency to form organisational 'networks'. According to Limerick (1992), most networks appear to have been established in attempts by organisations to divest themselves of, or avoid taking on activities and functions that they do not do well, so they can focus on activities in which they have a comparative advantage. Limerick (1992, p. 42) noted a range of types of networks that have been identified, including: '... internal networking, sub-contracting, strategic alliances, franchising, strategic networks, "hub" organisations, and "solar system" organisations'. He argued that these new, network style organisations will be best placed to flourish in the future business environment. With the new style of employee, which Limerick (1992, p. 51) referred to as 'Yiffies' (young, individualistic, freedom-minded and few), the focus will need to be on lateral career paths and negotiated objectives. In terms of career development, Limerick (1992) suggests that the human resources manager will need to adopt an essentially supportive role helping these employees map and develop their assets, develop their intuitive and empathetic capacities and develop their competencies in negotiation. However, the responsibility for career path planning will need to be transferred to the individual, with movement out of the organisation seen as just as normal as is movement within the organisation.

These general predictions may be useful in attempts to conceptualise how career development will be likely to occur in the future. Before deciding that some entirely new model is needed for the future, however, it may be useful to consider Barton's (1981) point that each new kind of career tends to be added to the existing variety rather than replace it. For example, farmers and manufacturers still exist, in spite of the decline in employment in these areas. Thus models of career development such as that proposed by Super (1942) will no doubt still be applicable to some careers in the future. When looking ahead to the future, however, it is worthwhile to consider some of the newer, alternative models of careers that have been developed. The following sections will consider two of these: Hearn's (1980) 'anarchic careers' and Driver's (1978, 1988) career concepts.

Anarchic careers

Hearn suggested in 1980 that many people had begun to doubt that most organisations, whether private or public sector, really had the best interests of their employees at heart. Thus, he felt that there had been a decline in the loyalty felt to one's employing organisation, and a loss of faith in its leaders. Recent experiences with massive redundancies and corporate takeovers have probably added to this disillusionment. The reduced levels of loyalty between organisations and their employees, coupled with lessened possibilities for promotion, was seen by Hearn (1980) as leading to an increase in the prevalence of four types of what he referred to as 'anarchic careers'. An **anarchic career** is one which lacks any clear pattern of development or relationship to organisational needs. Many anarchic careerists continue to work for traditional bureaucratic organisations, but have given up trying to get promoted and have lost any real interest in the work that they do.

Those Hearn (1980) calls **cop-out careerists** react to this frustration by trying to put as little energy as possible into their job, searching for satisfaction outside of work hours. In another type of anarchic career, those Hearn (1980) refers to as **non-careerists** also do as little real work as possible, but their major focus is on non-work aspects of the workplace. They may specialise in arranging social events, in office politics, or in another aspect of the workplace. While cop-out careerists are often seen as 'deadwood', non-careerists are more likely to become an accepted part of the work group.

A third type of anarchic careerist identified by Hearn (1980) is usually devoted to some external political or social cause, and sees their mission as one of trying to change or even revolutionise the organisation from within. These **guerilla careerists**, as Hearn (1980) calls them, may use methods ranging from union pressure through to outright sabotage to try to accomplish their ends. Management often refers to this type of careerist as a 'radical', or at least a 'stirrer'.

While all three of the above types choose to stay within the organisation, those whom Hearn (1980) refers to as **uncareerists** leave the organisation to strike out on their own or with a like-minded group. Many choose to develop alternative careers in the arts or crafts, in small-scale farming or as entrepreneurs or consultants in various areas. There is reason to suspect that this may be a growing pattern in the future, particularly for the victims of organisational downsizing. Indeed, the more optimistic of two post-service society scenarios developed by Jones (1982, p. 7) essentially saw a happy proliferation of what Hearn (1980) called uncareers in areas such as craftwork, gardening, research, sport, leisure, hobby and do-it-yourself activities.

Career concepts

Hearn (1980) clearly saw his anarchic careers as a supplement to more traditional types, and was not intending to give a comprehensive classification. Another writer has proposed a classification of career types that may be more generally applicable. **Driver (1978, 1988)** suggested four basic career concepts that appear to encompass both traditional and likely future career paths, and these concepts are outlined below.

The transitory career

In this pattern, the individual moves from job to job in reaction to their financial needs, interests and the opportunities available. Work may be interspersed with periods of unemployment and may span a wide range of occupations and geographical locations. This pattern has been fairly typical of young people in the past, as part of what writers such as Super (1942) called the exploration stage, prior to becoming established in a career. Some recent research, however, has found other groups pursuing a transitory pattern, including some entrepreneurs and troubleshooters (Brousseau 1990). The expected shortage of work in the future coupled with the growth of alternative work patterns may well see transitory work becoming a permanent career for many of those who lack high level skills as well as those who greatly value variety and independence.

The steady state career

This type of career normally sees the individual undergoing a period of study or training prior to entering an occupation, and then spending their working life in this occupation. Thus, the pattern is often similar to early models of career choice. Examples of occupations where this has long been the norm are the skilled trades and the professions. This type of career came in for some disparagement during the boom period prior to the 1970s, and no doubt some steady state careerists were made to feel like failures because they did not 'get ahead'. Some probably reacted to this frustration by adopting what Hearn (1980) referred to as cop-out careers or non-careers.

Although this may be the most traditional type of career, there are some indications that this pattern may become more rather than less common. Lansbury (1986, p. 22), for example, suggested that management is likely to become more than ever dependent upon the kinds of specialist skills that steady state careerists tend to develop.

The linear career

During the prolonged period of economic growth following the Second World War, the linear career came to be regarded as the ideal, and for many, the expected path. Linear careerists are typically less devoted to a particular occupation and more concerned with advancement to the top, and so look for established career ladders in moderate to large-sized organisations.

The linear career, with its period of advancement between 30 and 45 years of age, approximates that described by Super (1942). A survey of chief executive officers in Australia carried out by Mukhi (1982) found that the average age at appointment to a senior management position was 33.2 years, and the average age at appointment as a chief executive officer was 40.3 years. This pattern is strikingly similar to that suggested by Super in the USA forty years earlier. These linear careerists came from a variety of functional backgrounds, and had moved through an average of 3.5 organisations and 8.7 different job roles on their way to chief executive officer status.

Margerison & Smeed (1984) have also stressed the need for future top managers to gain cross functional experience, and the need for a career cross-over from technical work to managerial work between 30 and 40 years of age. The steady state careerist, on the other hand, may rise to Margerison & Smeed's (1984) level 3, team leadership, but their interest in their specific profession or trade tends to keep them at this level. Linear careerists are eager to move up into more generalist management positions.

While the transitory and the steady state careers tend to define themselves in relatively neutral terms, the linear career has become surrounded by value-laden terms, such as winner and loser. The periods of stagnation and recession that occurred from the late 1970s onward, however, have meant that successful linear careers have become harder to obtain. Since most forecasts see limited growth for the industrialised countries for the rest of this century, it might be appropriate to place less emphasis upon this pattern being the only successful one.

The spiral career

The spiral career is most closely related to what Maslow (1943) and other motivation theorists referred to as the process of self-actualisation. The spiral careerist seeks opportunities to develop and use their various abilities and interests. While they are interested in achievement, they are more likely to compete with themselves rather than with others. Spiral careerists tend to have little concern with status and organisational career ladders, and thus their motivation is often hard for linear careerists to understand. Although spiral careerists often move through a series of occupations, it is not done as part of a struggle to get to the top of the organisation, nor is it simply a drift through convenient jobs as in the transitory career. Spiral careers tend to unfold as the individual's self-concept and interests develop and elaborate.

Thus spiral careers rarely fit neatly into simple patterns such as Super's (1942) exploration, advancement and maintenance, and are even further removed from one-off career choice models. They may well spend at least a period in what Hearn (1980) refers to as an uncareer, and because they are internally rather than externally orientated, they may even adopt a guerilla career stance within some organisations. Spiral careerists are, however, unlikely to stay for long in jobs that they find unstimulating, so that they would rarely remain in a cop-out career or a non-career. Because of the inner-directed nature of spiral careers, a considerable amount of soul-searching may need to be involved. Thus, spiral careerists may experience something like the 'passages' discussed by Sheehy (1977) or the mid-life crises described by writers such as O'Connor (1981) and Hunt & Collins (1983).

Not surprisingly, Driver (1978, 1988) suggests that individuals with a particular type of career concept will fit most comfortably into an organisation that tends to offer a compatible career path. A transitory careerist, for example, will be readily accepted by an organisation that relies upon casual, temporary and part-time staff, and will feel some compatibility within a flexible, spiral career oriented organisation. They will tend to be seen as ill-disciplined within a steady state organisation, and as inadequate in an organisation that emphasises linear careers.

A number of relevant aspects of the career concepts proposed by Driver (1978, 1988) are summarised in Table 6.3.

Emerging career management programs

In the light of the changes in organisations and careers outlined above, some organisations have been experimenting with new programs which go beyond assisting employees with the traditional career stages. A number of these programs are described below.

Managing career concepts

If the predictions that current and future changes will call for a more flexible, multi-skilled workforce and that more people are likely to experience several career transitions within a lifetime are accurate, then spiral careers may become much more common, or even the norm. If this is the case, then individuals will need to become more inner-

Table 6.3 Career concepts compared

TYPE OF CAREER CONCEPT	TRANSITORY	STEADY STATE	VERTICAL	SPIRAL
Positive features	Flexibility, little long-term commitment or training required, often available at short notice.	Sense of identity, commitment to trade or profession, depth of knowledge and experience.	Drive and determination leads to likelihood of success. Occupational flexibility and broad view. Tends to show leadership.	Search for self-development leads to flexibility, variety, lateral thinking and creativity. High tolerance for ambiguity.
Work values	Variety and independence.	Expertise and security.	Power and achievement.	Personal growth, creativity and developing others.
Potential problems	May not have developed the depth of expertise needed for some highly skilled or high-level jobs.	Lack of flexibility when faced with redundancy or restructuring. Low tolerance for ambiguity and change. May resent the recognition given to vertical careerists. May choose the wrong career and become disillusioned.	Can be overly opportunistic, and become frustrated or disillusioned if goals cannot be met or career paths disappear. Possibility of burn-out.	Lack of long-term loyalty to the organisation or the occupation. May experience periodic crises and stressful changes. Often difficult for other types of careerists to understand, and even self-understanding may be difficult. May resent the success of vertical careerists.
Possible developments	May drift into a steady state cop-out, or non-career.	May move into an advisory or supervisory role. If a poor initial choice of career is made, may slide into a cop-out career or a non-career.	Search for new areas to achieve in if previously successful or if totally blocked. May become resigned to a steady state career.	May move into an uncareer at least for a time, or may act like a guerilla careerist if forced to stay in an unsuitable organisation.
Future viability	Expected shortage of work and reduction of employment in traditional unskilled areas are minuses. Growth of alternative work patterns and short-term contracts are pluses. Mixed prognosis.	Supply and demand for the trades and professions may fluctuate rapidly. Otherwise, generally reasonable prognosis.	Likely to be few clear career paths due to downsizing and elimination of middle management positions, and fewer growing organisations. Moderate prognosis at best.	Likely to be greater opportunities for multi-skilled, flexible people. Multiple careers likely to become commonplace. Good prognosis.
Implications for the organisation	May show low work commitment. Most useful in casual or temporary positions.	Content and productive in specialist positions with little promotional opportunities. Not typically executive material, and often hard to redeploy. Need to ensure that correct career choice has been made.	Need to have viable career paths and adequate assessment and reward systems. Best suited to growing organisations.	Must offer sufficient opportunities for self-development or will lose them quickly. Often difficult to assess their past record or to understand their motivation.

Source: Based on Driver 1978; 1988 & Brousseau 1990

directed and self-aware, rather than dependent upon organisations providing them with established career ladders. Thus an important role for HRM in the future may be in managing the career culture of an organisation and its employees so that alternative career paths, such as spiral ones, become seen as more of a legitimate expectation.

Unfortunately, surveys have found that at least the majority of managers in many organisations identify most strongly with the ideal of the linear career (Brousseau 1990). However, along with 'true linears' often exist those whose primary identification is with a linear career but who secondarily identify with the spiral career concept and those who have been 'brainwashed' by social norms into expecting to achieve a linear career even though their own values are closer to the spiral career orientation. Brousseau (1990) reports that some success has been obtained in using career awareness training and career counselling to assist both of these groups adjust to a reality of limited opportunity to reach the top level in an organisation. This training consists of an assessment of individuals' ideal and possibly past and expected future career orientation and work values.

Even though models such as Hearn's (1980) and Driver's (1978, 1988) provide useful additions to our understanding of careers, they still tend to focus mainly on the careers of what have traditionally been dominate groups in the industrialised countries. As shown in the Managing diversity discussion, although some initiatives aimed at career development for members of other groups have been reported, much still remains to be done to develop models of careers that will aid in the understanding and facilitating of careers for an increasingly diverse workforce.

Managing diversity

A growing trend in countries such as Australia, New Zealand and the USA has been increasing recognition of the need to develop more varied approaches to management so that employees from all backgrounds are encouraged to contribute effectively to the organisation (Rynes & Rosen 1995; Sauers 1993; Sloane & Deves 1995). In the USA, Gottfredson (1992) has described a number of initiatives taken by organisations to foster career development among minority groups. Pacific Bell, for example, conducts 6-day Efficacy Seminars, which are designed to assist minority employees to become more competitive for promotion and it has implemented a 2-year accelerated development track for managers from minority groups. Xerox has attempted to expand its pool of promotable women and minority group members by assigning them to pivotal jobs to gain essential experience and by supporting a variety of networking groups (Gottfredson 1992, p. 284).

One common innovation has been the creation of diversity training programs. Rynes & Rosen (1995, p. 248), for example, reported that around three-quarters of companies in the USA have or plan to begin such programs. They found very favourable responses in terms of immediate reactions to diversity training, but generally negative responses in terms of the extent to which the programs seemed to have any long-term effect (Rynes & Rosen 1995, p. 264). The major problem was seen to be a lack of real support for change on the part of management.

A consistent concern has been the slower progression rates of females than of males, particularly into top management positions (Hede & Ralston 1993; Limerick, Heywood &

Ehrich 1995). Morrison, White & Van Velsor (1987) originated the term 'glass ceiling' to refer to the finding that, in spite of the removal of visible barriers such as discriminatory polices, women were still under-represented in higher level positions, as if some invisible barrier was restraining them. In a recent report, Carmody (1995) chronicles the steps taken by one major Australian corporation in developing career development practices more suitable for female employees. Studies reported by Still, Guerin & Chia (1994), however, found that women's proportional representation in junior, middle and senior level management positions in the private sector in Australia had actually declined over the 1984 through 1992 period.

Some writers have also suggested that women often have different, although equally valid, perspectives on careers. Pringle (1994, p. 135), for example suggests that a feminist perspective on careers includes lateral as well as horizontal movements, acceptance of temporary plateauing to coincide with a time of life with greater non-work commitments and a general recognition and acceptance that many women's careers are cyclic or spiralling rather than simply linear. Marshall (1989) has contrasted an 'agency' perspective on careers, which seeks control, certainty and predictability with a 'communion' perspective which emphasises flexibility, openness to opportunities and right timing as the person and appropriate environment meet. These latter characteristics appeared frequently in her interviews with women who had satisfying and organisationally successful careers (Marshall 1989, p. 288).

Overall, while a number of initiatives have been reported and some analysis of differing perspectives on careers have taken place, as Sloane & Deves (1995) suggest, there still appear to be more questions than answers in the area of diversity management.

Work–family interface programs

Balancing work and family demands has become an increasingly important organisational issue (Grover & Crooker 1995; Smith 1992). The 'traditional' family with a husband who is the breadwinner, a wife who is a full-time home maker, and two children is coming to constitute a minority of households. In Australia, for example, Smith (1992, p. 21) reported that only 35 per cent of two-parent families now fit the traditional image of the wife as the primary homemaker and the husband as the sole income-earner and that in an estimated 60 per cent of two-parent families with dependent children, both parents are in the paid workforce. With the dramatic influx of women into the work force and the growing number of dual-career and two-wage couples, individuals are finding it difficult to avoid conflict between work and family areas. One suggestion, for example, has been the establishment of separate career tracks for those who have major child-care responsibilities (sometimes referred to as the 'mommy track'), so that these employees can work part-time or share jobs during this period (Butruille 1990; Schwartz 1989). Since work and family have been treated as 'separate worlds' in the past, however, many people feel that conflict is not supposed to happen; that they are the only people experiencing such problems and that the organisation will not be impressed if family problems are causing poor job performance.

In fact, career development can now be viewed as a family affair. Family-friendly organisations provide a setting for employees to discuss work–family issues and to identify coping strategies that can reduce the conflict. Thus a variety of family-friendly policies have been introduced. Grover & Crooker (1995, p. 272), for example, suggest that family-friendly policies tend to include: flexible work scheduling (e.g. part-time work, job-sharing and variable starting and quitting times); family-leave policies allowing periods away from work for employees to take care of family matters; and child care assistance. In their study, Grover & Crooker (1995, p. 283) found that employees had a greater commitment to their organisation if it offered family-responsive policies, regardless of the extent to which the employee might personally benefit from these policies. In another recent study, Moore (1996) found that 75 per cent of her sample of Australian organisations were seen as family friendly, with the average organisation providing nine out of nineteen family-friendly work practices considered.

Child-care assistance

The provision of various forms of child-care assistance is one area of family-friendly policies that has attracted considerable attention in Australia from governments, unions and employers (Ruzek 1990). Ruzek (1990) reported that a wide range of Australian organisations are now providing child-care programs. While some larger organisations are establishing their own child-care centres, others are taking advantage of a growing number of external companies which lease child-care places to organisations on an as-needed basis (Ruzek 1990). Kossek & Nichol (1992) estimated that about 12 per cent of organisations in the USA with at least 100 employees offered child-care benefits. In a study of child-care centre users, they found that users were more likely to hold positive attitudes towards managing their work and family responsibilities and were less likely to experience problems with care. They concluded that child-care benefits may be viewed as creating a favourable climate conducive to enabling good performance by alleviating problems and allowing employees to focus on their jobs (Kossek & Nichol 1992, p. 502). Butruille (1990) reported that in one major American company men made up nearly half of those using or planning to use child-care assistance, and that 25 per cent of men and 50 per cent of women had considered seeking an employer who offered more work or family flexibility.

Perhaps the most significant aspect of work–family programs is the recognition that work and family life are interdependent, that it is important to both society and to work organisations that they be interdependent, and that family issues can affect work performance and career development (Smith 1992).

Expatriate careers

As discussed further in Chapter 13 on International HRM, for many organisations, being competitive now means being globally competitive. One impact of this internationalisation on careers is the growing use of **expatriates** to run the businesses overseas. Stone (1991) reported a study of expatriate selection and failure which covered 60 major Australian, New Zealand, British and American organisations with operations in South Asia. Although there was some variation in opinions, seven criteria were ranked as highest in importance in selecting expatriates by all groups: ability to adapt, technical competence, spouse and family adaptability, human relations skills, desire to serve overseas, previous overseas experience, and understanding of host country culture (Stone 1991, p. 10). The leading causes of expatriate failure were: the manager's inability to adapt; the spouse's inability to adapt; inability to cope with larger responsibilities; other family-related problems; the manager's personality; and lack of motivation to work overseas.

Given the level of problems and failures reported in this and other studies, offering suitable support for expatriates would seem to be necessary to encourage individuals to become expatriates and for overseas postings to be successful. It appears from a recent survey, however, that Australian organisations are lagging far behind their counterparts in the USA in this regard (Davidson & Kinzel 1995). Problem areas identified included the nature and limited extent of training offered for both managers and their families. In addition, while 70 per cent offered career development and repatriation planning, only 52 per cent rated their own efforts as sufficient (Davidson & Kinzel 1995, p. 112). In another study, Pierce & Delahaye (1996) found that the increasing proportion of dual-career couples also frequently made relocation more difficult, with a growing resistance to relocations that did not provide career opportunities for both partners. Despite difficulties such as these, it is likely that the use of expatriates will continue to grow, so that more effort will need to be spent in the development of viable career paths for expatriates.

Managing change

While most organisational changes can have some effect on the career paths that are available, the trend for large-scale retrenchments under the labels of 'downsizing' and 'delayering' are perhaps the changes that have affected careers the most. O'Rourke (1995) suggests that Australian companies have downsized proportionally more than those in any other OECD country, with some two million Australians retrenched in the 1989–95 period. In an Australian survey conducted every two years since 1988, economic reasons for downsizing were once the majority (*HRMonthly* 1995). In this series of surveys, 39 per cent cited 'economic reasons' for terminating staff in 1988, which rose to 54 per cent and 59 per cent in 1990 and 1992, but fell to 15 per cent in 1994. 'Efficiency restructuring', however, was given as the most common reason for terminating staff in 1994, and more than half of the companies involved expected to terminate as many staff in the future as they had in 1994.

These efforts at improving performance through shedding staff are not always successful. O'Rourke (1995), for example, reported that of American companies that had downsized, 80 per cent found morale had lowered, two-thirds showed no immediate increase in productivity, less than half saw an improvement in short term profit, 30 per cent found that costs had increased, and 22 per cent discovered they had eliminated the wrong people.

Stratford (1996) noted these problems and emphasised the importance of maintaining a focus upon business strategy and communicating continually and effectively in any change effort such as downsizing. In terms of career issues, he recommended: realising that making change happen means making new 'contracts' with employees, change management initiatives to retain employee commitment, career profiling services to ensure more effective internal redeployments and the provision of outplacement services for the unavoidable casualties (Stratford 1996, p. 20).

Outplacement counselling

The retrenchments discussed in the Managing change discussion have often had a major effect on the careers of those involved, and a growing trend has been to provide outplacement counselling to those affected. *HRMonthly* (1995), for example, reports that only 15 per cent of executives and 8 per cent of managers were offered such counselling in 1988 compared to 65 per cent of executives and 47 per cent of managers in 1994. Stratford (1994) expects this percentage to continue to grow, noting that over 90 per cent of the Fortune 500 companies in North America regularly use outplacement services. He predicts: 'The role of outplacement in easing the pain of organisational change—in putting some professional skill and humanity into the agonising process of constant structural adjustment—will become more vital and more widely appreciated' (Stratford 1994, p. 19). Critchley (1996) suggests that the key learnings for many terminated employees include developing the skills needed to thrive on change, learning to manage their own careers and acquiring strategic competencies that organisations need. While employees made redundant may initially want to seek a similar job in the same industry, Stratford (1994) reports that, following outplacement counselling, moves such as retraining for a different function or industry sector, relocation to another state or overseas or shifting to self-employment by setting up one's own business, taking up a franchise or becoming a consultant have all become commonplace.

Sharing the responsibility: launching your career

Although many organisations provide at least some support in career planning for employees, by actively managing your own career, you will do better than by not managing it. 'Better' can be measured by any standard you choose—job security, self-esteem, growth, comfort, success in climbing to the top of the organisation, or salary level. By planning and managing, you will increase your chances of obtaining whatever you realistically identify as most important. Dalton (1989, p. 107), for example, at the end of a review of various models of career development concluded: 'Specialists cannot do career development for individuals, only individuals can do the hard work, make the choices, develop the relationships, and take the chances that will make the biggest differences in the way their careers develop'. Fundamental to this is the personal appraisal. Personal appraisal (or career self-appraisal) is really the basis of career planning activities. It consists of identifying the strengths and weaknesses an individual possesses (Dalton 1989).

Conducting a personal appraisal

This involves taking a personal inventory of the following:

- values
- goals
- skills
- strengths and weaknesses
- objectives.

Do this step by completing the career self-appraisal exercise shown in Figure 6.4.

Steps
1 List five goals you have for each of three categories—career, affiliations, and personal fulfillment (or create other categories).
2 Go back and rate them (1–little importance through 5–great importance). Which list has the most 4s and 5s?
3 Merge the three lists and rank all fifteen goals in order of importance to you.

4 Select your top goal and describe it on the top of the second sheet. Then, discuss it in terms of:
  a personal strengths and weaknesses
  b obstacles to prevent achieving the goal
  c strategies to circumvent obstacles
  d are the goals realistic, attainable, and measurable?
  e what are the rewards for achieving the goal?
  f steps for achieving the goal (do this for all your goals).

	Goal rating
Career Goals, e.g. become president by 45; become vice-president by 35, etc.	(1,2,3,4 or 5)

Career Goals, e.g. become president by 45; become vice-president by 35, etc.
1 _____ _____
2 _____ _____
3 _____ _____
4 _____ _____
5 _____ _____

Affiliation/Interpersonal, e.g. family, friends, clubs, group members, etc.
1 _____ _____
2 _____ _____
3 _____ _____
4 _____ _____
5 _____ _____

Personal fulfillment/achievements, e.g. master the piano, run a marathon, get an MBA degree, etc.
1 _____ _____
2 _____ _____
3 _____ _____
4 _____ _____
5 _____ _____

Goal ranking

Please list (in order of importance) the fifteen goals from above
1 _____ _____
2 _____ _____
3 _____ _____
4 _____ _____
5 _____ _____
6 _____ _____
7 _____ _____
8 _____ _____
9 _____ _____
10 _____ _____
11 _____ _____
12 _____ _____
13 _____ _____
14 _____ _____
15 (least important) _____ _____

Take one important goal, restate it here, and then continue by discussing your personal strengths and weaknesses.

_____
_____

Personal strengths in relation to attaining the goal
1
2
3
4
5

Personal weaknesses in relation to attaining the goal
1
2
3
4
5

Obstacles in the way to goal attainment	Strategy to overcome obstacles
1	1
2	2
3	3
4	4
5	5

Rewards for achieving the goal (rank in terms of value)
1
2
3
4
5

Indicators that you have achieved the goal (short and long term)
1
2
3
4
5

Steps for achieving the goal (starting now)	Time deadline
1	
2	
3	
4	
5	

Figure 6.4 Career self-appraisal

Source: Schuler 1995, pp. 136–37

Identifying types of jobs, organisations and industries

Because the job or jobs you choose will have such an impact on your life, it is important to carefully analyse what you want from your first job and your first organisation. You may want to start by first identifying industries or sectors in which you may want to work. Then within these industries or any others, you next need to gather information on particular organisations. You can gain direct information through summer work experience, internships, and part-time work; these are valuable ways to gain exposure to new organisations. Although some work experiences may be boring, you need to consider them as learning experiences, ways of getting to know yourself and the world of work better. Other sources of information are newspapers and professional magazines, university placement offices, libraries, direct mail, job-search firms, friends and family.

In thinking about the types of jobs, organisations, and industries, weigh the relative value to you of such things as more salary and fewer benefits versus less salary and more benefits and more opportunities to learn new skills.

There are many types of jobs to be considered, including self-employment and the more traditional entry-level jobs in larger organisations that are the first step in a series through promotions to senior management positions. Within larger organisations, these traditional paths are available in many functional areas such as human resource management, marketing, manufacturing, and finance.

Preparing for organisational life

It is one thing to know the type of job you might want and the type of industry or organisation in which you want to work, but it's an entirely different thing to know the realities of life and work in that organisation. Two facets of organisational life that you should be aware of are organisational expectation and disappointment. Most organisations expect a new employee to have the basic competencies to learn the job when assisted by training and to accept the way things are done within the organisation, including any negative aspects about the job.

For example, it is common for newcomers to the organisation to be initially assigned to a lower status or probationary job category for a certain period. They may also find that they are given more menial duties, less privileges and greater scrutiny than are longer-term employees (Meglino, Denisi & Ravlin 1993). While this may be reasonable from an organisation's point of view, turnover rates among new hires are frequently high due to unmet expectations. As noted earlier, some organisations have tried to overcome this clash of expectations through realistic job previews and realistic orientation training programs (Waung 1995). Even without such programs, however, individuals can do a number of things to facilitate successful organisational entry including the following:

Develop self-awareness

This activity, known also as self-assessment, involves an inventory of values, goals, skills, strengths and weaknesses, and objectives. Individuals must develop an awareness of themselves and their preferred work environment. You can use Figure 6.4 for this purpose.

Identify prospective employers

Because the job or jobs individuals choose have such an impact on their lives, they must analyse carefully what they want from their first job and their first organisation. Information about organisational realities can be gathered through summer work experience, internships, and part-time work.

Participate effectively in job interviews

'Selling' oneself to prospective employers requires a high degree of self-awareness. The interview is the individual's chance to create a favourable impression, emphasise past accomplishments, demonstrate initiative and leadership through extracurricular activities, and practice interviewing skills (perhaps through information interviews). However, the job interview should also be seen as 'a two-way street'. It should offer a chance to gather additional information about the organisation and the details of the position involved.

Choose a suitable organisation. Although choosing the best job offer may be more art than science, a career balance sheet can help. This involves listing the positive and negative aspects of each offer, making a separate balance sheet for each one. Individuals should consider how each aspect affects them and others such as their spouse, friends, or family. Balance sheets assist the decision-making process because they organise the information systematically.

Summary

One key idea of this chapter is that planning is a vital function to any successful organisation. Human resource planning by definition, however, is a derived function. That is, before an organisation can plan for its people needs, it must know something about its organisational goals and strategy. Thus, human resource planning takes on strategic importance because it requires that human resource strategy and objectives be linked to organisational strategy and objectives.

Human resource planning typically involves four phases: (1) forecasting supply and demand of labor, (2) estimating surpluses or shortages of people based on organisational strategy and objectives, (3) planning specific human resource activities based on Phase 2 forecasts—for example, recruitment if shortages are expected, layoffs if surpluses are expected, and (4) evaluating both the implementation and administration of programs.

However, it was suggested that human resource planning should itself be viewed in a more strategic and contingent way, and three alternatives to the long-range, detailed human resource planning approach outlined above were described. One of these is continuing use of the older Staff Replacement Approach, wherein staff are recruited or promoted when a vacancy occurs, unless there are obvious reasons for not doing so, with little if any attempt at long-term or formal human resource planning. A second option is short-term Human Resource strategy, where HR-related issues are seen as vital, but the future is too uncertain to place much faith in detailed long-range human resource planning. Speed of response and flexibility are emphasised and HRM issues are identified in reaction to rapidly evolving threats and opportunities. The third option is use of a vision-driven human resource development approach, often as the result of an apparent need for relatively major shifts in employee attitudes, skills and behaviours along with changes in the culture which pervades the organisation. Although also long term in its orientation, it is driven by vision or a sense of mission and lacks the detail and specific targets characteristic of the kind of detailed human resource planning described earlier.

Roadblocks exist that increase the challenge and difficulty of human resource planning. A primary barrier is the lack of top management support. Because human resource planning is derived from corporate strategy and objectives, this support is necessary as is the involvement of the human resources manager in corporate-level planning.

Secondly, this chapter has also traced the evolution of the field of career development and outlined a number of the models that have been proposed. The general argument throughout has been that newer types of career patterns and succeeding views of career development do not simply replace older patterns or views, but instead add to them.

The trait-factor, career choice view is still relevant, for example, when considering initial career choice, when selecting individuals to fit particular positions, and for those likely to desire a steady state type of career. The individually oriented view contributed a useful emphasis upon the individual's motivation, satisfaction and development, and career development models such as the one proposed by Super (1942) are still applicable in the case of linear careers. The associated emphasis upon individual career counselling led to the development of valuable services, which are likely to become even more widely needed in an uncertain and rapidly changing future. The systems view is a useful one for moderate to large-sized organisations that seek to grow or that can foresee changes in their environment. This approach also helps to establish the kind of career paths that attract linear careerists.

Thus, the future is seen as needing additional conceptions rather than the complete discard of these earlier approaches. Although no attempt was made to establish and justify a complete future scenario, it was suggested that many writers predict rapid and extensive changes, the further growth of alternatives to permanent full-time work, and the need for a larger percentage of flexible, multi-skilled workers who can expect a number of different career paths during their lifetime.

The four basic career patterns suggested by Driver (1978, 1988) were seen as the best existing attempt to classify current and likely future career types. Using Driver's (1978, 1988) typology, the expected future trends cited above may lead to an increase in the availability of transitory careers, fluctuation in the availability of steady state careers, reduced opportunities for vertical careers, and a considerable growth in the possibilities for spiral careers.

Hearn's (1980) four anarchic career types were also seen to be useful descriptions, especially in terms of possible kinds of reactions when there is a poor fit between an individual's desired career path and what the organisation offers.

The career typologies suggested by both of these writers should be useful to those involved in selecting employees, in organisational change, and in career counselling and planning. Ideally, preferred individual career paths as well as organisational receptiveness to these paths should be assessed. The degree of applicant–organisational match could be considered as part of the selection process, proposed organisational changes could be compared with staff career expectations, and career counsellors could help individuals to clarify their career expectations and to identify occupations and organisations likely to provide compatible paths. An enlarged understanding of alternative career types should also be of use to those undergoing mid-life crises or life stage passages.

Those in the HRM field have an important role to play in this pathfinding process. In most organisations, HRM practitioners are actively involved in the areas of recruitment, selection, staff appraisal, promotions, transfers and redundancies, in addition to any direct responsibilities they may have for career development. In all of these areas, an understanding of the various possible career types described in this chapter are important. Thus, a greater understanding of the complexities of the career development process should impact favourably upon most aspects of the HRM practitioner's role.

questions for discussion and review

1 In what circumstances is a major emphasis upon human resource planning likely to be worthwhile for an organisation?

2 Many Australian organisations are experiencing unprecedented levels of change in their environment. What effects are these changes likely to have on each of the four phases of human resource planning?

3 What kind of arguments are likely to convince senior managers to invest in human resource planning?

4 Responsibility for career management is shared by the individual and the organisation. What can each party gain from career management programs?
5 What can managers do to help keep employees motivated in the organisational entry, early career, midcareer and late career stages?
6 It can be suggested that careers as we have known them in the past will hardly exist in the 21th century. Why might this be so? What implications would this have for those hoping to enter the workforce?
7 What are likely to be some of the major effects of the growth in numbers of network organisations on human resource planning and career management programs?
8 It could be argued that the current changes in the Australian business environment make human resource planning an impossibility for many organisations. Discuss both sides of this view.
9 How can an organisation offer additional career opportunities to women and members of minority groups without disadvantaging members of other groups?
10 How can an organisation planning to significantly reduce the number of layers of its management (delayering) ensure its remaining staff have viable career paths?

case study

As discussed in this chapter, formalised mentoring programs are a relatively new innovation designed to provide personal career-related advice and support to assist employees who would not normally be part of an established network. Thus they may be particularly useful when targeted at women employees and members of minority groups within the organisation. One Australian company which has recently trialled such a program is QBE Insurance. Two participants in this program, one a mentor and the other a mentoree, describe their experience of it below.

Recognising the hidden talents

BY KAREN MCGHEE

Terry King jumped at the chance to join a facilitated mentoring program with her employer of 10 years, QBE Insurance.

'I saw it as a wonderful opportunity to learn more, gain better networking skills and find out what options were available within the company', she says.

King has moved a lot inside QBE for a long time, but mostly sideways. She is in a senior clerical position and believes that guidance may open opportunities upwards.

She's found that her mentor for the past six months, Bryan Riddell, QBEs manager for performance support, has not so much taught her *new* skills as shown her that she already has talents and abilities she isn't exploiting. 'For example, Bryan made me realise that I already had a very good business network but I wasn't using it to its full capacity', she says.

'It has definitely given me more self-confidence in my abilities and a lot more energy. I now know there are more places I can go within this company. The mentoring relationship has helped me realise my potential and that I've got more opportunities than I was aware of'.

Riddell also has gained in terms of improving his own personnel skills. 'Wherever two people interact, you find they both have something to learn if they listen', he says.

If it's successful, the mentoring role brings a great deal of satisfaction. 'It's quite exciting that someone sees an angle to their potential that they didn't know was there and that they've found that angle through the mentoring relationship'.

Riddell says QBE is very happy with the impact of facilitated mentoring. QBE has been trialing the strategy for the past 18 months with women employees as its primary target and plans to broaden it throughout the organisation. Mentoring sits well with the company's general ethos on staff development, particularly the way it 'grows' its manager.

Riddell says there aren't too many gains that the company can measure at the moment but they are likely to emerge in the longer term. 'For example (the pilot program) has already identified some talent that we may need in a couple of months' time and which may otherwise have been overlooked. I believe also that (formal mentoring) is just another way of maximising people's talents and that we are getting benefits from that straightaway'.

King says Riddell is an easy mentor—accessible, encouraging and letting her know that, although their relationship is formally coming to an end, he will continue to be available for her.

Source: *Sydney Morning Herald*, 24 February 1996, p. 1E.

Questions
1 What skills does a manager need to be a good mentor, and how can these skills be acquired?
2 How could a mentoring program such as the QBE one be related to human resource planning?
3 What other career development programs should an organisation have in place to support a formal mentoring program?

Resources

Academy of Management Executive (1996), vol. 10, no. 4, special issue: careers in the 21st century.

Arthur, M. B., Hall, D. T. & Lawrence, B. S. (1989), *Handbook of Career Theory*, Cambridge University Press, Cambridge.

Brousseau, K. R. (1990), 'Career dynamics in the baby boom and baby bust era', *Journal of Organisational Change Management*, vol. 3, no. 3, pp. 46–58.

Buller, P. F. (1988), 'Successful partnerships: HR and strategic planning at eight top firms', *Organisational Dynamics*, vol. 17 no. 2, pp. 27–43.

Carmody, H. (1995), 'EEO: From policy to practice', in G. L. O'Neill & R. Kramar (eds), *Australian Human Resources Management: Current Trends in Management Practice*, Pitman, Melbourne, pp. 243–51.

Kane, R. L. & Stanton, S. (1994), 'Human resource planning in a changing environment', in A. R. Nankervis & R. L. Compton (eds), *Readings in Strategic Human Resource Management*, Nelson, Melbourne, pp. 209–33.

New articles on human resource planning and on career development continually appear. Two worthwhile resources for new articles in these areas are the periodicals *Human Resource Planning* and the *Journal of Vocational Behavior*.

References

Anderson, G. & Ford, L. (1994), 'Nominal group technique and the formulation of competency standards', *Asia Pacific Journal of Human Resources*, vol. 30, no. 4, pp. 61–73.

Andrewartha, G. (1994), 'Certainty vanishes from career planning', *HRMonthly*, April, p. 23.

Arthur, M. B., Hall, D. T. & Lawrence, B. S. (1989), 'Generating new directions in career theory: The case for a transdisciplinary approach', in M. B. Arthur, D. T. Hall & B. S. Lawrence (eds), *Handbook of Career Theory*, Cambridge University Press, Cambridge, pp. 7–25.

Aubrey, R. F. (1977), 'Historical development of guidance and counselling and implications for the future', *Personnel and Guidance Journal*, vol. 55, pp. 288–95.

Bardwick, J. (1986), *The Plateauing Trap*, AMACOM, New York.

Barton, P. (1981), 'A perspective on work', in J. Wilkes (ed.), *The Future of Work*, Allen & Unwin Australia, Sydney, pp. 49–61.

Betz, R. E., Fitzgerald, L. F. & Hill, R. E. (1989), 'Trait-factor theories: Traditional cornerstone of career theory', in M. B. Arthur, D. T. Hall & B. S. Lawrence (eds), *Handbook of Career Theory*, Cambridge University Press, Cambridge, pp. 26–40.

Bowen, D. E. & Greiner, L. E. (1986), 'Moving from production to service in human resources management', *Organisational Dynamics*, vol. 15, no. 1, pp. 34–53.

Bowey, A. M., Jefferies, B. J., Porter, B. & Green, G. J. L. (1977), 'Human resource planning: An integrated approach to manpower planning and corporate planning', *Personnel Management*, Winter, pp. 32–39.

Boynton, A. C. & Victor, B. (1991), 'Beyond flexibility: Building and managing the dynamically stable organisation', *California Management Review*, vol. 34, no. 1, pp. 53–66.

Brousseau, K. R. (1990), 'Career dynamics in the baby boom and baby bust era', *Journal of Organisational Change Management*, vol. 3, no. 3, pp. 46–58.

Brush, V. J. & Nardoni, R. (1992), 'Integrated data supports AT&Ts succession planning', *Personnel Journal*, September, pp. 103–109.

Buller, P. F. (1988), 'Successful partnerships: HR and strategic planning at eight top firms', *Organisational Dynamics*, vol. 17 no. 2, pp. 27–43.

Butruille, S. G. (1990), 'Corporate caretaking', *Training and Development Journal*, April, pp. 49–55.

Byrne, J. A., Brandt, R. & Port, O. (1993), 'The virtual corporation', *Business Week*, 8 February, pp. 98–102.

Carmody, H. (1995), 'EEO: From policy to practice', in G. L. O'Neill & R. Kramar (eds), *Australian Human Resources Management: Current Trends in Management Practice*, Pitman, Melbourne, pp. 243–51.

Caro, P. C. (1983), 'Counselling in industry: A selected review of the literature', *Personnel Psychology*, vol. 36, no. 1, pp. 1–18.

Chao, G. T., Walz, P. M. & Gardner, P. D. (1992), 'Formal and informal mentorships: A comparison on mentoring functions and contrast with nonmentored counterparts', *Personnel Psychology*, vol. 45, no. 3, pp. 619–36.

Critchley, R. (1996), 'New paradigm aims for "sustainable employability" ', *HRMonthly*, April, pp. 22–23.

Dalton, G. W. (1989), 'Developmental views of careers in organisations', in M. B. Arthur, D. T. Hall, & B. S. Lawrence (eds), *Handbook of Career Theory*, Cambridge University Press, Cambridge, pp. 89–109.

Davidson, P. & Kinzel, E. (1995), 'Supporting the expatriate: A survey of Australian management practice', *Asia Pacific Journal of Human Resources*, vol. 33, no. 3, pp. 105–16.
Department of Employment, Education and Training (1991), *Australia's Workforce in the Year 2001*, Australian Government Publishing Service, Canberra.
Driver, M. J. (1978), 'Career concepts and career management in organisations', in C. L. Cooper (ed.), *Behavioural Problems in Organisations*, Prentice-Hall, Englewood Cliffs, NJ, pp. 77–139.
—— (1988), 'Careers: A review of personal and organisational research', in C. L. Cooper & I. T. Robertson (eds), *International Review of Industrial and Organisational Psychology—1988*, John Wiley & Sons, Chichester, UK, pp. 245–77.
Dunphy, D. & Mills, J. A. (1982), 'Human resource planning for major projects in Australia', *General Engineering Transactions*, pp. 61–64.
Dyer, L. (1982), 'Human resource planning', in K. M. Rowland & G. R. Ferris (eds), *Personnel Management*, Allyn & Bacon, Boston, pp. 52–77.
Fandt, P. M. (1988), 'Linking business strategy and career management', in G. R. Ferris & K. M. Rowland (eds), *Human Resources Management: Perspectives and Issues*, Allyn & Bacon, Boston, pp. 56–63.
Fitzgerald, l. (1986), 'Career counselling women: Principles, procedures, and problems', in Z. Leibowitz & D. Lea (eds), *Adult Career Development: Concepts, Issues and Practices*, National Career Development Association, Alexandria, Va., pp. 116–31.
Frantzreb, R. B. (1981), 'Human resource planning: Forecasting manpower needs', *Personnel Journal*, November, pp. 850–57.
Gottfredson, L. S. (1992), 'Dilemmas in developing diversity programs', in S. E. Jackson & Associates, *Diversity in the Workplace: Human Resources Initiatives*, Guilford, New York, pp. 279–305.
Greer, C. R. & Armstrong, D. (1980), 'Human resource forecasting and planning: A state-of-the-art investigation', *Human Resource Planning*, vol. 3, pp. 67–78.
Grover, S. L. & Crooker, K. J. (1995), 'Who appreciates family-responsive human resource policies: The impact of family-friendly policies on the organisational attachment of parents and non-parents', *Personnel Psychology*, vol. 48, no. 2, pp. 271–88.
Hearn, G., Smith, B. & Southey, G. (1996), 'Defining generic professional competencies in Australia: Towards a framework for professional development', *Asia Pacific Journal of Human Resources*, vol. 34, no. 1, pp. 44–62.
Hearn, J. (1980), 'Anarchic careerists rule, O.K.?', *Personnel Management*, vol. 12, pp. 37–39.
Hede, A. & Ralston, D. (1993), 'Managerial career progression and aspiration: Evidence of a "glass ceiling"'? *International Journal of Employment Studies*, vol. 1, no. 2, pp. 253–82.
HRMonthly (1995), 'Management and executive job losses will continue, survey finds', *HRMonthly*, April, pp. 16–17.
Hunt, J. W. & Collins, R. R. (1983), *Managers in Mid-Career Crisis*, Wellington Lane Press, Sydney.
Huselid, M. A. (1993), 'The impact of environmental volatility on human resource planning and strategic human resource management', *Human Resource Planning*, vol. 16, no. 3, pp. 35–51.
Jones, B. (1982), *Sleepers, Wake!: Technology and the Future of Work*, Oxford University Press, Melbourne.

Kane, R. L. (1994), 'Training and staff development in Australian organisations: Quick fix or long term investment', *International Journal of Employment Studies*, vol. 2, no. 1, pp. 158–69.

Kane, R. L., Abraham, M. & Crawford, J. (1990), *Training and Staff Development Strategies and Organisational Characteristics: Results of an Australian Survey*, Faculty of Business Working Paper Series, University of Technology, Sydney.

Kane, R. L. & Stanton, S. (1994), 'Human resource planning in a changing environment', in A. R. Nankervis & R. L. Compton (eds), *Readings in Strategic Human Resource Management*, Nelson, Melbourne, pp. 209–33.

Karpin, D. S. (1995), *Enterprising Nation: Renewing Australia's Managers to Meet the Challenges of the Asia-Pacific Century*, Report of the Industry Task Force on Leadership and Management Skills, Australian Government Publishing Service, Canberra.

Kossek, E. E. & Nichol, V. (1992), 'The effects of on-site child care on employee attitudes and performance', *Personnel Psychology*, vol. 45, no. 3, pp. 485–509.

Kram, K. E. (1983), 'Phases of the mentor relationship' *Academy of Management Journal*, vol. 26, pp. 608–25.

Kramar, R. (1986), 'The personnel practitioner and affirmative action', *Human Resource Management Australia*, vol. 24, pp. 38–45.

Lado, A. & Wilson, M. C. (1994), 'Human resource systems and sustained competitive advantage: A competency-based perspective', *Academy of Management Review*, vol. 19, no. 4, pp. 699–727.

Lang, G. (1976), *Australian Employee Manpower Study, 1976*, Management Development Centre, Royal Melbourne Institute of Technology, Melbourne.

Lansbury, R. D. (1986), 'Organisational change resulting from advances in technology', *Human Resource Management Australia*, vol. 22, pp. 22–30.

—— (1992), 'Managing change in a challenging environment', *Asia Pacific Journal of Human Resources*, vol. 30, no. 1, pp. 16–28.

Leibowitz, Z. B., Kaye, B. L. & Farren, C. R. (1990), 'What to do about career gridlock', *Training and Development Journal*, vol. 44, no. 4, p. 32.

Limerick, B., Heywood, E. & Ehrich, L. (1995), 'Women-only management courses: Are they appropriate in the 1990s?', *Asia Pacific Journal of Human Resources*, vol. 33, no. 2, pp. 81–92.

Limerick, D. (1992), 'The shape of the new organisation: Implications for human resource management', *Asia Pacific Journal of Human Resources*, vol. 30, no. 1, pp. 38–52.

Mackey, C. B. (1981), 'Human resource planning: A four-phased approach', *Management Review*, vol. 70, no. 5, pp. 17–22.

Manzini, A. O. (1985), 'Human resource planning and forecasting', in W. R. Tracey (ed.), *Human Resources Management and Development Handbook*, AMACOM, New York, pp. 507–29.

Margerison, C. & Smeed, B. (1984), 'Career choices and career paths', *Human Resource Management Australia*, vol. 22, pp. 22–30.

Marshall, J. (1989), 'Re-visioning career concepts: A feminist invitation', in M. B. Arthur, D. T. Hall & B. S. Lawrence (eds), *Handbook of Career Theory*, Cambridge University Press, Cambridge, pp. 275–91.

Maslow, A. H. (1943), 'A theory of human motivation', *Psychological Review*, vol. 50, pp. 370–91.

McGregor, D. (1960), *The Human Side of Enterprise*, McGraw-Hill, New York.

Meglino, B. M., Denisi, A. S. & Ravlin, E. C. (1993), 'Effects of previous job exposure and subsequent job status on the functioning of a realistic job preview', *Personnel Psychology*, vol. 46, no. 4, pp. 803–22.

Michelson, G. (1994), 'The effect of career stage on the work attitudes of union officials', *International Journal of Employment Studies*, vol. 2, no. 2, pp. 289–304.

Midgley, D. (1990), *Interim Report on the Benchmark Study of Management Development in Australian Private Enterprises*, National Board of Employment, Education and Training, Australian Government Publishing Service, Canberra.

Miles, R. E. & Snow, C. C. (1978), *Organisational Structure, Strategy, and Process*, McGraw-Hill, New York.

—— (1984), 'Designing strategic human resources systems', *Organisational Dynamics*, vol. 13, no. 1, pp. 36–52.

Miller, E. L. & Burack, E. H. (1981), 'A status report on human resource planning from the perspective of human resource planners', *Human Resource Planning*, vol. 4, no. 2, pp. 99–106.

Mintzberg, H. (1993), 'The pitfalls of strategic planning', *California Management Review*, vol. 36, no. 1, pp. 32–47.

Moore, T. (1996), 'Work and family: A balancing act', *Asia Pacific Journal of Human Resources*, vol. 34, no. 2, pp. 119–25.

Morrison, A., White, R. P. & Van Velsor, E. (1987), *Breaking the Glass Ceiling*, Addison-Wesley, Reading, Mass.

Mukhi, S. K. (1982), 'Leadership paths and profiles: Part 1: A survey of Australian chief executives', *Human Resource Management Australia*, vol. 20, pp. 20–23.

Nkomo, S. M. (1980), 'Stage three in personnel administration: Strategic human resources management', *Personnel*, July–August, pp. 69–77.

—— (1988), 'The theory and practice of HR planning: The gap still remains', in G. R. Ferris & K. M. Rowland (eds), *Human Resource Management: Perspectives and Issues*, Allyn & Bacon, Boston, pp. 30–37.

O'Connor, P. (1981), *Understanding the Mid Life Crisis*, Sun Books, South Melbourne.

O'Rourke, G. (1995), 'How to rebuild and preserve trust after the layoffs', *HRMonthly*, April, pp. 17–18.

Patrickson, M. & Hartman, L. (1992), 'Workforce participation choices of older males', *Asia Pacific Journal of Human Resources*, vol. 30, no. 3, pp. 40–48.

Peters, T. (1990), 'Prometheus barely unbound', *Academy of Management Executive*, vol. 4, no. 4, pp. 70–84.

Pierce, J. & Delahaye, B. L. (1996), 'Snakes and ladders: Relocation and the dual career couple', *Journal of the Australian and New Zealand Academy of Management*, vol. 2, no. 2, pp. 1–10.

Pithers, R. T., Athanasou, J. A. & Cornford, I. R. (1995), 'Development of a set of Australian occupational descriptors', *Asia Pacific Journal of Human Resources*, vol. 33, no. 3, pp. 140–46.

Pringle, J. (1994), 'Feminism and management: Critique and contribution', in A. Kouzmin, L. V. Still & P. Clarke (eds), *New Directions in Management*, McGraw-Hill, Sydney, pp. 127–42.

Rosen, B. & Jerdee, T. H. (1985), *Older Workers: New Roles for Valued Resources*, Dow Jones-Irwin, Homewood, Ill.

Ruzek, P. (1990), 'Childcare: A point of difference in the 1990s', *HRMonthly*, September, pp. 8–9, 12–13.

Rynes, S. & Rosen, B. (1995), 'A field survey of factors affecting the adoption and perceived success of diversity training', *Personnel Psychology*, vol. 48, no. 2, pp. 247–70.

Sahl, R. J. (1987), 'Succession planning: A blueprint for your company's future', *Personnel Administrator*, September, pp. 101–108.

Salmon. P. W. (1995), 'Information technology and human resource management', in G. O'Neill & R. Kramar (eds), *Australian Human Resources Management: Current Trends in Management Practice*, Pitman, Melbourne, pp. 303–324.

Sauers, D. A. (1993), 'Managing workforce diversity: A challenge for New Zealand business in the 1990s', *Asia Pacific Journal of Human Resources*, vol. 31, no. 3, pp. 44–51.

Schein, E. H. (1978), *Career Dynamics: Matching Individual and Organisational Needs*, Addison-Wesley, Reading, Mass.

Schuler, R. S. (1990), 'Repositioning the human resource function: Transformation or demise?', *Academy of Management Executive*, vol. 4, no. 3, pp. 49–60.

—— (1995), *Managing Human Resources*, 5th edition, West Publishing, St. Paul, Minn.

Schuler, R. S. & Walker, J. W. (1990), 'Human resources strategy: Focusing on issues and actions', *Organisational Dynamics*, vol. 19, no. 1, pp. 5–19.

Schwartz, F. (1989), 'Management women and the new facts of life', *Harvard Business Review*, vol. 67, no. 1, pp. 65–76.

Senge, P. M. (1990), *The Fifth Discipline: The Art and Practice of the Learning Organisation*, Random House, Sydney.

Sharratt, P. & Field, L. (1993), 'Organisational learning in Australian organisations: Hollow rhetoric or attainable reality', *Asia Pacific Journal of Human Resources*, vol. 31, no. 2, pp. 129–41.

Sheehy, G. (1977), *Passages*, Bantam, New York.

Smith, C. R. (1992), 'Dual careers, dual loyalties: Management implications of the work/home interface', *Asia Pacific Journal of Human Resources*, vol. 30, no. 4, pp. 19–29.

Sonnenfeld, J. A. & Peiperl, M. A. (1988), 'Staffing policy as a strategic response: A typology of career systems', *Academy of Management Review*, vol. 13, no. 4, pp. 588–600.

Stanton, S. (nee Maguire) (1986), *Human resource planning*, Unpublished Graduate Diploma Project, University of Technology, Sydney.

Still, L. V., Guerin, C. D. & Chia, W. (1994), 'Women in management revisited: Progress, regression or status quo?', in A. Kouzmin, L. V. Still & P. Clarke (eds), *New Directions in Management*, McGraw-Hill, Sydney, pp. 44–64.

Stone, R. J. (1991), 'Expatriate selection and failure', *Human Resource Planning*, vol. 14, no. 1, pp. 9–18.

Stratford, D. (1994), 'Change makes outplacement an all-climate service', *HRMonthly*, April, pp. 18–19.

—— (1996), 'Outplacement is but one part of corporate change strategy', *HRMonthly*, April, p. 20.

Super, D. E. (1942), *The Dynamics of Vocational Development*, Harper & Brothers, New York.

Ulrich, D. (1992), 'Strategic and human resource planning: Linking customers and employees', *Human Resource Planning*, vol. 15, no. 2, pp. 47–62.

Walker, J. W. (1990), 'Human resource planning, 1990s style', *Human Resource Planning*, vol. 13, no. 4, pp. 229–40.

Wallace, J. & Hunt, J. (1996), 'An analysis of managerial competencies across hierarchical levels and industry sectors: A contemporary Australian perspective', *Journal of the Australian and New Zealand Academy of Management*, vol. 2, no. 1, pp. 36–47.

Waung, M. (1995), 'The effects of self-regulatory coping orientation on newcomer adjustment and job survival', *Personnel Psychology*, vol. 48, no. 3, pp. 633–50.

Wilson, J. A. & Elman, N. S. (1990), 'Organisational benefits of mentoring', *Academy of Management Executive*, vol. 4, no. 4, pp. 88–94.

Wright, P. M., McMahan, G. C. & McWilliams (1994), 'Human resources and sustained competitive advantage: A resource-based perspective', *International Journal of Human Resource Management*, vol. 5, no. 2, pp. 303–26.

chapter 7

Job analysis and design

David Lamond

learning objectives

After studying this chapter, you will be able to:

1. Discuss the purposes and importance of analysing and designing jobs.
2. Describe and explain the main approaches to analysing and designing jobs.
3. Critically assess the main approaches to job analysis and design.
4. Write job descriptions and job specifications.
5. Make recommendations concerning different job designs.

chapter 7

chapter outline

- Understanding, creating and describing jobs — 265
  - Purposes and importance of job analysis and design — 265
- Job analysis and design in context — 266
  - Relationships with other HRM activities — 266
  - Relationships with the internal and external environment — 268
- Aspects of job analysis and design — 270
  - Collecting job information — 270
  - Job descriptions and employee specifications — 274
- Approaches to job analysis and design — 278
  - Job-focused techniques — 278
  - Person-focused techniques — 283
  - Team-based approaches — 289
  - Ergonomics — 290
  - Development of job families — 291
- Assessing job analysis methods — 292
  - Purposes of job analysis — 292
  - Practical concerns — 293
- Trends in job analysis — 294
  - Assessing job analysis — 294
  - Competency profiling — 295
  - Computer technology and HRIS in job analysis — 296
- Summary — 296
- Questions for discussion and review — 296
- Case study — 297
- Resources — 300
- References — 300

HRM IN THE NEWS

In late October 1995, there was a flurry of activity on the HRNET (an Internet bulletin board service run at Cornell University by John Boudreau) centred on whether, for many people and occupations, there were any longer such things as jobs or job descriptions and whether, in light of this question, there was still a need for the process of job analysis and design. The following provides snippets of the debate as an introduction to some of the key issues involved in the job analysis and design process. It also provides an interesting insight into the way academics and practitioners are now communicating their ideas and how new sets of skills are required if individuals are to take advantage of the opportunities that technological innovations are providing.

Dejobbing and the death of job descriptions: An Internet exchange

HRNET@LISTSERV.CORNELL.EDU.

Job analysis is the foundation for all the other human resource functions. You can't know what person to hire if you're not crystal clear about what you want that person to do now and in the immediate future. You can't set compensation appropriately or equitably without good job analysis. You can't do any kind of meaningful performance appraisal unless you have criteria by which to measure performance (these criteria come in the job description). You can't know what your training needs are unless you can measure what skills you want your employees to have (as stated in the job description) compared to what your workers are capable of doing. You can't pay proper attention to health and safety in the workplace unless you look at the ways people are expected to perform their jobs. These are the practical implications of job descriptions.

Source: Susan Herman, Keene, USA

Like most things, there are advantages and disadvantages to job descriptions. Doing a thorough job analysis and describing important tasks in detail is very helpful in ensuring that you get the right person into the job, but over-reliance on formal descriptions tends to lead to rigidity, turf problems, etc.

Source: Roger Keast, USA Public Sector

As a former employee of a major US corporation, I'd have to say that 'jobs' have been dead for some time, in some places. I suppose I could have had a full time 'job' just updating my job description ... if anyone could have agreed on what that description was at any given time!

This was true for the entire 16 years I spent there.

As for needing job descriptions for hiring ... well, there is a problem. No matter how well written the description is, what is needed will change ... often before the person even starts the job.

Somehow, the world doesn't want to slow down long enough to do things right ... so I guess we need to change what is right so we can actually *do* something.

Source: K. C. Burgess Yakemovic, USA

There are jobs that can be analysed and described using standard job analysis and position description procedures. These are the jobs that are increasingly being done by machines and are slowly but surely disappearing ... The whole job analysis edifice stands on the premise that there is something called a job which is independent and separable from the person doing it. Away from the assembly line, this is self-evidently nonsense.

Source: John J. Howard, NSW Public Sector

The series of arguments for and against the value of job descriptions and job analysis in the 'HRM in the news' discussion highlights many of the current debates about the process of trying to understand jobs. How do we come to understand jobs? This chapter discusses the processes by which we can understand jobs and their relationship to each other and to organisational success.

Understanding, creating and describing jobs

Job analysis and design involves the process of analysing, describing and recording the characteristics and qualities of jobs and specifying the skills and other requirements necessary to perform those jobs. The outputs of this process are the job description and the job specification. Typically described and recorded in the **job description** are the purposes of a job, its major duties or activities and the conditions under which the job is performed. Job descriptions may also include information about performance standards, task design characteristics and employee characteristics. On the basis of the job description (also referred to as the position description or the position specification), job specifications are developed and written. The **job specification** (or person specification) details the knowledge, skills, and abilities (KSAs) needed by individuals to perform that job. Additionally, job specifications could include information about individual characteristics, interests and preferences likely to be compatible with the job or satisfied during its performance.

Understanding what the job entails is a critical prerequisite to identifying the KSAs that a person must possess in order to perform competently in the role. Individual characteristics, interests and preferences are also important in the process of matching the person and the position. The provision of job descriptions and job specifications also serves to enable the organisation to comply with a range of legal regulations.

Purposes and importance of job analysis and design

Since the turn of the century, when Frederick Taylor's scientific management principles held sway, jobs have been designed for productivity and efficiency—maximising the output per human resource and physical input by finding the one best way to produce a product. Today, as many economies are described as post-industrial, focusing on the provision of services which require many different combinations of resources, there may be no best way. At the same time, organisations are employing workforces that are much more diverse in terms of age, gender, lifestyle and ability. There is a need, therefore, to understand and design jobs that not only contribute to organisational efficiency and productivity in meeting a disparate range of market requirements, but also are capable of attracting, accommodating and motivating this diverse workforce. In an era too, which emphasises the notions of job enrichment, empowerment and the creation of self-managed teams, careful job design is more important than ever.

Job analysis and design is the basis of the job descriptions and job specifications used in making employment decisions such as selection, promotion and performance appraisal. It is also important because it serves several other purposes including:

1. Providing a justification for the existence of the job and where it fits into the rest of the organisation
2. Determining the recruitment needs (when used together with the human resource planning needs discussed in Chapter 6) and the information necessary to make employment decisions
3. Determining the relative worth of jobs, which is necessary to maintain external and internal pay equity

4 Ensuring that companies do not violate equal pay for equal work legislative, award and enterprise agreement provisions
5 Providing potential job applicants with realistic job information regarding duties, working conditions and job requirements
6 Providing selection information necessary to make employment decisions consistent with the merit principle and relevant legislation
7 Aiding the supervisor and employee in defining the duties, responsibilities and reporting relationships of each employee
8 Serving as the basis for establishing career development programs and paths for employees
9 Identifying worker redundancies during mergers, acquisitions and downsizing
10 Guiding supervisors and incumbents in respectively writing references and preparing resumes for employees leaving and seeking new employment.

Job analysis and design in context

Job analysis has extensive relationships with other HRM activities and the internal environment and external environment (see for example Chorpade & Atchison 1980; Gael 1983; Grant 1988; McCormick 1979; Montminy 1994; Page & Van De Voort 1989; Sparks 1982, 1988; Vasbinder 1994; Verespej 1994). These are illustrated in Figure 7.1

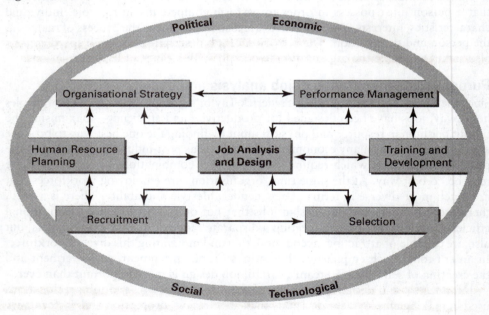

Figure 7.1 Job analysis and design: relationship with other HRM activities
Source: Based on Lamond 1995, p. 9

Relationships with other HRM activities

Almost all HRM activities are critically related to job analysis and design. Some of the most important are detailed below.

Recruitment and selection

On the basis of job analysis and in conjunction with human resource planning, the organisation knows who to recruit (Gordon, Hequet, Lee & Picard 1995). Without human resource planning and job analysis, the organisation would be unable to specify what types of job applicant are needed, and when and where. This in turn can have negative consequences for organisational productivity and the validity of its selection procedures and decisions. Only with job analysis information can an organisation show that its selection procedures are job-related.

Performance management and training

To effectively manage and evaluate employee performance, the methods used must reflect the important duties and skills of the job. Only by examining the skills required for a job (as defined in the job specification) can the organisation train and promote employees in conjunction with its human resource needs defined by the human resource planning activity. Additionally, identification of training needs and selection into training programs must be based on job-related criteria (Holton & Bailey 1995; Hong & Lin 1995; Piskurich 1994).

Remuneration

Job analysis and design also plays a vital role in one of the most important concerns of individuals in organisations—remuneration. It is on the basis of the job analysis and its design that a job is evaluated. Since this determines the worth or value of a job to the organisation, it is often used to help determine how much an employee gets paid for doing that job. Understanding the scope and responsibilities of a job is also important in ensuring that the level of pay for a job is fair in relation to others.

Organisation development programs

Programs to develop and enhance organisational productivity often involve changing the design of jobs. Regardless of the nature of the resulting job design, the new duties, purposes and conditions have to be analysed. While relatively straightforward for individually designed jobs, it is more complex to analyse group- or team-designed jobs. When the focus of doing work switches from the individual and a narrowly defined set of tasks to the group and a more broadly defined set of tasks related to a major portion of a final product, it becomes more difficult to analyse what each individuals duties are, and the necessary skills, knowledge and abilities. One consequence of this is to go from job evaluation and pay grades for specific jobs to skill evaluation and pay for knowledge possessed by employees.

Future organisational forms

> Informed by the realisation that human resources are the linchpin of a firms' capacity to adapt to future market opportunities, Wachter, Modrow-Thiel & Rossman (1994, p. 44) have developed an approach to job analysis aimed at anticipating future work situations under automation and evaluating them in terms of the skill content of labour required in the metal working industry. It is an approach predicated on the observed dynamic nature of work and the changing workplace and the view that it is important to prepare for new and different organisational forms rather than merely establish them. Wachter et al. (1994)

see an important lesson for job descriptions—the dynamic nature of work makes rigid job descriptions impossible—at most they are retrospective documents of the original job description used for comparative purposes (the original job requirements become redundant when the workers training and experience enhances their skills).

Relationships with the internal and external environment

Two key aspects of the internal environment with relevance for job analysis and design are the goals of top management and the technology used to pursue these.

Top management's goals

Because they are created by organisations, jobs are very explicit statements by top management of its goals, and what is determined to be the most appropriate means for accomplishing those goals. Furthermore, if the thoughts and beliefs that workers have regarding their organisation help determine their behaviour, then the stated goals and the subsequent standards of excellence that an organisation establishes give clear cues to employees about what is important and where their efforts are required.

Since goals help determine the products, services and environments of organisations, they also determine the criteria against which workers will be evaluated hence, their behaviours. The criteria and goals, in turn, also determine the kinds of individuals who will be attracted to the organisation, evaluated highly and promoted. Thus, organisational goals can help establish the reasons for jobs, the nature of the organisation's expectations from workers performing them, and even the legitimacy of job demands. Goals have several other consequences through their relationship with the structure of the organisation, which is in turn related to the design and redesign of jobs.

Technology

The type of technology being used by, and available for, an organisation is also critical because it determines what types of job design are possible and what types of job are appropriate for various organisational designs. For example, Australian car manufacturers have worked hard to convert their car-making technology from the segmented assembly-line jobs so that groups of workers make the cars. As such, it is the choice of assembly-line technology and the structure or design of the organisation which determine the most appropriate type of job design. In the banking industry meanwhile, the development of computer technology has changed dramatically the role of counter staff from simple financial transactions to the provision of a range of related customer services.

The example of the banking industry reminds us that the kinds of technology available for an organisation are also determined by changes in the external environment, including the political, economic and social environments in which the organisation operates.

Technological environment

The changes in banking services already mentioned have been accompanied by the proliferation of Automatic Teller Machines (ATMs), while checkouts at supermarkets have become defacto banks for transaction (withdrawal) purposes through the development of Electronic Funds Transfer at Point Of Sale (EFTPOS). Hong & Lin (1995) point out that these sorts of changes in manufacturing and service processes and technologies will take place more slowly if the workforce lacks the skills required to be effective. The workforce needs training and development to be equipped with appropriate knowledge and skills. In this context, job analysis seeks to examine workers' duties in order to determine the occupational knowledge and skills required to accomplish job goals.

Political environment

During the 1980s, a raft of equal opportunity and anti-discrimination legislation was passed throughout Australia. This legislation, based, inter alia, on the principles of merit and equity in selection and promotion was designed to prompt the re-examination of jobs in accordance with those principles. More recently, the unfair dismissal provisions of the *Industrial Relations Act 1994* have provided a further impetus to the production of job descriptions which clearly outline the duties and responsibilities of employees.

Economic environment

There have been many changes in the Australian economy over the last decade, as it has become more open to global competition. At the same time, the economy has experienced a boom and a recession, as well as changes in consumer and other markets. International competitiveness has forced firms to examine new ways of increasing productivity, while the recessionary times have been marked by organisational downsizing and the need to distinguish between the jobs and employees in terms of their importance to achieving the organisation's objectives.

Social environment

The workforce, is now older, more educated, more female, and comes from a diversity of cultural and ethnic backgrounds. Coupled with the international competition, these changes in employee characteristics have also further changed the concept of a 'job' by forcing firms to find better ways of motivating employees as well as tapping into individual abilities.

Managing change

Love, Bishop, Heinisch & Montei (1994) remind us that countries are increasingly part of a global economy and companies need to become familiar with other countries' customs, business practices, culture and traditions. They point out there is also a need to modify job analysis and personnel selection practices to meet other countries' job performance and cultural expectations. In this regard, they describe a case study of an American parts assembly company which had to adapt its traditional job analysis when it established a new plant in Japan. Where in the past the company had collected job-related data from the job incumbents and then asked them to rate the various characteristics, the standard questionnaire could not be used with the Japanese incumbents and their supervisors because it was culturally inappropriate. As a result, the job analysis was primarily based on observations of videotapes of Japanese workers performing the jobs and interviews with American managers completing their training in Japan. Combined with a separate importance rating scheme, 140 critical behaviours covering the sequence of steps in assembly, quality control checkpoints and related plan operations were identified and categorised. This became the basis of a work simulation that was successfully used as a primary method of evaluating job applicants.

Aspects of job analysis and design

Spurred on in part by organisational efforts to become more competitive and profitable, there has been a renewed interest in job analysis and design (Gael 1983; Sparks 1987). This is also based on the fact that job analysis and design serves so many purposes and has such an extensive set of system relationships in organisations. As a consequence, organisations are wanting to know about all aspects of job analysis, starting with collecting job information.

Collecting job information

As defined earlier, job analysis and design is the process of describing, analysing and recording many aspects of jobs. The aspects that can be described and recorded vary greatly, often depending on the purposes to be served. The possible aspects of jobs that can be described are illustrated in Table 7.1. It is important to know who collects the information and how it is collected.

Table 7.1 Types of job information obtained through job analysis and design

Work activities
- Job-oriented activities (usually expressed in terms of what is accomplished; sometimes indicating how, why and when a worker performs the activity)
- work activities processes
- procedures used
- activity records (films, etc.)
- personal accountability/responsibility
- Worker-oriented activities
- human behaviours performed in work (sensing, decision-making, performing physical actions, communicating etc.)
- elemental motions (such as those used in methods analysis)
- personal job demands (energy expenditure, etc.)

Machines, tools, equipment and work aids used

Job-related tangibles and intangibles
- Materials processed
- Products made
- Knowledge dealt with or applied (such as law or chemistry)
- Services rendered (such as laundering or repairing)

Work performance
- Work measurement (time taken)
- Work standards
- Error analysis
- Other aspects

Job content
- Physical working conditions
- Work schedule
- Organisational context
- Social, context
- Incentives (financial and non-financial)

> **Personnel requirements**
> - Job-related knowledge skills (education, training, work experience, etc.)
> - Personal attributes (aptitudes, physical characteristics, personality, interests, etc.)

Source: Based on McCormick 1976, p. 653

Who collects the information?

In large organisations, it is typically someone in the HRM department, along with a supervisor, who collects the job information. Increasingly it is becoming more common for the incumbent, or the person in the job, to also provide job information. Often a combination of the three is used. The exact combination, the information each provides, how it is used, and who has the final responsibility, often varies between different organisations. In smaller organisations, for example, the responsibility necessarily lies with supervisors and incumbents.

Obtaining information from as many sources as possible leads to a greater understanding of the jobs particular duties and knowledge, skills, and abilities needed to perform those duties. Given the importance of careful job design to the organisation, the data collector (whether HR specialist, supervisor or incumbent) should be trained and then allowed to practice the steps in gathering the information so that the data fulfils a number of important requirements. Not only must the information be accurate, detailed and complete, it must also be collected in a manner does not antagonise the workers or supervisors.

The launching of a job analysis and design exercise can be unpopular because it is not only time-consuming but also potentially threatening to the incumbents who perceive that it can lead to changes in job responsibilities, compensation and training (or even to the loss of the job itself if undertaken in the context of a downsizing program). To defuse potential resentment and misunderstanding, it is important to convey to all employees the purpose of the program, who will be involved, and exactly what will happen as a result of the program. Involving the incumbent and supervisor increases the perceptions of procedural fairness and reduces resistance to change.

Methods of gathering job information

The way or method by which job information is gathered is as extensive as its number of possible attributes to be described. Methods of collecting job information include:

1. Observation
2. Interviews with the job incumbent(s)
3. Conferences with job analysts/experts
4. Observations by job analysts
5. Diaries kept by job incumbents
6. Structured and unstructured questionnaires filled out by the incumbents or observers such as the supervisor or job analyst
7. Critical incidents written by incumbents or others who know the jobs
8. Mechanical devices such as stopwatches, counters and films
   An example of the diary method is contained in Table 7.2.

Table 7.2 Excerpts from Daily Diary used for Great Barrier Reef Marine Park Authority Project

Dear Staff Member,

As you probably already know, a review of the day-to-day management of the Great Barrier Reef Marine Park is currently being undertaken by a group of consultants from Macquarie University in NSW. A number of staff members have already taken part in various aspects of the review, which has included a pilot survey of Park users in December 1990–February 1991.

We would like marine park staff to contribute to the review by providing information about what they actually do, in terms of how much time they spend on various activities. We understand that rangers already complete a diary, and we would collect the information according to the existing categories. We would, however, like to get some more detailed information for analysis.

We are therefore seeking your co-operation in the review by filling out the attached work diary for the two-week period April 29, 1991 to May 10, 1991. For the analysis to work, you need to fill out the work diary during the day every day for the two weeks. This is, of course, a very short time for the analysis, but we want to ensure that people don't spend all their time filling in forms. Please follow the steps outlined below.

Step 1
At the beginning of the two week period, fill out the details about you and your position. If you are acting out of your substantive position, put in the title for your acting position.

Step 2
Whenever you start, change or complete a task, make sure that you record the code for that task in the diary. The diary breaks up each day into half-hour blocks, so if on Day 1, for example, you spent from 7.00 am to 7.30 am on equipment maintenance and then from 7.30 am to 10.00 am on vessel surveillance patrol, you would fill out the diary as per the example:

DAY	MON	TUES	WED	THURS	FRI	MON	TUE	WED	THURS	FRI
DATE	29/4	30/4	1/5	2/5	3/5	6/5	7/5	8/5	9/5	10/5
Hour of day										
7.00–7.30 am	5b									
7.30–9.00	2e									
9.00–9.30	2e									
9.30–10.00	2e									

If the tasks you perform are not adequately covered by the existing codes, assign a new code (6a, 6b, 6c etc).

Step 3
Keep filling out the diary for each day of the survey period.

Step 4
At the end of the two week period, forward your completed diary in the attached addressed envelope to the consultants.

Be assured that no identifying information will be passed on to the Authority and that all information collected will be confidential to the consultants. The Authority will be presented with aggregate data only, so that no individual can be identified. We should also stress that this part of the review is not an evaluation of any individual's performance. Rather, it is an evaluation of the *program*, its aims and objectives.

NAME: _____   POSITION: _____

DAY	MON	TUES	WED	THURS	FRI	MON	TUE	WED	THURS	FRI
DATE	29/4	30/4	1/5	2/5	3/5	6/5	7/5	8/5	9/5	10/5
Hour of day										
7.00–7.30 am										
7.30–9.00										
9.00–9.30										
9.30–10.00										
10.00–10.30										
10.30–11.00										
11.00–11.30										
11.30–12.00										
12.00–12.30 pm										
12.30–1.00										
1.00–1.30										
1.30–2.00										
2.00–2.30										
2.30–3.00										
3.00–3.30										
3.30–4.00										
4.00–4.30										
4.30–5.00										
5.00–5.30										
5.30–6.00										

Code description

Administrative support
1a Budgets
1b Reports
1c Audits

User liaison and management
2a Education/liaison
2b Permits
2c Law enforcement
2d Aerial surveillance/patrols
2e Vessel surveillance/patrols
2f User management research and monitoring

Planning
3a Planning

Resource protection, management and monitoring
4a Protecting Marine Life
4b Protecting Island Life

Estate development and maintenance
5a Infrastructure
5b Equipment

Other (specify)
6a
6b
6c
6d

Source: Gilmore et al. 1994

From all the data gathered in the job analysis and design process, two major outputs result: job/position descriptions and job/person/employee specifications. On the basis of the job description, performance appraisal forms can be developed and job classification systems can be established for job evaluation and compensation purposes. Because job specifications identify the education and training needed to perform a job, appropriate recruitment, selection, and training and development programs depend on this process.

Job descriptions and employee specifications

Job descriptions and specifications are generated from the data gathered in the job information collection process. Although the actual job descriptions used in many organisations contain information on employee specifications, analysing and describing jobs, then identifying the employee specifications for these, are two different activities. Because they are related, however, most of the job analysis and design techniques described below was used to gather information on both activities. Typically, a single job description is written, describing or at least listing, several aspects of a job along with the necessary skills, knowledge and abilities (i.e. employee specifications are often included in the job description). The final product of the job analysis and design process is likely to include:

1. **Job title.**
2. **Job number** and **job group** to which the job belongs (maybe using Australian Standard Classification of Occupations (ASCO) codes if appropriate).
3. **Department** and/or division where the job is located.
4. **Date** when the job is analysed and name of job analyst. This will provide a cue for subsequent analyses to update the description.
5. **Name of incumbent** (optional).
6. **Job summary** is an abstract of the job, useful for job positing, recruitment advertisements and salary surveys.
7. **Supervision received** and given identifies the reporting relationships. If the job is supervisory, the duties associated with the supervision should be detailed under work performed.
8. **Work performed** describes the major duties and underlying tasks that make up the job. A task is something that workers perform or an action they take to produce a product or provide a service. Duties are a collection of tasks that recur and are not trivial. For maximum information use, duties should be prioritised in terms of importance as well as percentage of time for each duty. They may take little time to complete but be critical to job success.
9. **Job requirements** (specifications) delineate the competencies (knowledge, skills and abilities) and experience, education, training and licenses, needed to perform a job. Competencies refer to the body of information in a particular subject area (knowledge) that, if applied, makes adequate performance of the job possible (e.g. knowledge of the word processing package or the Occupational Health and Safety Act) and the observable capabilities (skills and abilities) to perform a learned behaviour (e.g. to operate a drill or provide transaction services in a bank). Job requirements should be limited to the minimum qualifications a new employee would be expected to bring to the job. For example, a Master of Social Work degree may be an inappropriate qualification for the position of child protection worker if individuals without the degree have been shown to perform the job as well (to be just as competent). On the other hand, the degree may be necessary if required by state law. Similarly, a matriculation qualification is not necessary for the position of

cleaner, but the cleaner may need basic reading skills to identify cleaning agents. Thus the appropriate qualification or competency level would be the ability to read labels and instructions, not a higher school certificate.

10 **Job context** deals with the environment in which the job is performed. For example, work may be conducted outdoors (construction worker), in close quarters (film editor), in remote areas (national park rangers), in high temperatures (chef), or low temperatures (meat cutter). The job may involve extensive standing (sales person), sitting (data entry operator), exposure to fumes (fibreglass fabricator), noise (drill operator), electrical shocks (electrician), exposure to diseases (laboratory technician) or stress (police officer or nurse). Such details provide an understanding of the setting in which the job is conducted.

A common writing style of most job descriptions provides that:

1 A terse, direct style should be used.
2 Present tense should be used throughout.
3 Each sentence should begin with an active verb.
4 Each sentence must reflect an objective, either specifically stated or implied in such manner as to be obvious to the reader. A single verb may sometimes reflect both objective and worker action.
5 All words should impart necessary information; others should be omitted. Every precaution should be taken to use words that have only one possible connotation and that specifically describe the manner in which the work is accomplished.
6 The description of tasks should reflect the assigned work performed and, where possible, worker performance ratings (Jones 1984).

In writing or preparing job descriptions it should be kept in mind that the job should be described in enough detail so that the reader can understand:

1 What is to be done (the domains, the behaviours, the results and the duties)
2 What products or services are to be generated/provided (the purpose of the job)
3 What work standards are applied (standards such as quality and quantity)
4 Under what conditions the job is performed
5 The design characteristics of the job.

Note that the design characteristics are included in order that individuals might select and be placed in jobs that match or suit their personality, interests and preferences. An example of a typical job description containing many of these features is that of General Manager, Human Resources, shown in Table 7.3. Note that this job description does not provide information regarding performance standards, design characteristics, purpose of the job or job conditions. Purposes, however, are implied in the introductory section. Performance standards are typically not specified in job descriptions. Increasingly, however, these are being included in performance agreements prepared and signed as part of the performance appraisal process.

The writing style of the job description gives the impression of being an objective statement of the duties and requirements of a job which is, in turn, the product of an objective process of analysis. Job descriptions may not, however, be either the objective statements we take them to be or the result of an objective process. Before we examine the various approaches to job analysis and design, it is important to understand the social influences on the collection of job information and the production of job descriptions and employee specifications. In particular, the work of Clare Burton (see, for example, Burton 1988a, 1988b, 1991) highlights the influence of gender issues on how jobs are defined and evaluated.

Job evaluation schemes use quantitative methods as a basis for classifying jobs into wage and salary grades. Burton (1988b; 1991, pp. 93–104) summarises the biases in job evaluation:

1. **Choice, definition and weighting of compensable factors** (the job characteristics regarded as contributing to the overall worth of the job) for ranking of jobs. For example, where a set of factors emphasises experience in the job rather than training, physical effort rather than mental effort, and does not emphasise responsibility for people, the position of maintenance fitter (traditionally a male job) will be ranked significantly higher in terms of job worth than the position of a company nurse (a traditionally female job). When the set of factors emphasises basic knowledge, complexity of tasks, training and includes mental effort and responsibility for people, however, the company nurse position will be ranked higher than the maintenance fitter role (Burton 1991, p. 96).
2. **Collection and recording of job information.** For example, when job incumbents are providing information about their positions, women tend to be self-deprecating (under-estimating the demands of the position) while men tend to be self-enhancing (over-estimating the demands of the position) (Burton 1988, p. 7; 1991, p. 98).
3. **The evaluation process.** Evaluators frequently overlook important features of women's work and the requisite qualities and skills to carry out those tasks. For example, They may overlook the communication skills of receptionists (but not the manual skills of a maintenance fitter) or they may overlook the stressful conditions of working with people with serious mental health problems (but not the noise of machinery) (Burton 1988, pp. 9–10; 1991, pp. 98–99).

Clearly, as Burton (1991, p. 104) says, we have to constantly remind ourselves that there is no right answer in the sense of an evaluation being objectively correct and we should be careful to review our approaches in light of that acknowledgment.

Table 7.3 Position description and specification for General Manager, Human Resources

Functional title: General Manager, Human Resources
Department: Human Resources Department

Position profile
This position represents the personnel point of view in the strategic and operational direction of the business. The incumbent is expected to provide, with the support and concurrence of the CEO, a philosophy and guiding principles for managing the human resources of the company. Authority is limited to the protection of the company's interests in relation to laws and regulations pertaining to personnel. The position directly impacts all functions and areas of the company in matters of morale, management practices, employee well-being, remuneration, benefits, structure and development. The incumbent is expected to positively affect these matters through personal influence and professional credibility rather than vested authority.

This position requires an incumbent with broad managerial and professional knowledge and experience. From the managerial standpoint, the Human Resources group comprises ten interrelated yet disparate functional areas: employee relations, remuneration, benefits, training, organisational development, recruiting, personnel administration, field personnel services, corporate communications and head office personnel services. The current staff consists of 75 people, including 42 professionals. The incumbent also has functional responsibility for personnel services to four distribution centres. Budget administration responsibilities include annual expenditure of $29.7 million.

On the professional side, with the exception of the directors of remuneration and staffing and of human resource development, and the managers of benefits and media projects, virtually all staff members have been developed inside the company. Technical and professional direction and training rest with the incumbent. The incumbent is expected to provide the company with systems, programs, and processes that effectively support business goals and organisation values. The company's principal executives rely on the incumbents personal experience, skills and resources to bring the company to best practice status.

Critical competency requirements include preventative industrial relations, relevant employment and occupational health and safety legislation, remuneration and benefit practices, training and organisation development practices, and employee participation processes. The company's widespread training needs are especially important at this time. The incumbent must have highly developed consulting and communication skills. Although the incumbent is not expected to create or invent systems and programs, there is an expectation that successful practices will be introduced and adapted to the company's particular needs. The incumbent must be able to judge when to act and when not to act with patience and persistence an able and willing to modify actions to gain agreement and consensus. The incumbent must be able to place the priorities of the company over those of the personnel function. At the same time, the incumbent is expected to be a strong advocate for employee interests and well being.

Candidate qualifications

Broad experience is required in the following areas:
- Employee/industrial relations, including enterprise agreement negotiation and administration
- Personnel policy formulation, communication and administration
- Corporate culture change, including the facilitation of improved organisational effectiveness
- Human resource development with special emphasis on all facets of training but also including human resource planning (including succession planning), performance standards and review, assessment of management potential, personal/management development, career paths, and the recruitment/selection process
- Remuneration programs, including job evaluations, wage and salary plan design and administration, short- and long-term incentive plan design and administration
- Benefit programs, including the design and administration of health care, life and disability insurance and of defined benefit/contribution plans, sick/holiday pay and other policies
- Corporate communications, using print, video and other media, including booklets, newspapers and other publications, institutional and informational videos and meetings of management personnel
- Participatory and responsive management, including the use of employee participation processes, project management/task force/focus group techniques, attitude surveys and other forms of employee communications
- Human resource information systems, including the development and utilisation of cost/time effectiveness reports and analyses
- Departmental direction, management and administration, including staff selection, training/development and deployment, short- and long-term departmental planning, project management, program development and execution, delivery of human resource services, budget development and administration.

Approaches to job analysis and design

There are many ways organisations can choose to analyse and design jobs. That is, there are many ways or procedures which can be used to determine what job information to collect, how to collect it, from whom, and how to organise and present it in job descriptions. Most of the procedures are structured: fixed forms and procedures are used to gather the job data. When organisations use similar-structured methods to analyse and design jobs, they can (among other things) exchange compensation information and develop more valid methods of recruitment, selection and performance appraisal.

Structured techniques tend to divide into two types: one which is job (task) focused and one which is person (behaviour) oriented. The goal of work oriented approaches is to break down a job into very specific tasks, or things to be accomplished by the job incumbent, while person oriented approaches determine the specific activities, or behaviours, that a person engages in to carry out the job (Gatewood & Field 1994). Some of the typical job focused techniques, which make use of a scientific approach to job design, include Functional Job Analysis, the Management Position Description Questionnaire, the Hay Plan, and Methods Analysis. More behavioural focused techniques, which complement an individual approach to job design, include the Position Analysis Questionnaire, Critical Incidents, Extended Critical Incidents, and the Guidelines Oriented Job Analysis.

Job-focused techniques

The study of human work probably has not generally benefited from the systematic, scientific approaches that have been characteristic of other domains of enquiry such as the study of physical or biological phenomena, or of the behaviour of humankind (as through psychological and sociological research). The study of human work in the past, however, has not been entirely unsystematic and lacking in a scientific approach (McCormick 1979, p. 67).

The scientific approach

Under the scientific approach, job analysts take special pains to design jobs so that the tasks performed by employees do not exceed their abilities. The jobs designed this way often result in work being partitioned into small, standardised segments. These tasks lend themselves well to time and motion studies and to incentive pay systems, each for the purpose of obtaining high productivity.

Through meticulous human engineering, United Parcel Service (UPS) is highly successful in the USA despite stiff competition. In a business where a package is a package, UPS succeeds through its application of scientifically designed work standards. Their approach has been key to their continuing gains in efficiency and productivity since the privately owned company was founded in 1907. In the 1920s, UPS engineers cut away the sides of UPS trucks to study how the drivers performed. The engineers then made appropriate changes in techniques to enhance worker efficiency. Time and motion studies enable the company to closely monitor the performance of the workers. At UPS, more than 1000 industrial engineers use the time study to set standards for a variety of closely supervised tasks. In return, the UPS drivers, all of whom are represented by the Teamsters Union, earn above average wages and are offered better job security by the company (Bernstein 1993; Machalaba 1986).

Functional job analysis

The United States Training and Employment Service in the US Department of Labor developed this type of job analysis to describe the nature of jobs in terms of people, data and things, and to develop job summaries, job descriptions and employee specifications. It was designed to improve job placement and counselling for workers registering for employment at local state employment offices. The *Dictionary of Occupational Title*, which was the product of this effort, is now is its 4th edition (Department of Labor 1991).

In September 1986, the Australian Standard Classification of Occupations (ASCO) was introduced by the Australian Bureau of Statistics and the Commonwealth Department of Employment and Industrial Relations. ASCO is based on the kind of work performed, defined in terms of skill level and skill specialisation. An ASCO Dictionary has been released with detailed descriptions of about 1100 different occupations which relate to the major, minor, unit group and occupation levels of the classification. At the occupation or specific job level, information is provided on skill levels, tasks or duties performed, and related occupations or occupation titles which are specialisations of the particular occupation. ASCO classifications when used by the Australian Bureau of Statistics to produce such publications as the *Labour Force Survey* provide valuable information for general human resource planning.

Functional job analysis is both a conceptual system for defining the dimensions of worker activity and a method of measuring levels of such activity (Fine 1974; McCormick 1979; Markowitz 1981). The fundamental premises of functional job analysis are:

1 A fundamental distinction must be made between what gets done and what workers do to get things done. Bus drivers do not carry passengers; they drive vehicles and collect fares.
2 Jobs are concerned with data, people and things.
3 In relation to things, workers draw on physical resources; in relation to data, on mental resources; and in relation to people, on interpersonal resources.
4 All jobs require the worker to relate to data, people and things to some degree.
5 Although the behaviour of workers or the tasks they perform can apparently be described in an infinite number of ways, there are only a few definitive functions involved. Thus, in interacting with machines, workers feed, tend, operate and set up; in the case of vehicles or related machines, they drive or control them. Although these functions vary in difficulty and content, each draws on a relatively narrow and specific range of worker characteristics and qualifications for effective performance.
6 The functions appropriate to dealing with data, people or things are hierarchical and ordinal, proceeding from the complex to the simple. Thus, to indicate that a particular function, say compiling data, reflects the requirements of a job, is to say that it also includes the requirement of lower functions, such as comparing, and that it excludes the requirements of higher functions, such as analysis.

Management position description questionnaire

Although the functional job analysis approach is complete, it requires considerable training to use well and is quite narrative in nature. The narrative portions tend to be less reliable than more quantitative techniques such as the Management Position Description Questionnaire (Cascio 1982; Tornow & Pinto 1976). This is a method of job analysis that relies upon the checklist method. It contains 197 items related to the concerns and responsibilities of managers, their demands and restrictions, and miscellaneous characteristics. These 197 items have been condensed into 13 job factors including:

1 Product, market and financial planning
2 Co-ordination of other organisational units and personnel

3 Internal business control
4 Products and services responsibility
5 Public and customer relations
6 Advanced consulting
7 Autonomy of action
8 Approval of financial commitments
9 Staff service
10 Supervision
11 Complexity and stress
12 Advanced financial responsibility
13 Broad personnel responsibility.

The Management Position Description Questionnaire is designed for managerial positions, but responses to the items vary by managerial level in any organisation and also in different organisations. The Management Position Description Questionnaire is appropriate for determining the training needs of employees moving into managerial jobs, evaluating managerial jobs, creating job families and placing new managerial jobs into the right job family, compensating managerial jobs, and developing selection procedures and performance appraisal forms.

Supervisor task description questionnaire

While the Management Position Description Questionnaire can be used to describe, compare, classify, and evaluate management jobs at all levels, the Supervisor Task Description Questionnaire is limited to the work of first-line supervisors. The questionnaire describes 100 work activities of first line supervisors in these areas:

1 Working with subordinates
2 Planning subordinates work
3 Maintaining efficient production and quality
4 Maintaining safe and clean work areas
5 Maintaining equipment and machinery
6 Compiling records and reports.

A study of more than 250 first-line supervisors in 40 plants showed that job responsibilities are universal regardless of technology or product type (Dowell & Wexley 1978).

The Hay Plan

Another method of analysing managerial jobs is the Hay Plan which is used in a large number of organisations. Although less structured than the Management Position Description Questionnaire and Position Analysis Questionnaire, it is systematically tied into a job evaluation and compensation system. Thus, use of the Hay Plan allows an organisation to maintain consistency not only in how it describes managerial jobs but also in how it rewards them. The purposes of the Hay Plan are management development, placement and recruitment; job evaluation; measurement of the execution of a job against specific standards of accountability; and organisation analysis.

The Hay Plan is based on an interview between the job analyst and the job incumbent. The information that is gathered relates to four aspects of the incumbents job: the objectives; the dimensions; the nature and scope of the position; and the accountability objectives. Information about the objectives allows the reader of the job description to know why the job exists in the organisation and for what reason it is paid. Information about dimensions conveys to the reader how big a show the incumbent runs and the magnitude of the end results affected by his or her actions.

The real heart of the Hay job description is the information about the nature and scope of the position, which covers five crucial aspects:

1. How the position fits into the organisation, including reference to significant organisational and outside relationships.
2. The general composition of supporting staff. This includes a thumbnail sketch of each major function of any staff under the incumbents position—size, type and the reason for its existence.
3. The general nature of the technical, managerial and human relationship know-how required.
4. The nature of the problem solving required: What are the key problems that must be solved by this job and how variable are they?
5. The nature and source of control or the freedom to solve problems and act, whether supervisory, procedural, vocational or professional.

Information related to the accountability objectives tells what end results the job exists to achieve and the incumbent is held accountable for. There are four areas of accountability: organisation (including staffing, developing and maintaining the organisation); strategic planning; tactical planning, execution and directing the attainment of objectives; and review and control.

Because the Hay Plan is based on information gathered in an interview (as opposed to the checklist method in the Management Position Description Questionnaire), the success of the plan depends on the skills of the interviewer. Interviewers can be trained, however, enabling the information to be used for job descriptions, job evaluation and compensation. The Hay Plan results from one organisation can be compared with those in others to ensure external pay comparability. The Hay Plan is further discussed in Chapter 10.

Methods analysis

Conventional job analysis procedures and structured procedures generally focus on describing the job and its general duties, the conditions under which the duties are performed, and the levels of authority, accountability and know-how required. Equally important, however, is a description of how to do the job as efficiently and effectively as possible. This is the purpose of Methods Analysis.

Methods analysis focuses on analysing job elements, the smallest identifiable components of a job. The need for methods analysis often comes from changes in tools and equipment; changes in product design; changes in materials; modifications of equipment and procedures to accommodate handicapped workers; and health and safety concerns.

While human resource managers have downplayed the importance of methods analysis in recent years, it is still widely used in manufacturing settings. In fact, the use of new technologies, collectively referred to as programmable automation, has increased the need for methods analysis. These new processes include computer-aided design and computer aided manufacturing (CAD/CAM), computer aided engineering, (CAE), flexible manufacturing systems (FMS), group technology, robotics, and computer integrated manufacturing (CIM).

These new manufacturing technologies can create shock waves in an organisation because they require a quantum leap in precision and integration. Automated machine tools can produce parts to more exacting specifications than can the most skilled human machinist, but to do so they need explicit, unambiguous instructions in the form of computer programs.

The new hardware provides added freedom, but it also multiplies the ways to succeed or fail. It therefore requires new skills on the part of the managers, for example, an integrative imagination and a passion for detail. To prevent process contamination, for example, it is no longer possible to rely on people who have a feel for their machines, or to merely note on a blueprint that operators should remove iron filings from the part. When using the new automated machine tools, everything must be stated with mathematical precision: where is the blower that removes the filings, and what's the orientation of the part during the operation of the blower (Hayes & Jailkumar 1988).

Thus it is increasingly important to study and document work processes. A variety of techniques is available for conducting methods analysis.

Flow process charts

These are used to examine the overall sequence of an operation by focusing on either the movement of an operator or the flow of materials. For example, flow charts have been used in hospitals to track patient movements, in grocery stores to analyse the checkout process, in small-batch manufacturing facilities to track material flows from machine to machine, in banks to examine the sequence associated with document processing, and in supervisor–incumbent interactions during performance appraisal interviews.

Worker-machine charts

These are useful for envisioning the segments of a work cycle in which equipment and operator are busy or idle. The analyst can easily see when the operator and machine are working jointly or independently. One use of this type of chart is to determine how many machines or how much equipment an operator can manage. A team process chart is an extension of worker-machine charts. Rather than focusing on the operations of a single operator and machine, this chart simultaneously plots the worker-machine interfaces for a team of workers. Such charts are particularly useful for identifying equipment utilisation as well as for pinpointing bottlenecks in interdependent tasks.

Time and motion study

Also called motion study, the technique of time study has its origins in industrial engineering and the work of Frederick W. Taylor and Frank & Lillian Gilbreth. In essence, **work measurement** determines standard times for all units of work activity in a given task or job. Combining these times gives a standard time for the entire job. **Observed time** is simply the average of recorded times. **Normal time** is the observed time adjusted for worker performance. This is accomplished by determining a performance rating for observed performance. The performance rating is an estimation of the difference between the normal rate at which a worker can be expected to perform and the observed rate. The adjustment is necessary because workers may deliberately slow down or speed up the processes when observed. For instance, a performance rating of 1.20 indicates that an observed pace is much faster than normal. By comparison, a performance rating of 0.80 assumes that observed performance is slower than normal (a possible occurrence if the job is being studied to set rates of pay).

Standard time is the normal time adjusted for routine work interruptions. These delays may include personal delays (getting a drink of water, going to the toilet) as well as variable allowances specific to the job (mental or physical effort, lighting, atmospheric conditions, monotony, and detail). Industrial engineers have developed tables listing the allowances for different work delays.

These standard times can be used as a basis for wage-incentive plans (incentives generally are given for work performance that takes less than the standard time), cost determination, cost estimates for new products, and balancing production lines and work crews (Adam & Ebert 1986; Amrine, Huber & Hyer 1985). Establishing standard times is a challenge of some consequence, since the time it takes to do a job can be influenced as much by the individual doing the job and the effectiveness of the training received as by the nature of the job itself. Consequently, determining standard times often requires measurement of the actual effort the individual is exerting and the real effort required. This process, as you can imagine, often means trying to out-guess someone.

Common methods of collecting time data and determining standard times include the stopwatch times studies, standard data, predetermined time systems and work sampling for determining standard time.

Work sampling is not only a technique for determining standard times but also another form of methods analysis. Work sampling is the process of taking instantaneous samples of the work activities of individuals or groups of individuals McCormick 1979, p. 83). The activities from these observations are timed and classified into predetermined categories. The result is a description of the activities by classification of a job and the percentage of time for each activity.

Work sampling can be done in several ways: the job analyst can observe the incumbent at predetermined times; a camera can be set to take photographs at predetermined times; or, at a given signal, all incumbents can record their activity at that moment.

Person-focused techniques

The job-focused approach is not always effective, primarily because it does not take into account all the variables which impact on performance of the job (individual skills, the quality of training and so on). Indeed, as was discussed in regard to gender issues impacting on job evaluation, the job-focused approach can give the illusion of objectivity where it doesn't exist and paint an inappropriate picture of the work to be done and the skills required to do it. Organisations have, therefore, sought alternative job design approaches. One result is the individual contemporary design.

Individual contemporary design

As shown in Table 7.4, five positive personal and work outcomes—high motivation, quality work performance, satisfaction, and low absenteeism and turnover—result when people are allowed to function in an environment where work enables the individual to gain a sense of meaningfulness, responsibility, empowerment, and knowing the results.

According to researchers, these are critical psychological states that evolve from five core job characteristics:

1 **Skill variety**—degree to which tasks that are performed require different abilities and skills
2 **Job significance**—degree to which the job has substantive importance
3 **Job identity**—degree to which a whole and identifiable piece of work with a visible outcome is produced
4 **Autonomy**—degree of freedom and discretion in work scheduling and procedures
5 **Feedback**—amount of direct and clear information about performance effectiveness.

Table 7.4 The core job characteristics model

CORE JOB CHARACTERISTICS	CRITICAL PSYCHOLOGICAL STATES	OUTCOMES
• Skill variety • Job identity • Job significance	Meaningfulness of the work	• Less absenteeism • Less turnover • High satisfaction
• Job autonomy	Responsibility for outcomes of the work	
		• High motivation
• Feedback from the job	Knowing the actual results of work activities	• High-quality work performance

Source: Based on Hackman & Oldham 1980, p. 77

Job enrichment results when jobs are high on these core characteristics. When employees value feelings of meaningfulness, responsibility, empowerment and knowing the results, job enrichment leads to positive personal and work outcomes (Campion & Thayer 1985; Fried & Ferris 1988; Thomas & Griffin 1983).

Several different strategies can be used to stimulate core job characteristics. For example, job rotation does not change the nature of a specific job, but it does increase the number of duties an employee performs over time. This increases task variety and can also boost job identity and scope of purpose because the employee is performing several jobs (it can also have important ergonomic consequences which are discussed in a later section).

Job enlargement is the opposite of the scientific approach, which seeks to reduce the number of duties in any given job. Job enlargement seeks to increase skill variety. Task identity can also improve when the employee completes a whole and identifiable piece of work. One form of job enlargement is horizontal loading, which involves adding more duties with the same types of task characteristics. Vertical loading means creating a job with duties that have many different characteristics. While horizontal loading may increase skill variety, it may also foster resentment because the employee is expected to do more of the same. Vertical loading is more promising because it closes the gap between planning, doing and controlling the work. As a result, it affects job autonomy, skill variety and possible feedback.

Today, providing job autonomy appears to be a particularly effective way to obtain high worker commitment and quality—as a result of better education and changing social expectations, many employees value responsibility and empowerment. Yet providing autonomy depends on more than merely changing the job. Organisations with a high level of job autonomy usually have the following characteristics (Kerr 1993):

1 They invest a lot of time and effort in the recruitment and selection process to make sure new employees can handle workplace freedom
2 Their organisational structure is flat
3 They set loose guidelines, so employees know their decision-making parameters
4 Accountability is paramount; results matter more than process
5 High-quality performance is always expected

6 Openness and strong communication are encouraged
7 Employee satisfaction is a core value.

These job design approaches are the results of person-focused or behaviour-focused techniques of job analysis. These are behavioural statements resulting in the definition of the person oriented content of jobs. Among the techniques in this category are: Position Analysis Questionnaire, Physical Abilities Analysis, the Critical Incident Technique, the Extended Critical Incident Technique and the Guidelines Oriented Job Analysis. (Note that the job description in Table 7.3 is person-focused.)

Position analysis questionnaire

The Position Analysis Questionnaire (PAQ) is a structured questionnaire containing 187 job elements and 7 additional items relating to amount of pay that are for research purposes only. The Position Analysis Questionnaire is organised into 6 divisions, with each containing some of the 187 job elements. The divisions and a sample of elements include:

1 **Information input**—Where and how does the worker get the information used in performing the job? Examples are the use of written materials and near-visual differentiation.
2 **Mental processes**—What reasoning, decision making, planning and information-processing activities are involved in performing the job? Examples are the level of reasoning in problem-solving and coding/decoding.
3 **Work output**—What physical activities does the worker perform and what tools or devices are used? Examples are the use of keyboard devices and assembling/disassembling.
4 **Relationships with other people**—What relationships with other people are required in performing the job? Examples are instructing and contacts with the public or customers.
5 **Job context**—In what physical or social contexts is the work performed? Examples are high temperature and interpersonal conflict situations.
6 **Other job characteristics**—What other activities, conditions or characteristics are relevant to the job? (McCormick & Tiffin 1974, p. 53).

In addition to describing jobs on the basis of the 6 divisions and 187 elements, each element is also rated on 1 of 6 rating scales. These are:

1 Extent of use
2 Importance to the job
3 Amount of time
4 Possibility of occurrence
5 Applicability
6 Other.

Using these 6 divisions and 6 rating scales, the nature of jobs is essentially determined in terms of communication/decision making/social responsibilities; performance of skilled activities; physical activity and related environmental conditions; operation of vehicles and equipment; and processing of information. Using these 5 dimensions, jobs can be compared and clustered. The job clusters can then be used for, among other things, staffing decisions and the development of job descriptions and specifications (Sparks 1982, p. 87).

The Position Analysis Questionnaires reliance on person oriented traits allows it to be applied to a variety of jobs and organisations without modification. This, of course, allows organisations to more easily compare their job analyses with those of other organisations (Cornelius, DiNisi & Blencoe 1984; Shaw & Riskind 1983).

Job element inventory

Closely modelled after the PAQ, the 153-item Job Element Inventory has a readability index estimated to be at Year 10 level and is explicitly designed for completion by incumbents. The dimensional structure of the Job Element Inventory is similar to that of the PAQ. The advantage of this instrument lies in the cost savings associated with the fact that incumbents rather than trained analysts can complete the instrument (Harvey, Friedman, Hakel & Cornelius 1988).

Physical Abilities Analysis

A special subset of abilities and job demands used to analyse jobs is physical proficiency. The Physical Abilities Analysis uses nine abilities to analyse the physical requirements of tasks (Sparks 1982, p. 92). The nine abilities and examples of each include:

1 **Dynamic strength**—is defined as the ability to exert muscular force repeatedly or continuously over time.
2 **Trunk strength**—is a derivative of the dynamic strength factor and is characterised by resistance of trunk muscles to fatigue over repeated use.
3 **Static strength**—is the force that an individual exerts in lifting, pushing, pulling, or carrying external objects.
4 **Explosive strength**—is characterised by the ability to expend a maximum of energy in one or a series of maximum thrusts.
5 **Extent flexibility**—involves the ability to extend the trunk, arms and/or legs through a range of motion in either the frontal, sagittal or transverse planes.
6 **Dynamic flexibility**—contrasts with extent flexibility in that the ability involves the capacity to make rapid, repeated flexing movements in which the resilience of the muscles in recovering from distension is critical.
7 **Gross body co-ordination**—is the ability to co-ordinate the simultaneous actions of different parts of the body or body limbs while the body is in movement. This ability is frequently referenced as agility.
8 **Gross body equilibrium**—is the ability to maintain balance in either an unstable position or when opposing forces are pulling.
9 **Stamina**—is synonymous with cardiovascular endurance and enables the performance of prolonged bouts of aerobic work without experiencing fatigue or exhaustion.

In analysing jobs with the Physical Abilities Analysis, 7-point scales are used to determine the extent to which each job requires each of the 7 abilities (from maximum performance to minimum performance).

With the passage of such legislation as WorkCare, Equal Opportunity Acts and the creation of bodies such as the Victorian Accident Rehabilitation Council, the need for organisations to know the precise physical requirements for jobs is increasing. The information from the Physical Abilities Analysis can be instrumental, along with job design, in accommodating more workers to jobs. Other job analysis techniques also helping organisations to comply with legal requirements in hiring are the Critical

Incident Techniques, the Extended Critical Incident Technique and the Guidelines Oriented Job Analysis.

The Critical Incident Technique

One of the more frequently used job analysis techniques for developing behavioural criteria is the Critical Incident Technique (Flanagan 1954). This requires those knowledgeable about a job to describe to a job analyst critical job incidents, i.e. those that they have observed over the past 6–12 months that represent effective and ineffective performance. Sometimes the job analyst needs to prompt those describing the incidents by asking them to write down 5 key things an incumbent must be good at in the job to be analysed, or to identify the most effective job incumbent and describe that persons behaviour (Latham & Wexley 1981, pp. 49–51).

Those describing the incidents are also asked to describe what led to the incident, what the consequences of the behaviour were, and whether it was under the control of the incumbent. After the critical incidents have been gathered and described, they are rated by their frequency of occurrence, importance, and the extent of ability required to perform them.

Once the critical incidents and their characteristics are gathered, often a few hundred for each job, they can be clustered into job dimensions. These, which may often utilise only a subset of all the critical incidents obtained, can then be used to describe the job. They can also be used to develop performance appraisal forms, particularly Behavioural Anchored Rating Scales (described in Chapter 8). These in turn can be useful for appraising performance and spotting training needs. As with this job analysis method and those that follow, the major disadvantages are the time required to gather the incidents and the difficulty of identifying average performance, since these methods often solicit extremes of performance (e.g. ineffective or effective, or very bad or very good) and omit examples of average performance. This disadvantage, however, can be overcome by obtaining examples of all three levels of performance. This is what is done in the Extended Critical Incident Technique.

Extended Critical Incident Technique

Instead of beginning by having incumbents or others knowledgeable about jobs list examples of effective and ineffective behaviours, the Extended Critical Incident Technique begins by having incumbents identify **job domains** (Zedeck, Jackson & Adelman 1980). These (described further in the discussion of Guidelines Oriented Job Analysis) are essentially representations or umbrellas under which many specific tasks can be included. For example, a job domain for a manager may be *training*. Specific tasks that can be placed under this domain include: informally and formally teaching employees to learn new job skills, engaging in self-study on and off the job, and orienting new employees to the job and the organisation.

The specific tasks that come under a given domain may vary from organisation to organisation. Consequently, after the job domains have been identified (often between 10–20 per job) and defined, the job analyst lists the task statements that represent each. The analyst writes these tasks by asking the incumbents to give examples or scenarios that reflect three different levels of performance for each domain. In describing these, the incumbents list the main event, the behaviours of the people in the scenario, and the consequences of these. An example of a scenario depicting excellent performance for a manager in one domain is shown in Table 7.5.

Table 7.5 An example of excellent performance for a manager in one job domain

Domain: Management and supervision of personnel resources
Performance level: Excellent

Once a year, Mary completes the performance evaluations for her six clerical staff members. These are used to make decisions about promotions and merit increases. They are also used to provide feedback to workers. Recognising the importance of these evaluations, Mary considers the behaviour of each staff member carefully and tries to identify both the strengths and weaknesses of their performance. Mary is careful not to rely on global impressions when completing her evaluations. Instead, she provides examples of the behaviours that indicate a worker's performance level. Mary then uses these evaluations to provide feedback to members of her staff. She recommends improvements when they are needed and she acknowledges good performance as well. Thus Mary's evaluations help improve the effectiveness of her unit.

Why is this a useful scenario? Because it describes:

- Who: Mary, six staff members.
- Main event: Performance evaluations done once a year.
- Surrounding circumstances: Evaluations are used to make decisions about promotion, merit increases and for feedback.
- Behaviours: Identifies strengths and weaknesses; does not rely on global impressions; provides examples of behaviours that indicate performance levels; provides feedback; recommends needed improvements; acknowledges good performance.
- Consequences: Improves effectiveness of unit.

Using scenarios collected from incumbents, the analyst writes task statements. Each is essentially an example of one behaviour (or several) in a domain that is described in the scenarios. After these task statements are constructed, the incumbents (generally a different group from those writing the scenarios) indicate if they actually perform the tasks, how frequently, the difficulty in doing so, and the importance of the task.

With the information obtained thus far, job descriptions can be written. By adding another step, however, the Extended Critical Incident Technique can be used to develop performance appraisal forms to appraise performance and spot training needs. The step that is added to attain these benefits includes having the incumbents (again, a different group to ensure validity) estimate the level of performance each task statement represents and place it in one of the domains identified initially by a previous group of incumbents.

By next having the incumbents describe the abilities (physical and mental) necessary to perform the tasks in each domain, selection procedures can be developed. In this step the incumbents are presented with a list of abilities with short definitions, and asked to indicate the amount needed to satisfactorily perform the tasks in each domain. In addition to being useful in the development of selection procedures, the identification of these abilities can be used to write the employee specifications on a job description.

Although the Critical Incident Technique method takes time to develop, the Extended Critical Incident Technique takes even more time. The extended method, however, gathers a great deal more information from the incumbents, such as the needed abilities, performance levels and the domains of the jobs. In contrast with the Critical Incident Technique, the Extended Critical Incident Technique goes through several additional development steps. Both, however, are based on the identification of job behaviours and, as such, both are useful in performance appraisal and training. The same is true for the next job analysis method.

Guidelines Oriented Job Analysis

This is another behaviour focused job analysis technique which was developed in the US. There are several steps in it, each involving job incumbents. Before any of these steps begin, the incumbents indicate their names, length of time on the job, experience and the location of the job. In the first step, they list their job domains. Related duties in a job often fall into broad categories or groups. A secretary may type letters, contracts and memos. Since these duties are related, they are put into the same domain and we call it typing.

After the domains are identified, the incumbents list the important or critical duties typically performed for successful job performance in each domain. Duties are observable work behaviours and something that incumbents are expected to perform. Often each domain contains several duties. Once the critical duties are identified, the incumbents indicate how frequently they are performed. Then each duty's degree of importance is determined.

The fourth step is the incumbents determination of the skills and knowledge required to perform each duty.

The fifth step is the determination of the physical characteristics incumbents need to perform their job duties. Here the incumbents respond to five open-ended statements, each related to a physical characteristic.

The sixth and final step is a description of other characteristics necessary to perform the job, such as a listing of any legally required licences or degrees. It may also inquire about the necessity to work overtime and travel and, if so, when, where and how frequently.

The results of the six Guidelines Oriented Job Analysis steps are a job description, a set of individual knowledge, skills and abilities (KSAs) needed to perform the job, and a basis for developing job-related selection procedures and performance appraisal forms. As with the Extended Critical Incident Technique and the Critical Incident Technique, Guidelines Oriented Job Analysis, because it focuses on behaviours, is useful for developing performance appraisal forms and spotting training needs. In addition, since skills (physical and mental) and knowledge are identified, selection procedures can also be developed as described in Chapter 8. As with the Critical Incident Technique and the Extended Critical Incident Technique, Guidelines Oriented Job Analysis enhances employee understanding and validity of the job analysis since job incumbents are involved in the process. This involvement, however, takes time.

Team-based approaches

A third approach to job analysis and design is known as the team contemporary approach. Whereas the scientific and individual contemporary approaches design jobs for individuals, the team contemporary approach designs jobs for teams of individuals. These designs generally show a concern for the social needs of individuals as well as the constraints of the technology. Here teams of workers often rotate jobs and may follow the product they are working on to the last step in the process. If the product is large, for example an automobile, teams may be designed around sections of the final car. Each group then completes only a section and passes its sub-product to the next team. In the team contemporary design, each worker learns to handle several duties, many requiring different skills (also know as multi-skilling). Thus they can satisfy preferences for achievement and task accomplishment and some preferences for social interaction. When faced with decisions, teams that work well together will generally use teamwork, trying to involve all members. If their decisions and behaviours result in greater output, all team members share the benefits.

The team approach can be successful when establishing new plants or offices or when converting old plants. This is due in part to the flexibility of the people involved and their adaptability to change and to the fact that there are different degrees of teamwork. Typically, teams may start out making only a few decisions. After time, training, and familiarity, they begin to make many more decisions. Essentially, the team members pass through the stages of greater empowerment. In each new stage, they make more decisions, resulting in self-managed teams. The tasks about which these teams most often make decisions is shown in Figure 7.2. These decisions may be made by the team alone or in conjunction with the supervisor (Johnson 1993).

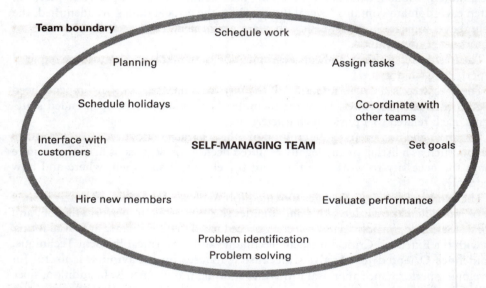

Figure 7.2 Self-managing teams: roles and responsibilities
Source: Based on Szwejczewski 1995, p. 14

Ergonomics

Ergonomics is concerned with fitting jobs to the basic physical abilities and characteristics of people so they can perform the jobs without undue effects on their health. Put another way, ergonomics is the science of making a workplace more comfortable and safer by reducing the physical stress that the task or the workstation place on the worker (Verespej 1994, p. 36). Studies have shown that when jobs are designed along ergonomic principles, worker productivity is greater.

For example, **job rotation**—changing jobs to change the parts of the body which are used—can reduce the likelihood of injury as well as offering more diversity on the job, because it reduces exposure to repetition, awkward posture and/or high forces (Vasbinder 1994). Vasbinder (1994) notes that in the sewn products industry, for example, to ensure that the person is moved to genuinely different tasks (and not just from one hand intensive job to another) one needs to understand jobs in terms of the frequency of finger, hand, wrist and arm motions as well as postures and object weights. One also needs to understand the product characteristics because of the pulling, pinching and pushing work done by the fingers with different materials. For example, lycra spandex and cotton sail cloth require different finger forces. It is job analysis which provides the basic structure for the job rotation scheme. Vasbinder (1994) identifies multiple benefits from job rotation since it not only reduces the risk of repetition injuries, it also increases the flexibility of the workforce because everyone learns multiple jobs and the knowledge developed through careful analysis of each job can be used for accommodating jobs for people with disabilities and developing balanced return-to-work programs for those undergoing occupational rehabilitation.

AT&T provides a good example of a company that sees the value of examining jobs for risk factors and applying some common sense to the way work is done (Verespej 1994, p. 37). By carrying out a job analysis, AT&T discovered that, to pack wire spools in boxes, each employee must:

- walk 3 metres to a stack of empty boxes
- stoop, reach and then carry the empty 500 gm box back to the work station, which had a bench height of 1 metre
- reach for a spool
- lower the 5 kg spool into a box
- reach for and then pull tape from a dispenser (with a pulling force of 2 kg) in order to seal the box
- lift the sealed box from a workstation
- carry the box 1 metre to a pallet with boxes stacked at heights ranging from 80 cm to 1 metre.

AT&T put the boxes on pallets to reduce the degree of stooping; gave workers who stood all day cushioned floor mats; and bought automatic tape dispensers to eliminate the stress on muscles from the pulling force that the employees needed to tear off the tape (Verespej 1994, pp. 40–42).

Managing diversity

The examples of an ergonomic approach to getting work done which are provided by Vasbinder (1994) and Veserpej (1994) highlight the importance of recognising that we manage people with quite different levels of skills and physical abilities, so that we can ensure the working environment is designed to take account of those differences. Job design is an important method by which organisations can accommodate the needs of their workers. It is also a way that organisations can increase the size of their recruitment pool of potential employees by making their workplaces more accessible to otherwise qualified individuals who may have previously been excluded.

Development of job families

The initial results of job analysis are typically many separate and unique job descriptions and employee specifications, as many as there are unique jobs. Often, however, not all these unique jobs are greatly different from each other: that is, it is likely that employees who perform one job can easily perform several others. It is also likely that these jobs are of similar value to the organisation. Consequently, organisations group jobs together into families or classes. They are placed in the same family to the extent they require similar employee specifications and are of similar value to the organisation (Pearlman 1980).

The use of job families provides many benefits. Many organisations use it in designing their compensation programs: it is sometimes difficult to justify paying jobs differently when they are nearly identical. In addition to their traditional use in compensation, job families can also be used to break down the walls between similar jobs and facilitate the movement of employees from job to job. This, coupled with employee agreement to job assignment flexibility, is critical to organisations offering employment security to employees. This also enables organisations to minimise overall staffing levels. Job families also enable organisations to be more efficient in their recruitment, selection, performance appraisal and training and development activities. For example, instead of developing several selection tests for several different jobs, it may be necessary to design only one or two.

Assessing job analysis methods

Confronted with several alternative job analysis methods, the question is: Which is the best to use? As with the selection of a job design approach, the appropriateness of a specific job analysis method depends upon two major sets of considerations. The first set represents the purpose job analysis serves and the second several practical concerns. The following discussion draws on evaluations undertaken by Ash & Levine (1980; 1981) and Levine, Ash & Bennett (1980).

Purposes of job analysis

A review of our earlier discussion indicates that the purposes job analysis serves include:

1. Job descriptions and employee specifications
2. Job classification and evaluation for compensation
3. Recruitment and selection information
4. Performance appraisal development
5. Training and development needs
6. Worker orientation
7. Human resource planning needs.

An assessment of how well these purposes are served by each method is shown in Table 7.6. The assessment of the methods is unique to each purpose. In relationship to job descriptions, the assessment of methods is determined by the extent to which it can be used to describe the jobs range of duties, the worker requirements necessary to perform them, and the conditions under which they are performed. In relationship to the job classification and evaluation purpose, each method is assessed by how easily and how directly the job information collected can be used to establish job classes and families and by how well internal equity distinctions are identified in using the method for job evaluation. In relationship to performance appraisal, each method is assessed by how well it provides behavioural examples of performance and identifies the quality of those examples. Similarly, in training and development, each method is assessed in relationship to how clearly behavioural examples of performance and the skills and abilities required for those behaviours are identified, thus allowing an evaluation of individuals against those requirements. Last, the assessment of each method against human resource planning reflects how well the method facilitates a needs analysis, one that can be used to identify specific current and future human resource training needs and the types of skills needed for future jobs.

Table 7.6 Assessment of several job analysis methods against purposes of job analysis

PURPOSES	FJA	MPDQ	HAY PLAN	PAQ	CIT	EXTENDED CIT	GOJA
Job descriptions	5	4	5	4	3	3	4
Job classification and evaluation	5	4	5	5	2	3	3
Recruitment and selection	4	4	4	4	4	5	5
Performance appraisal	3	3	4	3	4	5	5
Training and development	4	3	3	3	4	5	5
Human resource planning	4	4	3	4	4	4	4

1 Serves this purpose inadequately
2 Serves this purpose somewhat adequately
3 Serves this purpose adequately
4 Serves this purpose very adequately
5 Serves this purpose extremely adequately

Practical concerns

As with the purposes of job analysis, there are several practical concerns useful in assessing each job analysis method.

These are:

1 Versatility/suitability
2 Standardisation
3 User acceptability
4 User understandability/involvement
5 Training required
6 Readiness to use
7 Time to completion
8 Reliability and validity
9 Purposes served
10 Utility.

In assessing each method against these concerns, the following definitions of each concern are used: **Versatility/suitability** is the methods appropriateness for analysing a variety of jobs. **Standardisation** is the extent to which the method yields norms that allow comparison with different sources of job analysis data collection, at different times. **User acceptability** refers to the users acceptance of the method, including its forms. **User understandability/involvement** refers to the extent to which those who are using the method, or are affected by its results, know what it is about and are involved in the collection of job analysis information. **Training required** is that needed by those involved in using the method. **Readiness to use** is the extent to which it is ready. **Time to completion** is the time required for the method to be implemented and the results obtained. **Reliability and validity** refer to the consistency of the results obtained with the method and the accuracy of these in describing the duties, their importance, and the skills and abilities required to do them. **Purposes served** refers to the number of purposes listed above that are served by the method. To some extent, in summary, **utility** refers to the amount of overall benefit or value to be gained by the organisation in using the method in relationship to the costs incurred in its use.

Using these several practical concerns, the assessment of each job analysis method is presented in Table 7.7.

Table 7.7 Assessment of several job analysis methods several practical concerns

PURPOSES	FJA	MPDQ	HAY PLAN	PAQ	CIT	EXTENDED CIT	GOJA
Versatility/ Suitability	5	4	5	4	5	5	5
Standardisation	5	5	5	5	5	3	3
User acceptability	4	4	4	4	4	4	4
User understandability/ involvement	4	4	5	4	5	5	5
Training required	3	3	3	3	4	5	5
Readiness to use	5	5	5	5	3	3	3
Time to completion	4	4	4	4	3	3	3
Reliability and validity	4	4	4	4	4	5	5
Purposes served	4	3	3	4	3	4	4
Utility	4	4	4	4	3	4	4

1 Served to a very limited extent
2 Served to a limited extent
3 Served to an average extent
4 Served to an above average extent
5 Served to a great extent

The assessment of the job analysis methods presented in Tables 7.6 and 7.7 suggests that, overall, no method is clearly superior to others. Thus, in analysing jobs as in designing them, several considerations must be weighed and any potential constraints identified. It appears, however, that if the organisation really desires to use job analysis as a critical base upon which to develop and direct the remaining HRM activities, job analysis techniques providing extensive person focused information, such as the Extended Critical Incident Technique or Guidelines Oriented Job Analysis, may be most useful.

Trends in job analysis

Major trends in job analysis focus around assessing job analysis, the emerging notion of competency profiling, and the use of computer technology and human resource information systems.

Assessing job analysis

Assessment of job analysis can be done on the basis of how well it facilitates the organisation's staffing needs and whether or not it results in valid staffing procedures. Without job descriptions and worker specifications, potentially qualified job applicants cannot be identified and valid selection measures cannot be developed. The result may be rather expensive recruiting efforts and non-compliance with equal opportunity regulations. As such, these two measures can be used to assess the effectiveness of job analysis. Because some methods may be less expensive and more appropriate, it is important that this assessment of job analysis be done. The result may be a search for even more appropriate and less expensive methods. More recently, the underlying value of traditional job analysis has been called into question (Carson & Stewart 1996).

Carson & Stewart (1996) point out, rightly, that traditional job analysis techniques assume identifiable jobs exist in the organisation and they are independent of the individuals who are employed at any particular moment. Further, that they can be meaningfully described in terms of observable, or otherwise identifiable, behaviours (tasks) that lead to work outcomes important to the organisation. They argue however, that changing environmental conditions—the general movement from a manufacturing to an information society, rapidly advancing technology, increasing international competitiveness, and changing worker characteristics—have eroded the traditional conception of jobs and the conception of 'the job' (and therefore job analysis) has become less appropriate.

Carson & Stewart (1996) maintain that the move to an information society has created a workplace requiring employees to perform a wide variety of relatively complex tasks which are much less concrete than manufacturing work and so behavioural statements are less effective in capturing the activities of workers. At the same time, the rate of technological advancement is also becoming so accelerated that many jobs defined today will likely be obsolete such that workers will constantly be performing activities that go beyond formal job descriptions. Meanwhile, the increasing competitiveness of international organisations, coupled with changes in employee characteristics, has further changed the concept of a 'job' by forcing firms to find better ways of motivating employees as well as tapping into individual abilities. These observations by Carson & Stewart (1996) are, of course, focused on the same issues of dejobbing and the death of the job description that formed the basis of the HRNET interchange reported at the beginning of the chapter.

Competency profiling

Beyond the initial problems with traditional job analysis identified by Carson & Stewart (1996), it has been argued that job analysis methods yield inadequate information for other human resource activities because they require an inferential leap from job tasks and behaviours to specific individual characteristics of employees (Gatewood & Field, 1994). This leap is required because, while the various methods yield behavioural or task lists, they provide no direct information about the individual characteristics required to carry out the tasks or behaviours. As a consequence, human resource functions such as selection and training have to infer a list of desirable characteristics from the job analysis outcome.

In order to overcome this inferential leap, some recent job analytic methods have been proposed which ask job analysts to directly identify abilities necessary for successful job performance. This is often called competency profiling but, to the extent that a number of authors use the terms competency and knowledge, skill or ability interchangeably (Beardwell & Holden 1994, p. 286; Stone 1995, p. 22; Walker 1980, p. 154), it would seem the idea that this is merely old wine in a new bottle (Nankervis, Compton & McCarthy 1995, p. 158) has some currency. At the same time, insofar as the various discussions of the process stress the need to talk about the application of knowledge, skills and abilities in the context of the workplace, it serves to remind us that job analysis by whatever name is a strategic exercise which is necessarily informed by organisational objectives and that an individual's knowledge, skills and abilities can be seen to be competencies to the extent that they contribute to the achievement of those objectives.

Computer technology and HRIS in job analysis

The rapidly changing job environment and the vast amount of personnel information that is produced in job has prompted the development of computer technology aimed at managing the resultant databases, called Human Resource Information Systems (HRISs). This information, in turn, is critical for effective personnel management. For example, changing organisational requirements for particular blends of skills, knowledge and abilities, and personality, interests and preferences, can result in job descriptions and job specifications which do not accurately reflect current organisational needs.

Computer technology can be instrumental in avoiding mismatches between organisational needs regarding skills, knowledge and abilities, and personality, interests and preferences. Job description and job specification information crucial to job analysis components may be stored on the computer system and then used to match people with jobs (Dortch 1989).

The maintenance of timely job descriptions and job specifications is also useful in determining the worth of jobs to the organisation. By identifying compensable factors (job aspects to which monetary value is assigned), organisations may accurately develop equitable pay structures. This process can be greatly aided by the creation of job families that can be more readily constructed with computer technology.

Summary

An interesting postscript to the Internet debate which began this chapter is given by Robert J. Harvey (1996), webmaster of an Internet site at Virginia Tech (USA) devoted to job analysis. He was responding to the search for a citation to complete the reference list for this chapter and made the following observation in relation to that debate:

Many people have suggested we just drop the term 'job analysis' from our vocabulary, and make-up a new 90s-sounding buzzword that we can use instead. That may be true. However, sooner or later, any organisation that plans to stay in business has got to deal with the issue of what their employees are supposed to be doing, how they are supposed to be doing it, and what outcomes are to be expected. That's still job analysis whatever else you might want to call it!

Job analysis has a significant impact on the rest of the HRM activities and on the organisation's equal opportunity considerations. Although there is no magical way to do job analysis perfectly, it can, and furthermore must, be done. The challenge, therefore, is finding the best or most appropriate way to analyse jobs. Because there are so many ways, it becomes important to first identify what purposes are to be served. This is useful to know since different ways to analyse jobs serve different purposes, such as helping to develop tests for selection, criteria for performance appraisal, and needs for training programs. Once this is decided, the possible ways can be narrowed down. A final selection can then be made with the consideration of several practical concerns. The organisation can then start to establish its human resource needs and general staffing requirements. This, in turn, can be used to determine the organisation's recruitment and selection and placement needs, which will be discussed in the next chapters.

questions for discussion and review

1 What areas of human resource management are related to job analysis and design?
2 List several strategic purposes of job analysis and design.

3 In what ways is job analysis and design related to organisation goals and technology?
4 How can job analysis and design be affected by state and federal legislation?
5 Who has the responsibility for job analysis and design?
6 What is the difference between a job characterised by quantitative overload and one characterised by qualitative overload?
7 Identify and discuss the approaches to job analysis and design.
8 Discuss and review the important considerations in selecting job analysis methods.
9 In a nutshell, how might job analysis and design activities be assessed in terms of their importance to organisations?
10 Is job analysis dead?

case study

When Peter Brown was assigned to head the Internal Audit Department in March 1992, it had a staff of three senior officers. An accountant and an engineer were in charge of the audit of the financial systems and operational systems respectively. Another accountant, Janet Sim, was in charge of auditing five finance-related computerised systems. These five systems were considered by Top Management to be extremely important and had to be audited.

The Audit Department, however, did not appear to enjoy strong support from the General Manager. He understood that the Audit Department performed the 'watchdog' function in the organisation by ensuring that internal controls were in place, and ensuring operational departments maintained a high level of effectiveness and efficiency.

The General Manager was a person of vision who told his managers to look for quantum leaps. 'Look for projects which can double or triple the revenue or even improve it 30 times over! Don't just look at areas which improve productivity by just a few percentage points. Think Big!' he would say. Being a very busy man, he asked Mr Brown to report to one of his Assistant General Managers instead of directly to him. The other lower and middle managers soon adopted the boss's 'Think Big' mentality and consequently did not take the Audit Department seriously. 'Please don't disturb my department, go and audit someone else', they would hint when audit staff contacted them.

Mr Brown had been working in Tele-Info for over twenty years. He had been a manager in the Cost Management Department and was not exactly enthusiastic when he was told to move to the Audit Department. He did not really like the 'policeman' job. After all, as manager of the Cost Management Department, he too had not really liked being audited by the Audit Department. But he felt that he did not have a choice.

Mr Brown felt the need to add a System Analyst to his team and, after approval was granted, met his three senior officers to prepare a job description for the new officer. The final version is given in Appendix 1. Janet told Mr Brown that she wished to retain her existing duties. All computerised systems, besides those which she was handling, could be examined by the new Systems Analyst.

As a statutory board, the general guideline was that newly recruited officers should start at the lowest end of the salary scale. Because of this, the organisation generally engaged new graduates to fill its vacancies. However job advertisements usually included the phrase '2 or 3 years working experience in similar positions preferred'. The new position—Systems

Analyst (Internal Audit)—was advertised at the same time as the position of Systems Analyst (Development).

By the closing date, a fair number of applications for the post of Systems Analyst (Development) had been received. There were no applications for the post of Systems Analyst (Internal Audit). During the interviews, several applicants were asked if they would be interested in internal audit work. They all expressed their preference for the Development Department.

Florence Henderson was one of the applicants. She was told on 5 May 1993 that her application had been successful. She immediately resigned from the Multi-National Corporation where she had worked for 14 months. On 6 June 1993, she reported to Tele-Info for work.

Florence was surprised when she was told by the Personnel Officer that she had been appointed as Systems Analyst in the Audit Department. She was rather unhappy when she reported to Mr Brown for duty.

As Mr Brown briefed Florence, she soon realised that her main duties were to audit the software and application systems developed by other Systems Analysts in the organisation. By the end of the briefing session, she was very upset that the job was not what she had expected. She told Mr Brown directly that she had not expected her duties to turn out this way. Mr Brown was sympathetic but encouraged her to give the job a try.

That afternoon, as Florence sat in her office and reflected upon the morning's events, she became more and more upset. She arranged to see Mr Brown again to reject the appointment. Mr Brown contacted Personnel Department and Florence was posted to another department on her third day of work.

During the interviews for the next intake of Systems Analysts, the interviewing panel again asked the applicants whether they were interested in audit work.

Finally, one applicant, Joan Leeson, expressed her willingness. She reported for work on 1 October 1993.

Joan was a recent graduate from the local university. She had been looking for a job for sometime and, the place of work being only a short distance from her home, decided to accept the offer to work in the Audit Department.

Joan was an engineering graduate who did not know anything about auditing. Mr Brown told her to 'get used to the organisation, learn the company policies, the various functions of the company and the audit function'. Janet would give her some guidance at the beginning, and later she could start to audit the smaller systems on her own. After six months, Joan had attended courses on Advanced Programming, IBM Operating Systems, and the basics of Computer Audit. She had not started on an audit exercise on her own yet.

In May 1994, Joan started her first audit exercise. She prepared the audit program, studied the system being audited, and contacted the auditees for information. Contacting the auditees was particularly unpleasant for her as they were suspicious of her motives when they learnt that she was trying to check their internal controls. 'What are you going to do with your audit results?' 'So you're writing to the boss when you find weaknesses?' 'Why did you choose this system to audit?' they asked.

Joan examined two other systems in the next five months. The role of an internal policeman became more and more unpleasant to her. Some of her auditees happened to be former classmates and she found it very embarrassing to question their work. At times she ran into difficulties in her programming and had to consult her friends in the organisation. She felt that her friends and auditees were avoiding her. Furthermore, she had not found anything significantly wrong with the systems she audited. She questioned the value of her job and, in February 1995, she resigned.

Mr Brown was unhappy that, with Joan's resignation, the computer audit strength of the department had been further undermined. He discussed the problem with the Personnel Manager and asked him to search internally for Joan's replacement.

Betty Tandy was a Systems Analyst in the Systems Development Department. She had been there for a year and a half and believed that she was one of the better analysts in the department. In the latest promotion exercise, she believed that her Project Leader had promoted others less qualified than she was. She asked for a transfer to another department and was referred to Mr Brown.

Mr Brown was happy to accommodate Betty. After all, she had been a Systems Analyst in one of the departments computer audit was supposed to look into. Betty felt that she had nothing to lose by going to the Internal Audit Department. She was an accountancy graduate, and auditing was an area in which accountants were strong. She was transferred in April 1995.

As usual, Mr Brown asked Betty to take a few weeks to familiarise herself with computer audit methodologies and those audit exercises performed by Janet and Joan. After six weeks, Betty began to undertake audit exercises on her own.

Betty soon found that audit work was not suitable for her. She knew almost everybody in the EDP Division and it was quite awkward to examine their work for weaknesses. Often, she would compare her existing job with what she did in the Systems Development Department. There, she had been popular because she was better than average. Her colleagues had often consulted her when they had problems and she was in control of her work. Now she had to go around asking auditees for information on the systems she audited. Her friends seemed to avoid her. The job content was also less interesting. Training opportunities were reduced as in-house training for Systems Analysts was organised by EDP Division and, though staff from Internal Audit Department were also accommodated, she felt that she was treated as a 'second class' participant.

Betty was unhappy. When the Systems Development Department had a vacancy, she went to see Mr Brown to ask for a transfer back. Mr Brown failed to persuade her to stay and decided that it was not good to keep a discontented member of staff.

David Copperfield was a young engineer in another department. When he heard that a vacancy existed in the Internal Audit Department, he asked for a transfer there even though he had no audit experience. He was not happy with his existing assignment and believed he could gain some experience from a stint in audit work. Mr Brown also felt that internal staff would pick up the job faster so David was transferred to the Audit Department in October 1995.

David was aware that in the past all those appointed to the post of Systems Analyst (Audit) had not stayed long. He decided to take up the challenge 'to do a good job and make it interesting'. He started to learn relevant computer languages, to view self-study tapes in the computer library and initiated audit projects. It was not long before he realised that audit was, to put it plainly, 'checking others weaknesses'. He felt that most auditees were nice people and did not wish to find fault with them. David resigned in July 1996 to start a small business of his own. He had no regret leaving such a contentious job.

Mr Brown had to find a new person to do the job. He did not know where to look ...

Questions

1 Why was this the job nobody wanted?
2 What had Brown done that you would do differently?
3 What should Brown do before trying to find another incumbent for the position?

Systems analyst—job description

Responsible for:
1 Assisting Departmental Manager in planning the scope of computer audit
2 Designing, developing and implementing computer audit programs to ensure that there are proper controls
3 Designing and developing audit softwares and computer systems for audit analysis purposes
4 Providing consultation on computer-related matters and computer controls
5 Carrying out any other duties as directed by Departmental Manager.

Activities:
1 Prepare computer audit plans and audit programs
2 Interview auditees to understand their systems and controls
3 Review application systems, integrity controls of computer systems, operating systems and other EDP-related areas when deemed necessary
4 Design systems, write programs and maintain them for audit and analysis purposes
5 Prepare working appears on audit exercises conducted
6 Report audit findings and recommendations to Departmental Manager for improvements in controls, efficiency and effectiveness
7 Supervise staff and review their working papers
8 Provide technical consultation on computer-related matters to financial and operational audit sections of the department
9 Provide advice on control requirements as and when invited by other departments during the development of computer systems.

Source: Based on Putti & Toh (1990).

Resources

Burton, C. (1988a), *Monograph no. 2: Redefining Merit*, Australian Government Publishing Service, Canberra.
—— (1988b), *Monograph no. 3: Gender Bias in Job Evaluation*, Australian Government Publishing Service, Canberra.
Carson, K. P. & Stewart, K. P. (1996), 'Job analysis and the sociotechnical approach to quality: A critical examination', *Journal of Quality Management*, vol. 1, pp. 49–64.
Job Analysis and Personality Research Internet Site at http://harvey.psyc.vt.edu/ (webmaster Robert J Harvey).

References

Adam, E. E. & Ebert, R. J. (1986), *Production and Operations Management*, Prentice-Hall, Englewood Cliffs, NJ.
Amrine, H. T., Huber, V. L. & Hyer, N. L. (1985), 'The human factor in cellular manufacturing', *Journal of Operations Management*, vol. 5, pp. 213–27.
Ash, R. A. & Levine, E. L. (1980), 'A framework for evaluating job analysis methods', *Personnel*, Nov.–Dec., pp. 53–59.
—— (1981), *Evaluation of Seven Job Analyses*, Unpublished manuscript, University of South Florida, 17 July.

Beardwell, I. & Holden, L. (eds) (1994), *Human Resource Management: A Contemporary Perspective*, Pitman, London.

Bernstein, A. (1993), 'In the line of fire at the Teamsters', *Business Week*, August 30, p. 39.

Burton, C. (1988a), *Monograph no. 2: Redefining Merit*, Australian Government Publishing Service, Canberra.

—— (1988b), *Monograph no. 3: Gender Bias in Job Evaluation*, Australian Government Publishing Service, Canberra.

—— (1991), *The Promise and the Price: The struggle for equal opportunity in women's employment*, Allen & Unwin, Sydney.

Campion, M. A. & Thayer, P. W. (1985), 'Development and field evaluation of an interdisciplinary measure of job design', *Journal of Applied Psychology*, vol. 68, no. 1, pp. 29–43.

Carson, K. P. & Stewart, K. P. (1996), 'Job analysis and the sociotechnical approach to quality: A critical examination', *Journal of Quality Management*, vol. 1, pp. 49–64.

Cascio, W. F. (1982), *Applied Psychology in Personnel Management*, 2nd edition, Reston Publishing Company, Reston, Va.

Chorpade, J. & Atchison, T. H. (1980), 'The concept of job analysis: A review and some suggestions', *Public Personnel Management*, vol. 9, pp. 134–44.

Cornelius, E. T., DiNisi, A. S. & Blencoe, A. G. (1984), 'Expert and naive raters using the Position Analysis Questionnaire: Does it matter?', *Personnel Psychology*, Autumn, pp. 453–64.

Department of Labor (1991), *Dictionary of Occupational Titles*, 4th edition, Government Printing Office, Washington, DC.

Dortch, C. T. (1989), 'Job-person match', *Personnel Journal*, vol. 68, no. 6, pp. 49–57.

Dowell, B. C. & Wexley, K. N. (1978), 'Development of a work behavior taxonomy for first line supervisors', *Journal of Applied Psychology*, vol. 61, no. 3, pp. 563–72.

Fine, S. A. (1974), 'Functional job analysis: An approach to a technology for manpower planning', *Personnel Journal*, November, pp. 813–17.

Flanagan, J. C. (1954), 'The critical incident technique', *Psychology Bulletin*, vol. 51, pp. 327–57.

Fried, Y. & Ferris, G. R. (1988), 'The dimensionality of job characteristics: Some neglected issues', *Journal of Applied Psychology*, vol. 71, no. 3, pp. 419–26.

Gatewood, R. D. & Field, H. S. (1994), *Human Resource Selection*, 3rd edition, Harcourt Brace, New York.

Gael, S. (1983), *Job Analysis*, Jossey-Bass, San Francisco, CA.

Gilmore, A., Cunningham, J. & Lamond, D. (1991), 'Evaluation of the day-to-day management of the Great Barrier Reff Marine Park', Report prepared by the Great Barrier Reef Marine Park Authority, July.

Gordon, J., Hequet, M., Lee, C. & Picard, M. (1995), 'Job analysis: The foundation of employment tests', *Training*, April, pp. 23–25.

Grant, P. C. (1988), 'What use is a job description?', *Personnel Journal*, February, pp. 45–53.

Hackman, J. R. & Oldham, G. R. (1980), *Work Redesign*, Addison-Wesley, Boston, Mass.

Harvey, R. J. (1996), Internet communication, October 15.

Harvey, R. J., Friedman, F., Hakel, M. D. & Cornelius, E. T. (1988), 'Dimensionality of the Job Element Inventory: A simplified worker-oriented job analysis questionnaire', *Journal of Applied Psychology*, vol. 71, no. 3, pp. 639–46.

Hayes, R. H. & Jailkumar, R. (1988), 'Manufacturings crisis: New technologies, obsolete organisations', *Harvard Business Review*, Sept.-Oct., pp. 77–85.

Holton, E. F. & Bailey, C. (1995), 'Top-to-bottom curriculum redesign', *Training and Development*, March, pp. 40–44.

Hong, J. C. & Lin, Y. S. (1995), 'A model of job analysis on industrial occupations', *Work Study*, vol. 44, no. 1, pp. 11–13.

Jones, M. A. (1984), 'Job descriptions made easy', *Personnel Journal*, May, pp. 31–34.

Johnson, S. T. (1993), 'Work teams: What's ahead in work design and rewards management', *Compensation and Benefits Review*, March–April, p. 37.

Kerr, J. (1993), 'The best small companies to work for in America', *INC.*, July, p. 63.

Kulik, C. T. & Oldham, G. R. (1988), 'Job Diagnostic Survey', in S. Gael (ed.), *The Job Analysis Handbook for Business, Industry and Government*, vol. 2, John Wiley and Sons, New York, pp. 936–59.

Lamond, D. A. (1995), 'The art of HRM: Human Relationship Management', Paper presented at the ANZAM Annual Conference, Townsville, 4–6 December.

Latham, G. P. & Wexley, K. N. (1981), *Increasing Productivity Through Performance Appraisal*, Addison-Wesley, Reading, Mass.

Levine, E. L., Ash, R. A. & Bennett, N. (1980), 'Exploratory comparative study of four job analysis methods', *Journal of Applied Psychology*, vol. 65, no. 3, pp. 524–35.

Love, K. G., Bishop, R. C., Heinisch, D. A. & Montei, M. S. (1994), 'Selection across two cultures: Adopting the selection of American assemblers to meet Japanese job performance demands', *Personnel Psychology*, vol. 47, pp. 837–46.

Machalaba, D. (1986), 'United Parcel Service gets deliveries done by driving its workers', *The Wall Street Journal*, April 22, pp. 1, 23.

McCormick, E. J. (1976), 'Job and Task Analysis', in M. D. Dunnette (ed.), *Handbook of Industrial and Organizational Psychology*, Rand McNally College Publishing, Chicago.

—— (1979) *Job Analysis: Methods and Applications*, New York: AMACOM.

McCormick, E. J. & Tiffin, J. (1974), *Industrial Psychology*, 6th edition, Prentice-Hall, Englewood Cliffs, NJ.

Markowitz, J. (1981), 'Four methods of job analysis', *Training and Development Journal*, September, pp. 112–21.

Montminy, P. M. (1994), 'Managing', *Security Management*, February.

Nankervis, A. R., Compton, R. L. & McCarthy, T. E. (1995), *Strategic Human Resource Management*, 2nd edition, Thomas Nelson, Melbourne.

Page, R. & Van De Voort, D. (1989), 'Job Analysis and HR Planning', in W. F. Cascio (ed.), *Human Resource Planning, Employment and Placement*, Washington DC: Bureau of National Affairs, vol. 2, pp. 34–72.

Pearlman, K. (1980), 'Job families: A review and discussion of their implications for personnel selection', *Psychological Bulletin*, vol. 87, p. 127.

Piskurich, G. M. (1994), 'Developing self-directed learning', *Training & Development*, March, pp. 31–36.

Putti, J. M. & Toh, T. S. (1990), *Cases in Human Resource Management* (revised edition), Times Academic Press, Singapore.

Shaw, J. B. & Riskind, J. H. (1983), 'Predicting job stress using data from the Position Analysis Questionnaire', *Journal of Applied Psychology*, vol. 66, no. 2, pp. 253–61.

Sparks, C. P. (1982), 'Job Analysis', in K. M. Rowland & G. R. Ferris (eds), *Personnel Management*, Allyn and Bacon, Boston, pp. 78–100.

—— (1988), 'Job Analysis', in R. S. Schuler, S. A. Youngblood & V. L. Huber (eds), *Readings in Personnel and Human Resource Management,* West Publishing, St. Paul, Minn., pp. 108–20.

Stone, R. J. (1995), *Human Resource Management*, 2nd edition, John Wiley & Sons, Brisbane.

Szwejczewski, M. (1995), 'A quiet revolution', *Management Focus*, Cranfield School of Management, Cranfield, UK, pp. 13–14.

Thomas, J. & Griffin, R. (1983), 'The social information processing model of task design: A review of the literature', *Academy of Management Review*, October, pp. 672–82.

Tornow, W. W. & Pinto, P. R. (1976), 'The development of a managerial job taxonomy: A system for describing, classifying and evaluating executive positions', *Journal of Applied Psychology*, vol. 61, pp. 410–17.

Vasbinder, D. M. (1994), 'Ergonomic helpline', *Bobbin*, September, pp. 164–66.

Verespej, M. A. (1994), 'Ergonomics: An unfounded fear?', *Industry Week*, December 5, pp. 36–42.

Wachter, H., Modrow-Thiel, B. & Rossman, G. (1994), 'Work design and computer-controlled systems: Job analysis under automation—ATAA', *Logistics, Information Management*, vol. 7, no. 5, pp. 44–52.

Walker, J. W. (1980), *Human Resource Planning,* McGraw-Hill, New York.

Zedeck, S., Jackson, S. J. & Adelman, A. (1980), *Selection Procedures Reference Manual*, University of California Press, Berkeley, CA.

chapter 8

Recruitment, selection and placement

Peter McGraw

learning objectives

After studying this chapter, you will be able to:

1. Understand the strategic importance of recruitment, selection and placement to an organisation.
2. Understand the links between recruitment, selection and placement and other HRM activities.
3. Know the purpose of recruitment, and relationships influencing recruitment.
4. Identify the various sources and methods of obtaining job applicants.
5. Appreciate current trends in the recruitment process.
6. Recognise the advantages and disadvantages of different selection techniques.

chapter 8

chapter outline

- Recruitment — 310
  - Purposes and importance of recruitment — 310
- Relationships influencing recruitment — 311
  - Relationships with the external environment — 311
  - Relationships with other HRM activities — 312
  - Obtaining job applicants: sources and methods — 312
  - Increasing the pool of potentially qualified applicants — 316
- Trends in recruitment — 319
  - Recognition of diversity issues — 319
  - Assessing recruitment — 320
  - Behaviourally-based recruitment systems — 321
  - Rejection with tact — 322
- Selection and placement — 322
  - Purposes and importance of selection and placement — 323
  - Relationships influencing selection and placement: the internal environment — 324
  - Relationships with other HRM activities — 325
  - Considerations in choosing selection techniques — 325
  - Reference verification and background checks — 330
- Methods of using information for selection and placement decisions — 339
  - The single predictor approach — 339
  - The multiple predictor approach — 340
  - Australian data on selection practices — 340
- Biases in selection — 341
  - Training — 343
  - Decision aids — 343
  - Trends in selection and placement — 344
  - Assessing selection and placement decisions — 345
  - Use of computer technology — 345
- Summary — 346
- Questions for discussion and review — 346
- Case study — 347
- Resources — 347
- References — 348

HRM IN THE NEWS

Assessing 'real' candidates

BY MARK LAWSON

It's the first day on the job and you are meeting with a representative of a major customer who is not happy with the level of service, or with deliveries of your company's products.

Can you deal with those concerns, as well as discover the fact that the salary bonus of the visiting executive is also riding on having the problem solved, fast?

If you can't then no harm is done except, perhaps, to your own career prospects. For the visiting executive is simply an actor briefed beforehand and the whole session has been videotaped for later analysis by assessors.

Welcome to the growing trend towards assessment centres as a means of selecting personnel.

Instead of relying solely on a half-hour chat and a glance at a résumé as the basis for assessing applicants, organisations are using a range of new techniques, including psychological testing, structured interviews, active reference checking and assessment centres, often in combination.

That last technique involves putting the applicant through a management simulation, complete with a fully worked out scenario and actors playing the parts of visitors and colleagues. One of the major operators in the field in Australia is DDI-Asia/Pacific.

DDI consulting services manager Mr Peter Goldrick said the number of assessments done by the company over five years had risen from zero to 3000 a month, and was continuing to grow.

Most of those doing the assessment were people within large organisations who wanted promotion to managerial level, but its use in straight selection was also growing.

In the assessments by DDI and two of its major competitors, Wilson Learning and Saville & Holdsworth Australia, as well as assessment centres set up in major corporates such as BHP, participants are given a tough 'in tray' assignment.

One such DDI exercise, presented to the participant in the form of a videotape of a managing director giving a series of tasks to a divisional director, was exhaustive—designed to require a day and a half of intense work.

As the candidate's efforts are also videotaped and reviewed it's an expensive way of weeding out applicants but, properly done, can be effective.

DDI senior consultant Mr Andrew Gill said that after doing the exercises applicants freely admit that they were able to pretend for a time, but then the test proved too much.

'They will say, "that's the real me" ', he said.

Another effective point in dealing with the applicants afterwards is that their own recorded words can be repeated back to them.

Mr Gill and Mr Goldrick agreed that the tests were expensive, around $1500 per exercise for a line manager and several thousand dollars for a general manager test.

But the costs of selecting senior personnel were also very high, as much as one third of their annual salary (say, $50 000 for an $150 000-a-year executive), with the added cost and risk that the appointment might not work out, they said.

The apparent accuracy of assessment centres in separating the management wheat from the chaff, plus the fact that the participants themselves usually admit that the assessment is right, partly accounts for the acceptance of the method in the US and UK, says Mr Scott Ruhfus, managing director of Saville Holdsworth.

He said that assessment centres had become very big in those countries in order to counter draconian employment and discrimination legislation.

Their use had also been growing markedly in Australia since 1990 but management had to remember that the centres were one selection tool among many.

A behavioural test followed by an interview could be just as effective and was certainly cheaper. In fact, assessment centres should only be used in conjunction with tests and interviews, and the centres themselves had to be designed and run professionally.

Source: *Financial Review*, 2 August 1996, p. 15.

HRM IN THE NEWS

Why psych tests are just the job

BY MARK LAWSON

'Is your father your ideal male figure?'

The question's relevance to your work may not be immediately apparent, but it's the sort of thing you are asked when applying for a job.

Psychometric testing is one of a range of techniques now frequently used in the recruitment process in an effort to reduce the number of wasteful, misjudged appointments.

Given that the appointment of even a mid-rank executive on $60 000 can end up costing the company $60 000 to $90 000 if it does not work out, there is an obvious incentive to make the right choice.

Neil Jones, a director of recruitment consultancy Morgan & Banks, says that six years ago his company might have conducted 10 to 15 such tests each week on behalf of clients. Now the figure is nearer 40 or 50 a week, and growing by 20 per cent a year.

Psychometric tests have their detractors, but everyone in the recruitment industry acknowledges that they are an established feature of the selection process for larger companies trying to reduce the costs of personnel turnover.

Jones says the tests are part of his company's efforts to add value to its client's search for the right employees, but warns that they can be misused if too much is read into the results.

Morgan & Banks regards the selection process as 'a big pie', of which psychometric tests are just one piece, he says. Other important slices include the standard interview, reference checking and checking of academic qualifications.

The results of all these tests are raised with the hapless candidate in interviews that are much more probing than the traditional half-hour chat with a complete stranger.

The tests interact with the other techniques to highlight issues that can be raised with the candidate in the interview or with the candidate's referees.

Other recruitment experts contacted by the *Australian Financial Review* had mixed views on the usefulness of psychometric tests, but recognised that their use was growing—mainly among the large, blue-chip companies, rather than small to medium-sized enterprises.

Among known users of such tests are Macquarie Bank and Bankers Trust.

In response to an inquiry by the AFR, BT issued a statement saying that psychology testing was often used as a part, although not a major past, of the hiring process for BT marketing and some technology personnel. The tests were not used by the bank 'at large'.

The tests gave BT an insight into the candidate's work style, interpersonal skills and motivations, and whether or not the person was a team player, the statement said.

Mr Greg Savage, a director of Recruitment Solutions, said that his firm used tests both in their own selection procedures and at the request of clients.

He said that client requests for such tests had become more frequent in the past few years, as clients looked to improve their 'hit rate' of successful appointments, but they could never be used in isolation.

One technique often used in his firm was to ask in-depth questions of the applicant's referees, but ensuring that the questions they asked related to the job the applicant was going to, rather than the job the applicant had been doing.

Tests were useful in that they might show, say, that the candidate was weak in interpersonal skills, that is, dealing with people, and that point could be discussed with the referees and in the interview, he said.

Mr Richard Levine, managing director of Hays Personnel Services (formerly Accountancy Placements), said that his company routinely used a form of character profiling, and would arrange for other forms of tests if requested by clients.

He also agreed that psychometric testing of one form or another was 'quite widespread' but was mostly used by the larger companies. SMEs were 'less fixated' on the need for tests.

Otherwise the techniques used depended very much on the level of executive that was being hired, Mr Levine said.

Psychometric tests have their detractors, including Mr Grant Montgomery, managing director of El Australia Ltd.

Mr Montgomery said that the tests did have their uses, for example in hiring skilled and semi-skilled personnel where there were not many other factors to help judge the selection.

Such tests were also easy to administer, were not influenced by personal factors, such as the applicant's communications skills or accent, and passing a long test together could help a work team bind together.

But the tests also had a mathematical bias, and tested applicants for complex executive tasks on the basis of their ability to answer a lot of simple questions quickly.

The tests did not measure creative skills, people skills or lateral thinking, and test scores could be improved by doing tests regularly.

Although there was research to show a correlation between high IQ scores and job proficiency (though low IQ people can still do well and high IQ people may still do badly), there was no research showing correlations between job proficiency and personality tests.

Large-scale testing could even do some damage. Mr Montgomery knew of one company that IQ tested its employees but the results, including the fact that the leader of a very successful team had a lower IQ than the team members, leaked from the personnel department.

The result was to undermine the position of the leader and make for a much less effective team.

If the company did want to run tests then company executives had to be careful that they were testing for the characteristics that fitted the job—and not, say, testing mathematical skills for a job dealing mainly with other people.

Thus although interviewing was a far from perfect method of selection it remained 'the only game in town', and a great deal could be done by a skilled, experienced interviewer who also spoke with the referees and knew what skills the client wanted, Mr Montgomery said.

As noted, psychometric tests are just one of a number of sophisticated techniques used by an increasingly professional recruitment industry, selection centres and behavioural interviews.

Very little information is available about assessment centres, where several applicants may be put through a weekend of testing, as they are still quite new to Australia.

One group to practise the other technique of behavioural assessment interviewing is the specialist graduate recruitment group, the Sydney-based Accord Group.

> Accord spokeswoman, Ms Laraine Toms, said that behaviour interviews were a structured pattern of questions designed to test candidate's past behaviour in specific situations, selected for their relevance to the needs of the client.
>
> She said that, for example, the interview would look at how the applicant had reacted in various situations involving conflict and leadership in campus activities—a useful technique for graduates as there was no work record from which to judge their performance.
>
> One point on which everyone agreed was that the traditional method of interviewing was an unreliable guide to how the candidate was likely to perform in the job. The only thing interviewing appeared to measure was how well the candidate performed in an interview.

Source: *Financial Review*, 24 June 1996, pp 1, 7.

These two 'HRM in the news' items are indicative of the amount of attention that recruitment, selection and placement are receiving in modern Australian organisations. Many of the reasons for this attention, such as fear of litigation and the costs of incorrect selection decisions, are mentioned in the articles. However, a more fundamental reason for organisations to take great care in recruitment, selection and placement activities lies in a recognition that, as was discussed in Chapters 1 and 2, the extent to which an organisation achieves its strategic goals depends largely on the way in which people are managed within that organisation. Recruitment, selection and placement are key activities in managing people strategically. Getting the right people in the right jobs in the organisation is a fundamental basis for getting value added performance from people and a key mechanism for aligning the management of people with organisational vision and mission and hence ensuring that strategic goals are achieved. A US study analysing the productivity rates between employees in self-paced jobs concluded that the most productive employees were about twice as good as the least productive (Schmidt & Hunter 1983). Moreover, the writings on HRM best practice consistently cite selective recruiting as a key practice in achieving effective organisational performance. This is mirrored by the recruitment and selection policies of large numbers of best practice organisations (Pfeffer 1995). In Australia, a recent study by Dowling & Fisher (1995), which canvassed the views of nearly 2800 HR managers, identified recruitment and selection as key areas where new policy and systems had been developed in the last five years.

The translation of organisational strategy into selection decisions should work through a number of steps which involve the organisation forming a view or a vision of what it wants to be like, a broad plan of how to get there and detailed implementation strategies which will enact the desired change. The implications of these changes should then be assessed in relation to the technical system and culture within the organisation and this exercise in turn will yield information about the type of people required by the organisation. This is the process of job analysis and competency assessment which has been detailed in Chapter 7.

In addition to the challenge of getting the right blend of people to facilitate the achievement of organisational mission, organisations today also face numerous external challenges in the area of staffing. Skill shortages in some areas, the difficulty of dismissing staff who do not perform and the need to conform to stringent standards in terms of non-discriminatory selection procedures are obvious areas of concern. Other challenges arise from the ongoing need for organisations to systematically identify their human resource requirements and develop strategies to ensure that these needs are met.

In this chapter the critical HR functions of recruitment, selection and placement are reviewed. The purpose of each is discussed as well as relationships with other HRM activities, and current methods used.

Recruitment

Recruitment is generally defined as searching for, and obtaining, potential job candidates in sufficient numbers and quality, and at the right cost, for the organisation to select the most appropriate people to fill its jobs. In addition to job needs, the recruitment activity should be concerned with filling the needs of job candidates. Consequently, recruitment not only attracts individuals to the organisation but also increases the chance of retaining them once they are hired. Recruitment activity must also be conducted in compliance with an extensive set of Commonwealth and state rules and legal regulations. Thus *recruitment* is specifically the set of activities and processes used to legally obtain a sufficient number of the right people at the right place and time so that the people and the organisation can select each other in their own best short- and long-term interests. Reflecting all these aspects of recruitment is the fact that it serves several purposes in organisations.

Purposes and importance of recruitment

The general purpose of recruitment is to provide a pool of potentially qualified job candidates. More specifically, the purposes of recruitment are to:

1. Determine the present and future recruitment needs of the organisation in conjunction with the human resource planning activity and the job analysis activity
2. Increase the pool of job applicants with minimum cost
3. Help increase the success rate of the selection process by reducing the number of obviously underqualified or overqualified job applicants
4. Help reduce the probability that job applicants, once recruited and selected, will leave the organisation after only a short period of time
5. Meet the organisation's responsibility for equal opportunity programs and other social obligations regarding the composition of its workforce
6. Start identifying and preparing potential job applicants who will be appropriate candidates
7. Increase organisational and individual effectiveness in the short- and long-term
8. Evaluate the effectiveness of various techniques and locations of recruiting for all types of job applicant (Schneider & Schmidt 1977).

Several important activities are part of recruitment, including determining the organisation's short- and long-range needs by job title and level in the organisation, staying informed on job market conditions, developing effective recruiting materials, developing a systematic and integrated program of recruitment in conjunction with other personnel activities, and, with the co-operation of the line managers, obtaining a pool of qualified job applicants; recording their number and quality, as produced by the various sources and methods of recruiting, and following up on those hired or not hired, in order to evaluate the effectiveness of the recruiting effort. In addition, all of these must be done within a legal context that may affect an organisation's recruitment and selection policies and procedures.

Meeting all these purposes effectively enables the organisation to avoid legal problems and to select only those applicants who are qualified and will be productive. In essence, effective recruiting is crucial in helping the organisation to achieve its strategic objectives and helps an organisation attain the general purposes of HRM which are discussed in Chapter 1.

Relationships influencing recruitment

In achieving the purposes listed above, recruitment is influenced by many relationships with other HRM activities and with the external environment. The most important of these relationships are described next (see Figure 8.1).

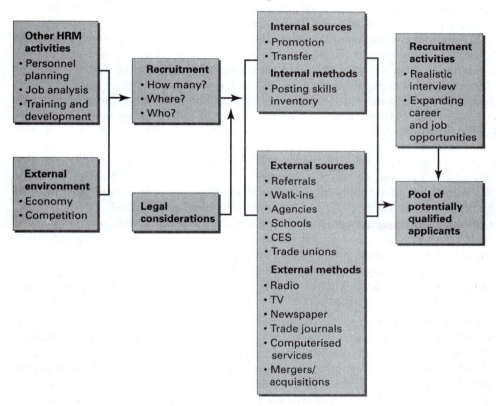

Figure 8.1 Relationships and aspects of the recruitment activity
Source: Schuler et al. 1992, p. 162

Relationships with the external environment

Often the type of employees an organisation needs depends upon the external environment. For example, the current shortage of skilled workers such as diagnostic radiographers, printing machinists, cabinetmakers, nuclear medical technicians, secondary school teachers (maths and science) and chefs is presenting many Australian organisations with a real challenge to recruit skilled workers in sufficient numbers (Australian Bureau of Statistics 1995, p. 3).

In addition to these external economic factors which influence an organisation's recruitment activities, are the considerations of equal opportunity legislation, which were discussed in Chapter 4. It has also been argued that stringent unfair dismissal legislation at the Federal level has encouraged some firms to remain small so as to reduce the potential for claims of unfair dismissal which may arise when a firm recruits new staff who turn out to be unsatisfactory.

Relationships with other HRM activities

While recruitment is affected by all aspects of HRM, three relationships are critical.

1 **Human resource planning.** To develop a strategic recruiting program, extensive planning is required. Recruiting programs are developed around three components of organisational planning: (1) strategic business planning, which determines the organisation's goals, future products and services, growth rate, structure, and location, (2) job-role planning, which specifies what will be done at different levels, and (3) human resource planning, which determines the types of jobs the organisation needs (or will need) to fill, as well as the skills, knowledge, and abilities that job applicants need. All three planning components are interrelated and necessary to determine how many individuals should be recruited to fill specific positions.

2 **Job analysis.** Job analysis is also important because it identifies the organisation's need for jobs and pinpoints the knowledge, skills and abilities qualified recruits need to possess. No internal or external recruiting should begin until there is a clear and concise statement of the education, skills, and experience requirements and the salary range for the job. In larger organisations, this information is readily available in job descriptions and salary structures. Yet numerous hours and dollars are spent in recruiting, particularly advertising, where the applicant is required to play a 'guessing game' about the job qualifications required (Acuff 1992).

3 **Training and development.** If recruiting activities produce a large pool of qualified job applicants, the need for employee training may be minimal. But recruiting activities may produce only a large, potentially unqualified pool of job applicants. At this point, the organisation may weigh the costs and benefits of selecting versus those of training. If the costs of selection are deemed greater than those associated with training, the organisation may hire all the applicants it needs and train them.

A further point related to this concerns how narrowly the organisation seeks to be in recruiting purely on the basis of skills as opposed to recruiting on the basis of attitudes of the candidates. It is often said that Australian organisations 'hire on the basis of skills and fire on the basis of attitudes', meaning that the major recruitment and selection criteria are narrowly, and more or less exclusively, linked to the position description and job specification rather than broader issues such as the attitudinal requirements of the job. In some Asian countries, notably Japan, there is a tendency to use broader recruitment criteria related to the whole person and then train extensively to provide the right skills.

Obtaining job applicants: sources and methods

The process of obtaining job applicants is essentially about two things; reaching people who the organisation considers qualified for the job, and generating sufficient interest that these people are motivated to apply for the job. There are two major sources: internal and external.

Internal sources

Internal sources include present employees, friends of employees, former employees, and former applicants. Promotions and transfers can also provide applicants for departments or divisions within the organisation. Current employees are a source of job applicants in two respects: they can refer friends to the organisation, and they can also become applicants themselves by potential promotion or transfer.

Promotions

The case for promotion from within rests on several sound arguments. One is that internal employees are better qualified. 'Even jobs that do not seem unique require familiarity with the people, procedures, policies, and special characteristics of the organisation in which they are performed' (Sayles & Strauss 1977). Another is that employees are likely to feel more secure and to identify their long-term interests with the organisation that provides them the first choice of job opportunity. Availability of promotions within an organisation can also motivate employees to perform, and internal promotion can be much less expensive to the organisation in both time and money.

By comparison, luring applicants from outside the organisation can be an expensive process. Often the new recruit is brought in at a salary higher than that of workers currently in similar positions, and the costs to the organisation of relocating the new recruit and his or her family may range from $10 000 to $50 000. Soon other employees will learn of this expensive new recruit. The result, especially if he or she fails to contribute as expected, is dissatisfaction among current employees. In addition, the incentive value of promotions may diminish. Disadvantages of a *promotion-from-within* policy may include an inability to find the best qualified person, infighting and inbreeding (the factors which lead to inbreeding are dealt with in greater depth later in this chapter in the section on selection bias). Moreover, an organisation with a promotion from within policy may also end up having to pressure candidates for the promotions.

Considering these advantages and disadvantages, it is not surprising to find organisations doing some internal promoting while obtaining some applicants from external sources. In addition, they tend to obtain particular types of employees from particular sources. For example, many organisations are more likely to hire highly-trained professionals and high-level managers from the outside than to promote from within. Further discussion of sources used for particular applicants is presented later in this chapter. Irrespective of whether internal or external sources of promotion are used, promotion considerations must incorporate affirmative action and equal employment requirements.

Transfers

Another critical way to recruit internally is by transferring current employees without promotion. Transfers are often important in providing employees with the more broad-based view of the organisation that is necessary for future promotions. A second reason for transferring employees focuses on the changing nature of organisations. For a variety of reasons the trend today is towards lean, flat organisations, and more and more mid-career employees are becoming plateaued in positions with little or no advancement opportunity.

With promotional opportunities blocked, a transfer may give these committed employees opportunities for learning new skills, enriching their jobs and avoiding the staleness that can come from remaining in the same job for too long. The slogan that captures this sentiment is that while most firms these days cannot 'guarantee employment' they can 'guarantee employability'.

Internal methods

Candidates for job vacancies can be located by a notice on the bulletin board, word of mouth, personnel records, promotion lists based on performance, potential ratings obtained from assessment activities, seniority lists, and lists generated by the skills inventory in an organisation's Human Resource Information System (HRIS). The most frequently used methods include **job posting** and **skills inventories**.

Job posting

Job posting, a method of prominently displaying current job openings, extends an open invitation to all employees in an organisation. It serves the following purposes:

1. Provides opportunities for employee growth and development
2. Creates a greater openness in the organisation by making opportunities known to all employees and thereby promotes equality
3. Increases staff awareness of salary grades, job descriptions, general promotion and transfer procedures, and what constitutes effective job performance
4. Communicates organisation goals and objectives and allows each individual the opportunity to find a personal fit in the job structure.

Although job postings are usually found on bulletin boards, they also appear in newsletters, and are announced at staff meetings. Sometimes specific salary information is included, but job grade and pay range are more typical. Job posting is beneficial for organisations because it improves morale, provides employees with the opportunity for job variety, facilitates a better matching of employee skills and needs, and fills positions at a low cost (Kleinman & Clark 1984; Levine 1984).

These benefits are not always realised. Conflicts are sometimes created if an 'heir apparent' in a department is passed over in favour of an outside candidate. Conversely, the system may lose credibility if the successful candidate within the department has apparently been identified in advance and the manager is merely going through the motions in considering outsiders. In addition, the morale of the unsuccessful candidates may suffer if feedback is not carefully handled. Finally, choices can be more difficult for the selecting manager if two or three equally qualified candidates are encountered.

Skills inventories

Another method of internal recruiting is to use skill-related information buried in personnel files; much time and effort is required to get at it. A formal skills inventory aggregates this information through the use of an HRIS. Any data that can be quantified can be coded and included in a skills inventory.

Common information includes name, employee, number, job classification, prior jobs, prior experience, specific skills and knowledge, education, licences, publications, and salary levels. The results of formal assessments, such as those obtained in assessment centres, during work-sample tests, and with job interest inventories, are usually included. Skill inventories should also include information regarding the employee's job interests, geographical preferences, and career goals. The inclusion of the latter information ensures that potential job assignments meet individual as well as organisational goals.

Skill inventories are only as good as the data they contain. They are also time-consuming and somewhat costly to maintain. However, a skill inventory helps ensure that *any* individual who has the necessary qualifications for a position is considered.

External sources and methods

Recruiting internally may not always be desirable and does not always produce enough qualified job applicants. This is especially true for organisations that are growing rapidly or have a large demand for high-talent professional, skilled and managerial employees. Therefore organisations need to recruit from external sources. Recruiting from outside has a number of advantages, including bringing in people with new ideas. It is often cheaper and easier to hire an already-trained professional or skilled employee, particularly when the organisation has an immediate demand for scarce labour skills and talents. External sources can also supply temporary employees who provide the organisation with much more flexibility than permanent ones. External recruiting sources include walk-in applicants, the Commonwealth Employment Service, private employment agencies, trade unions and schools. In addition to these, organisations use traditional recruitment methods such as advertising in newspapers, on radio and, to a lesser extent, on television. More recent methods of staff recruitment are through acquisitions and mergers and the use of computerised recruiting services.

In the last decade there has also been a massive growth in the use of consultants and external recruitment agencies. Estimates concerning the usage of these by Australian firms vary but Drake Consulting, recently estimated that somewhere between 20–30 per cent of Australian companies use recruitment firms to hire permanent staff and up to 50 per cent use recruitment firms to hire temporary staff. In 1994–95 the National Association of Personnel Consultants surveyed their members and concluded that they had placed 69 209 people in permanent and 372 685 in non-permanent positions. This equated to a wages bill of $1 522 262 999 and, including revenues from contracting, represented a total industry revenue of $2 107 662 909 (National Association of Personnel Consultants 1996).

In some industries the growth of agencies has had a major impact on employment patterns. In engineering, for example, agencies such as Skilled Engineering have grown rapidly in recent years and are now major employers in their own right. As an indication of size and growth in the 1995–96 report to shareholders Skilled Engineering reported a sales revenue of just under $300 million, an increase of 39 per cent from 1994–95 (Skilled Engineering 1996).

The recent expansion of the information superhighway has seen the emergence of recruiting on the Internet. It is now standard for newspapers to put their classified advertisements on the Internet and recruitment agencies, universities and some professional associations all now advertise positions on the Internet.

Internet recruitment postings are also becoming common among companies who have access to the system. This is expected to be a major growth area of recruitment in the next few years as more and more organisations connect to the Internet. Companies who already have home pages on the Internet include Intel, Sony, Siemens, Fujitsu, Heinz, Kellog's, Lloyds Bowmaker, Ericsson, AT&T, Procter and Gamble and UNISYS.

Future organisational forms

Lawyers find BOC selection system a gas

BY PETER ROBERTS

Objectivity is one of those things companies strive for when selecting their suppliers, but it is a state rarely achieved when choosing service providers such as lawyers and business consultants.

Now an innovative supplier selection process developed within BOC Gases Australia Ltd is showing that there can be something better than ad hoc choices based on gut feeling and the old boy network.

Last month BOC Gases chose national law firm Middletons Moore and Bevins to supply its legal needs for an open-ended period after an exhaustive supplier evaluation selection and performance appraisal (SESPA).

The SESPA system, developed by Craig Lardner, BOCs head of materials management, has since been adopted by 60 BOC group companies internationally as part of its global sharing of best practice.

While SESPA has already been used to select companies supplying BOC in Australia with $270 million worth of goods annually, the selection of Middletons is the first in the area of high-value services.

The SESPA process began with the formation of a three-person evaluation team led by BOCs in-house legal specialist, David Voet.

The team sent a detailed questionnaire to the 27 key users of legal services within the company, gleaning from their answers a total of 32 key competencies in four areas that users expected of an outside legal firm.

Only four of the competencies related to cost, with users focusing on the law firm's capabilities, customer focus, ability to innovate and continuous improvement and quality management skills.

Once the evaluation team understood the internal expectations of BOC gases, it was able to weigh the 32 competencies and include them in a tendering document sent to a wide range of legal firms.

A spreadsheet matrix of the competing firms' competencies was then used to guide an interview process score short-listing companies' ability to match BOCs needs.

Firms were invited to present their proposals to BOC in two-hour sessions and present a final 'come-back' document.

Middletons, which scored highly throughout the SESPA process, came out well ahead of its competitors—a result that David Voet admits was a surprise, given the pedigree of the competition.

'No-one can criticise the deal, it was very objective', Says Voet. 'Personal bias can't change the process'.

Several innovative features of the relationship were developed during the SESPA process as the client and supplier came to understand each other.

BOC has prepared an information pack given to all new Middleton's staff, for example, while the firm is providing one staffer to work at BOCs Chatswood head office one day a week. Key BOC managers are also able to telephone Middleton's experts for short, free-of-charge responses to emerging legal issues.

The single contract, which BOC expects to change only gradually over time, replaced a situation where BOC spent an average of $400 000 a year with up to 21 outside law firms.

While cost was only one of several criteria, BOC expects to save between $50 000 and $120 000 annually on better legal services.

Source: *Financial Review*, 11 September 1996, p. 29.

In general, organisations need to use both internal and external sources of recruitment. A summary list of the advantages and disadvantages of each is provided in Figure 8.2.

Increasing the pool of potentially qualified applicants

Effective recruitment goes beyond choosing between internal and external sources. To gain a competitive edge, organisations must also understand and meet the needs of job seekers. To increase the likelihood that high potential employees will be successfully recruited, hired, and retained, organisations can adopt a variety of strategies.

Conveying job and organisational information

The traditional approach to recruitment involves matching the job applicant's skills, knowledge and abilities with the demands of the job. The more recent approach to recruitment is also concerned with matching the job applicant's personality, interests,

External

Advantages
- Wider pool of applicants
- New perspectives, skills and ideas brought into the organisation
- Can be cheaper than training internal candidates
- External candidates are not part of the existing political structure
- in line with EEO/AA concepts.

Disadvantages
- Increased difficulty and risk associated with recruitment and selection process
- Lowered morale of those not selected
- Longer orientation and adjustment time for new employee
- New candidate may not fit organisational culture.

Internal

Advantages
- Organisation has more knowledge of candidates abilities
- Candidate has more knowledge of job requirements and organisation
- Employee morale is improved
- Organisation only needs to hire at base level
- Lower direct costs associated with recruitment
- Can facilitate a succession of promotions.

Disadvantages
- Problems of insularity and 'inbreeding'
- Can lead to political infighting for promotions
- Need for effective training and appraisal systems
- Unsuccessful candidates can become demotivated.

Figure 8.2   Advantages and disadvantages of internal v. external recruitment

and preferences with the job and with organisational characteristics, as the HRM in the news item 'Why psych tests are just the job' illustrates. For effective HRM, getting the job applicants to stay is as important as recruiting those who can do the job.

Achieving both is possible by: (1) devoting attention to the job interview, (2) carefully timing recruitment procedures, (3) developing policies regarding job offer acceptances, and (4) expanding career and job options.

HRM IN THE NEWS

Job hunters want facts, not hype, survey finds

Job hunters prefer hard facts rather than hype in job advertisement, according to the results of a new survey by recruitment advertising agency, Austin Knight.

The survey into the views of job applicants towards aspects of vacancy ads, was conducted among candidates who applied to anonymous Austin knight confidential ads during the three months to March 1991.

Job hunters rated a clear description of the duties involved as their top requirements (84 per cent). And job title, location and prospects were generally rated as more important inclusions than the salary. Less than 20 per cent felt it was essential to reveal the employer's identity.

As for applying for a job, 69 per cent of respondents favoured sending a résumé, probably because it is easier than filling in an application form, which only 4 per cent favoured. Nearly 50 per cent, liked the option of a telephone contact and 9 per cent said a facsimile would be a helpful response method.

One unexpected responses was that 91 per cent of respondents considered themselves to be committed job seekers as opposed to casual browsers.

In terms of ad placement and people's reading habits of weekend newspapers, 82 per cent of respondents said that they always read the early news pages and 63 per cent always read the employment sections.

Source: *HRMonthly*, May 1991, p. 25.

Job interview

A vital aspect of the recruitment process is the interview. A good interview provides the applicant with a realistic preview of what the job will be like. It can definitely be an enticement for an applicant to join an organisation, just as a bad interview can turn away many applicants.

The quality of the interview is just one aspect of the recruitment process. Other things being equal, the chances of a person accepting a job offer increases when interviewers show interest and concern for the applicant. The content of the recruitment interview is also important. Organisations often assume that it is in their best interests to tell a job applicant only about their positive aspects. But studies have reported that providing realistic (positive and negative) information actually increases the number of eventual recruits. In addition, those who receive realistic job information may be less likely to leave once they accept the job. The type of interview that conveys positive and negative information is referred to as a **realistic job preview**.

A realistic preview can be given as part of the recruitment process before an individual has accepted a job, or as part of the orientation or socialisation process that takes place after job acceptance. If the latter is the case, acceptance would be conditional on the basis of a satisfactory orientation period.

Such previews can take many forms, including written descriptions of the job, film or video tape presentations, and samples of the actual work. Although they may differ in form or mode of presentation, all realistic job previews are alike in presenting all relevant aspects of a job as accurately as possible. Since new or potential employees usually have inflated ideas or expectations about what a job involves, a realistic preview usually *reduces* these overly optimistic expectations. In effect, even though it presents a complete and accurate picture, a realistic preview primarily serves to acquaint new or prospective employees with the previously unknown *negative* aspects of a particular job (Breaugh 1983; Dean & Wanous 1984; Meglino & DeNisi 1987; Meglino, DeNisi, Youngblood & Williams 1988).

Assuming that job applicants pass on initial screening, they should be given the opportunity to interview with a potential supervisor and even with co-workers. The interview with the potential supervisor is crucial, because this is the person who often makes the final decision. Co-worker involvement in interviews is becoming increasingly common in Australian workplaces with the growth of team-based organisational structures.

Timing of recruitment procedures

In labour markets where recruiting occurs in well-defined cycles, (e.g. university graduates), organisations have the option of being either early or late entrants into the recruiting process. Assuming that most individuals evaluate job options sequentially, organisations enhance their chances of obtaining high-potential candidates through early entry into the recruitment process. In some cases, potential job holders are targeted via graduate sponsorship schemes to ensure a more certain and predictable supply of labour. In competitive labour markets, organisations that rely on traditional practices may find themselves in a less competitive position than that of their more aggressive recruiting rivals.

Policies regarding job offer acceptance

Employers can also influence job applicants' selection decisions through the amount of time they allow individuals to ponder their offer. Given unlimited time to ponder a job offer, most job seekers will delay decision making until they have heard from all the organisations in the job search net. While potentially advantageous to the job seeker, the lack of a deadline places the organisation at a distinct disadvantage. Unless job openings are unlimited, it cannot extend an offer to a second-choice candidate until a decision is made by the preferred one. Conversely, job applicants may want to delay making a commitment until they have completed all interviews. Thus, most organisations have recall policies, and job seekers find themselves in the dilemma of having to accept or reject a minimally acceptable alternative before receiving an offer from a preferred one. The short- and long-term effects of time deadlines need further investigation before definitive conclusions can be drawn about their effectiveness, and clearly much depends on the nature and the level of the job.

Expanding career and job opportunities

By providing career opportunities and child-care assistance, organisations can enhance their attractiveness while increasing their applicant pools. The decision to provide career opportunities involves several choices for the organisation. First, should it have an active policy of promotion from within? Second, should it be committed to a training and development program to provide sufficient candidates for internal promotion? If the answers to these questions are affirmative, then the organisation must identify career ladders consistent with organisational and job requirements and employees' skills and preferences. Increasingly, organisations will need to consider providing some kind of child care service for their employees and developing policies which preserve seniority in career ladders for women on maternity leave. The NRMA is one Australian organisation that has done this well as can be seen in the 'Managing diversity' discussion below.

Trends in recruitment

Four major trends in recruitment are the recognition of diversity issues, the assessment of recruiting, behaviourally based approaches and applicant rejection management.

Recognition of diversity issues

As has been discussed in Chapters 1 and 2, managing diversity is about achieving a workforce with a variety of talents, views, and values which can broaden and enrich decision making in an organisation and improve the quality of life. One of the key areas for promoting diversity is in the area of recruitment and retention of staff. The NRMA provides a good example of an organisation that has made a success of promoting diversity policies in this area.

Managing diversity

NRMA finds lowering staff turnover pays off

BY PETER ROBERTS

Australian managers have a peculiarly blasé attitude towards our generally high levels of staff turnover and absenteeism.

In the financial-services sector, for example, staff turnover of 35 per cent a year is typical and managers often blithely accept such a level as 'normal'.

Yet the loss of even one experienced staff member with accumulated knowledge, experience and training can be a blow to any business and at the very least necessitate the expensive recruitment and training of a replacement.

In the late 1980s, NRMA found that recruiting and training new staff to replace the 35 per cent of employees who left each year cost more than $6 million a year in direct, quantifiable costs.

Recruiting and training a middle-level manager cost $55 000, a specialist in information technology cost $44 000, and a front-line member of NRMAs branch staff $38 000.

NRMA spends the equivalent of 7 per cent of payroll on training its 5500 staff. New customer service staff, for example, undergo three months training before they face the public.

Alarmed by the wastage of talent and cash, NRMA conducted staff surveys and exit interviews and found that those leaving would generally have liked to stay. But NRMA was not flexible enough to cope with the varying circumstances employees found themselves in at various stages of their lives.

It launched a series of initiatives designed to make NRMA a flexible workplace that could accommodate such things as women returning to the workforce after having a baby.

Flexible working house, job-sharing, more child-care places, home-based training and the development of career paths for part-time staff helped boost the proportion of women returning to the company after childbirth from 35 per cent to 85 per cent.

At the same time, NRMA introduced a merit-based promotional system to replace the subjective, 'old boy network' that still decides most white-collar promotion.

Managers now carry out a yearly self-assessment in which they have to demonstrate examples of desirable managerial behaviours such as customer focus, team-working and staff development. The self-assessment is backed up by reviews by peers and each manager's subordinates.

As a result, the proportion of women executives in the company has risen quickly to 45 per cent.

NRMA has been careful to ensure its initiatives are not simply aimed at women, but at others who need at various time in their careers more flexibility in the job than was possible in the past.

Both male and female parents, for example, are allowed to take 12 months additional unpaid child care leave before their children reach the age of six. All staff are eligible for five days paid personal emergency leave to handle crises such as illness among children or elderly parents.

All training was redesigned for CD-ROM technology so it could be performed at home. And all staff are eligible for incentives to allow them to take on outside study.

The bottom line is a saving of $2 million a year in training as staff choose to remain with the NRMA.

Source: *Financial Review*, 1 May 1996, p. 29.

Assessing recruitment

The recruitment activity is supposed to attract the right people at the right time within legal guidelines, so that people and organisations can select each other in their best short- and long-term interests. This is how recruitment should be assessed. More specific criteria for assessing it are shown in Figure 8.3, grouped by the stage of the recruitment process to which they are most applicable.

Recruitment is not just concerned with attracting people. It is concerned also with attracting those whose personalities, interests and preferences will most likely be matched by the organisation, and who have the skills, knowledge and abilities to perform adequately. Another criterion by which to assess recruiting is legal compliance. Job applicants must be recruited fairly and without discrimination.

STATE OF ENTRY	TYPE OF CRITERIA
Pre-entry	Total number of applicants
	Number of minority and female applicants
	Cost per applicant
	Time to locate job applicants
	Time to process job applicants.
Offers and hires	Offers extended by source
	Total number of qualified applicants
	Number of qualified female, minority, and handicapped applicants
	Costs of acceptance versus rejection of applicants.
Entry	Initial expectations of newcomers
	Choice of the organisation by qualified applicants
	Cost and time of training of new employees
	Salary levels.
Post-entry	Attitudes towards job, pay, benefits, supervision, co-workers
	Organisational commitment
	Job performance
	Tenure of hires
	Absenteeism
	Referrals.

Figure 8.3 Some criteria for assessing recruitment

Source: Schuler et al. 1992, p. 169

In addition to assessing each benefit criterion of recruitment, each method or source of recruitment can be valued, or 'costed out', in terms of its short- and long-term benefit costs. First, the utility of each method is determined by comparing the numbers of potentially qualified applicants hired by each method and by occupational group. These comparisons are referred to as **selection ratios**. The method resulting in the largest number of qualified applicants at the lowest per-hire cost may be deemed the most effective in the short run. The important costs to compare are those associated with hires versus non-hires. *If an organisation is spending more than two-thirds of its recruiting budget on individuals who never join the company, the recruiting program needs serious revamping.* The items reviewed should include the salaries of recruiters and line managers involved in interviewing and selection; all expenses for postage, telephone, and recruiting materials; administrative support costs; and all recruiting advertising charges, including receptions, videos, and programs (Boudreau & Rynes 1985; Caldwell & Spivey 1983; Levinson 1988; London & Stumpf 1983).

Behaviourally-based recruitment systems

Behaviourally-based recruitment systems, some of which have been developed into proprietorial systems, are now being used with increasing frequency. Behavioural systems are based on the idea that a person's past behaviour is a good predictor of their future behaviour. Consequently, the whole recruitment and selection process is built around the idea that getting an accurate picture of past behaviours will increase the reliability of the process.

The claimed advantages of this system are that it:

1 Removes misunderstandings about the past experience of the candidates and thereby removes the necessity for the interviewer to play amateur psychologist

2   Reduces the impact of personal impressions as a source of selection data
3   Reduces the chances of the candidate faking since candidates are asked to describe not what they would do in a given situation in a broad sense but specifically what they did and the context that they did it in.

The first stage in this process is to define the behaviours that lead to success or failure in a given position. These behaviours, sometimes called dimensions, then form the platform for the collection of information in the selection process and the eventual acceptance or rejection of candidates. In many ways this is a comparable process to that of job analysis, which traditionally then leads to the development of a job specification (which defines the job in terms of the attributes required for successful performance) and person specification (which defines the special characteristics required by the ideal candidate for the job). In the behavioural approach, instead of describing a job in terms of the specific knowledge, skills and attributes that the job holder should possess, the job will be described in terms of performance statements. These performance statements can then be specifically tested against the candidates behaviour in the past as ascertained via an interview or their demonstrable competence in terms of a job simulation of some sort. In this respect behavioural approaches have much in common with competency approaches which are discussed in Chapters 7 and 11.

Rejection with tact

For consumer-oriented organisations, there's a new challenge to recruiting: rejection with tact. Consider a hundred applicants who apply for one position with a bank. Only one applicant will be accepted, leaving ninety-nine potential employees and/or customers. If these rejected candidates feel angry at the rejecting organisation, they may never again purchase goods or services from it. If procedures are viewed as unfair, too lengthy, or too impersonal, rejected candidates may also share their dissatisfaction with friends and associates.

While research on the rejection process is in its infancy, several characteristics of rejection letters make a difference. Statements that: (1) are friendly (e.g. 'thank you for applying', 'good luck in the future', (2) include a personalised address and correct salutation (Ms, Mrs or Miss—versus Mr to all), and (3) summarise the applicant's job qualifications, leave positive impressions. Including statements about the size and excellence of the application pool and the person who was offered the job (e.g. the person had ten years experience and an MBA) reduce disappointment and increase perceptions of fairness.

Including a statement that the applicant's résumé will be kept on file increases the likelihood that he or she will continue to use the organisation's services or buy its products. However, such promises made in rejection letters (e.g. to keep the résumé on file) should not be made lightly. Thus, a promise to keep an application on file should be made only if the organisation intends to do just that. The timeliness with which rejection letters are mailed also seems important. Not only should a recruitment and selection timetable be specified to applicants, but the organisation should also meet its self-imposed deadlines (Aamolt & Peggins 1988).

Selection and placement

Selection is the process of gathering legally defensible information about job applicants in order to determine who should be hired for long- or short-term positions. Placement is concerned with matching individual skills, knowledge, abilities, preferences, interests, and personality to the job. Effective selection and placement involve finding the match between organisational needs for qualified individuals and individual needs for jobs in which they are interested (Arvey & Faley 1988; Field & Gatewood 1988).

Line managers play an important role in the selection and placement activity. They help identify the need for staffing through the organisation's human resource planning activity, assist with job analysis, and evaluate employee performance.

The human resource department, however, is usually responsible for gathering information and should arrange interviews between job applicants and managers for several reasons:

1. Applicants have only one place to go to apply for a job and have a better chance of being considered for a greater variety of jobs
2. Outside sources of applicants can clear employment issues through one central location.
3. Operating managers can concentrate on their operating responsibilities—especially helpful during peak hiring periods
4. Hiring is done by specialists trained in staffing techniques so selection is often better
5. Costs may be cut because duplication of effort is avoided
6. With increased government regulation of selection, it is important that people who know about these rules handle a major part of the hiring process.

Purposes and importance of selection and placement

Selection and placement procedures provide the very essence of organisations—their human resources. And it is largely by effective selection and placement that organisations can obtain and retain the human resources most likely to serve their needs. Effective selection and placement are likely to improve organisational productivity. Since there are likely to be productivity differences between employees, selecting only those employees likely to perform well may result in substantial productivity gains. For example, in a study of budget analysts, the dollar value of the productivity of the superior performers (top 15 per cent) was $23 000 per year greater than that of lower performers (bottom 15 per cent). In another study of computer programmers the dollar value difference was $20 000 per year (Arvey & Faley, 1988).

Effective selection and placement are critical to any organisation. Serving the needs of the organisation and being effective with selection and placement means attaining several purposes, including:

1. To fairly, legally, and in a non-discriminatory manner, evaluate and hire potentially qualified job applicants
2. To evaluate, hire and place job applicants in the best interests of the organisation and the individual
3. To engage in selection and placement activities that are useful for initial hiring as well as future selection and placement decisions for the individual (e.g. in promotions or transfers)
4. To make selection and placement decisions with consideration for the uniqueness of the individual, the job, the organisation and the environment, even to the extent of adapting the job or organisation to the individual (Baysinger 1988; Podsakoff, Williams & Scott 1988).

In order to serve these purposes effectively, selection and placement activities must be integrated with several other HRM activities. This is necessary because selection and placement have such an extensive set of relationships with other personnel and human resource activities and the environment.

Relationships influencing selection and placement: the internal environment

To serve these purposes effectively, selection and placement must be congruent with the internal environment and integrated with other HRM activities (see Figure 8.4). Moreover, managers should be selected to fit the culture and strategy of the organisation that they are to work for. As Michael Porter (1990) has noted, different industries require different approaches to management, depending on the particular structures and practices of particular companies and businesses.

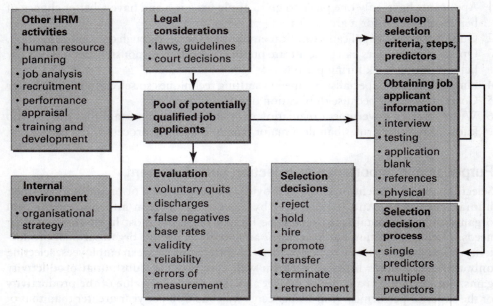

Figure 8.4 Relationships and aspects of selection and replacement
Source: Schuler et al. 1992, p. 171

Clearly, the characteristics, skills, abilities, values, and perspectives of executives need to be matched to particular types of business strategy (Olian & Rynes 1984; Szilagyi & Schweiger 1984). For example, a recently released study by the Hay Group reports that when a business is pursuing a growth strategy, it needs top managers who are likely to abandon the status quo and adapt their strategies and goals to the market. Because insiders are slow to recognise the onset of decline and tend to persevere in strategies that are no longer effective, top managers need to be recruited from the outside. In a recent address on strategic HRM the Human Resources Manager of Burns Philp, a company which has undergone a massive strategic shift in the last decade, referred to the changes among the ranks of senior international managers as replacing 'hunters with farmers', a move which was seen to be in keeping with the end of a period of corporate acquisition and the start of a period of consolidation (Dyer 1996).

However, recruiting outsiders is not always an appropriate solution. When a business is pursuing a mature strategy, what is needed is a stable group of insiders who know its intricacies. The results of the Hay study suggest that the staffing practices of top management should be tied to the nature of the business; different aspects of business demand different behaviours. The implication of this perspective is to select the right top manager for the nature of the business.

Relationships with other HRM activities

In addition to meshing with an organisation's culture, selection and placement procedures need to be integrated with human resource planning, job analysis, recruitment, performance appraisal, and training and development activities.

Human resource planning and job analysis

Human resource planning can facilitate the organisation's selection decisions by projecting when and how many such decisions will need to be made. When linked with job analysis, planning also helps indicate the worker qualifications necessary for these jobs. With essential worker qualifications known, selection procedures can be developed that are job related and consequently valid.

Recruitment

The success of selection and placement procedures depends on the effectiveness of the recruiting activity. If recruiting does not provide a large pool of potentially qualified job applicants, the organisation has difficulty selecting and placing individuals who will perform well and not leave. Even if recruitment does provide some applicants, if the pool is small, the potential effectiveness of the selection and placement procedures is lessened because the selection ratio tends to become large.

Performance appraisal

One of the functions of performance appraisal can be to serve as a source of feedback to show that the selection devices indeed predict performance. If the criteria used in performance appraisal are not job related (e.g. the appraisals are not built on job analysis or not communicated), the organisation has difficulty developing and using selection devices to predict meaningful employee performance. In other words, performance appraisals serve as criteria for evaluating the predictive and economic utility of selection procedures.

Training and development

If recruiting does not provide a large pool of potentially qualified job applicants, an organisation may hire underqualified job applicants and then train them. The trade-off between selecting the right individual versus training individuals to perform well centres around costs and time.

Considerations in choosing selection techniques

In choosing the appropriate selection devices to use, several technical factors need to be considered, including the choice of predictors and criterion scores and the relative usefulness of different devices.

Predictors

Selection decisions are generally made on the basis of job applicants' predictor scores, which predict how well applicants will perform. While a wealth of selection devices (background information, paper-and-pencil tests, work simulations, physical tests, interviews) can be used to predict job performance, the usefulness of these depends on their reliability and validity.

Reliability

The degree to which a measurement device produces dependable or consistent results indicates its reliability. Unreliable measurements produce one set of results at one time and a different set at another. When a selection device yields equivalent results time after time, it is considered reliable. For example, tests of physical attributes (height, weight, hearing) tend to be more reliable than tests of personality characteristics (neuroticism, flexible thinking, emotional stability).

Two types of reliability are relevant to selection. Consider a cognitive ability test administered to a hundred job applicants. It would be reliable if you retested these and received similar results the second time. This form of reliability is called test–retest reliability. Inter-rater reliability focuses on the consistency of ratings by different individuals. For example, unstructured interviews tend to be unreliable, with multiple interviewers perceiving the same applicant dissimilarly.

Validity

This refers to how well a measure actually assesses an attribute. The *validity* of a measure is not absolute; rather, it is relative to the situation in which the selection device is being used. For example, a test of aggression may be a valid predictor of police performance, but it may be useless in predicting job success for machinists.

Mathematically, validity refers to the correlation between the predictor score (selection device) and a criterion (job performance, job rating, number of absences, tardiness, or worker compensation claims). A correlation coefficient can range from –1.00 to 1.00. The closer the correlation coefficient to the absolute value of 1.00, the more valid the selection device. The validity coefficient of various selection techniques are given in Figure 8.5.

Criterion scores

The type of criterion against which a selection device is validated can vary greatly. At one end of the spectrum are direct measures of output (e.g. number of items produced, number of trades, number of absences, number of complaints). Unfortunately, for many jobs, direct output measures do not exist. Consequently, performance appraisal ratings become the criterion. As is discussed in Chapter 9, performance ratings need to be based on job related criteria if they are to be useful and valid measures of performance.

Selection techniques

A variety of selection techniques are available for obtaining applicant information. As Figure 8.5 shows, each selection technique varies in terms of costs, the number of firms using them, and their usefulness as predictors.

Application blanks and background information

Premised on the assumption that past behaviour is a good predictor of future performance, the **application blank** is a form seeking information about the applicant's background and present status. Usually this information is used as an initial or pre-employment screen to decide if the candidate meets the minimum job requirements. For many professional and managerial jobs, résumés prepared by the applicant replace application blanks as a means of gathering data for selection purposes. Unfortunately these résumés, like references indicated on application blanks, are increasingly less likely to reflect reality and should therefore be used only in conjunction with other information.

It should be noted that there is no direct legal prescription in Australia about what may be asked in an application form but certain enquiries are prohibited by relevant EEO or anti-discrimination legislation. This includes questions about the following:

- Age, sex, religion and national origin
- Number of children and who will care for them

- Height and weight, unless job related
- Marital status
- Conviction record unless strongly related to job
- Credit status
- Relatives and friends working for the employer.

TYPE OF TEST	COST	% OF FIRMS USING DEVICE	VALIDITY
Cognitive ability test	$5.00 – $100.00	42	0.53
Situational interview	25.00 – 50.00	5–20	0.54
Work sample test	50.00 – 500.00	75	0.44
Assessment centre	50.00 – 2000.00	6	0.44
Biodata	5.00 – 25.00	11	0.37
Background check	100.00 – 500.00	8–15	0.26
Experience rating	5.00 – 50.00	(no data)	0.18
Standard interview	25.00 – 50.00	70	0.07
Interest inventory	25.00 – 50.00	5	0.10
Education rating	5.00 – 50.00	(no data)	0.10
Personality test	1.00 – 100.00	5	0.10–.25
Handwriting analysis	50.00 – 250.00	5	0.00
Polygraph test	25.00 – 50.00	6	0.00
Drug screening	35.00 – 90.00	25	(varied estimates)
Alcohol screening	10.00 – 35.00	13	(varied estimates)
Genetic screening	35.00 – 450.00	1	(varied estimates)

Figure 8.5 Comparison of costs and benefits of various common selection devices

Source: Schuler et al. 1992, p. 174

Application blanks can yield a great deal of useful information. In order to make this information as job related as possible, organisations sometimes weight it or give it more importance than the rest as a predictor of criteria. This procedure produces a **weighted application blank**. These can be extremely effective in predicting criteria such as turnover and are often developed using multiple regression analysis. Based upon the results of such analysis, the relative importance (or weight) of the information on the application blank can be determined and used in selection decisions.

Education and experience evaluations

As part of the initial application process, applicants often complete a form that details their educational achievements and work experience. Validity evidence indicates that education requirements are predictive of job tenure (the average correlation of performance is 0.10). Like education, experience requirements may be useful in selecting individuals for high-level, complex jobs but not for jobs that require short learning periods (the average correlation is 0.18).

What is questionable is the *extent* of education and experience required for a specific job. In order to narrow down the application pool, some organisations impose inordinately high experience requirements (e.g. five years or more). Similarly, higher levels of education than needed are required for many jobs. These frequently form artificial barriers to minority applicants (e.g. women, migrants, Aborigines) who often have less opportunity to acquire education and experience.

Handwriting analysis

In addition to the application blank, an employer may request a special handwriting sample. Handwriting analysis, or graphology, is used by many European companies, particularly French, and has advocates in the US and Australia:

> Graphology is based on the premiss that the strokes of a person's handwriting are subconscious expressions of the individual's personality. In developing their assessments, graphologists examine such items as the slant or angle of letters in a handwriting sample; the spacing between letters and words; the size, shape and length of letters; and the way the writer uses the space on the sheet of paper. While an analysis cannot determine age, sex, or race, it can identify up to 300 different character traits (Ben Shaker et al. 1986).

Despite the testimonials, there is *no scientific evidence that graphology can predict job performance*. In one controlled study of sales success, applicants provided handwriting samples, and graphologists predicted job success. While there was limited evidence of inter-rater agreement on observed character traits, there was no relationship between the assessments and three measures of job performances (sales productivity and self and supervisory performance ratings). Given its poor predictive ability, it is *not* recommended as a selection device.

HRM IN THE NEWS

References come back to haunt

'We advise our clients against giving a reference which overstates an employee's abilities or gives a false indication of their character'—Lawyer, Mr Gary Rothville.

BY STEPHEN LONG

The phone rings. It's a manager at another company, thinking about hiring a troublesome ex-employee of yours.

You let fly, telling them in damning terms just what you think of the applicant's competence and attitude.

Stop right there.

Lawyers are warning employers to be very careful when giving references—written or oral—for employees and ex-employees, following a landmark court ruling.

The judgement by the House of Lords, Britain's highest court, established that employers have a duty of care to prepare accurate references—and that they may face huge damages payouts if they negligently fail to do so.

Experts at major Australian law firms believe Australian courts are likely to adopt the same principle.

Lawyers warn that companies may face damages claims not only from former employees, but from companies which suffer economic loss after recruiting an employee on the basis of a falsely glowing reference. The threat of civil liability may force Australian managers to stop the practise—common in unfair dismissal settlements—of agreeing to give a dismissed worker a good reference in return for their agreement to stop unfair termination proceedings.

Mr John Lunny, who specialises in human resources management law with solicitors Clayton Utz, said it was a matter of 'grave concern' that industrial tribunals routinely encouraged employers to give employees favourable references to settle unfair dismissal claims.

He said that these references may leave employers open to a damages claim from a subsequent employer 'on the ordinary principles governing misleading or deceptive representations'.

'Employers agree to give references that completely compromise their true feelings', Mr Lunny said. 'At best, they are economical with the truth; at worst, a form of agreed deception'.

Mr Gary Rothville, a partner with law firm Phillips Fox, said: 'We are advising our clients against giving a reference which strays from the truth in overstating an employee's abilities or giving a false indication of their character'.

'While it has been found that an employer owes a duty of care to a former employee when preparing a reference, it may not stop there'.

'An employer could face civil liability from a company which suffered economic loss as a result of hiring an employee on the basis of a false reference'.

'We sometimes get calls from ex-employees of our clients, raising concerns that their former manager has been making statements running them down'.

'We strongly advise our clients in these circumstances not to go to the other way and talk up a former employee. The best policy is to decline to comment, saying that the circumstances of the employment relationship are confidential'.

The concern about references arose after the landmark judgement last year in Spring v. Guardian Assurance PLC, where a four-to-one majority in Britain's House of Lords decided that an employer owes a duty of care to employees in relation to giving a reference, and in obtaining the information upon which the reference is based. This allows employers to sue for economic loss resulting from the reference, providing a wider potential remedy than a claim in defamation. Mr Spring, an insurance salesman, successfully sued for economic loss after guardian assurance supplied another firm, Scottish Amicable, with a reference which said that Spring was 'a man of little or no integrity who could not be regarded as honest'.

Guardian Assurance said spring would give bad advice, deliberately or ignorantly, in an attempt to gain maximum commissions from insurance sales. Mr Spring was unemployable in the insurance industry when word was spread. The same principle has been raised in less extreme cases, leading to a series of out-of-court settlements.

Some lawyers are not convinced that Australian courts will follow Britain in extending the duty of care in negligence to cover references, arguing that to do so would intrude on the domain of defamation law and conflict with high court decisions emphasising the right to free speech.

But an article in last month's *Australian Law Journal* argued that it was highly likely that the high court would find a duty of care when giving references.

'Employers are likely to continue giving references, and those who provide full and frank references will need to exercise more care', Mr Tom Thawley of the Australian National University wrote in the law journal.

'It is easy to imagine the high court finding a duty of care if it were presented with the facts in Spring'.

Traditionally, Australian courts have taken a more expansive view of tort law than British courts, he said. This made it more than likely the high court—faced with a claim for economic loss as the result of a negligent reference—would find a duty of care.

Indeed, labour lawyers such as Professor Greg McCarry of the University of Sydney argue that, in the new deregulated industrial relations environment, the high court may follow the British courts in finding that employers have a general common law duty to treat their employees fairly and reasonably.

This would give employees and unions a new avenue for challenging employment contracts. Already, a prominent federal court judge, Justice Peter Gray, had advocated this approach in the landmark case of Byrne v. Australian Airlines.

Source: *Financial Review*, 28 June 1996, pp. 1, 36.

Reference verification and background checks

Because some job applicants falsify their past and current qualifications, employers are stepping up efforts to check references. In the USA instead of relying on unstructured reference letters (which are always positive) many employers are using outside investigators to verify reference data and check claimed academic qualifications, which are commonly falsified. References can represent a useful selection technique in some circumstances but it is recommended that they be rigorously checked via personal contact with the provider. As the 'HRM in the news' article 'References come back to haunt us' notes, some employers are now reluctant to provide reference information because of fear of defamation actions and limit the information they provide. However, reference checks of prior employment records are not an infringement on privacy if the information provided relates specifically to work behaviour and to the reasons an applicant left a previous job.

Table 8.1 Question areas to probe when reference checking

- Length of service in position
- Work responsibility
- Number of people supervised
- Relations with co-workers
- Relations with management
- Quality of work
- Quantity of work
- Attitude
- Dependability
- Areas of excellence
- Areas where improvement was required
- Disciplinary issues
- Suitability for position/organisation

Source: Based on Centre for Professional Development 1995, p. 817

Written tests

Written testing is another important procedure for gathering, transmitting and assembling information about applicants. The most common types of written test measure ability (cognitive or mechanical and psychomotor), personality, and interests and preferences.

Cognitive ability tests

Ability tests measure the potential of an individual to perform, given the opportunity. These typically will test verbal comprehension, word fluency, numerical aptitude, inductive reasoning and memory. Used in the US and Europe since the turn of the century, these devices are useful and valid (see Figure 8.5). Recent studies further suggest that they are equally valid for black or white applicants, and that their use can be generalised to different jobs in different situations. Figure 8.6 shows sample items for measuring seven types of cognitive ability.

Psychomotor tests

Many jobs involve not only a wide range of cognitive ability but also psychomotor skills. For example, a bank teller needs the motor skills necessary to operate a computer or a ten-key calculator and the finger dexterity to manipulate currency.

Verbal comprehension involves understanding the meaning of words and their relationship to one another. It is measured by such test items as:

Which one of the following words means most nearly the same as 'dilapidated'?
(1) new   (2) injured   (3) unresponsive   (4) run-down   (5) lethargic

Word fluency involves the ability to name or make words, such as making smaller words from the letters in a large one or playing anagrams. For example:

Using the letters in the word 'measurement', write as many four-letter words as you can in the next two minutes.
_____   _____   _____
_____   _____   _____

Number aptitude involves speed and accuracy in making simple arithmetic calculations. It is measured by such test items as:

Carry out the following calculations:
   429   7983   721 x 52 = _____   4920 ÷ 6 = _____
  +762   -64279

Inductive reasoning focuses on the ability to discover a rule or principle and apply it to the solution of a problem. The following is an example:

What number should come next in the sequence of five numbers?
   1   3   6   10   15
  (1)22   (2)21   (3)25   (4)18

Memory relates to having the ability to recall pairs of words or lists of numbers. It is measured by such test items as:

You have 30 seconds to memorise the following pairs. When the examiner says stop, turn the page and write the appropriate symbols after each of the letters appearing there.
A@   C#   E   G?
B>   D*   F+   H$

Perceptual speed is concerned with the ability to perceive visual details quickly and accurately. Usually these tests are timed and include such items as

Make a check mark in front of each pair below in which the numbers are identical. Work as fast as you can.
1   755321.............. 753321
2   966441.............. 966641
3   334579.............. 334579

Motor Skill—Aiming involves the ability to respond accurately and rapidly to stimuli. For example, Place three dots in as many circles as you can in 30 seconds.
○ ○ ○ ○   ○   ○○   ○ ○

Figure 8.6 Samples of cognitive ability and psychomotor tests
Source: Based on Dunnette 1966, pp. 47–49

There are a variety of psychomotor abilities, each of which is highly specific and shows little relationship to other psychomotor abilities *or* to cognitive ability. For example, control precision involves finely controlled muscular adjustments (e.g. moving a lever to a precise setting), whereas finger dexterity entails skilful manipulation of small objects (e.g. assembling nuts and bolts).

Ability tests, then, are useful for selecting applicants in many occupations. However, only some categories of ability tests may be predictive of job performance in a specific position.

Personality tests

These are intended to measure an individual's personality traits or characteristics. They were originally developed for use in clinical settings as diagnostic instruments. Although personality questionnaires are most commonly called 'tests', the term 'inventory' is really more appropriate because, unlike a test, an inventory has no right or wrong answers. Personality questionnaires usually contain statements or questions relating to behaviour, attitudes or beliefs. Subjects are asked to respond to these as they apply to themselves and these responses to individual items are scored on each of several personality dimensions or traits. The best-known personality tests are the Cattell 16PF, the Minnesota Multiphasic Personality Inventory, the California Psychological Inventory and the Myers-Briggs Type Indicator. The latter is an instrument that is mainly used for self development and should not be used for selection purposes. The safest and least controversial use of psychological tests is as an aid to self understanding and a starting point for development and training.

The use of personality testing for selection purposes is a subject of continuing controversy in Australia. The 'pro' case rests on the view that personality tests can:

- add insight about job candidates' behaviour in critical areas such as decision-making ability, personal organisation, ability to cope with pressure, assertiveness and business acumen
- reduce subjectivity in selection decisions by introducing objectives standards against which to measure candidates
- measure specific aspects of personality required for the successful conduct of certain tasks
- usefully supplement data from other selection methods in order to reduce risk in selection decisions
- are valid and reliable so long as they are administered professionally and in controlled conditions

The case against personality testing is based on claims that personality tests:

- are not valid predictors of on the job performance
- are unreliable i.e. do not give accurate measures in test/retest trials
- are highly susceptible to faking
- are not good measures of personality, which is a nebulous concept that is hard to define and measure
- are based on the idea that there is an ideal personality for any job, whereas in practice most jobs permit varying styles or approaches towards achieving results
- are culturally biased and show marked disparity in test scores between different ethnic minorities.

Reviewers of this debate in the US have concluded that the case for testing basically rests on acceptance of the professional responsibility of personality test users, while the case against their use is based on the considerable body of evidence which indicates that these tests are seldom valid employment predictors (Ghiselli 1973; Gough 1976; Hunter & Hunter 1984).

In the UK a more recent review of the debate concluded with qualified support for personality testing:

> Routine large-scale personality testing is unlikely to be useful, whereas the focused application of personality tests, based on clear hypotheses about which scales are related to job performance will have the best chance of success (Fletcher, Blinkhorn & Johnson 1991, pp. 38–42).

A study conducted by Vaughan & McClean (1989) found that around two thirds of Australian employers rarely or never used tests although large firms were slightly more likely to use them than small firms.

As Stone (1985) has noted, it is likely that Australian employers will come under increasing pressure to demonstrate that personality tests are related to job performance.

HRM IN THE NEWS

Psychological testing leads to costly law suit

A US employer that required applicants to answer intimate personal questions in a pre-employment psychological examination agrees to pay more than $US 2 million to settle a lawsuit over the test.

The employer, which operates a chain of retail stores in California, administered the test to about 2500 applicants for security jobs. The test's true or false questions included the following:

- I have never indulged in any unusual sexual practices
- I have often wished I were a girl
- I am very strongly attracted by members of my own sex
- I believe my sins are unpardonable
- I feel sure there is only one true religion
- A minister can cure disease by praying and putting his hand on your head.

Before settling the suit, the employer argued that the test was necessary to screen out applicants who are emotionally unstable, unreliable, undependable, and not inclined to follow directions or established rules, as well as applicants with addictive or violent tendencies who might put customers or other employees at risk.

Under the settlement, the employer admits no wrongdoing but agrees to set up a $1.3 million fund to be divided among applicants who took the test.

Additionally, the employer agrees to pay $60 000 plus attorney's fees to the four individuals who actually pursued the lawsuit, as well as the costs of notifying the 2500 applicants (Soroka v. Dayton Hudson Corp. 1993).

Source: *Bulletin to Management* 1993, p. 226; cited in Schuler 1995, p. 274.

Work simulations

Often also referred to as **work sample tests**, these require applicants to complete verbal or physical activities, which are closely related to work tasks, under structured 'testing' conditions. Rather than measuring what an individual knows, they assess his or her ability to do. Although they have a high validity as selection devices, work sample tests are somewhat artificial because the selection process itself tends to promote anxiety and tension (Plumke 1980). Figure 8.7 shows three sets of work simulation tests.

PHYSICAL

Dental students	Carving dexterity
Machine operators	Lathe, drill press, and tool dexterity
Meat scalers	Meat weighing
Mechanics	Belt and pulley installation, gear box repair, motor installation and alignment, sprocket reaming
Miners	Two-hand co-ordination
Pilots	Rudder control, direction control, complex co-ordination
Administrative assistants	Word-processing on specific equipment, dictation, filing

MENTAL

Magazine editors	Writing skills, page layout, headline writing
Administrators	Judgement and decision making
Engineers	Processing mathematical data
Administrative assistants	Letter composition, proofreading

VERBAL

Telephone operators	Role play of telephone contacts
Construction supervisors	Construction error recognition
Administrative assistants	Telephone screening

Figure 8.7 Examples of physical, verbal, and mental work sample tests
Source: Schuler et al. 1992, p. 180; based on Asher & Sciarrino 1974

Because they replicate the actual work, work sample tests are not easy to fake. As a result, they tend to be more valid than almost all other types of selection devices. Additionally, they do not have an adverse impact on minority applicants. Unfortunately, because simulation tests are job specific, they are usually expensive to develop unless a large number of applicants are to be examined. However, by placing work sample tests at the end of a selection process, the number of applicants tested is smaller and the price lower.

Assessment centres

As the 'HRM in the news' article 'Assessing Real Candidates' (see front of chapter) outlines, this selection device evaluates applicants or current employees with regard to how well they might perform in a managerial or higher-level position. In the US, over 20 000 companies now use this method, and its use grows each year because of its validity in predicting which job applicants will be successful and which unsuccessful (Shippman, Hughes & Prien 1988). Despite this, studies conducted by Patrickson & Haydon (1988) and Vaughan & McClean (1989) both report a low usage of assessment centres in Australian organisations. However, as the 'HRM in the news' article indicates there has been a rapid growth in the use of assessment centres in Australia during the 1990s.

An assessment centre usually involves six to twelve people who have been chosen or have chosen to attend it. It is most often conducted off the premises by the organisation, for one to three days. The performance of the attendees is usually rated by managers in the organisation who are trained assessors. Typically, the purpose of an assessment centre program is to help determine potential promotability of applicants to a first-line supervisor's job.

At a typical assessment centre candidates undergo evaluation using a wide range of techniques. One important activity is the in-basket exercise, which creates a realistic situation designed to elicit typical on-the-job behaviours. Situations and problems encountered on the job are written on individual sheets of paper and set in the in-basket. The applicant is then asked to arrange the papers by priority. Occasionally the applicant may need to write an action response on the piece of paper. The problems or situations described to the applicant involve different groups of people—peers, subordinates, and those outside the organisation. The applicant is usually given a set time limit to take the test and is often interrupted by phone calls meant to create more tension and pressure.

Other tests used in managerial selection are the leaderless group discussion (LGD) and business games. In the LGD, a group of individuals is asked to discuss a topic for a given period of time. At IBMs assessment centre, participants must make a five-minute oral presentation about the qualifications of a candidate for promotion. During the subsequent group discussion, they must defend their nomination of the candidate with five or more other participants. Participants are rated on their selling ability, oral communication skill, self-confidence, energy level, interpersonal competency, aggressiveness, and tolerance for stress. LGD ratings have been shown to be useful predictors of managerial performance in a wide array of business areas. Additionally, prior experience in LGD does not affect present LGD performance. Business games are living cases. That is, individuals must make decisions and live with them, much as they do in the in-basket exercise.

Because in-baskets, LGDs and business games tend to be useful in managerial selection, they are often used together in an assessment centre (Petty 1974; Bass & Barnett 1981). As candidates go through these exercises, their performance is observed by a specifically trained team of observers or assessors drawn from the local management group. After the candidates have finished the program, the assessors meet to discuss them and prepare performance evaluations based on their combined judgements in such areas as organising and planning, analysing, making decisions, controlling oral communications, conducting interpersonal relations, influencing, and exhibiting flexibility. The composite performance on the exercises and tests is often used to determine an assessment centre attendee's future promotability and the organisation's human resource planning requirements and training needs, as well as to make current selection and placement decisions. This rating is generally given to the attendee, who in turn can use it for his or her own personal career planning purposes.

Assessment centres have been used effectively in a wide range of organisations. Assessment centres appear to work because they reflect the actual work environment and measure performance on multiple job dimensions. Additionally, more than one trained rater with a common frame of reference evaluates each participant's behaviour. In terms of cost-effectiveness, assessment centres are often criticised as being too costly at around $1500 per assessment for a mid-level manager and several thousand dollars for a senior manager. However, annual productivity gains realised by selecting managers via assessment centres have been shown to be on average well above administrative costs (Gaugler, Rosenthal, Thornton & Bentson 1987; Klimoski & Brickner 1987; Tziner & Dolan 1982). Moreover the costs of incorrect selection decisions particularly at senior levels can be enormous.

Interviews

Job offers go to applicants who *appear* most qualified because it is often impossible to determine from available data who really is. Though appearances can be deceptive, the job interview and the perceptions gained from it still comprise the tool most heavily used to determine who gets a job offer (Arvey, Miller, Gould & Burch 1987; Campion,

Pursell & Brown 1988; Dougherty, Ebert & Callendar 1985, Fear 1984; Hakel 1982; James, Campbell & Lovegrove 1984; Latham & Saari 1984; Maurer & Fay 1988; Raza & Carpenter 1987; Rodgers 1987; Weekley & Gier 1987). As shown in Figure 8.8, the interview is important at the beginning and the end of the selection procedure.

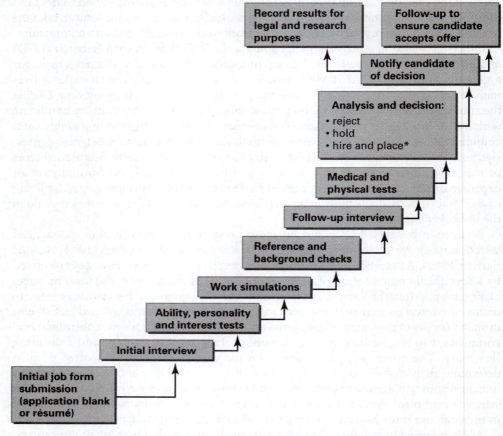

* Note: These decisions could be made in previous steps in the selection process; however, they would then be based on less information.

Figure 8.8 Possible steps in the selection process

Source: Schuler 1992, p. 183

The reliability and usefulness of interviews really depend on several factors; structure, job relevance, systematic scoring, number of interviewers and training.

Structure

The unstructured interview involves little preparation. The interviewer merely prepares a list of possible topics to cover and, depending on how the conversation proceeds, asks or does not ask them. While this provides for flexibility, the digressions, discontinuity, and lack of focus may be frustrating both to interviewer and interviewee. More importantly, unstructured interviews result in inconsistencies in the information collected about candidates.

Alternatively, in a structured interview, all applicants are asked the same questions in the same order. While structuring the interview restricts the topics that can be covered, it ensures that the same information is collected on all candidates. As a result, managers are less likely to make snap or erroneous judgements.

A compromise that still minimises such judgements is the semi-structured interview. Questions are prepared in advance, and the same questions are asked of all candidates; responses are recorded. However, follow-up questions are allowed to probe specific areas in depth. This approach provides enough flexibility to develop insights, along with the structure needed to acquire comparative information.

Job relevance

At one extreme, interviewers focus on generalities about qualifications. Such questions help them form an overall impression of the candidate's competence, but are not predictive of success in a specific job. A better approach is to use job analysis to generate questions about specific job skills and duties. For example, the critical incident method of job analysis (see Chapter 7) can be used to develop *situational questions*. Also appropriate here are the behavioural methods referred to earlier in this chapter.

Systematic scoring

Job interviews also vary in the degree to which results are scored. At one extreme, an interviewer merely listens to responses, forms an impression, and makes an accept, reject or hold decision. Alternatively, raters are given specific criteria and a scoring key to evaluate responses to each question. This latter approach is more rational because it helps ensure that applicants are evaluated against the same criteria. Systematic scoring also tends to minimise halo bias, in which an interviewer judges an applicant's entire potential on the basis of a single characteristic, such as how well the applicant dresses or talks.

Number of interviewers

Typically, applicants are interviewed by one person at a time. Unfortunately, managers sometimes overlap in their coverage of some job related questions and miss others entirely. An applicant may have not four interviews, but one interview four times. This is a time-consuming process in which the interviewer's *and* applicant's impressions may vary, depending on what was discussed in the one-on-one interviews. This problem can be overcome by using a **panel interview** in which several individuals simultaneously interview one applicant. Because all decision makers hear the same responses, panel interviews produce more consistent results. On the other hand, they are expensive because many people are involved. But, if applicants are to be interviewed by more than one manager anyway, panel interviewing may be more efficient and reliable and as cost-effective as individual interviews.

Training

Left on their own, interviewers tend to form their own impressions based on whatever criteria are most important or salient to them. For example, an applicant might be rejected by one interviewer for being 'too aggressive' but accepted by another for being 'assertive'. Consequently, it is important to train interviewers to interpret information consistently by providing a uniform frame of reference. Moreover interviewers need to be trained about what they can and cannot ask in relation to non-discriminatory recruitment, as referred to in the section in this chapter dealing with application blanks.

Physical examinations

The physical or medical examination is often one of the final steps in the selection process. Many employers give common physical examinations to all job applicants, whereas special examinations are given to only a subset of all the applicants. For example, production job applicants may receive back X-rays while office job applicants may not.

Physical examinations can be used in conjunction with physical ability tests to help ensure that proper job accommodation is made and to provide a record for the employer in order to prevent employees filing workers' compensation claims for pre-existing injuries (Novitt 1981). In the US a more recent use of the physical exam is to screen applicants based on their genetic make-up. **Genetic screening**, as it is called, is based upon the premise that some individuals may be more sensitive to workplace elements such as chemicals (Carmean 1985). The screening is done on the basis of an analysis of an applicant's blood sample. While genetic screening is still relatively new, it may grow in use in the 1990s. While cost-effective genetic tests have not yet been developed, 1 per cent of major US firms already use genetic screening and 15 per cent are considering its use in the future (Cropanzano & James 1990). As scientific research on genetic screening continues, the debate over the ethics of basing employment decisions on immutable traits is likely to grow. It also seems probable that pressure will be exerted on organisations to develop engineering controls that minimise or eliminate workplace pollutants. These controls will be the preferred alternative to genetic screening, a selection criteria over which the individual has no control.

Issues related to AIDS testing in the workplace are discussed in the 'Managing change' discussion below

 Managing change

> Although there is no specific legislation on AIDS testing in relation to employment, the 1992 federal Disability Discrimination Act outlaws discrimination on, among other things, the presence of 'disease causing organism'. However, because AIDS is such a challenge to today's workplace, many larger organisations have developed policies on it. Companies such as IBM or Johnson and Johnson have endorsed the following guidelines:
>
> - People with AIDS or who are HIV positive are entitled to the same rights and opportunities as people with other serious illnesses
> - Employment policies should be based on the scientific evidence that people with AIDS or HIV infection do not pose a risk of transmitting the virus through normal workplace contact
> - Employers should provide workers with sensitive and up-to-date education about AIDS and risk reduction in their personal lives
> - Employers have the duty to protect the confidentiality of employees' medical information
> - Employers should not require HIV screening as part of general pre-employment or workplace physical examinations.
>
> Despite these policies a report by the NSW Anti-Discrimination Board released in 1992 indicated that discrimination and violence against homosexuals and people with AIDS was widespread.

Drug and alcohol testing

In Australia pre-employment drug testing is not common although it is used by certain employers in industries where operatives have great responsibilities such as transportation, mining and chemical processing. The type of drug testing done in pre-employment situations is rather similar to that done on Olympic athletes in that the test is aimed at detecting residues which remain in the body after the user has stopped taking the drug. Like the Olympic tests though the tests are not infallible, particularly if potential employees know that they are to be done. Moreover, major problems of test reliability, security of samples and privacy of the individual arise in employment related drug testing. This has forced some commentators and employers to claim that testing is too controversial to be of any practical use.

Tests for alcohol and drug abuse are more common once employment has commenced and generally take the form of random breath testing, blood testing or urine testing. However, in most cases these are only done on a 'for cause' basis when some pre-agreed criteria are in evidence, for example, suspected drunkenness. Industries where the use of dangerous equipment is common are the most likely to have such policies and the federal Transport Administration Act specifically provides for testing. Once again these tests are controversial because drug residues such as those from cannabis may remain in the body for a long period of time and, it is claimed, have no impact on performance.

Regardless of what methods are used for drug testing, a key issue in adopting a drug policy is establishing a new disciplinary procedure. Essentially, a disciplinary policy must spell out clearly what disciplinary action will result if an employee breaches the drug and alcohol policy. If the consequences of a breach are not made clear then it is not worthwhile testing because employees will be able to appeal any disciplinary action on the basis of lack of procedural fairness.

Lie detector tests

While few organisations in Australia use such tests, in the US large numbers of organisations routinely ask job applicants to submit to a lie detector or **polygraph test** as part of the selection procedures. This is particularly true in situations where the applicant is being considered for a fiduciary position or has access to pharmaceuticals or any small consumer item that has resale value. Many critics of lie detectors question their reliability and claim that their use is an invasion of an applicant's right to privacy. New South Wales has prohibited the use of lie detector tests for employment purposes since the early 1980s (the *Lie Detector Act 1983*) and in the United States, the passage of the *Employee Polygraph Protection Act 1988* has begun to restrict the widespread use of these tests for employee selection (Labato 1988).

Methods of using information for selection and placement decisions

As shown above, many devices are available to make selection decisions. Their choice depends on job relatedness, costs, and time constraints. If more than one predictor is used, a decision must be made regarding the order in which selection devices will be administered and how information from the various sources should be combined. Additional considerations centre on controlling bias associated with making selection decisions.

The single predictor approach

When HRM managers use only one piece of information or one method for selecting an applicant, they are taking this approach. **Single predictors** are used by many organisations to select employees, especially when they can readily be validated. This occurs most frequently when a single predictor captures the essence or the major dimension of the job, thereby making it easy to validate (e.g. requiring a candidate for a keyboard operator's job to pass a typing test).

But for many jobs, a single predictor test cannot be used, nor can a single dimension duty, such as typing, be used to explain the essence of the job. Many jobs can be explained only with several job dimensions or duties. For such jobs, several predictors, such as written tests and application blanks, are used in making selection and placement decisions.

The multiple predictor approach

The multiple predictor approach is taken when more than one selection device is needed to elicit the essence of the various dimensions which are required in successful job performance. The information from multiple predictors can be combined in three ways.

Multiple hurdles approach

In such an approach, an applicant must exceed fixed levels of proficiency on all predictors in order to be accepted. A score lower than the cutoff score on one predictor test cannot be compensated for by a higher-than-necessary score on another predictor. Underlying this approach is the assumption that a specific skill or competency is so critical that inadequacy guarantees the person will be unsuccessful on the job. This assumption legitimately applies for some physical ability requirements (e.g. visual acuity for pilots) and for mandated licensing requirements (e.g. registration requirements for nurses).

Compensatory approach

Because most jobs do not have truly absolute requirements, this is more realistic. It assumes that good performance on one predictor *can* compensate for poor performance on another (e.g. a low score on a written examination can be compensated for by a high score on an interview). With a compensatory approach, no selection decisions are made until the completion of the entire process. Then a composite index is developed that takes into consideration performance on all predictors.

The advantage of this approach is that every applicant, regardless of race or ethnic background gets to participate in the *entire* selection process. While more time-consuming and costly than a multiple hurdles approach, a compensatory approach is less likely to cause legal problems.

Combined approach

Many organisations also use this approach, in which one or more specific requirements (e.g. qualifications in law or accounting) must be met. Once these hurdles are overcome, performances on the remaining predictors are combined into an overall measure of job suitability. Consider graduate recruiting. Many organisations only interview students with good academic records (first hurdle). The candidate must then pass a campus interview (second hurdle). At corporate headquarters, the applicant may take aptitude tests, participate in an assessment centre, and be interviewed. A composite index that considers performance in all three areas is used to make the final selection (compensatory).

Australian data on selection practices

There is not a great deal of Australian data on selection practices. However, three relatively recent small-scale studies point to a similar conclusion that selection practices are relatively unsophisticated. In a survey of thirty-nine Victorian businesses, Vaughan & McClean (1989) found that:

- Australian firms have tended to use selection methods which are ad hoc, subjective and non standard
- Selection practices were technically and scientifically unsophisticated and highly susceptible to error
- There was strong opposition in many firms to structured interview formats
- Most firms seldom used more than one interviewer at a time although most claimed to use more than one interview prior to a decision being made
- There was a reliance on unsupported interview information which was rarely checked against other source of information
- In excess of two thirds of the sample never or seldom used psychological testing.

Patrickson & Haydon (1988) in their study of management selection practices in South Australia came to similar conclusions although they noted that larger and longer established organisations tended to use more sophisticated selection practices and psychological testing was more likely to be used for more senior positions.

In research reported by CCH (1989) organisations were asked to estimate the complexity of their recruitment and selection techniques on a five point scale. Only 5 per cent responded that they use the most sophisticated techniques such as psychological testing, serial interview, weighted application blanks and selection interviewer training. Fourteen per cent said that they used basic techniques like interviews and reference checks, and the remainder were distributed throughout the middle of the range. Large and private organisations were slightly more likely to use more sophisticated techniques (CCH 1989, pp. 1461–93).

These findings confirm that Australian organisations on the whole use fairly basic selection techniques which are susceptible to error. This is despite an abundance of research indicating that selection errors are reduced when multiple and more sophisticated techniques are used. This is most likely related to the high incidence of small- to medium-sized organisations in Australia who are less likely to use more advanced techniques in any HR area. However, this does not necessarily mean that all these firms are making poor selection decisions. Smaller firms are much more likely to recruit people who are personally known to the owners or other staff members and in this situation references and other forms of personal recommendation are likely to be more reliable than in the somewhat more impersonal world of small business. Another practice which is likely to offset the consequences of poor selection decisions, and which is being adopted now by big and small businesses alike, is that of probationary periods. Probationary periods are very useful in allowing both employers and employees to decide if a long-term employment relationship is appropriate, on the basis of actually doing the job in question. Indeed a modified form of a probationary period is for an employer to actually pay a potential employee to come and do one or two days work for them in order to assess suitability. This practice is also becoming more common as employers become more aware of the pitfalls of incorrect hiring decisions.

Biases in selection

In addition to deciding on the order in which selection devices will be administered, managers should make a conscious effort to minimise biases associated with selection. Because of information processing limitations, managers tend to overuse inferential strategies. As a result, their selection decisions may be biased in a number of different ways. Figure 8.9 lists some of the specific biases that affect selection decisions.

BIAS	DEFINITION
1 Illusion of completeness	Decision makers perceive an information set as complete, even in the absence of important information or considerations. Consequently, decisions will be made with incomplete information. For example, a secretary will be selected on the basis of a typing test, even though typing accounts for only 15 per cent of work duties.
2 Over-confidence	Decision makers tend to be over-confident in their fallible judgements when answering moderately to extremely hard questions. Human resource managers have greater confidence in their selection decisions than objectively they should. Recall that the best selection devices (e.g. cognitive ability tests) have a validity coefficient of only 0.53, which means they account for approximately 25 per cent of the reason someone performs well or poorly on a job.
3 Confirmatory bias	Information that confirms one's hypothesis is taken at face value, while potentially unconfirmatory evidence is subjected to highly critical and sceptical scrutiny. For example, during the initial phase of an interview, a manager makes a judgement about the suitability of an applicant. Information that confirms this is retained, while non-confirming information is more likely to be ignored.
4 Base rate fallacy	Decision makers tend to ignore prior probabilities (base rates) when any—even worthless—situational information is available. For example, in determining whether to use a specific test, managers may fail to consider how many applicants could perform adequately if no test were used. As a result, they may view a test as more useful than it actually is.
5 Law of small numbers	In estimating probabilities, people tend to ignore the importance of sample size and attribute greater stability to results attained from small samples than is warranted. For example, human resource managers have inappropriately believed that small samples were sufficient to validate a test. Similarly, they have assumed that a 30-minute interview is a representative sample of an applicant's overall job behaviour.
6 Framing	Decision makers are likely to treat risks concerning perceived gains differently from risks associated with perceived losses. In the face of losses, they are risk-seeking; in the face of gains, risk-averse. For example, managers may not narrow down applicant pools sufficiently if they adopt a reject versus an accept selection strategy.
7 Illusion of validity	A good fit between the predicted outcome and input information produces unwarranted confidence. Information that appears consistent (redundant) is weighted more heavily than it should be. For example, managers may erroneously believe that two tests that are highly correlated (e.g. perceptual speed and error detection) predict better than a single predictor or uncorrelated predictors.
8 Anchoring and adjustment	The number of openings to be filled may inappropriately anchor selection decisions. That is, when there is more than one opening to be filled, marginal candidates may be viewed as

		qualified; if there is only one opening, managers adjust their evaluations upwards so that fewer candidates are considered qualified. Consequently, evaluations of candidates are based on the number of openings rather than on qualifications.
9	Career fixation	Following an initial judgement about an applicant's qualifications, an employee is later perceived as incapable of possessing or developing expertise in other areas. As a result, the employee may be pigeon-holed in a particular career track, even when qualified for other positions.

Figure 8.9 Description of cognitive biases affecting selection decisions
Source: Schuler et al. 1992, p. 186; based on Huber et al. 1988

A more general form of bias may lie in the tendency noted in many organisational studies for managers to show preference in selection for socially similar subordinates. This is often referred to as **homosociability** (or sometimes, more controversially, as 'homosexual' reproduction) and refers to situations where managers, through selection processes, reproduce themselves in their own image (Moss Kanter 1977, p. 48). Not surprisingly, this is a major source of discrimination in relation to selection. The reasons for homosociability stem mainly from the perceived need of managers to have subordinates that they can trust. This often involves conformity, loyalty and the acceptance of authority which can be shown in part by appearance. Moreover, when managers select people broadly in their own image they reinforce the belief that people of their own kind legitimately deserve authority. As Moss Kanter succinctly puts it:

> 'Homosocial' and 'Homosexual' reproduction provide an important form of re-assurance in the face of uncertainty about performance measurement in high-reward and high-prestige positions. So management positions again become easily closed to people who are 'different'. Finally, since uncertainty about evaluation also raises questions about who 'wins' in a competitive situation, the pressures for on-site and off-work lifestyle conformity also constitute as William Henry put it, a 'self-protective system assuring in some degree that competitive peers are held to some common standards' (Moss Kanter, 1977, p. 63).

Training

Despite the susceptibility of decision makers to these biases, distortions can be minimised in several ways. First, selection biases can be prevented or reduced by direct frontal assault—training decision makers to be aware of and to compensate for their susceptibility to judgemental influences. At a minimum, such training programs need to alert decision makers to the possibility of bias, offer alternative approaches, and give feedback regarding the frequency of bias in their judgements. Unfortunately, because of the range of decision biases, such training may be lengthy and costly.

Decision aids

Alternatively, selection biases can be reduced with decision aids. The advantage of decision aids is that they provide an 'organisational memory'. Because the procedures insulate the decision from the biases of the decision makers, decision aids reduce inappropriate cognitive influences for *any* decision maker who uses them. Decision aids may be as simple as a scoring key for interview questions or as complex as mathematically derived regression equations that indicate how the results from multiple selection devices should optimally be combined.

Unfortunately, few organisations rely exclusively on decision aids. This is because managers do not easily accept the fact that mathematical models provide better predictions than humans do. They contend that the nuances of good decision making simply cannot be captured adequately by decision models. This argument is personified in discussions about the viability of the interview as a selection device. Even though the interview is less reliable than cognitive ability tests, managers persist in using it as a primary selection device because testing cannot accurately assess interpersonal skills or whether an applicant will fit within an organisation's culture.

In sum, when developing a selection process, several questions need to be answered:

1. Which predictors are most valid?
2. Are predictors correlated with one another? (if so, only one should be used)
3. In what order will predictors be administered?
4. How will predictors be scored? (multiple hurdles, compensatory, or combined)
5. What strategies will be used to minimise bias in selection decisions?
6. Were the desired results attained?

Trends in selection and placement

Three important trends in selection and placement are the selection of contractors, assessment of decisions and the use of computer technology.

The selection of contractors

As has been noted in many places in this book, one of the key changes in organisational forms recently has been a shrinking of the 'core workforce' and a growth use of 'peripheral' employees. One of the main methods of achieving this change has been to increase the use of subcontractors. However, a major potential problem with subcontractors is the variable quality of service provided. Thus the selection of subcontractors has become a critical task. The building industry in Australia has had a long history of using subcontractors and has recently developed some innovative recruitment and selection techniques which provide good examples of how the relationship can be managed so that the subcontractors perform consistently to organisational standards.

At the Victorian branch of Multiplex, a pre-qualifying system has been established to screen subcontractors on their financial and technical strength and their health and safety record. In a recent project this system was used to reduce a field of twenty potential subcontractors to six (Roberts 1996). As can be seen from the 'Future organisational forms' discussion, 'Lawyers find BOC selection system a gas' similar practices are now being used outside the building industry.

The development of partnering relationships with subcontractors at Multiplex goes further however than just selecting carefully, as Roberts (1996) explains:

> Perth-based Multiplex now involves contractors in the early stages of bidding for contracts, and is working with 30 contractors to develop their internal strategies for continuous improvement. The company first invited its contractors' senior executives to a three-day intensive workshop where they learned Multuplex's techniques for continuous improvement.
>
> A group of a half dozen companies has since been selected to implement their own total quality management programs. In one case electrical contractor Elecraft Pty Ltd, has developed a team-based approach to continuous improvement.

One team at Elecraft studied how the company stored, located and used building tools on its sites. The team developed a new tool-management system that has cut the time needed to complete a job by 8 per cent ...

Multiplex is also encouraging small contractor to group together to bid for larger packages of work. In one case a plasterer, air-conditioning contractor and electrical contractor have formed Complete Building Services to deliver all services on major building projects. Complete has so far won work on two apartment block projects in central Melbourne.

Multiplex carries out its own on-site training for contractor construction workers, and has a partnership with Deakin University to develop a distance learning program aimed at managers and supervisors ...

There has always been some element of relationship building between major construction companies and their preferred contractors. But Multiplex has taken these relationships to a new level that emphasises the strategic benefits to contractor, builder and customer of formal ties and knowledge sharing ...

Assessing selection and placement decisions

The quality and effectiveness of selection and placement decisions depend on whether the organisation hires applicants who turn out to be good performers. If it can select and place applicants who turn out to perform well, organisational productivity will benefit. If applicants who would have performed poorly are not selected, organisational productivity will also benefit. The critical point is that when an organisation makes selection and placement decisions based on activities that benefit productivity, it is making them using predictors that are valid and serve its legal considerations. Organisations must use valid predictors, and must also be concerned with the overall costs of the selection devices and weigh these against the benefits.

Use of computer technology

On any given day, a human resource department will probably evaluate a number of candidates for a variety of positions. Deciding which predictors are valid for a particular case and administering a multitude of predictors make personnel work challenging. Effective management of predictors is critical in the face of extensive laws and regulations. Doing all these tasks effectively requires a great deal of information. Computer technology can enhance the ability of the human resources department to co-ordinate the scheduling, administration, and evaluation of predictors by processing this information in a variety of ways.

For example, the department could quickly do a validation study by correlating the current job performance data with any of several predictors, if these data were stored in a human resource information system and analysed by computer. Results of tests to measure job applicants' skills, knowledge, and abilities, as well as interests and preferences, can be stored in an HRIS and used together with job analysis data (also in the HRIS) to make better selection and placement decisions. This same information can then be used to help plot career paths for employees when they are hired.

Computers can also be used to reduce first impression biases inherent in interviews. Computer aided interviewing uses the computer to present a structured interview directly to an applicant, without an interviewer present. Although it does not replace the face-to-face interview, it complements it by providing a base of information about each applicant before the interviewer meets him or her. This provides a first impression based on information that is job relevant rather than anecdotal.

Computer interviewing is also faster. An applicant can complete a 100-question computer-aided interview in about 20 minutes. The same information would require a face-to-face interview of more than 2 hours. In addition to time savings, computer aided interviewing provides an automatic record of answers, so that they can be compared across applicants. More important, computer aided interviews have been validated in a number of settings, including manufacturing and service industries (Rodgers 1987).

Summary

In this chapter the three key aspects of the staffing function: recruitment, selection and placement have been examined. Recruiting is a major activity in an organisation's program to manage its human resources. After human resource needs have been established and job requirements have been identified through job analysis, a program of recruitment can be established to produce a pool of job applicants, from internal or external sources. As with other HRM activities, it is essential that recruitment be assessed. This can be done by evaluating the benefit and cost criteria associated with recruitment. For example, the benefits of reduced turnover or enhanced performance can be assessed and compared with the costs of the programs to recruit the job applicants. Costs of sources and methods can also be assessed and weighed against benefits such as ease of recruiting or number of qualified applicants obtained. After these assessments are made, recruiting methods and sources can be revised as appropriate. As with the assessment of the recruitment activity, this should be done with consideration for selection and placement, the other half of the staffing function.

The final part of this chapter examines what selection and placement procedures are and how they relate to other human resource management activities. Organisations want to ensure that they hire job applicants with the abilities to meet job demands. Increasingly, they also want to ensure that job applicants will not only perform well but stay with the organisation. Thus they may want to attain a match between the needs of the job applicants and the rewards offered by the job qualities and organisational context.

In order to match individual skills, knowledge and abilities to job demands and individual preferences to job and organisational characteristics, organisations need to gather information about job applicants. The three most common methods for doing so—interviewing, testing and application blanks—must operate within legal regulations. As a consequence of these legal concerns, the types of information and the methods used to obtain information for selection vary according to the type of job for which the applicants are being selected. For example, assessment centres are more apt to be used for managerial jobs, and physical ability tests are more apt for manufacturing jobs. Exactly how many predictors are used may depend in part upon the type of job, but is also likely to depend upon the selection ratio, the costs associated with the selection tests in comparison with their benefits, and the degree of validity and reliability of the predictors being used.

questions for discussion and review

1 What are the purposes of recruitment and how do these affect other organisational activities?

2 How does human resource planning contribute to effective recruitment? What are the roles of the line and HR manager in each of these activities?

3 Just-in-time inventory is a concept that enables manufacturers to assemble products from parts that are delivered as needed rather than kept in inventory, which is costly. Could this concept be applied to the recruitment function and human resources? Explain.
4 Why do some organisations use an external search, whereas others use an internal one? Can each be best for a particular organisation? Explain.
5 Assessment of recruitment activities requires an estimate of costs as well as benefits. Choose an organisation you are familiar with and describe how you would measure and compare the costs and benefits of its recruitment methods.
6 What are the best methods of recruiting potentially qualified applicants?
7 Successful selection and placement decisions are dependent on other HR functions. Identify these and their relationships to selection and placement.
8 A frequent diagnosis of an observed performance problem in an organisation is, 'John was a selection mistake'. What are the short- and long-term consequences of these so-called selection mistakes? Can you relate this question to your own experience with organisations?
9 How is an achievement test distinguished from an aptitude test? Give an example of each.
10 Given all of the weaknesses identified with the interview, why is it a popular selection device? How could you improve it to overcome some of these?

case study

Read the 'HRM in the news' items at the beginning of this chapter and answer the following questions.
1 What are the advantages and disadvantages of Assessment Centres as a selection method?
2 What are the advantages and disadvantages of psychological testing as a selection method?
3 What do these cases reveal about the nature of selection practices in Australia today?
4 What general conclusions can be drawn from these cases about the reliability and validity of different selection methods?

Resources

BBC (1995), *Right First Time: A Guide to Recruitment and Selection Skills* (Video and CD materials), Sydney, BBC Worldwide.

Compton, R. L. & Nankervis A. (1992), *Effective Recruitment and Selection Practices*, CCH Australia, Sydney.

Hicks, R. E. (1991), 'Psychological Testing in Australia in the 1990s', *Asia Pacific HRM*, vol. 29, no. 1, pp. 94–101.

Murdoch, V. J. (1992), 'Assessment Centres: Through the Glass Brightly', *Asia Pacific Journal of Human Resources*, vol. 30, no. 2, pp. 29–41.

Stone, R. J. (1991), 'Personality Tests in Executive Selection', in *Readings in Human Resource Management vol. 2*, John Wiley and Sons, Brisbane.

Vaughan, E. & McClean, J. (1989), 'A Survey and Critique of Management Selection Practices in Australian Business Firms', *Asia Pacific HRM*, vol. 27, no. 4, pp. 20–34.

References

Aamodt, M. J. & Peggans, D. L. (1988), Rejecting Applicants with Tact', *Personnel Administrator,* April, pp. 58-60.

Acuff, H. A. (1982), Improving the Employment Function, *Personnel Journal,* June.

Arvey, R. D., Miller, H. E., Gould, R. & Burch, P. (1987), 'Interview Validity for Selecting Sales Clerks', *Personnel Psychology,* Spring: 1–12.

Arvey, R. D. & Faley, R. H. (1988), *Fairness in Selecting Employees,* Addison-Wesley, Reading, Mass.

Asher, J. J. & Sciarrina, J. A. (1974), 'Realistic work sample tests: a review', *Personnel Psychology,* vol. 27, pp. 519–33.

Australian Bureau of Statistics (1990), *Yearbook Australia* (1990), Canberra.

—— (1995), *Skills Demand Bulletin,* March.

Australian Personnel Management, CCH, Sydney.

Bass, B. M. & Barnett, G. V. (1981), People, *Work, and Organizations,* 2nd edition, Allyn and Bacon, Boston.

Baysinger, R. A. (1988), 'Disparate Treatment and Disparate Impact Theories of Discrimination', in R. S Schuler, S. A Youngblood & V. L Huber (eds), *Readings in Personnel and Human Resource Management,* 3rd edition, West Publishing Company, St. Paul, Minn., pp. 162–77.

Bazerman, M, (1985), 'Norms of Distributive Justice in Interest Arbitration', *Industrial Relations Review,* vol. 38, pp. 558–70

—— (1994) *Judgement in Managerial Decision Making,* Wiley, New York.

Ben-Shakar, G, et al. (1986), Can Graphology Predict Occupational Success? Two Empirical Studies and Some Methodological Ruminations), *Journal of Applied Psychology,* November, pp. 645–53.

Ben-Shakar, G. et al. (1986), 'Can Graphology Predict Occupational Success?' (Two Empirical Studies and Some Methodological Ruminations', *Journal of Applied Psychology,* November, pp. 645–53.

Boudreau, J. W. & Rynes, S. L. (1985), 'Role of Recruitment in Staffing Utility Analysis', *Journal of Applied Psychology,* May, pp. 354–66.

Bulletin to Management (1993), 'Psychological testing leads to costly law suit', July 22, p. 226.

Breaugh, J. A. (1983), 'Realistic Job Previews: A Critical Appraisal and Future Research Directions', *Academy of Management Review,* October, pp. 612–23.

Cacioppe, R. (1988), 'AIDS in the Workplace: A Frightening Disease Poses Delicate Questions for Employers', *HRM Australia,* vol. 26, no. 3, pp. 52–67.

Caldwell, D. F. & Spivey, W. A. (1983), 'The Relationship Between Recruiting Source and Employee Success: An Analysis by Race', *Personnel Psychology,* Spring, pp. 67–72.

Campbell, J. P., Dunnette, M. D Lawler III, E. E. & Weick, Jr. K. E. (1970), *Managerial Behaviour, Performance, and Effectiveness,* McGraw-Hill, New York.

Campion, M. A., Pursell, E. D. & Brown, B. K. (1988), 'Structured Interviewing: Raising the Psychometric Properties of the Employment Interiew', *Personnel Psychology,* Spring, pp. 25–42.

Carmean, G. (1985), 'Preplacement Medical Screenings', *Personnel Journal,* June, pp. 124–32.

Centre for Professional Development (1995), *Recruitment and Termination: Essential Facts,* Kew, Victoria.

Cohen, S. L. (1980), 'Pre-Packaged vs. Tailor-Made: The Assessment Center Debate', *Personnel Journal,* December, pp. 989–95.

Cropanzano, R. & James, K. (1990), 'Some Methodological Considerations for the Behaviour Genetic Analysis of Work Attitudes', *Journal of Applied Psychology*, vol. 75, no. 4, pp. 433–39.

Dean, R. A. & Wanous, J. P. (1984), 'Effects of Realistic Job Previews on Hiring Bank Tellers', *Journal of Applied Psychology*, February, pp. 61–68.

Dougherty, T. W., Ebert, R. J. & Callendar, J. C. (1985), 'Policy Capturing in the Employment Interview', *Journal of Applied Psychology*, February, pp. 9–15.

Dowling, P. & Fisher, C. (1995), '1995 AHRI Survey Results', Australian Human Resources Institute.

Dunnette, M. (1966), *Personnel Selection and Placement*, Brookes/Cole Publishing, Monterey, CA.

Dyer, J. (1996), Address to Macquarie University Graduate School of Management, 18 June.

Farish, P. (1985), 'Cost Per Hire', *Personnel Administrator*, January, p. 16.

Fear, R. A. (1984), *The Evaluation Interview*, 3rd edition, McGraw-Hill, New York.

Field, H. S. & Gatewood, R. D. (1988), 'Matching Talent with the Task', in G. O. Ferris & K. M. Rowland (eds), *Human Resource Management: Perspectives and Issues*, Allyn and Bacon, Boston.

Fletcher, C. A. & Dulewicz, V. (1984), 'An Empirical Study of a UK based Assessment Centre', *Journal of Management Studies*, vol. 21, pp. 83–97.

Fletcher, C., Blinkhorn, S. & Johnson, C. (1991), 'Personality tests: the great debate', *Personnel Management*, vol. 23, no. 9, pp. 38–42.

Fombrun, C. (1982), 'An Interview with Reginald Jones', *Organizational Dynamics*, Winter, p. 46.

Gaugler, B. B, Rosenthal, D. B., Thorton, G. C. & Bentson, C. (1987), 'Metanalysis of Assessment Center Validity', *Journal of Applied Psychology*, vol. 72, pp. 493–511.

Ghiselli, E. E. (1973), 'The Validity of Aptitude Tests in Personnel Selection', *Personnel Psychology*, vol. 26, pp. 461–77.

Gough, G. (1976), 'Personality and Personality Assessment' in M. D. Dunnette (ed.), *Handbook of Industrial and Organizational Psychology*, Rand McNally, Chicago.

Hakel, M. D. (1982), 'Employment Interviewing', in K. M. Rowland & G. Ferris (eds), *Personnel Management*, Allyn & Bacon, Boston, pp. 129–55.

Heshizer, B. & Muczyk, J. P. (1988), 'Drug Testing at the Workplace: Balancing Individual, Organizational and Societal Rights', *Labor Law Journal*, June, pp. 342–57.

Huber, V. L., Northcraft, G. B. & Neale, M. (1992), 'Foibles and Fallacies in Organizational Staffing Decisions', in Schuler et al. *Readings in Personnel and Human Resource Management*, 3rd edition, West Publishing, St. Paul, Minn., pp. 193–205.

Hunter, J. E. & Hunter, R. F. (1984), 'Validity and Utility of Alternate Predictors of Job Performance', *Psychological Bulletin*, vol. 96, pp. 72–98.

James, S. P., Campbell, I. M. & Lovegrove, S. A. (1984), 'Personality Differentiation in a Police-Selection Interview', *Journal of Applied Psychology*, February, pp. 129–34.

Kleinman, L. S. & Clark, K. L. (1984), 'An Effective Job Posting System', *Personnel Journal*, February, pp. 20–25.

Kleinmutz, B. (1985), 'Lie Detectors Fail the Truth Test', *Harvard Business Review*, vol. 63, pp. 36, 42.

Klimoski, R. & Brickher, M. (1987), 'Why Do Assessment Centers Work? The Puzzle of Assessment Center Validity', *Personnel Psychology*, vol. 40, pp. 243–60.

Labato, S. (1988), 'Business and the Law: New Rules Limit Lie Detectors' Use', *New York Times*, 28 November, p. 22.

Latham, G. P. & Saari, L. M. (1984), 'Do People Do What They Say? Further Studies on the Situational Interview', *Journal of Applied Psychology*, November, pp. 569–73.

Levine, H. Z. (1982), 'Relocation Practices', *Personnel*, Jan–Feb., pp. 4–10.

Levinson, D. A. (1988), 'Needed: Revamped Recruiting Services', *Personnel*, July, pp. 50–52.

London, M. & Stumpf, S. A. (1983), 'Effects of Candidate Characteristics on Management Promotion Decisions: An Experimental Study', *Personnel Psychology*, Summer, pp. 241–60.

Masters, M. F., Ferris, G. & Ratcliff, S. L. (1988), 'Practices and Attitudes of Substance Abuse Testing', *Personnel Administrator*, July, pp. 72–78.

Maurer, S. D. & Fay, C. (1988), 'Effect of Situationai Interviews and Training on Interview Rating Agreement: An Experimental Analysis', *Personnel Psychology*, Summer, pp. 329–44.

Meglino, B. M. & DeNisi, A. S. (1987), 'Realistic Job Previews: Some Thoughts on Their More Effective Use in Managing the Flow of Human Resources', *Human Resource Planning*, vol. 10, no. 3, pp. 157–67.

Meglino, B. M., DeNisi, A. S., Youngblood, S. A. & Williams, K. J. (1988), 'Effects of Realistic Job Previews: A Comparison Using an Enhancement and Reduction Preview', *Journal of Applied Psychology*, May, pp. 259–66.

Moss Kanter, R. (1977), *Men and Women of the Corporation*, Basic Books, New York.

Mucyzk, J. P. & Heshizer, B. P. (1988), 'Mandatory Drug Testing: Managing the Latest Pandora's Box', *Business Horizons*, March–April, p. 14.

National Association of Personnel Consultants (1996), *Industry Activities and Revenues*.

Nichols, L. C. & Hudson, J. (1981), 'Dual-Role Assessment Center: Selection and Development', *Personnel Journal*, May, pp. 350–86.

Novit, M. S. (1981), 'Physical Examinations and Company Liability: A Legal Update', *Personnel Journal*, January, pp. 47–52.

Olian, J. D. & Rynes, S. L. (1984), 'Organizational Staffing: Integrating Practice with Strategy', *Industrial Relations*, vol. 23, pp. 170–83.

Patrickson, M. & Haydon, D. (1988), 'Management selection practices in South Australia', *Human Resource Management Australia*, vol. 26, no. 4, pp. 96–104.

Patton, A. (1982), 'When Executives Bail Out to Move Up', *Business Week*, 13 September, pp. 13, 15, 17, 19.

Petty, M. M. (1974), 'A Multivariate Analysis of the Effects of Experience and Training upon Performance in a Leaderless Group Discussion', *Personnel Psychology*, vol. 27, pp. 271–82.

Pfeffer, J. (1995), 'Producing sustainable competitive advantage through the effective management of people', *Academy of Management Executive*, vol. 9, no. 1, pp. 55–72.

Plumke, L. P. (1980), 'A Short Guide to the Development of Work Sample and Performance Tests', Pamphlet from the US Office of Personnel Management, February, Washington, DC.

Podsakoff, P. M., Williams, M. L. & Scott M. E. Jr. (1988), 'Myths of Employee Selection Systems' in R. S. Schuler, S. A. Youngblood & V. L. Huber, *Readings in Personnel and Human Resource Management*, 3rd edition, West Publishing, St. Paul, Minn., pp. 178–92.

Porter, M. (1990), *The Competitive Advantage of Nations*, Free Press, London.

Quick, J. C, Fisher, W. A., Schkade, I. J. & Ayers, G. W. (1980), 'Developing Administrative Personnel Through the Assessment Center Technique', *Personnel Administrator*, February, pp. 444–662.

Raza, S. M. & Carpenter, B. N. (1987), 'A Model of Hiring Decisions in Real Employment Interviews', *Journal of Applied Psychology*, November, pp. 596–603.

Rendero, T. (1980), 'Consensus', *Personnel*, Sept.–Oct., p. 5.

—— (1984), 'Job Posting Practices', *Personnel*, Nov.–Dec., pp. 48–52.

Roberts, P. (1996a), 'Multiplex builds on efficiency', *Australian Financial Review*, 13 March, p. 24.

—— (1996b), 'Lawyers find BOC selection system a gas', *Australian Financial Review*, 11 September, p. 29.

Rodgers, D. D. (1987), 'Personnel Computing: Computer-Aided Interviewing Overcomes First Impressions', *Personnel Journal*, April, pp. 148–52.

Rothman, M. (1988), 'Random Drug Testing in the Workplace: Implications for Human Resource Management', *Business Horizons*, March–April, p. 23.

Saxe, L., Dougherty, D. & Cross, T. (1985), 'The Validity of Polygraph Testing', *American Psychologist,* vol. 40, pp. 355–56.

Sayles, L. R. & Strauss, G. (1977), *Managing Human Resources*, Prentice-Hall, Englewood Cliffs, NJ.

Schein, E. H. (1977), 'Increasing Organizational Effectiveness Through Better Human Resource Planning and Development', *Sloan Management Review*, Autumn, pp. 1–20.

Schmidt, F. L. & Hunter, J. E. (1983), 'Individual Differences in Productivity: An Empirical Test of Estimates Derived from Studies of Selection Procedure Utility', *Journal of Applied Psychology*, vol. 68, pp. 407–14.

Schuler, R. S. (1995), *Managing Human Resources*, West Publishing, St. Paul, Minn.

Schuler, R. S., Dowling. P. J., Smart, P. J. & Huber, V. L. (1992), *Human Resource Management in Australia*, 2nd edition HarperEducational, Sydney.

Shippman, J. S., Hughes, G. L. & Prien, E. P. (1988), 'Raise Assessment Center Standards', *Personnel Journal*, July, pp. 69–79.

Skilled Engineering (1996), *Report To Shareholders*, Skilled Engineering, August.

Smith, L. (1978), 'Equal Opportunity Rules Are Getting Tougher', *Fortune,* June, p. 154.

Stone, R. J. (1985), 'Personality Tests in Executive Selection', *Human Resource Management Australia,* vol. 23, no. 4, pp. 10–14.

Szilagyi, A. D. & Schweiger, D. M. (1984), 'Matching Managers to Strategies: A Review and Suggested Framework', *Academy of Management Review*, vol. 9, pp. 626–37.

Taylor, M. S. & Bergman, T. J. (1987), 'Organizational Recruitment Activities and Applicants' Reactions at Different Stages of the Recruitment Process', *Personnel Psychology*, Summer, pp. 261–86.

The Melbourne *Age* (1996), *Employment*, 11 May.

Tziner, A. & Dolan, S. (1982), 'Validity of an Assessment Center for Identifying Female Officers in the Military', *Journal of Applied Psychology*, vol. 67, pp. 728–36.

Wagel, W. H. (1988), 'A Drug-Screening Policy That Safeguards Employees' Rights', *Personnel*, February, pp. 10–11.

Weekley, J. A. & Gier, J. A. (1987), 'Reliability and Validity of the Situational Interview for a Sales Position', *Journal of Applied Psychology*, August, pp. 484–87.

chapter 9

Performance management

Robin Kramar

learning objectives

After studying this chapter, you will be able to:

1. Describe the roles and purposes of performance appraisals.
2. Describe the relationship between performance appraisals, other human resource activities and the environment.
3. Describe the processes and procedures in performance appraisals.
4. Identify and assess the main approaches and types of performance appraisals.
5. Examine the way performance appraisals systems can be designed and used effectively.
6. Identify strategies to improve performance.
7. Describe future trends in performance appraisal.

chapter 9

chapter outline

- Performance management defined — 356
  - Performance appraisal — 356
  - Performance appraisal system — 356
  - Superior rater and subordinate ratee — 356
- Roles and purposes of performance appraisals — 356
  - Roles of performance appraisals — 357
  - Purposes of performance appraisals — 357
  - Ethical considerations — 358
- Relationships and performance appraisals — 358
  - Relationships with other HRM activities — 358
  - Relationships with the internal environment — 359
  - Relationships with the external environment — 359
- Performance appraisals as a set of processes and procedures — 361
  - Criteria and standards — 361
  - Performance criteria — 362
  - Choice of raters — 364
- Performance appraisal approaches — 366
  - Comparative standards — 366
  - Absolute standards — 367
  - Objectives-based approaches — 374
  - Direct index approach — 378
  - Accomplishment records — 378
  - Means-based approach — 379
- The design and use of performance appraisals — 379
  - Assessing performance appraisal forms: which is best? — 379
  - Criteria for assessment — 379
  - Which form is best? — 379
  - The context of performance appraisal — 382
  - Using the performance appraisal data — 384
  - Designing the appraisal system — 387
- The performance appraisal interview — 388
  - Before the interview — 388
  - Choose an interview style — 389
  - Interview effectiveness — 390
  - Interview follow-up — 391
- Performance appraisal and performance improvement — 393
  - Identifying gaps in performance — 394
  - Identifying the causes of deficiencies — 395
  - Strategies for improving performance — 397
- Trends in performance appraisal — 399
- Summary — 402
- Questions for discussion and review — 403
- Case study — 403
- Resources — 404
- References — 405

HRM IN THE NEWS

Realising the Karpin vision
Performance appraisal to build an enterprise culture.
BY LIZ COUSENS & TED COUSENS

The following ideas show how performance appraisal can help to develop the management competencies suggested in the (Karpin) Report [people skills, strategic thinking, visioning and flexibility/adaptability to change] and achieve the success-imperatives proposed, namely:

- Increased management and leadership knowledge and skills
- Development of a learning organisation approach
- Greater emphasis on quality in management, HRD, business processes and products and services
- Greater return achieved by companies on their investments
- Greater level of success in attempting to meet world's best standards and benchmarks.

Performance appraisal can help to build a learning culture once we see appraisal as a necessary condition of learning.

Once performance appraisal is seen as a developmental tool, its importance in a learning organisation is clear. This is where visioning comes in.

Whenever people set out to develop skills, they visualise what they will be able to do once they have the skill. This type of visioning leads to performance agreements that 'go somewhere' and map the journey to exemplary achievement. So appraisees know what skills to develop to get to where they want.

There are two powerful outcomes of mapping the path to exemplary achievement:

- The continuum of descriptors that traces your map visualises best practice and shows how to get there.
- The descriptors along the continuum are succinct and so unambiguous that reliability and validity come within kicking distance.

An appraisal scheme can be used to develop a quality culture if that's what an organisation needs. The organisation simply distils some key competencies that are essential to deliver quality and then purposefully develops and appraises them.

It is relatively easy to identify generic quality-based competencies that can be applied to any job description in an organisation which is building a quality culture.

They need to be sufficiently flexible to enable all staff to slot their job responsibilities into them.

All performance agreements need a strategic focus if they are to help appraisees and appraisers work towards organisational outcomes that matter.

A two-fold approach works. First, performance agreements need to be designed 'from the other end', so to speak.

Instead of starting from a specific job or 'job family', more energy, corporate awareness and needed skill are generated by starting from strategic priorities.

This can be done by building-in participative operational planning sessions that link strategic goals with work unit plans and performance agreements.

Visioning plays an important part in the process, particularly in setting performance indicators and planning contingency communication lines to handle problems or opportunities that emerge. This planning session also becomes the first step for managers to find out from staff where their leading and enabling skills will most be needed.

Second, the simple corporate measures set to measure achievement need to be closely aligned with strategic priorities.

These measures enable performance levels for each job responsibility to progress from *novice impact & contribution*, through *fully effective impact & contribution* to *exemplary impact & contribution*.

So the performance descriptors become constant reminders of where everyone's work is leading, as well as benchmarking best practice.

Because they are common measures, they help reliability and validity.

Appraisees and appraisers can map what the essential skills for the year's targets look like as they improve to deliver more corporate impact and contribution. The performance descriptors that result provide a development plan, while the agreement provides an action plan.

Another important outcome of this planning process is that appraisers have tangible ways to build their leading and enabling management skills. The performance agreements give clear guides for useful feedback.

An appraisal system needs to give a lot of elbow room to different types of strengths, personalities and aspirations. It can give this elbow room if reliability is facilitated via explicit achievement goals, results-oriented feedback, shared competencies that have become second nature to everyone, and common performance measures.

References

AIM, (1995), 'Setting The Agenda: Management Reform In Australia—A Discussion Paper Concerning *Enterprising Nation*'.

Briggs-Myers, I. with Myers, P. B. (1980), *Gifts Differing*, Consulting Psychologists Press Inc. CA.

Cousens, L. & Cousens, T. (1994), *Performance Appraisal: Making It Work*, Australian Education Network [Aen], Springwood, NSW.

Deming, W. Edwards (1982), *Out Of Crisis*, Cambridge University Press, Melbourne.

Karpin Taskforce (1995), *Enterprising Nation: Renewing Australia's Managers To Meet The Challenges Of The Asian-Pacific Century*, AGPS, Canberra.

Saul, P. (1992), 'Rethinking Performance Appraisal', *Asia Pacific Journal Of Human Resources*, vol. 30, no. 3.

Senge, P. M. (1990), *The Fifth Discipline*, Doubleday, New York.

Source: *Management*, October 1995, pp. 11–13.

The 'HRM in the news' feature suggests how performance appraisal systems can be used to improve organisational performance through building a learning organisation with an enterprising culture. It claims the establishment of performance agreements which are linked with strategic goals and which give clear guides for useful feedback are an important part of the performance appraisal process. The process of improving employee performance through the use of performance appraisals involves the two key activities of identifying deficiencies and developing strategies to remove deficiencies. Unfortunately, there are inherent conflicts associated with this process.

Performance management systems and appraisals are increasingly being used in Australian organisations. In order to understand the process of performance appraisal it is important to understand a number of key concepts. These include:

- performance management
- performance appraisal
- performance appraisal system
- superior rater
- subordinate ratee

Performance management defined

A performance management process or system involves a series of processes designed to manage employee performance. It includes a number of components including work and job design, reward structures, the selection of people to do the work, the training and induction of these people into the way work is done, the assessment of how employees are doing their work and policies for rewarding and improving performance. Performance appraisal is only one part of a performance management system.

Performance appraisal

Although employees may learn about how well they are performing through informal means, such as co-workers telling them what a great job they are doing or their superiors giving them an occasional pat on the back, performance appraisal is defined here as a formal, structured system of measuring, evaluating and influencing an employee's job-related attributes, behaviours and outcomes to discover at what level he or she is presently performing on the job: that is, how productive the employees are and whether they can perform more effectively in the future. It is a dynamic and multidimensional process (Latham & Wexley 1981; Carroll & Schneier 1982).

Performance appraisal system

To account for all of the factors that affect this formal, structured system of measuring and evaluating performance, the term performance appraisal system (PAS) is used. In essence, the performance appraisal system refers to:

1. The form or method used to gather the appraisal data
2. The job analysis conducted to identify the appropriate criteria against which to establish standards to be used in evaluating the appraisal data
3. Establishing the validity and reliability of the method(s) used
4. The characteristics of the rater and ratee influencing the appraisal and the appraisal feedback and interview processes
5. The processes involved in utilising the appraisal information for development and evaluation
6. The evaluation of how well performance appraisal is doing in relation to its stated objectives.

Superior rater and subordinate ratee

In this chapter, the terms supervisor and manager are generally discarded because both the appraiser and the appraisee may be managers or supervisors. Thus, the term superior or rater is used to denote the person doing the appraising, and the term subordinate or ratee is used to refer to the employee whose performance is being appraised. The terms superior and subordinate are used in this chapter only for clarity; they do not imply that the person doing the appraising (the rater) is 'better' than the appraisee (ratee) or that the subordinate is 'inferior' to the superior.

Roles and purposes of performance appraisals

Performance appraisals perform a number of roles including acting as a means of improving organisational performance and success, and serving as a contract between the employer and employee. The results of the performance appraisal can be used for two purposes. These roles are:

1 developmental
2 evaluative.

Roles of performance appraisals

Productivity improvement is of concern to almost all organisations, especially when the rate of productivity increases is relatively small. Although the productivity of most organisations is a function of technology, capital and human resources, many organisations have not sought to increase productivity through improving the performance of their human resources (Latham & Wexley 1981, p. 2). Nevertheless, what employees do or do not do influences the productivity of organisations. What employees do can be measured and evaluated, particularly those critical aspects of productivity such as job performance (e.g. the level of the quality and quantity of what an employee does) and absenteeism. In other words, employee job performance (or simply performance) describes how well an employee performs his or her job while absenteeism refers to whether the employee is in attendance to perform the job. Although both may be important job criteria, employee job performance and absenteeism are often discussed separately; nevertheless, they are discussed together in this chapter. Emphasis is placed on job performance since performance appraisal forms are generally developed to measure this, although occasionally absenteeism is also included. Performance appraisal refers to appraising both job performance and absenteeism. Job performance can be measured by an employee's job-related attributes (e.g. the extent of co-operativeness or initiative), behaviour (e.g. making a loan), or outcomes (e.g. quantity of output).

Performance appraisal also has importance because an effectively designed form serves as a contract between the organisation and the employee, and helps act as a control and evaluation system.

Purposes of performance appraisals

The results of performance appraisals can provide information which is used to make decisions in two areas. The first area involves developing the individual, while the second area involves evaluating the individual.

Developmental purposes include research, feedback, management and career development, human resource planning, performance improvement and communication. Specifically some of the developmental processes are:

- **Management development**—it provides a framework for future employee development by identifying and preparing individuals for increased responsibilities.
- **Performance improvement**—it encourages continued successful performance and strengthens individual weaknesses to make employees more effective and productive.
- **Identification of potential**—it identifies candidates for promotion.
- **Feedback**—it outlines what is expected from employees against their actual performance levels.
- **Human resource planning**—it audits management talent to evaluate the present supply of human resources for replacement planning.
- **Communications**—it provides a format for dialogue between superior and subordinate and improves understanding of personal goals and concerns. This can also have the effect of increasing the trust between the rater and ratee.

Evaluative purposes include decisions on pay, promotion, demotion, retrenchment and termination. Specifically some of the evaluative processes are:

- **Performance measurement**—it establishes the relative value of an individual's contribution to the company and helps evaluate individual accomplishments.
- **Remuneration and benefits**—it helps determine appropriate pay for performance and equitable salary and bonus incentives based on merit or results (Cummings & Schwab 1973; Beer 1981, pp. 24–36).

Ethical considerations

The design and conduct of performance appraisals involve ethical and legal considerations. Unethical assessment procedures can not only undermine organisational morale and employee confidence, but could also lead to legal action. Employment and EEO law establish standards of behaviour regarding the nature and conduct of performance appraisals. Employees have the opportunity to undertake litigation in circumstances when employers fail to give an accurate assessment of their employee's work performance in the course of a performance appraisal.

Relationships and performance appraisals

Performance appraisal is associated with several aspects of the internal and external environment and with several other HRM activities. The most important of these relationships are highlighted.

Relationships with other HRM activities

Performance appraisal has some of its most critical relationships with job analysis, selection, remuneration and benefits, and training.

Job analysis

The foundation in the development of the performance appraisal form is job analysis, which should include an analysis of the important work behaviours which are required for successful performance. A performance appraisal form which does not have a basis in such job analysis may lack validity (Budford, Burkhalter & Jacobs 1988, pp. 132–40).

Selection

To help increase the likelihood that those selected from the job applicant pool are more likely to perform well on the job than those who are not selected, valid selection tests are used by organisations. Since empirical validation of a selection test is the correlation between test and performance scores, having performance appraisal results is necessary because, without them, performance scores cannot be established. When performance appraisal is used in this way it is particularly important that the forms are based upon job analysis.

Remuneration and benefits

One of the purposes of performance appraisal is to motivate employees. One of the ways in which performance appraisal can be used to motivate employees to perform, is by serving as a basis upon which to distribute salaries and benefits. A valid appraisal of employee performance is necessary in order for an organisation to provide contingent rewards (i.e. those based on performance) (Latham, Cummings & Mitchell 1981, pp. 4–23). Performance appraisal information can be used in the determination of pay increments under merit pay and performance-based pay plans.

Training

Training can improve employee performance because performance is in part determined by employee ability, employee motivation and the situation. Training can improve employee performance by enhancing employee ability. In order to provide the appropriate training, however, it is necessary to know the employee's current level of performance and on which aspects of performance the employee is performing at an undesirable level. It is also necessary to know if the undesirable performance is caused by ability, motivation or situation. Performance appraisal, used in conjunction with job analysis, is also necessary in order to establish and implement effective pre-employment training programs.

Relationships with the internal environment

Aspects of top management, organisational strategy and culture have important relationships with performance appraisal (Serpa 1984, pp. 41–46). In addition to influencing how much time and attention is paid to performance appraisal and keeping employees informed as to where they stand, the internal environment influences how performance appraisal is done. For example, top management may emphasise employee participation. Consequently, employees are likely to be involved in performance appraisal through self-appraisal and appraisal of others. Top management may also decide to use product quality and employee performance as a way to gain competitive advantage for the organisation. If this is the case, performance appraisal is used to help shape the strategy of the organisation. This, however, may also influence the way performance appraisal is done. Short-term criteria may be used in performance appraisal in organisations pursuing a stable, exact profit strategy. Longer-term criteria may be used in those pursuing a growth strategy.

Relationships with the external environment

Factors in the external environment have a major impact on the use and nature of performance appraisals. Developments in the international and Australian economies and legislation have encouraged the use of performance appraisals.

Domestic and international competition

The intensity of domestic and international competition is making it more difficult, yet more necessary, for organisations to survive, grow and be profitable. Consequently, they are seeking as many ways as possible to improve. Although there are many, improving employee performance is seen as critical in most organisations. To facilitate the improvement of performance, it is useful to be able to measure it, and seek reasons for any performance deficiencies. Because this is the essence of gathering and using performance appraisal data, the entire performance appraisal system takes on greater importance. This has been happening in organisations and will continue to as long as competition remains such a significant part of the external environment.

Surveys of Australian organisations in 1976, 1985 and 1990 indicate an increase in the use of performance appraisal systems for executive/managerial, forepersons/supervisors, scientific/technical, sales and trades/production/labourer employees during this fourteen year period. However, there was evidence of a slow down in the introduction of performance appraisal systems and the continuing failure to allocate sufficient resources for the adequate use of performance appraisal systems (CCH 1995, pp. 12–700).

Future organisational forms

The new deal

What companies and employees owe one another.

BY BRIAN O'REILLY

Note the wording. Many companies tell workers they are responsible for their own careers. That's what Intel used to say. But 'career' implied constant, upward movement through one broad discipline. Intel's organisation chart has become so flat, there aren't many upper berths to aspire to. Anybody who wants to keep a job must be prepared to go anywhere. Lest anyone ignore that gospel, it is coming home to its in-house evangelists. After a SLRP last year, Dyess realised her HR operation had been growing faster than the company and would have to be cut back. In April 1993, a year before the cut-backs would start, she met with her staff to explain the cuts and to tell them they should keep an eye out for new work. Says Dyess: 'Some people are concerned. Some are excited—it's a chance to get into a whole new line of work'.

At Reuters, which had a more conventional contract with workers for many years, managers found that switching to a new employment arrangement requires explanation, sensitivity, and time. 'Because we were doing well financially, employees' first reaction was, "Why are you doing this to us?"' says Celia Berk, who heads employee programs and training for the company's operations in North and South America.

'But we decided that if you measure yourself just by financial results, you can't tell if you're creating an opportunity for rivals'. Now the company measures itself on client satisfaction, employee effectiveness and satisfaction, operating efficiency, and contribution to shareholder value, in that order. Employee satisfaction is deliberately not at the top of the list. Berk explains, 'You could argue that IBM had satisfied employees. It's obviously not enough'.

That new measurement system is changing much of how business gets done at Reuters, and the company is exploring ways to link it to employment security and pay. 'But we recognised you can't just announce the end of job security without explaining what you'll do in its place', says Berk. 'The company isn't entitled to blind loyalty'. The company held workshops to explain the new approach and to teach employees how to think about their careers. Reuters developed a set of explicit brochures that show what is expected of managers (for example: 'encourages continuous improvement ... looks beyond the short term') and another set for senior managers ('promotes innovation ... defines and implements strategy beyond a 12-month time frame').

In the absence of job security, it turns out, targeted firings are far more palatable to workers than wide-swath layoffs. Companies should probably do more firing—most employees feel it's necessary. Sirota & Alper Associates, a New York City firm that measures employee sentiment, among other things, found that failure to get rid of nonperformers damages morale.

But firing people fairly means evaluating them fairly, and evaluation and measurement remain large failures of the new employment model. Even the best-intentioned companies flub it. At an AT&T division near Bedminster, New Jersey, employees were told that those with the poorest evaluations over the past two years would have to go.

Pay and job security are tied in part to how the team performs, and while she feels

> no loyalty to management, she is willing to work hard to help her teammates.
> Not everyone gets a gold watch. What may evolve are two or three classes of employees, all with varying degrees of connectedness to the organisation, and each getting a very different package of compensation and reward.

Source: *Fortune*, 13 June 1994, pp. 30–35.

The extract from the article 'The new deal', describes the changing nature of the relationship between employees and employers. It highlights the implications of employers requirements for flexibility in the nature and use of employee performance appraisals and how these appraisals are used.

Anti-discrimination legislation

The nature and conduct of performance appraisals are also influenced by anti-discrimination legislation. State and federal legislation requires employers to treat employees equally in the employment context, and this includes the conduct of performance appraisals.

In New South Wales an employee of TAFE was found to have been discriminated against when her name was not placed on a promotion list. In the case, D. Harrison v. Department of TAFE, before the Anti-discrimination Board, it was found Ms Harrison met the requirements for promotion and that if she had been a man in the same circumstance she would have been placed on the promotion list. Ms Harrison had not been placed on the list because of her 'authoritarian attitude' which was manifested by 'aggressive and abrasive conduct'—described as 'pushiness'. She claimed, however, that although she 'was somewhat forceful and aggressive' she was 'not unduly so and certainly no more than was and is acceptable in male applicants'.

The Anti-discrimination Board held that both human resource procedures and the raters' attitudes and behaviours were relevant factors in their decision. It drew attention to the fact that the discrimination was not the result of a conscious and intentional purpose to discriminate, but resulted from sub-conscious assumptions which translated into unlawful behaviour (Kramar 1988, p. 318). The case demonstrates that organisations are accountable for their performance appraisals and highlights the essential requirement for the criteria used in appraisals to be job-related.

Performance appraisals as a set of processes and procedures

Figure 9.1 shows many processes and procedures that are essential for an organisation to do well in order to attain evaluation purposes and meet the many legal requirements (Landy & Farr 1980, pp. 72–107). It is important to discuss these processes and procedures, starting with the establishment of criteria and standards (Ilgen & Feldman 1983, pp. 141–97).

Criteria and standards

To serve the organisation's purposes and meet legal challenges, a performance appraisal system must appraise current employee performance. If the system is to

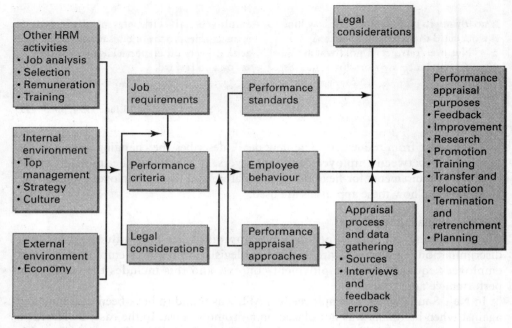

Figure 9.1 Relationships, processes and procedures of appraising employee performance

Source: Schuler, Dowling et al. 1992, p. 210

uncover employees' potential for greater responsibilities and promotion, it must also provide accurate data about such potential. In addition, the system must yield consistent data (i.e. it must be reliable) about what it is supposed to measure (i.e. it must be valid) (Lazer & Wikstrom 1977).

A reliable performance appraisal system produces the same appraisal of a subordinate regardless of who is doing the appraising at any one point in time. Over different periods of time, a reliable performance appraisal system produces the same results from the same rater if the actual performance of the subordinate has not changed. An appraisal system may not be reliable due to numerous errors in rating, as described in a later section in this chapter on superior–subordinate relationships.

Performance criteria

A valid performance appraisal system must specify performance criteria that are job related and important, criteria that can most easily be determined through job analysis. Then, employees' contributions to the organisation can be evaluated based on the degree to which they perform those criteria and attain those results specified in the job analysis. For example, if selling 100 units per month is the only important result of an employee's job, then the appraisal system should only measure the number of units sold. There is only one performance criterion.

Generally, job analysis identifies several performance criteria that reflect employees' contributions. For example, selling 100 units per month may be accompanied by such criteria as 'effects of remarks to customers', 'consistency in attendance', and even 'effects on co-workers'. If all these criteria are found in the job analysis to be important, they all should be measured by the performance appraisal.

If the form used to appraise employee performance lacks the job behaviours and results important and relevant to the job, the form is said to be deficient. If the form includes appraisal of anything either unimportant or irrelevant to the job, it is contaminated. Many performance appraisal forms actually used in organisations measure some attributes and behaviours of employees unrelated to their jobs. These forms are contaminated and in many cases also deficient (Cummings & Schwab 1973; Carroll & Schneier 1982).

Depending on the organisation's strategy and its ability to measure performance, criteria that relate to individual or group behaviour outcomes, or overall organisational effectiveness (e.g. profitability, having high quality, and meeting customer service goals) can be developed. Consider the corporate loan assistant's job. Behavioural criteria for this job may include such things as 'prepares follow-up documentation in a timely manner'. By comparison, outcome criteria refer to the product or output produced such as 'helps generate $5 million in loans each month'. Organisational effectiveness involves an inferential leap. It entails aggregating individual and group outcomes in order to determine how well the organisation is functioning. For example, an organisational effectiveness criteria for a Director of Finance might relate to total profitability of the bank for a specific quarter.

Single, multiple and composite criteria

To avoid performance appraisal deficiency it may be necessary to use more than a single criterion to appraise performance. Then the issue is to determine which criteria to combine and how best to combine them.

Although the use of multiple criteria recognises individual differences and the fact that most job performance is multidimensional, it also presents the problem of how to combine the criteria into a single index that permits comparisons across people. Two major ways to combine the criteria are: (1) to set equal weights for each criterion, and (2) to set relative or differential weights for each criterion based on subjectively determined weights or dollar value to the organisation (Bernardin & Cascio 1987). Once done, performance comparisons can be made more easily.

Standards

In addition to determining the performance criteria and deciding how they are combined, standards must be identified to evaluate how well employees are performing. By using standards, performance criteria take on a range of values. For example, selling 100 units per month may be defined as excellent performance and selling 80 units may be defined as average. Organisations often use historical records of how well employees have done before (essentially to determine what is really possible) to establish what constitutes average or excellent performance. Standards can also be established by time and motion studies and work sampling. Whereas these methods are often used for blue collar, non-managerial jobs, many organisations evaluate how well their managers do by how well or how many goals are attained. Often these are part of an entire performance appraisal method called Management by Objectives (MBO), to be discussed later. Increasingly, managers are also being evaluated against standards of profitability, revenues, or costs.

Although the standards used are determined in part by the nature of the job, they may also be influenced by the way employee performance is measured. That is, if employee performance is appraised by management by objectives, then the level of goal attainment can be used as a standard. Information can also be gathered from a variety of sources.

Choice of raters

While many different sources can be used to gather performance data, the relevance of these sources needs to be considered prior to the choice of rating method. Appraisal sources include supervisors, peers, subordinates, self appraisal, customers and computer monitoring.

Appraisal by superiors

The superior is the immediate boss of the subordinate being evaluated. The assumption is that the superior knows the subordinate's job and performance better than anyone else. But appraisal by the superior has drawbacks. First, since the superior may have reward and punishment power, the subordinate may feel threatened. Second, evaluation is often a one-way process that makes the subordinate feel defensive. Thus little coaching takes place; justification of action takes prevails. Third, the superior may not have the necessary interpersonal skills to encourage high performance or give good feedback. Fourth, the superior, by giving punishments may alienate the subordinate.

Because of the potential liabilities, organisations may invite other people to share the appraisal process, even giving the subordinate greater input. Allowing other people to gather performance appraisal data creates greater openness in the appraisal process, thus helping to enhance the quality of the superior–subordinate relationships.

Self-appraisal

The use of self-appraisal, particularly through subordinate participation in setting goals, was made popular as an important component in management by objectives. Subordinates who participate in the evaluation process may become more involved and committed to the goals. Subordinate participation can also clarify employees' roles and reduce the uncertainty about what to do ('Daily Labor Letter', *The Wall Street Journal*, 1 May, 1990, p. A2).

Self-appraisals are effective tools for programs focusing on self-development, personal growth, and goal commitment. However, self-appraisals are subject to systematic biases and distortions when used for evaluations. There is evidence that self-ratings are more lenient or higher than those obtained from supervisors. Self-ratings will correspond more closely to supervisory ratings when extensive performance feedback is given and when employees know that their performance ratings will be checked against objective criteria.

Team member appraisal

Team member involvement in the appraisal process can take many forms. One way this can occur is for team members to individually set performance standards for themselves and identify the consequences of low performance, and to then agree on the standards and consequences. Team members could also serve as evaluators. In circumstances where a co-worker is at an individual's side all day, an excellent opportunity is provided for observing employee behaviour. Performance dimensions on which team members have evaluation expertise include:

1 Attendance and timeliness
2 Interpersonal skills—willing to give and take on issues; not unreasonably stubborn
3 Group supportiveness—offers ideas/suggestions for the group to use on the project, supports group decisions

4 Planning and co-ordination—contributes input to assist other team members in performing their assignments (Schuler 1995, p. 314).

Team members can also provide useful information for evaluating how well the team as a whole is functioning. Figure 9.2 contains questions that firms can use to assess overall team productivity, cohesiveness, and motivation. Using this instrument, comparisons between groups can be used to determine the relative degree of productivity, cohesiveness and motivation. Comparisons can also be made within group ratings at specific intervals to determine which ones performs effectively and which ones are dysfunctional.

Cohesiveness
1 People in this work group pitch in to help one another.
2 People in the work group don't get along with one another. (R)
3 People in this work group take an interest in one another.
4 There is a lot of team spirit among members of my work group.
5 The members of my work group regard each other as friends.
6 The members of my group are very co-operative with one another.
7 My group's members know that they can depend on each other.
8 Group members stand up for one another.
9 Members of my group work together as a team.

Drive
10 My group tackles a job with enthusiasm.
11 The group I work with has quit trying. (R)
12 The group is full of vim and vigour.
13 The work of my group seems to drag. (R)
14 My group works hard on any job it undertakes.
15 The group shows a lot of pep and enthusiasm.

Productivity
16 My group turns out more work than most groups in the company.
17 My group turns out as much work as our supervisor expects.
18 My group has an excellent production record.
19 My group gets a job done on time.
20 This work group has an excellent production record.

Items are scored on a 1–7 scale with '1' being strongly disagree and '7' being strongly agree.
Items marked with an (R) should be reverse-scored.

Figure 9.2 Representative appraisal questions to measure team or work group cohesiveness, drive, and productivity

Source: Schuler 1995, p. 315; based on Stogdill 1965

Upward or reverse appraisals

Upward or reverse appraisals involve subordinates rating their superiors' performance. This form of appraisal can be used to improve the management of operations, make organisations less hierarchical and develop better managers (Kiechel 1989, p. 201). While subordinates often do not have access to information about all dimensions of supervisory performance, they do have access to information about supervisor–subordinate interactions. When asked, subordinates usually complain that they do not get enough feedback. They want a pat on the back for doing well and honest criticism—even when it is unfavourable. Employees also complain that their supervisors play lip-service to their input—that suggestions are not taken seriously and are seldom acted upon. Subordinates also want their superiors to support them more in the wider organisation, particularly when it comes to salary, promotion and allocation to jobs. A fourth common comment is that subordinates would like their supervisors to delegate more responsibility.

One problem with upward or reverse appraisal is that subordinates might not evaluate performance objectively or honestly. This is particularly likely, if subordinates feel threatened, for example, 'If I give my boss a low rating, she will reciprocate and give me a low rating too'. To protect anonymity, evaluations need to be made by at least three or four subordinates and turned in to someone other than the supervisor being evaluated. Alternatively, the evaluations can be scored by computer.

Appraisal by customers

Another source of appraisal information comes from clients and customers of the employees. These appraisals are appropriate in a variety of contexts. Appraisals by customers can include a variety of techniques including asking customers to rate employees on a variety of performance indicators such as courtesy, promptness and quality of service, or using mystery customers to use the service and then evaluate it, or surveying customers about the quality of service they received.

Computer monitoring

In the US, a recent development in performance appraisals has been the gathering of performance data by computers. This is known as computer monitoring. Advances in technology make it possible for employers to continuously collect and analyse information about work performance and equipment. More managers are using this type of data to plan workloads, reduce costs, and find new ways to organise work. Although this method may be fast and apparently objective, it has raised a number of critical issues in the management and use of human resources. These issues include employees' right to privacy, health and safety issues, the proportion of casual to full time workforce and the preference for particular types of employees (Wright & Lund 1996).

Performance appraisal approaches

There are six major approaches to performance appraisal:

1 Comparative standards
2 Absolute standards (quantitative and qualitative)
3 Objectives-based
4 Direct or objective indices
5 Accomplishment records
6 Means-based.

Within each of these approaches a variety of appraisal forms may be used.

Comparative standards

All comparative standards of evaluation compare one subordinate to the others. In straight ranking, the superior lists the subordinates in order from best to worst, usually on the basis of overall performance. The first step in alternative ranking is to put the best subordinate at the head of the list and the worst subordinate at the bottom. Then the superior selects the best and worst from the remaining subordinates; the best is placed second on the list and the worst next to last. The superior continues to choose the best and worst until all subordinates are ranked. The middle position on the list is the last to be filled by this method.

Other comparative methods are more time consuming but may provide better information. In the paired comparison method, each subordinate is compared to every other, two at a time, on a single standard or criterion such as overall performance. The subordinate with the second-greatest number of favourable comparisons is ranked second, and so on.

The comparative methods discussed so far give each person a unique rank. This suggests that no two subordinates perform exactly alike. Although this may be true, many superiors say that subordinates' performances are too close to differentiate. Another method—the forced distribution method—was designed to overcome this complaint and to incorporate several factors or dimensions (rather than a single factor) into the ranking of subordinates. The term 'forced distribution' is used because the superior must assign only a certain proportion of subordinates to each of several categories on each factor. A common forced distribution scale may be divided into five categories. A fixed percentage of all subordinates in the group falls within each of them. A problem with this method is, of course, that a group of subordinates may not conform to the fixed percentage. In fact, all comparative methods assume that there are good and bad performers in all groups. You may know from experience, however, of situations where all the people in a group actually perform identically. If you encountered such a situation, how would you evaluate these people?

Regardless of the specific comparative approach, all are based on the assumption that performance is best captured or measured by one criterion—overall performance. Since this single criterion is a global measure and is not anchored in any objective index, such as units sold, the results can be influenced by ratee subjectivity.

Absolute standards

In the comparative approach to performance evaluation, the superior is forced to evaluate each subordinate in relationship to the others, often based on a single overall dimension. In contrast, the absolute standard approach allows superiors to evaluate each subordinate's performance independent of the other subordinates and often on several dimensions of performance. These approaches can take either a qualitative or a quantitative form.

Qualitative forms

The qualitative forms of performance appraisal are the narrative essay, the critical incidents form, weighted checklist and the forced choice form.

Narrative essay
One of the simplest absolute standards forms is the narrative essay. In this form the rater can describe, generally in sentences, the ratee's strengths and weaknesses and what could be done to improve the ratee. Since these essays are unstructured, they often vary in their length and detail. Consequently, comparisons of rates within a department or across departments in a company are difficult. Furthermore, the essay

form provides only qualitative data. Thus, it is difficult for these appraisals to be used in making zero sum-type decisions (i.e. salary increases, promotions and retrenchments). This also applies to several other qualitative forms of appraisal, however, including critical incidents, behavioural checklists and forced-choice forms.

Critical incidents form

In the critical incidents form, the superior observes and records things that subordinates do that are particularly effective or ineffective in accomplishing their jobs (Flanagan 1954). These incidents generally provide descriptions of the ratees' behaviours and the situation in which these occurred. Then when the superior gives feedback to the subordinate, it is based on specific behaviours rather than personal characteristics or traits such as dependability, forcefulness or loyalty. This feature of the critical incidence can increase the chances that the subordinate will improve since he or she learns more specifically what is expected. Drawbacks of the critical incident technique include the fact it is time consuming for the superior to keep records ('little black books') on each subordinate, it is non-quantitative and the incidents are not differentiated in terms of their importance to job performance. It is also hard to compare subordinates because the incidents recorded for each one can be quite different.

Weighted checklist

The weighted checklist technique eliminates some of the drawbacks of the critical incident one. The weighted checklist can be developed using the critical incident technique. After several critical incidents of subordinate behaviours are gathered from several superiors or expert raters knowledgeable of the job, they can be used to construct checklists of weighted incidents. An example of one is shown in Figure 9.3. Raters using the form are unaware that each of the incidents has been weighted (i.e. its relative importance to job performance has been determined by the expert raters). The rater merely has to check the incidents each subordinate performs. Alternatively, the form may be designed to include frequency response categories, e.g. 'always', 'very often', and 'infrequently'. Then the rater checks the frequency category for each incident for each subordinate. Nevertheless, the rater does not know the relative importance of each incident, thus making feedback more difficult for him or her to give. It does save the rater time, however, and it is based on behaviours rather than personal attributes and can yield a summary score.

Forced choice form

To reduce the potential for leniency rating error (to be discussed below) and to establish a form with more objective standards for comparison of ratees, the forced choice form was developed. This method differs from the weighted checklist because it forces superiors to evaluate each subordinate by choosing which of two items in a pair better describes the subordinate. The two items in a pair are matched to be equal in desirability but of differential relevance to job performance (discriminability). The degrees of desirability and discriminability are established by individuals familiar with the jobs. A sample form is shown in Figure 9.4. As a consequence of this format, leniency error is minimised and validity and reliability may be enhanced. Although the forced-choice scale can be very useful, the raters are essentially unaware of how their ratings of their subordinates are interpreted. This not only makes feedback difficult, it also reduces the trust the rater has for the organisation (Flanagan 1954, pp. 327–58).

ITEM	SCALE VALUE
Occasionally buys some of the competitor's products	6.8
Never consults with the head salesperson when making a bake order	1.4
Belongs to a local merchants' association	4.9
Criticises employees unnecessarily	0.8
Window display is usually just fair	3.1
Enjoys contacting customers personally	7.4
Does not know how to figure costs of products	0.6
Lacks a long-range viewpoint	3.5
Products of uniformly high quality	8.5
Expects too much of employees	2.2
Weekly and monthly reports are sometimes inaccurate	4.2
Does not always give enough thought to bake orders	1.6
Occasionally runs a selling contest among salespeople	6.8
Baking in the shop continues until 2 pm or later	8.2
Has originated one or more workable new formulas	6.4
Sometimes has an unreasonably large inventory of certain items	3.3
Employees enjoy working for the manager	7.6
Does not delegate enough responsibility to others	2.8
Has accurately figured the costs of most of the products	7.8
Wishes he or she were just a baker	0.8
Shop is about average in cleanliness	4.4
Is tardy in making minor repairs in the salesroom	1.9
Periodically samples all of the products for quality	8.1

Figure 9.3 Sample weighted checklist for bakery managers
Source: Knautt 1948, pp. 63–70

Prepares credit reports accurately	Likes the customers		Analyses credit histories thoroughly	Makes friends with others quickly
Desirability index			Desirability index	
4.30	4.45		4.39	4.48
Discrimination index			Discrimination index	
4.70	1.15		4.15	1.65

Figure 9.4 Forced choice pairs with equal desirability and differential discriminability for the corporate loan assistant
Source: Schuler & Dowling et al. 1992, p. 214

Quantitative forms

In addition to these qualitative forms there are several quantitative ones. Quantitative forms differ from the qualitative forms by generally requiring the rater to assign or check a specific numerical value to a personal attribute (trait) or behaviour shown by the ratee, rather than simply indicating whether or not a ratee has ever exhibited the attribute or behaviour. There are three quantitative forms: the conventional or graphic rating scale, the behaviourally anchored rating scale, and the behavioural observation scale.

Conventional rating

The conventional rating is the most widely used form of performance evaluation (see Figure 9.5) (McGuire 1980, pp. 744–46; Beer 1981, pp. 24–36; Carroll & Schneier

Name		Date of birth	Date of employment	Office location Branch Department	Date completed Department
Present job title		Years in present position	Post no	Education	

Quality of work General excellence of output with consideration to accuracy—thoroughness—dependability—without close supervision.	☐ Exceptionally high quality. Consistently accurate, precise, quick to detect errors in own and others' work.	☐ Work sometimes superior but usually accurate. Negligible amount needs to be redone. Work regularly meets standards.	☐ A careful worker. A small amount of work needs to be redone. Corrections made in reasonable time. Usually meets normal standards.	☐ Work frequently below quality. Inclined to be careless. Small amount or work needs to be redone. Excessive time to correct.	☐ Work often almost worthless. Seldom meets normal standards. Excessive amount needs to be redone.
Quantity of work Consider the amount of useful work over the period of time since the last appraisal. Compare the output of work to the standard you have set for the job.	☐ Output consistently exceeds standard. Unusually fast worker. Exceptional amount of output.	☐ Maintains a high rate of production. Frequently exceeds standard. More than normal effort.	☐ Output is regular. Meets standard consistently. Works at steady average speed.	☐ Frequently turns out less than normal amount of work. A low producer.	☐ A consistently low producer. Excessively slow worker. Unacceptable output.
Co-operation Consider the employee's attitude towards the work, the employee's fellow workers and supervisors. Does the employee appreciate the need to understand and help solve problems of others?	☐ Always congenial and co-operative. Enthusiastic and cheerfully, helpful in emergencies. Well liked by associates.	☐ Co-operates well. Understands and complies with all rules. Usually demonstrates a good attitude. Liked by associates.	☐ Usually courteous and co-operative. Follows orders but at times needs reminding. Gets along well with associates.	☐ Does only what is specifically requested. Sometimes complains about following instructions. Reluctant to help others.	☐ Unfriendly and un-cooperative. Refuses to help others.
Knowledge of the job The degree to which the employee has learned and understands the various procedures of the job and their objectives.	☐ Exceptional understanding of all phases. Demonstrates unusual desire to acquire information.	☐ Thorough knowledge in most phases. Has interest and potential towards personal growth.	☐ Adequate knowledge for norm performance. Will not voluntarily seek development.	☐ Insufficient knowledge of job. Resists criticism and instruction.	☐ No comprehension of the requirements of job.

Dependability The reliability of the employee in performing assigned tasks accurately and within the allotted time.	☐ Exceptional. Can be left on own and will establish priorities to meet deadlines.	☐ Very reliable. Minimal supervision required to complete assignments.	☐ Dependable in most assignments. Normal supervision required. A productive worker.	☐ Needs frequent follow up. Excessive prodding necessary.	☐ Chronic procrastinator. Control required is out of all proportions.
Attendance and punctuality Consider the employee's record, reliability and ability to conduct the job within the unit's work rules.	☐ Unusual compliance and understanding of work discipline. Routine usually exceeds normal.	☐ Excellent. Complete conformity with rules cheerfully volunteers time during peak loads.	☐ Normally dependable. Rarely needs reminding of accepted rules.	☐ Needs close supervision in this area. Inclined to backslide without strict discipline.	☐ Unreliable. Resists normal rules. Frequently wants special privileges.
Knowledge of company policy and objectives Acceptance, understanding and promotion of company policies and objectives in the area of employee's job responsibilities.	☐ Thorough appreciation and implementation of all policies. Extraordinary ability to project objectively.	☐ Reflects knowledge of almost all policies related to this position.	☐ Acceptable but fairly superficial understanding of job objectives.	☐ Limited insight into job or company goals. Mentally restricted.	☐ Not enough information or understanding to permit minimum efficiency.
Initiative and judgement The ability and interest to suggest and develop new ideas and methods; the degree to which these suggestions and normal decisions and actions are sound.	☐ Ingenious self-starter. Superior ability to think intelligently.	☐ Very resourceful. Clear thinker, usually makes thoughtful decisions.	☐ Fairly progressive, with normal sense. Often needs to be motivated.	☐ Rarely makes suggestions. Decisions need to be checked before implementation.	☐ Needs detailed instructions and close supervision. Tendency to assume and misinterpret.
Supervisory or technical potential Consider the employee's ability to teach and increase skills of others, to manage and lead, to organise and assign work, and to communicate ideas and instructions.	☐ An accomplished leader who earns their respect and can inspire others to perform. An articulate and artful communicator, planner and organiser.	☐ Has the ability to teach and will lead by example rather than technique. Speaks and writes well and can organise and plan with help.	☐ Fairly well-informed on job related subjects but has some difficulty communicating with others. Nothing distinctive about spoken or written word.	☐ Little ability to interpret or implement. Seems uninterested in teaching or helping others. Careless speech and writing habits.	☐ Unable to be objective or reason logically, inarticulate and stilted in expression.

Figure 9.5 Conventional form employee performance appraisal

Source: Schuler & Dowling et al. 1992, p. 216–17

1982). Conventional forms vary in the number of dimensions of performance they measure. The term performance is used advisedly here because many conventional forms use personality characteristics or traits rather than actual behaviours as indicators of performance. Frequently used traits are aggressiveness, independence, maturity and sense of responsibility. Many conventional forms also use indicators of output such as quantity and quality of performance. Conventional forms vary in the number of traits and indicators of output they incorporate. They also vary in the range of choices (only one of which is to be checked) for each dimension and the extent to which each dimension is described.

Conventional forms are used extensively because they are relatively easy to develop, permit quantitative results that allow comparisons across rates and departments, and include several dimensions or criteria of performance. But because the rater has complete control in their use, they are subject to several types of error, including leniency, strictness, central tendency and halo (to be discussed below). Nevertheless, they have been shown to be as reliable and valid as more complicated forms such as forced-choice (Landy & Trumbo 1980).

A Summary of current performance:
1. Employee's strongest points
2. Employee's weakest points
3. What steps have been taken to modify weak points?
4. Is employee properly placed in present job? Explain

B Employee's potential:
1. In what significant way has this employee demonstrated improvement in past 12 months?
2. Have you made any suggestions for the employee's self-development?
                                               Yes ☐   No ☐
      a If 'Yes',   1 What was the suggestion?
                      2 How did the employee react?
3. In your opinion, is the employee limited to the work in present job?
                                               Yes ☐   No ☐
4. a If your answer to no. 3 is 'No', what have you considered as a possibility to improve the employee's position in our Company?
      b   What has been done about it?
5. If your answer to no. 3 is 'Yes', please explain.

C Employee's Reactions: Enter reactions or comments after you have discussed this appraisal with the employee. Are there any changes in your evaluation as a result of your interview?

Supervisor's signature		Date
Reviewed		
Department Head	☐	Date
Supervising Officer	☐	Date
Personnel Dept	☐	Date

Figure 9.6 Modification of the conventional form shown in Figure 9.5

Source: Schuler & Dowling et al. 1992, p. 218

In addition to their potential for errors, conventional forms are criticised because they are difficult to use for developmental purposes, e.g. they fail to tell a subordinate how to improve and they are not useful for the subordinate's career development needs. Consequently, when actually used, organisations often modify the conventional form and add space for short essays so that the appraisal results can be used for developmental as well as evaluative purposes. An example of how one company modified a conventional form (shown in Figure 9.5) is shown in Figure 9.6; but even when essays are added to the conventional forms, the results are still subject to the errors of the conventional forms and the essay forms described earlier. Thus, even the modified form is not the most appropriate for giving feedback and improving the subordinate's performance.

Behaviourally-anchored rating scale

The behaviourally-anchored rating scale was developed to provide results subordinates could use to improve performance. It was also designed so superiors would be more comfortable giving feedback. The development of a behaviourally anchored rating scale generally responds to the first steps in the critical incidents method of job analysis, i.e. incidents describing competent, average and incompetent behaviour for each job category are collected. After these are collected, they are categorised into broad overall categories or dimensions of performance, e.g. administrative ability or interpersonal skill. Each dimension serves as one criterion in evaluating subordinates. Using these categories, another group of individuals lists the critical incidents pertinent to each category. An example of one such criterion or category, transacting loans, and the critical incidents listed as pertinent to it are shown in Figure 9.7 (Landy & Farr 1980). Also shown in this figure is the next step, the assignment of a numerical value (weight) to each incident in relation to its contribution to the criterion.

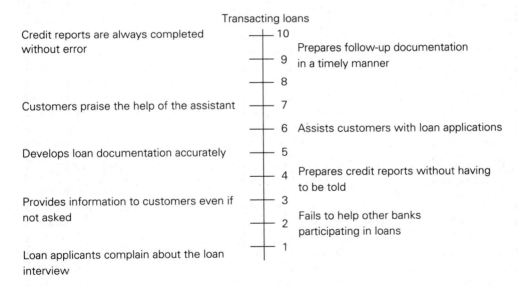

Figure 9.7 Sample behaviour anchored rating scale for one dimension of the work performance of the corporate loan assistant

Source: Schuler & Dowling et al. 1992, p. 219

Armed with a set of criteria with behaviourally anchored and weighted choices, the superiors rate their subordinates with a form that is relatively unambiguous in meaning, is understandable, justifiable and relatively easy to use (Latham & Wexley 1981). Yet it has its limitations or shortcomings. Since most behaviourally-anchored rating scale forms use a limited number of performance criteria, e.g. seven, many of the critical incidents generated in the job analysis stage may not be used. Thus the raters may not find appropriate categories to describe the behaviours—the critical incidents—of their subordinates (Latham & Wexley 1981). Similarly, even if the relevant incidents are observed, they may not be worded in exactly the same way on the dimension, thus the rater may not be able to match the observed behaviours with the dimension and anchors. A procedure that overcomes these and other limitations but retains its advantages is called the behavioural observation scale (Latham & Wexley 1977, pp. 255–68; Loar, Mohrma & Stock 1982, pp. 75–86).

Behavioural observation scale

The behavioural observation scale and the behaviourally-anchored rating scale are essentially the same except in the development of the scales or dimensions, the scale format, and scoring procedures. But they are even similar in this area to the extent that expert raters or judges rate the incidents from the job analysis in terms of the degree to which each incident represents effective job behaviour. The behavioural observation scale and behaviourally-anchored rating scale are most different in their scale development in the use of statistical analysis to select items for building each dimension of performance. For the behavioural observation scale, statistical analysis is used to identify those behaviours or critical incidents which most clearly differentiate effective from ineffective performers. For the behaviourally-anchored rating scale, expert raters perform this function. The major ways the behavioural observation scale differs from the behaviourally-anchored rating scale are the rating scale format and summated scoring procedure used for each dimension, as shown in Figure 9.8, based on the critical incidents from the job description of the corporate loan assistant.

The advantages of the behavioural observation scale are several, including: (1) it (like the behaviourally-anchored rating scale) is based upon a systematic job analysis; (2) its items and behavioural anchors are clearly stated; (3) it, in contrast to many other methods, allows participation of employees in the development of the dimensions (through the identification of critical incidents in the job analysis) that facilitates understanding and acceptance; (4) it is useful for performance feedback and improvement since specific goals can be tied to numerical scores (ratings) on the relevant behavioural anchor (critical incident) for the relevant performance criterion or dimension; and (5) the behavioural observation scale appears to satisfy issues of validity (relevance) and reliability (Latham & Wexley 1981, p. 63). The limitations of the behavioural observation scale are connected with some of its advantages, especially the time and cost for its development as compared with forms such as conventional rating. Remember that the scale is developed and used across several job categories. This cost may be greater than all the benefits. Furthermore, several dimensions which are essentially behaviours may miss the real essence of many jobs, especially managerial and highly routinised ones where the essence of the job may be the actual outputs produced regardless of the behaviours used to obtain them. When these conditions exist, some argue that a better method is one that is goal-oriented or that appraises performance against output measures.

Objectives-based approaches

The two most common types of output performance measuring systems for managerial employees are Management by Objectives and responsibility centres. Another approach

```
                           Effective performance
1  The corporate loan assistant prepares credit reports accurately
Almost                                                              Almost
never                                                               always
1              2              3              4                      5
2  The corporate loan assistant is friendly when interviewing loan applicants
Almost                                                              Almost
never                                                               always
1              2              3              4                      5
3  The corporate loan assistant is effective when interviewing job applicants
Almost                                                              Almost
never                                                               always
1              2              3              4                      5

                          Ineffective performance
1  The corporate loan assistant fails to prepare follow-up documentation
Almost                                                              Almost
never                                                               always
1              2              3              4                      5
2  The corporate loan assistant does not help customers with loan applications
Almost                                                              Almost
never                                                               always
1              2              3              4                      5
   The corporate loan assistant needs to be told to prepare credit reports
Almost                                                              Almost
never                                                               always
1              2              3              4                      5
```

Figure 9.8 Sample behavioural observation scale items for the corporate loan assistant illustrating both effective and ineffective performance

Note: On an actual form the items would neither be grouped nor identified as effective and ineffective performance.
Source: Schuler & Dowling et al. 1992, p. 220

similar to Management by Objectives is the work standards approach, and it is usually applied to the assessment of non-managerial employees.

Management by Objectives

Management by Objectives (MBO) is probably the most popular method used to evaluate managers (CCH Australia 1995, pp. 12–700). Figure 9.9 shows the results of a survey in Australian organisations in 1990 and demonstrates that MBO is the most common approach to performance appraisal in three industries. This appears to result from its identity with commonly held personal values, especially the philosophy that it is important to reward people for what they accomplish. Management by Objectives is also popular because it can attain greater individual–organisational goal congruence and reduce the likelihood that managers will be working on things unrelated to the objectives and purposes of the organisation (goal displacement) (Carroll & Schneier 1982, p. 141).

PERFORMANCE APPRAISAL CRITERIA BY SELECTED INDUSTRY SAMPLES

INDUSTRY	TRAITS	CRITICAL INCIDENTS	MBO	BEHAVIOURALLY- ANCHORED RATING SCALES (BARS)	BEHAVIOURAL OBSERVATION SCALES (BOS)
Finance	42%	7%	65%	9%	2%
Manufacturing	45%	9%	62%	5%	2%
Public sector	29%	7%	43%	7%	29%

Figure 9.9 CCH PA + MBO results
Source: CCH 1995, pp. 12–700

Management by Objectives can be described in four steps. The first is to establish the goals each subordinate is to attain. In some organisations, superiors and subordinates work together to establish goals; in others, superiors establish goals for subordinates. The goals can refer to desired outcomes to be achieved, means (activities) for achieving the outcomes, or both.

The second step involves the subordinates' performance in a previously arranged time period. As subordinates perform, they know fairly well what there is to do, what has been done, and what remains to be done.

The third step is a comparison of the actual level of goal attainment against the agreed-on goals. The evaluator explores reasons for the goals not being met and for goals being exceeded. This step helps determine possible training needs. It also alerts the superior to conditions in the organisation that may affect a subordinate's performance but over which the subordinate has no control.

The final step is to decide on new goals and possible new strategies for goals not previously attained. At this point, subordinate and superior involvement in goal-setting may change. Subordinates who successfully reach the established goals may be allowed to participate more in the goal-setting process the next time (Olivas 1981, pp. 75, 78).

The goals can refer to a desired outcome, the means of activities for achieving the outcome, or both. The goals can also relate to routine activities that comprise day-to-day activities, the identification and solution of problems that hamper individual and organisational effectiveness, or they can be innovative and have a special purpose. Regardless of their focus, the objectives are more effective if they include the following characteristics:

1 **Specificity**—objectives must identify how well the behaviour must be performed or how high the output must be to be considered acceptable. Specificity reduces variability in performance and ratings.
2 **Timeliness**—the deadline for completion of the task or attainment of the output level must be identified.
3 **Conditions**—any qualifications associated with attaining the objective need to be detailed since many factors beyond the control of employees may hamper goal attainment.
4 **Prioritisation**—for behaviour to be directed towards desired ends, employees need to understand which objectives are most important. Supervisors and employees can weight them, or weights can be derived from the job description.
5 **Consequences**—the consequence of attaining or not attaining the specified level of performance must be spelled out.
6 **Goal congruence**—it is important for managers performing similar jobs to assign comparable goals. Individual goals must be congruent with departmental goals.

Although the use of goals in evaluating managers is effective in motivating their performance, it is not always possible to capture all the important dimensions of a job in terms of output. How the job is done (i.e. job behaviours) may be as critical as the outcomes. For example, it may be detrimental to an organisation if a manager meets a personal selling goal by unethical or illegal means. But even if output measures accurately describe the job, the concern still exists to establish goals that are of equal difficulty for all managers and that are sufficiently difficult to be challenging.

Responsibility centres

To help avoid some of the problems encountered in establishing goals in the Management by Objectives approach, some organisations have implemented the use of responsibility centres. These centres appear to be most relevant in appraising the performance of managers. Under this approach, profit, cost or revenues centres are established (and become criteria), and the performance of the managers of those centres is evaluated in relation to one or a combination of the criteria. To develop the centres, an organisation essentially creates many little independent sub-organisations.

To the extent that real independence cannot be created, however, the responsibility centre approach becomes a less appropriate form by which to evaluate managerial performance. And lack of real independence seems to be more typical of departments in organisations than otherwise. For example, suppose there are three departments in an organisation—production, sales and finance. It would seem that setting standards for appraising these divisions would be straightforward. For the production department, quantity, quality, time and cost can be considered. The sales department is concerned with total sales. The finance department can be evaluated on the amount lost to bad debts and the like.

The difficulty here is that the performances of these departments are not independent. For example, the production department could operate most efficiently with a limited product line that varies little in size or colour. The sales department, of course, wants as much variety as possible, and these are mutually exclusive needs. Similarly, the sales department could, through very large sales, overtax the production department which would increase equipment fatigue, increase overtime payments, and so on. To be effective, the finance department requires sound fiscal policies. So, for large sales, finance would request a relatively high down-payment and a reasonably accelerated payback period. The sales department, on the other hand, would prefer to sell at a dollar per week forever.

The point is that if you appraise the performance of just one department, you may undermine the efforts of another. The performance of all divisions, departments and groups must be reasonably congruent. And appraisal systems must tap the performance of individuals and groups without encouraging behaviours and attitudes that are dysfunctional to the organisation as a whole. These considerations are a major concern and a serious challenge for higher-level management. If independence can be established, however, responsibility centres are a useful way to evaluate and motivate managers. The centre concept gives each manager a great deal of freedom—to succeed or fail.

Works standards approach

The work standards approach, which is similar to Management by Objectives, uses more direct measures of performance and is usually applied to non-managerial employees. Instead of asking subordinates to set their own performance standards or goals as in management by objectives, organisations determine them through past experience (e.g.

what's done on this job before), time study data and work sampling. Data are collected pertaining to how long it takes a worker to do a certain task under particular circumstances to produce time study data (e.g. how long it takes a secretary to type a business letter in an office setting with only normal interruptions from the telephone and visitors). If job circumstances can be ignored, more standard data can be used to establish standards and goals. Although the standard data approach is more efficient than time study because each job does not have to be examined, if job circumstances are important, the standard data may produce inapplicable results. Time study and standard data are useful on jobs that are relatively repetitive and non-complex. With jobs that are less repetitive and more complex, the work-sampling technique is more appropriate. Using this technique, it is determined how workers allocate their time among various job activities.

The disadvantages of these work standards are that they require time, money and co-operation to develop. Often co-operation of the job incumbents is necessary, and there can be problems inherent in this. Without co-operation, however, the data are neither reliable nor valid. What workers do, a necessary ingredient in work sampling, may reflect what tasks they like and dislike instead of the importance of the tasks and what they should do (Locke 1968, pp. 157–89). As with Management by Objectives, the essence of job performance may not be captured entirely by set standards and goals. Consequently, important job behaviours may be ignored in the evaluation process. And although set standards may provide clear directions to the employees and the goals may be motivating, they may also induce undesirable competition among employees to attain their standards and goals. If this competition does not lead to undesirable consequences and if the employees do not want to participate in the standard- and goal-setting process, this method can prove to be good motivation.

Direct index approach

This approach differs from the first three primarily in how performance is measured. The first three approaches, except the objective-based approach, depend on a superior evaluating a subordinate's performance. There is a certain amount of subjective evaluation in these cases. However, this approach measures subordinate performance by objective, impersonal criteria such as productivity, absenteeism and turnover. For example, a manager's performance may be evaluated by the number of employees working for him or her who resign, or by the absenteeism rate of that manager's employees. For non-managers, measures of productivity may be more appropriate. Productivity measures can be divided into measures of quality and quantity. Quality measures include scrap rates, customer complaints and the number of defective units or parts produced. Quantity measures include units of output per hour, new customer orders and sales volume.

Accomplishment records

A relatively new type of output-based appraisal is called an accomplishment record. It is suitable for professionals who claim 'my record speaks for itself' or who claim they are unable to write standards for their job because every day is different. For this approach, professionals describe their achievements relative to appropriate job dimensions on an accomplishment record form. Their supervisor verifies the accuracy of the accomplishments to determine their overall value. While time-consuming and potentially costly because outside evaluators are used, this approach has been shown to be predictive of job success for lawyers. It also has face validity because professionals believe it is appropriate and valid (Hugh 1984, pp. 135–46).

Means-based approach

The means-based approach to performance appraisal focuses on the way in which individuals achieve performance outcomes. This approach provides a way of determining the extent to which performance outcomes are the results of an individual's behaviour and actions, rather than the efforts of other individuals or aspects of the organisations environment. It also explicitly acknowledges that the achievement of performance outcomes in the short term is not to build a successful organisation in the long term.

Competency-based assessment is a form of means-based assessment. This approach views performance in terms of the processes employees use to achieve their job results. It seeks qualitative assessment orientated to the future and focussing on development.

Competency models identify distinguishing characteristics of superior performers in a job in terms of a number of groups of competencies which are described in terms of three to six behavioural indicators.

A performance management system can combine both output-based and means-based approaches. Such a 'mixed' model can assess and reward both what employees actually deliver and how they did it. In many 'mixed models', the achievement of performance results is quantified, focuses on the past, based on the short term and used to make compensation decisions. Competency assessment is more long term, future orientated and used for employee development and career planning (Spencer & Spencer 1993, p. 266).

The design and use of performance appraisals
Assessing performance appraisal forms: which is best?

Although performance appraisal is a set of processes and procedures of which the appraisal form or method is just one component, the performance appraisal system often revolves around the form. Consequently, attention is often focused on assessing the available appraisal forms to enable organisations to choose the best one (McAfee & Green 1977, pp. 61–64; Yager 1981, pp. 129–33).

Criteria for assessment

Determining which appraisal form is best prompts the question: Best for what? That is, what criteria or criterion of assessment is the appraisal form going to use? They include the purposes of performance appraisal, namely evaluation and development, but an effective appraisal form should also be free from error, be reliable and valid, and allow comparisons across subordinates and departments in an organisation. Each of these goals can be used as a criterion. Each form should also be evaluated by its influence on the superior–subordinate relationship. Does the form encourage superiors to watch their subordinates in order to collect valid data for evaluation and developmental purposes, and does it facilitate the appraisal interview? All these criteria must be counter-balanced by one other major criterion: economics. The cost of developing and implementing a form must be compared with its benefits, or how well it does on the other criteria. The costs and benefits of all forms should be compared to arrive at an estimate of the utility of each (Schmidt, Hunter & Pearlman 1982, pp. 333–48).

Which form is best?

Research on this question is limited. It does, however, reinforce the necessity of first identifying the purpose of performance appraisal for the organisation (Kavanagh 1982). Each form can then be assessed in relation to the following criteria:

1 **Developmental**—motivating subordinates to do well, providing feedback, and aiding in human resource planning and career development
2 **Evaluational**—promotion, discharge, retrenchment, pay and transfer decisions and, therefore, the ability to make comparisons across subordinates and departments
3 **Economic**—cost in development, implementation and use
4 **Freedom from error**—halo, leniency and central tendency, and the extent of reliability and validity
5 **Interpersonal**—the extent to which superiors can gather useful and valid appraisal data that facilitates the appraisal interview
6 **Practicality**—the ease with which the system can be developed or implemented
7 **User acceptance**—the degree to which users accept the appraisal format as being reliable, valid and useful.

 Managing diversity

Esso Australia—building a supportive workplace where women can achieve their potential

BY FIONA KRAUTIL, EQUAL OPPORTUNITY MANAGER, ESSO AUSTRALIA LTD.

In 1991, after a major review of 12 years of equal opportunity program, the company identified that we were not achieving the success we had expected from the program; that is, a critical mass of women building successful careers with the company.

Our statistical analysis showed that we have been very successful at recruiting professional women into the organisation. Since 1986, on average, 40 per cent of our professional hires have been female, reflecting their presence in the marketplace. In 1992 and 1993 50 per cent of our graduate engineers have also been female.

But after 12 years, retention rates of female engineers were still one half that of male engineers, and only a small number of women had been successful in moving up the ranks in the administrative areas of the company.

This was despite a high quality equal employment opportunity program with high visibility and strong senior management commitment that has been in place since 1979.

Why is capturing the talents of our female workforce important to the company?

There are a number of key aspects of our business and the external environment in which we operate, that make capturing the potential of our increasingly diverse workforce a key human resource issue for Esso in the 1990s. It is important to understand these business issues to understand why providing a workplace that supports all our employees is a key business issue for us.

How has our diversity process been implemented and linked to the business?

Our diversity process is linked directly to our mission statement. Our mission is to be Australia's most successful petroleum exploration and production company.

To achieve this mission the company has six core values, three of which are relevant to the effective management of employee diversity. Two of the three, *teamwork* and *concern for the individual* are specifically targeted at people. A key success factor for achieving the third core value, *business excellence*, is to maximise the productivity of our people.

Each year the critical priorities for the business are identified. Each employee

receives a copy of these. In 1994, priorities have been grouped in three areas:
1. Achieving performance objectives e.g. safety, production volumes (2 of 6)
2. Improving organisational effectiveness e.g. to increase employee effectiveness by managing and valuing diversity (1 of 3)
3. Implementing business programs e.g. building a quality inventory of exploration acreages (1 of 9).

The effective management of employee diversity is one of our mainstream business issues and is about increasing the effectiveness of our people. Managers are accountable to company directors through our systems and processes, and are responsible for implementing change and achieving the results that address these priorities.

To manage our diverse workforce, we have recognised that we have to shift our management style from treating everyone the same (based on the old rules that worked well for our homogenous white male workforce) to managing people as individuals.

Culture audit

A company-wide culture audit provided us with a gap analysis of how well we 'walked our talk'. This questionnaire measured employee perceptions of:
- How well we walk our six core values
- Successful people in Esso
- Effectiveness of our formal and informal people management systems and processes.

Twenty seven per cent of the workforce, who were randomly selected, completed the questionnaire with a 100 per cent return rate. A task force of eight employees, selected from across various sites and employment categories (including a director), developed the questionnaire with the assistance of a consultant and analysed the findings.

For a 'numbers based' organisation like ours, the data provided was invaluable. Managers were unable to rationalise the data, and based on the employee perceptions data, could identify priority areas for action.

A key issue that emerged was that to 'live' our core values there was a need to better balance the task focus with the people focus of the company, to maximise workforce effectiveness. Gaps were identified and areas were prioritised for action.

Next steps

The culture assessment provided us with a huge amount of data from which we had to determine our next steps. This was not an easy process.
1. Systems

The first system to be reviewed has been our highly regarded performance management and employee development systems, that are all highly individually focused. The data indicated that the linkage of performance to reward needs to be better aligned and that there are opportunities to improve our career development processes. One of our first initiatives is to set up a system of upwards feedback for supervisors that will help them improve their working partnerships with their teams.

Over the next few years some of the systems that will need to be reviewed to ensure they deliver fair results to a diverse workforce include: recruitment, training, working conditions, compensation, hiring, benefits, termination and transfers/promotion.
2. Communication/training
3. Policies and practices
4. Culture change
5. Management accountabilities

As part of the planning process for 1995 departments will develop diversity initiatives that fit with their business priorities. Employee relations will work in a consultancy role with department managers to help them develop these plans.

In our culture you only get what you measure. The challenge in this process is to create some measurable outcomes or milestones that will help our managers measure their progress and which they can be held accountable to deliver.
6. Traditional EEO initiatives

Source: Esso Australia Ltd 1995.

The extracts from the article 'Esso Australia—building a supportive workplace where women can achieve their potential' explains the way the concept of managing diversity is linked to improving organisational performance and discusses the implications for performance appraisals.

The context of performance appraisal

Regardless of the form or method used to gather performance appraisal data, the validity and reliability of the data and even the feasibility of gathering it may be influenced by the superior–subordinate relationship, the nature of the job and organisational conditions (Lefton, Buzzotta, Scerberg & Karraker 1978; Ilger & Favero 1985, pp. 311–21).

Superior–subordinate relationships

Important aspects of the superior–subordinate relationship are personal characteristics of the superior; characteristics of the superior in relation to those of the subordinate; the superior's knowledge of the subordinate and the job; and the subordinate's knowledge of the job. For ease of discussion, these can be grouped into problems with the superior, and problems with the subordinate.

There are basically four problems with the superior that may arise.

1 Superior not knowing what employees doing

The first is that superiors may not know what employees are doing or may not understand their work well enough to appraise it fairly. This particular problem occurs more frequently when a manager has a large span of control—a large number of responsibilities and possibly a large number of employees working in different areas. This problem also occurs when the tasks of the employees are varied and technically complex or changing.

2 Superiors don't have performance standards

The second problem is that even when superiors understand and know how much work subordinates do, they may not have performance standards for evaluating that work. As a result, subordinates may receive unfair (invalid) evaluations because of variability in standards and ratings. This unfairness may be particularly obvious when comparing the evaluations of subordinates working for different superiors. This problem can occur in any organisation, regardless of size, complexity, or the amount of change going on.

3 Superiors don't use performance standards

The third problem is that superiors may use inappropriate standards. They may allow personal values, needs or biases to replace organisational values and standards. The general result is any one of several errors in evaluation. The most common errors occur when superiors rate an employee or group of subordinates on several dimensions of performance. Frequently a superior will evaluate a subordinate similarly on all dimensions of performance just on the basis of the evaluation of one dimension, the one perhaps perceived as most important. This effect is the halo error. When superiors tend to give all their subordinates favourable ratings, they are said to be committing an error of leniency. An error of strictness is just the opposite. An error of central tendency represents a tendency to evaluate all subordinates as average. A recency-of-events error is a tendency to evaluate total performance on the last or most recent part of the subordinate's performance. This error can have serious consequences for a subordinate who performs very well for six months or a year but then makes a serious or costly error in the last week or two before evaluations are made (Cooper 1983, pp. 489–502; Kraigen & Ford 1985, pp. 56–65). These errors may occur intentionally or unintentionally. Some superiors, for example, may intentionally evaluate their best performers as slightly less than excellent to prevent them from being promoted out of the superior's group. On the other hand, some superiors may unintentionally evaluate certain subordinates less favourably than others merely because they 'don't look like good performers'. A female subordinate, for instance, may be perceived by a male superior as having such traditional female qualities as dependence, passiveness and kindness—an unfortunate contrast to the qualities he perceives as required to be a good performer such as independence, initiative and impersonalism. Thus, this superior may evaluate this subordinate less favourably. A superior may also incorrectly evaluate a subordinate because of personal likes or dislikes the superior has for the subordinate.

Even the most valid and reliable appraisal forms cannot be effective when superiors commit these all-too-common errors. But many such errors can be minimised if:

- Each performance dimension addresses a single job activity rather than a group of activities
- The rater can observe the behaviour of the ratee while the job is being accomplished on a regular basis
- Terms like 'average' are not used on a rating scale, since different raters have various reactions to such a term
- The rater does not have to evaluate large groups of employees
- Raters are trained to avoid such errors as leniency, strictness, halo, central tendency and recency of events
- The dimensions being evaluated are meaningful, clearly stated and important (Gibson, Ivancevich & Donnelly 1979, p. 361).

4 Superiors don't like making ratings

The last major problem related to the superior, although important in itself, is also so because it often leads to some of the errors listed above, particularly the halo and leniency errors: superiors do not like and, where possible, resist making ratings, especially ones that need to be defended or justified in writing. The result is often inadequate or inaccurate evaluations. Superiors may consider performance appraisals a time conflict. For example, they may perceive that appraisals take time away from their 'real job'. It may also be the case that superiors fail to see how performance appraisals really fit into the mainstream of knowledge about the behaviour of people in organisations. Halo and leniency errors are easy to make when superiors do not want to take time to consider each performance criterion separately for each subordinate. The leniency error is often committed by superiors because it is difficult for them to give negative feedback, especially when sufficient justification is lacking.

The problems for superiors in performance appraisal are difficult indeed. However, subordinates also present problems. For one thing, they may not know what's expected of them. It's not that they don't have the ability; they just don't know how to apply it. This is true regardless of the level of difficulty of their jobs and whether they work in hospitals, government agencies or private organisations.

The second problem is that subordinates may not be able to do what's expected. Of course, this may be corrected by training or job matching. But it is not always easy to spot performance inabilities. The personnel and human resource manager can play an important role in these cases, working with superiors to spot reasons for performance deficiencies.

The nature of the job
'To a considerable extent, the potential value of any performance appraisal system is dependent upon the nature of the subordinate's job' (Wexley 1979). On many jobs, the quality or quantity of performance may be outside the subordinate's control. This is particularly true on very routine jobs and where the pace of the jobs is controlled by machines. And when jobs are highly interdependent, it is difficult to separate the individual's performance from that of the group.

Organisational conditions
Organisational conditions over which subordinates may have little control but are likely to influence their performance (more often negatively than positively) include tools, equipment and supplies availability, and heat, light and noise levels (Peters & O'Connor 1980, pp. 391–99). If only the subordinates' outcomes, not their behaviours, are appraised, and if organisational conditions are adversely affecting performance, the subordinates are likely to either quit the job or lower their commitment (Latham & Wexley 1981, pp. 42–44). A condition that may not so much inhibit performance as the use of performance appraisal is whether the subordinates are unionised. If they are, performance appraisals may not even be used. Unions have traditionally favoured the use of seniority to determine wage increases, promotions, transfers and demotions. In addition to the performance appraisal form and the context in which appraisal occurs, the determination of who gathers the performance appraisal data must be considered.

Using the performance appraisal data
Using performance appraisal means using the appraisal data for their intended purposes: evaluation (salary, promotion, demotion and retrenchment decisions) and development (counselling, coaching, improving and career-planning decisions). The major way organisations use performance appraisal is through an interview between superior and subordinate. Although the performance appraisal interview may be used to gather additional performance data, its major use as discussed here is to feed back performance appraisal data to the subordinate. On the basis of this feedback, the intended purposes of performance appraisal are served. How effectively they are served depends upon how the appraisal system is designed and how the interview(s) is (are) conducted. An understanding of the inherent conflicts in performance appraisal is useful in discussing the design of the system and the conduct of the interview.

Inherent conflicts in performance appraisal
Performance appraisals draw poor reviews from employees, employers and experts alike; with the cost of doing performance appraisals so high, why are they not done well?

The several purposes of goals of performance appraisal presented at the beginning of the chapter can be categorised as evaluative or developmental. Although the performance appraisal system should serve both sets of purposes for organisations, doing so often creates inherent conflicts (Porter, Lawler & Hackman 1975). These conflicts revolve around the organisation's goals for performance appraisal and those goals of the individual. Although the organisation's goals have been identified already, those of the individual have not. Goals of individuals are to obtain feedback so they know where they stand with the supervisor and the organisation, to learn how to improve their performance and to obtain important rewards in the organisation such as pay and promotions. Additionally, individuals want to affirm their self-image as being competent (Beer 1981, p. 26).

Conflicts in organisational and individual goals

From organisational and individual goals come three sets of conflicts. One is between the organisation's evaluative and developmental goals. When pursuing the evaluative goal, superiors have to make judgements affecting their subordinates' careers and immediate rewards. Communicating these judgements can lead to the creation of an adversarial, low-trust relationship between superior and subordinate. This in turn precludes the superior from performing a problem-solving, helper role that is essential if the organisation wants to serve the developmental goal.

A second set of conflicts arises from the various goals of the individual being evaluated. On the one hand, individuals want valid feedback which gives them information about how to improve and where they stand in the organisation. On the other hand, they want to verify their self-image and also obtain valued rewards. In essence, the goals of individuals imply a necessity to be open (to give valid feedback for improvement), yet to be protective (to maintain a positive self-image and obtain rewards).

The third set of conflicts arises between the goals of the individual and the goals of the organisation. One conflict is between the organisation's evaluation goal and the individual's goal of obtaining rewards. Another conflict is between the organisation's developmental goal and the individual's maintaining self-image. The nature of these conflicts is shown in Figure 9.10.

Consequences of inherent conflicts

Among the several consequences of the inherent conflicts described above are ambivalence, avoidance, defensiveness and resistance (Beer 1981, pp. 27–29).

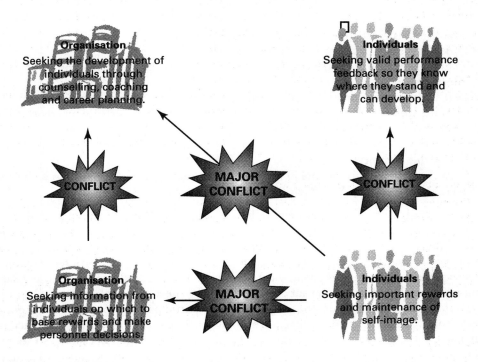

Figure 9.10 Conflicts in goals

Source: Beer 1981, p. 27

Ambivalence is a consequence for both the superiors and the subordinates. Superiors are ambivalent because they must act as judge and jury in telling subordinates where they stand, both because the organisation demands it and because the subordinates want it. Yet, they are uncertain about their judgements and how the subordinates will react upon receiving negative feedback. This feeling is intensified when superiors are not trained in giving feedback. Subordinates are equally ambivalent because they want honest feedback, yet they also want to maintain their self-image (i.e. they really want only positive feedback) and to receive rewards. Additionally, if they are open with their superiors in identifying undeveloped potential, they risk the chance that the superiors may use this to evaluate them unfavourably.

A consequence of this joint ambivalence is avoidance. Subordinates, to avoid the risks of negative feedback, reduce their initiative to seek appraisal data and through talk, diminish the importance of performance appraisal data. The superiors, meanwhile, avoid giving appraisals by implicitly colluding with the subordinates who really would rather not know anyway. This process has given rise to the term 'vanishing performance appraisal' (Hall 1976). If organisational demands do not allow superiors to engage in the vanishing performance appraisal process, and if they must give negative feedback (to support current and future decisions regarding retrenchment, termination and demotion), they may resort to the 'sandwich approach'. Here the superiors squeeze the negative feedback between two pieces of positive feedback. When this is done, subordinates may report never having received negative feedback, even though superiors will report giving it.

Subordinates and superiors also may become defensive in performance appraisals. The subordinate becomes defensive in responding to negative feedback which threatens his or her self-image and chances for gaining rewards. This is corroborated by the results of a study at General Electric in the US where it was found that:

- Criticism has a negative effect on achievement of goals
- Praise has little effect one way or the other
- The average subordinate reacts defensively to criticism during the appraisal interview
- Defensiveness resulting from critical appraisal produces inferior performance
- The disruptive effect of repeated criticism on subsequent performance is greater among those already low in self-esteem
- The average GE employee's self-estimate of performance before appraisal placed him at the 77th percentile
- Only 2 out of 92 participants in the study estimated their performance to be below average (Meyer, Kay & French 1965, p. 125).

Accordingly, subordinates attempt to blame others for their performance, challenge the appraisal form, and demand that their superiors justify their appraisals. Initially at least, subordinates are not inclined to apologise for their behaviour and seek ways to improve; in fact, they resist efforts by the superiors to engage in problem solving. Consequently, the superiors spend most of their time trying to defend their appraisals and resisting the efforts of the subordinates to have their appraisals altered. Overall, the appraisal process is uncomfortable for both participants, especially when poor performance and negative feedback are involved. But even if good performance is involved, the superiors are still going to have to make evaluation decisions, so somebody may still have to get less and come out looking like a poor performer. Because appraisals are uncomfortable yet necessary, it is important to seek ways to improve the process. Possible ways include the design of the appraisal system and the characteristics of the performance appraisal interview.

Designing the appraisal system

Based upon the inherent conflicts in performance appraisal, several features can be incorporated into the design of the appraisal process to reduce likely consequences.

Separate evaluation and development

Because subordinates react defensively to evaluations that are negative, they block out from consideration, at least at that time, ways to improve. Consequently, attempts by superiors to engage in developmental activities such as problem solving are likely to be futile, since for it to be effective, subordinates have to be open and superiors have to play the role of helper, not judge or defender. If organisations want to serve both the evaluation and development purposes effectively, there should be two appraisal interviews. One can focus on evaluation and the other, at a different time of year, on development (Schuler 1981, pp. 8–13). The interview can also be done by different people e.g. the line managers and the HR manager or career counsellor.

Use appropriate performance data

Even when there are two interviews, the subordinates will still become defensive to negative evaluations. Because such defensiveness makes the superiors uncomfortable, they can help minimise it by utilising performance data that focus on specific behaviours or goals. Performance data that focus on personal attributes or characteristics are likely to prompt more defensiveness because they are more difficult for the superior to justify and because more of the subordinate's self-image is at stake.

Superiors can facilitate specific performance feedback through their selection and use of the appropriate appraisal forms. Specifically, if superiors want to use performance data on behaviours, a critical incident form or a behavioural observation scale method would be facilitative, while a management by objectives or work standards approach may be more facilitative in using performance data on goals. Using these appraisal forms allows the supervisors to manage what subordinates are doing as well as how they are doing.

Separate current and potential performance appraisal

Current performance of subordinates may have little to do with their performance potential. Yet superiors may unconsciously incorporate evaluations of performance potential into evaluations of current performance unless there exists a specific and separate form for appraisal of potential. One consequence may be an appraisal of current performance that represents an averaging of current and potential performance appraisal. This can result in unfair appraisals, especially for subordinates who may not be interested in being promoted yet perform adequately on their present jobs. Thus a separation of the appraisal process for current and potential performance could help eliminate the averaging effect and unfairness that may result for some subordinates. Separation would also allow superiors to avoid appraising the potential performance of subordinates not interested in promotion (Lawler III, Mohrman & Resnick 1984, pp. 20–24). This separation is consistent with the importance of recognising and incorporating individual differences into the appraisal process (Beer, Carroll, Schneier & Kavanach 1982, pp. 187, 226).

Empower employees

Part of the difficulty in managing the appraisal system is collecting and maintaining information on all employees. As the span of control increases in size, the tasks grow to unmanageable levels. One way to resolve this problem and simultaneously increase perceptions of fairness is to shift the responsibility for performance record keeping to the subordinate. To enact this process, employees first need training in writing performance standards and in collecting and documenting performance information. Also, the two-way communication process needs to operate effectively so employees feel free to renegotiate performance standards that have become obsolete or unattainable due to constraints.

There are several advantages to delegating responsibility for performance planning, goal setting and record keeping to subordinates. First, they are no longer passive participants reacting to supervisor directives. Second, since it is their responsibility to identify performance hurdles and bring them to the attention of their manager, defensiveness is reduced. Third, the supervisor is free to manage and coach rather than police. Finally, the subordinate feels ownership of the process.

Encourage appropriate degree of participation

Many companies view worker participation as the key to improved performance. Many managers feel that allowing employees to set or participate in the development of their own goals will result in higher commitment and performance. However, participation in and of itself, does not lead to higher performance. More important is the development of specific performance standards and an explanation for their existence. Participation is only useful if it helps employees identify an appropriate strategy to attain performance. That is, as long as performance standards are specific, time-bound, job-relevant, and communicated, motivated employees will perform well (Latham, Erez & Locke 1988, pp. 753–72).

The performance appraisal interview

Because of the inherent conflicts in the performance appraisal, the actual interview between the superior and subordinate is generally unpleasant, which is why it is often avoided. It may be even more unpleasant if the appraisal system does not have the design features just described. But now you know how to reduce some of the unpleasantness and the attendant defensive, avoidance and ambivalent reactions on the part of the superior and the subordinate. To further enhance the effectiveness of the performance appraisal, several considerations should be made regarding the actual performance appraisal interview. The four stages that need to be addressed are:

1 Before the interview
2 Choose the interview style
3 Effective feedback
4 Interview follow-up.

Before the interview

As mentioned previously, performance appraisal is an on-going process of which the interview is only one component. Prior to the interview, the supervisor and subordinate need to prepare. At least three issues need to be addressed:

1. The scheduling of the interview
2. Self-review
3. Gathering relevant information.

Scheduling the interview

The best way of scheduling the interview is for the supervisor to personally notify the subordinate of the time, date and place of the interview. By personally scheduling the interview, there is less chance of misunderstanding about the purpose and content of the session and unnecessary formality, misunderstanding and ambiguity are avoided.

In setting up the interview, both parties should agree on the purpose and content of the interview. For instance, issues such as whether the subordinate will have the opportunity to appraise the performance of the supervisor; will future training and education issues and future career developments be discussed. Ideally, a neutral location for the interview should be chosen so that both parties feel they are operating from an equal power base and that they will not be interrupted.

Self-review

Advance notice of an interview will give subordinates an opportunity to update their performance records and do a self-review. In situations where employees formally review their own performance, comparisons of self-ratings and ratings by supervisors can actually be made by each party to the session and then used for subsequent discussion in the interview.

Gather relevant information

Both the rater and ratee must gather information which will have a bearing on discussions. Critical incident files of behavioural diaries and job descriptions can be reviewed. Ideally, an agenda could be developed so the subordinate can examine it, and make additions or deletions.

Choose an interview style

There are essentially four major types of interview: (1) tell-and-sell (2) tell-and-listen (3) problem solving, and (4) mixed (Maier 1958).

Tell-and-sell

The tell-and-sell, or directive interview is to let subordinates know how well they are doing and sell them on the merits of setting specific goals for improvement, if needed. It is efficient and effective in improving performance, especially for subordinates with little desire for participation (Latham & Saari 1979; Erez, Earley & Hulin 1985). This type of interview may be most appropriate in providing evaluation; however, the subordinates may become frustrated in an attempt to convince their superiors to listen to reasons or justifications for their levels of performance.

Tell-and-listen

The tell-and-listen interview provides subordinates with chances to participate and set up a dialogue with their superiors. The purpose of the tell-and-listen interview is to communicate the superior's perceptions of the subordinate's strengths and weaknesses and let him or her respond to these. The superiors summarise and paraphrase the responses of their subordinates but generally fail to establish goals for performance improvement. Consequently, the subordinates may feel better but their performance may not change.

Problem solving

In the problem solving, or participative problem solving, interview, an active and open dialogue is established between the superior and the subordinate. Not only are perceptions shared, but also solutions to problems or differences are presented, discussed and sought. Goals for improvement are also established mutually by the superior and the subordinate. This type of interview is generally more difficult for most superiors to do; thus, training in problem solving is usually necessary and beneficial (Latham & Wexley 1981, pp. 154–55).

Mixed interview

Conducting a mixed interview also requires training. This is because it is a combination of the tell-and-sell and the problem solving interviews. Skills are needed to do both, and to make the transition from one to the other. It is desirable to use the tell-and-sell for evaluation, and the problem solving for development, but separate interviews for each purpose may not be feasible. Corporate policies, time and expectations may prevent separation of purposes. Consequently, a single interview must accomplish both purposes. In the single interview, the subordinate may start out listening to the superior provide an appraisal of performance but then take a more active role in determining what and how performance improvements can be made (problem solving), concluding with agreed-upon goals for improvement.

Interview effectiveness

Although a mixed interview may prove to be an effective format by which to structure an interview, it fails to specify all the necessary characteristics for an effective interview. These include preparation for and aspects of the actual interview, which in turn include:

1 Scheduling so that subordinate as well as superior are aware of, and agree on, an appropriate time for the interview
2 Agreeing upon the content of the interview: foremost should be whether the interview is for evaluation or development, or both
3 Agreeing upon the process, e.g. how differences are to be resolved, how problems are going to be solved, and the flow of the interview
4 Selecting and using a neutral location in which the interview can be held, including neither the superior's work location nor the subordinate's (Beer 1981, pp. 34–35: *Bulletin to Management* 1984, pp. 2, 7).

Aspects of the interview necessary to facilitate the effectiveness of the appraisal interview include:

1 High levels of subordinate participation. This increases the subordinate's acceptance of the superior's appraisal and enhances satisfaction (Nemeroff & Wexley 1977; Wexley, Singh & Yukl 1973, pp. 54–59; Mount 1983, pp. 99–110).
2 Superior's support of and trust in the subordinate help increase the openness of the interview and the subordinate's acceptance of the appraisal and the superior (Latham & Saari 1979; Greller 1975, pp. 544–49).
3 Open, two-way discussion of performance problems and joint problem solving can increase the subordinate's performance (Wexley, Singh & Yukl 1973).

4 A setting of specific and hard goals to be achieved by the subordinate serves to increase the chances for improved performance (Meyer, Kay & French 1965, Latham & Yukl 1975, pp. 824–45).
5 Provision for effective feedback rather than criticism can enhance the quality of the subordinate-superior relationship and the subordinate's performance.

The whole process of effective feedback is easier when a supervisor is comfortable giving the feedback. The survey in Figure 9.11 can be used to determine your comfort level. The lower your score the more comfortable you are.

Interview follow-up

Even with the most useful feedback, follow-up is essential to ensure that the behavioural contract negotiated during the interview is fulfilled. Because changing behaviour is hard work, supervisors and subordinates both tend to put the agreement on the backburner. Consequently, a supervisor should verify that the subordinate knows what's expected, has a strategy to performance as desired, and realises the consequences of good and bad behaviour.

Additionally, immediate reinforcement for any new behaviour on the job that matches desired objectives is important. If reinforcement is delayed, new behaviour is less likely to become a habit. Reinforcement can be as simple as a pat on the back or a pleasant comment, or as tangible as a note placed in the employee's file indicating performance improvement.

HRM IN THE NEWS

Upward feedback
The neglected wisdom
An upward feedback process is a chance to break down barriers created by misunderstanding.

BY DR RONALD FORBES

Today, while we say we are seeking full and open communication at every level, upward feedback is usually neither sought nor welcomed. And yet it is precisely in those organisations that have barriers of any kind between levels that the feedback is most necessary and valuable.

Useful feedback of this kind must be confidential. Any sense of risk changes the ratings, therefore *the feedback must be processed by a trusted and impartial third party*. One concern is what the feedback is about.

These questions raise a great deal of discussion and complexity. They have been answered by Peter Farey, one time senior manager with British Airways, who says, 'We must measure behaviours [not competencies] as perceived by the team'. This raises the question of the range of behaviours to be considered. Working through over fifty years of leadership and management research, Peter Farey concluded that there are two ways generally used in determining leader/manager behaviour. The first is the one favoured by Blake & Mouton, and Hersey & Blanchard. It refers to the degree to which the manager is people focused or task focused. They measure people management versus task management.

The second way is that proposed originally by James MacGregor Burns, and refers more specifically to leadership. It measures transformational leadership [as opposed to transactional leadership (negotiating improvement)], and it also relates to both people and task. Making the assumption that managers must both lead and manage. Peter Farey used these definitions:

Management is about goals, strategies, resources, organisation, control, reward ...

Leadership is about the future, new directions, risks, influencing, values ...

A map of behaviours

The framework he developed combines these four areas of behaviour, allowing us to consider two kinds of management and two kinds of leadership, as shown in Figure 1.

He used this to sort his collection of one thousand behaviours of leaders and managers, gathered over more than two decades, down to one hundred questions describing twenty vectors, in sequence. This became the leader/manager map. And so *we acquire a set of descriptions broad enough to cover every significant behaviour of leaders and managers.*

While the leader/manager map does not set out to measure competencies, it does include behaviour in all of the areas [and more] that good competency models of leader and manager behaviour currently measure [excluding some very industry-specific details].

Since the map is used as a tool of management development, it inevitably leads to the development of competencies—specifically the ones required by the manager in managing their team in their organisation.

Giving the feedback

Each person indicates their view that the boss should be doing 'more', 'less' or 'as now' and their responses are computer processed to produce a map.

A dialogue is facilitated between manager and team that leads to the breaking down of barriers of fear, misunderstanding and frustration.

The outcome of the process is not necessarily all change for the manager. It may also mean change for the team. Managers may be unaware that the pressure they are exerting on the team is slowing the development they want.

And then again, the team may have to learn how to lift its game!

Feedback to the manager

Together the manager and team consider what is required to work more productively together. There must be action plans for both team and manager.

We have operated throughout the recorded history of organisations on the myth that managers are the best ones to tell their subordinates how to improve. Peter Farey's research has convinced him that it is the team's feedback that is the most effective. Neither peer groups nor more senior managers can ever actually know what it is like at the coalface.

Towards self-management

Managers faced with the process of upward feedback often feel distinct apprehension—what are they going to hear? Will they be criticised? Will it weaken their position with their staff, or in the organisation? One factor that makes the experience easier for them is that the process is usually started when their boss gets *their* confidential feedback.

Upward feedback does represent a new paradigm in management development, it does require a little courage but, in one form or another, the best managers have always been willing to learn from it.

Figure 1: The leader/manager map.

References

Farey, Peter (1993), *Mapping The Leader/Manager*, Lancaster University, UK: Management Education and Development, vol. 24, part 2.

Forbes, Ron (1995), *What Karpin Forgot*, Sydney: Australian Institute Of Company Directors, *The Company Director*, August.

Humphries, Edwin & Ron Forbes (1993), *The Challenge Of Mandated Organisational Change*, Proceedings of Qualcon, Brisbane, QLD.

Karpin, D. S. (1995), *Enterprising Nation, Renewing Australia's Managers To Meet The Challenges Of The Asia-Pacific Century*, Canberra: Australian Government Publishing Service.

Source: *Management*, October 1995, pp. 16–17.

The extract from the article 'Upward feedback—neglected wisdom' explains some of the benefits of employees providing feedback to managers. It also provides some useful ideas about the way in which this process can be used in an effective way.

Performance appraisal and performance improvement

Performance appraisals can be an important part of improving employee performance. Performance can be improved by identifying gaps in performance, identifying causes of the performance deficiencies and developing strategies for performance improvement. For these processes to work effectively, it is important the information in the appraisal is accurate.

Indicate the degree of discomfort *you* would feel in the following situations. Answer as candidly as possible by indicating what is true for you. Use the following scale to write in one number in the blank to the left of each item.

5 = High discomfort
4 = Some discomfort
3 = Undecided
2 = Very little discomfort
1 = No discomfort

_____ 1 Telling an employee who is also a friend that he or she must stop coming to work late.
_____ 2 Telling an employee that his or her work is only satisfactory, when you know that he or she expects an above-satisfactory rating.
_____ 3 Talking to an employee about his or her performance on the job.
_____ 4 Conducting a formal performance appraisal interview with an ineffective employee.
_____ 5 Asking an employee if he or she has any comments about your rating of his or her performance.
_____ 6 Telling an employee who has problems in dealing with other employees that he or she should do something about it (e.g. take a course, read a book).
_____ 7 Telling a male subordinate that his performance must improve.
_____ 8 Responding to an employee who is upset over your rating of his or her performance.
_____ 9 Having to terminate someone for poor performance.

_____ 10 Letting an employee give his or her point of view regarding a problem with performance.
_____ 11 Giving a satisfactory rating to an employee who has done a satisfactory (but not exceptional) job.
_____ 12 Letting a subordinate talk during an appraisal interview.
_____ 13 Being challenged to justify an evaluation in the middle of an appraisal interview.
_____ 14 Being accused of playing favourites in the rating of your staff.
_____ 15 Recommending that an employee be discharged.
_____ 16 Telling an employee that his or her performance can be improved.
_____ 17 Telling an employee that you will not tolerate his or her taking extended coffee breaks.
_____ 18 Warning an ineffective employee that unless performance improves, he or she will be discharged.
_____ 19 Telling a female subordinate that her performance must improve.
_____ 20 Encouraging an employee to evaluate his or her own performance.

Figure 9.11   Performance appraisal discomfort scale
Source: Abbott et al. 1994; based on Villanova et al. 1993

Identifying gaps in performance

Gaps in the performance of employees, units and departments can be identified through comparisons with goals, peer/departmental comparisons and time comparisons.

Job performance is appraised in terms of attributes, behaviours, outcomes and goals. For example, outcomes and goals can identify deficiencies by showing how well an employee does in relation to the goals set. If an employee had a performance goal of reducing the scrap rate by 10 per cent but actually reduced it by only 5 per cent, a performance gap exists. The discrepancy between set goals and actual outcomes can thus be used to spot gaps. This method is valid as long as the goals are not contradictory and can be quantified in measurable terms and the subordinate's performance can be measured in the terms in which the goals are set (Latham, Cumings & Mitchell 1981, pp. 4–23; Greengard 1993, pp. 81–91). Figure 9.12 is a checklist of symptoms associated with performance problems: more than one yes indicates a need to probe deeper.

Read the following questions about an employee's performance. If you are thinking 'yes' in response to a question, place a tick next to that item. If not, leave it blank.

Do peers complain that:
_____ 1 She is not treating them fairly?
_____ 2 He is not carrying his own weight?
_____ 3 She is rude?
_____ 4 He is argumentative and confrontational?
_____ 5 She is all talk and no action?

Do customers:
_____ 1 Always ask for someone else to help them?
_____ 2 Complain about her attitude?
_____ 3 Complain that he has made promises to them that he's never fulfilled?
_____ 4 Say she is bad-mouthing you, the organisation, or its products?
_____ 5 Complain that he is too pushy?

Do you:

___ 1 Find it difficult to get your own work done because you spend so much time with him on his problems and mistakes?
___ 2 Worry about what she will say to customers and clients?
___ 3 Check his work often because you are afraid of mistakes?
___ 4 Do work yourself that you should have delegated to her?
___ 5 Assign work to others because they can do it faster or better than he can?
___ 6 Hear about her mistakes from your boss or others?
___ 7 Sometimes find out that he has lied to you or stretched the truth?
___ 8 Seldom think of her when you're deciding who should get an important assignment?

Does he/she:

___ 1 Infrequently complete assignments on time?
___ 2 Often show up to work late or not at all?
___ 3 Always have an excuse for poor performance?
___ 4 Wait to be assigned additional work rather than asking for more work when an assignment is completed?
___ 5 Rarely complete assignments in the way you want?

Figure 9.12 Checklist for identifying performance problems
Source: Schuler 1995, p. 359

The performance of employees, units or departments can also be compared with one another. For example, organisations with several divisions often measure the overall performance of each division by comparing it with all other divisions. The divisions that are ranked on the bottom become identified as problem areas (i.e. they have performance gaps). Efforts can then be expected from these divisions.

A third method of identifying performance deficiencies is by comparing performance over time. For example, it would appear that a performance gap exists in a situation where a manager sold 1000 record albums last month but only 800 albums this month. Although performance has declined, the supervisor needs to examine whether this gap represents a deficiency that should or can be corrected, or whether it is a normal fluctuation.

Regardless of the method used to discover whether a performance deficiency exists, once detected managers will want to remove it. In order to improve employees' performance, however, they must begin by examining the causes underlying the actual gaps.

Identifying the causes of deficiencies

One way of identifying the causes of performance deficiencies is to ask a number of questions based on a model of determinants of employee behaviour in organisations (Mager & Pipe 1970). This model enables the human resource manager to diagnose deficiencies and correct them in a systematic way. In general, the model says that employees perform well if the following determinants are present:

- ability
- interest in doing the job
- opportunity to grow and advance
- clearly defined goals
- feedback on how well they are doing
- rewards for performing well
- punishments for performing poorly
- power to get resources to do the job.

Figure 9.13 shows these determinants and the specific questions to ask in locating causes. Negative responses indicate that the item is probably a cause, and based on a series of responses, the likely causes for a performance deficiency begin to take shape.

Check which of the following factors affecting an individual's performance or behaviour apply to the situation you are analysing	Yes	No
I Skills, knowledge, and abilities of the individual		
A Does the individual have the skills to do as expected?		
B Has the individual performed as expected before?		
II Personality, interest, and preferences of the individual		
A Does the individual have the personality or interest to perform as expected?		
B Does the individual clearly perceive what's actually involved in performing as expected?		
III Opportunity for the individual		
A Does the individual have a chance to grow and use valued skills and abilities?		
B Does the organisation offer career paths to the individual?		
IV Goals for the individual		
A Are there goals established?		
B Are the goals very specific?		
C Are the goals clear?		
D Are the goals difficult?		
V Uncertainty for the individual		
A Is the individual certain about what rewards are available?		
B Is the individual certain about what to do?		
C Is the individual certain about what others expect?		
D Is the individual certain about job responsibilities and levels of authority?		
VI Feedback to the individual		
A Does the employee get information about what is right and wrong (quality or quantity) with performance?		
B Does the information received tell the employee how to improve performance?		
C Does the employee get information frequently?		
D Is there a delay between the time the employee performs and receiving information on that performance?		
E Can the information be easily interpreted by the employee?		
VII Consequences to the individual		
A Is it punishing to do as expected (immediate)?		
B Is it punishing to do as expected (long term)?		
C Do more positive consequences result from taking alternative action (immediate)?		
D Do more positive consequences result from taking alternative action (long term)?		
E Are there no apparent consequences for performing as desired?		
F Are there no positive consequences for performing as desired?		
VIII Power for the individual		
A Can the individual mobilise resources to get the job done?		
B Can the individual influence others to get them to do what is needed?		
C Is the individual highly visible to others higher up in the organisation?		

Figure 9.13 Diagnosing performance deficiencies
Source: Schuler 1995, p. 362; based on Mager et al. 1970

Strategies for improving performance

There are a number of strategies which can be used to improve performance. These include:

- Positive reinforcement system
- Positive discipline programs
- Employee assistance programs
- Employee counselling
- Negative behavioural strategies.

Positive reinforcement system

This involves the use of positive rewards to increase the occurrence of the desired performance. It is based on two fundamental principles:

1 People perform in ways that they find most rewarding to them
2 By providing proper rewards it is possible to improve performance.

A Positive Reinforcement (PR) system or program focuses on the behaviour that leads to desired results rather than on the results. It uses rewards rather than punishments or the threats of punishment to influence behaviour and attempts to link specific behaviours to specific rewards. This model operates according to the law of effect, which states that behaviour that leads to a positive result tends to be repeated while behaviour that leads to a neutral or negative result tends not to be repeated. Thus an effort is made to link behaviour to its consequences.

A PR system is installed in four basic steps, as shown in Figure 9.14. These four steps are:

1 Conducting a performance audit
2 Establishing performance standards or goals
3 Giving feedback to employees about their performance
4 Offering employees praise or other rewards tied directly to performance (Bandura 1969, pp. 375–401).

This is a linear diagram. From a systems point of view, each step may have unintended consequences.

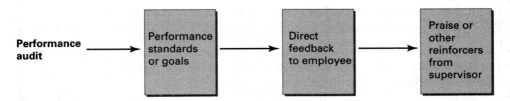

Figure 9.14   Steps in a positive reinforcement system
Source: Schuler 1995, p. 362

A performance audit examines how well jobs are being performed. It provides the basis for the establishment of performance standards or goals. Performance standards or goals should be tied directly to the job, be measurable, attainable, precise and challenging, but not impossible to meet. Ideally employees should be involved in the establishment of these standards. Performance should then be measured against these standards and an employee given direct feedback. When performance justifies rewards or praise, these should be given as soon as possible after the behaviour takes place. They should also be more frequent at the beginning but become less frequent and more unpredictable after the desired performance level is reached.

Positive discipline programs

A positive discipline program puts the responsibility for the employee's behaviour into the hands of the employee. In circumstances when discipline discussions have failed to produce the desired results, the employee is put on paid decision-making leave for a day. During this time the employee is asked to decide whether they will give a 'total performance commitment' to the job or find work elsewhere. Continued tenure is conditional on the individual's decision to solve the immediate problem. These programs appear to be effective (Campbell, Fleming & Grote 1985, pp. 162–78).

Employee Assistance Programs

Employee Assistance Programs (EAPs) are specifically designed to assist employees with chronic personal problems which hinder their job performance and attendance. The most common EAPs provide assistance with alcohol and drug abuse and issues such as marital and family problems, mental disorders, stress, dependant care, bereavement counselling and financial problems. These programs seek to help individuals help themselves within a context of fairness yet firmness.

Employee counselling

Another method of improving employee performance is the process of employee counselling. This technique stresses problem solving and goal-setting techniques. It consists of a series of steps which involve the employee being made aware of the problem and of the organisation's performance standards. At the same time it provides the employee with the opportunity to explain the reasons for the poor performance. Discussions with the employee are documented and if the employee shows no improvement in performance this documentation supports a dismissal decision.

Negative behavioural strategies

Punishment is sometimes used because it is perceived to correct poor performance, absenteeism and rule violation. Discipline or punishment is an effective management tool for the following reasons:

1. Discipline alerts the marginal employee that his or her low performance is unacceptable and a change in behaviour is warranted.
2. Discipline has vicarious reinforcing power. When one person is punished, it signals other employees regarding expected performance and behavioural conduct.
3. If discipline is viewed as appropriate by other employees, it may increase their motivation, morale, and performance (Wylie & Grothe 1981).

Although it has been shown that managers who used the disciplinary system more frequently than their peers had higher department performance ratings, punishment may not always be effective. Employees can resent the punishment and become angry.

The performance may even get worse. The negative effects of punishment can be reduced by incorporating several 'hot-stove' principles, including:

- provide ample and clear warning
- administer the discipline as quickly as possible
- administer the same discipline for the same behaviour for everyone, every time
- administer the discipline impersonally.

Trends in performance appraisal

Two major trends in performance appraisal are evident. First, performance appraisals are increasingly becoming strategically aligned so they can assist in the achievement of organisational goals. Second, greater interest is being shown in 360 degree feedback. A third trend which is developing is a rethinking of the value of formal performance appraisals.

Performance appraisals are increasingly being seen as a way of achieving organisational goals. Employees do tend to do what is expected of them, so that if criteria such as teamwork and customer satisfaction are included into performance appraisals this type of behaviour is encouraged. The several components of a strategically aligned performance appraisal are identified in Figure 9.15 and compared to the components of a traditional performance appraisal.

APPROACH COMPONENTS	TRADITIONAL	STRATEGIC
Goal	Evaluation	Achievement
Manager	Controls program	Partnership
Employee	Passive	Initiator
View	Review mirror	Prospective
Outcome	Performance rating	Improved performance
Timing	Once a year	Ongoing
Links	None	Corporate goals
Rewards	Based on rating	Based on contribution
Theme	Control	Sharing
Criteria	Determined by manager	Suggested by and mutually determined by employee
Customer	No input	Provides input
Development plan	No input	Essential element
Individual vision	Not discussed	Basis for the plan
Atmosphere	Often confrontational	Supportive

Figure 9.15 Two approaches to performance appraisal

Source: Schuler 1995, p. 336; based on *Personnel Journal*, 119, p. 74

A more complete picture of performance can be achieved when feedback is obtained from a variety of sources. The process of 360 degree feedback involves obtaining feedback from subordinates, peers, boss, self and customers. This gives everyone more information about their behaviours, thus enhancing the potential for improvement.

Managing change

The power of 360 degree feedback

BY LARRY CIPOLLA & CHRIS TRAFFORD

What is 360 degree performance-based feedback? Unlike a performance appraisal review, where the individual receives feedback from one person, typically the boss or team leader, 360 or multi-rater feedback allows that same individual to receive feedback from people at all levels above and below, internal or external to the organisation. The individual is, in effect, surrounded by feedback about his/her performance effectiveness (see diagram).

Credible, relevant feedback can help individuals recognise areas of performance that need improvement. Performance-based feedback helps people understand the consequences of their actions.

It enables them to create self-directed action plans that move them in the direction of the performance expectations of others.

The competitive trend in the marketplace is not simply to appraise performance, but to improve upon it. Multi-rater feedback helps eliminate bias by providing more balanced feedback from different sources. People anonymously assess an individual on a wide variety of skills and practices necessary for performance effectiveness. To help identify any bias, the feedback reports should identify the distribution of responses for each question. This keeps each person's input confidential while identifying clusters of strengths, weakness, or skewed responses.

How is it used?

Organisations in business, industry, government and educational institutions use multi-rater feedback for a variety of applications: team building, career development, counselling, diversity awareness, succession planning, and introducing organisational change. They use it to identify high-potential performers, complement their internal training programs, and conduct needs analyses. It is used to help drive their culture and values, and reinforce their leadership, sales, and sales management effectiveness efforts.

The employee benefits by receiving a variety of feedback from different sources. The organisation benefits when the employee creates and implements self-directed action plans linked to the feedback. Both benefit when the developmental feedback focuses on performance-related issues, rather than style. Through a carefully planned and implemented 360 degree process, individual team and organisational effectiveness can be enhanced.

Who should you assess?

What happens at the top influences what happens throughout the organisation.

Implementation checklist

- Ensure support and involvement of top-level management.
- View the purpose of 360 degree feedback as developmental.
- Take great care when considering 360 degree feedback data for direct input into the reward process.
- Eliminate any concerns about confidentiality of data and possible bias.
- Pilot 360 degree feedback on your most effective performers.
- Consider the use of front-end 360 degree positioning sessions for raters.

- Provide those being rated with the first look at feedback results.
- Use a skilled and trained facilitator to review results with feedback participants.
- Develop a process that ensures the feedback is operationalised via developmental planning, manager coaching, etc.
- Consider re-assessment to measure changes in performance effectiveness.

Source: *HRMonthly*, October 1995, pp. 10–15.

The extracts from the article 'The power of 360 degree feedback' describes the process of 360 degree feedback and the ways in which it can be used in organisations. However, the process of 360 degree feedback requires an environment of trust, honesty and openness if it is to result in constructive feedback.

Constructive feedback is difficult to achieve when there are personality clashes, a climate of 'them and us' and competition between organisational members. People can also find receiving critical feedback uncomfortable and emotionally traumatic.

Other developments which could occur are the use of team-based criteria and a review of the use of performance appraisals. If companies want employees to work together in teams in their pursuit of a total quality management strategy, they must adjust several human resource activities. One of the important ones is the performance appraisal system. Typically, the basis for appraisal begins to reflect team-oriented criteria rather than solely individual-oriented criteria. Longer-term criteria become included with more traditional, shorter-term criteria. Peer review is incorporated, along with the traditional supervisory review.

As is usually the case, these changes do not take place overnight; they take place gradually. People need to get comfortable with the new ways. Just as important, organisations need to experiment with what they are doing. New ways of doing things generally have to be adapted to specific conditions facing a given company. In the instance of performance appraisal, companies may continue to make the types of changes described in the above paragraph. At some point, they may ask, 'Do we even need performance appraisal?'

Firms have used performance appraisal systems for a long time now. It is unlikely that they will abandon them wholesale, but some are starting to ask, 'Why do we do appraisals?' As firms address these questions, they must see that they do it more to *control* than to develop or improve employee performance—and they do it because they assume they need to. (If employee goals are different from organisational goals, then—the assumption goes—firms have to monitor and control what employees do. In some cases, firms are finding that this assumption is wrong: employees can have goals that coincide with the organisation's.) W. Edwards Deming, a pioneer in the field of quality management and statistical process control, acted on the assumption that employees will do their best when managers treat them accordingly. In fact, he argued that, in terms of performance problems, managers—not the employees—are largely responsible for the problems. This questioning could eventually result in the disappearance of performance appraisal as most organisations use it today, at least as a method for evaluating employees. Deming strongly maintained until his death in 1993 at the age of 93 that appraisal can be useful, but only to help an employee develop and improve.

Summary

Appraising employee performance is a critical human resource management activity. This chapter examined performance appraisal as a set of processes and procedures consisting of developing reliable and valid standards, criteria and performance appraisal forms. In it a discussion of who gathers the performance appraisal forms was also provided. To ensure its effectiveness, human resource managers must be concerned with implementing and monitoring all of these aspects of the performance appraisal system.

Although a substantial amount of organisational experience and research with performance appraisal exists, not all the questions have been answered sufficiently. For example, neither the advantages of the behavioural observations scale are uncritically expected by all, nor have all the criticisms of behavioural observation scales been resolved. Additionally, the question, 'What is the best form of performance appraisal?' remains unanswered.

We do, however, know that the effectiveness of performance appraisal depends upon several components of appraisal, not just one, such as the appraisal form. Recognition of the importance of the role of the system in performance appraisal has helped focus attention on such components of appraisal as the superior–subordinate relationship, job qualities and organisational conditions. Another important quality of the system is the raters themselves, particularly how the raters process appraisal information and make evaluation decisions.

In this chapter, two critical components of using the performance appraisal data were discussed: feeding back the data to the subordinate via the performance appraisal interview, and spotting performance deficiencies and developing strategies for improvement.

It was suggested that in providing effective feedback to subordinates, superiors should use the appropriate and specific performance data, that the purposes of evaluation and development should be served separately, that current and potential performance appraisal discussions should be separated, and that there should be multiple appraisals.

With effective feedback and valid performance appraisals, it is easier to engage in programs of spotting and correcting performance deficiencies. These should begin with a model or paradigm for determining the causes of the performance deficiencies. When these deficiencies are traced to employee motivation rather than ability, several programs designed either to control or prevent the deficiencies can be developed and implemented. In so doing, all the reasons for performance appraisals and performance appraisal systems can be attained.

Facilitating the effectiveness of the performance appraisal and the performance appraisal system is the assessment of the entire system and its specific components. Such assessments are necessary to help determine how well the evaluational and developmental purposes are being attained and if legal considerations are being observed. On the basis of these, revisions in current appraisal methods can be made and more effective strategies for improving performance can be developed and implemented. Once done, an organisation has a much better basis upon which to make other personnel/human resource management decisions, particularly those associated with remuneration and benefits, and training and development, topics which are addressed in the following chapters.

questions for discussion and review

1. In what ways can a performance appraisal system help an organisation?
2. What are the purposes of performance appraisal?
3. How can performance appraisal forms be developed so that supervisory errors in performance appraisal can be minimised?
4. What relationship does performance appraisal have to other HRM activities?
5. What is the primary difference between the behavioural observation scale and the behaviourally-anchored rating scale?
6. What is involved in the successful use of performance appraisal?
7. What kinds of conflict emerge when assessing performance?
8. Identify and discuss several types of interviews used in performance appraisal.
9. What characteristics of the interview are likely to enhance and facilitate the effectiveness of performance appraisal?
10. What information is critical in determining how to improve employee performance?
11. What are the critical issues in determining the utility of a specific performance appraisal system?

case study

Ron Gates propped his feet on the desk, leaned back on his chair, and let his imagination run. Ron, a district sales manager for a Melbourne-based distributor of computer hardware and related office equipment which specialised in finance-related industries, had just finished reading the front page story in the *Australian Financial Review*. It had summarised the major changes and rapid expansion. It concluded that the rapid expansion was likely to continue and that the future for related computer hardware and office equipment was very rosy.

At that moment Ron's phone rang and brought him up out of his chair and back to the reality of his job. It was Jack Hale, one of the 5 field representatives of a staff of 18 people whom Ron managed. Jack was calling in during the afternoon, as was his custom, because the field representatives need to check periodically on customer calls and additional assignments that Ron may have received. Jack informed Ron that he was going well and was presently in Geelong preparing to make a call on the last customer of the day. (Geelong is approximately 86 kilometres from Melbourne.)

As Ron hung up, he glanced at the clock. It was 4.45 pm and he knew that if he was going to airfreight a facsimile machine to a customer in Portland he would have to leave now for the Ansett terminal in the city. As he drove towards it he passed the Melbourne Cricket Ground and did a double-take when he saw Jack Hale's car, with its company logo on the side, pulling into the car park outside the members' bar.

Ron was furious, but he couldn't stop if he was going to make it to the Ansett terminal in time to deliver his machine. However, the ride into the city would give him enough time to contemplate a confrontation with Jack Hale. As far as he was concerned this was the proverbial last straw that was going to break his back.

Six months ago Ron had been promoted to district sales manager in charge of an 18-member staff, responsible for service to the organisation in the state of Victoria. When Ron arrived, he decided not to make any changes in staff or operating procedures for at least 6 months so that he could 'get a feel' for the job and the people on his staff. Jack Hale was one person whom Ron felt he had begun to understand. Although the company did not have a formal appraisal system, Ron felt that his experience with Jack dictated some form of evaluation.

Field representatives were paid a salary plus commission. What Ron learned when he arrived, was that all 5 of his field representatives earned the maximum commission because the finance industry had been expanding over the previous few years and business had been booming. After about 3 months on the job though, Ron decided to 'document' a file on Jack Hales's performance because of a number of disturbing incidents. Although the nature of the field representative's job renders direct observation by the supervisor virtually impossible, some data on Jack's job behaviour had filtered its way back to Ron. For example, when he visited some customers he noticed that the office managers never asked about Jack, although their organisations were in Jack's territory. In Ron's estimation, this was clear indication of a lack of communication and salesmanship on Jack's part. He also recalled the Friday afternoon he had to track Jack down to deliver another printer because he had previously delivered a printer which was incompatible with the system used in an organisation. Finally Ron had noticed that within the past 3 months he had become a victim of job enlargement on Jack's account. An important component of the field representative's job is the paperwork associated with customer orders. In Jack's case, Ron found himself consistently redoing Jack's incomplete paperwork in order to make a delivery on time, or spending time on the phone with the dispatch department to straighten out delivery paperwork that Jack had incorrectly submitted.

Enough was enough, he decided. As Ron completed his delivery at the Ansett terminal and headed home for dinner, he had resolved his dilemma. Tomorrow morning he was going to call Jack in and inform him that his commission was to be cut by 50 per cent, beginning immediately. For starters that ought to get old Jack's attention, Ron thought, with a satisfied smile on his face.

Questions
1 Assess Ron Gates' planned method of addressing Jack Hales' performance deficiency.
2 Explain why this planned approach will be effective or ineffective in addressing the performance deficiency.
3 Describe the way in which you would deal with this matter.
4 Now that Ron has been in the job for six months, describe the form of appraisal system you would recommend he use. Explain the reasons for your suggestion.
5 Identify the skills Ron Gates will need to use when he appraises Jack Hales' performance.

Resources
Books and articles
CCH Australia Ltd (1994), *Employee Assessment, Appraisal and Counselling*, 3rd edition, CCH Australia Ltd, North Ryde.

Lansbury, R. (1995), 'Performance appraisal: The Elusive Quest?', in G. O'Neill & R. Kramar (eds), *Australian Human Resources Management: Current trends in management practice*, Pitman Publishing, Melbourne, pp. 123–44.

Saul, P. (1992), 'Rethinking Performance Appraisal', *Asia Pacific Journal of Human Resources*, vol. 30, no. 3, pp. 25–40.

Videos

Video Train (1994), 'Performance Appraisal and Personal Development', Mount Waverley, Victoria.

BBC (1994), 'Marking the managers', London.

References

Abbott, J. R. & Bernardin, H. J, (1984), 'The Development of a Scale of Self Efficacy', Working paper, Florida Atlantic University.

Bandurra, A. (1969), *Principles of Behaviour Modification*, Holt, Rinehart and Winston, New York.

Beer, M. (1981), 'Performance Appraisal: Dilemmas and Possibilities, *Organizational Dynamics*, Winter, p. 27.

Beer, Carroll, Schneier & Kavanach, M. (1982), 'Evaluating Performance' in K. M. Rowland & G. R. Ferris (eds), *Personnel Management*, Allyn and Bacon, Boston, pp. 187–226.

Bernardin, H. J. & Cascio, W. (1987), *Performance Appraisal and the Law—Readings in Personnel and Human Resource Management*, 3rd edition, West Publishing, St. Paul, Minn.

Budford Jnr, J. R., Burkhalter, B. B. & Jacobs, G. T. (1988), 'Assessment: Link Job Descriptions to Performance Appraisals', *Personnel Journal*, June, pp. 132–40.

Bulletin to Management, 18 October 1984, pp. 2, 7.

Campbell, D. N., Fleming, R. L. & Grote, R. C. (1985), 'Discipline Without Punishment at Last', *Harvard Business Review*, July–August, pp. 162–78.

Carroll Jnr, S. J. & Schneier, C. E. (1982), *Performance Appraisal and Review (PAR) Systems*, Scott-Foresman, Glenview, Ill.

CCH Australia Ltd (1995), *Human Resources Management*, CCH Australia Ltd, North Ryde.

Cooper, W. H. (1983), 'Internal Homogeneity, Descriptiveness, and Halo: Resurrecting Some Answers and Questions about the Structure of Job Performance Rating Categories', *Personnel Psychology*, Autumn, pp. 489–502.

Cummings, L. L. & Schwab, D. P. (1973), *Performance in Organisations: Determinants and Appraisal*, Scott-Foresman and Company, Glenview, Ill.

'Daily Labor Letter', Wall St Journal, 1 May, 1990, p. A2.

Erez, M., Earley, P. C. & Hulin, C. L. (1985), 'The Impact of Participation in Goal Acceptance and Performance: A Two-Step Model', *Academy of Management Journal*, March, pp. 50–66.

Flanagan, J. C. (1954), 'The Critical Incident Technique', *Psychological Bulletin*, vol. 51, pp. 327–58.

Gibson, J. L., Ivancevich, J. J. & Donnelly, J. H. (1979), *Organizations: Behaviour, Structure, Processes*, 3rd edition, Business Publications, Inc., Dallas, Tex., p. 361.

Greengard, S. (1993), 'Theft Control Starts with HR Strategies', *Personnel Journal*, April, pp. 81–91.

Hall, D. T. (1976), *Careers in Organizations*, Scott, Foresman and Company, Glenview, Ill.

Hugh, L. (1984), 'Development of the Accomplishment Record Method of Selecting and Promoting Professionals', *Journal of Applied Psychology*, vol. 69, pp. 135–46.

Ilgen, D. R. & Favero, J. L. (1985), 'Limits in Generalization from Psychological Research to Performance Appraisal Process', *Academy of Management Review*, April, pp. 311–21.

Ilgen, D. R. & Feldman, J. M. (1983), 'Performance Appraisal: A Process Focus', in B. Staw & L. L. Cummings (eds), *Research in Organizational Behaviour*, vol. 5, pp. 141–97.

Kavanagh, M. J. (1982), 'Evaluation Performance', in K. M. Rowland & G. R. Feris (eds), *Personnel Management*, Allyn and Bacon, Boston, pp. 187–225.

Keichell III, W. (1989), 'When Subordinates Evaluate the Boss', *Fortune*, June. pp. 201.

Knauft, E. B. (1948), 'Construction and use of weighted checklist ratings scales for two industrial situations', *Journal of Applied Psychology*, vol. 32, pp. 63–70.

Kraiger, K. & Ford, J. K. (1985), 'A Meta-Analysis of Ratee Race Effects in Performance Ratings', *Journal of Applied Psychology*, February, pp. 56–65.

Kramar, R. (1988), 'Discrimination and the Development of Personnel management', in G. Palmer (ed.), *Australian Personnel Management: A Reader*, Macmillan, Melbourne.

Landy, F. S. & Farr, J. L. (1980), 'Performance Rating', *Psychological Bulletin*, January, pp. 72–107.

Landy, F. J. & Trumbo, D. A. (1980), *Psychology of Work Behaviour*, revised edition, Dorsey, Homewood, Ill.

Latham, G. P. & Saari, L. M. (1979), 'The Importance of Supportive Relationships in Goal Setting', *Journal of Applied Psychology*, vol. 64, pp. 163–68.

Latham, G. P. & Yukl, G. A. (1975), 'A Review of Research on the Application of Goal Setting in Organizations', *Academy of Management Journal*, vol. 18, pp. 824–45.

Latham, G. P., Cummings, L. L. & Mitchell, T. R. (1981), 'Behavioural Strategies to Improve Productivity', *Organizational Dynamics*, Winter, pp. 4–23.

Latham, G. P., Erez M. & Locke, E. (1988), 'Resolving Scientific Disputes by the Joint Design of Crucial Experiments by the Antagonists: Application to the Erez-Latham Dispute Regarding Participation in Goal Setting', *Journal of Applied Psychology*, vol. 73, pp. 753–72.

Latham, G. P. & Wexley, K. (1977), 'Behavioural Observation Scales for Performance Appraisal Purposes', *Personnel Psychology*, vol. 30, pp. 255–68.

—— (1981), 'Increasing Productivity Through Performance Appraisal', Addison-Wesley, Reading, Mass.

Latham, G. P., Cummings, L. L. & Mitchell, T. R. (1981), 'Behavioural Strategies to Improve Productivity', *Organisational Dynamics*, Summer, pp. 20–42.

Lawler III, E. E., Mohrman, A. M. & Resnick, S. M. (1984), 'Performance Appraisal Revisited', *Organizational Dynamics*, Summer, pp. 20–24.

Lazer, R. I. & Wikstrom, W. S. (1977), *Appraising Managerial performance: Current Practice and Future Directions*, Conference Board Inc., New York.

Lefton, R. E., Buzzotta, V. P., Scerberg, M. & Karraker, B.L. (1977), *Effective Motivation Through Performance Appraisal*, Wiley, New York.

Loar, M., Mohrman, S. & Stock, J. R. (1982), 'Development of a Behaviourally Based Performance Appraisal System', *Personnel Psychology*, vol. 35, Spring, pp. 75–88.

Locke, E. A. (1968), 'Toward a Theory of Task Motivation and Incentives', *Organizational Behaviour and Human Performance*, vol. 3, pp. 157–89.

Mager R. F. & Pipe P. (1970), *Analysing Performance Problems or 'You Really Oughta Wanna'*, Fearon Pitman.

Maier, N. R. F. (1958), *The Appraisal Interview*, Wiley, New York.

McAfee, B. & Green, B. (1977), 'Selecting a Performance Appraisal Method', *Personnel Administrator*, June, pp. 61–64.

McGuire, P. J. (1980), 'Why Performance Appraisals Fail', *Personnel Journal*, September, pp. 744–46, 762.

Meyer, H. H., Kay, E. & French Jnr, J. R. P. (1965), 'Split Roles in Performance Appraisal', *Harvard Business Review*, January–February.

Mount, M. K. (1983), 'Comparisons of Managerial and Employee Satisfaction with a Performance Appraisal System', *Personnel Psychology*, Spring, pp. 99–110.

Olivas, L. (1981), 'Adding a Different Dimension to Goal Setting Processes', *Personnel Administrator*, October, pp. 75–78.

Personnel Journal (1991), 'A new focus on achievement', p. 74.

Peters, L. H. & O'Connor, E. J. (1980), 'Situational Constraints and Work Outcomes: The Influence of a Frequently Overlooked Construct', *Academy of Management Review*, vol. 5, pp. 391–79.

Porter, L. W., Lawler, E. E. & Hackman, J. R. (1975), *Behavior in Organizations*, McGraw-Hill, New York.

Schmidt, Hunter, J. E. & Pearlman, K. (1982), 'Assessing the Economic Impact of Personnel Programs on Workforce Productivity', *Personnel Psychology*, Summer, pp. 333–48.

Schuler, R. S. (1981), 'Taking the Pain Out of the Performance Appraisal Interview', *Supervisory Management*, August, pp. 8–13.

Schuler, R. (1995), *Managing Human Resources*, West Publishing, St. Paul, Minn.

Serpa, R. (1984), 'Why Many Organisations—Despite Good Intentions—Often Fail to Give Employees Fair and Useful Performance Reviews', *Management Review*, July, pp. 41–46.

Spencer, L. M. & Spencer, S. M. (1993), *Competence at work: Models for Superior Performance*, John Willey and Sons, New York.

Stogdill, R. M. (1965), *Group Productivity, Drive and Cohesiveness*, Bureau of Business Research, Columbus, OH.

Villanova, P., Bernardin, H. J., Dahmus S. A & Sims, R. L (1993) 'Rater leniency and performance appraisal discomfort', *Educational and Psychological Measurement*, vol. 53, pp. 789–99.

Wexley, K. N. (1979), 'Performance Appraisal and Feedback', in S. Kerr (ed.), *Organizational Behaviour, Grid*, Columbus, OH, p. 256.

Wexley, K. N., Singh, J. P. & Yukl, G. A. (1973), 'Subordinate Personality as a Moderator of the Effects of Participation in Three Types of Appraisal Interviews', *Journal of Applied Psychology*, vol. 58, pp. 54–59.

Wright, C. & Lund, J. (1996), 'Best Practice Tayorism; "Yankee Speed-Up" ' in Australian Grocery Distribution', *Journal of Industrial Relations*, vol. 38, no 2, pp. 196–212.

Wylie, P. & Grothe, M. (1981), 'Problem Employees: How to Improve their Performance', Pitman Learning, Belmont, CA.

Yager, E. (1981), 'A Critique of Performance Appraisal Systems', *Personnel Journal*, February, pp. 129–33.

chapter 10

Reward management

Graham O'Neill

learning objectives

After studying this chapter, you will be able to:

1. Appreciate the role and importance of pay and other employer provided rewards.
2. Understand how total reward management fits with other human resource activities, and the key internal and external factors that influence reward management.
3. Identify the four key issues in reward planning and management.
4. Understand how a pay structure is established.
5. Describe the link between pay and performance, including the arguments for and against linking pay to performance.
6. Be familiar with non-wage and salary benefits provided by employers, and their role in the overall reward system.

chapter 10

chapter outline

- Role of total reward management — 411
- Relationships of total reward management — 413
  - Relationships with other HRM activities — 413
  - Relationships with the internal environment — 415
  - Relationships with the external environment — 417
- Remuneration planning and management — 420
  - Determining the relative value of jobs — 420
  - Establishing the pay structure — 428
  - Building a link with performance — 431
- Linking pay to performance: the great debate — 447
  - Communication and administration of reward — 449
  - Employee participation — 449
- Employee benefits — 451
  - Social welfare and security — 452
  - Workers' compensation — 452
  - Private employee welfare programs — 452
  - Superannuation and retirement benefits — 452
  - Insurance — 453
  - Employee services and perquisites — 453
  - Administrative issues in employee benefits — 454
- Summary — 456
- Questions for discussion and review — 457
- Case study — 458
- Resources — 459
- References — 459

HRM IN THE NEWS

Designing a compensation program that's right for your organisation

It involves more than compensation.

Designing a successful dynamic pay program today involves more than compensation. The 'secret' of dynamic pay is really the alignment of individual competencies with the core competencies of the business through a measurement system that reinforces the right behaviours.

'Pay for performance' really means 'performance for pay'. It is not internal equity, external competitiveness, or personal motivation that enables the organisation to maximise its corporate competencies, but rather how individual and group values and behaviour work to create a unique performance-oriented culture.

Pay can no longer be viewed as separate from an organisation's culture, but must be *fully* and *positively* incorporated into it. A successful pay program cannot be built on external values alone. Instead, it must complement and reinforce the values of the organisation and the individuals within that organisation.

Before a dynamic compensation program can be designed and implemented, many questions must be answered. For example:

Is the organisation homogenous or heterogenous?

If heterogenous, will it tolerate different pay schemes?

If different pay schemes are developed, are the mechanisms—the ability to price differently, to measure different kinds of performance, to develop different pay vehicles—in place?

Questions, issues demand attention

At the same time, a number of issues much broader than pay itself must be explored. These include:

- The design of work systems that are understandable, practical, and friendly for both individuals and work teams
- The design and creation of work cultures—combinations of work design and employment relationships—that support the organisation's strategy
- Identification of capabilities—proficiencies and competencies that support and enhance work system effectiveness and success
- Selection and development of people who fit the work and culture
- Empowerment of people to act in ways that are advantageous for both themselves and the organisation
- Motivation of people, including both psycho-social and material remuneration, to act in ways that help the organisation.

Compensation must continue to evolve

The specific elements of a compensation program, depend on the individual organisation. At one end of the spectrum are organisations that need to completely rebuild their programs. At the other end are those that can successfully maintain their traditional compensation systems with only minor adjustments. In the middle are the vast majority of organisations that need to continually evolve their programs.

One thing is certain, though. There are no pat answers or trendy, quick-fix solutions to the compensation issues that organisations face today. The single universal valuing system, which worked well when organisational structures and strategies were less varied, must—in many cases—evolve into diverse yet sound concepts for measurement and reward that incorporate highly reliable data. Monochromatic approaches must be replaced with a variety of bold, creative, yet carefully thought-out solutions. And the concept that compensation is a one-dimensional, static, and independent element of the organisation must be replaced with a vision that pay is ever evolving, fully integrated, and multi-faceted.

Source: The Hay Group May 1993, pp. 11–12.

The 'HRM in the news' article indicates three important issues associated with remuneration. First is the need to relate pay directly to performance. It is the performance of employees, both individually and in their work groups, that determines how effective the enterprise will be in meeting its business objectives and priorities. Second, relating performance and pay is essentially an issue of organisational culture: an effective pay program is one that directly reinforces the values of the company. Third, to achieve this requires attention to broader issues ranging from the way that work is designed, through to the style of management required to empower and motivate employees.

In this respect, there is no one answer. What works for one company may be totally inappropriate for another. As a result, pay—and reward systems generally—need to be specifically tailored to the needs of the individual organisation. This requires stepping away from the traditional notion of 'one size fits all', and designing innovative and flexible approaches that directly support the needs of the business.

Role of total reward management

Total reward management is the process by which organisations distribute direct and indirect monetary and non-monetary rewards to employees. Work is a central activity in the lives of most people: nevertheless, no matter however central or important work is to people, they are unlikely to be satisfied if their employer does not pay them well enough. All things being equal, people prefer to work for an organisation that provides better rewards than others.

Once on the job, employees generally want to do a 'fair day's work for a fair day's pay'. Consequently, one of the typical key accountabilities of the human resource function is to develop reward structures and processes that ensure employees are paid fairly. Fairness in this respect refers to what other people in the organisation are paid, and what people with similar jobs in other work places are paid.

Many organisations seek to tie their **direct remuneration** (i.e. the direct cash elements of pay) to individual, team, business unit, or overall company performance. These approaches (often referred to as **performance-based pay**, variable pay, or incentive pay) aim to strengthen and expand the linkages between performance, individual and work group contribution to that performance, and the distribution of rewards.

Although employees are concerned with being paid fairly, and in line with their respective contribution, the **indirect rewards** provided are also important. As shown in Figure 10.1, indirect rewards include those things that a company must by law provide its employees (e.g. superannuation, holiday and sick leave), as well as those things provided at the discretion of the employer (e.g. additional leave, flexible working hours, purchase discounts on company products, health insurance, employee share plans).

Reward management serves the following important organisational purposes:

1 **It attracts potential job applicants**—in conjunction with the organisation's recruitment and selection efforts, the reward management program can help assure that direct and indirect rewards are sufficient to attract the right people at the right time for the right jobs.
2 **It retains good employees**—unless the reward program is perceived as internally equitable and externally competitive, good employees (those the organisation wants to retain) are likely to leave.
3 **It motivates employees**—all organisations seek to be profitable, productive and have a committed and motivated workforce. Effective reward management can help produce such a workforce by providing a share in profits, tying rewards to productivity and other key performance measures that recognise employee effort and contribution.

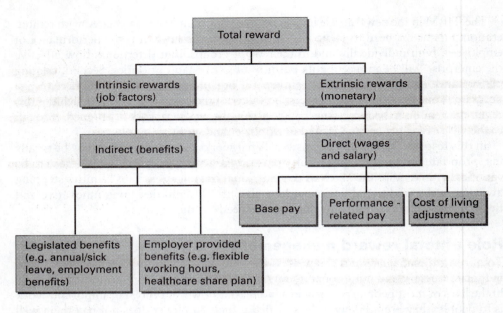

Figure 10.1 Components of total reward

4 **It administers pay within legal requirements**—there are important legal regulations relevant to direct and indirect rewards; organisations must be aware of them and avoid violating them in their reward management programs.
5 **It facilitates achievement of human resource and business objectives**—a company may want to create a particularly rewarding and competitive climate, or it may want to be perceived as a 'good employer' so it can attract the best applicants. The reward management program can be designed with these specific objectives in mind, and can also result in furthering other organisational objectives such as rapid growth, survival or innovation.
6 **It helps gain a competitive edge**—total reward costs can be a significant cost of doing business. Depending on the industry, remuneration, benefits and related costs can range from 10 to 80 per cent of total operating costs. An organisation may develop a range of reward-based strategies to control these costs. For example, the firm may choose to relocate to areas where labour is cheaper, or it may develop variable pay plans linked to company results.

The capacity to attract, retain and motivate individuals is largely related to the value that the reward structure has for people. Remuneration, both direct and indirect, has the potential to serve several preferences; because individuals differ in their preferences, money can take on varying degrees of importance. However, employees are often willing to join an organisation for reasons other than just the money. They are often willing to join for the non-monetary rewards an organisation may offer (e.g. opportunity to travel, generous superannuation or convenient work arrangements). Table 10.1 lists some of the monetary and non-monetary rewards that are provided by Australian organisations. These can vary from basic employment arrangements (e.g. job sharing, flexitime and extra leave) to work design (challenging work, job variety performance feedback and opportunities for self-development) through to such perquisites as a company supplied vehicle and status symbols such as office furniture.

Table 10.1 Organisational rewards

MONETARY REWARDS AND FRINGE BENEFITS		STATUS SYMBOLS	SOCIAL REWARDS	TASK-SELF REWARDS
Pay	Medical care, including free physical examinations	Office size and location	Friendly greetings	Interesting work
Pay raise				Sense of achievement
Share plan	Company vehicle	Office furnishings	Informal recognition	
Profit sharing	Produce discount plans	Formal awards/ recognition	Praise	Job of more importance
Bonus plans	Reserved company parking		Evaluative feedback	Job variety
Provision and use of company facilities	Superannuation		Compliments	Job-performance feedback
	Club memberships and privileges		Non-verbal signals	Self-recognition
Pay and time off for attending work related training programs and seminars	Discount purchase privileges		Invitations to coffee/lunch	Self-praise
	Personal loans at favourable rates		After-hours social gatherings	Opportunities to schedule own work
	Free legal advice			Participation in new organisational ventures
	Free personal financial planning advice			Choice of geographical location
	Moving expenses Home-purchase assistance			Autonomy in job
				Flexible working hours

Source: Schuler et al. 1992, p. 258; based on Podsakoff et al. 1987

Relationships of total reward management

Reward management has a significant relationship with a range of other important HRM activities, as well as the internal and external environments. The breadth of these relationships is shown in Figure 10.2.

Relationships with other HRM activities

Reward management either relies upon other HRM activities for input into determining remuneration and benefits (e.g. job analysis and performance assessment), or is a key influence on other areas (e.g. the capacity to attract and retain employees and union–management relations).

Job analysis

Remuneration is highly dependent on the outcomes of **job analysis**. The job evaluation process determines the relative worth of jobs. Job evaluation results are heavily dependent on the outcomes of job analysis, typically described in the formal job description. The relative ranking of one job to another, as done in the job evaluation process, is the prime determinant of pay grades, and therefore individual pay rates.

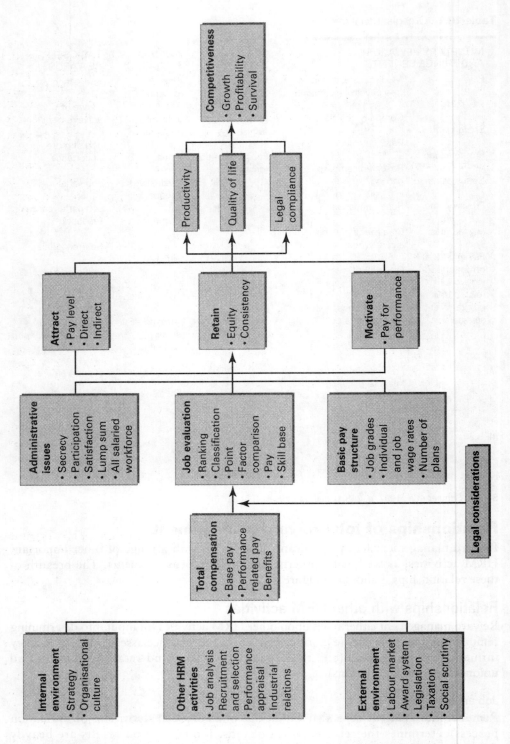

Figure 10.2 Relationships, administrative issues, and process of total compensation

Source: Schuler 1995, p. 384

Recruitment

Organisations need to compete for skilled resources. The level of remuneration offered, together with other direct and indirect rewards, are important considerations for employees when they are contemplating job opportunities. Firms with highly competitive reward policies will generally be highly selective in whom they recruit. Conversely, a company that does not pay well, or has minimal benefits, may find difficulty in attracting people of the calibre required for its business. It is also true that employees differ in the value they put on pay. Some jobs may be very interesting but pay modestly, whereas other jobs may be quite routine but pay very well. It is not always true that the most competitive pay levels need be offered. Individuals make employment decisions on the basis of several factors, including the location of the organisation, its reputation as a place to work, and the general community image of the company. Consequently, rather than taking the job that pays the most, individuals may take that which satisfies, or does as well as possible across all these factors.

Performance assessment

In many organisations there is a direct link between the performance assessment process and remuneration. Employees are given a rating (e.g. Outstanding, Commendable, Satisfactory) as a result of the performance assessment process. This rating then determines what their respective pay increase will be for the coming year. In companies where this approach to performance-based pay exists, results of the performance assessment can be very significant to employees. Where the ability to plan, measure and assess performance is seen by employees as reliable and valid, linking pay and performance may be viewed as highly positive and help create a motivating work environment.

Union–management relations

A significant number of Australian employees are covered by Enterprise Agreements and Awards. These agreements and awards define a wide range of employment conditions, including pay and related issues (e.g. pay progression, pay-performance linkages and benefits). In this respect, reward issues are frequently a major part of union-management negotiations.

Relationships with the internal environment

The provision of employee rewards represent significant expenditure in any organisation. Pay and benefit costs are the largest single operating expense for most service companies, and are typically the second or third highest expense category in manufacturing operations. Reward processes are increasingly being influenced by aspects within the organisation as companies seek to maximise their return on this investment.

Corporate strategy

Reward processes and mechanisms can be a key support to an organisation's business objectives. A growing number of Australian firms use a deliberately defined reward strategy as a means of positioning each of the reward elements (e.g. base pay, bonus payments, share plans, benefits) against their business plans. The purpose is to ensure that each reward element has a defined role in supporting the operating objectives. O'Neill (1995a) describes the process and issues involved in developing a reward strategy for an organisation. Figure 10.3 is an example of the type of reward matrix that an organisation might develop for this purpose. Each reward component is specifically designed to match one or more of the company's key business objectives.

Reward component	Reward objectives					
	Attract	Retain	Productivity	Individual contribution	Employee security	Company performance
Base salary	Prime	Prime				
Gainsharing plan			Prime			
Performance incentive			Secondary	Secondary		Secondary
Corporate profit share			Secondary	Secondary		Secondary
Superannuation		Secondary			Prime	
Other benefits		Secondary			Prime	
Career planning		Secondary		Secondary		

Legend: ■ Of prime importance ▨ Of secondary importance □ Not relevant

Figure 10.3   Illustrative reward strategy matrix
Source: O'Neill, 1995a, pp. 103–117

The matrix shown in Figure 10.3 provides a direct link between the reward system, human resource strategies and organisation objectives. For example, the company may decide to use its **base pay** as a prime tactic in recruiting and retaining key performers. It will therefore aim to be the pay leader in its industry or geographic area. Or it may be that the company aims to hold its fixed costs down by paying low in the market, but provide for very attractive indirect compensation (e.g. superannuation, share ownership plan, health care) to increase company loyalty and retention rates of employees. Another firm may want to focus on specific business objectives (e.g. profit, market growth, shareholder returns), and consequently use these as the basis for performance-based bonus payments. There is no one answer: which tactic is better, or more appropriate, depends on the nature of the business. Reward structures based on short-term criteria should be used where the market conditions dictate short-term concerns for survival. Reward systems based on long-term criteria need to be used where market conditions dictate long-term concerns for survival. An organisation with businesses operating in different markets, or at different stages of maturity, is likely to have a range of reward approaches tailored to the specific needs of each of its operations.

Organisational culture

Reward systems can influence employee behaviour. They can also be used to underpin the management philosophy, values, attitudes and styles desired by the organisation (see for example, O'Neill 1995a). Many organisations place a strong value on employee involvement and commitment as a means of developing a work environment and climate where all employees share a common set of goals. This is the central theme of a paper by Cook (1993) promoting the sharing of financial success with employees. Reward systems can be used to support this value by providing a share in the financial success of the enterprise. This is a major reason Australian firms show an interest in **profit sharing plans** such as gain sharing (Carey 1993), productivity incentives, and employee share schemes (Stradwick 1992). Similarly, many organisation change processes are initiated by a desire to develop a strong culture around such issues as team-based work, total quality management, customer service or continuous improvement. Specific pay systems can be developed to support these sorts of work cultures; useful examples are described in articles by Cornish & Adams (1993) and O'Neill (1993). These cultures influence employee values, attitudes and behaviour; it is therefore important that an organisation is systematic in articulating its reward practices with its desired culture.

Managing change

Across the board, Australian private and public sector organisations are being forced to develop flexible, adaptive practices to compete in a cost-conscious and highly competitive environment. This has led to the development of a wide range of innovative human resource responses in structuring organisations, designing work, and the development and utilisation of employees.

Reward planning and management is no exception. Line managers are continually looking for reward systems that will support the management values and philosophy, and the operating objectives of the business. As firms move to a flatter structure, remuneration specialists are asked to design systems with fewer pay grades to allow for the flexible (often lateral) utilisation of employees, without the barriers associated with the traditional 'promotional hierarchy'. As companies adopt a 'lean and mean' profile, remuneration specialists are asked to design pay alternatives that recognise and reward individuals for the acquisition and utilisation of broader skills, in place of traditional job size relativities. As enterprises adopt clear mission and values statements that emphasise their move toward a 'performance-oriented culture', remuneration specialists are being asked to design reward systems that have a clear and credible link between pay and performance. As we promote a committed and loyal workforce as the key to success, remuneration specialists are asked to review profit sharing, employee share plans, and a range of other alternatives, all aimed at providing employees with a financial stake in the outcomes of their employer.

The purpose of the reward system is not to drive change; that comes from the management direction in philosophy and values, and the business plans and strategies. The role of the reward system is to facilitate change by reinforcing the key actions and elements that will drive change.

Relationships with the external environment

The labour market

Wage and salary surveys are used to determine rates for comparable work within the relevant labour market. In this respect, the relevant labour market might be the industry generally (as it often is for managers, professional and specially skilled employees), or it may be the geographic area for provincial cities and rural areas. In addition to the market wage and salary levels, other criteria for wage and salary determinations are labour market conditions (the level of unemployment); particular professional or skill shortages, and indices such as inflation and the general economic outlook.

The market can be used directly or indirectly for determination of wage rates. Used directly, it provides comparisons for organisations to facilitate them establishing their own pay rates for 'benchmark' jobs. These 'benchmark' rates are then used to establish pay rates for other jobs within the company. When used indirectly, organisations first establish a basis of ranking their existing jobs (typically by using a means of job ranking or sizing); then, on the basis of the resulting hierarchy of jobs, establish pay grades that gather jobs of approximately equal size within discrete pay bands. The next step is to gather survey data to see what other organisations pay for similar sized jobs or job grades. The final pay rates used generally represent a composite of market-rate information and answers to pay-policy questions such as 'Does the organisation want to be a pay leader?', 'What can the organisation afford?' and 'What does the organisation want to pay for: job content, seniority, performance or cost of living?' These usually are the central issues in base pay determination in most organisations.

The industrial relations system

Some 70 per cent of Australia's workforce have their wages and conditions determined by awards. In the past decade Australia has moved from a centralised system for determining awards to an enterprise-based system. Previously, federal or state awards prescribed a wide range of employment conditions from job and pay classification systems through to specific work arrangements including areas of skill demarcation, rostered hours, part-time employment issues, types and amounts of leave entitlements and the like. The enterprise focus provides for the individual organisation to negotiate directly with its employees—or employee associations such as unions—to develop specific employment conditions consistent with the need of the company. In this environment, firms seek to introduce and negotiate processes that are flexible, adaptable and consistent with their particular business objectives. This can be seen in the way that many manufacturing organisations have introduced skill-based pay systems to encourage employees to acquire and apply a wider range of skills. Similarly, many companies have introduced performance management, together with performance-based pay, as part of their enterprise awards. A very important aspect of the Enterprise Bargaining process is that pay increases must be linked to sustainable productivity increases. If this cannot be demonstrated, it is likely that the Industrial Relations Commission would not approve a proposed agreement.

The enterprise award process still leaves a wide sphere of influence for unions (or other agents) to act and negotiate on behalf of their members in individual companies. There remains also a key role for the Industrial Relations Commission in resolving disputes and approving Enterprise Agreements. Here, the industrial relations arena remains a key part of the external environment that has a direct impact on rewards and related conditions of employment.

Government legislation

There is a wide range of federal and state government legislation that affects employee rewards and the process for determining those rewards. The relevant legislation ranges from guaranteeing protection to individual employees, through to determining the way that pay and other employer-provided benefits will be treated for taxation purposes.

Legislation provides public protection in areas ranging from social welfare (e.g. provision of unemployment benefits), to prescribed minimum standards for employers (e.g. minimum rates of pay and conditions such as annual and sick leave) and prevention of discrimination in the work place as detailed in various state and Federal Government Acts related to Equal Employment Opportunity. Of particular interest is the 1991 introduction of legislation to make employer-provided superannuation compulsory. Superannuation was first introduced as a benefit, provided at the discretion of the company, to reward long and loyal service to the employer. However, a concern that the eligibility for many people was insufficient and therefore maintained reliance on social welfare (in the form of age pensions) to fund retirement, prompted the previous Labor Government to make universal superannuation provisions compulsory for all employers—and for employees to contribute to their own retirement from 2000.

There is a range of legislation that affects the taxation of pay and benefits. The most obvious is that which relates to the pay-as-you-earn (PAYE) tax scales and regulations covering deductions from the employee's pay. Fringe benefit tax (FBT) applies to the employer on a wide range of benefits and payments that may be made to employees. The FBT legislation played a major role in prompting employers to move to a total employment cost for calculating employee rewards. While FBT is levied on the employer, the vast majority of employers pass the cost of the tax on to the employee; thus, the cost of the benefit is 'grossed up' to cover any FBT applicable, and it is this total that represents the total reward, or total employment cost.

Social and political scrutiny

There has always been a degree of public commentary on remuneration issues. Media reports regarding the amounts paid to executives and managers especially attract significant attention. Such scrutiny is to be expected given that these are occupations often paid five to ten times average weekly earnings. The first formal step in monitoring amounts paid to executives, and annual movements in their pay, came with the 1986 amendment to the Companies Code. This required salaries at specified levels paid to executives and directors of publicly listed companies to be reported in the annual reports to shareholders. In the USA, executive salaries above one million dollars per annum cannot be claimed as a tax deduction unless the amounts in excess of this figure have been awarded against a formal performance contract, approved by shareholders and set at the beginning of the period for which performance is to be measured.

Individual organisations are often influenced in their remuneration decisions by social sensitivity. Not-for-profit organisations, especially those established for charity or social welfare purposes and relying on public donations for their funding, often provide below average salaries and benefits. This is to avert any possible criticism of their funds being used for other than the public welfare. At the same time, these organisations need to compete in the market to attract and retain employees capable of achieving their objectives. Similarly, the issue of pay raises for public sector employees is often met with press reports of 'fat cats', despite the fact that public sector pay rates are significantly behind private sector levels for similar sized jobs.

Taxation

Taxation issues, especially tax on benefits and perquisites, has a significant impact on reward issues. The Fringe Benefit Taxation Legislation (FBT) was introduced in 1986 to counter the trend towards a 'cafeteria' approach to remuneration where a growing number of employees were trading off salary against motor vehicles and various cash allowances (e.g. travel, entertainment, school fees). Prior to the introduction of FBT, the administration of existing tax laws largely failed to collect taxation due on such items. Over the years, the FBT rates have moved such that there is now virtually no advantage in having remuneration 'packaged' with the exception of a motor vehicle and superannuation.

In early 1995 the federal government withdrew a proposed bill that sought to bring a wide range of employee share plans under the FBT net. The bill as originally drafted would have severely limited the use of employee share plans as part of a company's reward processes. As a result of strong lobbying by many private sector firms and other political parties, the proposed legislation was changed to capture only those share plans that were designed to evade, or minimise, rightful taxation obligations.

Remuneration planning and management

There are four key issues in planning and managing an organisation's basic reward program. These issues are: (1) determining the relative value of jobs, (2) establishing the pay structure, including job grades or classes and individual wage determination, (3) building a link with performance, and (4) communication and administration.

Determining the relative value of jobs

Most organisations offer rewards to employees on the basis of their personal performance and individual contributions. However, the basic pay structure implicitly recognises job-related contributions by assigning pay in accordance with the perceived value of the job itself. This issue is often referred to as **internal equity**—the overall fairness and consistency of the way that the remuneration structure is applied throughout the company. All employees expect that their pay is going to be about the same as that which others receive for jobs that require a similar degree of training, effort, skill and application. The purpose of internal equity is to provide systems and processes that rate the relevant aspects of a job, and as a result, rank jobs in a hierarchy according to their assessed 'size' and value.

The most common process for determining internal equity is by using some form of job 'sizing' or **job evaluation**; that is, the use of formal and systematic procedures to compare the relative worth of jobs within the organisation. After jobs are formally evaluated, they are grouped into job classes or grades for pay purposes. Job evaluation and the job grade structure are thus critical elements in the determination of employee pay.

There are four sequential steps in the job evaluation process. The first is to gain a thorough understanding of the role, its requirements and the expected outcomes. This is commonly referred to as **job analysis** (see Chapter 7) and provides full details about the job duties and responsibilities, and employee requirements for successful performance.

The second step is to determine the criteria against which job comparisons are to be made. In effect, these are the 'yardsticks' used to measure the relative ranking and size of jobs within the company. As these factors help determine how each job is rated—and consequently, how much it will be paid—they are sometimes called **compensable factors**. The factors used by organisations vary widely, but they are all presumed to reflect significant job-related contributions. Typical job factors include such elements as education and training required, decision-making, breadth of management, impact on end results, problem-solving, responsibility for supervising others and physical effort. Regardless of which factors a company uses to evaluate its jobs, those chosen should meet several criteria:

1. They need to represent all major aspects of job content for which the company is willing to pay (i.e. compensable factors)
2. There is a need to avoid overlap or duplication between factors
3. The factors chosen need to be clearly definable and measurable, and reliably discriminate between different jobs

4 It is important that all employees understand what the factor is, and what it is measuring
5 Measurement or assessment of the factors should not cause excessive job evaluation installation or administrative cost
6 The factors need to be consistent with legal requirements and considerations.

The next step is to determine the relative weight each factor contributes to the final job size. In its simplest form, this is reflected in differential points assigned to each of the compensable factors. The weights assigned should be determined by a judgement of the relative importance of each factors to the end objectives of the organisation. An example of differential weightings is shown below in Table 10.2.

Table 10.2 Sample of point rating method

COMPENSABLE FACTOR	1ST DEGREE	2ND DEGREE	3RD DEGREE	4TH DEGREE	5TH DEGREE
Basic knowledge	15	30	45	60	—
Practical experience	20	40	60	80	—
Complexity and judgement	15	30	45	60	—
Initiative	5	10	20	40	—
Probable errors	5	10	20	40	—
Contacts with others	5	10	20	40	—
Confidential data	5	10	15	20	25
Attention to functional detail	5	10	15	20	—
Job conditions	5	10	15	—	—
For supervisory positions only					
Character of supervision	5	10	20	—	—
Scope of supervision	5	10	20	—	—

Source: Schuler et al. 1992, p. 264

The third step is to choose a system for conducting the actual evaluation of jobs according to the compensable factors chosen. There are a variety of job evaluation methods that can be adapted to the specific needs of each organisation. Typical approaches used by Australian private and public sector organisations are discussed below.

The final step is to decide who will do the job evaluation. Where the system used is a proprietary system (i.e. a standard job evaluation system, designed and marketed by a consulting firm), the consultants will usually work with a committee selected from the client organisation. Most companies conduct the job evaluation process using a committee process chaired by a senior representative of the human resource function, typically the remuneration manager. The initial committee is usually responsible for establishing a **benchmark evaluations**, representing a sample of jobs across the entire organisation. The remaining jobs are often matched (or 'slotted') against this benchmark by job analysts in the human resource department.

Clearly, job evaluation is a major determinant of pay; as such, it is the focus of significant discussions regarding equal pay and **comparable worth**. This is particularly so with respect to gender bias in jobs. Gender bias is mainly a result of two factors: first, segregation of women into a narrow range of jobs, often seen as traditional female roles (e.g. nurse, secretary, personal assistant); and second, undervaluation of women's work and skills (Lander & O'Neill 1991). The issue of comparable worth is concerned with ensuring that the relationship between job content and pay is the same for males and females—that is, gender is eliminated as a determinant of pay. Burton (1990) argues that discrimination in the form of gender bias in work value assessment could account for half of the difference between average male and female earnings. In an earlier work, Burton drew attention to the way that similar male and female roles are described, and the differences in male and female titles (Burton 1987). For example, a male-held job involving public contact may be described as requiring negotiation and liaison skills. A similar female-held role may be more likely described as requiring patience, tact and common sense! As you read the discussion on job evaluation, think about the issue of ensuring gender equity in job evaluation. For a full review of issues related to gender equity in job evaluation see Lander & O'Neill (1991).

Managing diversity

More and more organisations are stepping away from the 'one size fits all' notion of remuneration management and administration; instead they are actively developing and implementing reward structures tailored to their unique needs as a business. This tailor-made approach has also increased awareness of the potential for reward systems to be flexible enough to meet the specific needs of different segments of the workforce. Part of this is driven by the need to adhere to legislated requirements: for example, job evaluation and related pay systems must conform to EEO requirements. Other companies are using the potential for flexibility in rewards to maintain and attract employees, and to build a loyal and committed workforce by allowing substantial employee choice.

In these circumstances, the choices employees make will depend on their particular needs. Some older employees, whose financial security is assured, may wish to trade off a pay increase in favour of extra leave; others, not so financially stable, may elect extra superannuation savings in favour of direct pay. Employees wanting to balance home and work commitments may favour permanent part-time work through job sharing; this retains the benefits of permanent employment, while allowing the time necessary for non-work obligations or interests. Employees building for their own financial security may opt for discounted shares in their employer, thus meeting their need for wealth creation, and the employer's need for employee commitment.

Job evaluation methods may be described as qualitative or quantitative. The essential distinction is that qualitative methods provide a job hierarchy or grouping based on 'whole-job' comparisons against the compensable factors; quantitative methods provide a comparative points score, usually the sum of scores for individual factors, for each job (the respective job 'size'). The most common qualitative methods of job evaluation are ranking and job classification. The point rating and **factor comparison methods** are the most used quantitative approaches.

Job ranking

Information from job analysis is used to develop a hierarchy or ladder of jobs against the selected factors. This is the core of the **job ranking** method, and establishes the relative worth of jobs to the organisation. Ranking is a 'whole-job' method in which the total job is considered overall against the factors; for this reason, ranking typically uses a standard description based on only one or two factors.

This method is most convenient and effective where there are a limited number of jobs to evaluate, and the job analyst is familiar with them all. As the number of jobs increases, and the likelihood of one or a few individuals knowing all jobs declines, detailed job analysis information becomes more important and ranking is often done by committee. When a large number of jobs are to be ranked, key or benchmark jobs are used for comparison. At the completion of the ranking process, jobs that are seen to be approximately the same are grouped into job grades for pay purposes.

Job classification

Job classification is similar to ranking, except that the process commences by establishing job classes or grades; jobs are then allocated to a class or grade depending on a comparison of each job with the general class descriptor. Again, this is a 'whole-job' process, typically using a brief summary description of the factors as a basis for comparing and allocating jobs to a classification. The classification to which the job is allocated is then used as a basis for establishing pay rates.

A particular advantage of this method is that it can be applied to a large number and variety of jobs. As the number and variety of jobs in an organisation increase, however, classification tends to become more subjective. This is particularly true when an organisation has a large number of plant or office locations, meaning jobs with the same title may differ widely in content. As a consequence, the job title may default to become a more important guide to classification than the actual job content because it is difficult to evaluate each job separately in such cases.

A major disadvantage of the job classification method is the reliance on a whole-job comparison against a limited number, or overall summary, of factors. The problem with using only one, two or three factors is that they may not effectively discriminate between the range of jobs. For example, some jobs may require a great deal of skill, but others may require a great deal of responsibility. Does this mean that jobs requiring much responsibility should be placed in a lower classification than jobs requiring much skill? Not necessarily. Perhaps both factors could be considered together. Thus each factor becomes a compensable factor valued by the organisation. Jobs would be evaluated and classified on the basis of both factors. However, balancing off the compensable factors to determine the relative equality of jobs can make the overall process confusing to communicate to employees, and difficult for job analysts at a later stage to understand and replicate as they extend the process to other work roles. To deal with this disadvantage, many organisations use more quantifiable methods of evaluation.

Point factor

Probably the most widely used method of job evaluation in Australian organisations is the point factor or point rating method. This consists of assigning point values for a job against previously determined compensable factors, and then adding those values to arrive at a total job score. There are several advantages of this method.

1. Proprietary point factor systems provided by consulting firms are widely used in private and public sector organisations. This permits reliable and consistent job and pay comparisons with other firms.
2. The point factor approach is the simplest form of quantitative method, and is relatively easy to communicate to employees at all levels.
3. The point values for each job are easily converted to pay grades with a minimum of confusion and distortion.
4. A well-conceived point factor plan has considerable stability. It is objective, consistent and uniform, and as such the process is applicable to a wide range of jobs over an extended period of time.
5. The point factor method requires separate and distinct judgement decisions against each factor. In this respect it is a more systematic and precise approach than the 'whole-job' methods.

The limitations of the point factor method are few, but an especially critical one is the assumption that all jobs can be described with the same factors. Many organisations avoid this limitation by developing additional (or different) factors for different groups of employees.

In Table 10.2 there are nine compensable factors used by one organisation to evaluate jobs in supervisory, non-supervisory and clerical categories. The same nine factors are used to evaluate supervisory positions, but there are also two additional factors related to the character and scope of supervision required. The lower part of Table 10.2 breaks down one factor (Complexity and Judgement) to show how the specifications for each degree (or level) of Complexity and Judgement differ within that one factor. A similar description as that shown for Complexity and Judgement is written for each of the compensable factors. The table also shows the different weightings of the factors: for example, the second degree of Practical Experience is worth four times as much as the second degree of Job Conditions.

Once the job evaluation benchmark has been set, the system is maintained by job analysts from the HRM department: within the confines established by the benchmarks, they determine the appropriate factor degree for jobs, and then sum the points assigned to each degree of each factor to give a total job score. Pay levels are then determined on the basis of the total job size.

The point factor method, as with most other job evaluation plans, incorporates the possibility of subjectivity of the job analyst. As such it has the potential for wage discrimination. Bias or subjectivity can affect the job evaluation process in three main ways: (1) in the selection of the factors, (2) in the relative weight assigned to factors, and (3) in the assignment of degrees, and thus points, to the jobs being evaluated. What is at stake here is equal pay and job comparability. Typical job evaluation processes allow for input from the job incumbent, the supervisor and job analysts; the purpose is to minimise the likelihood of potential bias, and to ensure the system is implemented as objectively and consistently as possible.

The **Hay Guide Chart Method**, also known as the 'Hay System' or the 'Hay Plan', is probably the best known point factor method in Australia. In Australia it is used extensively for evaluating administrative, professional, supervisory, managerial and executive positions across such diverse private and public sector organisations as Alcoa, Australian Defence Force, BHP, Colonial, Curtin University, Hoechst, National

Australia Bank, NRMA, Pizza Hut, Shell, Southcorp and Telstra. The system is based on three factors (Know-How, Problem Solving and Accountability) assumed to be the most important aspects of professional and managerial work (see Table 10.3). Although the Hay System is said to use three factors, there are eight in reality: Know-How is the sum of three distinct sub-factors (Specialised or Technical Knowledge, Management Breadth and Human Relations Skill); Problem Solving is the sum of two sub-factors (Thinking Challenge and Thinking Environment); and Accountability is the result of scores on three further sub-factors (Accountability, Freedom to Act and Impact). However, only the three major factors are assigned point values for the purpose of scoring a job.

Table 10.3 HAY guide chart factors

KNOW HOW	PROBLEM SOLVING	ACCOUNTABILITY
The sum total of all knowledge and skills, however acquired, needed for satisfactory job performance. Know-how has three dimensions: • The amount of practical, specialised or technical knowledge required • Breadth of management or the ability to make many activities and functions work well together, (the job of company president, for example, has greater breadth than that of a department supervisor) • Requirement for human relations skills in managing people. Using a chart, a number can be assigned to the level of know-how needed in a job. This number—or point value—indicates the relative value of know-how required by the job being evaluated.	The amount or original self-starting thought required by the job for analysis, evaluation, creation, reasoning and arriving at conclusions. Problem solving has two dimensions: • The degree of freedom with which the thinking processes is used to achieve job objectives without the guidance of standards, precedents, or direction from others • The thinking challenge involved requiring complexity, abstractness, or originality of thought. Problem solving is expressed as a percentage of know-how for the obvious reason that people think with what they know. The percentage judged to be correct for a job is applied to the know-how point value; the result is the point value given to problem solving.	The contribution made by the job on company objectives. Accountability has three dimensions: • Freedom to act, or relative presence of personal or procedural control and guidance, determined by answering the question, 'How much freedom has the job holder to act independently?' For example, a plant manager has more freedom than a supervisor under his or her control. • Dollar magnitude, a measure of the sales, budget value-added, or any other significant annual dollar figure related to the job. Impact of the job on dollar magnitude; a determination of whether the job has a primary impact on end results or has a sharing, contributory, or remote effect. Accountability is given a point value independent of the other two factors.

The total evaluation of any job is arrived at by adding the points (not shown here) for know-how, problem solving and accountability.

Source: The Hay Group 1993, pp. 11–12

Factor comparison

The point factor method, regardless of the number of factors and degrees of each factor, derives a point total for each job. Several very different types of job can have the same total points. After the total is determined, jobs are priced, often according to groups or classes similar to the job classification method. The factor comparison method avoids this step between point totalling and pricing by assigning dollar values to factors and comparing the amounts directly to the pay for benchmark jobs. Factor comparison is similar to point rating in that both use compensable factors: where they differ is that the point factor method uses the job size (i.e. total points score) to measure jobs and establish their relative value, whereas factor comparison uses benchmark jobs and money values on individual factors.

The 'price' or wage rates for the benchmark jobs are determined with reference to general labour market rates of pay. Although this is a quick and convenient method for setting wage rates, it has the potential to perpetuate existing pay differentials between jobs. Furthermore, this approach is also open to potential wage discrimination because the process of determining the wage rates of other jobs is itself somewhat subjective, and highly dependent on the skills of the respective wage and salary analyst. As such it has come under attack from job comparability advocates for claims of pay discrimination.

Skill-based evaluation

Whereas the job evaluation plans described previously 'pay for the job', **skill-based evaluation** is derived from the notion of 'paying for the person'. As such, this type of evaluation, also called 'pay for knowledge', is concerned with employee skills and in developing training programs to facilitate skill acquisition.

O'Neill & Lander (1993) provide a comprehensive overview of the different approaches to skill-based pay plans, of which skill-based evaluation is one. A typical skill-based evaluation plan might have all new employees on a single starting rate. As they acquire specific, job-related skills employees are advanced through the pay grade. Skills may be related to breadth of job knowledge (e.g. a factory worker who learns how to operate a variety of equipment); or the skills might be related to depth of knowledge (a plant operator who can work the equipment as well as strip it down for routine maintenance). Some systems combine both breadth and depth of skills as a means of promoting a highly skilled and flexible workforce. The design of the skill-based evaluation plan may allow for skills to be learned in any order, or it might prescribe a specific sequence to be followed. In a factory environment it is sometimes the case that members of the employee's work team ensure that the skills are learned proficiently. Alternatively, the training department may have the role of assessing and accrediting the employee's skill level. Employees reach the top pay grade after learning all jobs in the plant. While there are clear differences in the work requirements of a factory operator and a professional employee or manager, skill-based evaluation plans can be tailored to a wide range of employees.

The idea of paying for the person, or at least the person–job combination rather than just for the job, is not new. Many professional organisations such as legal, accounting and management consulting firms, engineering companies and research laboratories have been doing this for a long time. Skill-based evaluation plans for professional employees are often referred to as 'career ladders' and recognise that the more skilled and experienced an employee is, the greater their individual worth and value to the organisation. Career ladders also offer professional employees continued pay progression within their specialist field, rather than having to seek a broader management role.

Table 10.4 Comparison of skill-based pay components with conventional job evaluation

COMPONENT	SKILL-BASED EVALUATION
1 Determination of job worth	Tied to evaluation of skill blocks
2 Pricing	Difficult because the overall pay system is tied to the market
3 Pay ranges	Extremely broad; one pay range of entire cluster of skills
4 Evaluation of performance	Competency tests
5 Salary increases	Tied to skill acquisition as measured by competency testing
6 Role of training	Essential to attain job flexibility and pay increases for all employees
7 Advancement opportunities	Greater opportunities; anyone who passes competency test advances
8 Effect of job change	Pay remains constant unless skill proficiency increases
9 Pay administration	Difficult because many aspects of pay-plan (training, certification) demand attention

Source: Based on Ledford 1990, pp. 11–23 & Those & Tosi 1986

An increasing number of companies are exploring skill-based pay plans as an alternative to traditional job-based pay. Skill-based evaluation is compared with traditional job evaluation methods in Table 10.4. A survey of US firms conducted by Gupta, Ledford, Jenkins & Doty (1992) indicates that the results for companies that have taken this approach are promising in terms of advantages to both the organisation (more flexibility in meeting bottlenecks, highly skilled workforce) and to employees (greater opportunities for pay growth, more varied work opportunities, more effective communication).

Choosing a job evaluation method

Job evaluation methods differ in several respects. Some methods evaluate the whole job while others evaluate jobs using compensable factors. Job evaluation approaches also vary in the type of output produced. For example, the factor comparison method expresses the relativities between jobs directly in dollar values; the point factor system requires a conversion of job points to dollars. An organisation's choice of method depends on several factors.

1 **Legal requirements**—clearly, the method must comply with the law; this is particularly so with regard to issues of discrimination in the workplace.
2 **Organisation structure**—in small firms, simple systems such as ranking may be appropriate. However, in larger and more diverse companies, plans are likely to be more complex.
3 **Management style**—management styles vary from autocratic to democratic. Management style will primarily affect the scope of employee participation in the design and implementation of the system.
4 **Employee relations**—the job evaluation system is only likely to succeed if it is accepted by employees. Indeed, the results of many a job evaluation program have

been totally rejected because of union opposition. To prevent this happening, many organisations make the job evaluation process a joint union–company exercise.
5. **Cost in time and money**—job evaluation, as with many other important HR activities, costs time and money. There is the cost of designing a tailor-made plan, or the fees involved in using a proprietary system. As a rule of thumb, installing a full job evaluation plan for a firm with 500 or more employees will take up to six months.

Establishing the pay structure

Once job evaluations are finalised, and before salaries are determined, job classes or job families are created. This means grouping together all jobs of similar size; for example, grouping all clerical/administrative or all managerial roles together. The jobs within the same class may be quite different, but they should be of comparable worth to the organisation.

Why group jobs into classes? One reason is that each job class will eventually have a salary range attached to it; this makes for ease and efficiency in managing and administering salaries. Also it can be hard to justify the small differences in pay that might exist between jobs if job classes are not created. Finally, small errors that occur in evaluating jobs can be overcome by grouping jobs of approximately the same size into a single pay range. Of course, employees can also find fault with the classification results if their jobs are grouped with others they feel are smaller in size. Sometimes the jobs that are grouped together are too dissimilar. This may occur because there are too few job classes being used for the total number of jobs. Using only a few classes is appropriate, however, if many of the jobs in the organisation are of similar value. It is when there is a wide range of job values that too few classes may lead to employee complaints of perceived inequity.

Determining pay rates

Having established the job classes, wage rates or ranges need to be determined for each class. Although job classes are determined for the purpose of establishing wage rates, job classes are often based on wage rates already established (often through awards or enterprise agreements). Apart from industrially determined pay rates, organisations are already paying their employees, and need to determine job classes only when there is an influx of many new jobs, or if the organisation is introducing a formal job analysis program for the first time. In such cases there is a need to group jobs for salary administration purposes.

Surveys are an important component of determining a wide range of reward issues. They are used to develop remuneration levels for jobs, overall pay structures and even benefit plans that include both direct and indirect rewards. Whereas job evaluation helps ensure internal equity, wage surveys provide information to help ensure **external equity**, that is parity with general market practices. Internal and external equity are both important if an organisation is to be successful in attracting, retaining and motivating its employees. In addition, survey results can also be used to indicate the different reward philosophies and practices of competing organisations. For example, a company may adopt a policy of paying 10 per cent above the average market rate (the average of all rates for essentially the same job in an area), it may choose to pay exactly the average of the market rate, or indeed it may decide to pay below the market average.

Most organisations use wage and salary surveys extensively. Specialist consulting firms publish a wide range of market surveys. These include specialist occupational groupings (e.g. accountants, sales and marketing senior executives) and industry data (e.g. banking and finance, manufacturing, pharmaceutical, information technology). As a result of the data available, larger organisations subscribe to a wide range of commercially available surveys data. Separate surveys are conducted not only because there are such wide differences in skill level (and therefore pay rates), but also because labour markets are so different. An organisation surveying clerical workers may need only to survey companies within a 10 kilometre radius, whereas a survey of managerial salaries may cover the entire country.

Once the survey data is collected wage and salary analysts must decide how it is going to be used. For example, will the organisation set its own rates based on the survey averages, or should the data be 'weighted' by comparative size of participating companies (e.g. number of employees, asset value, sales turnover)? Remuneration data from surveys can be analysed by a variety of mathematical processes ranging from simple descriptive statistics (e.g. histograms, graphs and scattergrams) through to more sophisticated analyses (e.g. sample variance, standard deviations, least squares and multiple regression). The wage and salary analysts must also decide whether to use wage and salary ranges from all participating companies to determine the firm's own wage and salary ranges, or whether a sub-set of the participants is more appropriate. A sub-set of the data may provide a more specific comparison of companies of similar size, in the same industry, or in the same geographic area. After deciding upon the wage and salary information to be used, the next step is to develop a pay grade structure with wage and salary rates for the various job classes.

Pay grade structure

A typical example of a grade structure is shown in Figure 10.4. This is based on job evaluation points derived from a point factor method of evaluation. The boxes shown are pay grades determined on the basis of job evaluation points (the job class) and a range of pay. In essence, these pay grades are the job families or classes described previously. Consequently, there may be several different jobs within one box, but they are of similar job size. The boxes vary in shape but generally increase from left to right. This reflects increased job size, and consequently higher pay levels as shown on the vertical axis, for more valued jobs. The pay levels are established from the survey data to help ensure parity with the market information (i.e. external equity).

The wage rate for each job is then determined by locating its grade (based on the job size), and then moving across to the vertical axis, as illustrated by Job A in Grade II. The structure provides a minimum and a maximum pay level for each pay grade. Staying within this salary range is essential to maintain internal equity. This of course assumes that the job evaluation process has been accurate in locating the job within its respective grade. For employees to obtain a significant salary increase they must move into a job in a higher grade. However, employees may also receive pay raises within a given grade, thus moving them further up the available pay range. Generally, each job has its specific pay range as shown in Figure 10.4. For example, the range for Job A is from $150 to $300 per week, with a midpoint of $225. These aspects of the salary range are important for salary administration purposes. Many organisations prefer the average salary of employees in a job to equal the midpoint of the range. If the average salary is higher than the midpoint it suggests that a number of employees may no longer be able to receive meaningful salary increases unless they are promoted to a higher pay grade.

Occasionally jobs fall outside the established pay grades (see Jobs B and C in Figure 10.4). When a job falls below the minimum of the pay grade, it is noted and, at the

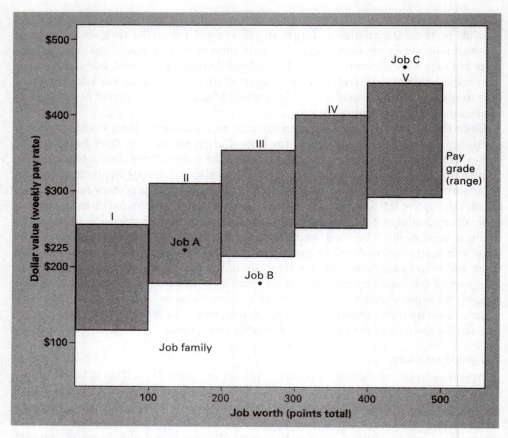

Figure 10.4 Establishing a grade structure based on job evaluation

Source: Schuler et al. 1992, p. 270

regular pay review period, suitable adjustment is made to bring it within the grade. Conversely, a job may be overpaid relative to its grade (see Job C in pay Grade V). One means of dealing with this is often called 'red circling' the job. That is the pay rate is unchanged for as long as the current incumbent remains in the job—in fact, the employee may even receive the normal increases that other employees receive. However, when the incumbent leaves the job, the rate is adjusted downwards to into the established pay range. Sometimes the entire salary structure has to be adjusted upward to bring jobs within established pay grades, thereby moving the midpoints up for all pay grades: this is most likely to occur when an organisation has not been monitoring market rates effectively, and is beginning to lose employees to other firms.

Initially an employee is likely to start at the bottom of the range and progress through the range over time. The rate at which an employee's wages rise depends on factors related to individual wage determination.

Individual wage determination

Once the wage structure has been determined, the question arises as to how much to pay each individual. For example, consider Anne and John, both of whom work in different, but similar sized, jobs for the same company. Their pay grade range is from

$1500 to $2000 per month; Anne is paid $2000 and John $1750. What might account for this pay differential? Performance contribution is perhaps the logical answer; however, seniority, skill shortages and market demand, age, and experience will also influence individual wages. Age and seniority are frequently critical determinants of individual wage determination in some Asian cultures such as Japan and South Korea, but less likely to be so in Western societies such as Australia, USA and the UK.

In practice, individual wage determinations combine personal contributions and performance. Thus, age and seniority, as well as performance, may influence Anne and John's pay. However, remuneration specialists argue that pay differences based on performance and contribution are more equitable than those based on personal attributes such as age and seniority (e.g. Lawler 1990; Schuster & Zingheim 1992).

But if performance is the criterion, is it past, current, or future performance? Many employees are given a pay raise on the basis of their performance potential. There are several difficulties in pay based on past performance. One is the employees' perceptions of their own performance. Anne and John, like many people, are likely to rate themselves in the top 50 per cent in terms of performance. Both are likely to believe that they performed reasonably well. Using performance as the sole explanation for the pay differential may therefore upset John—unless he recognises and accepts that he has a significantly lower level of performance than Anne. More issues related to paying for performance are discussed in the following section.

The answer to the question of how much to pay Anne and John can be as varied as the number of people answering the question. Remuneration managers need to ask such questions as: 'What does the rest of the reward program look like?', 'What was the initial understanding, or contract, with Anne and John?', and 'Can I defend my decisions?' Overall, defensibility and consistency are perhaps the two most important aspects of reward management. Some employees will always be dissatisfied with their performance rating, regardless of the method used or the decision reached. Being able to defend the decision by demonstrating consistency in the treatment of other employees goes a long way toward maintaining credibility and trust in the system.

Building a link with performance

The trend to relating rewards in general—and pay in particular—to individual and organisation performance is a prominent feature of remuneration in most Western economies. Influential texts such as Lawler's (1990) *Strategic Pay* and Schuster & Zingheim's (1992) *New Pay*, together with Kanter's (1989) references to contribution-based pay, all share a common theme: traditional approaches to the way that we plan and implement reward systems are not consistent with the need to more closely align the interests and financial well-being of employees with those of owners and shareholders. A consistent message coming from these writers is the need to strengthen and expand the linkages between an organisation's performance, individual and work group contribution to that performance, and the distribution of available rewards.

In general, there are four outcomes sought from developing and implementing performance-based reward structures:

1. Provide a clear focus and direction for employees
2. Ensure that high performing employees are recognised for their contributions
3. Provide processes for employees to identify with, and share in, the success of the enterprise, and
4. Control the fixed remuneration costs by having variable payments related to performance.

Building a direct link between the reward structure and performance is probably the most topical area of reward planning and management for Australian organisations in the 1990s. Private sector organisations have used performance-based pay for their executives, managers and salaried employees for some time. More recently, there have been significant examples in a variety of state government departments and federal and state government-owned enterprises where performance contracts and performance-related pay structures have been introduced for senior executives and managers.

HRM IN THE NEWS

Assessing & rewarding achievements in TQM: linking TQM, performance & pay

The roles of performance appraisal and individuals' incentives remain one of the most controversial issues in the Total Quality Management (TQM) movement. Followers of the Deming philosophy are often vehemently opposed to traditional notions of performance appraisal and merit pay in total quality environments. Others argue that there is a natural and important link between quality, employee performance and pay.

Deming and others have described several conflicts between TQM and traditional performance appraisal systems. The key criticisms are outlined below.

Performance appraisal systems focus on employee effect rather than work systems and processes. Performance appraisal assumes that the person begin evaluated is primarily responsible for the results. This ignores a basic tenet of the TQM movement—the system or process determines performance and is the source of variance. Any attempt to measure individual performance based on the output of the system is unfair.

Individual performance appraisal undermines teamwork. Traditional performance appraisal systems focus on the individual's personal performance as evaluated by the supervisor. Teamwork is actively undermined when employee performance appraisal is combined with individual rewards.

Performance appraisal overlooks continuous improvement. Appraisal systems establish goals and objectives as performance standards for employees to achieve. This has three disadvantages. First, there is little incentive to exceed the set standard. Second, the importance of continuous improvement is reduced (or even neglected) when the focus is on setting absolute standards. Third, when pay is linked to goal achievement, the incentive is to keep the goal as low as possible. Deming's argument is that performance should be analysed to learn how it an be improved—not for the purpose of comparing it to standards or goals.

Performance appraisal has a short-term focus. Appraisal systems involving individual objectives place the primary emphasis on short-term (e.g. quarterly, half-yearly or annual) performance issues. This encourages employees to focus on short-term achievements at the expense of longer-term success.

Appraisal systems blame the individual. Employee performance is often on factors outside their control. Most people are dependent on co-workers, equipment, operating policies and procedures and a range of other factors that can adversely affect performance. By concentrating on the individual, there is a tendency to overlook the impact of these other factors.

Successful TQM processes don't just happen. They require a significant shift in the management style of most organisations. In particular, three things need to be emphasised.

1. **Customer satisfaction must become a business strategy.** The challenge is for organisations to strike the appropriate balance between the financial performance indicators and the customer service components of the business strategy.
2. **Develop employee commitment.** Having employees 'on-side' is one thing, building a collaborative, highly participate organisation with an emphasis on employee commitment—rather than employer control—is a qualitatively different thing. Commitment requires a shared vision of the future, delegated decision making and responsibility combined with a timely, accurate and constructive two-way performance feedback process.
3. **Management processes must support customer satisfaction and employee commitment.** Deming's argument is that traditional approaches to performance measurement and performance rewards are wrong. The question here is how to design performance management and reward mechanisms that support TQM strategies.

Table 1 Overcoming traditional criticisms of performance appraisal and merit pay

CRITICISMS OF TRADITIONAL APPROACHES	PERFORMANCE MANAGEMENT RESPONSES	PERFORMANCE REWARD RESPONSES
Focuses on people rather than systems & processes	Plan and manage the bridge between performance of the system and processes and the the team and individuals.	Determine systems and process baseline (e.g. scrap, customer complaints, response time) and reward for improvement in baseline measures.
Undermines teamwork	Focus on individual's contribution to the team and its goals.	Relate rewards closely to team performance. Reward individuals for contribution to team performance.
Overlooks continuous improvement	Manage through goal-setting *not* goal achievement.	Ensure reward structures emphasise and pay for continuous improvement.
focus	Define goals in terms of corporate mission, business strategy and customer service criteria.	Design reward systems that pay on corporate mission, business strategy and customer service criteria.
Blames the individual	Assess team performance. Allow multi-assessment by customer, team and individual self-ratings.	Relate base pay to skill differences. Use group incentives based on quality achievements to predetermined formula performance.

Performance management & reward in high commitment organisations

Recent research suggests that many organisations involved in TQM also have an effective link between managing and paying for performance. Successfully dealing with these issues in a work environment and climate where employees have an active commitment to a common set of values and goals. These high involvement organisations will always expect to outperform their competitors because their entire resources are focused on the same, shared outcome. However, building a successful, high commitment organisation requires more than the effective communication of corporate vision, values and business objectives. Management processes—such as goal setting, performance management and reward mechanisms—need to be in place to support the high commitment approach.

Table 1 summaries some typical approaches taken by high commitment organisations to support their TQM initiatives and overcome the weaknesses of traditional performance appraisal and merit pay.

Table 2 Comparison of traditional & high involvement/TQM performance management processes

	TRADITIONAL PERFORMANCE APPRAISAL	HI INVOLVEMENT/TQM PERFORMANCE MANAGEMENT
Who appraises and plans performance levels?	Supervisor/manager	Individual, supervisor, co-workers, team, internal & external customers
Who performance is planned and appraised	Individual employee	Individual, supervisor, work team, work systems & processes
What is the basis for setting performance standards	Individual job goals & standards set for employee	Performance levels set for work team and defined on on the basis of business mission/objectives, customers, & nature of work process & systems
What is the process for planning & managing employee performance?	Focus on review of individual's past performance	Focus is on review of past, planning ahead & ensuring resources required are provided
	Supervisor-directed and one-way	Mutual review encouraging two-way feedback
	Minimum training—where provided is aimed at supervisor	Training provided to all participants
	Done annually & administratively driven	Periodic, as-needed and on natural performance cycles
Why is the performance management process undertaken?	Personal development, identify training needs, succession planning & pay	Personal development, identify training needs, succession planning & pay
		Provide feedback to the team to help identify & correct structural problems in work process & systems that lead to variance in output
		Provide feedback to the individual on contribution to team

TQM, pay & employee involvement

Deming's concern with merit pay is consistent with the questioning of traditional merit pay systems by a range of writers and practitioners. The traditional approach provides an annual salary increase, the amount of which is dependent of the employee's performance appraisal. The employee is then paid that amount in perpetuity, regardless of performance in future years. This is not particularly a TQM issue but Deming's criticism is a timely addition to the voices demanding a review of these traditional merit pay practices.

For high commitment organisations the reward system is a critical element in creating a clear line-of-sight between employees and TQM goals and strategies. These organisations have high expectations of their reward systems: not only must each component be cost-effective, but it must send the right messages to employees and work teams about the organisation's priorities and performance expectations.

One approach to linking pay and quality, and still provide employees the opportunity to increase their level of pay, is through skill-based pay systems. Each organisation can define the skills it requires to reach its objectives. The employee's contribution and value is directly related to his or her proven acquisition and performance of these skills. Thus, paying people to acquire skill required in the business—including specific customer services and quality skills—ensures that individual pay progression is linked to increased resources (i.e. skills) available to the enterprise.

Another approach to linking pay and quality is through the use of specifically designed variable pay or incentive systems. Incentive systems have two significant advantages. First, the TQM emphasis on team or group performance provides a simple and logical basis for an incentive pay system. Second, the payout to employees is a one-off payment made on the basis of results achieved; it is not folded back into pay to become a perpetual annuity. Incentive payments can be linked to almost any measure of organisation, workteam or individual performance.

For example, an incentive plan could be designed solely around improvement in outcome measures such as defects, scrap or other measurable process improvement. Alternatively, the design might combine outcome criteria with some other measure (e.g. customer satisfaction or reduced cycle time).

The TQM emphasis on employee involvement is a strong argument for providing direct input from employees in the program design. Their input is often essential for credibility and testing. While management will typically retain authority over the final plan design, especially where there are cost implications, genuine employee involvement is necessary for final acceptance. It is also consistent with TQM principles that those affected by the system have a dominant say in its design.

TQM requires that an organisation forms a partnership with its customers and suppliers. The basis of this relationship is financial benefit to all the parties. It is unlikely that such a partnership can be successful unless there is a prior partnership between the organisation and its employees. This relationship is similarly built on financial benefit—payment for skills and performance. Making this clear and defined link between pay and TQM is consistent with the objectives of the overall quality movement.

Source: The Wyatt Company 1993.

The 'HRM in the news' article highlights several important aspects of linking performance and pay, especially in a team-based work environment. First, there must be some means of measuring and evaluating performance. But traditional performance management systems focus on the individual, not the team. Clearly, there is a need to tailor the performance measures to meet the demands of the work place. Second, the way in which incentives are tied to performance must be consistent with the business objectives and operating environment. Individual rewards in a team environment run a serious risk of presenting team members with conflicting messages, 'Do I maximise my individual reward, or work to boost team performance?' Finally, the article suggests that a well thought out performance-based pay plan can support employee involvement and commitment by providing employees with a financial stake in the organisation's achievements.

Performance-based pay systems

These are the processes by which performance is related to pay. The two most common ways of linking pay and performance are merit and incentive pay plans. **Merit pay plans** are generally dependent on individual performance assessments made by supervisors, usually on the basis of an overall rating of the past year's performance. **Incentive pay plans** are more likely to use a more direct measure of performance, such as productivity, volume, quality and profitability. Another aspect of some incentive pay plans is that a significant portion of individual pay may be derived from the incentive plan. This is true for salespeople on commission who may be dependent on the incentive plan for the majority of their earnings. Similarly, it is not unusual for management and executive bonus plans to provide 20–30 per cent of pay as a result of performance against business targets such as profit or return on shareholder funds. Because the overall level of remuneration with incentive and bonus plans varies directly with performance against the objectives, pay can vary greatly. On the other hand, merit pay plans affect a relatively small percentage of an individual's total salary because such pay is generally used to move an individual's wage or salary within the given range for the job, and this adjustment is made only once a year. Thus, merit pay plans are likely to represent only a small percentage increment in an employee's direct remuneration.

Future organisational forms

Reward systems are undergoing substantial change. This change is driven by competitive pressures that require rapid response to market changes, better management of costs, the introduction of new technologies, and the introduction of re-engineered work processes.

Current trends in Australian organisations suggest that future reward systems will have the following characteristics:

1. More emphasis on the company's capacity to pay, rather than annual adjustments based solely on market surveys
2. Increased recognition of the 'individual market value' component of specialist professionals and senior executives in salary planning
3. Greater incidence of job evaluation systems, that reflect the specific values, philosophy and needs of the individual organisation
4. More innovative approaches to designing pay structures specific to the work design (e.g. skill-based pay, team-based incentives)
5. A growing proportion of pay dependent on individual, work group and organisation performance at all levels
6. Increased facility to trade-off wage and salary increases to superannuation, extra leave, sabbaticals and study leave the like, and
7. Greater use of equity, in the form of shares and share options, particularly for managers and executives.

Although many people are rewarded by performance-based pay, merit pay plans are by far the most common in Australia. Consequently, much of the direct pay that employees receive is heavily reliant on the results of job evaluation and the steps in the pay ranges discussed previously. Nevertheless, it is frequently argued that effectively designed and implemented performance pay plans, especially incentive-based systems, can get employees to perform at high levels. This is why they are important in the design and management of the reward system.

There is an ongoing question with regard to the use of performance-based pay systems for clerical, administrative and service workers, particularly in the public sector. The key issue asked is, 'How can productivity in these occupations be effectively measured?' There are two ways of approaching this. First, from a traditional job analysis point of view, every job exists to achieve some outcome. It is relatively straightforward for the job analyst to define outcomes for a sales person (e.g. volume and value of sales, new accounts, bad debts), or in a manufacturing environment (volume and quality of production). The principle remains the same for clerical and service areas. A useful question for job analysts to ask of the position's supervisor is, 'What tells you if the job is being done extremely well, poorly, or if indeed the job is being done at all?'. In many instances the response to this question will focus on qualitative issues such as client satisfaction, service standards or quality of recommendations coming forward; other measures may be much more quantitative (e.g. accuracy or error rates, time schedules and overall service costs). Inevitably, there will be some outcomes expected of the role, and relative performance can be assessed against them.

A second approach recognises that in many roles the key performance indicators are to be found in the inputs the person brings to the role. Inputs refer to the knowledge, skills and other capacities that the person uses to perform the activities of the job. In essence, this approach says that if the requisite skills, competencies and behaviours are in place, then the necessary job outcomes will follow. This approach is increasingly being used to define development needs in professional roles (Hearn, Close, Smith & Southey 1996), as well as for differentiating pay based on the level of competence and skill acquired and demonstrated by the employee (Cofsky 1993; O'Neal 1995).

Merit pay plans

There are several basic building blocks necessary for developing a merit pay plan. These include the need to establish guidelines for determining the size of merit pay raises, the timing of when increases are given, and the relationship between the increments and the employees place in the salary range. During times of high inflation it is also particularly important that remuneration planners address the relationship between merit pay and cost-of-living adjustments.

Merit pay guidelines

Most medium to large private organisations have some type of merit plan. A typical plan is shown in Table 10.5 where annual pay increments are dependent on two things—the rating of individual employee performance, and the respective employee's current position in the salary range. Position in the range is determined by expressing the employee's current salary as a percentage of the midpoint salary for the range of salaries for that job; this is known as the **compa-ratio** for that individual. The lower the position in the range (the first quartile is the lowest), the larger the percentage of current salary given as the merit raise. The approach shown in Table 10.5 ensures that employees whose performance is rated highest, but who are currently low in the pay range for their jobs, will receive the largest percentage increase.

Table 10.5 Sample merit pay plan

PERFORMANCE RATING	CURRENT POSITION IN SALARY RANGE			
	FIRST QUARTILE	SECOND QUARTILE	THIRD QUARTILE	FOURTH QUARTILE
Outstanding	13–14% increase	11–12% increase	9–10% increase	6–8% increase
Above Average	11–12% increase	9–10% increase	7–8% increase	6 increase or less
Good	9–10% increase	7–8% increase	6% increase or less	delay increase
Satisfactory	6–8% increase	6% increase or less	delay increase	no increase
Unsatisfactory	No increase	No increase	No increase	No increase

An important aspect of administering the merit pay plan shown in Table 10.5 is monitoring the number of people in each quartile. Although the percentage of merit increases is greater in the lower quartiles, the dollar size of increases is likely to be larger in the higher quartiles. Consequently, the more people there are in the higher quartiles of the salary ranges, the larger the budget necessary for merit increases. Therefore, the remuneration manager must monitor the number of employees moving to the top of their respective pay ranges. This is one of the areas where the remuneration manager has the important role of auditing line managers' compliance with remuneration policies, especially in highly centralised corporations. This role is necessary for overall budget purposes, and to ensure equity for all employees in the implementation of remuneration policies. Employees who perform equally well in similar sized work roles will generally expect to be paid similar salaries and given approximately the same merit increases.

Incentive pay plans

In general, it is more likely that incentive plans will be used if labour costs are large, the market is cost-competitive and where clear performance targets can be set and monitored. These factors may influence whether or not incentive plans are used, as well as which type of plan is most suitable.

The objectives, and therefore design, of incentive plans vary widely. The easiest way to describe them is with reference to the level at which they are applied—individual, group or organisation. Each type of plan is generally unique to a specific level. Regardless of the level at which a plan is implemented, the intended beneficiaries are always the organisation and the individuals covered by it.

Individual-level incentive plans

These are plans that provide an incentive for individual employees to achieve, or exceed, some defined target level of performance (often referred to as target-based incentives).

Some plans are specific to 'blue-collar' work as typically found in a manufacturing environment, others plans are directed towards 'white-collar' work (e.g. sales incentives) or managerial roles. Examples of various plans are described below.

Piecework plan

Piecework is an incentive pay plan commonly used in manufacturing operations. Under this plan, employees are guaranteed a standard pay rate for each unit of output. The rate per unit is typically determined by time-and-motion studies and the current base pay for the job. For example, if the existing base pay is $20 per day, and the employee can produce 20 units a day at a normal rate, the piece rate may be established at $1 per unit. Thus the incentive pay rate is based on the standard output and the base wage rate as these are supposed to represent 100 per cent efficiency in the use of labour and plant. The final rate also reflects the bargaining power of the employees (or their unions), profitability of the enterprise, prevailing economic conditions, and general industry pay rates.

Standard hour plan

This is essentially a variation on the piecework plan. Under a standard hour plan, the required performance standards are defined in terms of manufacturing time per unit of output, rather than money per unit. Tasks are broken down by the amount of time it takes to complete them. This can be determined by historical records, time-and-motion studies, or a combination of both. The time to perform each task then becomes the 'standard time' for production with incentive payments related to a comparison of 'actual time' to standard times for a production period.

Measured day work

An individual-level incentive plan that removes some of the relationship between pay rates and work standards is measured day work. Again, formal production standards are established and employee performance is judged against them; but with measured day work, the typical standards are less precise. For example, standards may be determined by the results of a rating or ranking procedure (e.g. target daily production volume) rather than by an objective index such as standard time.

Sales incentive plans

The most usual incentive plans for salespeople is a sales commission. A sales commission plan works on the basis of returning some percentage of the volume of sales (measured either by sales volume or dollar value) to the salesperson. About half of Australian companies with field sales staff have some form of incentive plan in addition to fixed salary. Door-to-door sales people tend to have most of their remuneration based on a commission plan (sometimes as high as 80 per cent). In high technology areas such as computer hardware and telecommunications, the fixed component of pay is usually higher than that provided by the incentive plan. In the sales function, the ratio between fixed and variable pay is very much related to the nature of the sales process. For example, the variable component of pay (as a percentage of total pay) is higher in sales situations where the products are high volume and low unit cost, and where the sale is made to the end consumers. On the other hand, where products require significant technical expertise (including after-sales service), are high unit cost and low sales volume, and where the sales cycle may take considerable amounts of time and effort, the variable component is usually lower as a percentage (e.g. 70 per cent fixed to 30 per cent variable). This is typical of industrial plant and equipment, commercial telecommunications and some sophisticated computer hardware sales environments.

Executive and managerial incentive plans.

Bonus and incentive plans for executives and managers are generally related to the performance of their respective department, division or business unit, and the organisation as a whole. Table 10.6 shows the incidence and size of incentive payments received by various categories of Australian management as reported in a national survey in 1995.

Table 10.6 Incidence of variable pay in Australia, 1995

POSITION	FIXED PAY *	VARIABLE PAY **
CEO	75%	25%
Direct reports	82%	18%
Middle management	90%	10%
Professional and supervisory staff	95%	5%
Customer service/sales	97%	3%

* as an average % of total remuneration
** as an average % of total remuneration

Source: Towers Perrin 1995

At this level of the organisation, incentive payments may be in cash, company shares, share options, or some combination of the three. A share option is an opportunity for a manager to buy shares in the organisation at a later date, but at a price established when the option was granted. Granting shares and share options is based on two premises: first, that senior executives and managers can exert a direct effect on the performance of the company, and those parts of it under their control; and second, that they will work harder to increase the performance and profitability in their areas of responsibility (thus increasing the price of the company shares) if they are able to participate financially over the long term. If the market price of shares increases over time, managers can use their options to buy shares at the lower price, thus realising personal financial gain.

Most major corporations have special share schemes for their senior management group, and receipt of shares alone can result in a substantial financial gain. Examples of Australian companies operating executive and management share plans include: ANZ Bank, BHP, Coles-Myer, CSR, Pacific Dunlop, Mayne Nickless, National Australia Bank, North Broken Hill, James Hardie, David Jones, TNT, Lend Lease and Westpac.

Group incentive plans

As organisations become more complex, a growing number of jobs become interdependent. Some work roles are part of a sequence of operations: their capacity to perform well relies on the quality and timeliness of work that precedes their involvement; and conversely, the effectiveness of employees following them in the process is dependent on how well they have done themselves. Other jobs require joint efforts to achieve results (e.g. a mixed group of technical and professional specialists engaged on a major project). In either case, measurement of individual performance is at best difficult, and often impossible. Individual-level incentives are not appropriate under these conditions because they do not recognise the interdependencies and fail to reward co-operation (see the previous 'HRM in the news' article). Group-level incentives can do this at the work team, department or organisation level. Thus individual-level incentive plans may become less common as changing technologies and work structures make jobs even more interdependent and individual performance more difficult to measure and evaluate.

Although both individual-level and group-level incentive plans attempt to tie pay to performance, by giving employees incentives for an increase in output or profit or a decrease in costs, they differ significantly. The most obvious difference is that individual incentives are based on the sole performance of the respective employee. More importantly, group incentives are usually related directly to current results compared with some historic baseline, whether it be production volume, quality, cost or profit. Group incentives based on accounting period profit comparisons are referred to as profit-sharing plans. These are usually paid out in cash, but in some instances may be distributed wholly or partially in shares.

Group-level incentive systems should have an objective measure of performance if they are to effectively influence employee behaviour and motivate performance. Employees must believe that they can affect the performance measure by their work output. The plan must also be perceived as rewarding co-operation among all participating employees. This requires the organisation to have a culture and core values congruent with employee co-operation. The results can be highly favourable to the company and its employees when genuine conditions of open communication and employee participation exist.

One particular approach to group-based incentives that is highly effective when these aspects of management philosophy and values are in place is known as **gainsharing**. Gainsharing originated in the USA but has been used by many Australian manufacturing firms (see Carey (1993) for a detailed description of gainsharing and its general application in Australian industry; and Carey (1995) for a case study based on an Australian metal manufacturer). Two popular gainsharing plans using cost-savings comparisons are the Scanlon Plan and the Rucker Plan.

The Scanlon Plan

The Scanlon Plan is named after Joe Scanlon, a US union official who proposed his original plan to save a metal manufacturing company, for which he was a union representative, from closure. His approach represents as much a philosophy of management–employee relations as it does a company-wide incentive system. It emphasises employer–employee participation and sharing in the operational decision making and profitability of the company. Scanlon Plans are adaptable to a wide variety of manufacturing style companies and are used extensively in union and non-union plants in the US.

The Scanlon Plan reflects the fact that efficiency of operations depends on company-wide co-operation, and that bonuses derived from cost savings encourage this co-operation. The bonus is determined on the basis of savings in labour costs measured by comparing the payroll to the sales value of production on a monthly or bimonthly basis. Previous months' ratios of payroll-to-sales value of production help establish expected labour costs. Savings in such costs are then shared between employees and the company (a common ratio is in the order of 75 per cent to employees and 25 per cent to employers). The employees' share is paid into a bonus pool: a large proportion of the bonus pool is distributed to workers immediately (usually 70–80 per cent) and the balance kept as a 'bonus bank' to cover poor months, and limit wide variations in employee pay. Any excess in the 'bonus bank' at the end of the year is distributed to employees prior to the start of the next plan year.

Each individual employee's bonus is determined by converting the bonus pool to a percentage of total payroll and applying this percentage to the employee's pay for the month. All employees share in equal proportion in the bonus pool (i.e. percentage of his or her pay); thus, no one group can gain at the expense of another.

Although Scanlon Plans can be successful, their real incentive value may be short-lived. This can occur if employees feel they cannot improve upon previous months' payroll-to-sales-value-of-production ratios. At this point, performance levels off and the Scanlon Plan loses its incentive value. This effect is greatly minimised where work methods and products are always changing. Under these conditions employees are more likely to feel they can always find better ways to improve their work methods and find savings.

The Rucker Plan

The Rucker Plan is similar to the Scanlon Plan in operation and distribution of the bonus pool, although the basis for determining the size of incentives is more complex. Here a ratio is calculated that determines the value of production required for each dollar of the total payroll costs. For example:

- Assume accounting records show that it costs the company $0.60 worth of raw materials (including power) to produce $1.00 worth of product. The value added is $0.40 for each $1.00 of sales value. Assume also that records show that 45 per cent of the value added is attributable to labour; then a productivity ration (PR) can be allocated from the formula:

    PR x 45 per cent = 1.00. Solving yields PR = 2.22.

- If the wage bill is $100 000, the *expected* production value is the wage bill

    ($100 000) x PR (2.22) = $222 222 22.

- If *actual* production value equals $280 000, then the savings (actual production value—expected production value) equals $57 777 78.
- Since the labour contribution to value added is 45 per cent, the bonus to the workforce should be 0.45 x $57 777 78 = $26 000.

Profit-sharing plans

In contrast to gainsharing, profit-sharing plans are based on period to period profit comparisons. The amount distributed to employees may be a percentage of absolute profit, or it may be a percentage of the increase in profit from the previous period, or from some baseline standard. As a result, these plans are easier to communicate and administer than gainsharing. Employee involvement is not a necessary aspect of profit-sharing plans, and payment may be made to employees irrespective of their individual performance. On the other hand, an employee may perform very well and still not receive a bonus payment because the firm is not profitable.

Some companies in Australian that have had profit sharing plans in place for some time include:

- WL Allen Foundry Company Pty Ltd
- Dynavac Pty Ltd
- Fletcher Jones and Staff Pty Ltd
- Lend Lease Corporation Ltd
- The Lincoln Electric Company (Australia) Pty Ltd
- Siddons Industries
- Thomson and Scougall
- Walter Reid and Co Ltd
- Weston Hart Ltd (SW Hart & Co Pty Ltd).

Planning & management issues in performance-based pay

There are three common issues related to the planning and management of performance-based pay systems. One is the identification of potential obstacles that may limit the plan's effectiveness; the second has to do with the need to audit the company's merit pay system; and finally, the issue of determining who should participate in the plan.

Obstacles to performance pay effectiveness

Potential obstacles in the design and implementation of performance-based pay plans can be grouped into three general categories: (1) difficulties in specifying and measuring job performance, (2) the need to carefully consider the available rewards that will be valued by plan participants (where monetary rewards may be just one of a range of possible rewards), and (3) methods for linking rewards to job performance.

Prerequisites for rewarding job performance include specification of the required job outcomes (what will be measured?); accurate measurement of job performance (how will it be measured?); and what is to be the relationships between levels of job performance and rewards (how will it be paid for?). This aspect of plan design may be difficult because of the often multidimensional and changing nature of work, technological developments, lack of supervisory training, and the manager's value system ('Why pay people an incentive for doing the job they're paid to do?'). These are presented in more detail in Table 10.7, together with the implications for plan design.

The second issue relates to choosing the appropriate reward structure; this highlights the importance and value of using rewards other than pay to recognise desired behaviours. In certain circumstances non-monetary rewards may have more motivational value than pay. This is a common issue where pay increments for employees may be largely consumed by increased taxation. Other employees may prefer extra leisure time, opportunities for further study at company expense, or to be rewarded in kind (e.g. fully paid travel). Consequently, it is important for the plan designers to understand the needs of participants and to learn which rewards are most likely to be most valued by employees. Clearly, this needs to result in a system that is administratively simple and easy for participants to understand. The implications for plan deign are shown in Table 10.7.

Table 10.7 Obstacles in the design of effective reward systems and their implications for management

OBSTACLES	CAUSES	IMPLICATIONS FOR MANAGEMENT
A Difficulties in specifying and measuring performance.	1 Changes in the nature of work: • Increase in service oriented jobs • Increase in white-collar, managerial and professional jobs • Increases in the interdependencies and complexity of work. 2 Multidimensional nature of work: • Single item measures of performance are often inadequate • In many jobs today, multiple criteria are necessary to assess performance. 3 Technological developments: • Technological developments often result in new and untested methods of work • Machine paced jobs permit little variation in performance. 4 Lack of supervisory training: • Use of untrained, inexperienced supervisors in the evaluation process • Perceptual biases. 5 The manager's value system: • Lack of interest or in inability to differentiate among high and low performers • Failure to see long-range outcomes of differential rewarding.	1 Develop techniques for specifying desirable behaviours and clarifying the objectives of the organisation 2 Use evaluation procedures which recognise the multi-dimensional nature of performance 3 Develop a valid and reliable performance appraisal system based on results and/or behavioural standards 4 Train supervisors to use the PA system appropriately and to understand potential sources or bias 5 Clearly define long-term consequences of performance-contingent and non-contingent reward practices.
B Problems in identifying valued rewards.	1 Choice of rewards • Choosing a reward that is not reinforcing. 2 Utilising rewards of size or magnitude: • Lack or resources • Company policy. 3 Poor timing of rewards • Size of organisation, bureaucracy • Standardisation/formalisation of feedback mechanisms • Complexity of feedback systems.	1 Make managers award of the effects of rewards on employee performance and satisfaction 2 Train managers to identify rewards for their subordinates 3 Administer rewards of sufficient magnitude 4 Administer rewards as quickly after desirable responses as possible.

C Difficulties in linking rewards to performance.	1 Failure to create appropriate contingencies between rewards and performance • Lack of knowledge, skill, experience • Belief system • Difficulty of administration. 2 Creating inappropriate contingencies: • Rewarding behaviour which does not increase performance • Rewarding behaviour A, but hoping for B. 3 Nullifying intended contingencies: • Using improper PA instrument • Improper use of PA instrument • Failure to use information obtained • Inconsistently applied. 4 Employee opposition: • Individually: mistrust, lack of fairness, inequity • Socially: restrictions due to fear of loss of work • Outside intervention: union.	1 Make managers award of the effects of rewards on employee performance and satisfaction 2 Train managers to identify rewards for their subordinates. 3 Administer rewards of sufficient magnitude 4 Obtain employee participation in the design and administration of the pay plan.

Source: Podsakoff, Greene & McFillen 1987

The third set of obstacles refers to linking rewards to job performance. The major issues here include creating inappropriate relationships between pay and performance; using an unreliable or inaccurate performance measure; and dealing with an existing or potential lack of employee credibility in the performance–pay relationship. Employee opposition is often a major obstacle to successfully implementing performance based pay, especially incentive plans. Plan designers therefore need to understand the work climate and employee attitudes towards performance-based pay. The following examples are typical of the initial attitudes that employees may have about the introduction of performance-based pay.

- rates are cut if earnings under the plan increase too much
- incentive plans encourage competition among workers and the discharge of slow workers
- employees don't get their fair share of increased productivity
- the plans are too complex
- performance standards are set at levels that are too hard to achieve
- incentive plans increase strain on workers and may impair their health
- earnings fluctuate, making it difficult to budget household expenditures and even to obtain home mortgages
- performance-pay plans are used to avoid a deserved pay increase
- incentive plans imply a lack of trust in workers by management.

The last belief, that incentive plans imply a lack of trust in workers by management, pervades most of the other beliefs as well. This lack of trust has immediate implications for the establishment of rates and standards that incentive systems are based on. Workers may plan elaborate charades for the benefit of time-study engineers doing work measurement, but these manoeuvres do not entirely fool engineers who know that workers may try to mislead them. Therefore they include estimates of potential slack in the system, combining scientific observation and measurement with a professional 'guesstimate'. The result may result in rates that reduce the incentive value of the system, the profitability of the company, or both. The implications for management in removing these causes of difficulties in linking rewards to job performance are also shown in Table 10.7.

Auditing the merit pay system

It is critical to the success of any merit pay system to administer it in a way that maintains its credibility and integrity with employees. This suggests that merit pay be administered consistently across employees, units or divisions within the company, and within the pay structure for all salary grades. That is, it is important for all employees to know that their merit raise is being determined in the same way regardless of the supervisor, and that the determination is based on a credible measure of job performance. Accuracy of the actual performance appraisals may be effectively addressed by a behavioural based performance appraisal method, such as the behaviourally anchored rating scale (BARS) or behavioural observation scale (BOS). Fair and consistent administration within the pay structure is done through the use of compa-ratios and performance ratios.

Compa-ratios and performance ratios, used together, can highlight pay and job performance relationships by individual employee, by salary grade, by level in the organisation or by department or division in the company. The compa-ratio is the measure of an individual's salary in relation to the midpoint of the range for a salary grade. This ratio is determined by expressing the individual salary as a percentage of the salary range midpoint. Thus, a ratio of 110 means that the individual is being paid 110 per cent of the range midpoint. Assuming a normal distribution of employee performance and experience, the average compa-ratio in any department or division should be close to 100. Ratios above or below 100 may suggest 'soft' or 'tough' appraisals respectively; alternatively, the causes may be related to inconsistencies in administration of the merit pay system.

Similar conclusions can be drawn from the use of performance ratios. These indicate where the performance rating of any employee stands relative to others, and is determined by expressing an individual employee's performance rating as a percentage of the midpoint of the performance rating range. Again, assuming normal performance distributions, the average performance ratio for a department or division should be close to 100. Variations from 100 may also be indicative of inconsistent performance evaluation processes.

Participation in performance-based pay plans

Employee participation can take place in the design and the administration stages of performance-based pay plans.

Design stage participation

Many pay plans are designed by management, or consultants commissioned by management, and installed with minimal (if any) employee consultation. However, there is a sound argument for employees to have more active involvement at all stages of the plan design and implementation. First, they are closest to the work and are highly likely to understand the key issues leading to performance variations. Research also indicates that people are more likely to accept and be committed to things that they have had a stake in designing. In this respect, employee participation in plan design helps to reduce the potential resistance that accompanies most organisation change processes. Consequently, the plan is more likely to succeed because employees will be more motivated to increase performance.

Administration participation

There is some evidence to suggest that employees can responsibly determine when and if other workers should receive pay increases. This was previously discussed in reference to skill-based pay plans where team members assess whether an employee has gained suitable competence in new skills. There is also some anecdotal evidence to suggest that some individuals are capable and effective in determining their *own* pay increases. Nevertheless, employee participation may not work in all cases, nor is it appropriate under all circumstances. Employee involvement in pay decisions may be appropriate in organisations with a strong commitment to employee participation, and with strong values in workplace democracy. It is unlikely to be accepted by managers in companies with a belief in strong centralised control systems.

Linking pay to performance: the great debate

The process of linking some portion of an employee's pay to his or her performance is based on the notion that this will lead to greater effort, and consequently productivity. But is there any evidence to prove this is the case? Certainly, the issue is debatable, and most recently Alfie Kohn (1993; 1992) has been a major spokesperson against the use of variable, performance-based pay plans. His essential position is that performance-based pay fails to achieve its intended objectives because of the inadequate psychological assumptions underlying such plans.

Kohn's criticisms fall under four key points. First, **extrinsic rewards** (i.e. rewards applied by one person to influence another's behaviour) do not alter the fundamental attitudes that underlie behaviour. Consequently, they bring temporary compliance rather than enduring change or commitment. According to Kohn, the evidence for this can be seen in the frequency with which incentive systems need to be revised as the targeted behaviour decreases over time. His second point is that incentive systems treat symptoms, not underlying causes. He argues that managers rely on incentive systems as substitutes for effective management behaviour such as appropriate job design, providing feedback to employees, and seeking opportunities for genuine involvement and participation. The third argument against performance-based pay is that it reduces risk-taking and reinforces a rigid focus on behaviour. By definition, performance-based pay systems specify the behaviours or outcomes required for the reward to be paid. This has the effect of detracting from the intrinsic value of work and limiting employee efforts to the goals and outcomes specified. As such, issues of quality, creativity and individually motivated improvement are jeopardised when employee behaviour is governed by contingent reward processes. Finally, according to Kohn's review of a variety of published studies, there is no consistent empirical evidence for a causal link between incentives and performance.

Does this mean that linking pay to performance has a limited—if any—effect on behaviour? In an article titled 'Linking Pay to Performance: Conflicting Views and

Conflicting Evidence', O'Neill (1995b) reviewed Kohn's case against incentive systems and questions his conceptual framework and the interpretation of the research evidence he cites. O'Neill argues that the only area where Kohn is on firm ground is his final point, that is the lack of empirical evidence to support the relationship between financial incentives and performance. The fact is that the available evidence regarding the link between pay and performance is equivocal. Researchers concerned with robust, scientific evidence regarding a causal link between incentives and employee behaviour refer to 'insufficient experience to support any strong judgements' (Blinder 1990, p. viii), and the 'generally disappointing and mixed results' (Gomez-Mejia & Balkin 1992).

A major review undertaken by Jenkins (1986) looked at twenty-eight laboratory experiments, experimental simulations and field experiments that met an extremely rigorous selection criteria. On the basis of his analysis of the collected data, Jenkins drew the following conclusions:

1. The results of linking pay to performance, in the studies reviewed, were generally positive
2. Knowledge of the impact of financial incentives on performance are largely confined to clerical and production tasks
3. It is reasonable to conclude that linking pay to performance can lead to an average 30 per cent improvement in performance under certain task and environmental parameters
4. Overall, there are too few empirically reliable studies for strong conclusions (either way) to be drawn, and
5. There is an absence of studies relating financial incentives and jobs that have a strong component of cognitive, problem solving and heuristic qualities (e.g. management positions).

The fact is that most of the available studies fall between professional magazine reports and quasi-empirical studies. It is an area that does not lend itself readily to experimental field studies with carefully designed control groups and neutralised environmental conditions. As a result, where empirical data is available, authors often reach opposite conclusions testing the same hypothesis, even when using identical data (see Gomez-Mejia & Balkin 1992, p. 177).

In his review, O'Neill suggests that human resource practitioners have a key role to play in the design of variable pay plans. He also suggests some minimal criteria for the design of performance-based pay plans. These design criteria include the following:

- **Funding**—performance-based reward systems ought to be self-funding.
- **Distribution**—the process for distribution of rewards must be consistent, equitable and defensible. Plans ought to minimise arbitrary discretion in favour of open, and clearly communicated, guidelines.
- **Financial analysis**—the draft plan should be tested with a financial impact analysis of anticipated results and costs under a variety of scenarios. This will give a clear indication of the likely costs to the business and pay-off to employees.
- **Integration**—plans must be designed to be consistent with the organisation structure, work design and other human resource processes (e.g. performance management).
- **Communication**—the implementation must be accompanied by full communication to all participating employees to ensure they understand the objectives, and potential rewards.
- **Evaluation**—each plan must incorporate a viable process for testing and evaluating the plan against its objectives.

4. Communication and administration of reward

In any organisation the management and administration of reward systems have the potential to be very visible and significant forms of employee communication. The amount that an employee is paid, how this amount is determined and delivered, the additional benefits provided during employment—and in the case of superannuation, post-employment—send clear signals about the human resource values, goals and priorities of the enterprise. Much of the criticism that employees have of current reward management processes often stems from a lack of communication about the reward policies and structures.

This is an area where human resource managers and remuneration specialists can provide a significant contribution. First, those HR practitioners involved in planning and managing reward processes need to be fully aware of the business trends affecting their industry in general, and their own organisations in particular. This allows for the design and implementation of structures and systems that focus directly on relevant operating priorities. Second, there is a need to raise the understanding and appreciation of executives and line managers about remuneration and reward planning issues—especially with reference to the overall business and HR objectives. Finally, there is a need to clearly communicate the reward policies and systems to employees so that they understand how their pay and benefits are determined, and how company's reward processes fit within the business generally. This is not to suggest that other aspects of the workplace (e.g. security, work satisfaction, social relationships) are not important. However, as Lawler (1987) points out, if one doubts the essential role of financial and related rewards, remove all of the psychological rewards and people will continue to work, however grudgingly and dissatisfied they may be. Remove the financial rewards and see how long employees stay on the job!

In terms of key reward management and administrative issues to be determined, four are of particular significance: (1) To what extent should employees be able to participate in choosing their forms of pay and in setting their own wages? (2) What are the advantages and disadvantages of pay secrecy? (3) What is needed for employees to be satisfied with their pay? and (4) Should all employees be on an annual salary?

Employee participation

The total reward package for many employees generally represents a mixture of direct remuneration (wage or salary) and indirect benefits. Depending on the level in the organisation, benefits can represent as much as 30–40 per cent of total direct and indirect financial reward. However, employees generally have no choice as to what indirect benefits they receive. Management defends this policy on the grounds that all employees are covered for basic benefits (e.g. superannuation) and there is a cost advantage in standardising the benefits available to all employees. Yet the proliferation of indirect pay arrangements has created a kind of smoked glass effect through which the attitudes and desires of the recipient can be seen only darkly, if at all. Employees often receive costly benefits they may not want or, given a choice, particularly need; and in some cases, they do not recognise as a benefit (workplace parking often falls into this category). Even in cases where employees have full knowledge of what they are receiving, they tend to underestimate the cost and value the benefits (see Dyer, Schwab & Fossum 1978).

What are the alternatives? The popular form of employee participation is a **flexible reward** approach (often referred to as the cafeteria reward system) in which individuals select from a menu of available benefit items. Another form incorporates employee–management negotiations on the essential reward format. These approaches are based on the fact that employees are more likely to be satisfied with their reward package under situations where they are permitted some degree of choice. This also helps increase their understanding of the monetary value of the items provided by their employer. Nevertheless, these approaches are generally restricted to the proportion of the total cash value of their reward package to be taken in remuneration or benefits, and provide a relatively limited menu for selection.

Pay secrecy

Ask anyone who works for a living how much money he or she makes and you are likely to encounter a range of responses from polite evasion to outrage at such a personal question. Such responses are not surprising; according to organisational etiquette, it is generally considered bad form to ask others what they earn. Nevertheless, a considerable amount of information about pay is public knowledge.

The majority of Australian employees are covered by some form of Award that stipulates pay rates. Unless there is considerable overtime being worked, or significant 'over-award' payments are being made, then it is possible to determine what an award-covered person is being paid. Similarly, under section 5 of the Corporations Act, public companies are required to detail the remuneration of senior executives paid over $100 000 per annum in bands of $10 000 (e.g. $100 000 to 110 000, $110 000 to 120 000). Although the executives are not identified by name, simply by the number of people paid within each respective pay band, it is possible to estimate what the most senior executives of public corporations are paid.

Some other organisations, particularly in the public sector, are quite open about a range of salary administration issues, including the grade and pay range for each job. In federal and state public service departments, and many government-owned corporations in Australia, open salary administration of this type is a fact of life designed to ensure open and equitable treatment of all employees.

Open salary administration is less frequent in private sector organisations: first, there is not the requirement for openness and public accountability that exists in government employment; and second, issues of individual performance may cause significant variation in pay rates between employees. Some private sector companies disclose the pay ranges for an employee's grade, but few make public the grade that each job is in. The issue of how much of the remuneration structure to make public and how much to be kept confidential, inevitably causes debate, even among HR and remuneration practitioners. The essential issues are concerned with 'open and honest communication' on the one hand versus personal confidentiality and the use of management discretion in pay issues on the other.

Satisfaction with pay

Employees need to express satisfaction with their pay if the reward system is to have an impact on absenteeism and turnover. It is therefore necessary to know the determinants of pay satisfaction. Three major determinants of pay satisfaction are internal pay equity, external pay equity and pay administration practices.

Internal pay equity

This refers to what people feel they deserve to be paid in relationship to what others deserve. The tendency is for people to determine this by comparing what they give to the organisation with what they get out of it. In comparing themselves with others, people may decide whether or not they are being paid fairly, i.e. what they deserve in relationship to others. If they regard this comparison as fair or equitable, they are more likely to be satisfied. If they see it as unfair they are likely to be dissatisfied.

External pay equity

The other reference point that is an important determinant of pay satisfaction is comparison with general community wage levels. Again, people make an intuitive judgement about the level of pay they receive from their employer, in comparison with what they perceive as general pay rates for similar sorts of work in other organisations. Another component of this comparison has to do with the overall level of pay received in relation to the cost of living. The question here is whether or not the pay rate is sufficient to maintain a reasonable standard. The result of these comparisons will determine the overall 'felt fairness' of the employee's own pay level compared with the rest of the community.

Pay administration practices

This refers to the policies, processes and systems by which the organisation manages such as issues as internal and external pay equity, relates pay to performance, and reviews its pay rates against the external market. In effect, it is the tangible experience that the employee has of the firm's administration of its remuneration and reward policies and practices. This is very much dependent on each individual's perception of consistency in the system: a high degree of consistency leads to employee confidence and trust; inconsistent reward administration leads to a lack of confidence and trust. Where employees perceive that the organisation is looking out for their interests as well as its own, pay satisfaction will be high. Where this is not the case, pay satisfaction is not only low, but remuneration policies and their administration become a target for complaints and affect other areas of morale and climate.

Employee benefits

Almost all organisations offer some form of benefits to their employees. In recent times, the cost of providing benefits has risen significantly and many organisations question whether this investment is worthwhile. The answer depends on what is defined as a benefit, and the objective sought by the company in offering benefits to employees. In general, benefits may be defined as those cash, near-cash and deferred-cash rewards (apart from pay and pay-related amounts such as bonuses and incentives) provided to employees in return for their membership in the organisation. They can be divided into three categories:

- employee welfare programs
- pay for time not worked
- employee services and perquisites.

A significant number of benefits are mandated by federal and state legislation and administered within specific laws and regulations. On the other hand, a range of benefits are provided voluntarily by organisations. The objective is to enhance the organisation's image as an attractive employer, and to aid the process of building commitment with the workforce. In this respect, organisations seek to attain various goals in return for benefits. These goals include:

- attracting good employees
- increasing employee morale

- reducing turnover
- increasing job satisfaction
- gaining the longer term commitment of employees
- enhancing the organisation's image as a 'good' employer.

The potential range of benefits that may be provided is quite diverse; similarly, employees' preferences are varied and dependent on personal issues such as lifestyle, age and individual preferences. As a result, benefits are not equally valued or seen as a reward by all employees. The objectives of providing benefits are more likely to be attained when the actual benefits available are matched with employee preferences.

Another important reason why some of the purposes of benefits are not attained is that employees regard benefits as natural conditions (or rights) of employment. Some benefits may be regarded as safeguards against insecurity (e.g. long-term sickness, family care, post-employment financial security, or general wealth creation) because these issues are not adequately provided by federal or state legislation.

Social welfare and security

One of the major functions of the Australian federal government's Department of Social Security is income maintenance. This is undertaken through the administration of the *Social Security Act 1947* and its amendments. A major aspect of this Act relates to income maintenance provided through various pensions, benefits and allowances. The Department of Social Security pays pensions for age, invalidity, deserted wives, supporting parents and widowhood. Other benefits paid by the department include: unemployment, sickness and 'special' (an all-embracing category to capture people not eligible for other benefits, but still unable to earn a sufficient livelihood for themselves and their dependants). Further allowances are paid to assist families in need and those entitled to a special pensioner benefits (e.g. free pharmaceuticals)

Workers' compensation

All employees in Australia are subject to workers' compensation legislation and must be covered by workers' compensation insurance by their employers. The insurance provides a scale of benefits for employees who are injured at work or who incur a work-related illness. The aim of the legislation is to maintain employees' income and employment benefits for the period that the employee is unable to perform his or her usual work. Payment is usually at the full rate for a period and then at a reduced amount. Recent legislation, particularly in New South Wales and Victoria, has tended to emphasise rehabilitation and retraining in addition to accident compensation.

Private employee welfare programs

These are benefits offered voluntarily by private and public sector organisations, although their administration may be regulated by law. Additional retirement and insurance benefits (including health insurance) are the major types of private employee welfare benefits.

Superannuation and retirement benefits

In the past, superannuation in Australia has traditionally been a benefit available to higher salaried staff and not usually provided to lower-paid employees. This is evidenced by a 1984 survey (Australian Bureau of Statistics 1984) showing that:

- 39 per cent of all employees were covered by superannuation
- 32 per cent of employees earning less than $240 per week received superannuation
- 70 per cent of employees earning more than $240 received superannuation.

The mid-1980s saw an acceleration of movement towards the establishment of superannuation for all employees. The Australian Council of Trade Unions was a major influence in the campaign to extend superannuation coverage to all union members. Initially, 3 per cent of wages was prescribed as a minimum level of superannuation support for award-covered employees as a direct result of the 1987 National Wages Case.

The Australian government has also been influential in the development of superannuation coverage for all employees . A range of legislative changes was introduced under the federal Labor government from 1983. These changes affected the taxation of superannuation benefits, but more importantly, made the provision of superannuation compulsory for every Australian employee. This included a prescribed level of contribution that all employers must provide for their employee. Initially, this was set at 4 per cent of pay in 1992, rising to 9 per cent by the year 2002. A comprehensive summary of the development of superannuation in Australia, including the current legislation and its impact on employers and employees is provided by Dillon (1995). It is important to note that the federal Liberal government, elected under John Howard in 1996, maintained support for superannuation coverage of all employees.

Insurance

Private employee welfare programs offering life, health and disability insurance in Australia are generally available for professional and managerial employees, but less commonly for normal blue- and white-collar employees. However, one direct implication of the extension of superannuation to all employees, is that these forms of personal protection are most often provided as part of superannuation coverage.

Pay for time not worked

Pay for time not worked is not as complex to administer as benefits from employee welfare programs, but is almost as costly to the organisation. Annual leave and paid public holidays are the major components of time not worked. The most common, paid 'off-the-job' components are annual leave, sick leave, holidays and personal days off. Paid benefits, for time not worked 'on-the-job' include rest and lunch periods, wash-up time and 'get-ready' times.

Employee services and perquisites
Fringe benefits

The introduction of the **Fringe Benefits Tax (FBT)** to Australia in July 1986 resulted in changes to the services and perquisites available to employees. Prior to July 1986 services and perquisites consisted of such things as employee discounts, day-care centres, employee counselling and advisory services for legal, tax and personal problems, employer-sponsored scholarships and tuition assistance for employees and their dependants, low-cost loans, and company provided vehicles for business and personal use. Additional benefits were often provided at management levels, and these included annual company paid medical examination, memberships in business, social and sporting clubs and the use of company expense accounts to cover personal travel, meals and entertainment.

These items are now fully taxable under the current FBT rules. The impact has been for the majority of companies to closely examine the business need and cost of providing many of these benefits. This has led to a more restricted availability of the traditional 'perks' available to managers and executives compared with the pre-FBT times. In many cases, the only perquisite to survive has been the company-provided vehicle.

Golden employment practices

Although many benefits are provided to almost all employees, golden employment practices are only provided to those considered indispensable to the organisation. The nature of these benefits is such that they are often quite expensive.

Arrangements providing financial protection for top corporate executives in the event of a change in control of the company are often referred to as **golden parachutes**. This protection is either in the form of guaranteed employment, or severance pay upon termination or resignation. The need for golden parachutes came about with the rapid flurry of mergers and acquisitions in the early 1980s. Because mergers or acquisitions can financially help some companies and shareholders, the parachutes were devised to soften top management resistance to take-over attempts. Top managers who might be replaced as the result of a take-over would still be financially well off.

Golden handcuffs are meant to retain key people by making it too costly for them to leave the company. Typically, **golden handcuffs** consist of shares, share options and retirement packages. The executive forfeits these financially attractive benefits in the case of resignation. Judicious use of golden handcuffs can be a significant retention device for highly valued employees.

Employee share plans

Many large corporations have **employee share ownership plans** (**ESOPS**) that allow employees to purchase shares, usually at a discount and often with company provided financial assistance. The aim is to encourage greater employee commitment to the enterprise by sharing in the company's financial performance as reflected in growth in the share price over time. A well-designed employee share plan can be an effective tool in supporting other HR initiatives related to employee commitment, morale and overall productivity. An employee with a long service record, and who takes advantage of such a share plans can add quite significantly to his or her personal savings—assuming always that the company performs well over time.

Administrative issues in employee benefits

Organisations provide benefits to employees as part of the overall reward structure; however, the recipients do not always see them in that way—often they are viewed as a right and an entitlement. This causes organisations to become concerned with their package of employee benefits and how it is communicated and administered. This raises two important issues with respect to the administration of benefits.

Determining the benefits package

The benefits package needs to balance the needs of the employee and the employer, as well as meet any legislative requirements. Benefits packages are best designed with a knowledge of employee preferences, and a fair degree of flexibility in meeting these—often diverse—needs. Examples of preferences include: trading pay (or other benefits) for additional time off work; the preference for older employees to sacrifice current wages and salaries for higher superannuation benefits; and greater medical and health insurance benefits for employees with young families.

Communicating the benefits package

Providing benefit flexibility is worthwhile, because it gives employees what they want, and makes them aware of the specific benefits they are provided with. Many employees are unaware of the costs of benefits and what is available to them. There is little reason to believe that the organisation's benefit program objectives will be attained if employees are unaware of their entitlements and choices. Many organisations indicate that they assign a high priority to telling employees about their benefits, although a majority spend only a small amount per employee per year doing this.

Trends in benefits

Currently, the major issue in corporate benefits revolves around managing the total program cost. Trends of assessing benefit plans and using computer technology to aid this assessment certainly enable companies to better understand and manage this element of personnel costs. This is also true for the trend towards the strategic involvement of benefits. As such, these three trends of developing choices in benefits can also reduce or contain costs.

Assessing and managing benefit costs

This issue has to do with balancing the impact of providing benefits on employee morale with the cost associated with the benefit program. An organisation can determine the dollar value of the costs of benefits in a variety of ways; the following four are merely examples:

1. Total costs of benefits annually for all employees
2. Benefit cost per employee per year divided by the number of hours worked
3. Benefit cost as a percentage of payroll divided by annual payroll
4. Cost of benefits per employee per hour, divided by employee hours worked.

These costs can be compared with HR records such as reduced turnover and absenteeism, or from survey data related to perceptions of company image among employees. The dollar value of these results (e.g. reduced absenteeism, turnover, employee satisfaction) may be extrapolated to provide some measure of effectiveness by comparing these HR costs with the direct dollar value of providing benefits. This sort of human resource accounting is seen by many as an effective way of measuring the impact of a range of HR programs and initiatives (see Cascio 1991 for a detailed approach to costing various aspects of the HR function).

Strategy and choice in benefits

A major trend in all reward planning is to ensure that the reward structure directly supports the strategic and operating objectives of the firm. With regard to benefits, this can range from the development of a very deliberate reward philosophy and strategy, to highly specific tactical issues such as the potential use of superannuation funds to fend off corporate takeovers. More than this, there are a range of steps that organisations can take in overall reward planning; the following are adapted from Williams (1984).

Review other employers' programs

There is a need to regularly review the benefit program against the external market. Such a review needs to take account of trends within the particular industry, general community expectations and other relevant comparisons (e.g. what are other companies providing graduates, executives and other selected jobs?).

Current compensation and benefits trends

What are the trends that are emerging with regard to the provision of benefits? This may include such issues as benefit cost management, provision of health care security to retirees, extending health care to employees' aged dependants and changing trends in family care. Similarly, remuneration managers need to keep abreast of potential and pending legislation that may affect the benefits offered by their organisation.

Financial impact of benefit design

It is important that the introduction of new benefits, or revisions to existing benefits, are preceded by a financial impact analysis. This is particularly relevant to benefits that involve long-term commitments by the company. A major aspect of the financial analysis is the taxation implications for both the organisation and employees. Some benefits may have a strong link to employee morale, be tied directly to HR strategy but have immediate consequences for an employee's personal taxation planning (e.g. share plans).

Employees' perception of the value of their benefits

Internal surveys can help determine the level of employee knowledge of benefits, the relative value that the employee puts on various components of the program, and the allocation of benefit dollars among options offered under a flexible plan. This, and similar employee feedback, is a valuable contribution to the monitoring and assessing the effectiveness of the benefits program.

Summary

An organisation's reward system serves many purposes; these are often summarised as 'the need to attract, retain and motivate employees'. But it is also broader than this: the total reward structure involves base pay, performance-based pay, compulsory employer provided benefits (such as superannuation and various paid time off such as sick leave, annual holidays and long service leave), as well as those benefits provided at the discretion of the employer (e.g. employee share plans, health care, study leave and the like). These are factors that can have a direct impact on employee productivity and morale; for this reason, the design of a total reward structure must be consistent with the management philosophy and values of the enterprise, and deliberately support its business objectives.

Pay equity is an important building block in establishing the salary and wages part of rewards. From an internal perspective, employees want the comfort of knowing that their pay is determined in a systematic and objective way relative to the pay of other employees. From an external perspective, the various federal and state governments have equal employment opportunity legislation providing safeguards against discrimination in establishing pay systems. There is a variety of job evaluation techniques available to provide a systematic and objective approach to determining pay relativities. These vary from whole job approaches (e.g. ranking and classification) to points-factor comparison and tailor-made systems. An important decision is whether to introduce a standardised proprietary method (such as the Hay Guide Chart method), or to design your own so that the particular needs and values of the company are embodied in the way that job relativities are established. Alternatively, many organisations are turning away from traditional job-based pay systems and looking for more direct ways of establishing person-based pay (e.g. pay-for-knowledge, skill-based and competency-based pay).

Having determined the relative ranking of jobs, the next step is to group jobs of similar classification or size within common pay bands. This is often referred to as the pay grade structure and will usually contain jobs from various functions (e.g. accounting, sales, manufacturing). The next step is to establish the price to be paid for each job grade (i.e. wage and salary rates). Most organisations use some form of market survey data, especially for those jobs that are widely represented in the labour market. Typically, the market data is used to structure a range from a minimum to a midpoint and maximum pay level for each grade.

Another important aspect of reward is to link it with performance. Performance-based pay systems are attracting the attention of many organisations in the Australian public and private sectors, and across all industries. The experience of human resource managers and line managers prompts some doubt as to whether traditional merit pay plans do a good job of rewarding and motivating top performing employees. On the other hand, there is some evidence to suggest that a well designed incentive plan, combined with effective job design, can impact performance positively. Incentive plans vary from individual plans to sales incentives, managerial and group plans; similarly the rewards may be paid annually or more frequently, and may be in cash or, as often applies to senior executives, in shares. However, problems may arise due to obstacles that are often associated with the implementation of incentive plans.

Which performance-based pay plan is appropriate depends on several factors such as whether job performance is best measured at the individual, work team or organisation level, the need for co-operation and interdependence between employees and work teams, the extent to which employees actually influence business goals and operating objectives of the firm, and the level of trust between management and employees.

Even when companies adopt some form of incentive plan, they still need to provide employees with certain indirect rewards or benefits. Some of these are mandated by legislation; this includes superannuation, sick leave and annual holidays. Other benefits are provided by the organisation as a means of building and reinforcing its image as an attractive employer. The potential range of benefits is quite diverse, as is the choice of employees. The maximum impact of the company's benefit program will occur when the benefits provided is closely matched with employee preferences.

questions for discussion and review

1. What is meant by the term 'total reward' and what are the key components you might expect to be provided by an organisation?
2. What are the main external influences on planning and managing a company's reward program?
3. Describe the link between job analysis, job evaluation and pay.
4. Distinguish between job-based pay and person-based pay.
5. What are the major outcomes companies seek from introducing performance-based reward structures?
6. How might a company's total reward program provide it with a competitive edge?
7. How do team-based work structures differ from traditional work designs in terms of performance management and pay?
8. Will the introduction of a performance-based pay systems necessarily lead to increased motivation and higher productivity? What are some other issues that need to be considered?
9. Who should be responsible for the post-employment financial security of employees? Is this an individual, employer or government responsibility?
10. What are some of the ways that an organisation might use to evaluate the impact and acceptance of its reward structure?

case study

Elite Manufacturers Pty Ltd is a manufacturing and sales organisation consisting of a corporate head office, and three relatively independent business units. The business units make unrelated products for different market segments. The company employs 590 people across the business and has annual sales of $380 million, with an annual profit before tax of $47.5 million.

There are 20 employees in Elite's head office. They include the Chief Executive Officer and his corporate staff headed by the General Manager Finance & Administration, Company Secretary, General Manager Marketing & Distribution and the General Manager Human Resources. Apart from these head office positions, the three business unit managers also report directly to the Chief Executive.

The corporate staff positions are accountable for overseeing the total group operations that fall within their respective portfolios. Each division is treated as an individual profit centre and has its own manufacturing, accounting & administration, sales & marketing and human resource functions. The divisional functions report directly to the respective business unit head, but have a strong 'dotted line' reporting relationship to the relevant corporate function manager.

- **Elite cutlery**. The Cutlery division manufactures and markets domestic and industrial steel kitchen cutlery (e.g. carving knives and forks, skewers). The business has an annual sales turnover of $95 million and employs some 120 people. Elite products are recognised as the premium band and have a leading market share. Elite Cutlery is the company's original business and has been continually profitable over the years.
- **Elite fasteners**. This division manufactures, imports and distributes fasteners (e.g. nails, screws etc.) to the hardware industry. Annual sales turnover is $135 million and the business unit has 240 employees. This is a tightly competitive market with low profit margins; however, divisional management believes there is significant scope for cost reductions from productivity improvement off existing plant, machinery and work processes. Achievement of these productivity gains is important if this business unit is to make inroads into its poor profit performances of the past few years.
- **Elite heating appliances**. The Heating Appliance division is a relatively new acquisition by Elite. The original owners made a considerable investment in developing an innovative new domestic heater with considerable cost reductions for user power bills. Elite management assessed the company as having a significant profit potential and are now in the third year of manufacture and distribution of the product. Sales are currently at $150 million per annum and returning good profitability; however, with improved marketing strategies, and greater marketing penetration, revenue and profitability have the potential to double within five years. This division has 230 employees.

Although Elite executives are familiar with such practices as self-managing work teams, total quality management, flat organisation structures and the like, they are quite comfortable with their rather traditional, although 'enlightened' top-down management style. Generally speaking, the corporation operates quite successfully in this way. Overall Elite is essentially a manufacturing and marketing business where labour costs are a critical determinant of the organisation's profitability. Similarly, individual performance effectiveness—at all levels—is a critical driver of business success. At a recent General Managers' meeting, the executive group developed what they saw as the core principles that should be built into any changes to Elite's remuneration and reward structure.

- Pay increases will be based on job performance
- Performance of all employees will be assessed regularly, and employees will be told how they are performing
- Organisational pay levels will reflect the relevant competitive market place
- Success of the business will influence pay levels throughout the corporation
- Individuals will be paid fairly, based on the nature of the work that they do, and on pay rates for similar work in other organisations
- Elite wishes to provide a better than average range of benefits to its employees to encourage staff loyalty.

You have just been appointed as the new General Manager Human Resources and the Chief Executive has asked you to treat a review of the reward system as a top priority. Next month you are expected to present your preliminary recommendations to the General Managers' Committee.

Questions

1. What issues will you consider in recommending a base pay program?
2. Will a performance-based pay system be appropriate? How might it be designed?
3. What type of benefits might you suggest, and how would these link to legislative requirements and company objectives?

Resources

American Compensation Association Journal—A quarterly journal published by the ACA containing timely and high quality articles on all aspects of reward planning, management and administration.

Blinder, A. (ed.) (1990), *Paying for Productivity: A Look at the Evidence*, The Brookings Institute, Washington DC.

Lawler, E. (1990), *Strategic Pay: Aligning Organisational Strategies & Pay Systems*, Josey Bass, San Francisco, CA.

Rock, M. & Berger, L. (1991), *The Compensation Handbook: A State-of-the-Art Guide to Compensation Strategy & Design*, McGraw-Hill, New York.

Schuster, J. & Zingheim, P. (1992), *The New Pay: Linking Employee & Organisational Performance*, Lexington, New York.

References

Australian Bureau of Statistics 1984, *Employee Benefits*, Catalogue no. 6334.

Blinder, A. (ed.) (1990), *Paying for Productivity: A Look at the Evidence*, The Brookings Institute, Washington DC.

Burton, C. (1987), *Women's Worth: Pay Equity & Job Evaluation in Australia*, Australian Government Publishing Service, Canberra.

—— (1990), *Pay Equity—Obligations, Costs and Benefits. Preventing Discrimination in the Workplace*, IRR Conference, Sydney.

Carey, P. (1993), *Productivity Gainsharing*, Longman, Melbourne.

—— (1995), *Gain sharing: A Metal Industry Case Study* in G. O'Neill & R. Kramar (eds), *Australian Human Resources Management: Current Trends in Management Practice*, Pitman, Melbourne.
Cascio, W. (1991), *Costing Human Resources*, PWS-Kent, Boston, Mass.
Cofsky, K. (1993), (Critical keys to competency-based pay), *Compensation & Benefits Review*, Nov.–Dec., pp. 46–52
Cook, F. (1993), 'The Ascendancy of Capital: Sharing Capital Returns with Employees who Create Value', *American Compensation Association Journal*, vol. 2, no. 2, pp. 6–13.
Cornish, G. & Adams, G. (1993), 'Trends in Remuneration', *Asia Pacific Journal of Human Resources*, vol. 31, no. 2, pp. 75–86.
Dillon, A. (1995), 'Superannuation: Managing a Changing Environment', in G. O'Neill & R. Kramar (eds), *Australian Human Resources Management: Current Trends in Management Practice*, Pitman, Melbourne.
Dyer L., Schwab, D. & Fossum, J. (1978), *Impacts of Pay on Employee Behaviours and Attitudes: An Update*, Personnel Administrator, p. 56.
Gomez-Mejia, L. & Balkin, D. (1992), *Compensation, Organizational Strategy, and Firm Performance*, South-Western Publishing, OH.
Gupra, N., Ledford, G., Jenkins, D. & Doty, D. (1992), 'Survey-based Prescriptions for Skill-based Pay', *American Compensation Association Journal*, vol. 1, no. 1, pp. 48–58.
Hay Group Pty Ltd (1993), 'Designing a compensation program that's right for your organization', in *Dynamic Pay for a changing world of work*, pp. 11–12, Melbourne.
Hearn, G., Close, A., Smith, B. & Southey, G. (1996), 'Defining generic professional competencies in Australia: Towards a framework for professional development', *Asia Pacific Journal of Human Resources*, vol. 34, no. 1, pp. 44–62.
Jenkins, D. (1986), 'Financial Incentives', in E. Locke (ed.), *Generalising from Laboratory to Field Settings*, D. C. Heath, Lexington.
Kanter, R. M. (1989), *When Giants Learn to Dance*, Unwin, London.
Kohn, A. (1992), *Punished by Rewards: The Trouble with Gold Stars, Incentive Plans, A's, Praise and Other Bribes*, Houghton Mifflin, Boston.
—— (1993), 'Why Incentive Plans Cannot Work', *Harvard Business Review*, Sept.–Oct., pp. 54–63.
Lander, D. & O'Neill, G. (1991), 'Pay Equity: Apples, Oranges and a Can of Worms', *Asia Pacific Human Resource Management*, vol. 29, no. 1, pp. 16–28.
Lawler, E. (1987), 'Pay for Performance: A Motivational Analysis', in H. Nalbatian (ed.), *Incentives, Co-operation and Risk Sharing: Economic & Psychological Perspectives on Employment Contracts*, Rowan & Littlefields, Savage.
—— (1990), *Strategic Pay: Aligning Organisational Strategies & Pay Systems*, Josey Bass, San Francisco, CA.
Ledford, G. E. (1990), 'Three case studies on skill-based pay: an overview', *Compensation and benefits Review*, April, pp. 11–23.
O'Neal, S. (1995), 'Competencies and pay in the evolving world of work', *American Compensation Journal*, vol. 4, no. 3, pp. 72–79.
O'Neill, G. (1993), 'Linking TQM and Pay', *Corporate Review*, November, pp. 32–36.
—— (1995a), 'Framework for Developing a Total Reward Strategy', *Asia Pacific Journal of Human Resources*, vol. 33, no. 2, pp. 103–17.
—— (1995b), 'Linking Pay to Performance: Conflicting Views and Conflicting Evidence', *Asia Pacific Journal of Human Resources*, vol. 33, no. 2, pp. 20–35.

—— (1995c), 'Trends and Issues in Pay Design and Management', in G. O'Neill & R. Kramar (eds), *Australian Human Resources Management: Current Trends in Management Practice*, Pitman, Melbourne.

O'Neill, G. & Lander, D. (1993), 'Linking Employee Skills to Pay: A Framework for Skill-based Pay Plans', *American Compensation Association Journal*, Winter, pp. 36–49

Podsakoff, P. M., Greene, C. N. & McFillen, J. M. (1987), 'Obstacles to the effective use of reward systems', in R. S Schuler & S. A. Youngblood (eds), *Readings in Personnel and Human Resource Management*, 3rd edition, West Publishing, St. Paul, Minn.

Schuler, R. S. (1995), *Managing Human Resources*, West Publishing, St. Paul, Minn.

Schuler, R. S., Dowling, J. P., Smart, J. P. & Huber, Vandra, L. (1992), *Human Resource Management in Australia*, 2nd edition, HarperCollins, Sydney.

Schuster, J. & Zingheim, P. (1992), *The New Pay: Linking Employee & Organisational Performance*, Lexington, New York.

Stradwick, R. (1992), *Employee Share Plans*, Longman Professional, Melbourne.

Towers Perrin (1995), 'Remuneration Survey Database', July.

Williams, T. (1994), 'Total Compensation Strategies', *Bulletin of Management*, 4 October, p. 8.

Wyatt Company (1993), 'Assessing & Rewarding Achievements in Total Quality Management: Linking TQM, Performance & Pay', *Human Resources Update*, April.

chapter 11

Training and development

Andrew Smith

learning objectives

After studying this chapter, you will be able to:

1. Describe the purposes and importance of training and development.
2. Determine training and development needs.
3. Answer questions about setting up training and development programs.
4. Describe the different approaches to training and development.
5. Identify the importance of management development.
6. Recognise the key features of training policy reform in Australia.

chapter 11

chapter outline

- Training and development — 465
- Why training and development is important — 467
- Determining training and development needs — 469
  - Organisational-needs analysis — 470
  - Job-needs analysis — 470
  - Person-needs analysis — 470
- Where and how training is conducted — 472
  - Location of training—on-the-job — 473
  - Location of training—off-the-job — 475
- Training methods — 477
  - Role playing — 477
  - Behaviour modelling — 477
  - Simulation — 478
  - Outdoor training — 478
- Training technologies — 479
  - Video — 479
  - Interactive video — 479
  - Computer-based training — 479
- Evaluating training and development programs — 480
  - Evaluation criteria — 480
  - Evaluation designs — 480
- Management development — 482
  - Common approaches to management development — 483
  - The Karpin Report — 485
- Organisational learning — 487
  - What is a learning organisation — 487
  - Barriers to organisational learning — 489
- Training and corporate strategy — 490
- International comparisons — 492
  - Japan — 492
  - Germany — 492
- Training policy — 493
  - Reactions to the training reforms — 494
- Summary — 495
- Questions for discussion and review — 495
- Case study — 496
- Resources — 497
- References — 498

HRM IN THE NEWS

How training beat the bushfires

The NSW bushfires may have been defeated by a 'ragtag army of volunteers' *(The Age*, 11/1/93) but these men and women were primed for battle by a professional approach to training and HR management. NSW Bushfire Services introduced competency-based training in 1983—well before most organisations in Australia recognised its value, and nine years before CBT was adopted as the model for Australia's national vocational education system. A decade of CBT and enlightened people management has seen most of the state's 70 000 volunteer fire fighters gain basic training and the skills needed to make decisions in the field independently. 'The old saying used to be "All you need is one expert to direct the group and a bunch of chooks to follow orders" ', says Phil Robeson, NSW Bushfire Services Manager, Training Services. 'Now you've got teams who all have an understanding of basic fire behaviour'.

The NSW Department of Bushfire Services has no power to compel volunteers to undertake training because the brigades are 'owned' by local councils—and it wouldn't enforce compulsory training even if it could. It believes training fails unless the participants recognise and embrace its value. Even so, in 1991, a survey of about 60 per cent of local councils from all bushfire regions in NSW showed that 86 per cent had implemented basic bush fire training programs, 65 per cent had implemented crew leader training programs and 45 per cent had implemented specialist bush fire training. Those figures are likely to be higher now.

Training Services Manager for NSW Bushfire Services, Phil Robeson, says the strength of the training system is its success in empowering people at low levels to make decisions with confidence.

CBT is used to ensure volunteer fire fighters have the basic knowledge of fire behaviour and equipment needed to act independently. When fire fighting used to rely on 'one expert and a bunch of whackers', the burden was carried by a talented few, who wasted time coaching, correcting and closely supervising fire fighters.

'Today, if you ask them to do a parallel attack on a fire, everyone will know what to do', says Robeson. 'Fifteen years ago you would have had to explain in detail what you meant. that takes the pressure off the crew leaders. Volunteers can go onto the fire ground and be an asset rather than a liability'.

Robeson says CBT appeals to volunteers because it recognises existing skills, and is assessed through practical demonstrations rather than formal 'class room type' tests. Fire fighters aren't enthusiastic about training if they think it is going to be like going back to school, if it covers things they already know, or if it forgets they are volunteers.

The service has overcome these pitfalls of formal assessment by introducing a flexible training management system, with a common set of standards recognised statewide but tailored to meet the needs of specific areas. It takes a 'train the trainer' approach with three full-time head office staff preparing standards, then training volunteers from the hundreds of brigades as instructors for their own region. Fire fighters are trained to different levels: basic fire fighters, who work consistently under supervision and receive 16–20 hours training; advanced fire fighters who can work without supervision; crew leaders; and group leaders who control several units. While battling a bushfire is a military style operation and necessarily hierarchical, Robeson says the day-to-day running of the brigades is very democratic. Volunteer fire fighters elect their own crew leaders.

National competency standards are currently being prepared for all Australian fire services, and some of these have already been ratified by the National Training Board. Once these are completed, says

> Robeson, it will ensure that fire fighters from around the country 'talk the same language' and can work together effectively to fight bushfires. This was one of the key advantages of the state-wide training system in the battle against the NSW blazes.

Source: *Human Resources Report* no. 71, 18 January 1994, p. 1–2.

This feature underlines how essential good training can be to organisations where performance is critical. You can think of other examples such as the airline industry, the health industry and so on. In all these cases, training and even retraining of staff is often literally a matter of life or death. In recent years, other organisations and industries in the private and public sectors have begun to realise how critical training is to the performance of their staff and to the prosperity of the companies themselves. This chapter examines how and why training and development has become so important a part of the HR policies of so many organisations in Australia.

Since the mid-1980s the world of the training and development practitioner has literally been undergoing something of a quiet revolution. Thrust into the centre stage of the industrial reforms of recent years by the Structural Efficiency Principle in the 1988 National Wage Case decision, training has assumed increasing importance in Australian enterprises as they seek to obtain competitive advantage in a deregulated and increasingly internationalised economy. Traditional sources of competitive advantage based on tariff protection or technological innovation have disappeared within the global economy and managers of Australian enterprises are increasingly aware that competitive advantage lies with the creativity and resourcefulness of their employees. The skills of the workforce can only be nurtured by a more effective provision of training both public and private. Yet it would appear that Australia has traditionally lagged behind its major trading partners in this respect.

Training and development obviously serves many purposes. This chapter analyses those purposes in detail. It discusses the types of needs analysis that should be conducted to determine who should receive training, what skills are necessary and at what level they should be taught. The effectiveness of training can only be assessed through an evaluation procedure. This is discussed. **Management development** has become the focus of interest in the training community recently and this is discussed along with international comparisons of training and development.

Training and development

The field of training and development has become confused by the number of terms which describe aspects of the activity but also overlap to a considerable extent. In particular, 'training', 'development', 'education' and the popular term, 'human resource development' are used almost interchangeably in discussions of training and development.

The notion of Human Resource Development (HRD) originated in the USA and is a much broader concept than that of training, development or education. It is generally seen to subsume these other activities (Nadler & Nadler 1989) and reach beyond the 'traditional' notion of training. The American Society for Training and Development has defined HRD as:

> ... the process of increasing the capacity of the human resource through development. It is thus a process of adding value to individuals, teams or an organisation as a human system (McLagan 1989, p. 10).

In this sense, HRD encompasses the broad set of activities that improve the performance of the individual and, hence, the organisation. The central notion is that of 'development' and HRD may involve traditional training and development, organisation development and career development. The notion of HRD is illustrated in the 'human resource wheel' in Figure 11.1.

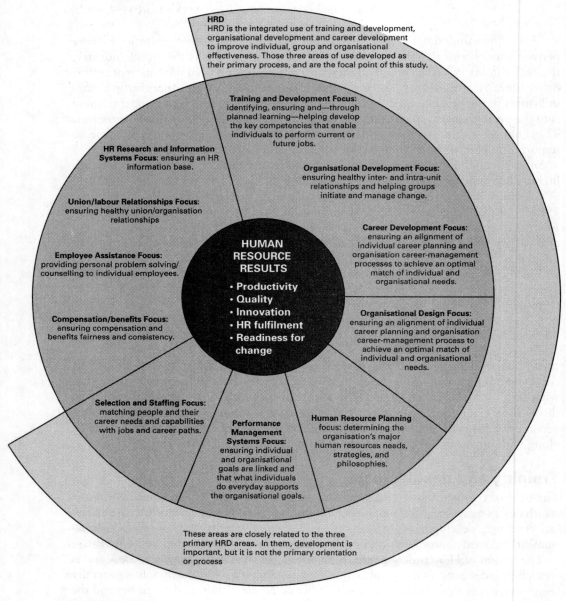

Figure 11.1 Human resource wheel
Source: McLagan 1989, p. 53

The more specific concepts of training, development and education can be placed within this overarching HRD framework. Thus training is concerned with knowledge, skills and attitudes relevant to performing a current job. Education is the process of preparing individuals for a future position and development is concerned with the overall growth of individuals, groups and organisations—the realisation of potential. In this chapter the term **training and development** will be taken to cover all these three activities.

A further term in the training and development context is that of **learning**. As training and development has come to be viewed as a lifelong activity, rather than the front-end acquisition of qualifications, the focus of concern has shifted from what the trainer does to what the learner requires. Moreover, learning occurs not only within the individual but at the organisational level also. The ultimate aim of the training and development process has been characterised as the creation of the learning organisation, constantly reviewing its mistakes and successes and adapting its activities appropriately (Senge 1990).

Why training and development is important

Training and development has a positive impact for the individual, the organisation and the nation.

For individuals, there is little doubt that training and development increases the earnings and opportunities open to people. Economists have shown how earnings profiles are positively linked to skills, whether acquired through the public education system or through training provided by the employer. The highest wages are earned by those with the highest skills; a fact which many employers use as a reason for making trainees bear some of the cost of their training in lower wages during the training period (Maglen 1990).

The acquisition of skills also opens up opportunities for career development. Promotion is increasingly determined by the possession of qualifications and skills. In Australia, the process of **award restructuring** has created career paths for workers through which progression is controlled by skill. Training and development has, therefore, assumed vital importance to individual opportunity.

Investment in education and development also repays the individual in terms of earnings and job security. In times of economic downturn, organisations will tend to lay off their least skilled workers first. It is not in the interests of the organisation to risk losing the workers who may be able to make the most contribution to corporate recovery. Skilled and qualified workers also tend to retain their earnings differentials more effectively than non-skilled workers. It has been shown in the USA that high school dropouts saw their average earnings decrease by up to 40 per cent in the 1980s while those with a college degree suffered only an 11 per cent decrease in earnings over the same period (Carnevale et al. 1990a).

For organisations, the importance of training and development lies in its links to performance and competitiveness. Although the debate over evaluation in training and development indicates the difficulties of demonstrating the impact of training and development activities on corporate performance, there is little doubt that training and development is a key ingredient in competitive success. UK research has shown how top performing companies are distinguished by their higher spending on training and development (Sparrow & Pettigrew 1985).

Although the mechanisms are not yet entirely clear, it appears that training and development contributes to organisational performance in three key areas. Firstly, training and development has the potential to improve labour productivity. Training in better ways of doing things whether it be the operation of a machine on the shop floor or the implementation of the corporate plan in the boardroom, increases the output of members of the organisation i.e. their productivity.

Managing change

Investment in people the turning point for NEC

A massive investment in employee training has been one of the major drivers behind the success of telecommunications manufacturer NEC Australia. John Ring, national manager training and development, said the decision to invest in people came about with a realisation that, despite NECs superior technology and substantial market share, profit levels were not meeting expectations. NEC soon realised that it had to focus on customer satisfaction, which could only be realised through boosting the skills and commitment of the workforce.

The organisation officially launched 'Improving Quality Together' in April 1991, after several years of working on various productivity and efficiency improvement measures. The next year was spent educating, developing and training the company's 250 managers, from the managing director through to middle management and supervisory levels. John Ring says much of the success of NECs quality improvement process rested with the level of commitment from the top—hence the full year spent on management training courses to ensure senior management was totally committed to the quality improvement process.

One of the company's most successful initiatives has been to select employees with good leadership and organisation skills for TAFE-accredited, train-the-trainer courses. Employees with proven ability from across all sections of the organisation are chosen for the sought-after accreditation, regardless of seniority or job function. Fifty employees have already attained accreditation, including engineers, shop floor people, and staff from the finance and accounting departments. Ring says people are chosen for the course if they have good communication skills, leadership qualities, and have the ability to plan their own work and the work of others. Employees are chosen on the basis of individual annual appraisals, the profitability of work units, and other appraisal methods. Participation is always voluntary.

Another initiative has been the establishment of customised MBAs for a select group of middle managers. NECs corporate service division spent 18 months developing an MBA program with the Monash Mt Eliza Management program. Ring says the program has been designed in a way that is 'totally NEC work related'.

Participants go to a 3-day workshop, for example, and develop material which they then use in their own business unit. The first group of 17 managers have just completed their first year of the 3-year MBA, attaining the graduate certificate level.

In terms of future goals, Ring says the company is now changing its focus from TQM—with its more common focus on product quality—to TQS, or total quality service, which is customer driven.

Source: Human Resources Report no. 92, 8 November 1994, pp. 4–5.

Secondly, training and development can improve the quality of that output. A more highly trained employee is not only more competent at the job but also more aware of the significance of his or her actions. Thus, the trained worker realises that the ability of others to do their jobs to a quality standard depends on the standard of his or her own work. This customer–supplier notion is the basis of modern total quality management processes.

Finally, training and development improves the ability of the organisation to cope with change. The successful implementation of change whether technical (in the form of new technologies) or strategic (new products, new markets etc.) relies on the skills of the organisation's members. Change is, perhaps, the single most important reason why organisations fund training and development programs.

Clearly training and development plays a central role in our experience of work. Individuals, organisations and nations have much to gain from the successful implementation of training and development policies.

Determining training and development needs

The three major phases of any training and development program are the **assessment phase** which determines the training and development needs of the organisation; the **implementation phase** (actual training and development) in which certain programs and learning methods are used to impart new attitudes, skills and abilities; and the **evaluation phase** (Goldstein 1986). Their relationships are shown in Figure 11.2.

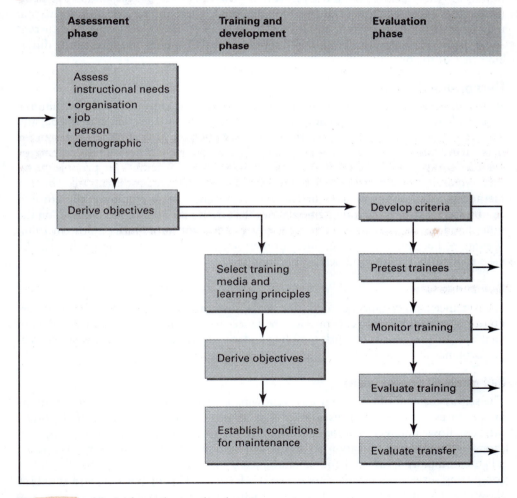

Figure 11.2 Model for an instructional system
Source: Based on Goldstein 1974

Organisational-needs analysis

This begins with an examination of the short-term and long-term objectives of the organisation and the trends that are likely to affect these. According to one expert, organisational objectives should be the ultimate concern of any training and development effort. In addition to examining the organisation's objectives, the organisational needs analysis also consists of human resource analysis and analyses of efficiency indices and organisational climate. Although analysis of the efficiency indices and the organisational climate help to locate **training needs**, they are primarily useful in the evaluation of training and development programs. Thus they are discussed later in this chapter.

Job-needs analysis

Because the organisational needs analysis is too broad to identify detailed training and development needs for specific jobs, it may also be necessary to conduct a job-needs analysis. Essentially, this analysis provides information on the tasks to be performed in each job (the basic information contained in job descriptions), the skills necessary to perform those tasks (from job specifications) and the minimum acceptable standards (sometimes excluded from traditional job analysis). These three pieces of information may be gathered from current employees, the human resources department or current supervisors. They may also be gathered simultaneously from teams representing different areas of the organisation.

Person-needs analysis

After information about the necessary skills and their importance and the minimal acceptable standards of proficiency has been collected, the analysis shifts to the person. This can be accomplished in two different ways. Employee performance discrepancies may be identified either by comparing actual performance with minimum acceptable standards of performance or by comparing an evaluation of employee proficiency on each required skill dimension with the proficiency level required for each skill. The first method is based on the actual, current job performance of an employee; therefore, it can be used to determine training needs for the current job. The second method, on the other hand, can be used to identify development needs for future jobs (Goldstein 1986; Wexley & Latham 1991). Regardless of method, several different approaches can be used to identify the training needs of individuals.

Output measures

Performance data (e.g. productivity, accidents, customer complaints), as well as performance appraisal ratings, can provide evidence of performance deficiencies. Person analysis can also consist of work sampling and job knowledge tests that measure actual performance and knowledge.

Self-assessed training needs

The self-assessment of training needs is growing in popularity. A recent study of training practices in major US firms showed that between 50 and 80 per cent of all corporations allow managers to nominate themselves to attend short-term or company-sponsored training or education programs. Self-assessment can be as informal as posting a list of company sponsored courses and asking who wants to attend, or as formal as conducting surveys regarding training needs (McAfee & Champagne 1988). Table 11.1 shows sample questions from a managerial self-assessment survey.

Table 11.1 Sample questions from a self-administered needs survey

Please indicate in the blanks the extent to which you have a training need in each specific area. Use the scale below.
To what extent do you need training in the following areas?

To no Extent				To a very Large Extent
1	2	3	4	5

Basic management skills (organising, planning, delegating, problem solving)

　_____ 1   Setting goals and objectives
　_____ 2   Developing realistic time schedules to meet work requirements
　_____ 3   Identifying and weighing alternative solutions
　_____ 4   Organising work activities

Interpersonal skills

　_____ 1   Resolving interpersonal conflicts
　_____ 2   Creating a development plan for employees
　_____ 3   Identifying and understanding individual employee needs
　_____ 4   Conducting performance appraisal reviews
　_____ 5   Conducting a discipline interview

Administrative skills

　_____ 1   Maintaining equipment, tools, and safety controls
　_____ 2   Understanding local agreements and shop rules
　_____ 3   Preparing work flowcharts
　_____ 4   Developing department budgets

Quality control

　_____ 1   Analysing and interpreting statistical data
　_____ 2   Constructing and analysing charts, tables, and graphs
　_____ 3   Using statistical software on the computer

Source: Schuler 1995, p. 512; based on Ford & Noe 1987, pp. 40–53

Self-assessment is based on the assumption that employees, more than anyone else, are aware of their skill weaknesses and performance deficiencies. Therefore, they are in the best position to identify their own training needs. One drawback of self-assessment is that individuals who are fearful of revealing any weaknesses may not know or be willing to accurately report their training needs. Consequently, they may not receive the education necessary to remain current in their fields. On the other hand, managers forced to attend programs that they believe they do not need or that do not meet their personal training needs are likely to become dissatisfied with training and lack the motivation to learn and transfer skills.

Attitude surveys

Attitude surveys completed by a supervisor's subordinates and/or by customers can also provide information on training needs. For example, when one supervisor receives low scores regarding his or her fairness in treatment as compared with others in the organisation, this may indicate that the supervisor needs training in that area (Latham 1988). Not only does this format provide information to management about service, but results can also be used to pinpoint employee deficiencies.

Surveys can be completed by managers' subordinates and their bosses. For managers, such surveys can be used to pinpoint which skills are important for managerial effectiveness. Differences in opinions can serve as the basis for discussion about what is really needed for success in today's environment.

Competency-based assessment

This is a type of needs assessment which is growing in importance. This approach involves five major steps:

- **Step 1**—develop broad competency categories. The initial step is to develop a set of broad competency areas, i.e. to determine the critical skills that employees at a given level or job classification in the organisation need to be most effective.
- **Step 2**—develop specific competencies. Once broad categories are selected, the next step is to further define each and develop a list of more specific competencies.
- **Step 3**—develop a resource guide and a competency rating form. The third step involves the development of resource guides or competency manuals that will aid employers and employees in developing skills.
- **Step 4**—prepare a developmental plan for each employee. Once each has been evaluated, the next step would be for the boss to work with each of his/her subordinates to develop a specific improvement plan.
- **Step 5**—evaluate employee progress and develop a new plan. Periodic assessment of an employee's progress skill development is essential.

Demographic needs analysis

In addition to organisational, job and person analyses, organisations may conduct demographic needs analysis to determine the training needs of a specific population of employees. Research indicates that different groups have different training needs. For example, front-line supervisors need more technical training (recordkeeping, written communications), while middle managers rate human resources courses as most important for meeting their needs, and upper level managers rate conceptual courses (goal setting, planning skills) as critical to their development (Gist, Bavetta & Stevens 1990; Schmitt, Schneider & Cohen 1990). In a study of male and female managers in the United States, male managers were found to need training in listening, verbal skills, non-verbal communication, empathy and sensitivity; women managers, on the other hand, need training in assertiveness, confidence building, public speaking and dealing with male peers and subordinates.

Where and how training is conducted

There are a wide variety of training arrangements found in Australian organisations (Smith et al. 1995). The most common ways in which training programs vary are based on:

- **Location**—where the training is conducted. This usually divided into on-the-job training and off-the-job training.
- **Training methods**—what techniques are used in the training?
- **Training technologies**—the extent to which the training uses technological solutions such as video or computer-based training.

Location of training—on-the-job

On-the-job training (OJT) occurs when an employee is taught a new job under the direct supervision of an experienced employee or trainer. The trainee learns the job by observing the experienced employee or trainer and by working with the actual materials and/or machinery that comprise the job. The experienced employee/trainer is expected to provide a role model and to take time from regular job responsibilities to provide the instruction and guidance. One advantage of OJT is that the transfer of training is high. Because trainees learn the job skills in the actual environment in which they will work, they are more apt to apply the skills on the job. Assuming the trainer works in the same area, the trainee receives immediate feedback on performance. The quality of OJT, however, depends on the skill of the person conducting the training.

Job instruction training

The disadvantages of on-the-job training can be minimised by making the training program as systematic and complete as possible. Job instruction training represents such a systematic technique. It was developed to provide a guide for giving on-the-job skill training to white and blue-collar employees as well as technicians (Carnevale et al. 1990b). Since job instruction training is a technique rather than a program, it can be adapted to training efforts for all employees in off- as well as on-the-job programs.

Job instruction training consists of four steps:

1. Careful selection and preparation of the trainer and the trainee for the learning experience to follow
2. A full explanation and demonstration by the trainer of the job to be done by the trainee
3. A trial on-the-job performance by the trainee
4. A thorough feedback session between trainer and trainee to discuss the trainee's performance and the job requirements.

Job rotation

Job rotation is used to train and expose employees to a variety of jobs and decision-making situations. Although job rotation does provide employee exposure, the extent of training and long-run benefit it provides may be overstated. This is because the employees are not in a single job for a long enough period to learn very much and are not motivated to learn because they know that they will have to move on in the near future. As a personal career development strategy, you may want to avoid job rotation and opt instead for job assignments that are more fixed but that provide greater challenge.

Apprenticeship and traineeship training

Another method used in minimising the disadvantages of on-the-job training is combining it with off-the-job training. Apprenticeships and traineeships are programs based on this combination. Apprenticeship training is mandatory for admission into any of the skilled trades, such as plumbing and gas-fitting, and jobs such as electrician, carpenter and boilermaker.

Traditional approaches to apprenticeship have been challenged by the Carmichael Report in 1992 (Employment and Skills Formation Council 1992; see below). The federal government plans to introduce a new system of apprenticeships which will replace both traditional apprenticeships and the newer Australian Traineeship System (ATS). Apprenticeships are still the most important form of entry-level training in

Australia, and their regulation is the responsibility of state and territory governments. Apprentices are normally between 16 and 23 years old and are indentured to an employer, normally for four years. They usually spend three to four days a week on the job and one or two days in off-the-job training, normally at a local technical (TAFE) college. Apprentices are overwhelmingly male (Curtain 1993) reflecting the traditional nature of the trades that support the system. Although the numbers of apprenticeship commencements varies with economic conditions, the number of new starts has never dropped below 34 000 per year and is usually in the range of 45 000 to 60 000. Apprenticeship is, therefore, a highly resilient form of youth training.

Somewhat less formalised and extensive than apprenticeship training is the Australian Traineeship System (ATS). The concept of youth traineeship was a major recommendation of the report of the Committee of Inquiry into Labour Market Programs (Kirby 1985) released in 1985. The Commonwealth government subsequently set up the Australian Traineeship Scheme. Modelled on the British Youth Training Scheme, traineeships involve a one year program of on and off-the-job training and are supported by government subsidies to employers. The ATS has never reached the target of 70 000 commencements envisaged for the system when it was established but has remained steady at between 15 000 to 20 000 per year (Keating 1995).

As with apprenticeship training, individuals in traineeship programs earn while they learn, but at a rate that is less than that paid to full-time employees or master tradespersons. The traineeship functions not only as a source of training, but also of exposure to job and organisational conditions. Students on traineeship and apprenticeship programs are often able to see the application of ideas taught in the classroom more readily than students without any work experience.

Coaching

Coaching is the name generally given to those developmental activities that take place in the workplace setting under the control of the manager. Coaches have been defined by Shore & Bloom:

> ... managers who help employees grow and improve their job competence on a day-to-day basis. Coaches set challenging goals, inform employees what is expected of them, and evaluate progress towards those goals (Shore & Bloom 1986, p. 362).

It is no coincidence that coaching takes its name from the sporting arena. In a sports setting, the coach does not act as a formal trainer but rather as one who aims to improve performance continuously through effective leadership (Stowel 1988). In the organisation, coaching becomes the day-to-day activity of the manager who uses the workplace to provide learning experiences for employees so that performance is continuously improved.

Generally, the coaching role involves the manager using certain distinct behaviours. The effective coach seems to display supportive behaviours such as showing concern and consideration for employees and initiating behaviours such as structured problem-solving discussions rather than non-supportive behaviours such as aggression and the use of power. Coaching highlights the crucial role of the manager in helping employees to learn at work.

Mentoring

A mentor is an older, more experienced person in the organisation who takes on a younger member of the organisation as a protégé and through the relationship that is developed, helps the protégé to advance in his or her career. The role of the mentor is ordinarily considered to be wider than that of the coach and will normally be performed by someone other than the direct superior of the protégé. Often the role of the mentor is split into two functions.

The career function of the mentor includes the usual developmental activities associated with coaching but also extends beyond that into the realm of corporate sponsorship. Thus mentors not only teach protégés how to advance in the organisation but also actively promoting their careers by advocating their ability and gaining them exposure and visibility to those who make important decisions in the organisation. The second function of mentors is more akin to that of the counsellor and is usually referred to as the psychosocial role of the mentor. In this capacity mentors build up the confidence and self esteem of proteges by providing them with counselling, friendship and roles on which to model their own behaviour.

The mentoring relationship typically follows a four stage chronology (Kram 1983).

1 **Initiation**—during the first 6–12 months the relationship becomes established and both parties adjust to their new roles
2 **Cultivation**—for a period of about 2–5 years the mentor relationship is at its most productive.
3 **Separation**—as a result of changes in the relationship (tensions) or external conditions (promotion of one party etc.) the relationship ceases to function
4 **Redefinition**—protege and mentor may develop a peer relationship if the feelings engendered by separation can be accommodated

There has been an explosion of formal mentoring programs in larger organisations in the last few years, particularly to assist women in their careers. A survey of training and development practices in Australian organisations showed 18 per cent of respondents were operating a mentoring program in 1991 compared to 9 per cent in 1986 (Collins & Hackman 1991).

Location of training—off-the-job

When the consequence of error is high, it is usually more appropriate to conduct training off-the-job. For example, most airline passengers would readily agree that it is preferable to train pilots in simulators than in the cockpit of a plane. Similarly, it is equally useful to have a bus driver train on an obstacle course before taking to the roads with a bus load of children. Off-the-job training is also used where complex skills have to be mastered or when the focus of the job is on interpersonal skills.

However, the costs of off-the-job training are high. There is also concern over the transfer of training to the workplace. As research has shown, the more dissimilar the training environment is from the workplace, the more likely it is that trainees will not be able to apply the skills learned to their jobs. For example, the transfer of training problem is minimal for vestibule training in which trainees learn in an environment that is very similar to their work environment. However, it may be difficult to apply teamwork skills learned in an outdoor training program to the job because the training environment is so different from the workplace.

Formal courses

The formal course method of training and development can be accomplished either by self-training which is facilitated by programmed instruction, computer-assisted instruction, and reading and correspondence courses, or by others-training, as in formal classrooms and lectures. Although many training programs use the lecture method because it efficiently conveys large amounts of information to large groups of people at the same time, it does have several drawbacks:

- it perpetuates the authority structure of traditional organisation and hinders performance because the learning process is not self-controlled
- except in the area of cognitive knowledge and conceptual principles, there is probably limited transfer from the lecture to the actual skills and abilities required to do the job
- the high verbal and symbolic requirements of the lecture method may be threatening to people with low verbal or symbolic experience or aptitude
- the lecture method does not permit individualised training based on individual differences in ability, interests and personality.

Because of these drawbacks, the lecture method is often complemented by other training methods.

Managing diversity

Literacy program a crucial precursor to work teams

Organisations with large numbers of blue-collar workers often experience problems in devolving management responsibilities down the line because of poor communication skills among shop floor employees. The situation worsens when employees come from primarily non-English-speaking backgrounds (NESB workers). Printing parts manufacturer, Columbia Pelikan, found itself in this situation: it had a long-term goal of implementing self-directing work teams and breaking down demarcations, but management realised the majority of the 110-strong factory workforce—90 per cent of whom are NESB workers—was not equipped with sufficient communication and literacy skills to handle the change.

Columbia Pelikan is the largest supplier of typewriter and printing ribbons in the Australian market. Its manufacturing plant is located in Milperra, south-western Sydney. In 1992, the company implemented its first literacy training program at the Milperra factory. It was initially a basic English skills program targeting NESB workers with a need to improve oral communication skills. Later, team leaders were targeted to enable more effective communication in the company with all workers. The aim of the program was to enable employees to understand written and spoken information and to improve all employees' ability to provide feedback and input on workplace issues—a crucial aspect of bottom-up workplace reform. The next target competency will be operators' writing and reading skills.

How was the program implemented? Training sessions were held in 4-hour blocks—three hours of company time and one hour individual's time. Presentations were held on the completion of courses, with employees making speeches. The company says there has been a noticeable improvement in self-esteem and assertiveness.

Some employees initially resisted the program, but the results have calmed their fears. Management says people in the company other than factory staff have since come forward of their own accord to request training after seeing the results.

The program has been managed by the plant manager—supported by the company management team. The multi-skilling of staff, in conjunction with the language and literacy training, has enabled greater flexibility in the company as people can now work in both the factory and the warehouse. Training in literacy and language has run side-by-side with other training, including training geared towards the establishment of self-directed work teams. Management says that without the language and literacy program other changes would not have been possible.

Source: Human Resources Report no. 87, 30 August 1994, p. 2.

Induction training

One of the most common forms of formal training in companies is induction or orientation training given to new employees when they start employment.

There are a number of reasons why induction takes place in organisations. There is evidence to show that labour turnover is highest among those who have most recently joined an organisation. Induction training, by helping to socialise the new entrant may help to reduce that level of turnover. A study of labour turnover and absenteeism in the Australian car industry demonstrated that both phenomena were strongly correlated with the degree of commitment of employees to the company (Automotive Industry Council 1990). If induction generates greater commitment on the part of the trainee, then it may be a powerful tool in reducing turnover. Legislative concerns are also of increasing importance. The employer has a duty to inform employees of occupational health and safety rules in the organisation, equal employment opportunity policies and general work rules that govern conduct in the organisation. The formal induction is a convenient forum for this activity and provides a record that employees have received that information in the case of litigation.

Training methods

A number of methods are used in formal training. This section will examine four methods that are often used in formal, company training programs—role playing, simulation, behaviour modelling and outdoor training.

Role playing

Role playing generally focuses on emotional (i.e. human relations) issues rather than on factual ones. The essence of role playing is to create a realistic situation, as in the case discussion method, and then have the trainees assume the parts of specific personalities in a situation. The usefulness of role playing depends heavily on the extent to which the trainees really 'get into' the parts they are playing. If you have done any role playing, you know how difficult this can be and how much easier it is to do what amounts to just 'reading' the part. But when the trainee does get into the role, the result is a greater sensitivity on his or her part to the feelings and insights that are presented by the role.

Behaviour modelling

Behaviour modelling has grown in popularity since the mid-1970s. The process of learning new behaviours through modelling has been applied since in a number of situations—training salespersons, job interviewees, eliminating racial prejudice at work. However, the technique of modelling has been most frequently used in the context of leadership, particularly for first-line supervisors.

Behaviour modelling involves the creation of a model which trainees observe and imitate in subsequent simulations. (Bandura 1977). The repetition of the simulations under the control of the trainer and the feedback received from other trainees reinforces the desired behaviour in the mind of the trainee to the point where it becomes an automatic response in similar situations. A typical behaviour modelling program might focus on handling difficult supervisory situations with employees such as dealing with grievances or correcting unacceptable behaviour. The session would begin with the trainer outlining a simple step-by-step approach to dealing with the situation. This outline would be followed by a model of the situation being handled correctly, usually recorded on video. Trainees would observe the video model and afterwards practise handling similar situations in one to one simulations controlled by the trainer. After the simulation, the trainee would receive feedback on their performance in terms of using the approach defined at the outset from both trainer and trainees. The emphasis in the feedback is on providing positive reinforcement, highlighting what the trainee did right.

Simulation

Simulation, a training and development technique that presents participants with situations that are similar to actual job conditions, is used for both managers and non-managers. A common technique for non-managers is the vestibule method, which simulates the environment of the individual's actual job. Since such an environment is not real, it is generally less hectic and safer than the actual one. As a consequence, there is the potential for adjustment difficulties in going from the simulated training environment to the actual one. Because of this some organisations prefer to do the training in the actual job environment. But the arguments for using the simulated environment are compelling: it reduces the possibility of customer dissatisfaction that can result from on-the-job training; it can reduce the frustration of the trainee; and it may save the organisation a great deal of money because fewer training accidents occur. Even though these arguments may seem compelling, however, not all organisations, even in the same industry, see the situation the same way. Some banks, for example, train their tellers on the job, whereas others train them in a simulated bank environment.

Outdoor training

Outdoor programs use the challenge of physical tasks and group activities in the natural environment to help trainees learn about themselves and their impact on others. The concept of outdoor programs originated with the Outward Bound movement whose original mission was to assist in the vocational preparation of young people. There are now some thirty-four centres throughout the world and its activities have extended into adult and management development.

The basic premise of an outdoor management program is the notion of setting trainees a problem or individual challenge (e.g. abseiling) for which they have no ready answer. The learning takes place through the process of working out a group solution to a problem or overcoming the challenge. After the exercise, the facilitator helps the trainees to reflect upon and analyse what happened. This type of program is enjoying increasing popularity in Australia and a number of large organisations use some form of outdoor training, often in conjunction with other forms of training, in their management development programs. A survey of training and development practices carried out by the Australian Graduate School of Management indicated that the number of organisations using outdoor programs increased from 8 per cent in 1986 to 23 per cent in 1991 (Collins & Hackman 1991). However, considerable criticism has been levelled at outdoor programs. This arises on two counts. Firstly, there is the difficulty of transferring skills learned in a non-work environment to the job as noted earlier in the chapter. Just because a team works well in the outdoors does not mean that it will work as well under the conflicting political pressures that characterise the work environment for many managers. There is also an ethical question. Does the company have the right to insist that unfit managers risk their health on hazardous outdoor activities when the training that they receive is of questionable benefit? Many companies are now are now moving away from outdoor training and, recognising the diverse abilities within their management ranks, using other forms of team-based activities such as community aid to train their executive teams.

Training technologies

In recent years, the world of the training practitioner has been invaded by new technologies which can significantly enhance the effectiveness of many conventional training programs. This section will discuss three such technologies—video, interactive video and computer-based training.

Video

Video presentations have generally replaced films as the visual medium of choice of organisational training. At its most basic level, video training includes taped instruction that can be stopped and started at any point. Because videos are less expensive than traditional training films, their use has increased rapidly in recent years. In fact, it was estimated that organisations spent $7 billion on video-based education in 1990 in the United States. An advantage of video is that instruction can be standardised. In the US for example, Pizza Hut faced the task of training 10 000 employees in various locations on such matters as competing with Domino's Pizza in the home delivery market, new products (e.g. pan pizza), safe driving, and customer service. Professionally prepared video presentations were mailed out to its individual locations, and the training was then provided on-site to each shift of workers. Cost savings over traditional training were substantial.

Interactive video

Interactive Video Training (IVT) combines the best features of programmed instruction with the best attributes of video instruction. Interactive video programs present a short video and narrative presentation and then require the trainee to respond. Usually, the video program is attached to a personal computer, and the learner responds to video cues by using a keyboard or touching a screen. This sequence—packaged program, learner response, and more programmed instruction—provides for individualised learning.

Computer-based training

Computer-based training covers a wide variety of applications of computers in training. Three major applications are usually distinguished. Firstly, computers can be used to control and manage the training process. Computer Managed Instruction (CMI), also known as Computer Managed Learning (CML) generates information about the students that are in training. Typically this information would be concerned with student records, the test results of the students and their progress through the training program.

Secondly, the computer can be used to instruct, a process known as Computer Assisted Instruction (CAI). In CAI the power of the computer is used to directly instruct the trainee, taking the place of the trainer. CAI systems usually revolve around two strategies. Drill and practice substitutes for the practice sessions so important in many skill training programs. Typical of these drill and practice programs would the typing tutor sessions that are now available with most word processing packages. In the tutorial mode, the computer gives information to the trainee. In the early days of computer-based training in the 1970s and 1980s, most tutorials were little more than 'page turning' programs in which the trainee simply sat in front of the computer screen and read information in the same way as a book. With the development of more sophisticated computer graphics and animation, information can be presented in a much more interesting way for the trainee and involve the trainee in an interactive way.

Finally, the computer can be used as a broader tool of learning in which the learner is more in control of the process and is using the computer in a real sense rather than being led by it. Computer Assisted Learning (CAL) is associated with more open-ended uses of the computer. The most common method associated with CAL is the simulation or game. The ability of the computer to store information and calculate the effect of changing the value of one variable on a series of others makes it an excellent tool for simulating the business environment of a company for the purposes of management training or steps to be used in operating a new machine.

Evaluating training and development programs

The evaluation of training and development programs is a necessary and useful activity, though in practice it is often not conducted. However, without an evaluation of results, it is impossible to tell if the training and development program met its objectives.

Evaluation criteria

There are many ways of evaluating training and development programs. Among the many options are changes in productivity, attitude survey results (covering, for example, satisfaction with supervisor, job satisfaction, stress, role conflict, and knowledge of work procedures), cost savings, benefit gains, and attitudes toward training (Smith 1992).

Traditionally training evaluation takes place at four levels (Kirkpatrick, 1975):

1 **Reaction to training**. Did the trainees like the program? Was the instruction clear and helpful? Do they believe they learned the material?
2 **Learning.** Did they acquire the knowledge and skills that were taught? Can they talk about things they couldn't talk about before? Can they demonstrate appropriate behaviours in training (role play)?
3 **Behaviour or performance change**. Can trainees now do things they couldn't do before (e.g. negotiate, conduct an appraisal interview)? Can they demonstrate new behaviours on the job? Is performance better?
4 **Production of results.** Were there tangible results in terms of productivity, cost savings, response time, quality, or quantity of job performance? Did the training program have utility?

The choice of criteria hinges on the level at which the training evaluation is to be conducted. For example, a short attitude survey could be used to assess the response of trainees to the course. However, such a survey would not provide information regarding learning, behaviour and results. In fact, when learning has been stressful or difficult, the trainees' reaction may even be negative.

If the objective is to assess what was learned, then paper-and-pencil tests can be used to determine knowledge acquisition. These may be used to analyse the content of responses to such training exercises as in-basket tests, role plays, or case analyses. While this may indicate that learning has occurred, it will not reveal whether learning has been transferred to the job.

To assess whether behaviour or performance has changed, output measures, performance evaluation reports, and employee attitude surveys provide better information. For example, if employees report more positive attitudes towards supervisory communications *after* they complete an interpersonal skills program, it may be deduced (assuming other hypotheses can be ruled out) that the training resulted in behavioural change. Finally, bottom-line results might be assessed by examining work group or unit output measures.

Evaluation designs

In addition to determining the appropriate criteria to evaluate the program, the human resources manager must select an evaluation design. These are important because they help the human resources manager determine if improvements have been made and if the training program caused the improvements. In addition to aiding in the evaluation of training programs, evaluation designs can (1) aid in evaluating any personnel and human resource program to improve productivity and the quality of work life, and (2) aid in evaluating the effectiveness of any personnel and human resource activity. Combining the data collection tools (i.e. organisational surveys) with knowledge of evaluation designs can prove essential for HRM in demonstrating its effectiveness, and that of any of its programs and activities, to the rest of the organisation. Because the combination of data collection and evaluation design is vital for HRM, evaluation design is discussed in more detail here. Review the assessment sections of all the other chapters to see how these evaluation designs might be used with data collection techniques to help measure human resource management effectiveness.

The three major types of evaluation designs are pre-experimental, quasi-experimental, and experimental. Although each can be used to evaluate the effectiveness of an HRM program, it is preferable to use experimental design, which is the most rigorous. Evaluation using this allows the human resources manager to be more confident that:

- a change has taken place—for example, that employee productivity has increased
- the change is caused by the program or HRM activity
- a similar change could be expected if the program were done again with other employees.

Because of many organisational constraints, however, the human resource manager is generally not able to use the experimental design and must settle for the moderately rigorous **quasi-experimental design**. Even when quasi-experimental designs are feasible, most evaluations that are done rely on the **pre-experimental design**. This is used because it is easier and quicker. Unfortunately, it is a poor one for most purposes. Figure 11.3 illustrates all three designs. This Figure is also used to convey how programs can be evaluated using these designs, and what is required. In Figure 11.3, X indicates that the program was administered. T1 indicates that a measure of the variable against which the program is to be evaluated (e.g. productivity or the level of accidents) is taken. T2 indicates that a second measure is taken on the same variable after training has occurred. Then the results of T1 and T2 are compared. Note that the two designs in the experimental class are different from those in the other two classes because all the individuals used in the evaluation are randomly assigned. Thus, if there are differences between T1 and T2, the human resource manager can be more confident that the changes were due to the program (X) and that the results can be repeated in future programs.

Pre experimental	Quasi-experimental	Experimental
1 One-shot-case study design $X \quad T_2$	1 time-series design $T_1 \ T_2 \ T_3 \ X \ T_4 \ T_5 \ T_6$	1 Pretest/post-test control group design $T_1 \quad X \quad T_2$ $T_1 \quad \quad T_2$
2 One-group pretest/post-test design $T_1 \quad X \quad T_2$	2 Non-equivalent control groups $T_1 \quad X \quad T_2$ $T_1 \quad \quad T_2$	2 Solomon four-group design $T_1 \quad X \quad T_2$ $T_1 \quad \quad T_2$ $\quad X \quad T_2$ $\quad \quad T_2$

Figure 11.3   The three major classes of evaluation designs to help determine program effectiveness

Source: Based on Goldstein 1974, pp. 49–65

As indicated, although using the experimental design is desirable, many organisations find it difficult to randomly assign employees to training programs. Organisations generally want all employees in a section trained, not just a few who are randomly selected. Consequently, the pre-experimental design is more typical of the type of evaluation that organisations use.

Management development

There are a number of reasons why management development is an increasingly important issue for human resource managers in the 1990s.

Despite corporate downsizing there are still a significant number of managers in Australia. Recent estimates put the managerial population at about 770 000, requiring about 30 000 new managers to be appointed per year simply to replenish the stock (Dawkins 1991).

Management is becoming an internationalised occupation as increasing numbers of managers are posted overseas to supervise the operations of transnational corporations. In the international context, however, it is clear that Australian managers do not match the educational and training profiles of their overseas counterparts. Only 21 per cent of Australian senior managers possess an undergraduate degree compared with more than 60 per cent of European managers and over 80 per cent of US and Japanese managers (Dawkins 1991). Training for managers in Australia also appears low by international standards, with Australian managers receiving an average of 4 hours training per year compared to an estimated 42 hours for managers in the USA (Cacioppe et al. 1990).

The performance of Australian managers has also been criticised. The short-term, profit orientation of management in this country has been unfavourably compared with the longer-term, strategic framework adopted by managers in competitor countries such as Germany and Japan (Dawkins 1991). Studies of major change programs such as Award Restructuring have left little doubt that it is the performance of local managers that is largely responsible for the success or failure of corporate change programs and thus change needs to be predicated upon the development of managers in the enterprise (McKenzie, Milner & Rimmer 1990).

If the case for management development in Australia is strong, the practice may be weakened by the rather conventional approaches that are taken to the problem. It appears that formal education and training programs are the order of the day with the emphasis on classroom-based training programs supplemented by external programs run through specialist institutes (such as the Institute for Administration in Sydney or Mount Eliza College in Melbourne) or Graduate Schools of Management in the university system. Doubt has been cast on the effectiveness of this largely American model of management training by studies in the UK which compared the management development experiences of managers in selected British and Japanese organisations. To the surprise of the researchers, British managers, almost without exception, reported receiving more management training than their Japanese counterparts. Indeed the very concept of management development appeared alien to the Japanese managers surveyed (Storey et al. 1991).

Further investigation, however, revealed that this counter-intuitive response indicated a fundamental difference in the approach taken to management development in the two countries. Whereas for British organisations management development was viewed as an 'add-on', given to the manager as a sign of favour in the organisation, in Japan, development was simply an integrated part of the manager's job. The emphasis on self-study, job rotation to create generalist managers and career 'mentoring' for senior managers was so well accepted within Japanese organisations, that the managers had difficulty in distinguishing management development as a separate category of activity.

In an attempt to make the mechanics of management development more relevant to the actual practice of management, competency-based approaches have become increasingly popular both overseas and in Australia (Saul 1989; Armstrong 1991). Originating in the USA with the work of Boyatzis (1982), an increasing number of organisations have attempted to define the exact competencies required of their managers. Boyatzis originally identified nineteen competencies which he grouped into five clusters:

1 Goal and action management
2 Leadership
3 Human resource management
4 Directing subordinates
5 Focus on others.

Boyatzis was careful, however, to state that competencies alone were not a sufficient condition of management effectiveness; they had to operate within a favourable organisational context to result in performance.

The major problem with the development of management competencies is the inherent complexity of the job and the lack of any universally applicable definition of what a manager does. As a result, lists of management competencies often become lists of mere activities or attributes, implying a return to the days of the 'traits' approach to management development when it was assumed that managers were born rather than made (Woodruffe 1991).

Nevertheless, the problem of the relevance of management development programs has continued to influence the development of new techniques in the field. In particular, techniques which emphasise the role of the individual manager in determining his or her own training needs and accepting the responsibility for meeting these needs have become popular.

Common approaches to management development

Action learning

Action learning stresses the importance of activity and problem solving to the development of managerial skills. In an action learning situation, managers taken from different organisational backgrounds are formed into groups to work on specific organisational problems. The multi-perspective approach of such a group helps the manager to learn not only about problem solving but also to question any operating assumptions made which result in less than effective behaviour (Revans 1982).

Self-development

Problems of releasing managers for formal training have made the notion of self-development very popular. The title, however, may be misleading. The self refers to the acceptance by the manager of responsibility for his or her own learning. This may involve attendance at formal training programs, but will also involve the formulation of training and a plan for meeting those needs through the use of work situations. The role of the training and development practitioner is very much one of a facilitator/counsellor, helping the manager to work out his own program of development and persisting with it.

Development centres

These are a refinement of the assessment centre process used in the selection and appraisal of managers in many larger organisations. The construction of the centre remains broadly similar, that is, a series of individual and group exercises observed by assessors who meet after the centre activities to produce an individual assessment of each candidate. However, the development centre is specifically geared toward the identification of development needs and the construction of an individualised training program for each candidate. This is considered to be a much less threatening process for those who go through the process.

 Future organisational forms

Restructuring management at Myer Grace Brothers

Myer Grace Brothers is the department store division of retailing conglomerate, Coles Myer Limited. Myer Grace Brothers was formed by the merger of Myer Stores Group and the Grace Brothers Stores Group in Coles Myer in the late 1980s. But in recent years the company's performance has been flagging with declining sales and profits.

Since 1993 the company has adopted a new strategy to reposition itself in the market and increase profitability. This has involved a major change in the organisational structure of the company. The new structure is based on a drastic reduction of management staff, a new role for managers in the stores and the implementation of teamwork on the sales floor. The role of the Store Manager has been changed to one of facilitator to employee teams.

Training is playing a key role in bedding down the new organisational structure. Store Managers and team leaders now see their jobs primarily in terms of coaching and training staff on the job. This idea of informal, on-the-job training has become known as *coaching on the run* and has been the focus of recent training for managers. Coaching on the run is seen as particularly important in helping staff adjust to the new expectations imposed on them as a result of the team system. As one Store Manager explained 'the strategies are obviously still important but the business of coaching and developing in all aspects of customer service, selling, merchandising is my primary focus'.

Much of the training and development for the teams takes place in the weekly communication meetings that the teams hold with the Store Manager. This is the forum for airing problems and solving them. Sometimes these weekly meetings are supplemented by half-day team development sessions which are attended by all the staff in a business unit.

Myer Grace Brothers managers feel that this type of training generates a level of commitment and enthusiasm that would not otherwise be there. As one manager said: 'I think from the style of training we do, informal mixed with the formal training, you gain a lot more commitment from the staff. And if you don't have the commitment, it's not going to happen'.

The switch to more informal training, coaching on the run, provides a powerful means of constantly improving the performance of staff and reinforcing the culture and the values of Myer Grace Brothers as the new organisational structure comes into being.

The Karpin Report

It was the level of concern about the capabilities of Australian managers and management development practice that led the then Minister for Employment, Education and Training, Kim Beazley, in 1992 to establish the Industry Task Force on Leadership and Management Skills, commonly known as the Karpin Committee after its chairman, David Karpin, Executive Director of resources giant, CRA. The Karpin committee's research has confirmed the pessimistic picture of Australian management presented above. But the Karpin committee has also shown how the role of the Australian manager has changed in the last 20 years and how it is likely to change in the next 20 (Table 11.2).

Karpin paints a picture of the evolving Australian senior manager as a globetrotting, corporate executive, managing workforces in several parts of the world. Whether this will be true of all Australian managers or simply the corporate executives that formed the samples for much of the research underpinning Karpin's deliberations is a matter of some debate. However, this is the basis on which Karpin based his main recommendations. These include:

- The development of an 'enterprise culture' starting at the level of primary and secondary schooling
- Capitalising on the talents of diversity and, particularly, those of women
- Measures to improve the management of small business by using, among other things, a system of qualified mentors or advisers to provide advice to small business managers
- Developing a new, front-line management development program for the estimated 180 000 frontline managers in Australia who have not received any formal, management training
- The development of a framework of management competency standards for use across all industries so that all managers gain a common core of skills
- Measures to improve the standards of management education offered by university business schools including moving away from the traditional, gendered focus of management education, the accreditation of MBA programs and the establishment of a new National Management School
- The promotion of best practice in management through measures such as international study tours for up to 1500 Australian managers each year

Table 11.2 The emerging senior manager profile

1970 **THE AUTOCRAT**	TODAY **THE COMMUNICATOR**	2010 **THE LEADER/ENABLER**
• Male.	• Male.	• Male or female.
• Anglo-Celt, British or Australian citizenship.	• Anglo-Celt, Australian citizenship.	• Wide range of ethnicities, citizenships.
• Started as message boy, rose through ranks. All management training on-the-job.	• Graduate, possibly postgraduate qualification. Career in corporate centre. Product of internal management development program.	• Graduate, probably MBA or AMP as well. Wide ranging career, many placements. Product of major development program including placements.
• Very local focus, possibly one Australian state. Has travelled once, to England.	• Expanding focus, travels regularly to Asia, United States of America, Europe.	• Global focus, travels regularly. Has lived in two or more countries.
• Established competitors, cartels.	• Recently deregulated marketplace, rapidly changing competitors.	• Manages in both regulated and deregulated economies.
• Paternal view of workforce.	• Sees workforce as stakeholder in business, working hard on communication and information sharing.	• Manages workforces in several countries. Shares information and delegates heavily.
• Stable environment. Relatively low stress, home to see kids most nights, long term position.	• Turbulent environment. High stress, long hours, fears burnout.	• Environment typified by rapid change. Limited term appointment, high pressure, results driven.

Source: Karpin 1995, p. 3

- The establishment of the Australian Council for Management Development which would oversee the implementation of many of Karpin's proposals and maintain a national focus on management development.

Karpin's views about the role of the manager have attracted some criticism. In particular, Karpin has been accused of under-estimating the changing nature of managerial work as a result of the introduction of teamwork in many organisations (Emery 1995). In many cases, teams are taking over the role of the traditional manager and making many decisions for themselves. In this situation, managers may become facilitators rather than leaders. It is not clear what the final impact of Karpin will be on management education in Australia. Although the report received widespread publicity at the time of its release, most of its recommendations have not been put into practice. The idea of a new national management school, in particular, was quickly dismissed by the federal government for whom this proposal represented an unnecessary increase in public resources. Furthermore, the election of a new, Coalition federal government in March 1996 considerably reduced the impact of the recommendations.

Organisational learning

Many organisations undergo a number of change programs in an attempt to improve competitiveness. Culture change, quality circles and TQM become almost fads or fashions which organisations subscribe to without any lasting impact on their effectiveness (Abrahamson 1996). Over time, however, some organisations continue to change and improve while others find it more difficult. A learning process would therefore appear to take place within organisations which enables them to survive in changing environments. Fiol & Lyles have described organisational learning as:

> ... the process of improving actions through better knowledge and understanding (Fiol & Lyles 1985, p. 810).

The concept of organisational learning is not new. It originated with economists who noted that successful organisations became better at what they did, over time. For instance, car manufacturers learnt to make cars cheaply and more quickly; retailers learnt how to keep constant supplies of goods on the shelves. In this way the organisations became more efficient and more profitable.

What is new is the increasing emphasis being placed on organisational learning as a process. It is now being seen not just as something that happens naturally, but as something that should be made explicit and should be fostered. In other words, in a rapidly changing economic environment, organisations need to learn and adapt quickly and efficiently.

What is a learning organisation?

As Kim (1993) has said, all organisations learn. However, organisational learning does not, necessarily imply that what is learned is good for the organisation. Organisations may learn bad habits as well as good. There are a number of elements that comprise the effective learning organisation.

Systems thinking

Systems thinking forms the basis of many commentators' views on learning organisations (e.g. Senge 1990). People working within organisations need to know that one part or process within an organisation never functions in isolation; change always leads to effects elsewhere. Therefore people taking actions need to take account of all the possible effects. An organisation does not just form a system of and by itself. It is also part of a wider system (in fact, of many wider systems) or an 'environment'.

Senge et al. (1994) suggest that it is hard for people to think in systems terms, because the way in which language is constructed can only have one (or a few) causes for one effect and vice versa. They also suggest that thinking in systems terms enables managers to avoid seeing organisational change as only a top-down process. Change can be initiated at any level of an organisation and should be participative in nature, because everyone is affected by any change.

Changes to the system, either internally or externally, have wide-ranging effects on the organisation. The organisation reacts and this process is almost involuntary. But the organisation has a choice: it can learn from these changes. Like an individual learner, it notes the experience and reflects on it. Next time, the reaction need not be involuntary and the organisation can anticipate the changes and move to pre-empt them.

Changes in the way in which work is organised

The concept of the learning organisation is gaining popularity because the environment in which organisations operate is seen as becoming increasingly complex and fast-changing. Some of these changes include:

- decentralisation of operations
- a move to flatter organisation structures
- the introduction of cultural change programs
- technological innovation
- increased networking between organisations
- the breakdown of demarcations
- multi-skilling of the workforce
- the increasing use of casual or otherwise 'loosely attached' workers
- an increased use of autonomous workteams at many levels of production, working without supervision and making their own decisions (Dunphy & Stace 1990).

Lepani believes that:

> ... employees are increasingly being defined by what they do, or by what they contribute, rather than the position they hold (Lepani 1995, p. 19).

Organisational learning is the ability of the organisation to adopt these changes in response to changes in the marketplace and to learn and improve as time goes on. Thus, the ability of the organisation to learn underpins the effective implementation of organisational change.

The way in which individuals learn

Organisations can only learn through their individual members. Individuals can undergo learning outside their organisations but organisations do not learn except through individuals. Kim (1993) suggests a model of learning that adds the role of memory to experience. He adds the concept of individual mental models, which are deeply ingrained assumptions, generalisations, or even pictures or images that influence how we understand the world and how we take action (Senge 1990). While the models help people to make sense of the world, they can also confine the way in which we understand things, and may be dangerous if we assume they are reality.

The relationship between individual learning and organisational learning

Organisational learning is not simply the sum of the learning of each of the individuals in the enterprise. Organisational learning implies a capacity to transmit the lessons from one generation of employees to another and to adapt as a result of the learning process. Organisational learning is a much deeper process involving the development of insights and knowledge over a long period of time and the ability to critically assess the assumptions on which the organisation is basing its actions.

For individual learning to become organisational learning, the role of memory is crucial. An organisation's memory is stored in its mental models, which function as individuals do—there will be frameworks and routines. There will also be written-down materials; databases, reference manuals, personnel procedures, plans, copies of letters, technical manuals, pro-formas. As Field & Ford suggest:

> ... it is organisational memory that ensures that lessons learnt are not subsequently forgotten, and that there is continuous improvement (rather than one step forwards, one step backwards) (Field & Ford 1995).

Learning theory for individuals cannot simply be transposed into learning theory for organisations. However, it seems that organisations have the capacity to learn from their experiences. One model of describing this, which is consistent with systems thinking, was suggested by Daft & Weick (1984, in Kim 1993), who suggested that organisations learn in a three-step manner:

- **Scanning**—monitoring and obtaining data about the environment
- **Interpreting**—translating events and developing concepts consistent with prior knowledge of the environment
- **Learning**—understanding the interrelationship between the organisation's actions and the environment, and taking actions.

Barriers to organisational learning

There are many barriers to effective organisational learning.

Field & Ford (1995) have identified four critical dimensions within the organisation that have to co-ordinated if effective organisational learning is to take place. These include employee relations, work organisation, skill formation and technology and information systems. These dimensions are interrelated and are depicted in Figure 11.4.

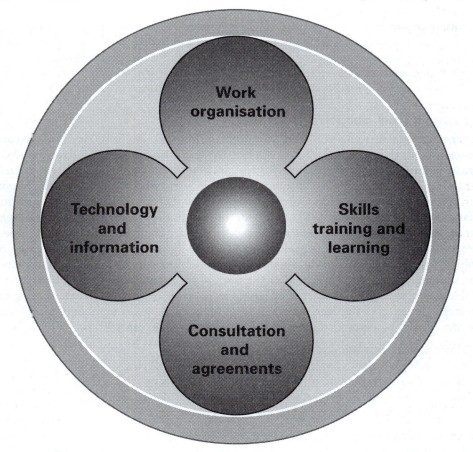

Figure 11.4 Factors which affect organisational learning

Source: Field & Ford 1995, p. 23

- **Employee relations**—if the employee relations climate is adversarial, every change will be approached with suspicion and no-one will be willing to become flexible outside their normal working conditions. Many opportunities for learning—by management and workers—will be lost.
- **Work organisation**—if work is organised in too structured a manner, people won't have the chance to learn anything new or to help other people in other departments.
- **Skill formation**—training may be carried out in a very conventional manner e.g. sending employees to a training centre for a course. Their learning is not shared and they feel frustrated because they see no chance of trying out what they've learned. In cases like this training can actually be bad for learning.
- **Technology/information systems**—knowledge about new technology may be jealously guarded by certain people and training may be inadequate. People cannot access the new technology themselves to make their own work better and more interesting.

Some other barriers to learning (Kim 1993) include:

- **Superstitious learning**—incorrect connections are made between what the organisation does and the response in the environment. Usually the interpretation is made to suit people's own agendas.
- **Situation learning**—in individual solves an immediate problem and moves on to the next thing, without thinking about what has been learned. The individual's mental model has not changed, so neither can the organisation's mental model.
- **Fragmented learning**—parts of the organisation learn, but the others do not. Learning is not spread evenly through the organisation.

Training and corporate strategy

If organisational learning emphasises the organisation-wide implications of training and development, then training should have a strong relationship to the strategy of the organisation. However, until recently it appears that training took a highly reactive role in the business. The discussion of training needs analysis earlier in this chapter highlights this reactive posture well. Most of the processes described are predicated on the notion that analysis is focused on the 'ground floor' of organisations i.e. the individual and the group levels. Tools for needs analysis at these levels are comparatively well developed. Processes for analysis at the organisational level are less sophisticated. In any case, the overall strategic direction of the organisation is rarely questioned in the analysis phase; the training practitioner tends to take the strategy for granted and work within it.

However, the notion that training has an important part to play in determining the strategic direction of the organisation is beginning to emerge. A number of factors can be identified that are contributing to this emergence (Garavan 1991):

- difficulties in recruiting skilled managers
- the need to develop a more flexible and adaptable skill base
- the need to align the potential of employees with business objectives
- the greater emphasis on performance evaluation and management
- the need for human resource and succession planning.

These are activities that are carried out at the strategic level in organisations i.e. senior level, long-range planning. In so far as these are viewed as strategic issues by managers, then the training policies to address them will be fashioned at the strategic level.

Research by Andrew Pettigrew and his colleagues at the UK-based Centre for Corporate Strategy and Change outlined a possible model for relationship between corporate strategy and training (Hendry 1991). The model is illustrated in Figure 11.5.

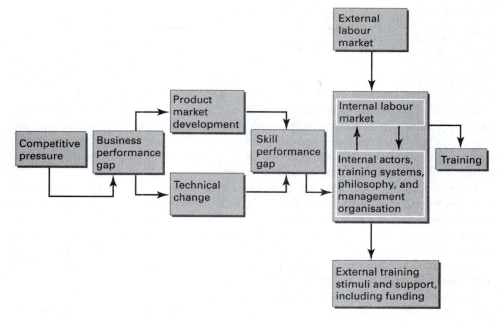

Figure 11.5 Factors which trigger and stabilise training
Source: Hendry 1991, p. 81

In this model, there are a variety of forces which act to trigger and/or stabilise training in organisations. These include the strategic position of the organisation, the nature of the external labour market (whether skills are available outside), external stimuli to training such as government grants, legislation etc. and internal organisational factors such as the presence of an internal labour market and the general philosophy of management (i.e. training orientation).

Recent research in Australia has added to our understanding of the relationship between corporate strategy and training (Smith et al. 1995; Hayton et al. 1996). Although most senior managers in Australian organisations claim that training is important to the long-term survival of their business, it appears that the reality of training provision in most enterprises does not reflect this senior management rhetoric. In fact, the key decisions about training in enterprises are taken at the operational level, by middle and junior managers. These managers are often working to tight deadlines with few resources to spare. In this situation, training receives a much lower priority than senior managers may claim. Training appears to be an operational rather than a strategic concern in modern Australian organisations.

The challenge to training practitioners is to move away from training which occurs as a 'burst of enthusiasm' in response to a temporary skills shortage or external encouragement and consolidate training as part of the way in which the organisation is run.

International comparisons

In contrast to companies in Australia and the Unites States, Japanese companies appear to offer far more extensive training for their employees. This also appears to be the case in Germany, particularly regarding apprenticeship training.

Japan

According to studies of vocational training in Japan, as many as 80 per cent of all business enterprises conduct in-company job training. Broken down according to employee classification, job training is made available to new regular employees in 75 per cent of all companies, and to non-regular employees in 52 per cent of them.

If classified according to the size of the firm, training increases with organisational size. Every firm with more than 5000 employees provides its own training. Vocational training in small- to medium-sized companies depends to a greater extent on cooperative centres established through the effort of the government's employment promotion agency, aided by state, municipal, and town agencies.

The in-company form of training is looked upon as the key to each company's productivity and managerial control. Regular employees generally have academic training but few, if any, vocational skills. Training is thus the means by which an employee is shaped to the company's needs. It is not unusual for new employees to have anywhere from one to six months of training before being integrated into the work force. Supplemental training usually continues throughout the first three years of an employee's career, with additional training provided as needed.

Descriptions of training programs generally reveal a greater emphasis on the company as a whole—its role in society (including the community, the nation, and the world), its relationship to the competition, its marketing goals and objectives. In short, training constantly seeks to develop the individual worker as a fully rounded worker who not only sees the whole picture, but is also able to respond to it. The payoffs of this philosophy are minimal levels of turnover and absenteeism.

Actual job training teaches workers to apply skills to a variety of situations, thereby permitting worker rotation. All blue-collar workers are expected to be multi-skilled within four or five years after joining the company. Many believe that this orientation toward skills enrichment and labour mobility is a crucial factor in the rapid growth of the Japanese economy.

However, the enterprise focus of much training in Japan has opened the system up to the criticism that the training activities are not is much about passing of skills as 'brainwashing' employees into accepting the company's policies and engaging the commitment of the workforce. Certainly, there is little public provision of vocational training in Japan and this reduces the ability of Japanese workers to use gain recognition for their skills outside the company. This effectively ties the Japanese worker to their company and restricts the free movement of labour between employers. There is some evidence that this is beginning to change as the Japanese government introduces public tests for the accreditation of skills (Curtain 1994).

Germany

Germany's economy is based on providing high-priced, high-quality goods. German executives say a key factor in their industrial success is a sophisticated workforce. 'You need highly qualified people when you produce high-quality goods,' says Hans-Peter Kassai, chief economist with Daimler-Benz.

A relatively unique feature of the training and development of employees in Germany is an extensive and successful apprenticeship system. The three-and-a-half-year apprenticeship program gives employees wide expertise on many machines. The program costs about $15 000 per apprentice, and each year German companies spend about $20 billion on their programs. Apprenticeship training for almost a half million German students begins at age 15 when compulsory schooling ends. At that point, young people select one of several programs. By comparison, in Australia, many machine operators receive just a week or two of training.

Even though the apprenticeship programs are costly, German firms believe it pays off because workers end up being more loyal and more willing to stay. Once the companies take on apprentices as permanent employees, they often stay for years, giving a stability and maturity to the work force that many countries lack. However, demographic shifts are impacting the future supply of skilled workers. In 1993, for the first time, the number of students entering university in Germany exceeded those entering apprentice programs. As a consequence, a number of apprentice slots went unfilled.

Training policy

It was comparisons with countries such as Germany and Japan that persuaded the federal government in the mid-1980s that Australian organisations were not providing enough training for their employees and that government intervention was necessary to rectify this situation. The direction of these training reforms was initially set by three major reports that were commissioned by the Department of Employment, Education and Training in the early 1990s.

The Finn Review (Australian Education Council 1991) advocated the convergence of general and vocational education and set ambitious targets for the retention of young people in the education and training system until Year 12 or equivalent. The Mayer Report (Australian Education Council/MOVEET 1992) developed the notion of 'key competencies' that had been introduced by Finn as specific vocational skills that should form the basis of curricula within the education and training system. Finally, the Carmichael Report (Employment and Skills Formation Council 1992) proposed a new competency-based, entry level system of training which would eventually subsume and/or replace the existing apprenticeship and traineeship arrangements at a national level.

The reforms that have taken place as a result of these reports have become known collectively as the National Training Reform Agenda (NTRA). Broadly speaking, the NTRA is based on six principles (Smith 1993):

1. Competency-based rather than process-oriented training (a concern with outcomes rather than length of time spent training)
2. The creation of flexible pathways so that trainees can move between different training programs with ease and with credit for training already undertaken
3. National recognition of training through the National Framework for the Recognition of Training (NFROT)
4. Articulation and credit transfer of skills
5. Greater convergence between general and vocational education
6. The introduction of the new apprenticeship and traineeship systems.

The implementation of the reforms led to the creation of a number of bodies to facilitate the reform process. Principal amongst these were the National Training Board (NTB) and the Australian National Training Authority (ANTA). The NTB has supervised the establishment of industry competency standards through a series of competency setting bodies (usually existing Industry Training Advisory Bodies). ANTA, the outcome of an agreement in 1992 between state and federal governments to rationalise funding to the TAFE systems, has increasingly taken the role of a policy setting body for the establishment of a national education and training system.

In order to encourage organisations to increase their expenditure on training directly, the federal government introduced the Training Guarantee Scheme. Under this scheme, organisations were obliged to spend a minimum of 1.5 per cent of their total payroll costs on structured training for employees. The scheme was introduced in 1990. However, there is little evidence that the Training Guarantee played a major role in increasing training expenditure. As a result of this and the successful lobbying of employer groups, the scheme was suspended for two years in the White Paper on Employment and Growth—Working Nation (Keating 1994) in 1994 and finally abolished by the incoming Coalition federal government in 1996.

Reactions to the training reforms

The NTRA generally has come under fire from both employers and educationalists. Educationalists have objected to the emphasis on competency-based training in the NTRA (Porter et al. 1992; Collins 1993) claiming that the notion of competency is too narrow and too behavioural-based to secure a general, liberal education for those undergoing competency-based education and training programs.

Employers have been more concerned with the perceived bureaucratic nature of the reforms and the slow speed of implementation (Curtain 1994, p. 48). There is little doubt that the training reforms have given rise to a plethora of bureaucratic bodies concerned with the implementation of different aspects of the NTRA.

Concerned that the impetus behind the NTRA might be stalling, the Australian National Training Authority (ANTA), the country's peak training policy agency, commissioned a review the progress of the reforms (Allen Consulting Group 1994). The ANTA review concluded that progress had indeed been very slow and that industry had been insufficiently involved in the process. As a result, the NTRA had focused on the supply of the training (from bodies such as the Technical and Further Education [TAFE] Colleges) without a clear view about the demand for training from industry. The review claimed that the title of 'agenda' was appropriate to the mixed bag of reforms it contained:

> While there is a discernible and coherent strategy lying behind the introduction of competency-based training the relationship between this, the open training market, entry level training, funding of training and access and equity goals is not clear ... the power of the reforms lies in the extent to which, together, they provide a comprehensive and complete response not to a random set of smaller goals but to the big goal of making Australia's enterprises and industries more competitive through the integrated use of a range of skill formation strategies (Allen Consulting Group 1994, p. 48).

Apart from the abolition of the Training Guarantee, the Coalition federal government has taken a far less interventionist role in the training market. Many of the labour market training programs aimed at the unemployed that bloomed in the 1980s and early 1990s have been cut back and the training market opened up to private training providers that compete directly with state-based providers such as TAFE. The Coalition government has also carried on the reform the apprenticeship system started by the Carmichael report and has pulled the apprenticeship and traineeship systems into a single national system.

Summary

The training and development of employees is becoming an increasingly important and necessary activity of human resource management. Rapidly changing technologies make employees obsolete more quickly today than ever before. As employee training and development becomes more important, it must also be more effective. This requires careful attention to the three phases of training and development: assessment or needs analysis, program development and implementation, and evaluation. The three types of needs analysis discussed in this chapter are a careful and systematic diagnosis of the short- and long-range human resource needs of the organisation; a determination of the skills and abilities necessary for specific jobs in the organisation; and an analysis of the current and expected performance levels of employees in the organisation compared with the performance levels desired of them. This difference between actual and desired employee performance defines a training and development need.

The final question then remaining is who should be trained. In general, any one with an important performance discrepancy should be trained. A program is then chosen that matches skills needed with the type of employee or group to be trained.

The last major phase of training and development is the evaluation phase. This phase compares data to see whether a change has occurred and to determine whether the change is due to the training and development program.

The importance of training and development has been recognised in recent years by governments, employers and unions. The Training Reform Agenda is a series of initiatives designed to improve Australia's training system and improve the skills of the workforce.

An emerging issue for training practitioners is management development. This was the subject of the Karpin Committee Review which made recommendations for major changes to the ways in which Australian managers are educated and trained.

Training and development programs will continue to be important as the emphasis on continual education increases and as companies make radical changes in their approaches to their business.

questions for discussion and review

1. Describe and explain the three major phases of any training and development program.
2. Reflect for a moment on your own work experience. What benefits did your former (or present) employer receive by training you? Why didn't your employer just hire someone who could perform the job without training?
3. Why do training specialists enjoy so little influence in Australian organisations?
4. What are some design principles that can enhance the learning that takes place in training and development programs?
5. You have been asked to train employees to use personal computers. What factors would you consider in designing the program?
6. What relationship does training and development have with other activities of human resource management?
7. How do companies decide whether to invest in training? What factors would influence a company not to invest in training?
8. Can poor managers be trained to perform better?
9. Discuss the strategic involvement of training and development.
10. How will the training reforms improve the competitive position of Australian organisations?

case study

IBM has had a presence in Australia since 1932. The company only started manufacturing in Australia, however, in 1976 when it opened the Wangaratta plant to produce the 'S' electric typewriter for the protected Australian market. In 1984 the plant changed over to the production of the PC computer and now produces planar boards (PCBs), the RISC 6000 and the PS/2 personal computer. Some 70 per cent of the plant's production goes to export principally to Japan, Korea and SE Asia. The plant employs some 240 full-time staff and a further 300 casual staff who make up the majority of the shop floor production workforce. Casual employment of shop floor staff has helped the company to keep its production costs low and remain competitive in the export markets it serves.

IBM Australia has a structured approach to training involving the extensive provision of in-house courses for permanent IBM staff and a systematic, on-the-job training process for shop floor employees at the Wangaratta plant. This is undergoing some change as the company has decentralised its training in the wake of internal restructuring and is planning more extensive provision of formal training for shop floor employees.

Management staff are required to undertake 3–5 days formal training per year. Usually this training takes the form of management seminars held at the Sydney HQ. With the cut back in the central training function, these management seminars are now held at the plant level using local training staff.

Technical and professional staff
The bulk of staff employed at the plant are engineers mostly concerned with the manufacturing needs of running the factory. Engineers are recruited directly from university, the company does not sponsor engineering students. After recruitment, the engineers are given opportunities to participate in formal training courses, many of which are run at the plant using IBM training staff, specialist IBM staff or local training providers such as TAFE. The company also operates a professional year program with Swinburne University. Under this arrangement, up to 24 engineering students a year from Swinburne are placed at the Wangaratta plant for a year's business experience in their third year, returning to Swinburne to finish their degree.

Operator training
Among the casual workforce there is a high level of specific job-related training which is an on-going process as a result of the relatively high turnover of casual staff. New staff receive a half day general induction to the plant from the training instructor in their area where they are given information that is directly relevant to their job. This covers basic health and safety, the importance of wearing protective clothing to eliminate the risk of electrostatic discharge and some basic product knowledge.

The new recruits are then taken to the production areas where their on-job training is handled by the supervisor and other IBM staff who are specialists in the processes involved. The training that the operator receives for each task is carefully documented in a manual that is given to the new operators to help them master each new task. As operators achieve the required standards on the tasks which they are doing they are 'signed off' by Engineering. Engineering sign off involves observation and questioning of the operator by an engineer who will then 'qualify' the operator on the tasks observed on the basis of their performance. The aim of the training is to achieve a fully qualified casual workforce. Operator training at Wangaratta is a lengthy and highly structured activity. The use of casual staff and the quality standards that the company has to meet have compelled the company to adopt this structured approach to manage the problems associated with a large, shifting workforce.

There are a number of powerful factors driving the provision of training at the Wangaratta plant. These include:

- The general philosophy of employee development that pervades the whole company
- The clear link between the Wangaratta plant's strategy of low cost production combined with very high levels of product quality
- The pressures exerted by the expansion of production at the plant in the last few years and the need for shop floor employees to become more responsible and self directing
- The introduction of new technology and equipment, and
- The need for greater business skills among management staff as the plant takes on more highly value added work and expands its marketing drive into Asia.

Although the plant's training needs are growing quickly as the plant expands and changes the nature of its activities, there are considerable bottlenecks in the supply of training which are limiting the ability of the company to develop its staff quickly to cope with the new environment. These include the difficulty of release, especially for professional and management staff for training and the lack of competent local training providers to service the plant.

Training planning is undertaken on an individual basis at the Wangaratta plant. Employees are assessed against six key skill areas:

1. Customer relations
2. Business acumen
3. Knowledge of the IBM environment
4. Project management
5. Knowledge of products/systems
6. Personal skills.

These key skills form the basis of a skills matrix which employees and their managers can rate themselves against— each skill rated from 1–5 depending on its importance to the particular job in question. The analysis covers all IBM staff and results in individual profiles which are used to draw up individual training plans.

The company has traditionally spent about 5 per cent of payroll on training. This figure is likely to increase as new training initiatives come on stream in future years.

Source: Smith et al. 1995.

Questions

1. Is the balance of on-the-job and off-the-job training right at IBM?
2. How well is IBMs training integrated with its business strategy?
3. How is training likely to change in the future at IBM?

Resources

Adler, P. (ed.) (1992), *Technology and the Future of Work*, Oxford University Press, New York.

Allen Consulting Group (1994), '*Successful Reform: Competitive Skills for Australians and Australian Enterprises*', Report to the Australian National Training Authority, Allen Consulting Group, Melbourne.

Applebaum, E. & Batt, R. (1994), *The New American Workplace*, Cornell University Press, Ithaca.

Collins, R. & Hackman, K. (1991), *National Survey of Training and Development Practices*, July 1991, CCH-AGSM, Sydney.

Brown, C., Reich, M., & Stern, D. (1993), 'Becoming a High-performance Work Organisation: The Role of Security, Employee Involvement and Training', *International Journal of Human Resource Management*, vol. 4, no. 2, pp. 247–75.

Burns, R. (1995), *The Adult Learner at Work*, Business and Professional Publishing, Sydney.

Cappelli, P. (1994), *Training and Development in Public and Private Policy* (International Library of Management), Dartmouth, Brookfield, USA.

Carnevale, A., Meltzer & Gainer, A. (1990), *Workplace Basics: The Skills that Employers Really Want,* Jossey-Bass, San Francisco, CA.

Field, L. & Ford, B. (1995), *Managing Organisational Learning: From Rhetoric to Reality*, Longman, Melbourne.

Finegold, D. (1992), 'The Changing International Economy and its Impact on Education and Training', *Oxford Studies in Comparative Education*, vol. 2, no. 2, pp. 57–82.

Ryan, P. (ed.) (1991), *International Comparisons of Vocational Education and Training,* Falmer Press, London.

Sloan, J. (1994), 'The Market for Training in Australia', *Working Paper 131,* National Institute of Labour Studies, Flinders University of South Australia, Adelaide.

Stevens, J. & Mackay, R. (eds) (1991), *Training and Competitiveness,* Kogan Page, London.

Smith, A. (1992), *Training and Development in Australia,* Butterworths, Sydney.

Smith, A., Hayton, G., Roberts, P., Thorne, E. & Noble, C. (1995), *Enterprise Training: The Factors that Affect Demand,* Office of Training and Further Education, Melbourne.

Wexley, K. N. & Latham, G. P. (1991), *Developing and Training Human Resources in Organizations*, 2nd edition, Harper Collins, New York.

References

Abrahamson, E. (1996), 'Management Fashion', *Academy of Management Review*, vol. 21, no. 1, pp. 254–85.

Allen Consulting Group (1994), *Successful Reform: Competitive Skills for Australians and Australian Enterprises,* Report to the Australian National Training Authority, Allen Consulting Group, Melbourne.

Armstrong, A. (1991), 'Management Skills and Performance Audit', *Asia-Pacific HRM,* vol. 29, no. 4, pp. 25–39.

Australian Education Council / MOVEET (1992), *Putting General Education Together* (The Mayer Report), Australian Government Publishing Service, Canberra.

Australian Education Council Review Committee (1991), *Young People's Participation in Post-compulsory Education and Training: Report of the AEC Review Committee* (The Finn Review), Australian Government Publishing Service, Canberra.

Automotive Industry Council (1990), *Labour Turnover and Absenteeism: Costs and Causes in the Australian Automotive Industry,* Australian Manufacturing Council, Melbourne.

Bandura, A. (1977), *Social Learning Theory*, Prentice-Hall, Englewood Cliffs, NJ.

Boyatzis, R. E. (1982), *The Competent Manager: A Model for Effective performance*, Wiley, New York.

Cacioppe, R., Warren-Langford, P. & Bell, E. (1990), 'Trends in Human Resource Development and Training', *Asia-Pacific HRM,* vol. 28, no. 2, pp. 55–72.

Cappelli, P. & Rogovsky, N (1994), 'New Work Systems and Skill Requirements', *International Labour Review*, vol. 133, no. 2, pp. 205–20.

Carnevale, A. P., Gainer, L. J. & Meltzer, A. S.(1990a), *Workplace Basics: The Essential Skills Employers Want*, Jossey-Bass, San Francisco.

—— (1990b), *Workplace Basics: Training Manual,*Jossey-Bass, San Francisco.

Collins, C. (1993), 'Competencies: For and Against', Keynote address presented to the Australian Curriculum Studies Association National Conference, QUT, Brisbane, 1 July, 1993.

Collins, R. & Hackman, K. (1991), *National Survey of Training and Development Practices: July, 1991*, Australian Graduate School of Management, Sydney, p. 13.

Curtain R. (1993), *Has the Apprenticeship System a Future? The Impact of Labour Market Reform on Structured Entry Level Training*, Unpublished report commissioned by the Department of Employment Education and Training.

—— (1994), 'The Australian Government's Training Reform Agenda: Is It Working?', *Asia-Pacific Journal of Human Resources*, vol. 32, no. 2, pp. 43–56.

Dawkins, J. S. (1991), *The Australian Mission on Management Skills: vol. 1: Report*, Australian Government Publishing Service, Canberra.

Dunphy, D. & Stace, D. (1990), *Under New Management: Australian Organizations in Transistion*, McGraw-Hill, Sydney.

Emery, F. (1995), 'Managers Look Past Snake-oil for Ideas', *Business Review Weekly*, October, vol. 16, p. 76.

Employment and Skills Formation Council (1992), *The Australian Vocational Certificate Training System* (The Carmichael Report), Australian Government Publishing Service, Canberra.

Field, L. & Ford, B. (1995), *Managing Organisational Learning: From Rhetoric to Reality*, Longman, Melbourne.

Fiol, C. & Lyles, M. (1985), 'Organizational learning', *Academy of Management Review*, vol. 10, no. 4, pp. 803–13.

Ford, J. K. & Noe, R. A. (1987), 'Self Assessed Training Needs: The Effects of Attitude Toward Training, Managerial Level and Function', *Personnel Psychology*, vol. 40, pp. 40–53.

Garavan, T. N. (1991), 'Strategic Human Resource Development', *Journal of European Industrial Training*, vol. 15, no. 1, pp. 17–30.

Gist, M. E., Bavetta, A. G. & Stevens, C. K. (1990), 'Transfer Training Method: Its Influence on Skill Generalization, Skill Repetition and Performance Level', *Personnel Psychology*, vol. 43, pp. 501–23.

Goldstein, I. (1974), *Training: Program Development and Evaluation*, Brooks/Cole Publishing Company, Monterey, CA, pp. 49–65.

Goldstein, I. L. (1986), *Training Program Development and Evaluation*, 2nd edition, Brooks/Cole, Monterey, CA.

Hayton, G., McIntyre, J., Sweet, R., MacDonald, R., Noble, C., Smith, A. & Roberts, P. (1996), *Enterprise Training in Australia*, Final Report to the Office of Training and Further Education, Victoria, University of Technology, Sydney.

Hendry, C. (1991), 'Corporate Startegy and Training', in J. Stevens & R. Mackay, (eds), *Training and Competitveness*, Kogan Page, London.

—— (1991), 'Training and Corporate Strategy', in J. Stevens & R. Mackay (eds), *Training and Competitiveness*, Kogan Page, London.

Karpin, D. S. (1995), *Enterprising Nation: Reviewing Australia's Managers to meet the challenges of the Asia Pacific Century, Executive Summary*, Australian Government Publishing Service, Canberra, p. 3.

—— (1995), *Enterprising Nation: Renewing Australia's Managers to Meet the*

Challenges of the Asia-Pacific Century, Report of the Industry Taskforce on Leadership and Management Skills, Australian Government Publishing Service, Canberra.

Keating, J. (1995), *Australian Training Reform: Implications for Schools,* Curriculum Corporation, Melbourne.

Keating, P. J. (1994), *Working Nation: The White Paper on Employment and Growth,* Australian Government Publishing Service, Canberra.

Kim, D. (1993), 'The Link between Individual and Organizational Learning', *Sloan Management Review,* Fall, pp. 37–50.

Kirby, P. (1985), *Report of the Committee of Inquiry into Labour Market Programs* (The Kirby Report), Australian Government Publishing Service, Canberra.

Kirkpatrick, D. L. (1975), *Evaluating Training Programs,* American Society for Training and Development Inc., Washington, DC.

Kram, K. E. (1983), 'Phases of the Mentor Relationship', *Academy of Management Journal,* vol. 26, no. 4, pp. 608–25.

Latham, G. P. (1988), 'Human Resource Training and Development', *Annual Review of Psychology,* vol. 39, pp. 545–82.

Lepani, B. (1995), *Vocational Education and Training (VET) 2005,* Report prepared for NSW TAFE, November.

Maglen, L. (1990), 'Challenging the Human Capital Orthodoxy: The Education-Productivity Link Re-examined', *The Economic Record,* vol. 66, p. 195, December.

McAfee, R. B. & Champagne, P. J. (1988), 'Employee Development: Discovering Who Needs What', *Personnel Administrator,* pp. 92–93, February.

McKenzie, D., Milner, S. & Rimmer, M. (1990), 'Award Restructuring: The First Stage Adjustment', *Working Paper no. 3,* National Key Centre in Industrial Relations, Monash University, Melbourne.

McLagan, P. (1989), *Models for HRD Practice,* ASTD Press, St. Paul, Minn.

Nadler, L. & Nadler, Z. (1989), *Developing Human Resources,* 3rd edition, Jossey Bass, San Francisco, CA.

Porter, P., Rizvi, F., Knight, J. & Lingard, R. (1992), 'Competencies for a Clever Country: Building a House of Cards?', *Unicorn,* vol. 18, no. 3, pp. 50–58.

Revans, R. W. (1982), *The Origin and Growth of Action Learning,* Chartwell-Bratt, Bickley, Kent.

Saul, P. (1989), 'Using Management Competencies to Improve Management Performance and Stimulate Management Self-Development', *Asia-Pacific HRM,* vol. 27, no. 3, pp. 74–85.

Schmitt, N., Schneider, J. R. & Cohen, S. A. (1990), 'Factors Affecting Validity of a Regionally Administered Assessment Center', *Personnel Psychology,* vol. 43, pp. 1–12.

—— (1990), 'Factors Affecting Validity of a Regionally Administered Assessment Centre', *Personnel Psychology,* vol. 43, pp. 1–12.

Senge, P. (1990), *The Fifth Discipline: The Art and Practice of the Learning Organization,* Random House, Sydney.

Senge, P., Kleiner, A., Roberts, C., Ross, R. & Smith, B. (1994), *The Fifth Discipline Handbook: Strategies and Tools for Building a Learning Organization,* Doubleday, New York.

Shore, L. M. & Bloom, A. J.(1986), 'Developing Employees through Coaching and Career Management', *Personnel,* vol. 63, no. 8, quoted in W. French (1990), *Human Resources Management.* Houghton Mifflin, Boston. p. 362.

Smith, A. (1992), *Training and Development in Australia,* Butterworths, Sydney.

—— (1993), 'Australian Training and Development in 1992', *Asia-Pacific Journal of Human Resources*, vol 33, no.2, pp. 65–74.

Smith, A., Hayton, G., Roberts, P., Thorne, E. & Noble, C. (1995), *Enterprise Training: The Factors that Affect Demand*, Office of Training and Further Education, Melbourne.

Sparrow, P. R. & Pettigrew, A. M. (1985), 'Britain's Training Problems: The Search for a Strategic Human Resources Management Approach', *Human Resource Management*, vol. 26, no. 1, pp. 109–27.

Storey, J., Okazaki-Ward, L., Gow, I., Edwards, P. K. & Sisson, K. (1991), 'Managerial Careers and Management Development: A Comparative Analysis of Britain and Japan', *Human Resource Management Journal*, vol. 1, no. 3, pp. 33–57.

Stowell, S. J. (1988), 'Coaching: A Commitment to Leadership', *Training and Development Journal*, June, pp. 34–38.

Wexley, K. N. & Latham, G. P. (1991), *Developing and Training Human Resources in Organizations*, 2nd edition, Harper Collins, New York, p. 15.

Woodruffe, C. (1991), Competent by any Other Name', *Personnel Management*. September, pp. 30–33.

part 3

The international environment

chapter 12
Cross-cultural management

chapter 13
International HRM

chapter 12

Cross-cultural management

Bruce Stening

learning objectives

After studying this chapter, you will be able to:

1. Appreciate the growing importance that managers in general, and human resource managers in particular, understand and be able to manage matters related to cultural difference and diversity, both cross-nationally and in the context of their own countries.

2. Understand several theoretical frameworks which can assist managers in identifying areas of cultural difference.

3. Understand the many ways in which cultural differences can create challenges and difficulties for human resource and other managers.

4. Understand how to go about solving cross-cultural management difficulties.

chapter 12

chapter outline

- Cultural frameworks — 508
  - Kluckhohn & Strodtbeck's variations in value orientations — 509
  - E.T. Hall's communication and culture — 509
  - Hofstede's dimensions of culture — 511
  - Trompenaars' 'waves of culture' — 512
  - Brake, Walker & Walker's *Framework of Cultural Orientations* — 513
- Cross-cultural management problems — 517
- Managing cultural differences — 524
- Summary — 528
- Questions for discussion and review — 529
- Case study — 529
- Resources — 535
- References — 535

HRM IN THE NEWS

Sri Lankan workers hold Australian bosses

BY CAMERON STEWART

The ACTU is investigating a bizarre incident involving an Australian company in Sri Lanka in which 10 Australian managers and 1200 local workers were trapped in a factory for almost two days by disgruntled employees.

The investigation follows allegations by Sri Lanka's peak trade union body that the Australian company, Ansell Lanka (a subsidiary of Pacific Dunlop), was not paying workers enough and that the Australian High Commissioner in Colombo had acted improperly by becoming involved in the industrial dispute.

... For more than 36 hours local workers and 10 Australian managers were trapped inside the factory with dwindling supplies of food and drinkable water in what union officials described as 'an extremely tense' stand-off.

... Mr Boon (the managing director of Ansell International) said he believed the lock-in of the Ansell management was politically motivated.

... The dispute is already believed to have cost Ansell at least $1 million in lost revenue.

... Ansell, which manufactures rubber products including gloves and condoms, is one of the most significant foreign investors in Sri Lanka, having invested around $80 million in its Sri Lankan factory during its six years of operation.

Source: *The Australian*, 31 August 1994, pp. 1, 6.

In 1995, the Industry Task Force on Leadership and Management Skills, a major government-sponsored inquiry into Australian management needs chaired by David Karpin, presented its findings. The title of its report, *Enterprising Nation—Renewing Australia's Managers to Meet the Challenges of the Asia-Pacific Century* (1995) was significant insofar as it clearly linked the required competencies of Australian managers to the challenges that we face in being part of a newly-formed global economy, the most important part of which for us is, and will continue to be, the Asia-Pacific region. Those challenges reside in the need to be much more responsive in an increasingly competitive environment, one which is not just 'out there' in the sense of being markets beyond our shores, but 'here', too, since the distinction between the two is, in a world of much more open global competition, fairly meaningless. The issue of globalisation is discussed more fully in Chapter 13 on international HRM.

The issue of cross-cultural managerial competence is not, however, only the concern of companies competing internationally. Australia has one of the most multicultural workforces in the world and thus local managers also need cross-cultural sensitivity and competence to effectively manage within domestic boundaries. This is obviously the case for HR managers since many of the cross-cultural managerial problems that can arise, do so in the domain of people management. Clearly, HR professionals need the kind of cross-cultural competence outlined in this chapter. However, in view of the trend to increasingly devolve HR to line managers referred to earlier in this book, all managers will benefit from enhanced competency in cross-cultural interaction.

The Karpin Report devoted a great deal of attention to how Australian organisations might equip themselves to more successfully undertake business internationally, including explicitly recognising the need for a much improved understanding of, and skills in respect of, cross-cultural management. The Task Force's commissioned research highlighted various needs in this regard. Among the research conducted was a study of how a large sample of Asian managers in countries with which we actively trade compare Australian managers with managers in five competing countries also active traders in Asia. The results are presented in Table 12.1. It can be seen that Australian managers do not rank particularly highly in most areas, including cross-cultural skills.

Table 12.1 How do others see our managers?

In a blind survey, 502 Asian managers in five countries with which we actively trade were asked to compare Australian managers to managers in five competitor countries identified as being particularly active in our region. The results were not encouraging:

QUALITY	AUSTRALIA	GERMANY	JAPAN	TAIWAN	UK	USA
Ability to look well into the future	6	3	1	5	4	2
Acceptance of responsibility	5	3	1	6	4	2
Management skills	5	3	2	6	4	1
Entrepreneurial skills	6	4	1	3	5	2
Leadership skills	4	=3	2	5	=3	1
Technical skills	6	2	1	5	4	3
Cross-cultural skills	4	5	2	=3	=3	1
Adaptability skills	=5	4	1	3	=5	2

Rankings: 1 = Best; 6 = Worst

Source: Industry Task Force 1995, p. 599

What, then, are these cross-cultural management skills? How and why are they important? How do we improve our abilities in this regard? Essentially, cross-cultural management is concerned with the issues that arise in the context of the relationships of individuals, groups and organisations of different cultural backgrounds. It recognises that the chances of misunderstandings between such parties is made more likely by virtue of the communication difficulties between them. Such difficulties may be those associated with the fact that the two parties speak different languages, but equally might be associated with problems created by their different cultural lenses, that is their divergent values, assumptions and so forth, differences that might not be immediately obvious.

The fundamental objective of this chapter is to provide an understanding of how and why cross-cultural management problems may occur and what might be done to overcome them. It should be stated from the outset that while managing and doing business across cultural boundaries is often difficult, the skills necessary for successfully undertaking such endeavours can be learned, not only through the painful route of practical experience but also by approaching such problems systematically.

In summary, while the emphasis in this chapter will be on difficulties that arise in international business relationships, many of the lessons to be learned will be applicable to problems that occur in the workplace in a multicultural society such as Australia. It is interesting to note that more recently there has been recognition that the cultural diversity that exists in Australia can be used productively to, among other things, create and sustain international business links.

Managing change

In *Megatrends Asia*, futurist John Naisbitt outlines eight Asia megatrends which he claims are changing the world. All have profound implications for the cross-cultural management of organisations. The eight shifts he discerns are these:

From nation states to networks: '... the power of Japan as a nation-state is giving way to the dynamic collaboration of the Chinese network ... it is the overseas Chinese network that will dominate the region'.

From export-led to consumer-driven: 'built on exports, Asian economies will increasingly be fuelled by consumer spending and, with it, the emerging middle class'.

From Western influence to the Asian way: 'The most significant development of the 1990s and the following few decades will be Asia's modernisation ... [n]ew options in all aspects of life are now open to Asians'.

From government-driven to market-driven: 'Central government control and direction of the economies of the region have shifted to market economies ...'.

From villages to supercities: '[the] urban shift is transforming Asia, moving it to the next era of development away from agricultural societies to those where telecommunications and the information age dominate'.

From labour-intensive to high technology: 'We are witnessing a dramatic shift from labour-intensive agriculture and manufacturing to state-of-the-art technology in manufacturing and services ...'.

From male dominance to the emergence of women: 'Women are participating in all aspects of Asian life in unprecedented ways, as voters, consumers and members of the workforce'.

From West to East: 'It is becoming apparent to those in the East and to some in the West that we are moving towards the Asianisation of the world. The global axis of influence has shifted from West to East. Asia was once the centre of the world and now the centre is again returning to Asia'.

Source: Naisbitt 1995, pp. xii–xiii.

Cultural frameworks

For a considerable time now, cultural anthropologists and others have sought to identify the characteristics of particular cultures and, in many cases, make comparisons between cultures in terms of those characteristics. The result has been that for most cultures in the world, we have detailed and rich descriptions and some understanding of how they differ, one from another. In this section we will examine the work of several authors who have sought to provide conceptual frameworks that can serve as the basis for over-arching comparisons of cultures. The objective of such frameworks, and their usefulness to others such as those of us interested in studying cross-cultural management, is to condense the essence of culture to its fundamentals in terms of dimensions of difference. The frameworks that will be considered (those of Kluckhohn & Strodtbeck (1961), Hall (1959; 1990), Hofstede (1980; 1991), and Trompenaars (1993) are the better-known ones, but there are others). To a large extent they are complementary, each looking at the issues from a somewhat different angle; in certain situations one might be a useful diagnostic tool, in another situation one of the others. Following a description of each of these frameworks, a recently-developed model which seeks to combine many of the elements of the individual frameworks will be outlined.

Kluckhohn & Strodtbeck's variations in value orientations

All societies are confronted with some basic issues or problems, yet deal with these issues in different ways, reflecting what Kluckhohn & Strodtbeck (1961) refer to as variations in value orientations. There are five such common problems faced by all human societies, they argue, and variations between societies along the following lines:

- Relationship of humans to nature, the variations being mastery over nature, subjugation to nature and harmony with nature
- Time orientation, where the society may be past-, present- or future-oriented
- Belief about basic human nature, the possible designations being good, good-and-evil, neutral, and evil
- Activity orientation, with the possible variations of being, being-in-becoming, and doing
- Relationships among people, where the variations are lineality, individualism and collaterality.

The value orientation that exists in a society for any of the five issues will have a significant impact upon the way that organisations are managed in that society. To take the first issue, the relationship of humans to nature, one of the most seriously affected aspects will be the function of planning and goal setting. If the perspective taken is that humans can control nature, or are masters of their own destiny, a belief which would characterise Australia, for example, then planning and goal setting is a very meaningful exercise. However, in many societies there is a predominant view that humans are subjugated by nature, that there is much that is out of our control, fate, destiny or luck being more likely to determine outcomes than whatever we might plan. In such a society, goal setting is to a large extent a meaningless, fanciful or even irreligious exercise. Attempts by, say, Australian companies to introduce strategic planning into their organisations in such countries may be a frustratingly futile exercise for all concerned.

E. T. Hall's communication and culture

Edward T. Hall is an American anthropologist who has contributed a great deal to our understanding of culture, and potential problems in the interactions of people from different cultures, through his work on proxemics and communication.

Proxemics is the study of the use of space, and Hall (1966; 1976) has done much to show how different cultures have different notions of what is public and private space and in matters such as the appropriate interpersonal distance in various social situations. For example, every culture will have well-understood norms about what is an appropriate distance between two colleagues engaged in a normal business discussion. To stray outside these norms (i.e. moving in too close or moving away too far) is likely to lead the other party to apply various attributions to this behaviour, such as intimacy, hostility, aloofness, and so on. In a cross-cultural situation, the norms governing such matters may not be well understood with an increased likelihood that the behavioural intentions of one party are misunderstood by the other.

At a much broader level, Hall (1959) has shown how there are many ways in which there can be communication problems between people of different cultural backgrounds, based on different rules governing such matters as time (the importance of punctuality, for example is fairly important in Australia, but much more relaxed in some other countries), friendships (who one makes friends with and what obligations are implied by that relationship) and agreements (the importance of written contracts as against giving one's word, for instance). Hall (1960) refers to these matters as the silent language in intercultural relations, in the sense that though they are frequently not discussed explicitly and may be difficult to 'read', they carry an enormous amount of meaning, communication that may well be misunderstood.

One of the conceptual tools developed by Hall that many managers engaged in cross-cultural situations find helpful is his distinction between high-context and low-context cultures (see Hall & Hall 1990). The essential difference between the two, as conveyed in Table 12.2, is that the former tend to be relationship-oriented while the latter are more task-oriented. In a task-oriented country such as Australia we are used to 'getting down to business' very quickly, without the need for a great deal of preliminary 'getting to know you' activity. By contrast, in a culture where relationships are paramount, for example, Japan, there is necessarily much time invested in understanding the larger context in which the business is being undertaken. The potential for serious cross-cultural misunderstandings in the relationship between people from cultures with different contextual frameworks is obvious.

Table 12.2 High and low context cultures

HIGH-CONTEXT CULTURES:
- Relationships between individuals are relatively long lasting and individuals feel deep personal involvement with each other.
- Because so much is communicated by shared code, communications can be economical, fast and efficient.
- People in authority are responsible for the actions of subordinates. This places a premium on reciprocal loyalty.
- Agreements tend to be spoken rather than written.
- Insiders and outsiders are tightly distinguished.
- Cultural patterns are slow to change.

LOW-CONTEXT CULTURES:
- Relationships between individuals are relatively shorter in duration and *in general* deep personal involvement with others is valued less. These cultures tend to be more heterogeneous and prone to greater social and job mobility.
- Messages must be made more explicit and the sender can depend much less on the receiver inferring the message from the context.
- Authority is diffused.
- Agreements tend to be written rather than spoken.
- Insiders and outsiders are less closely distinguished.
- Cultural patterns are faster to change.

Source: Based on Mead 1994, pp. 57–60

Hofstede's dimensions of culture

In what has in a fairly short time become one of the most widely-cited pieces of social science research, Geert Hofstede (1980; 1991) set out to identify the underlying dimensions of culture. His work was empirical, with more than 116 000 questionnaires being completed by employees in 72 national subsidiaries of IBM at two points in time, around 1968 and 1972. The questions in the survey were principally concerned with the employees' personal values in relation to their work situation. Using a statistical data-reduction technique known as factor analysis, Hofstede uncovered four dimensions that could provide the basis for a comparison of employees from different countries:

- **Power distance**—'the extent to which the less powerful members of institutions and organisations within a country expect and accept that power is distributed unequally'.
- **Individualism versus collectivism**—which Hofstede defines thus: 'Individualism pertains to societies in which the ties between individuals are loose: everyone is expected to look after himself or herself and his or her immediate family. Collectivism as its opposite pertains to societies in which people from birth onwards are integrated into strong, cohesive ingroups, which throughout peoples' lifetime continue to protect them in exchange for unquestioning loyalty'.
- **Masculinity versus femininity**—countries high on masculinity tend to rate achievement and success much more highly than caring for others and the quality of life, characteristics of a country high on femininity.
- **Uncertainty avoidance**—reflects the extent to which members of different cultures are socialised into accepting ambiguity and tolerating uncertainty about the future.

Subsequent to Hofstede's IBM study, Michael Bond, a cross-cultural psychologist based in Hong Kong, undertook a study of values from the starting point of Chinese values, using a questionnaire called the Chinese values survey (CVS) (Hofstede & Bond 1988; The Chinese Culture Connection 1987). His survey included data from twenty of the countries surveyed by Hofstede, permitting a comparison of the two sets of data. Though Bond found correlations between his and Hofstede's data, he also uncovered a further (fifth) unrelated dimension which he labelled 'Confucian dynamism'. Essentially, this dimension is one related to a long-term versus a short-term orientation taken by different cultures. The data indicated that, of the twenty-three countries surveyed, the countries with the highest long-term orientation were China, Hong Kong, Taiwan, Japan and South Korea, while the Anglo-Saxon countries included in the study were ranked much lower: Australia, 15; New Zealand, 16; USA, 17; Great Britain, 18; Canada, 20.

Though Hofstede's work has attracted various criticisms, principally in relation to its methodology (particularly the fact that it was conducted within one company), it is immensely impressive both in terms of its breadth (a large number of countries and large employee samples within those countries) and depth of analysis. Its value to practising managers is that it provides a thumbnail analysis of many countries in which they might be doing business. Accordingly, they can be informed as to the areas of contrast between their own and the other culture(s) and, thus, matters that might be problematic in the relationship. One caution is, however, in order. It must not be assumed that the cultural profiles provided by the Hofstede work can be applied at the level of the individual; to make the jump from country-level data (even though that data was based, obviously, on the responses of individuals) to individual analysis is to succumb to the ecological fallacy. This is probably the most common misuse of the Hofstede material.

Trompenaars' 'waves of culture'

Though his work is concerned with a wider range of issues, Trompenaars (1993) has contributed in highlighting a distinction between cultures in terms of particularism versus universalism. In essence, some cultures are concerned with consistently applying a set of general (universal) principles, procedures and rules to situations, largely in the interests of consistency and equity. Other cultures, by contrast, are more concerned with relationships than with rules, to which exceptions must be made in order to preserve those relationships.

The contrasts between cultures has been highlighted by Trompenaars in the responses that individuals from different cultures provided to various scenarios. One such scenario, designed to highlight the particularistic–universalistic dimension, was as follows:

You are riding in a car driven by a close friend. He hits a pedestrian. You know he was going at least 35 miles per hour in an area of the city where the maximum allowed speed is 20 miles per hour. There are no witnesses. His lawyer says that if you testify under oath that he was only driving 20 miles per hour it may save him from serious consequences.

What right has your friend to expect you to protect him?

1a My friend has a definite right as a friend to expect me to testify to the lower figure.
1b He has some right as a friend to expect me to testify to the lower figure.
1c He has no right as a friend to expect me to testify to the lower figure.

What do you think you would do in view of the obligations of a sworn witness and the obligation to your friend?

1d Testify that he was going 20 miles an hour.
1e Not testify that he was going 20 miles an hour (Trompenaars 1993, p. 34).

While, at one extreme, 96 per cent of Canadian respondents opted for the universalistic response (answers c or b + e), at the other, only 26 per cent of South Koreans did. (Australia was the fourth most universalistic country of those 38 surveyed, on 93 per cent.)

Besides the particularistic–universalistic dimension, the work of Trompenaars also draws distinctions between cultures based on the following dichotomies: individualism–collectivism (essentially the same as the Hofstede dimension); affective–neutral, the question of whether emotions are displayed openly in relationships or not; specific–diffuse, focusing on the segregation (or not) between the aspects of one's life, typified by the relationship between public and private space and the contrasts between cultures in this respect; achievement–ascription, whether one's status in society is determined primarily by what one has achieved oneself (doing) or by whom one is by virtue of age, class, gender and the like (being); internal–external, essentially the Kluckhohn & Strodtbeck relationship of humans to nature dimension, in which people are either controlled by their environment (externals) or control their environment (internals); and orientations towards time.

It should be noted that despite the current popularity of the work of Trompenaars, it has been subjected to quite severe criticism in relation to the empirical and content validity of the various dimensions. Hofstede (1996, p. 198) accuses Trompenaars of riding the waves of commerce, attuning his messages to what he thinks the customer likes to hear, concluding that, 'The result is a fast food approach to intercultural diversity and communication.' We wait for Trompenaars' rejoinder!

Brake, Walker & Walker's *Framework of Cultural Orientations*

A recent publication has sought to combine the key elements of several previous frameworks, including those discussed above. Though not empirically verified as a comprehensive model, it is useful as a further distillation of some key dimensions on which cultures may differ. The Brake et al. (1995) framework comprises ten dimensions, as illustrated in Figure 12.1, the definitions for each of which are provided below (see Brake & Walker 1995, section 2-A, pp.10–24).

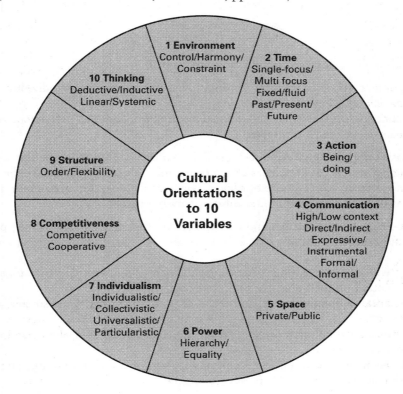

Figure 12.1 Framework of cultural orientations

Source: Brake et al. 1995, p. 45

1 Environment

Fundamentally, cultures may believe that they either have control over their environment, that it should be changed to fit human needs; or should live in harmony with their environment; or are constrained by their environment.

2 Time

This dimension is comprised of three sub-dimensions, along these lines: in terms of time, people gravitate toward one of two types: single-focus—high concentration on one task or issue at a time with commitment to schedules; multi-focus—greater emphasis on multiple tasks with concentration on relationship building rather than deadlines.

In terms of punctuality expectations, cultures can be categorised in two ways: fixed—punctuality is defined precisely; or fluid—punctuality is loosely defined.

Cultures can also be categorised according to their orientation to: past—high value placed on continuance of traditions; or present short-term orientation aimed at quick results; or future—willingness to trade short-term gains for long-term results.

3 Action

Cultures are either 'being' cultures in which stress is placed on working for the moment, job and personal satisfaction, release from tension, and relationships; or 'doing' cultures in which stress is placed on action and accomplishments, achieving goals, and improving standards of living.

4 Communication

This dimension is comprised of four sub-dimensions:

- **Low context**—little contextual information is needed about an individual before business is transacted; or
- **High context**—a great deal of contextual information about an individual is needed before business can be transacted.

Business is done through relationships. Information is transmitted not just in words, but through a variety of contexts, such as voice tone, body language, facial expressions, eye contact, speech patterns, use of silence, past interactions, status, common friends, etc. The verbal message in communications is more implicit.

- **Direct**—unmediated conflict and face-to-face conflict management is the norm; or
- **Indirect**—mix of conflict avoidance and face saving, or use of third parties to manage conflict.
- **Expressive**—communication is emotional and demonstrative rather than impersonal and is centred on relationships; or
- **Instrumental**—communication is problem-centred, pragmatic, impersonal and goal-oriented.
- **Formal**—in such cultures there is great emphasis on following business protocol and social customs; or
- **Informal**—people from informal cultures feel more comfortable dispensing with ceremony and conducting business more casually.

5 Space

Cultures can be categorised according to their distinctions between public and private spaces. People in different cultures have contrasting needs in their personal space requirements—for example, distances between individuals; the degree to which physical space is demarcated public or private; and the rules governing the use of each type.

6 Power

In some cultures, inequality is a given. The culture satisfies a need for dependence, and it gives a sense of security to the powerful and those in lower positions. In other countries, inequality is thought to be an unsatisfactory state of affairs. While it may be unavoidable, it is considered correct to minimise it through legal, economic and political means.

7 Individualism

This aspect of cultural orientation is subdivided into two further dimensions:

- **Collectivistic**—characterises those cultures in which individual interests are subordinate to group interests. Cohesive groups protect their members in exchange for loyalty and obedience. Social control is based upon the fear of losing face and the possibility of shame.

- **Individualistic**—characterises those cultures in which the bonds between individual members are independent and expected to take care of themselves only, or at most the nuclear family. Guilt and fear of losing self-respect are central to social control.

When individualism is valued, the 'I' predominates over the 'We'. Individual identity is a key value, and speaking one's mind is a sign of honesty. Laws and rights are the same for everyone, and political power is exercised by individual voters.

When individualism is not highly valued, identity is based on the social network to which the person belongs. Harmony, rather than speaking one's mind, is a key value. Laws and rights differ by group, and political power is wielded by interest groups. The in-group expects loyalty in exchange for security and protection.

- **Universalistic**—these cultures stress the consistent application of generalisations, rules and procedures, and the manufacture of universal products and services.
- **Particularistic**—these cultures emphasise difference, uniqueness and exceptions. Rules are secondary to relationships.

8 Competitiveness

On this dimension, cultures may be dichotomised as either competitive or cooperative.

- **Competitive**—characterises cultures in which achievement, assertiveness and competition are reinforced. Social and gender roles tend to be distinct. Often, men are expected to be assertive, tough, and driven by material success. Women, on the other hand, are expected to be modest, nurturing, and concerned primarily with the quality of life. In many Western industrialised societies this distinction between the gender roles is breaking down.

When competitiveness is valued, the culture is predominantly materialistic with an emphasis on assertiveness and the acquisition of money, property, goods, etc. High value is placed on ambition, decisiveness, performance, speed and size. One lives to work.

- **Co-operative**—characterises cultures that value the quality of life, sympathy, nurturing and relationships. One works to live. High value is placed on collaboration, consensus and intuition.

9 Structure

Structure is expressed as a need for predictability and rules, written and unwritten.

Cultures that value structure seek to reduce ambiguity and make events predictable and interpretable. Conflict is threatening, and there is a perceived need for rules and regulations. Anxiety and stress are high. Cultures with low need for structure are more tolerant of unknown situations, people and ideas. Anxiety levels are lower and tolerance of deviance is higher. Dissent is acceptable.

10 Thinking

This dimension is subdivided into two further dimensions:

- **Inductive cultures**—derive principles from the collection and analysis of data. Models and hypotheses are based on empirical observation and experimentation.
- **Deductive cultures**—emphasise abstract thinking and the reality of ideas and theories and the principles that can be derived from them. Gives priority to the conceptual world and symbolic thinking.

- **Linear cultures**—emphasise the dissection of events and concepts into pieces which can be linked in cause/effect and logical chains.
- **Systemic cultures**—stress a more integrated approach, sometimes called 'holistic' or synthetic.

The usefulness of the various frameworks is that they provide us with a basis for disaggregating particular cultures in terms of various key characteristics, thereby providing the basis for an analysis of likely areas of tension in the relationships between people from different cultures. As stated earlier, the virtue of the Brake et al. (1995) framework is that it combines the elements of several of the most important frameworks thus providing a more comprehensive model than any of the others alone.

It will be appreciated from the cultural frameworks which we have examined in this chapter that, fundamentally, culture is the ideals, values and assumptions about life that each of us learns as a member of one cultural group or another, passed on from one generation to another. There are several additional observations that need to be made in that regard. First, each of us has, in Hofstede's (1991) terms, been mentally programmed by various cultural agents, our family, schools, society at large; the important point here is that, though we may later question certain of the ideals, values and assumptions about life that were ingrained in us as children, a complete restructuring is unlikely and, indeed, significant deviation is rare. For that reason, culture is an enduring phenomenon, changing, as it is often put, at a glacial pace. In this regard, it is important to distinguish various levels of culture, as illustrated in Table 12.3. While changes in manifest culture (the fact that a certain group may now dress like us or eat frequently at McDonald's) may reflect various changes in outlook, at the level of expressed values and basic assumptions things may have changed relatively little. As a Thai market researcher has commented recently about youth in his country, 'Superficially they may look Western ... (b)ut inside they hold lots of values that they get from their parents that are hard to change: respect for age, respect for the family, collective not individual action and so on' (Elegant & Cohen 1996, p. 52). That is not to say, however, that cultures do not change; some difference in values between parents and their off-spring is a real phenomenon, not confined to Australia!

Table 12.3 Levels of culture

1	**Manifest culture**
	This level comprises the physical, visible elements of culture. It includes dress, art, technology and audible and visible behaviours.
2	**Expressed values**
	This level reveals how people communicate, explain, rationalise and justify what they say and do as a community. It represents how they make sense of and comment on the first level.
3	**Basic assumptions**
	This level consists of people's ideas and assumptions that ultimately govern what they do at the other two levels. These are primary assumptions about the world and how it works that guide people's thinking and actions. They are deeply rooted, have come to be taken for granted and are largely unconscious.

Source: Sathe 1985, p. 10

It should also be appreciated that culture is in many respects invisible, particularly to people from outside the culture. It becomes part of the basic fabric of our existence and is not discussed frequently by people in their daily lives. Of course, not every person in any culture is exactly the same. This recognises that an individual's attitudes and behaviour are a function not merely of culture but also personality. It also raises the issue of cultural homogeneity, the extent to which there is, in a technical sense, deviation around the cultural norm. A multicultural society such as Australia, with a population drawn in significant numbers from many other countries, would, by definition, be expected to have a much wider spread around the national mean on any cultural characteristic than a relatively homogeneous country such as Japan. (However, as we shall discuss in the next section, we should be wary, in the case of any cultural group of developing over-simplified stereotypes.)

Cross-cultural management problems

As will become clear in this section, there is a multitude of ways in which culturally-based differences in the attitudes and behaviour of managers can create problems in organisations. Indeed, it will be seen that culture impacts on virtually all aspects of organisations, from the values that individual managers bring to their work, to the manner in which decisions are made, negotiations are conducted, jobs are designed, disputes resolved, and so on.

Let us begin our exploration of how culture intrudes into organisational behaviour with a specific illustration, the introduction of a Management by Objectives (MBO) scheme in the overseas subsidiaries of an Australian firm. MBO is a method developed in the United States, the essential aim of which is to involve managers at all levels in the setting of specific targets (for sales or whatever) for themselves and their organisational unit, for a finite period, typically one year, in the context of the overall strategic plan and tactical plans of the organisation. The targets are established by mutual agreement between each manager and his or her superior. At the end of that period, an assessment and evaluation is made of performance in relation to the targets which is then fed back into the planning cycle for the organisation as a whole. The process is then repeated incorporating judgements and decisions as to how shortfalls in performance might be avoided in the future, including the possible requirement for management development.

Many organisations in the United States, Australia and elsewhere have found MBO to be a useful device for improving overall organisational performance. An Australian manager, having witnessed its effectiveness in their domestic operation might be inclined to introduce it in the firm's overseas operations. Before they do, however, they would be well advised to consider various difficulties this might present, based on the culturally-based assumptions inherent in MBO. What, then, are some such assumptions? (Hofstede 1980b; Schneider 1988):

- Goals can and should be set, implying that people have control over their environment
- Goals can and should be given specific, often short-term, time parameters, implying that time can be managed and that a short-term view is better than a long-term view
- Goal attainment can be measured, in the sense that reality is objective
- Superiors and subordinates can engage in a two-way dialogue to agree on what is to be done, when and how, making the assumption that Power Distance is small
- Both superiors and subordinates are prepared to take risks, implying weak Uncertainty Avoidance

- The subordinate will assume responsibility to meet the agreed-upon goals, implying that the subordinate has sufficient power to accomplish those goals and will exercise self-control in seeking to achieve them
- The reward set is contingent upon the performance achieved, implying that abilities and skills are more important in deciding rewards than traits, personal characteristics or need.

It is often astonishing to Australian managers to learn that there are many cultures in which these assumptions do not hold. Yet, as the frameworks discussed in the previous section revealed, for each of the assumptions above it is possible to find a culture or cultures in which a completely contrary view is held:

- People are controlled by, rather than control, their environment or, at least should seek to live in harmony with their environment
- The long-term view is better than a short-term perspective
- Objective reality is a myth—'reality' is subjective, a matter of perception and interpretation
- Managers are there to give orders, not engage in discussions with subordinates about what might be done (i.e. Power Distance is—and should be—large)
- It is unwise, personally and organisationally, to take risks
- It is the responsibility of managers to monitor their subordinates' performance and impose remedial action if it is required
- In rewarding individuals, the most important criteria are their personal traits, their personal characteristics including, say, their relationships to others and their needs.

Additional examples of contrasting values that can create problems in cross-cultural management situations are provided in Table 12.4.

It should be clear from Table 12.4 and the MBO example that numerous management functions are affected by these basic differences in the way different cultures view the world: planning and scheduling; motivation and reward systems; recruitment, selection and promotion systems; decision-making processes; accountability, performance and organisational effectiveness measurement; and others. Fundamentally, these are matters that must be acknowledged and actively taken into account not just by traditional line managers but by human resource managers in the way that they develop HRM policies and design HRM systems. As Dowling et al. (1994, p. 44) point out, 'The repositioning of the HR function to include strategy formulation, rather than being confined to strategy implementation, is particularly important in the international context'. An international corporate strategy that relies integrally on the implementation of a human resource practice that is not transferrable abroad (e.g. merit-based promotion in a society which is strongly wedded to promotion based on ascribed characteristics such as age, gender or the like) is clearly flawed.

Such tensions are not confined, of course, to cross-national situations. In multicultural societies such as Australia and New Zealand, sub-cultural differences also have to be managed both in the context of relationships within the workplace and between organisations and sections of the wider community. In the latter regard, relationships between Australian mining companies such as BHP and CRA and Aboriginal communities that have title to the lands on which they wish to mine, and relationships between New Zealand fisheries companies and Maoris with traditional fishing rights, have required careful attention in respect of conflicting values. As the recent Hindmarsh Bridge development in South Australia illustrated, the management of such situations can,

Table 12.4 Australian values and possible alternatives

AUSTRALIAN VALUE/ BELIEF/ATTITUDE/ ASSUMPTION	ALTERNATIVE VIEW	EXAMPLE OF MANAGEMENT FUNCTION AFFECTED
• Intuitive aspects of decision making should be reduced and efforts should be devoted to gathering relevant information.	• Decisions are expressions of wisdom by the person in authority. Any questioning would imply a lack of confidence in his judgement.	• Decision-making process.
• A person is expected to do whatever is necessary to get the job done. (One must be willing to get one's hands dirty.)	• Various kinds of work are accorded high or low status and some work may be below one's 'dignity' or place in the organisation.	• Assignment of tasks, performance and organisational effectiveness.
• The performance of individuals should be evaluated.	• Persons are evaluated but in such a way that individuals who are not highly evaluated will not be embarrassed or caused to 'lose face'.	• Rewards and promotion, performance evaluation and accountability.
• The individual can influence the future. (Where there is a will there is a way.)	• Life follows a pre-ordained course and human action is determined by the will of God.	• Planning and scheduling.
• We must work hard to accomplish our objectives. (Puritan ethic.)	• Hard work is not the only prerequisite for success. Wisdom, luck and time are also required.	• Motivation and reward systems.
• Commitments should be honoured. (People will do what they say they will do.)	• A commitment may be superseded by a conflicting request or an agreement may only signify intention and have little or no relationship to the capacity of performance.	• Negotiating and bargaining.
• A primary obligation of an employee is to the organisation.	• The individual has a primary obligation to his family and friends.	• Loyalty, commitment and motivation.
• The best qualified persons should be given the positions available.	• Family connections, friendships and other considerations are as or more important than formal qualifications.	• Employment, promotions, recruiting, selection, rewards.

Source: Based on Harris & Moran 1987, pp. 76–77

even with the best will in the world, be very complicated. However, it is encouraging to note that some organisations have begun extensive programs to educate and train their managers to cope with cultural differences; CRA, for example, is currently running a series of intensive three-day workshops for almost one thousand of its senior and middle managers under the rubric, 'Understanding Cultural Diversity'.

The task for managers should not be under-estimated. As summarised in Table 12.5, the overall impact of culture on various facets of organisational behaviour is enormous, there being scarcely any part of either macro (organisational-level) or micro (individual and group-level) behaviour that is unaffected by its influence.

Table 12.5 What things does culture impact upon in organisations?

ORGANISATIONAL LEVEL:	INDIVIDUAL AND GROUP LEVELS:
• Goals	• Attitudes
• Strategy	• Perceptions and attributions
• Structure	• Problem-solving styles
• Power and political behaviour	• Methods of learning
• Decision making	• Motivation
• Job design	• Goal setting
• Career planning and development	• Intra- and Inter- group processes
• Change processes	• Leadership
• Negotiation	• Interpersonal communication
• Ethics	• Ethics
• Dispute resolution	

Besides their initial inability to conceive that the members of other cultures might have assumptions at variance with their own, managers are often inclined to conclude that those other cultures are, in a sense, deviant and dysfunctional. This is a manifestation of the fact that most of us, from whatever culture we hail, are inherently and, in some cases, deeply ethnocentric, believing that our way of thinking or of doing things is the best (or only) way.

As suggested earlier, rationality is a rather subjective thing. The author was recently lunching with a very wealthy Chinese businessman in Hong Kong. The businessman stated that he was thinking of buying a house in Sydney, overlooking the harbour. When asked if the house was located in Kirribilli, an expensive suburb located on the North Shore directly opposite the Opera House, the businessman's response was effusively and unambiguously in the negative. The feng shui (the Chinese equivalence of geomancy, the relation of physical objects to one another), he explained, was very bad because one's wealth could flow directly and quickly across the harbour to be eaten by the jaws of the Opera House on the other side. Given the disparity in wealth between the businessman and the author, the latter was inclined to suspend judgement on what constitutes rational behaviour!

The kinds of management problems that might occur in cross-cultural situations can be analysed, understood and, to some extent, anticipated, using the various conceptual frameworks outlined in the previous section. By way of illustration, Figures 12.2 and 12.3 provide an analysis of Australia and Japan, respectively, using the Brake et al. (1995) framework. Assuming that one accepts the validity of the analysis contained in them (there may always be arguments at the margin), it is apparent that in respect of most of the ten dimensions there are differences in cultural orientations that might create cross-cultural management problems, especially if those areas of difference are not well understood and managed accordingly. For example, the orientation of managers in the two societies to communication is very different:

whereas Australian managers operate within a low-context environment and prefer direct and informal communication, their Japanese counterparts are likely to be much more comfortable with a less confrontational and more formal style of communication in which the ability to appreciate the larger context within which the communication is taking place is highly important. Similarly, while Japanese are very group-oriented and particularistic in their relationships, Australians are extremely individualistic and are universalistic in the sense that rules and so forth should be applied consistently, giving little importance to the relationships of people to one another.

The last-mentioned of these (the universalistic/particularistic distinction) has made for some difficult problems between Australian and Japanese organisations where the enforcement of contracts is concerned. The Japanese view of the world inclines them to believing that contracts should be flexible enough to accommodate the changing circumstances of the contracting parties while Australians generally believe that 'a deal's a deal'. In one of the most high-profile and problematic cases in the history of the trading relationship between our two countries, there was a major dispute concerning the purchase of Australian sugar by Japanese companies. The agreement was negotiated and agreed at a time when there was a worldwide sugar shortage. Within a relatively short time, however, a sugar glut evolved on the world market. The Japanese wanted to renegotiate the deal on the basis of changed circumstances, a perspective not shared by the Australians. Though the dispute was eventually resolved by a compromise, the bruises remained for some considerable time and had an adverse effect not only on the contracting parties but on the two nations themselves.

Figure 12.2 Australian cultural orientations

Source: Based on Brake & Walker 1995, pp. 2A–5

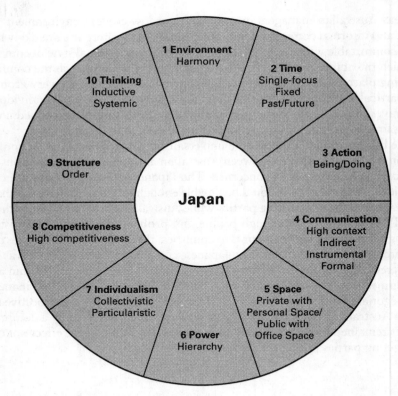

Figure 12.3 Japanese cultural orientations

Source: Based on Brake & Walker 1995, pp. 2–B, 46

The paragraphs above have used the Brake et al. (1995) framework to analyse cross-cultural difficulties arising in international settings. Equally, though, the framework might be used to analyse problems or potential problems within a company comprised of a multinational workforce (particularly those in industries such as automobile manufacturing in which the numbers are large enough for sizeable informal groups to form based on ethnicity) or, as discussed earlier, between a company and a community within the nation (say, a mining company and an Aboriginal community).

While the frameworks can be of assistance in identifying broad areas of potential difficulty, there is a danger, too, in our developing stereotypes which are either inaccurate or applicable to only a limited proportion of the population. Indeed, stereotyping is the cause of many complications and problems in cross-cultural contact situations. Put simply, stereotyping is a syllogistic form of reasoning that results from the inability or unwillingness of individuals to distinguish between individuals in a particular group. By whatever means, a generalisation is constructed for a particular group around some characteristic such as diligence; it might be, say, that Japanese are industrious. An Australian meeting Mr Suzuki quickly determines that he is Japanese. Accordingly, he judges that Mr Suzuki is industrious. There are at least two potential difficulties here. First, the stereotype may be inaccurate in broadly describing the group, perhaps being based on poor information or prejudice. Second, Mr Suzuki may not be a 'typical' member of that group, acknowledging that by their nature such generalisations will not apply to everyone.

There are those who claim that, for those reasons, stereotypes are inherently bad and should be avoided at all costs. On the other hand, this is both unrealistic and, to some extent, unnecessary: unrealistic in that people will resort to stereotypes in the absence of more refined information and in situations of information overload; and unnecessary insofar as it is possible for people to use stereotypes to good effect, provided those stereotypes are accurately reflective of a large segment of the population (and in that sense are sociotypes) and are treated with caution by those using them, such that they realise that they will not apply to everyone in the group. Stereotypes should only be used as a crude 'entry-level' strategy in cross-cultural contact and should always be open to modification both with respect to the group itself and the individuals comprising the group. Used injudiciously, stereotypes can create enormous problems in cross-cultural management situations.

It should be apparent that the potential for cross-cultural management problems exists in relation to many matters. Though such problems can occur in many different situations, even simple transactions between managers from different cultural backgrounds seeking to do a 'one-off' deal, they are seen most dramatically in circumstances where the relationship is more all-embracing. This is the case, for example, when a manager is assigned to work in another country as an expatriate. In this capacity they will not only be working in the host country but living there as well, in all likelihood with other members of their family. It is highly probable that the magnitude of the challenges of coping in the host culture will cause what is generally termed **culture shock** and will be manifested in reduced job performance, low levels of life satisfaction and many other dysfunctional phenomena. With training (and to some extent through the process of culture learning through experience, though without deliberate intervention through training the expatriate may be destined to a cycle of repeating their mistakes) the expatriate can be expected to improve their ability to deal effectively in the culture and, correspondingly, to both perform better and be happier living in the host culture. Interestingly, the difficulties which are encountered by managers returning from expatriate assignments are frequently as great as those they experience in entering the foreign country, intensified perhaps because people do not expect to have problems adapting to their own country. The issue is not just that of adapting to a home country that has changed during one's absence but dealing with that in relation to the changes that have occurred to the expatriate and his/her family during that time, too. On the job front, it is not uncommon for repatriates to find that they have missed out on promotional opportunities in their absence, that there is not a job for them to fit into when they return, that they are placed into a position with considerably less authority than the one they had overseas, and so on.

Another set of circumstances in which cross-cultural management problems are likely to be brought to the surface is in international joint-venture operations. In this case there will the dual difficulties of making a cultural fit and, additionally, of achieving a coincidence of interests on the business front. Perhaps the best parallel would be an intercultural marriage, since there is the expectation of an on-going, long-term relationship in which there is the need to accommodate different perspectives, values and so forth and in which the result is a sum greater than the individual parts. There are likely to be many dimensions along which the parties will be different and about which some agreement must be reached. (It is no accident that the case study included at the end of this chapter is focused on the operation of an international joint venture.) Cultural clashes might even occur in situations of merger between corporations based in the same national culture which have distinctly different corporate cultures. As Cartwright & Cooper (1993, p. 57) point out, 'selection decisions (vis-à-vis mergers and acquisitions) are generally driven by financial and strategic considerations, yet many organisational alliances fail to meet expectations because the cultures of the partners are incompatible …'. To a large extent these cultural differences pertain to the people management philosophies which exist in the respective organisations. A culture audit of the two organisations to assess compatibility in these philosophies might be much less expensive than a messy divorce later.

It should not be assumed that problems only arise between managers from quite disparate cultures; indeed, even between managers from Australia and the United States, there are many issues about which misunderstandings or disagreements based on different attitudes, values and behaviour may and do occur (Renwick 1991). How, then, can we seek to manage cultural differences in the managerial situation?

 Managing diversity

The honeymoon is over

BY ADAM SCHWARTZ

Australian miner Clive Pearson had every reason to be pleased. As he looked forward to the New Year's holiday last December, his company, Westralian Sands—one of the few foreign mining companies to invest in Vietnam—was expecting to show a profit in its second year … 'I thought we were doing pretty well', Pearson says.

But soon after, the wheels came off. Westralian Sands had a falling-out with Austinh's [the joint venture 50 per cent owned by Westralian Sands] general director, Vu Kim Cu.

Since April, Austinh's equipment imports have been impounded, its ilmenite exports suspended, and its bank account frozen. Even its gas supplies have been cut off, exit visas for some Australian employees have been revoked, and the Vietnamese police have threatened criminal smuggling charges. Westralian Sands has taken a hammering in the local press, and its local partners are petitioning the State Committee for Cooperation and Investment to withdraw Westralian Sands' investment licence.

While Austinh is an extreme example, the venture's troubles illustrate a worrying trend. Tensions between foreign firms and their Vietnamese partners are rising, bankers, businessmen and lawyers say. After an initial rush of enthusiasm many foreign investors are getting bogged down in an alien corporate culture.

Source: *Far Eastern Economic Review*, 14 July 1995.

Managing cultural differences

It should be apparent from the discussion earlier in this chapter that there are a number of lessons which need to be learned by managers who are already involved (a large number) or who are likely to be involved (a very large number) in cross-cultural relationships. To begin on an optimistic note, it is clear that cultures and the rules that apply to successfully operating within them, can be learned by outsiders, barring the extremely bigoted or exceptionally stupid. That is not to under-estimate the difficulties that might exist, for example, in learning another language; however, effective functioning in another culture does not always call for linguistic skills. In this section we will explore some of the ways in which a manager can prepare him/herself (or be prepared through training provided by the organisation) to do business cross-culturally. As we shall see, to a large extent what is required is an attitude change on the part of the manager, an openness and receptivity to new ideas and a willingness to learn.

Perhaps the most fundamental thing to be understood is that management practices do not always transfer across cultural boundaries. As the MBO example discussed earlier illustrated, most management concepts and practices are heavily laden with cultural assumptions, making it essential to assess whether, in a different environment, they are likely to be successful. We must begin to appreciate, then, that there is no 'one best way' to manage and set about learning the cultural expectations and assumptions which are attached to the role of 'manager' in other cultures. This, in turn, implies that, in a sense, we may have to 'unlearn' some attitudes and behaviours, while learning others. One of the biggest hurdles for managers setting out on this journey is to accept that there are good reasons for why people behave the way they do in different cultures and it is not a question of right or wrong, only of differences. We must endeavour to understand the other culture in its own terms and not keep comparing it (favourably or unfavourably) by reference to our own. One of the attributes that may need to be developed in this regard is that of tolerance; the manager must be encouraged to resist making judgements. This is often easier said than done: not infrequently do we revert to accusing 'those bloody foreigners' of being stupid, deceitful or even crazy for failing to see things our way. What is even more extraordinary is how some managers, through this attitude, treat people as foreigners in their own country. Especially when one is in another person's country, it is imperative that one respects the host culture by accommodating and adjusting one's style. This should not be taken to suggest that it is a matter of giving in or adopting holus bolus the perspectives of the other culture but rather that one understands those perspectives and takes them into account in deciding on one's own course of action.

A logical place to begin the process of more effective cross-cultural interactions is to undertake a cultural analysis of the type suggested by the Brake et al. (1995) wheel of cultural orientations. There are two comments to be made at the outset in this regard. First, for this to be effective it is necessary to have an understanding of one's own culture so that one can identify areas of potential friction or misunderstanding. Many people are ignorant of what they are communicating to other people through their own normal behaviour (Hall 1959) and for that reason some conscious attempt at self-insight is important. It is also important to recognise your own stereotypes of members of the other culture and, for that matter, their stereotypes of your group. This is not a straightforward matter: many people do not have the capacity, without expert help, to undertake such an analysis. Having been raised in an informal and individualistic society, it is frequently difficult for Australians to understand that directness, individuality and initiative are not revered in all cultures. Second, it is necessary to obtain accurate information about the other culture. Again, this may not be readily available and, in any event, expert help may be required in interpreting and explaining that information. Thus, while a self-learning approach through reading various materials might be helpful, in many instances a more structured approach using cultural experts is necessary or desirable. If the manager is going to be working in another culture, getting the help of a local (ideally in the organisation in which one is working) to give informal advice can help a great deal. It is very hard to be sensitive to local cultural values if we do not know what they are and, for this reason, the local adviser can be invaluable. Such a person can help in many areas, particularly advice about taboos and non-verbal behaviour. Of course, getting the assistance of such a local may, itself, not be easy. Often, managers seek the advice of others from their own culture who have experience of the foreign culture. While this can be very useful, it can be dangerous to rely too heavily on the 'war stories' or anecdotes of others, especially if they have (for whatever reason) developed a jaundiced view of the other culture. Indeed, at all times the manager should try to keep an open mind in relation to the foreign culture.

There are a number of training methods which have developed to assist managers in adjusting to different cultures and there is now a fairly large body of literature describing and critiquing such techniques (e.g. Black & Mendenhall (1990); Black et al. (1992); Mendenhall et al. (1987)). As Mendenhall et al. (1987) point out, the length of training provided and the broad approach adopted will depend on various circumstances, such as, in the case of expatriates, the length of stay abroad. As illustrated in Figure 12.4, Mendenhall et al. (1987) distinguish between three types of training: information-giving (or cognitive) approaches, which are relatively low-level; affective approaches which, as suggested by the name, address people's feelings as well as providing 'facts'; and immersion approaches which are in-depth methods covering a broad range of topics and methods. It is now apparent from empirical research which has been conducted (Stening & Hammer, 1992) that any training must take into account both the country being trained for and the country of origin of the trainee, for the reason that we all carry cultural baggage as a result of our own cultural conditioning.

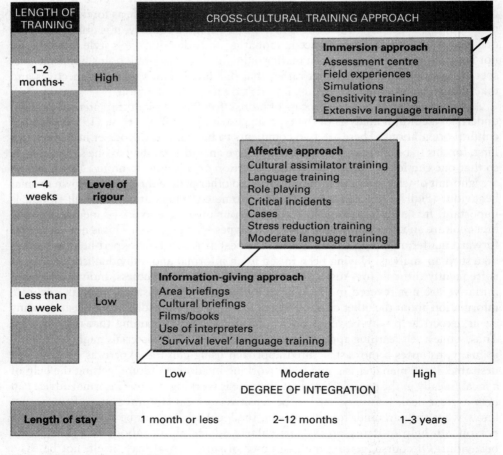

Figure 12.4 1 Relationship between degree of integration into the host culture and rigour of cross-cultural training 2 Relationship between length of overseas stay and length of training and training approach

Source: Mendenhall, Dunbar & Oddou 1987, p. 340

In addition to dealing with the difficulties posed by cultural differences, human resource managers need to be educated to consider how cultural diversity can be used proactively to enhance the effectiveness of their organisations. The diversity that exists within many Australian organisations could, in most instances, be used as a positive force instead of always being thought of as a constraint or weakness. For example, the linguistic and cultural skills of the workforce might be used very effectively in expanding the activities of the organisation into international markets. The Australian Public Service has recently turned its attention to the ways in which this might be achieved in the public sector in a publication entitled, 'Productive Diversity in the APS' (Public Service Commission and the Office of Multicultural Affairs 1995). Cox (1991) makes the point that while multicultural organisations can potentially suffer higher costs in terms of greater labour turnover, interpersonal conflict and communication breakdowns, such diversity can also bring considerable potential benefits such as better decision making, greater creativity and innovation and more successful marketing to different types of customers. To achieve such benefits, Cox argues that organisations must learn to value diversity and to promote it at all levels in the organisation. In a subsequent article, Cox & Blake argue that one of the keys to transforming traditional organisations into those which take advantage of their multicultural character is attention to their human resource management systems:

> A comprehensive analysis of the organisation culture and human resource systems such as recruitment, performance appraisal, potential assessment and promotion, and compensation should be undertaken. The primary objectives of this audit are: (1) to uncover sources of potential bias unfavourable to members of certain cultural groups, and (2) to identify ways that corporate culture might inadvertently put some members at a disadvantage (Cox & Blake, 1991, p. 53).

All of the above suggests that making the transition to being a competent cross-cultural manager is not a particularly easy task but that the necessary skills can be acquired. It is important, though, to be realistic about the magnitude of the task: the culture learning process takes time and one must be patient, setting realistic expectations about learning in this arena just as one would in other endeavours. Inevitably, mistakes will be made and that must be accepted; as in many situations, what is more important than the mistake itself is how one recovers from it; in cross-cultural situations, a certain level of gracefulness is highly desirable. Perhaps above all, it is critical that the manager maintains a sense of humour about such matters and is not weighed down by either their own or others' cultural baggage.

Future organisational forms

Tearing up today's organisational chart

BY PAULA DWYER

It's 7 am Friday in a specially rigged conference room at the head office of GE appliances in Louisville. CEO J. Richard Stonesifer, a fresh pot of coffee by his side is ready to roll. The speakerphone hums, and Stonesifer greets his management staff in Asia ... For the next five hours, Stonesifer follows the sun across the globe, holding phone meetings or video conferences with aides in Europe and the Americas. These talks 'allow us to make immediate adjustments', Stonesifer says.

Across the ocean, in Richard J. Callahan's London office overlooking fashionable Berkeley Square, a similar scene takes place. The US West International chief picks up his phone and begins a turbocharged conference call with seven division presidents in five countries. They hash over cellular phone sales in the Czech Republic, forecast long-distance hookups in Russia, and give a thumbs-up to opening an office in Japan.

Stonesifer and Callahan have never met and are in very different businesses but they have a lot in common. Both are trying to manage a revolution. They're racing to stay abreast of markets from Latin America to Russia and China that are accelerating in growth and leaping ahead in sophistication. New markets, rapid advances in communications, and new sources of brainpower and skilled labour are forcing businesses into their most fundamental reorganisation since the multidivisional corporation became standard in the 1950s. 'We're talking about a new order, a sea change, that will go on for the rest of my career', says Callahan. 'It's almost like Halley's comet arriving unannounced'.

Source: *Business Week*, 12 December, 1994.

Summary

Working in a cross-cultural environment presents a manager with a number of challenges additional to those which they confront in 'normal' circumstances. He or she must be sensitive to the fact that the assumptions, beliefs, values and so forth of those with whom they will be interacting may be rather different from those held by their own group. Such a manager must be equipped with the knowledge and skills to avoid what could be conflictive situations based on misunderstandings arising from such differences. However, this poses the question of what are 'normal circumstances'. Increasingly, as a result of many fundamental changes in the world (such as, but not confined to, the emergence of the global economy) all managers are being required to have the ability to operate effectively in cross-cultural situations. Managers are much more likely today than even ten years ago to be interacting with people from other countries. In the case of Australia, the existence of a multicultural society implies that for many managers interactions involving individuals from different cultural backgrounds will very likely be a daily occurrence.

In this chapter we have endeavoured to show that it is possible to go about dealing with cross-cultural circumstances in a systematic manner designed to minimise tensions. While it may take many years for someone to fully appreciate the nuances in another culture and to operate with the highest level of efficiency and effectiveness in that culture, almost all people can acquire sufficient skills to enable them to markedly improve their performance. Some of these skills can be learned in a self-help fashion, for example, by reading more about another culture. The most effective way of becoming a better manager in cross-cultural situations is, however, to undertake more formally structured learning activities under the tutelage of those who already know a great deal about the other culture. As we have seen, one of the primary reasons for why this more organised learning is effective is because it is very hard for anyone to shake off their ethnocentric perspective and begin to look at the world through glasses other than our own. The tools and techniques are available. It is incumbent on all of us who aspire to be effective human resource managers in the global economy to avail ourselves of them.

questions for discussion and review

1 In what broad types of situation might cross-cultural management problems be faced by an organisation?
2 Discuss the similarities and differences between the various theories of culture outlined in this chapter.
3 What is the problem of ecological fallacy in the context of empirical studies of culture?
4 How would you define culture? Where does it come from and how is it sustained?
5 Think of a couple of situations in which stereotyping is common. What are the positive and negative connotations and consequences of the stereotypes being used? How might negative stereotypes be changed?
6 Outline a strategy for how an HRM manager might go about extracting the advantages of cultural diversity in a multicultural organisation.
7 Use the Brake et al. (1995) framework of cultural orientations to analyse the culture of a country other than those discussed in this chapter.
8 Outline four HRM practices common in Australia that might be difficult to transfer to another (defined) culture, explaining what features of the other culture would make the transfer difficult.
9 Research a situation in which cross-cultural problems have emerged between an Australian or New Zealand company and indigenous people in either country. What was the character of the problem(s)? How was the situation resolved? How might it have been avoided in the first place?
10 Research a situation in which an Australian or New Zealand company has confronted a cross-cultural problem in its international business relations. What created the problem? How was it resolved? How might it have been avoided in the first place?

case study

Mike Flynn, president of the International Division of Information Network Services Corporation, was undecided as to how he could best approach several delicate issues with his Japanese joint venture partner. He needed to develop an agenda for his trip to Japan, scheduled for the following day. In many ways, he considered this trip of vital importance. For one thing, the problems to be discussed were likely to affect the long-term relationship between his company and the Japanese partner in the management of their joint venture. Moreover, this was his first trip to Japan in the capacity of president of the International Division, and he was anxious to make a good impression and to begin to build a personal relationship with senior executives of the Japanese firm.

Flynn had assumed the position of president several months previously in May of 1988. He was 40 years old and was considered to be one of the most promising executives in the company. After 2 years of military service followed by business school, he had joined a consulting company for several years prior to accepting a position with Information Network Services Corporation (INS). Prior to his promotion to the presidency of the International Division he had served as managing director of INSs wholly owned subsidiary in Canada.

INS was a major provider of value added network (VAN) services in the United States. Its principal products included high-speed data communications (packet switching), database management, transaction processing services, and a variety of industry-specific information services. The company's total sales for 1988 were roughly $250 million, and it had recently established successful presences in the United Kingdom and other European countries. International operations accounted for roughly 25 per cent of the company's total sales, and the company's top management felt that international markets represented a major field for future growth.

The company's management recognised that in order to capitalise on the rapidly growing Japanese market, a direct presence was needed. By the mid-1980s, the company began to receive a number of inquiries from major Japanese corporations concerning licensing possibilities. INS was particularly interested in the possibility of establishing a joint venture to provide VAN services.

The company, after 2 years of demanding negotiations, was successful in establishing a joint venture in Japan with Suji Company, a leading Japanese telecommunications equipment manufacturer. The arrangement was formalised in the summer of 1987.

Suji was one of the companies that approached INS initially to arrange a licensing agreement involving VAN technology and expertise. It appeared to be an attractive potential partner. Suji was a medium-sized telecommunication equipment vendor that was directly tied to one of the major Japanese industrial groups. The company had only limited sales to Nippon Telegraph and Telephone (NTT), the national telephone company. About half of its sales were exported, and the remainder went largely to other Japanese firms within the same industrial group. Suji had established a reputation for high quality, and its brands were well established.

In the mid-1980s, as the Japanese telecommunications market was deregulated, Suji began to explore opportunities in the telecommunication services market, particularly in paging and mobile phone services. Prior to deregulation, telephone and related services were monopoly markets served only by NTT. Under the terms of the 1984 New Telecommunications Law, other Japanese firms were permitted to offer these services to the general public. VAN services in particular could be initiated simply by notifying the Ministry of Posts and Telecommunications. The Ministry of International Trade and Industry had established several programs to provide incentives for new VAN services, including tax breaks and low-cost loans. Suji's management felt that VAN services would be a major growth area. Suji's management, after some investigation, concluded that the quickest and most efficient way to achieve entry into these markets was through either licensing or a joint venture with a leading US company. Suji's management felt that timing was of particular importance, since its major competitors were also considering expansion into these markets. Suji's expression of interest to INS was timely, as INS had become increasingly interested in Japan. Suji was at first interested in a licensing arrangement, but INS, anxious to establish a permanent presence in Japan, wished to establish a joint venture.

The negotiations concerning this joint venture were difficult in part because it was the first experience of the kind for both companies. INS had virtually no prior experience in Japan, and for Suji this was the first joint venture with a foreign company, although it had engaged in licensing agreements with several US and European firms.

The ownership of the joint venture was divided between the two companies, such that Suji owned two-thirds and INS one-third of its equity. Japanese law limited foreign ownership in telecom services vendors to one-third equity participation. In addition to a predetermined cash contribution, the agreement stipulated that INS was to provide network technology and the Japanese partner was to contribute facilities and network equipment. The joint venture was first to market data communication services and later was to introduce transaction processing services.

The services were to be marketed under the joint brands of INS and Suji. The agreement also stipulated that both companies would have equal representation on the board of directors, with four people each, and that Suji would provide the entire personnel for the joint venture from top management down to production workers. Such a practice was quite common among foreign joint ventures in Japan, since given limited mobility among personnel in large corporations, recruiting would represent a major problem for foreign companies. The companies also agreed that the Japanese partner would nominate the president of the joint venture, subject to approval of the board, and the US company would nominate a person for the position of executive vice president. INS also agreed to supply, for the time being, a technical director on a full-time basis.

INS had four members on the board: Flynn, Jack Rose (INSs nominee for executive vice president of the joint venture), and the chair and the president of INS. Representing the Japanese company were the president and executive vice president of Suji, and two senior executives of the joint venture, the president and vice president for finance.

By the Fall of 1988, the venture had initiated tests of its data communication services, and a small sales organisation had been built. Although the venture was progressing reasonably well, Flynn had become quite concerned over several issues that had come to his attention during the previous 2 months. The first and perhaps the most urgent of these was the selection of a new president for the joint venture.

The first president had died suddenly about 3 months before at the age of 68. He had been a managing director of the parent company and had been the chief representative in Suji's negotiations with INS. When the joint venture was established, it appeared only natural for him to assume the presidency; INS management had no objection.

About a month after his death, Suji, in accordance with the agreement, nominated Kenzo Satoh as the new president. Flynn, when he heard Satoh's qualifications, concluded that he was not suitable for the presidency of the joint venture. He became even more disturbed when he received further information about how he was selected from Jack Rose, the executive vice president of the joint venture.

Satoh had joined Suji 40 years previously upon graduating from Tokyo University. He had held a variety of positions in the Suji company, but during the previous 15 years, he had served almost exclusively in staff functions. He had been manager of Administrative Services at the company's major plant, manager of the General Affairs Department at the corporate headquarters, and personnel director. When he was promoted to that position, he was admitted to the company's board of directors. His responsibility was then expanded to include overseeing several service-oriented staff departments, including personnel, industrial relations, administrative services, and the legal department.

Flynn was concerned that Satoh had virtually no line experience and could not understand why Suji would propose such a person for the presidency of the joint venture, particularly when it was at a critical stage of development.

Even more disturbing to Mr Flynn was the manner in which Satoh was selected. This first came to Mr Flynn's attention when received a letter from Rose, which included the following description:

> 'By now you have undoubtedly examined the background information forwarded to you regarding Mr Satoh, nominated by our Japanese partner for the presidency of the joint venture.
> I have subsequently learned the manner in which Mr Satoh was chosen for the position, which I am sure would be of great interest to you.

I must point out at the outset that what I am going to describe, though shocking by our standards, is quite commonplace among Japanese corporations: in fact, it is well-accepted.

Before describing the specific practice, I must give you a brief background of the Japanese personnel system. As you know, the major companies follow the so-called lifetime employment where all managerial personnel are recruited directly from universities, and they remain with the company until they reach their compulsory retirement age, which is typically around 57. Career advancement in the Japanese system comes slowly, primarily by seniority. Advancement to middle management is well-paced, highly predictable, and virtually assured for every college graduate. Competence and performance become important as they reach upper middle management and top management. Obviously, not everyone will be promoted automatically beyond middle management, but whatever the degree to which competence and qualifications are considered in career advancement, chronological age is the single most important factor.

A select few within the ranks of upper-middle management will be promoted to top management positions, that is, they will be given memberships in the board of directors. In large Japanese companies, the board typically consists exclusively of full-time operating executives. Suji's board is no exception. Moreover, there is a clear-cut hierarchy among the members. The Suji board consists of the chair of the board, president, executive vice president, three managing directors, five ordinary directors, and two statutory auditors.

Typically, ordinary directors have specific operating responsibilities such as head of a staff department, a plant, or a division. Managing directors are comparable to our group vice presidents. Each will have two or three functional or staff groups or product divisions reporting to them. Japanese commercial law stipulates that the members are to be elected by stockholders for a 2-year term. Obviously, under the system described, the members are designated by the chair of the board or the president and serve at their pleasure. Stockholders have very little voice in the actual selection of the board members. Thus, in some cases, it is quite conceivable that board membership is considered as a reward for many years of faithful and loyal service.

As you are well aware, a Japanese corporation is well known for its paternalistic practices in return for lifetime service, and they do assume obligations, particularly for those in middle management or above, even after they reach their compulsory retirement age, not just during their working careers. Appropriate positions are generally found for them in the company's subsidiaries, related firms, or major suppliers where they can occupy positions commensurate to their last position in the parent corporation for several more years.

A similar practice applies to the board members. Though there is no compulsory retirement age for board members, the average tenure for board membership is usually around 6 years. This is particularly true for those who are ordinary or managing directors. Directorships being highly coveted positions, there must be regular turnover to allow others to be promoted to board membership. As a result, all but a fortunate few who are earmarked as heir apparent to the chair, presidency, or executive vice presidency must be 'retired'. Since most of these executives are in their late fifties or early sixties, they do not yet wish to retire. Moreover, even among major Japanese corporations, the compensation for top management positions is quite low compared with the US standard, and pension plans being still quite inadequate, they will need respectable positions with a reasonable income upon leaving the company. Thus, it is common practice among Japanese corporations to transfer senior executives of the parent company to the chair or presidency of the company's subsidiaries or affiliated companies. Typically, these people will serve in these positions for several years before they retire. Suji had a dozen subsidiaries, and you might be interested in knowing that every top management position is held by those who have retired from the parent corporation. Such a system is well routinised.

Our friend, Mr Satoh is clearly not the calibre that would qualify for further advancement in the parent company, and his position must be vacated for another person. Suji's top management must have decided that the presidency of the joint venture was the appropriate position for him to 'retire' into. These are the circumstances under which Mr Satoh has been nominated for our consideration'.

When he read this letter, Flynn instructed Rose to indicate to the Suji management that Satoh was not acceptable. Not only did Flynn feel that Satoh lacked the qualifications and experience for the presidency, but he resented the fact that Suji was using the joint venture as a home to accommodate a retired executive. It would be justifiable for Suji to use one of its wholly owned subsidiaries for that purpose, but there was no reason why the joint venture should take him on. On the contrary, the joint venture needed dynamic leadership to establish a viable market position.

In his response to Rose, Flynn suggested as president another person, Takao Toray, marketing manager of the joint venture. Toray was 50 years old and had been transferred to the joint venture from Suji, where he had held a number of key marketing positions, including regional sales manager and assistant marketing director. Shortly after he was appointed to the latter position, Toray was sent to INS headquarters to become acquainted with the company's marketing operations. He spent roughly 3 months in the United States, during which time Flynn met him. Though he had not gone beyond a casual acquaintance, Flynn was much impressed by Toray. He appeared to be dynamic, highly motivated, and pragmatic. Moreover, Toray had a reasonable command of English. While communication was not easy, at least it was possible to have conversations on substantive matters. From what Flynn was able to gather, Toray impressed everyone he saw favourably and gained the confidence of not only the International Division staff but those in the corporate marketing group as well as sales executives in the field.

Flynn was aware that Toray was a little too young to be acceptable to Suji, but he felt that it was critical to press for his appointment for two reasons. First, he was far from convinced of the wisdom of adopting Japanese managerial practices blindly in the joint venture. Some of the Japanese executives he met in New York had told him of the pitfalls and weaknesses of Japanese management practices. He was disturbed over the fact that, as he was becoming familiar with the joint venture, he was finding that in every critical aspect such as organisation structure, personnel practices, and decision making, the company was managed as though it were a Japanese company. Rose had had little success in introducing US practices. Flynn had noticed in the past that the joint venture had been consistently slow in making decisions because it engaged in a typical Japanese group-oriented and consensus-based process. He also learned that control and reporting systems were virtually nonexistent. Flynn felt that INSs sophisticated planning and control system should be introduced. It had proved successful in the company's wholly owned European subsidiaries, and there seemed to be no reason why such a system could not improve the operating efficiency of the joint venture. He recalled from his Canadian experience that US management practices, if judiciously applied, could give US subsidiaries abroad a significant competitive advantage over local firms.

Second, Flynn felt that the rejection of Satoh and appointment of Toray might be important as a demonstration to the Japanese partner that Suji-INS was indeed a joint venture and not a subsidiary of the Japanese parent company. He was also concerned that INS had lost the initiative in the management of the joint venture. This move would help INS gain stronger influence over the management of the joint venture.

Rose conveyed an informal proposal along these lines to Suji management. Suji's reaction to Flynn's proposal was swift; they rejected it totally. Suji management was polite, but made it clear that they considered Flynn unfair in judging Mr Satoh's suitability for the presidency without even having met him. They requested Rose to assure Flynn that their company, as majority owner, indeed had an important stake in the joint venture and certainly would not have recommended Satoh unless it had been convinced of his qualifications. Suji management also told Flynn, through Rose, that the selection of Toray was totally unacceptable because in the Japanese corporate system such a promotion was unheard of and would be detrimental not only to the joint venture but to Toray himself, who was believed to have promising future in the company.

Flynn was surprised at the tone of Suji's response. He wondered whether it would be possible to establish an effective relationship with the Japanese company. Suji seemed determined to run the venture on their own terms.

Another related issue which concerned Flynn was the effectiveness of Rose as executive vice president. Flynn appreciated the difficulties he faced but began to question Rose's qualifications for his position and his ability to work with Japanese top management. During the last visit, for example, Rose had complained of his inability to integrate himself with the Japanese top management team. He indicated that he felt he was still very much an outsider to the company, not only because he was a foreigner but also because the Japanese executives, having come from the parent company, had known each other and in many cases had worked together for at least 20 years. He also indicated that none of the executives spoke English well enough to achieve effective communication beyond the most rudimentary level and that his Japanese was too limited to be of practical use. In fact, his secretary, hired specifically for him, was the only one with whom he could communicate easily. He also expressed frustration over the fact that his functions were very ill-defined and his experience and competence were not really being well utilised by the Japanese.

Flynn discovered after he assumed the presidency that Mr Rose had been chosen for this assignment for his knowledge of Japan. Rose graduated from a midwestern university in 1973, and after enlisting in the Army was posted to Japan for 4 years. Upon returning home, he joined INS as a management trainee. In 1984, he became assistant district sales manager in California, Oregon, and Washington. When the company began to search for a candidate for executive vice president for the new joint venture, Rose's name came up as someone who was qualified and available for posting to Japan. Rose, although somewhat ambivalent about the new opportunity at first, soon became persuaded that this would represent a major challenge and opportunity.

Flynn was determined to get a first-hand view of the joint venture during his visit. He had many questions, and he wondered whether he had inherited a problem. He was scheduled to meet with Mr Ohtomo, executive vice president of Suji Corporation, on the day following his arrival. Ohtomo, who had been with Suji for over 40 years, was the senior executive responsible for overseeing the joint venture. Flynn had not met Ohtomo, but he knew that Ohtomo had visited the United States and spoke English reasonably well. He wondered how best to approach and organise his meetings and discussions with Mr Ohtomo. He also wondered if his planned stay of 1 week would be adequate to achieve his objectives. While practising with chopsticks, he returned to reading *Theory Z*, a popular book on Japanese management, in the hope of gaining insight for the days ahead.

Source: Mendenhall & Oddou 1991, pp. 290–97.

Questions
1 What should be Flynn's primary objectives and how can he go about accomplishing them?
2 What, specifically, should Flynn do about Suji's proposal to appoint Satoh as president of the joint venture?
3 Should Flynn leave Rose in his present position in the joint venture?
4 What mistakes, if any, did INS make in setting up the joint venture and how might such errors be avoided in the future?

Resources

Landis, Dan & Bhagat, Rabi S. (eds), *Handbook of Intercultural Training*, 2nd edition, Sage Publications, CA.
Martin J. Gannon & Associates (1994), *Understanding Global Cultures: Metaphorical Journeys Through 17 Countries*, Sage Publications, CA.
Milner, A & Quilty, Mary (eds), *Comparing Cultures: Australia in Asia*, Oxford University Press, Melbourne.
Morrison, T., Conway, W. A. & Borden, G. A. (1994), *Kiss, Bow, or Shake Hands: How to do Business in Sixty Countries*, Bob Adams Inc. Mass.
Puffer, Sheila M. (1996), *Management Across Cultures: Insights From Fiction and Practice*, Blackwell, Cambridge, MA.

References

Adler, Nancy J. (1991), *International Dimensions of Organizational Behavior*, 2nd edition, PWS-Kent Publishing, Boston, Mass.
Black, J. S., Gregersen, H. B. & Mendenhall, M. E. (1992), *Global assignments: successfully expatriating and repatriating international managers*, Jossey-Bass, San Fanncisco, CA.
Brake, Terence, Walker, Danielle (1995), *Doing Business Internationally: The Workbook to Cross-Cultural Success*, Princeton Training Press, Princeton, NJ.
Cartwright, S. & Cooper, C. L. (1993), 'The role of culture compatibility in successful organizational marriage', *Academy of Management Executive*, vol. 7, no. 2, pp. 57–70.
Cox, Taylor (1991), 'The multicultural organization', *Academy of Management Executive*, vol. 5, no. 2, pp. 34–47.

Cox, Taylor & Blake, Stacy (1991), 'Managing cultural diversity: Implications for organizational competitiveness', *Academy of Management Executive*, vol. 5, no. 3, pp. 45–56.

Dowling, Peter J., Schuler, Randall S. & Welch, Denice E. (1994), *International Dimensions of Human Resource Management*, 2nd edition, Wadsworth, Belmont, CA.

Elegant, S. & Cohen, M. (1996), 'Asia's New Generation: Just Like Their Parents', *Far Eastern Economic Review*, December 5, 1996, p. 52.

Griggs, Lewis Brown & Louw, Lente-Louise (eds) (1995), *Valuing Diversity: New Tools for a New Reality*, McGraw-Hill, New York.

Hall, Edward T. (1959), *The Silent Language*, Anchor Press/Doubleday, New York.

—— (1960), 'The silent language in overseas business', *Harvard Business Review*, May–June, pp. 87–96.

—— (1966), *The Hidden Dimension*, Anchor Press/Doubleday, New York.

—— (1976), *Beyond Culture*, Anchor Press/Doubleday, New York.

Hall, Edward T. & Hall, Mildred Reed (1990), *Understanding Cultural Differences*, Intercultural Press, Yarmouth, Maine.

Hampden-Turner, Charles & Trompenaars, Fons (1993), *The Seven Cultures of Capitalism*, Doubleday, New York.

Harris, Philip R. & Moran, Robert T. (1987), *Managing Cultural Differences*, 2nd edition, Gulf, Houston, Tx.

Hofstede, Geert (1991), *Cultures and Organizations: Software of the Mind*, McGraw-Hill, London.

—— (1980), *Culture's Consequences: International Differences in Work-Related Values*, Sage Publications, Beverly Hills, CA.

—— (1980b) 'Motivation, leadership, and organization: Do American theories apply abroad?', *Organizational Dynamics*, Summer, pp. 42–63.

—— (1996), 'Riding the waves of commerce: A test of Trompenaars' model of national culture differences', *International Journal of Intercultural Relations*, vol. 20, no. 2, pp. 189–98.

Hofstede, Geert & Bond, Michael Harris (1988), 'The Confucius connection: From cultural roots to economic growth', *Organizational Dynamics*, vol. 16, no. 4, pp. 4–21.

Industry Task Force on Leadership and Management Skills (Karpin Task Force) (1995), *Enterprising Nation: Renewing Australia's Managers to Meet the Challenges of the Asia-Pacific Century*, Australian Government Publishing Service, Canberra.

Kluckhohn, Florence Rockwood & Strodtbeck, Fred. L. (1961), *Variations in Value Orientations*, Peterson, New York.

Lane, Henry W. & DiStefano, Joseph J. (1992), *International Management Behavior: From Policy to Practice*, 2nd edition, PWS-Kent Publishing Company, Boston, Mass.

March, Robert M. (1989), *The Japanese Negotiator: Subtlety and Strategy Beyond Western Logic*, Kodansha International, Tokyo.

Mendenhall, Mark E., Dunbar, Edward & Oddou, Gary (1987), 'Expatriate selection, training and career-pathing: A review and critique', *Human Resource Management*, vol. 26, no. 3, pp. 331–45.

Mendenhall, M. & Oddou, G. (1991), *Readings and cases in International Human Resource Management*, PWS-Kent, Boston, Mass.

Mead, Richard (1994), *International Management: Cross-Cultural Dimensions*, Blackwell Publishers, Cambridge, Mass.

Naisbitt, J. (1995), *Megratrends Asia: The Eight Asian Megatrends that are changing the world*, Nicholas Brealey Publishing, London.

Public Service Commission and the Office of Multicultural Affairs (1995), *Productive Diversity in the APS*, Australian Government Publishing Service, Canberra.

Renwick, George W. (1991), *A Fair Go For All: Australian/American Interactions* (Revised by Reginald Smart & Don L. Henderson), Intercultural Press, Yarmouth, Maine.

Sathe, V. (1985), *Culture and Related Corporate Realities*, Richard D. Irwin, Homewood, Ill.

Schneider, Susan C. (1988), 'National vs corporate culture: Implications for human resource management', *Human Resource Management*, vol. 27, no. 2, pp. 231–46.

Stening, Bruce W. (1994), 'Expatriate management: Lessons from the British in India', *International Journal of Human Resource Management*, vol. 5. no. 2, pp. 385–404.

Stening, Bruce W. & Hammer, Mitchell R. (1992), 'Cultural baggage and the adaptation of expatriate American and Japanese managers', *Management International Review*, vol. 32 no. 1, pp. 77–89.

The Chinese Culture Connection (a team of 24 researchers) (1987), 'Chinese values and the search for culture-free dimensions of culture', *Journal of Cross-Cultural Psychology*, vol. 18, no. 2, pp. 143–64.

Trompenaars, Fons (1993), *Riding the Waves of Culture: Understanding Cultural Diversity in Business*, Nicholas Brealey Publishing, London.

chapter 13

International human resource management

Peter McGraw

learning objectives

After studying this chapter, you will be able to:

1. Identify the differences between domestic and international HRM (IHRM).
2. Identify the forces driving the expansion of global business and the impact on organisations and their HR policies and practices.
3. Understand the historical growth pattern of international organisations
4. Understand the link between strategy and structure in international organisations.
5. Understand the pattern of internationalisation of Australian organisations.
6. Understand the issues, concepts and research findings in three key areas of international HRM: (1) Recruitment and selection, (2) Training and development, and (3) Remuneration.

chapter 13

chapter outline

- Introduction to IHRM — 542
- The pattern of globalisation — 543
- The growth of international organisations — 547
- A strategic and structural typology of multinational organisations — 548
- International recruitment and selection — 550
  - Executive nationality policies — 551
  - Issues related to policy choice — 553
  - Expatriate failure rates — 554
  - Predictors of expatriate success — 557
  - Repatriation — 562
- International training and development — 563
  - Training to avoid expatriate failure — 564
  - A model of international training and development — 566
  - Multinational training practices — 567
  - Policy aspects of international training and development — 569
- International remuneration — 572
  - Issues in international remuneration — 573
- Summary — 575
- Questions for discussion and review — 576
- Case study — 577
- Resources — 582
- References — 582

HRM IN THE NEWS

Blending one culture with some local spice

Burns Philp needs the right mix of central policy and local flexibility to run businesses in 33 countries.

BY ADELE FERGUSON

Burns Philp's group performance reports for the December quarter show a higher rate of absenteeism at its European businesses. A comparison of workplace accidents between geographical centres showed there was a comparatively high rate in South America. Burns Philp has to overcome such cultural idiosyncrasies each time it makes an overseas acquisition.

But if it is to maintain its place as a player in global business, overseas acquisitions are part of the game. The group has operations in 33 countries and it is expanding its food and ingredients operations. John Dyer, general manager of personnel, says management of human resources is a key issue because Burns Philp is such a large organisation operating in so many countries. He says its human resources policy is important because Burns Philp does not want to operate as an Australian company with satellites. It also does not want the various operations to develop a feeling of remoteness. Rather, it wants its staff to behave as an international team, and each business acting as part of the same family.

Developing a team-style culture for a worldwide operation is no mean feat, but Dyer is confident that Burns Philp can achieve it. He says the company is centralised but it allows its overseas operations to run with a high degree of independence so long as each operation does not contradict the group's broad human resources policy. The group maintains a degree of autonomy in each operation by appointing locals to run the businesses. Dyer says it is much cheaper and the local staff prefer to work under a local boss rather than an expatriate. However, he says, in some cases expatriates are appointed for career development or because the local staff do not have an adequate management line.

Once an acquisition is announced and appointments made, the Burns Philp human resources team attempts to integrate the staff into the group's culture. Dyer says that even with operations in 33 locations there is not a feeling of remoteness by staff. He says the company has established product boards—yeast, consumer ingredients and spices—with representatives from the various worldwide operations, which meet three or four times a year to share ideas.

Dyer says each acquisition is different by the rule of thumb is that it takes one to two years to align any acquisition to the group. The time taken largely depends on the dominance of the culture but he says most companies have the sort of systems that are easily adapted to Burns Philip's broad human resources policy. Even so, most acquisitions are subject to some degree of rationalisation and changes in management systems. In the United States, for example, Burns Philp is closing two of its spice processing plants to concentrate all manufacturing operations at a single plant.

Each quarter, Burns Philp board members are supplied with a detailed analysis of the performance of each operation and each geographic region. Such details include productivity, the level of absenteeism, accidents, industrial action and staff turnover. Dyer says the quarterly reports are an important tool in assessing the effectiveness of management programs. He says the high level of absenteeism in Europe reflects a cultural attitude that Burns Philp has yet to overcome. Argentina's high rate of injuries stems from the cavalier attitude prevalent in the country, although, he says, Burns

Philp has dramatically cut the accident rate there through an education campaign that focuses on the benefits of safer workplaces.

'One area that is going to be hard is Russia', Dyer says. 'The people are not used to business. They were accustomed to operating in informal networks where people did each other favours and there was no concept of professional management. It will be a challenge to introduce a framework of management, but we are confident that we can'.

Although Burns Philp operates a 'top down' management structure it allows each operation the freedom to adapt broad company philosophies to suit local requirements. For instance, in the US, affirmative action policy differs from that in countries such as China. With a staff of 10 000, some as far away as Ireland, Spain, Russia, Argentina and China, the company has had its human resources team at head office develop a tight-knit framework for various operations to follow.

'It is not difficult overlaying different country cultures and company cultures with a core Burns Philp culture', Dyer says. 'We do this by running management training programs throughout the year to teach senior and middle management our systems'. Each business has a charter that acts as a framework for management to devise one-year and three-year plans. Each job at Burns Philp is given a grading and a job specification. Each job has annual goals that are reviewed and salaries adjusted accordingly.

Dyer says the human resources policy of the group has not changed since its decision in the early 1980s to abandon its conglomerate structure, divest non-core food businesses and become globalised. Since then, it has divested more than 300 businesses, including the BBC Hardware chain, and moved into 33 countries. The latest annual report shows that more than 70 per cent of group revenue is generated overseas. This is expected to increase as the group embarks on a strategy to maintain its status as a world leader in yeast and spices. Burns Philp is now the world's biggest producer of baker's yeast and vinegar and the second largest spice manufacturer.

Having its head office in Sydney is not a problem. Dyer says, 'Through various education campaigns and satellite links, managements around the world are taught the Burns Philp culture'.

'Each region operates autonomously but is given guidelines from head office. The role of the human resources department in Sydney is to facilitate the development of its people', Dyer says.

Individuals are measured according to their skills and knowledge and they are assessed to make sure they have the right cultural attitude.

Dyer says: 'The aim is to have a core culture so that different country cultures will not be eliminated, but overlaid with Burns Philp's culture. This is done through management training programs that are run three times a year in one of the four geographical regions we operate in: South America, North America, Europe and Asia-Pacific'.

Besides defining its own human resources policies, the company also draws on the Australian Human Resources Institute for knowledge about where the profession is heading. He describes the institute as a network that allows members to tap into international practices and learn about the latest techniques.

The need to define a cohesive and universal corporate culture is critical for companies pursuing a global growth strategy. Burns Philp's international expansion has occurred far more rapidly than most other companies, and with each acquisition it has made reviewing and repositioning human-resources policy a priority.

Staff are very important to us. We want people to feel they belong to a company that is unified yet flexible enough to absorb individual ideas', Dyer says.

Source: *BRW*, 5 June 1995, pp. 80–81.

Introduction to IHRM

It is widely accepted that the future health of Australia's economy depends upon the global competency of its companies and their ability to become efficient producers and exporters of manufactured products and services. For many companies this has involved setting up operations outside Australia. One of the key issues for the Australian economy identified in the Karpin Report (Commonwealth of Australia 1995) was that of meeting the challenges of the 'Asia-Pacific Century'. Implicit in any discussion of successful internationalisation is the assumption that international operations require specific management skills. As Duerr has noted:

> Virtually any type of international problem, in the final analysis, is either created by people or must be solved by people. Hence, having the right people in the right place at the right time emerges as the key to a company's international growth. If we are successful in solving that problem, I am confident we can cope with all others (Duerr 1986, p. 43).

International HRM (IHRM) involves the same functions as domestic HRM but is more complicated as a result of the addition of two major factors: the countries which are involved in the organisation's operations and the types of employees in the organisation. Thus in the case of Burns Philp there are operations in 33 locations around the globe and many nationalities are represented (See 'HRM in the news'). In view of this diversity, one of the key tasks for the HR manager in Burns Philp is to overlay headquarters policies, systems and culture on widely diverse international subsidiaries, with many different nationalities and ethnic cultures represented among the employees. Not surprisingly, this is a very complex operation. Such complexity is well summarised in Morgan's model of IHRM, which is shown in Figure 13.1

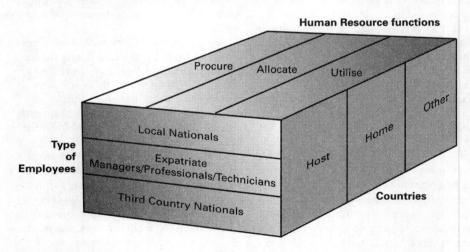

Figure 13.1   Model of International HRM

Source: Morgan 1986, p. 44

As can be seen from Figure 13.1 there are three broad HR functions which are the same in the domestic and international arenas; procurement, utilisation and allocation of staff. However, an international organisation has the opportunity to employ staff who are not just **Parent Country Nationals** (PCNs) but may also be **Host Country Nationals** (HCNs) or **Third Country Nationals** (TCNs). Moreover, IHRM must also take into consideration the different countries involved in HRM activities. There is the host country where an international subsidiary may be operating, a home country where and international organisation has its head office and other countries which may be a source of labour or finance. Morgan defines IHRM as the interplay among these three dimensions.

The layering of these two major additional variables on the operation of HR in international companies leads to much greater complexity. The major differences have been summarised in Dowling, Schuler & Welch (1994) as:

- **More functions and activities**—taxation, international relocation/orientation, expatriate administrative services, host government relations, language translation issues
- **Broader perspective**—co-ordination of international compensation, benefits and superannuation
- **More involvement in employee's lives**—housing, health care, education, family issues
- **HR changes** resulting from changes in the mix of PCNs and HCNs: career development, training
- **Risk exposure**—expatriate failure, physical risk
- **More external issues**—host government regulations (Dowling et al. 1994).

There are three further variables that either accentuate or diminish the differences between domestic and IHRM. These are the cultural environment, the industry in which a company is involved and the attitudes of senior management. The first of these, the cultural environment, is dealt with separately in Chapter 12. The second and third, the industry and senior management attitudes, are dealt with below in the section headed 'A strategic and structural typology of multinational organisations'.

The pattern of globalisation

The increased emphasis and usage of the term globalisation reflects the reality of the ever-increasing volume and complexity of world trade and markets. Economic activity now no longer overlaps neatly with the political and cultural entities defined by nation states. Whereas political space has remained defined by nations and the space defining cultural identity seems to be shrinking daily, with widespread conflict between ethnic communities in various parts of the globe, economic activity on the other hand has enlarged to cover the globe (Adler 1995, p. 10). According to Shenkar the growth in world trade is outpacing the growth of global goods and services by a margin of around two to one and in 1990 exceeded US$3.3 trillion (Shenkar 1995, p. 1). It is estimated that unregulated currency exchanges amount to almost a trillion US Dollars per day (Adler 1995). In addition, foreign direct investment is growing at the rate of 30 per cent per year and by 1990 had reached an accumulated value of US$ 1.3 trillion (Shenkar 1995, p. 1). Reflecting these figures, the decade of the 1990s has seen a huge growth in international joint ventures and the expansion of international businesses. An inevitable side effect of this growth has been the increasing employment of people outside their home country. For example:

- half the employees of the Ford Motor Company are employed outside the United States
- three quarters of the Phillips workforce is employed outside the Netherlands
- half of Matsushita Electric's employees are outside Japan
- over half of Ericsson's staff work outside Sweden (Dowling et al. 1994, p. 1).

Furthermore, it is estimated that 5 million Americans (5 per cent of the business sector workforce) are employed by the affiliates of foreign firms while 'At the same time US firms employ more than 6.5 million people in other countries: 3.5 million in Western Europe, 1.5 million (and growing rapidly) in Asia, and almost as many in Latin America ... at the end of this decade, roughly one out of six workers in the United Kingdom will be working for a Japanese company' (Shenkar 1995, p. 2).

In the case of Australia, the largest businesses earn, on average, nearly a third of their income overseas and have almost one third of their assets outside Australia. For major mining and industrial companies these figures rise to in excess of 40 per cent (Boston Consulting Group in Commonwealth of Australia 1995, p. 1236).

The Burns Philp case referred to in 'HRM in the news' is an example of how one company has embraced international business opportunities and the HR issues that flow from such a business strategy. Burns Philp is not alone; nearly 70 per cent of Australia's top twenty companies have major investments in Asia. The Asian activities of a number of Australian companies are summarised in Figure 13.2.

COMPANY	ASSETS OFFSHORE (%)	INCOME OFFSHORE (%)	ACTIVITIES IN ASIA
BHP	30	31	Coal, steel and transport subsidiaries in Asia. Joint ventures in PNG, Indonesia, Vietnam.
Coles Myer	0	0	—
News Corp	73	85	Major media interests in Hong Kong.
Westpac	28	22	Branch operations in Asia-Pacific.
NAB	44	44	—
ANZ	25	26	Branch operations in Asia-Pacific.
Woolworths	0	0	Predominantly Australian operations.
CBA (1)	14	13	Branch operations in Asia-Pacific.
Foster's Brewing	66	53	—
Pacific Dunlop	44	34	Latex products and batteries subsidiaries in Malaysia, Thailand, Sri Lanka. Joint venture in China and Malaysia.
STR Nylex	49	45	Production subsidiaries in Malaysia, Taiwan, Japan, Indonesia and Mexico
CRA	15	25	Gold and Aluminium subsidiaries in Indonesia. Joint ventures in PNG and Indonesia.
Pioneer International	35	26	Aggregate and concrete subsidiaries in Hong Kong, Macau, Singapore, China, Malaysia and Thailand.
Amcor	18	21	Container subsidiaries in Singapore. Joint ventures in Hong Kong, Singapore and Malaysia.
Goodman Fielder	40	43	Subsidiaries in Singapore, Indonesia and The Philippines.

Figure 13.2 Asian activities of Australia's largest companies
Source: Boston Consulting Group 1995, in Karpin Report, p. 1239

Australia is the fifth largest investor in China's special economic development areas of Shenzen, Guangzhou and Zhuhon (Harris 1994) and, according to Austrade, the seventh largest investor in Vietnam. The top ten Australian companies increased their offshore investment by 22 per cent annually between 1987–91. This compares with an onshore investment rate of only 9 per cent in the same period (Chong 1992). Moreover, a McKinsey/AMC study (1993) showed that 13 per cent of a sample of over 300 exporters had already established overseas production facilities and a further 50 per cent were considering doing so.

The impact of establishing international operation is profound for any organisation; some of the key trends are discussed in the 'Future organisational forms' section. One of the most affected areas is that of human resource management. For example, according to a Booz, Allen & Hamilton survey (cited in Shenkar 1995, p. 2), the problem of hiring quality staff is one of the main factors inhibiting the expansion of foreign investment in Japan. Ironically, according to the *Wall Street Journal* (cited in Shenkar, 1995, p. 2), the Japanese rate conflict between expatriates and their local workforces as the number one concern in relation to globalisation. In Indonesia many international organisations experience managerial turnover rates between 30–40 per cent p.a. (Stace 1996c) and 'job hopping' is a major problem for companies in international business centres such as Hong Kong and Singapore. Further challenges in international HRM are discussed in the 'Managing change' discussion.

Future organisational forms

Some of the key trends in the globalisation of business which are forcing international organisations to restructure are:

1 Managing organisations in the era of regional trade blocs and the loss of traditional sources of comparative advantage such as proximity to market.
2 Managing new organisational forms such as network or virtual organisations, which have been enabled largely through the growth of sophisticated communications technology.
3 Attempts by most organisations in the nineties to get closer to the customer, yet at the same time, and often paradoxically, extract more global synergy through better co-ordination and integration of operations. That is to simultaneously become more centrally co-ordinated and locally responsive, or, to use the cliché, 'think globally, act locally'.
4 Concerted efforts by the majority of global organisations to localise their foreign affiliates.
5 Attempts to develop multiple pathways for the diffusion of innovation or best practice within the organisation so that local affiliates do not merely follow management practices in corporate centres but also influence the operation of corporate centres and other affiliates, i.e. creating learning organisations on a global scale.
6 A large increase in the number of mergers, takeovers, strategic alliances and joint ventures which start to dissolve, or bring into question the boundaries of organisations.
7 The changing patterns of employment in the developed world versus the non developed world.
8 The challenge of managing multicultural and diverse workforces.

More fundamentally, global organisations can shift patterns of employment around different countries in order to maximise competitive advantage without much opposition from politicians. While we may not yet live in an era of free trade, we certainly live in an era of globally mobile capital. Adler (1995) reports that in a recent survey of 1500 CEOs surveyed for the 21st Century Report, the majority reported that they planned to reduce employment in their home countries during the 1990s. It is now clear that the economic viability of nations rests on their ability to construct competitive infrastructures for business which attract capital which will otherwise go elsewhere. As the Karpin Report noted:

> While they still form the majority of companies around the world, even those enterprises whose focus is entirely toward their domestic market now face more and more competition from overseas companies entering these markets. No Australian company, be it BHP operating in many countries around the globe, or a small services company operating solely in the western suburbs of Sydney, is now completely immune from the forces of global competition.
>
> *Globalisation has profound implications for the way Australian enterprises need to be managed* (Commonwealth of Australia 1995, p. 16).

This chapter examines key issues facing managers and employees in global work environments. The first part of the chapter reviews the growth of international organisations. This is followed by a discussion of the structural and strategic issues facing international organisations where a typology is outlined which examines the different types of international organisations and the HRM issues facing them. Australian organisations are then analysed in the context of this typology. The balance of the chapter looks in depth at key IHRM issues: recruitment and selection, training and development and remuneration.

Managing change

The key change issues confronting IHRM practitioners have been confirmed in a recent survey by Cascio of 110 senior HR professionals from multinational companies operating on four continents (Cascio 1993). In response to questions asking managers to identify the most important issues in IHRM the following three within-firm issues were identified as most important:

1 The role of human resources in international operations
   · 'exporting' home country culture overseas
   · managing expatriates
   · instilling a global orientation among managers and workers
2 Managing multicultural workforces
3 Developing managers in a global business environment.

Three critical external challenges were noted as:

1 Human resources issues in international alliances
2 The impact of the social dimension of the new Europe
3 The future role of Japan in Asia and the world.

From an Australian perspective we might add to this list the recent signing of the Asia Pacific Economic Co-operation Agreement on free trade within the region, and the continued rapid pace of growth in the Asia Pacific. As an illustration of this, Department of Foreign Affairs and Trade statistics on trade volumes between Australia and the APEC countries indicate that exports have jumped from $13.8 billion in 1990/91 to $52.4 billion in 1994/95. In the same period, imports have increased from $33 billion to $50.7 billion.

The growth of international organisations

International business has been with us for a long time. Ancient civilisations such as the Egyptians and Greeks traded with other groups and learned to do business across cultures. Ever since then people who have engaged in commerce beyond their own boundaries have had to grapple with the complexities of international business and the complex people and related organisational issues that go along with it. According to Robinson (cited in Ronen 1986) the period from 1500 to 1970 had four main eras of international business, each characterised by different business motivation and each seeing a different relationship between business and government.

The first of these was the Commercial Era from 1500 to 1850. In the first part of this era, individual entrepreneurs sought to maximise their own fortunes through trade in exotic commodities such as spices, fabrics and precious metals from foreign lands. In the second part of this era, governments became involved in this trade and established organisations which became autonomous colonial monopolies with widespread political as well as commercial power. Examples of such organisations included the British India Company, the Dutch East India Company and the Hudson's Bay Company.

The second era was the Explorative Era which lasted from 1850 to 1914. This period was characterised by the construction of industrial empires in Europe which required cheap and reliable supplies of raw materials. Thus, the emphasis in this era shifted from trade in exotic goods to raw materials for industrial processing such as mineral ores and plantation crops. The crucial importance of these commodities saw European nations become colonial powers controlling large tracts of Asia, Africa and Latin America. Because of the nature of the enterprises during this era large numbers of expatriate technical staff were sent overseas for the first time, and third country nationals were used to supplement the local unskilled labour force where local labour was considered inadequate to be trained.

The third, or Concessionary Era, lasted from the beginning of the first to the end of the second world wars, and saw international companies assume paternalistic responsibilities as traditional indigenous leaderships in the colonies continued to decline in the face of political and cultural domination from colonial governments. This resulted in Western companies being granted very substantial concessions within which they became virtually all powerful and all providing local administrations as well as the major source of economic activity. Examples from this era would include the Lever Concession in the Congo, various oil concessions in the Arab Middle East and the United Fruit Company's agreement in Central America. Ironically, the different ideas and approaches associated with economic development and introduced by these organisations in their virtually autonomous areas, sewed the seeds for the later downfall of colonialism; the depression led many organisations to replace expensive expatriates with cheaper local managers who eventually became nationalists when they rejected their employers as they fell short of expectations in the provision of paternal care.

The fourth, Nationalist Era, was ushered in with the Second World War and saw the emergence of two factors which changed power relations between the colonial and host countries. These factors were the emergence of locally responsible political leaders and the growing availability of alternative sources of capital and technical skills. During this era many countries became independent from colonial rule and set out to compete, economically, with their former colonial masters. Nevertheless, this period was also one of growth for international organisations and was a formative era for many of today's multinational corporations. The years 1954–70 saw widespread global expansion of business activity as international companies started to develop new markets and seek out new productive inputs. The rapid improvement in worldwide communication and transportation infrastructure underpinned this internationalisation as previously isolated geographic entities became easily accessible.

A strategic and structural typology of multinational organisations

There are numerous factors which influence the structure of multinational organisations. Some of the major factors are the international business strategy of the firm, industry type, operational requirements, company culture/values and the time period during which the organisation became international, which gives the organisation a distinct 'administrative heritage' (Bartlett & Ghoshal 1989). The standard typology of multinational organisations identifies three major types: multidomestic, international and global.

A multidomestic organisation gains its main competitive advantage from sensitivity to local market needs and speed of response to changing circumstances. Each national branch of the company operates with a high degree of independence, which has often led to their being thought of as local companies. According to Bartlett & Ghoshal, the classic multidomestic organisation is typically European and is likely to have a history extending back to the Concessionary Era mentioned above. Examples of such organisations would be Phillips, Unilever and ITT (Bartlett & Ghoshal 1992, p. 14). As will be discussed later, the majority of Australian multinational firms are in this group.

The typical US company expanded into international operations in the period of US economic hegemony following the Second World War. According to Bartlett & Ghoshal the strategy of this group is based mainly on transferring and adapting parent country knowledge and expertise into overseas markets thereby following an international product lifecycle. These companies are categorised by Bartlett & Ghoshal as following an international strategy. Such companies typically exhibit much stronger central control than multidomestic organisations (they often started life as part of an international divisions of the parent company) but nonetheless often adapt products and ideas coming from the corporate centre. Examples of such companies would be General Electric and Proctor & Gamble.

The third type of organisation is the typical Japanese organisation which emerged onto the international stage in the 1960s following an export-oriented strategy based on strong central control, global product lines and classic economies of scale. Such organisations, which Bartlett & Ghoshal describe as global, were typified by very strong control from the centre with very little autonomy at local level. Examples of global organisations would be NEC, Matsushita and Kao.

In the past, each of these structures gave these organisations pronounced strategic advantages. The main strength of the multidomestic lay in sensitivity to local markets and the development of a strong local identity. International organisations exploited parent company knowledge and product innovation and were able to diffuse and adapt this worldwide. Global organisations enjoyed the cost advantages which stemmed from centralisation and classic economies of scale (Bartlett & Ghoshal 1992, p. 15).

Clearly, industry type is crucial to the structuring of an international organisation since patterns of international competition vary widely across industries. As Porter (1986; 1990) has pointed out, retailing and distribution are typical examples of industries where a multidomestic strategy traditionally applies whereas aircraft, photocopiers and semiconductors would be examples of global industries where competitive position in one market is influenced by its position in other markets. As Dowling et al. (1994, p. 15) have noted there are clear implications for HR in this. In a multidomestic industry the HR function will closely resemble a domestic HR function in the countries in which it operates, since there is a relatively low requirement for international co-ordination. In a global industry, on the other hand, the high need for international co-ordination will make the role of HR more complex and critical to organisational success. As Desatnick & Bennett (1978) have pointed out:

> The primary cause of failure in multinational ventures stems from a lack of understanding of the essential differences in managing human resources, at all levels, in foreign environments. Certain management philosophies and techniques have proved successful in the domestic environment: their application in a foreign environment too often leads to frustration, failure and underachievement. These 'human' considerations are as important as the financial and marketing criteria upon which so many decisions to undertake multinational ventures depend.

Notwithstanding the differences in industry type and 'administrative heritage' which have led to divergent structures and strategies in the past, each of these organisations is, according to Bartlett & Ghoshal (1992, p. 16), now facing a new set of intense competitive circumstance which render their previous structures problematic. They argue that the combined forces of global integration, local differentiation and worldwide innovation have become simultaneously compelling and can no longer be ignored. Whereas in the past the industry type and 'administrative heritage' of these different organisations gave them strategic advantage which could offset any disadvantages, by the late 1980s this no longer applied. Thus even in markets which were previously isolated from one another and suitable for a multidomestic strategy, the forces of globalisation; the increased speed of the diffusion of technology, the reduction of trade barriers and the convergence of consumer preferences has tended to make the industry more global in character.

As Bartlett & Ghoshal (1992) argue, there is emerging pressure for convergence with each type facing the challenge of developing multiple strategic competencies by being simultaneously locally responsive, administratively efficient and globally innovative. The solution to the problems facing these organisations is to develop what they refer to as 'transnational capability' which primarily concerns an alteration to the 'mentality' of the managers within an organisation. Put another way this is about developing a global mindset amongst managers. Commenting specifically on HRM, Laurent (1986) has argued that a fully international conception of HRM would require:

- A recognition by the parent company that its way of managing HR partly reflects the values and assumptions of its home country culture
- A recognition that its approach to managing people is neither universally better or worse but has strengths and weaknesses, particularly when applied in other countries
- A recognition by the parent company that its international branches may have ways of managing people which are different but possibly more effective locally
- A willingness from the parent company to acknowledge cultural difference and make it usable

- The building of a belief by all that more creative and effective ways of managing people could be developed by cross-cultural learning.

For Bartlett & Ghoshal developing 'transnational capability' requires changes in the 'anatomy' (structure); 'physiology' (information flows); and 'psychology' (culture) of the organisation. This requires a move away from formal and inhibiting structures in each of these areas and highlights the need for managers to operate flexibly but towards a common purpose. Bartlett & Ghoshal characterise this as the creation of a 'matrix in the mind of the managers'.

Yetton & Craig (1995) in their research on the international growth of Australian firms have concluded that they mainly follow the multidomestic pattern with a few global exporters recently emerging onto the scene. The majority of Australia's large and successful manufacturers have established relatively independent operations in overseas locations and a small number of, mainly high technology, companies export their product direct from Australia. On the basis of this finding Yetton & Craig (1995, p. 1357) argue that the prescriptions of the IHRM literature, which are based mainly on research done in US, European or Japanese need to be treated with some caution. For example, the focus on developing international cadre of managers who can operate in a global or transnational organisation is somewhat redundant in view of the predominantly multidomestic pattern in evidence in Australian organisations. This view is supported by Stace (1996b) in his case study of Telstra.

Notwithstanding the predominantly multidomestic character of Australian overseas producers, the co-ordinating role of the HR function is vital and growing in importance as the forces of convergence described by Bartlett & Ghoshal force organisations to look for global synergy, avoid duplication and build core values in all areas of operation. The HR role in Burns Philp which is outlined in the 'HRM in the news' article is a good example of this. Similarly, in BHP Steel, which is broadly following a multi-domestic strategy, Corporate Human Resources plays an important role in providing strategic integration,

> ... and ensuring uniformity across several key areas of company focus—the global leadership program; executive compensation; expatriate policy; the employee share scheme; safety; management succession and business ethics. These are referred to as the BHP 'HR tights'—areas where BHP worldwide operates cohesively and with leadership. Other corporate requirements are that all capital projects must be accompanied by a HR implications analysis, and that a HR facilitator/manager should be appointed at the same time as the project or general manager of a new project. Beyond this, there is not significant intervention by corporate HR. Within the region/local operation it is expected that HR practitioners will recruit, remunerate and develop local and regionally sourced staff, with the aim of nationalising staff positions as soon as possible (Stace 1996a, p. 21).

Thus developing international capability, even following a multidomestic strategy, throws the HR function into centre stage, since developing the required flexibility and informality in key areas requires choosing the right managers, training and developing them appropriately, putting them in the right place at the right time and maintaining their motivation. The balance of this chapter develops these key HR areas in depth.

International recruitment and selection

The effective use of human resources is, of course, one goal of most organisations, domestic or international. However, there are a number of international staffing issues such as executive nationality policies, expatriate failure and predictors of expatriate success that are not present in a domestic environment. We shall discuss these issues in some detail.

Executive nationality policies

With regard to executive nationality policies, a multinational company can choose from five options: (1) ethnocentric (2) polycentric (3) geocentric (4) mixed, and (5) ad hoc/patchwork. It is important to consider these policies in some detail because each option has important implications for a multinational organisation's recruitment and selection practices.

The ethnocentric approach

An ethnocentric approach to staffing results in all key positions in a multinational company being filled by parent country nationals (PCNs). This practice is common in the early stage of internationalisation where a company is setting up a new business, process or product in another country and prior experience is essential. Other reasons for pursuing an ethnocentric staffing policy are a perceived lack of qualified host country nationals (HCNs) and the need to maintain good communication links with corporate headquarters.

An ethnocentric policy also, however, has a number of disadvantages. Zeira (1976) has identified a number of major problems. First, an ethnocentric staffing policy limits the promotion opportunities of HCNs. This may lead to reduced productivity and increased turnover among HCNs. Second, the adaptation of expatriate managers to a host country can be a long process. During this time, PCNs often make mistakes and poor decisions. Third, serious remuneration equity issues often arise when PCN and HCN remuneration packages are compared. The often considerable income gap in favour of PCNs is viewed by HCNs as unjustified. Finally, for many expatriates, a key overseas position means new status, authority and an increase in standards of living. Zeira (1976, p. 36) states that these changes 'tend to dull expatriates' sensitivity to the needs and expectations of their host country subordinates—and is not conducive to objective self-evaluation'. In addition, expatriates are very expensive with a common estimate being that the real costs of employing an expatriate are approximately three times the salary cost.

Polycentric staffing policy

A polycentric staffing policy is one where HCNs are recruited to manage subsidiaries in their own country, and PCNs occupy positions in corporate headquarters. There are four main advantages of a polycentric policy. First, employing HCNs eliminates language barriers, the adjustment problems of expatriate managers and their families, and removes the need for expensive training programs. Second, employment of local nationals allows a multinational company to take a lower profile in sensitive political situations. Third, the employment of local nationals is less expensive, even if a premium is paid to attract high-quality applicants. Fourth, a polycentric policy gives continuity to the management of foreign subsidiaries. Fifth, having an 'insider' run the business can confer real business advantages particularly in countries in Asia where relationships are so important for business success.

While a number of these advantages address some of the shortcomings of an ethnocentric policy, there are also a number of disadvantages which may develop from a polycentric approach. Perhaps the major difficulty is that of bridging the gap between the local national subsidiary and the parent country managers at corporate headquarters. Language barriers, conflicting national loyalties and a range of cultural differences (e.g. personal value differences and differences in attitudes to business) may leave the corporate headquarters staff relatively isolated from the various foreign subsidiaries. The end result may be that a multinational firm could become a 'federation' of independent national units with nominal links to corporate headquarters. Such a situation would make strategic shifts such as a move to production sharing very difficult to achieve.

A second major problem associated with a polycentric staffing policy concerns the career path of HCN and PCN managers. HCN managers have limited opportunities to gain experience outside their own country and cannot progress beyond the senior positions in their own subsidiary. PCN managers also have limited opportunities to gain overseas experience. Since headquarters positions are only held by PCNs, this means that the senior corporate management group responsible for resource allocation decisions between subsidiaries and overall strategic planning will have little overseas work experience on which to draw. In an increasingly competitive international environment this lack of expertise is a liability.

Geocentric staffing

A third approach to international staffing is the **geocentric** approach, where the best people are sought for key jobs throughout the organisation, regardless of nationality. There are two main advantages of a geocentric staffing policy. First, it enables a multinational firm to develop an international executive cadre. Second, this policy reduces the tendency of national identification of managers with units of the organisation. However, as Phatak has noted the success of a geocentric approach is based on five assumptions:

> (a) highly competent employees are available not only at headquarters, but also in the subsidiaries; (b) international experience is a condition for success in top positions; (c) managers with high potential and ambition for promotion are constantly ready to be transferred from one country to another; (d) competent and mobile managers have an open disposition and high adaptability to different conditions in their various assignments; (e) those not blessed initially with an open disposition and high adaptability can acquire these qualities as their experience abroad accumulates (Phatak 1989).

There are a number of difficulties in implementing a geocentric policy. The first is that most host countries want foreign subsidiaries to employ their citizens, and utilise their immigration laws to achieve this goal by requiring the employment of local nationals if adequate numbers and skills are available. Most Western countries (including Australia and the US) require companies to provide extensive documentation if they wish to hire a foreign national instead of a local national. This can be a time-consuming, expensive and, at times, futile process, particularly if a work permit is also required for an accompanying spouse. Second, a geocentric policy can be expensive to implement because of increased training and relocation costs and the need to have a remuneration structure with standardised international base pay which may be higher than national levels in many countries. Finally, to successfully implement a geocentric staffing policy, longer lead times and more centralised control of the staffing process are required. This necessarily reduces the independence of subsidiary management in these issues and this loss of autonomy may be resisted.

Regiocentric staffing

A fourth approach to international staffing is to adopt a mixed policy with regard to executive nationality. The best example of this approach is a regiocentric policy, which Heenan & Perlmutter (1979) define as functional rationalisation on a more-than-one-country basis. The specific mix will vary with the nature of a firm's business and product strategy. Robock & Simmonds (1983) give three examples of how the nature of a business or product strategy influences staffing policies. First, if regional or area expertise is important (e.g. consumer goods and/or limited product lines), then the need for PCNs will be low relative to the need for experienced HCNs and TCNs (third country nationals). A second example would be where product expertise is important and/or industrial markets are being served. In such a situation, PCNs would be used more frequently because of the need for quick access to parent country sources of supply and technical information. A third example is that of service industries such as banking which tend to use relatively large numbers of PCNs—particularly where a firm is serving parent country multinationals in foreign locations.

The final staffing option has been described as ad hoc or patchwork. In a sense it is a misnomer to label this staffing option as a policy because in fact it is policy by default. A better description may be corporate inertia. Robinson has succinctly summarised how an ad hoc approach often develops:

> The danger is that the firm will opt for a policy of using parent country nationals in foreign management positions by default, that is, simply as an automatic extension of domestic policy, rather than deliberately seeking optimum utilisation of management skills (Robinson 1978, p. 297).

A multinational firm that would be described as following an ad hoc staffing approach will clearly have difficulty developing a consistent organisational human resources strategy which fits with the overall business strategy of the enterprise. Consequently it will often be poorly placed to either anticipate threats or profit from opportunities.

Issues related to policy choice

The choice of policy in international staffing can clearly be related to company strategy and structure as discussed earlier. A company following a multidomestic strategy would clearly be most likely to follow a polycentric staffing policy with many HCN managers and some senior PCNs. A company that is concerned with control and central co-ordination, the approach typically taken by many Japanese multinationals in the past, is more likely to follow an ethnocentric approach to staffing. If Bartlett & Ghoshal are correct, however, and more companies move towards a transnational approach then we can expect to see more geocentric, or at least regiocentric approaches emerging. A key element in a move towards a geocentric approach is to overcome previous historical balances in an organisation's recruitment practices. Usually these are manifest in bias towards a PCN or ethnocentric selection practices which have automatically limited the pool of available talent. As an example of this short sightedness Bartlett & Ghoshal (1990, p. 142) cite Proctor & Gamble's practice of promoting managers from its domestic operations into key positions in overseas subsidiaries, a practice which culminated in several notable marketing failures in Japan. The implication of this is that past success must not be the only criteria for selection and promotion and that, because of the subtlety and sensitivity usually required for senior overseas posts, there is a role for very senior management to be involved in the selection process. In very large organisations this process is often linked to career management with potential senior managers being streamed into special 'fast track' development lists which are often overseen by the most senior managers in the organisation.

In practice, the choice of a policy on executive nationality will tend to reflect organisational need which may vary in different operational areas. Many companies do not operate with a uniform approach but may employ different approaches in different areas of the globe with typically a geocentric or polycentric approach in the first world but a more ethnocentric approach in developing countries.

In discussing BHP Steel's international staffing strategy (see end-of-chapter cases) which is probably best described as multidomestic, Stace (1996a) notes that there are two approaches dependent on geography. In the US, BHP appoints a minimal number of expatriates, preferring instead to recruit from the surplus of steel skills in the US, or use staff from their joint venture partner. However, in Asia, which is the major area of international growth, BHP plants are, initially, heavily staffed by expatriate Australians. This is particularly true in 'core' areas of the business such as operations management, finance and marketing. BHPs strategy though is to replace expatriates with employees of national extraction as soon as possible (Stace 1996a, p. 17).

Similarly, Telstra in its international businesses has, up until now been primarily ethnocentric. Like BHP Steel, however, Telstra is in the long term, planning to move to a polycentric model where local staff run the business (Stace 1996b, p. 19).

Expatriate failure rates

A prominent issue in the international recruitment and selection literature is that of expatriate failure, which may be defined as the premature return of an expatriate manager or technical expert. Expatriate failure represents a false positive selection error (see Chapter 8). The costs of such an error are both direct and indirect. In the case of expatriate recalls, the direct costs include salary, training costs and travel and relocation expenses. The importance of indirect or 'invisible' costs rises with the level of position being considered. For many expatriate positions, these indirect costs may be considerable. For example, an expatriate head of a foreign subsidiary who subsequently proves to be unsuitable for this job may damage relations with the host country government and other local organisations and customers. This may result in various outcomes such as loss of market share, difficulties with host government officials, and demands that PCNs be replaced with HCNs. Zeira & Banai (1984) argue that multinational corporations should consider these factors as the real cost of failure of international executives rather than direct expenses such as salary and repatriation costs. The likely deleterious effects on the expatriate and the family of the expatriate also need to be considered in assessing the costs of failure.

The international literature has traditionally indicated that expatriate failure is a persistent and recurring problem. Mendenhall & Oddou (1985) reported that the estimated expatriate failure rate for the previous twenty years had fluctuated between 25 and 40 per cent. Desatnick & Bennett (1978) stated that this figure rose to 70 per cent in developing countries. However, recent work by Brewster (1991) and Harzing (1995) has cast doubt on the research base supporting these figures and suggested that US expatriate failure rates may have been over-estimated in the literature and that European rates are lower. Recent work in Britain has suggested that expatriate failure rates there average around 5 per cent (Brewster 1991; Hamill 1989; Scullion 1991). This is not to suggest though that expatriate failure is not a problem. Even if the low failure rates noted in the British studies are proved generally correct, it must be remembered that the measure of premature return from assignment, which these studies are reporting, is a poor measure of expatriate failure. A better measure of failure should also include measures of expatriate underperformance and possible repatriate failure.

One of the few empirical studies on expatriate failure rates is reported by Tung (1982) who surveyed a number of US, European and Japanese multinationals. Her results are summarised in Table 13.1

Table 13.1 Expatriate failure rates

RECALL RATE %	% OF COMPANIES
US multinationals	
20–40	7
10–20	69
<10	24
European multinationals	
11–15	3
6–10	38
<5	59
Japanese multinationals	
11–19	14
6–10	10
<5	76

Source: Tung 1982, pp. 57–71

As Table 13.1 shows, US companies have both higher expatriate failure rates and a higher percentage of companies reporting recall rates of 10 per cent or more, than European or Japanese multinationals. However, these national differences should not obscure the fact that all multinationals in this sample have a significant expatriate failure problem. Recent studies reported in Dowling et al. (1994, p. 60) confirm the European expatriate failure rates reported in Tung and note very low rates of expatriate failure in more recent studies of British, Scandinavian and Australian organisations. However, caution needs to be exercised in concluding that US organisations are more prone to expatriate failure, since the more recent studies were conducted several years after Tung's study and her results may reflect an earlier era when awareness of the problem of expatriate failure was lower and preventative measures had not been put in place. While there are no data available which compare international and domestic false positive selection error rates, it would seem reasonable to assume that few companies would report domestic error rates of the relative magnitude shown in Table 13.1.

An indication of some of the differences between domestic and international selection is apparent when reasons for expatriate failure are examined. Tung asked her sample of multinational managers to indicate reasons for expatriate failure in their companies. For US multinationals, the reasons given, in descending order of importance were:

1. Inability of spouse to adjust
2. Manager's inability to adjust
3. Other family problems

4 Manager's personal or emotional maturity
5 Inability to cope with larger overseas responsibility.

For European companies, only one reason was consistently given by respondents as being important for explaining expatriate failure: the inability of the manager's spouse to adjust to a new environment. For the Japanese sample the reasons for expatriate failure in descending order of importance were:

1 Inability to cope with larger overseas responsibility
2 Difficulties with new environment
3 Personal or emotional problems
4 Lack of technical competence
5 Inability of spouse to adjust.

Tung notes that the finding that inability of spouse to adjust was a major reason for failure for US and European companies but not for Japanese ones: unsurprising, given the status to which Japanese society relegates the spouse. However, we should also note here that a number of other factors may contribute to the Japanese finding the inability of spouse to adjust; the fact that Japanese wives will often remain in Japan to supervise the children's education; the fact that the average Japanese assignment is four years, not two as in many US firms; and the fact that Japanese are often not expected to perform to their full potential until the third year of posting.

As with false positive selection error rates, there is no data available which compares reasons for international and domestic false positive selection errors. But it is a plausible hypothesis that relational and environmental adjustment difficulties would not be the major reasons for explaining failure of domestic managers as they are for international managers.

As noted above, expatriate failure is a prominent issue in the international recruitment and selection literature, but there are few empirical studies on expatriate failure. A study by Dowling & Welch (1988) examining the international HRM policies of four MNCs operating internationally from Australia (two were Australian, one was European, and one was American), found that expatriate failure was not a major concern. All companies in this study reported a small proportion of early recalls, which were attributed as much to lack of technical skills as to the failure of the spouse to adjust. One US personnel director who was interviewed for the study pointed out that attributing expatriate recall to 'failure of spouse to adjust' was at times a simplistic explanation. He postulated that, apart from the probability of the expatriate blaming his wife (all the expatriates in the study were male) for his own failure to adjust, some astute spouses might see the expatriate's poor performance and trigger the early recall to limit damage to the expatriate's career.

In an updated review of the common denominators of successful performance of European and Japanese multinationals in relation to expatriate failure Tung (1987) identified:

- a long-term orientation in relation to planning and performance assessment
- more extensive use of training programs for overseas assignments
- provision of extensive expatriate support systems
- the choice of well-qualified candidates for overseas appointments
- restricted job mobility, which was mainly as a result of company loyalty
- international orientation
- long history of international operations
- language capability.

Predictors of expatriate success

Ideally, it seems he should have the stamina of an Olympic swimmer, the mental agility of an Einstein, the conversational skills of a professor of languages, the detachment of a judge, the tact of a diplomat, and the perseverance of an Egyptian pyramid builder ... And if he is going to measure up to the demands of living and working in a foreign country, he should also have a feeling of culture; his oral judgements should not be too rigid; he should be able to merge with the local environment with chameleon-like ease; and he should show no signs of prejudice (Heller 1980).

In view of the high costs of expatriate failure, selecting the right managers for overseas postings is critical. Certain characteristics or traits have been identified in the research literature as predictors of expatriate success: technical ability, managerial skills, cultural empathy, adaptability, diplomacy, language ability, positive attitude, emotional stability and maturity, and adaptability of the family. Murray & Murray (1986) have noted that while managerial or technical competence is the baseline for expatriate success, the expatriate manager must be able to translate those skills into a foreign environment and also cope with the rigours of life overseas. Whether or not these characteristics or traits can be accurately measured by psychological tests is an issue of some controversy. The perennial questions of reliability and validity are raised in regard to such tests and questions are also directed at whether or not the tests are 'culture bound', given that most of them have been developed in the US or other Western countries. Also, there is the issue of the extent to which attitudes influence manifest behaviour. People may believe themselves to be tolerant and evaluate themselves accordingly on a psychological test but this might not be reflected in actual judgements of their behaviour made by others. Nonetheless, the development of models stemming from this approach have some utility in setting guidelines and criteria for the selection process even if too much reliance cannot be placed on the results of the actual tests. As the end-of-chapter case, 'Lend Lease's Approach to Staffing' indicates, Lend Lease is a user of specialist consultants in the expatriation area and has a pro-active and systematic approach to expatriate selection.

One of the empirical studies looking at expatriate selection is that conducted by Tung (1987) which looked at selection practices in 80 US multinationals. Based on a review of the literature on expatriate success, Tung grouped the variables that contribute to expatriate success into four general areas: (1) technical competence on the job, (2) personality traits or relational abilities, (3) environmental variables, and (4) family situation.

In all, Tung identified eighteen variables, or criteria for selection. The respondents (vice-presidents of foreign operations) were asked to indicate whether these criteria were 'used and very important', 'used but not important', or 'not used' in their organisations. Using categories reported by Hays (1974) Tung classified overseas job assignments as: (1) chief executive officer (CEO), (2) functional head, (3) troubleshooter, and (4) operative.

Some criteria such as 'maturity and emotional stability' and 'technical knowledge of the business' were commonly used, and were seen as very important for all four job categories. It is clear from the results, however, that for each category, some criteria were judged to be more important than others. For example, 'communicative ability' was less important for technical jobs (troubleshooter) than for a CEO, although 'knowledge of host country language' was not as important for either of these job categories as for functional head and operative. Presumably, individuals in these latter job categories have limited access to translators or are more likely to work with HCNs who do not speak English. Despite the obvious differences in demand between domestic and international operations, a notable proportion of respondents used 'the same criteria as other comparable jobs at home' for CEOs, functional heads and operatives. The evolution of Telstra's approach to international staffing (see end-of-chapter case) is an interesting example of an organisation, and the HR department specifically, coming to grips with these issues.

Tung also asked respondents to indicate the procedures used by each firm to assess the eighteen selection criteria considered in the study. Few companies formally assessed technical competence—a predictable result, as most expatriates are internal recruits, and ample documentation of technical competence is available from performance appraisal data and personnel records. With regard to assessing family situation, 52 per cent of companies interviewed both candidate and spouse for management positions, and 40 per cent of companies interviewed both candidate and spouse for technical positions. Only 1 per cent of firms conducted no interviews with either candidate or spouse. These figures for interviews with both candidate and spouse may seem high, but are less impressive when one considers the fact that inability of the spouse to adjust is the most frequently cited reason for expatriate failure.

The most surprising finding was for assessment of relational ability. Although most companies indicated that relational abilities were important, only 5 per cent of firms assessed a candidate's relational ability through a formal procedure (e.g. judgement by seniors or psychological appraisal). The research literature shows that relational abilities are positively related to expatriate success, so this failure to assess candidates' relational abilities is an obvious deficiency in the expatriate selection procedures of most of the companies in this study. This deficiency probably reflects top management's judgement either that relational abilities are not important or that technical abilities are more so.

A final aspect of Tung's paper that warrants discussion is her selection and training model, shown in Figure 13.3. There are a number of notable features to her model. First, it raises the issue of executive nationality by first requiring information about whether the position could be filled by a HCN. Second, the model follows a non-compensatory selection strategy that Newman, Bhatt & Gutteridge (1978) note is a lower-risk strategy with regard to selecting expatriates. Third, the model takes a contingency approach to selection and training by recognising that different expatriate jobs involve varying degrees of interaction with HCNs and durations of stay, and that foreign assignment locations vary widely in terms of similarity with the expatriate's own culture. Using this model, Tung analysed the relationship between type of selection and training procedure used and expatriate failure rate for the companies in her sample. She reports a correlation of –0.63, indicating that the more rigorous the selection and training procedures used, the lower the failure rate.

A second important paper is a review of the expatriate acculturation literature by Mendenhall & Oddou (1985). In reviewing problems in expatriate selection, they state that a major problem area is the ingrained practice of personnel directors, when selecting potential expatriates, to use the 'domestic equals overseas performance equation'. The effect of this practice is that little else is of importance in the selection process other than technical expertise and a successful domestic track record. They conclude that the field of expatriate selection and training suffers from two interdependent problems. First, there is an inadequate understanding of the relevant variables of expatriate acculturation, which leads to a second problem: the use of inappropriate selection and training methods. The purpose of their paper was to review the literature to determine the key dimensions involved in the expatriate adjustment process and to examine the implications of these for the selection and training of expatriates. From their review of the literature, Mendenhall & Oddou conclude that there are four key dimensions in the expatriate adjustment process: (1) self oriented, (2) others oriented, (3) perceptual, and (4) cultural toughness.

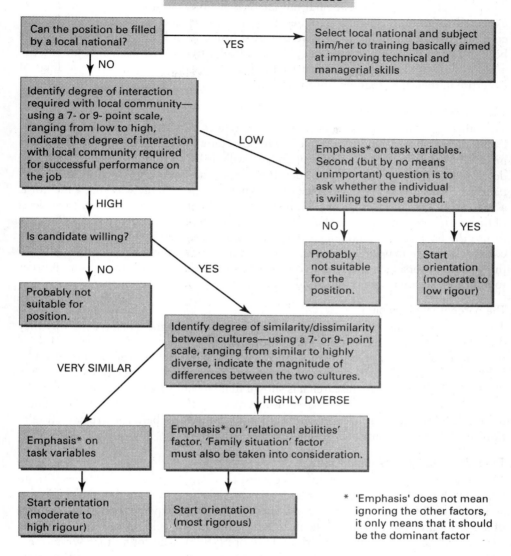

Figure 13.3 Flow chart of the selection process
Source: Based on Tung 1981, pp. 68–78

The self-oriented dimension

This dimension is concerned with activities and attributes that serve to strengthen the expatriates' self-esteem, self-confidence, and mental hygiene. It is composed of three sub-factors: (1) reinforcement substitution, (2) stress reduction, and (3) technical competence. Reinforcement substitution involves replacing pleasurable home culture activities and interests with parallel substitutes in the host culture. Thus, an expatriate who is able to adapt his or her interests in food, sports and music is more likely to be successful in adjusting to the new culture. Stress reduction refers to the need to engage in temporary withdrawal activities (e.g. keeping a diary or engaging in favourite activities or hobbies) that allow the expatriate to gradually adjust to the demands of a new cultural and physical environment. The final sub-factor is technical competence. Expatriates are expected to accomplish their assigned task. Possessing the necessary expertise and confidence in one's ability to achieve this goal (often with little or no assistance) has been shown to be an important part of expatriate adjustment. Mendenhall & Oddou cite a number of studies that found that well adjusted expatriates report more feelings of expertise in their jobs than do poorly adjusted ones.

The others-oriented dimension

The others-oriented dimension encompasses activities and attributes that enhance the expatriate's ability to interact effectively with host country nationals. Two sub-factors are involved: (1) relationship development and, (2) willingness to communicate. Relationship development refers to the ability to develop long-lasting friendships with host country nationals. This ability is of assistance to an expatriate in the same way that a mentor is able to assist a neophyte employee. Willingness to communicate does not refer to the level of fluency in a foreign language but rather to the expatriate's confidence and willingness to use the host culture's language. Thus, an expatriate who is not fluent in the host country language may collect 'conversational currency' (local phrases, comments about the weather, sporting terms, and so on) that he or she can use in conversation in order to indicate a desire to understand and relate with host country nationals.

The perceptual dimension

This dimension refers to the ability to understand why foreigners behave the way they do. The ability to make correct attributions about the reasons or causes of HCNs behaviour is important because it allows the expatriate to predict future HCN behaviour—and reduces the stress of uncertainty in interpersonal relations. According to Mendenhall & Oddou, research has shown that well adjusted expatriates tend to be non-judgemental and non-evaluative in interpreting the behaviour of host country nationals, which leads to clearer information exchange and better interpersonal relationships between expatriates and nationals.

The cultural toughness dimension

The dimension of cultural toughness recognises the fact that how well the expatriate adjusts to his or her overseas experience appears to be in part related to the country of assignment. The research literature indicates that Western expatriates find the cultures of some countries to be more difficult to adapt to than the cultures of other countries. Mendenhall & Oddou cite the work of Torbiorn (1982), who found that Western expatriates expressed high levels of dissatisfaction with their overseas assignments in India and Pakistan, South-East Asia, the Middle East, North Africa, East Africa, and Liberia in the areas of job satisfaction, levels of stress and pressure, health care, housing standards, entertainment, food, and skill of co-workers. It is also important to note that some cultures that emphasise a male-dominated value system may be 'extra culturally tough' for Western expatriate women, although Adler's research (1987) tends to refute this.

Mendenhall & Oddou derive two major propositions from their study. First, expatriate acculturation is a multidimensional process rather than a unidimensional phenomenon. Thus, selection procedures of multinational firms should be changed from their present one-dimensional focus on technical competence as the primary criterion to a multidimensional focus based on criteria relating to dimensions identified in their review. Second, comprehensive acculturation training programs incorporating each of the four dimensions outlined above should be designed for expatriates. To carry out these propositions, Mendenhall & Oddou suggest a number of proposals for enhancing the expatriate selection process. Specifically, they recommend that the expatriate selection process should focus on evaluating the applicant's strengths and weaknesses in the dimensions of expatriate acculturation identified in their review:

1. For the self oriented dimension, a number of psychological tests are available to measure stress levels and Type A behaviour patterns (Price 1982). Technical expertise is already assessed in most organisations.
2. For the perceptual dimension, psychological tests with established validity could assess the flexibility of an individual's perceptual and evaluative tendencies. They could be used in conjunction with in-depth evaluations from other sources, such as a consultant psychologist, and the applicant's superiors. Use of testing may also encourage self-reflection regarding motivation for the assignment.
3. The above approach could also be used to gauge degree of others-orientation.
4. The toughness of the culture of the country to which a future expatriate will be assigned can be assessed by comparing the host country's political, legal, socio-economic and business systems to those in the parent country. If there is considerable disparity (that is, if the host country is 'culturally tough'), only applicants with high scores on the battery of evaluation devices should be considered for the assignment. For assignment to countries similar to the parent country (for example, an assignment to Australia from the United States), applicants with more marginal evaluation scores may be considered. This point is very similar to the notion of similarity/dissimilarity between cultures as a selection factor in Tung's model (see Figure 13.2).

Managing diversity

A factor worthy of note in relation to expatriate success, and one which relates directly to the issue of managing diverse workforces, is the contribution of the family, particularly the spouse. Black & Stephens in their study of 220 US expatriates found that a positive opinion about the assignment by the spouse was positively related to the spouse's adjustment 'and that the adjustment of the spouse is highly correlated to the adjustment of the expatriate manager'. (Black & Stephens 1989). Notwithstanding this, the same study reported that only 30 per cent of the firms sought the spouse's opinion in relation to the international assignment. Australian research into this topic has found that the degree of control felt by the partner of the expatriate in the decision to relocate was correlated significantly with expressed satisfaction early in the assignment (De Cieri, Dowling & Taylor 1991). These studies, and others, clearly indicate that the involvement of the spouse and family in the selection process will reduce the risk of expatriate failure. An emerging issue in this regard is the rise of dual career families where the relocation of one partner disrupts the career of the other. It would seem reasonable to assume that the rise of dual career families will significantly reduce the number of people willing to undertake expatriate assignments. Evidence to support this is now emerging with a recent study by Coyle (1995) of Australian companies indicating that 59 per cent of companies surveyed had experienced difficulty in relocating dual career couples. Moreover, in a large proportion of these the transferee refused, or almost refused, to relocate. The issue of company assistance to the spouse of transferee is now a major concern with companies offering incentives such as counselling, internal job offers, external job search assistance, CV preparation, and financial compensation (Coyle 1995).

Repatriation

Another issue that is frequently not sufficiently addressed in the international recruitment and selection literature is that of repatriation of expatriates to their home locations at the conclusion of the international assignment. The repatriated employee, and indeed the entire family, may experience 'reverse culture shock' upon return to the home country, as the environment is no longer familiar to them and they may feel somewhat alienated from their surroundings (Harvey 1982). The repatriated employee may experience professional as well as personal re-entry difficulties. Research (Adler 1991) has indicated several factors that may cause difficulties for such people:

1. The experience of being 'out of sight, out of mind' of the parent company may limit chances for promotion upon re-entry. Often the company has done little or no planning for the manager's repatriation and career progression.
2. Managers may experience negative career progression upon re-entry if they return to a less challenging job with less responsibility and status than their previous international assignment entailed. Research by Tung (1988) has indicated that negative career moves after international experience are evident in many US multinationals. This phenomenon is in contrast to the majority of European, Japanese and Australian companies, which place more importance on international experience. (The US companies tend to focus more readily on the domestic market, while the companies operating from countries with smaller domestic markets must rely more heavily on international markets for revenue.)
3. Technological advances in the company may render the repatriate's functional skills and knowledge obsolete.
4. Changes in the formal and informal operations and information channels in the organisation may cause adjustment difficulties, particularly if there was insufficient contact with the expatriate during the overseas assignment. Lack of contact creates a sense of isolation and 'exile' for the expatriate.

Adler (1991) has reported that 20 per cent of employees who complete overseas assignments want to leave their company on their return. Black & Gregersen (1991) have suggested that the turnover rate among repatriates is as high as 25 per cent. Failure to address repatriation problems may lead to disillusionment and turnover, particularly when many other companies are willing to pay a premium for an expatriate's experience and expertise (Kendall 1981). The costs to MNCs of expatriate turnover are considerable, in terms of both the loss of valuable employees with international experience to competitors and the investment required to recruit suitable replacements. An additional problem is that fellow employees who witness the difficulties that many repatriates face may become more reluctant to accept international assignments. BHPs policy on repatriation is noted in the following article

HRM IN THE NEWS

This article is used by permission from D A Stace – *Reaching out from Down Under: building competence for global markets*, McGraw Hill, Sydney.

BHPs experience with repatriation

An emerging, but not yet critical issue is that of expatriate repatriation. As in other companies, the level of challenge in offshore assignments is typically above that

> available in the home corporation. Offshore interviewees frequently remarked on the excitement of working in expanding markets, while exercising significant levels of authority. Several also remarked that 'the thought of going back (to Australia) to less responsibility and challenge does not excite me'. BHP has a policy that expatriate staff should preferably not stay in one location longer than five years. This raises significant issues for the company if it is not to lose staff who have been key to its international growth. There are three options:
>
> - staff returning to Australia, preferably to equal or greater levels of skill and authority so that offshore work is seen as part of the career stream in an international company
> - staff being posted to other regional offshore operations
> - staff leave the company, either in the offshore location, or on returning to Australia.
>
> In BHPs case, the intention is to maximise the first two of these options, while minimising the third.

For the expatriate spouse and family, re-entry may involve difficulties and disillusionment. People may feel alienated in their own country, particularly if they have been out of contact with family, friends and local events. Their international experience may have distanced them socially and psychologically from their home environment. Expatriates and their families may have enjoyed participation in a social and economic elite during their international assignment, and the return home may bring with it some measure of social disappointment—as well as a compensation package that does not include expatriate premiums. In addition, repatriates may have developed a broader cultural perspective, as they can compare home country conditions with other ways of life and environments. Many repatriates report that people show little interest in hearing about their expatriate experiences, which can make conversation uncomfortable.

Feldman & Thomas (1992) suggest that there are seven strategies that organisations can pursue through through career development programs that may increase expatriate adjustment to international assignments and may impact upon retention rates:

- giving employees a chance to accept or reject an expatriate assignment
- having a mentor program
- ensuring that the assignment does not inhibit the employee's career
- ensuring that there is a job for the employee upon return
- using the expatriate's newly developed skills upon return
- providing realistic job previews
- ensuring that the assignment is part of a total career plan.

Findings from research by Stroh (1995) also support the view that organisations should plan for repatriation well before employees arrive back from their overseas assignment. (Harvey 1983) proposes repatriation programs to assist in the development of organisational policy and job definition for repatriates and to provide financial and career counselling and family orientation. Such solutions have relatively low costs (particularly when compared to the costs of losing the employee) and are essentially based on improved planning and communication. Until such programs are offered, MNCs lose the knowledge and experience that repatriates can impart to the organisation.

International training and development

Traditionally, the main focus of attention for training in international organisations has focused around the training needs of expatriate managers going out from headquarters into overseas subsidiaries. This is still an important area. However, reflecting the discussion on the evolution of strategy and structure earlier in this chapter the training area is now undergoing considerable evolution. In recent times the training and development agenda in international organisations has started to reflect the shifts to a global marketplace and more attention is now being paid to HCN and TCN training and development as well as confronting issues such as the development of international teams and the 'acculturation' role of training in an organisation that aspires to a transnational form and which is looking to create the 'matrix in the mind of the managers' which was discussed earlier. Table 13.2 neatly summarises the difference between the competencies required by the traditional international manager and the manager operating in a global environment.

Table 13.2 Globally competent managers

TRANSNATIONAL SKILLS	GLOBALLY COMPETENT MANAGERS	TRADITIONAL INTERNATIONAL MANAGERS
Global perspectives	Understand worldwide business environment from a global perspective	Focus on a single foreign country and on managing relationships between headquarters and that country
Local responsiveness	Learn about many cultures	Become an expert on one culture
Synergistic learning	Work with and learn form people from many cultures simultaneously	Work with and coach people in each foreign culture separately and/or sequentially
Transition and adaption	Adapt to living in foreign cultures	Integrate foreigners into the headquarters' national organisation structure
Cross-cultural interaction	Use cross-cultural skills on a daily basis throughout one's career	Use cross-cultural interaction skills primarily on foreign assignments
Collaboration	Interact with foreign colleagues as equals	Interact within clearly defined hierarchies of structural and cultural dominance
Foreign experience	Transpatriation for career and organisation development	Expatriation or inpatriation primarily to get the job done

Source: Adler 1995, p. 11

Training to avoid expatriate failure

As with recruitment and selection, the traditional rationale for international companies investing resources in training and development programs rests primarily on the cost of expatriate failure. As Robock & Simmonds (1983) have noted, 'However imperfect training may be as a substitute for actual foreign living experience, it is valuable if it can reduce the often painful and agonising experience of transferring into another culture and avoid the great damage that culture shock and cultural misunderstanding can do to a firm's operating relationships' (Robock & Simmonds 1983, p. 562). The overall training needs of expatriate managers and their families is summarised in Table 13.3.

Table 13.3 Training options for expatriate managers

TYPE OF TRAINING	EXAMPLES
Technical training	Technology level, opportunities for technology transfer, cultural and attitudinal constraints on technology transfer?
Management training	Organisational structure, spans of control, reporting relationships, communication structures, administrative procedures, government–business relationships, business environment, marketing issues, HRM issues, investment issues, ethical considerations?
Domestic information	Accommodation, schools, hospitals, medical and social services, shopping facilities and domestic services, issues related to vehicles, customs regulations and procedures, insurance?
Cross cultural training How to adjust to the other culture. Issues related to job performance in the other culture (Black & Mendenhall, 1990) Who gets cross cultural training? Employee, spouse, family?	Information about the other culture.
Language training Basic competence? Proficiency? Use of interpreters?	Few words and phrases?

The need for international training and development becomes more apparent if we examine the complexity of the role of the PCN manager as is shown in Table 13.4. Torbiorn has described the task of the PCN manager as one of 'realising the expectations of a psychologically close, but physically distant, stakeholder in an environment containing other role senders who are psychologically distant, but physically close' (Torbiorn 1985, p. 59).

Table 13.4 Role of PCN manager

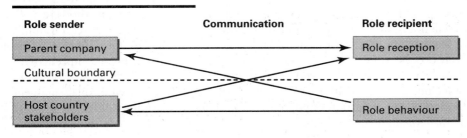

Source: Torbiorn 1985, p. 60

Two feedback loops are shown. The top loop transmits parent country expectations of the PCN manager while the bottom loop transmits host country stakeholder (e.g. colleagues, customers and government authorities) expectations of him or her. Because of the close link between parent company expectations and rewards, the PCN manager will naturally pay close attention to the top loop, but in the absence of suitable training may well lack both the skills and motivation to attend to the bottom one. Since HCN co-operation is invariably a precondition for PCN success, such behaviour is clearly dysfunctional.

Two additional problem areas concerning the expatriate assignment make the task of international training and development more complex than that for domestic assignments. First, since the stress associated with a foreign assignment falls on all family members, training programs directed towards the expatriate should also include family members. Second, in addition to initial culture shock at the start of an expatriate assignment, many expatriates also experience re-entry or repatriation shock when they return to the parent company environment. To overcome repatriation problems, international companies must develop training programs to facilitate the re-entry of expatriate executives into domestic operations.

A model of international training and development

Much of the above discussion may be conveniently summarised by examining a comprehensive model of international training and development. Rahim (1983) has developed such a model, and this is shown in Figure 13.4.

A strength of this model is the clear recognition of both international and external influences on the training and development process as is evident in the problem recognition and development objectives segments of the model. With regard to assessment of development needs, the literature on expatriate selection clearly indicates the need to assess the environment in which the expatriate will be working as well as individual factors. Thus, for example, using Tung's model, if the degree of dissimilarity between the parent and host cultures was high and the required level of interaction with the local community was high, a rigorous training program would be required. On the other hand, if the cultures were relatively similar and the required level of interaction with the local community was low, then the rigour of the training required would be correspondingly low. While this model is useful in assessing the rigour of the training required and the level of emphasis on culture needed in the program, it does not specify the methods of training required, the length of the program or the what constitutes rigour. The model presented by Mendenhall, Dunbar & Oddou (1987) (see Figure 12.4, p. 526) provides more specific information on each of these as well as the two elements discussed by Tung.

With regard to development methods, as Zeira (1976) has noted, the expatriate should only be exposed to those which fit both the corporation's goals and the expatriate's needs. In addition, it is also important to note that some training methods (e.g. T-Groups) will not be appropriate for all cultures (Jaeger 1986). A final feature of Rahim's model is feedback of results for evaluation. However, Rahim does not elaborate on the evaluation process other than to note that ideally there should be a comprehensive evaluation by an outside expert every three to five years. Two key criteria which Rahim does not include in the evaluation process are expatriate failure rate while on assignment and retention rate of expatriates upon return to domestic operations. With the support of top management, a comprehensive training program should be able to demonstrate improved results on these two important criteria.

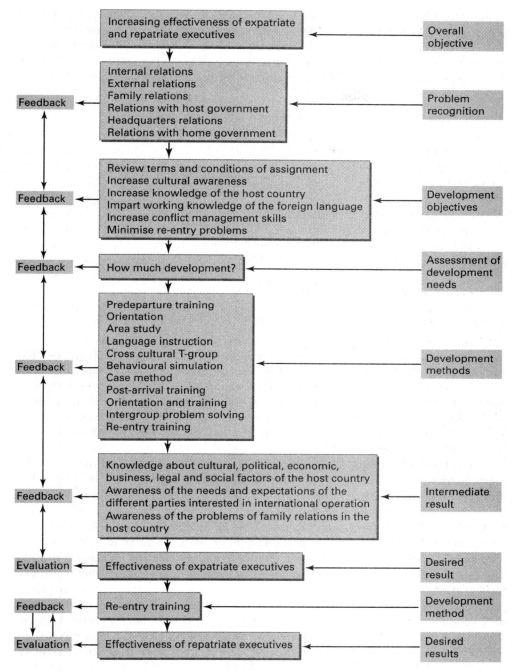

Figure 13.4 International training and development model
Source: Rahim 1983 pp. 312–17

Multinational training practices

A study of multinational training practices in the 1980s is reported by Tung (1982). The sample consisted of 144 American, European and Japanese multinational companies. One of the more striking findings of this study is the difference between the national sub-samples in terms of use of training programs for expatriates: only 32 per cent of the US companies had formal training programs compared with 69 per cent of European companies and 57 per cent of Japanese. All companies reporting no formal training programs were asked to give reasons for omitting these. The results for US companies were:

1. Trend towards employment of local nationals (45 per cent)
2. Temporary nature of such assignments (28 per cent)
3. Doubt about effectiveness of such training programs (20 per cent)
4. Lack of time (7 per cent).

The reasons given by European companies were:

1. Temporary nature of such assignments (30 per cent)
2. Lack of time (30 per cent)
3. Trend towards employment of local nationals (20 per cent)
4. Doubt about effectiveness of such programs (20 per cent).

The responses from Japanese companies were:

1. Lack of time (63 per cent)
2. Doubt about effectiveness of such programs (37 per cent).

Those firms which did have training programs were asked to indicate what types of training programs were used for the job categories of CEO, functional head, troubleshooter and operative. These data indicate the US and the European companies place more emphasis on training for CEOs and functional heads, while Japanese companies tend to provide similar training across job categories and give relatively more emphasis to operative training than do US or European companies. European companies also tend to place more emphasis on field experience for CEO and functional head positions than do US companies.

With regard to evaluation of training, 32 per cent of US companies used some form of evaluation, while the figures for European and Japanese companies were 26 and 33 per cent respectively. No company reported using evaluation procedures other than subjective ratings of trainees and supervisors.

Commenting on Tung's study, Ronen (1986) notes that the low percentage of US companies reporting use of expatriate training programs is consistent with early research by Baker & Ivancevich and that 'this figure has remained virtually unchanged over the last two decades even though large numbers of overseas managers have indicated that proper predeparture preparation is absolutely necessary to improve overseas performance' (1971, p. 548). Another study (Feldman 1989) looked at the relocation policies of US firms and found that only 13 per cent of respondents said that they offer expatriate orientation programs. Given this relatively low level of training, the higher expatriate failure rates experienced by US executives (see Table 13.1) are less surprising. Part of the reason for this may be found in Baker's 1984 survey of 1000 US multinational which indicated that, in the area of language training, senior managers were much less likely to consider it important than the expatriates themselves. Commenting on the same phenomena of senior management insensitivity, Black & Mendenhall (1991) note that US executives tend to ignore culture and assume that a good manager can operate anywhere in the world with equal effectiveness. Clearly, this is not the case.

Policy aspects of international training and development

A number of writers have suggested that the decision to transfer a manager may be for a number of reasons (Edstrom & Galbraith 1977; Prahalad & Doz 1981). The first and most obvious reason may be to fill a vacancy which has occurred. A second reason for a transfer may be to provide an opportunity for management development. A third reason may be that the organisation is using transfers as a co-ordination and control strategy to develop an international cadre of managers. The dimensions of each of these policies are shown in Table 13.5.

Table 13.5 Dimensions of transfer policies

		REASONS FOR TRANSFERS	
DIMENSIONS	FILL POSITIONS	DEVELOP MANAGERS	DEVELOP ORGANISATION
Relative numbers	Few	Moderate	Many
Specialities transferred	Technical plus a few managing directors	Technical and administrative	All
Location of host	Developing countries	Developing countries and countries with a unique competence	All countries
Direction of flow	From central offices to subsidiaries	To and from central offices and subsidiaries	Between subsidiaries and between central office and subsidiaries
Age of expatriate	Young	Young to middle age	Throughout career
Frequency	One or two moves	Several moves	Many moves
Nationality of expatriate	Nationality of ownership	Nationality of ownership plus select group from subsidiaries	All nationalities
Personnel information system	List of likely candidates from central office	Candidates from central office plus subsidiaries	Extensive lists of candidates and jobs monitored by personnel department
Power of personnel department	Weak	Moderate	Strong
Strategic placement and distribution	Absent	Absent	Extensive

Source: Edstrom & Galbraith 1977, p. 253

As the reason for transfer changes, so do the various dimensions involved (e.g. frequency of transfer and personnel information system requirements). A number of studies have confirmed that some multinational organisations use all three transfer policies. In the past though, the third organisation development option tended to be restricted to PCN employees only. However, under the competitive pressures noted at the beginning of this chapter this is now beginning to change. In the search to become more efficient, innovative and responsive many organisations are introducing management systems which result in:

- strategic decision-making responsibilities being devolved to line executives in business units throughout the organisation
- information gathering and sharing becoming critical elements of managerial work
- the development, training and career management of HCN and TCN employees as well as PCNs
- more responsibility being given to teams, both cross functional and geographic, to ensure the smooth implementation and coordination of change programs
- the consideration of wider perspectives during the decision making process
- greater tolerance of ambiguity and uncertainty in decision making.

The introduction of these management systems has clear and direct implications for the type of training undertaken in these organisations, much of which is aimed at the creation of 'the matrix in the minds of the managers'.

Bartlett & Ghoshal in their discussion of the training needs of transnationals are quite specific about this.

> The most successful development efforts have three aims that take them well beyond the skill building objectives of classic training programs: to inculcate a common vision and shared values; to broaden management perspectives and capabilities; and to develop contacts and shape management relationships.

> To build common vision and values, white-collar employees at Matsushita spend a good part of their first six months in what the company calls 'cultural and spirit training' ... they learn how to translate these internalised lessons into daily behaviour and even operational decisions ... Phillips has a similar entry level training practice (called 'organisational cohesion training'), as does Unilever (called straightforwardly 'indoctrination') ... broadening management perspectives is essentially a matter of teaching people how to manage complexity instead of merely to make room for it. To reverse a long and unwieldily tradition of running its operations with two- and three-headed management teams of separate technical, commercial and sometimes administrative specialists, Phillips asked its training and development group to de-specialise top management trainees. By supplementing its traditional menu of specialist courses with more intensive general management training, Phillips was able to begin replacing the ubiquitous teams with single business heads who also appreciated and respected specialist points of view ... developing contacts and relationships is much more than an incidental by-product of good management development, as the comments by a senior personnel manager at Unilever suggest: 'By bringing managers from different countries and businesses together ... we build contacts and create bonds that we could never achieve by other means'. The company spends as much on training as it does on R&D not only because of the direct effect it has on upgrading skills and knowledge but also because it plays a central role in indoctrinating managers into a Unilever club where personal relationships and informal contacts are much more powerful than the formal systems and structures (Bartlett & Ghoshal 1990).

The BHP 'Global leadership' programs which were introduced in 1994 have been specifically designed to build and develop a culture of commitment to the company's international strategy.

HRM IN THE NEWS

This article is used by permission from D A Stace (1997), *Reaching out from Down Under: building competence for global markets*, McGraw Hill, Sydney

Global leadership: creating alignment

As mentioned at the commencement of the study, the change in BHPs management development strategy is perhaps one of the most visible internal symbols of change in the corporation. In 1994, the Residential Management Courses (RMCs) which had been part of the benevolent paternalism and career structure of the old BHP were disbanded. In their place, a series of boldly titled 'Global Leadership' programs were introduced, offered at five levels:

- **Global Orientation**—for professional employees, a 2 or 3 day comprehensive introduction to BHP.
- **Global Leadership Program 1**—a five-day residential program for supervisory and professional staff with 5 to 8 years experience post graduation—focusing on leadership, BHP business strategy, management skills, cross-corporate linkages, and networking.
- **Global Leadership Program 2**—a two-week residential program for middle managers.
- **Global Leadership Program 3**—two ten-day residential modules, one in Melbourne and the other elsewhere in the world for BHP senior managers. The two modules are separated by a three month period in which participants work on a live strategy project for BHP.
- **Global Leadership Program 4**—the most advanced management program for executive management. This program has a formal residential component and a series of ongoing seminars and workshops in topic specific areas, e.g. risk management and doing business in countries offshore.

The Global Leadership Programs are used as agents of change. The learning styles are different at each level, with the more senior level programs involving self-directed learning. In one senior course, a group was asked to go to India to do a country study on how BHP could develop a successful business in that country. A budget of $100 000 was provided for the project. This type of action learning is typical of the approach used in these programs.

These are, therefore, more than development courses for staff. They are part of a broad ranging organisation development strategy for the corporation, aimed at acculturating managers/professional staff into the ethos of the company and developing strategic alignment through cross-divisional participation. An internal document states '... in communicating 'BHP Glue', that is, BHPs vision, mission and values widely, the intention is to arrive at a point of critical mass, where the majority of employees in BHP understand and are committed to the company's strategic objectives and values'. During 1995, 29 Global Leadership programs were scheduled, several of which were held offshore. BHPs managing director, John Prescott, addresses many of these programs.

A key challenge for BHP is in keeping the company as tightly knit culturally as it has been historically. The management development strategy is a key part of this, the intention being that every 4 to 5 years all 5000 managers will be re-visited via the Global Leadership Program. The symbolism of the Global Leadership programs is now being extended by the physical development of BHPs state-of-the-art multi million dollar Global Leadership Centre on the outskirts of Melbourne.

International remuneration

International remuneration policies are a key issue for multinationals. Robock & Simmonds (1983) state that an effective remuneration policy for expatriates should strive to meet the following objectives:

1 Attract and retain employees qualified for overseas service
2 Facilitate transfers between foreign affiliates and between home country and foreign affiliates
3 Establish and maintain a consistent and reasonable relationship between the remuneration of all employees of any affiliate, whether posted at home or abroad, and between affiliates
4 Arrange reasonable remuneration, in the various locations, in relation to the practices of leading competitors.

To achieve these objectives, most remuneration packages have some or all of the following components.

1 Base salary

This serves a number of functions in an expatriate manager's remuneration package. First, it represents a home country payroll value for that individual in terms of repatriation upon the expiration of the foreign assignment. This base salary may equal or exceed the host country rate for the position the expatriate will be assuming. While the base salary may be determined using a similar job evaluation plan for domestic and foreign employees, this is frequently problematic because many positions in foreign subsidiaries require considerably more autonomy of action than comparable domestic positions. A second function of the base salary is to provide the basis upon which various allowances and special benefits are calculated.

2 Expatriate premium

This is a general term used to describe payments made to expatriates to increase the attractiveness of foreign posts and to compensate for hardship or danger in the country involved. Two components or allowances are involved: an adjustment allowance to encourage mobility and a hardship allowance. These may be paid as separate allowances or as a single expatriate premium. For example, a large New York-based bank pays all expatriate staff a foreign assignment premium of 10 per cent of base salary and a hardship allowance of zero to 50 per cent, depending on location, while a leading US oil company pays an overall premium which varies from 5 to 65 per cent of base salary according to host country standard of living and the socio-political stability of the region or country.

3 Cost-of-living allowances

Allowances paid under this category include general cost of living, education, housing and tax equalisation. The overall purpose of these allowances is to allow expatriates to maintain their normal pattern or standard of living. With regard to cost-of-living allowance, this reflects market conditions and exchange rate fluctuations in the expatriate's host country. Generally the amount paid is based on spendable income curves and not base salary. Many companies use the US Department of State *Index of Living Costs Abroad* as a guide, but as Ruff & Jackson (1974) have noted, there are many problems involved with international comparisons of the cost of living.

An education allowance is paid to cover tuition expenses of school-age dependants at the nearest school which offers instruction in the dependant's primary language. If there is no school nearby or it is agreed that no adequate local facilities exist, most companies will pay part or all of the cost for tuition at either a home country or third country school. With regard to housing, an allowance is calculated on the basis of comparable housing within the expatriate's home country, or housing is provided by the company in lieu of an allowance. Housing is often a relatively large expense item for many companies.

A final allowance which is often a high expense item is tax equalisation. This is a particularly difficult problem for American companies, because the US is one of the few countries that taxes the income of its citizens that is earned abroad. Thus US expatriates are frequently faced with the situation of double taxation (i.e. host country and home country tax liabilities). Many US companies use a tax equalisation policy to ensure that there is no tax incentive or disincentive associated with an overseas assignment. A hypothetical tax burden is calculated on the base salary according to US tax provisions. The expatriate pays this amount and any additional foreign or US taxes are paid by the company (Pinney 1982).

4 Additional fringe benefits

Companies frequently offer other perquisites in addition to the expatriate premium and various cost-of-living allowances. Three common benefits are home country visits, car allowances and payment of part of base salary in home currency or a third country currency. Depending on local country conditions (i.e. tax laws, exchange-rate fluctuations, currency controls), these benefits can be of significant value to an expatriate.

Issues in international remuneration

There are a number of issues in the international remuneration field. One of the major issues is that of equity between PCN, HCN and TCN employees in terms of their remuneration packages. Typically the PCN employee of a multinational working in a foreign location will receive a higher level of remuneration than a TCN or HCN employee doing a similar job. The reason for this is that most multinationals opt for 'keeping the PCN expatriate whole' (i.e. maintaining relativity to PCN counterparts plus compensating for the costs of overseas service) rather than equal pay for equal work. The main advantage of the former policy is that it allows multinationals to achieve the first objective of an effective international remuneration policy as outlined earlier in this chapter: to attract and retain employees qualified for overseas service.

However, HCN employees tied to lower local wage rates and TCN employees tied to wage rates in their home country will invariably react negatively to these salary differences since they will use an equal pay for equal work equity standard. Short-term responses to this equity problem include keeping remuneration practices secret, paying PCN expatriates in both local and home currency so that the amount of local currency available to the PCN expatriate will match HCN disposable income patterns, and limiting the use of PCN expatriate assignments to relatively short-term consulting or training assignments.

Perhaps the best long-term solution to this dilemma is to ensure that remuneration policies match the organisation's international staffing policies. Such a strategy recognises that there is no ideal approach to international remuneration. Rather, policies should complement overall staffing policies so that advantages are optimised. Thus, if a multinational opts for an ethnocentric staffing policy for its foreign operations, the logical remuneration policy would be to keep the PCN expatriate whole because an ethnocentric policy (if consciously adopted) indicates that PCN employees have skills and experience which HCN and TCN employees do not possess. The dysfunctional side of this policy (perceived lack of equity by HCN/TCN employees) would be less important or significant than the functional outcome of satisfied PCN employees.

Similarly, a multinational which adopts a polycentric staffing policy would opt to keep PCN expatriates whole. This would be less controversial with HCN employees, since a polycentric staffing policy implies that most PCN assignments would be short-term consulting or training assignments. However, if a multinational aims to develop an international executive cadre via a geocentric staffing policy, it is not logically consistent to keep PCN employees whole and ignore HCN and TCN dissatisfaction. For example, most large US oil companies do not delineate between domestic and international operations since most product and regional subsidiaries have international activities. To develop a worldwide selection pool of managers, it is necessary to have a remuneration structure with standardised international base pay, with allowances and premiums based on the country of assignment. A system of international base pay would need to match the average parent country salary for each pay grade or particular position. This would be a major cost for the multinational company, but it is a precondition which must be met if a geocentric staffing strategy is to be successfully implemented.

A second issue in international remuneration is that of taxation and currency-rate fluctuations. As we have already indicated, tax equalisation programs are an important component of international remuneration packages which must be regularly reviewed to account for changes in US and foreign tax laws. Many companies now have fairly well-developed procedures for dealing with tax equalisation or seek advice from consultants. A less obvious problem area is that of incentive remuneration plans for foreign based executives. As Brooks (1985) has recently pointed out, multinationals that rely on the performance of overseas operations for long-term success need to assess the appropriateness of their incentive remuneration plans outside the US, because the value of awards to foreign based executives (both US expatriate and HCN or TCN ones) is largely determined by local tax codes and currency exchange rates and regulations. For example, Table 13.6 shows the impact of local taxes on a $10 000 cash bonus for six countries and details tax treatment on stock options in four.

As Table 13.6 shows, the value of a cash bonus or stock-option plan can be considerably diminished or enhanced by local tax treatment. Brooks reports a similar pattern of national variation for stock-based plans when the effect of inflation and exchange rates is examined. To overcome these problems, Brooks suggests that multinationals may either adapt corporate incentive plans to local conditions by adding specific enhancements for non-US participants, set up separate incentive plans, or set up a single 'contingent unit award' program which can be uniformly applied in all countries while allowing significant flexibility in the delivery of incentive awards. Regardless of which option is selected, all involve more flexibility than is currently available in most corporate incentive plans.

A further issue in international remuneration concerns the administration of the international remuneration and benefits function. Changes in the external environment (e.g. national tax codes, floating exchange rates) and a growing number of PCN and TCN executives are making the management of the remuneration process increasingly complex. An empirical study of this process was conducted by Toyne & Kuhne (1983). The focus of this study was to determine how multinational companies organise the three principal management tasks associated with international remuneration: policy and procedure

Table 13.6 Tax treatment of incentive compensation in various countries

IMPACT OF LOCAL TAXES ON $10 000 CASH BONUS[1]

COUNTRY	NETT AWARD	COUNTRY	NETT AWARD
Australia	$4000	Mexico	$4600
Canada	5300	United Kingdom	4640
Japan	5300	United States	6705

TAX TREATMENT OF STOCK OPTIONS IN FOUR FOREIGN COUNTRIES

COUNTRY	TAXATION AT DATE OF GRANT	TAXATION AT DATE OF EXERCISE[2]	TAXATION AT DATE OF SALE[3]
Australia	No	Yes	No
Brazil	No	No	No
France	No	Yes	Yes; capital gains rates
Japan	No	Yes	Yes; 50% of long-term gains

1. Executives in each country are assumed to earn US$50 000 or the equivalent in local currency. Nett awards reflect only national/federal income taxes for all countries, except that the figure for Canada takes into account Ontario provincial income tax.
2. Tax on the difference between the price paid for the shares and the market value at date of exercise.
3. Assuming certain conditions are met.

Source: Brooks 1985, p. 46–53

development, financing, and supervision and control. A majority of the 83 chief remuneration officers who responded to the survey indicated that both policy/procedure development and supervision/control were centralised at US headquarters, while financing was less centralised and as likely to be located in a foreign subsidiary as the US. With regard to financing, total worldwide sales were inversely related to the centralisation of the financing task, suggesting that multinational companies may decentralise this task as their financial system becomes more sophisticated. Further research should be conducted to determine whether these findings are indicative of how most multinational companies manage their international remuneration function.

Finally, there is the issue of how effective a remuneration plan is as a managerial reward system. Many multinational enterprises, have developed elaborate expatriate remuneration packages, 'However, the task ahead is to move from transfer-incentive remuneration packages to reward systems designed to elicit managerial actions in line with corporate long-term competitive strategy' (Pucik, 1984, p. 414). There is a dearth of research on how organisations achieve this objective.

Summary

The aim of this chapter was to critically review the international HRM field. Within the context of a structural and strategic typology, three functional HRM areas—international recruitment and selection, international training and development, and international remuneration—were reviewed and future research issues for each area were discussed. A number of general points emerge from these specific reviews.

First, sufficient research work has been done in the field of international HRM to define a future research agenda for researchers interested in the field.

Second, it is clear that there are some important differences between domestic and international HRM of which researchers and managers need to be aware. Mendenhall & Oddou (1985) were explicit on this point when they declared that one of the major problems in expatriate selection was the ingrained practice of many personnel directors of using the 'domestic equals overseas performance equation' when selecting potential expatriates—thus ensuring that little else is of importance in the selection process other than technical expertise and a successful domestic track record. One important difference is that many expatriate jobs require greater autonomy of action than comparable domestic positions. This needs to be considered when evaluating candidates for such a position, and when techniques such as job evaluation are being used to determine salary levels for nominally equivalent domestic and expatriate positions. Other differences between domestic and international personnel include the role of relational skills in expatriate effectiveness; the importance of spouse and family in the expatriate adjustment process; the degree of similarity/dissimilarity of parent country and host country cultures as an important variable in the expatriate selection and training process; host country national reactions to perceived remuneration inequities vis-à-vis PCNs as an important issue in international remuneration; and the need for multinational companies to operate in diverse national economic, political and legal systems.

Third, the literature reviewed in this chapter suggests that the planning process is of particular importance in the international HRM field. For example, to successfully implement a geocentric staffing policy (or any form of staffing or development program which aims to develop a more international executive cadre), a multinational company must use a more comprehensive personnel database which includes HCN and TCN employees in addition to PCN employees, and exercises more centralised control over the staffing process in foreign subsidiaries.

To overcome problems such as lack of a pool of qualified and suitable expatriate candidates, the frequent need to resolve a staffing crisis in an overseas subsidiary and dealing with expatriate re-entry problems, multinational companies need to increase the lead times involved in the human resource planning process.

questions for discussion and review

1 What do you think are the main differences between international and domestic HRM?
2 What are some of the forces of globalisation and what impact are they having on international HRM?
3 What is meant by the term 'administrative heritage' and what, according to Bartlett & Ghoshal, are the consequences of the 'administrative heritages' of multidomestic, international, and global companies in today's competitive environment?
4 How have Australian companies tended to internationalise?
5 Using a company in Australia, give examples of PCN, HCN and TCN appointments.
6 You have been asked to design an orientation program for personnel being transferred on a two-year assignment to a less-developed country (you select the country). The program must be completed by the participants in three weeks of full-time study. What are the several most important subjects that should be included in the program and why?

7 How can training and development facilitate strategic goal achievement in IHRM?
8 Why is the repatriation process often a difficult issue for both employees and organisations?
9 Discuss the various problem areas associated with international remuneration and suggest means by which these may be overcome.
10 In what ways can international remuneration policy be linked to international strategy?

case study

Case materials are used by permisssion from D A Stace (1997), *Reaching out from Down Under: building competence for global markets*, McGraw Hill, Sydney.

BHP steel's staffing strategy for offshore ventures

In Asia, BHP works to several key principles in the initial staffing of its offshore ventures:
- When a project manager for the venture is appointed, the next appointee if a BHP Human Resources (HR) Manager, from the home corporation, or the Regional Office. One of the priority tasks of the HR Manager is to recruit staff for the start up phase of the operation, and to locate and train a local successor.
- For joint ventures, the project manager and the Chief Financial Officer are normally BHP employees with experience of the BHP way of operating and reporting requirements.
- BHP hires all offshore staff, national or international, directly. It does not depend on joint venture partners to provide staff, although this occurs from time to time. As an example, in the US North Star development, the President and Human Resources Manager were North Star appointees.
- The initial phases of a project are dominated by short-term BHP assignees, working with country national employees.

Beyond the start-up phase, BHP International Steel sources its people in several ways:
- BHP expatriates—these are people sourced primarily from BHPs Australian or New Zealand operations, on 2–3 year offshore assignments, potentially renewable for one further term. BHP corporation currently has in excess of 500 people undertaking expatriate assignments worldwide, of whom approximately 90 are in International Steel.
- National employees—hired directly by BHP in the country of operation. These are predominantly younger, educated personnel or line staff for whom BHP provides operational training.
- Internationalist employees—third country nationals (e.g. British, Canadians, or Australian working for other companies) who are typically sourced from countries in the Region, and who can be posted anywhere in BHPs operations. A senior BHP HR executive estimated that this category of staff would soon constitute a growing percentage of the non-national staff in off-shore locations.
- Regional Asian employees—experienced specialists (e.g. Finance) from other countries in Asia-Pacific, appointed to BHP posts in other than their home country. BHP is just commencing this mode of employment. A variation of this is BHPs Singapore-based Asian Graduate program (in Engineering, Finance and Marketing). In 1995, it employed 20 Asian graduates from a total of 6000 applicants: these staff undertake Global Leadership programs in Australia, and must be willing to work anywhere in the Asia-Pacific Region, despite their country of origin.
- Short-term employees—these are typically Australian/New Zealand/US-based staff appointed for project specific tasks of several weeks to

several months duration, after which they return to their home base. In other organisations, this is referred to as the 'bungey' model of staffing.

There are several key issues in staffing within Asia-Pacific. First, conditions of entry to most countries require that foreign companies must Asianise their workforces as quickly as possible. BHP has detailed plans for Asianisation of its workforce and expects that, although the absolute numbers of expatriate/internationalist employees will grow as a percentage of BHPs total offshore staff, they will decline proportionately as BHPs offshore business expands. However, the task of finding in-country nationals with the appropriate skills, and then encouraging their on-going performance, has been problematic. Second, one of the most serious potential issues is the rate of national staff turnover, particularly in the most buoyant Asian economies. Several BHP interviewees spoke about the practice of blatant poaching by other employers, and the relative lack of company loyalty by national employees—'graduates in particular are very mobile, and we are working hard to make BHP a preferred company of employment through our training programs, and the BHP Employee Share Scheme'. It seems that most employers are vulnerable to poaching just after the yearly bonus (typically 2–4 months pay) payments. Related to this are the high expectations of national staff, many of whom have higher levels of education than equivalent staff in the Australian domestic businesses.

A third major issue is a variant of the expatriate allowance/package issue: what location allowances, if any, should be offered to regional Asian employees or internationalist employees, the former whom do not often volunteer in moving to other Asian Pacific countries? BHP has found it essential to offer inter-Asian regional location allowances but, because of the variations of individual cases, it is difficult to have any standardisation in this area of HR practice.

A compounding factor is the variation between Asian countries in standards of living, schooling and education and, importantly, the frequent non-acceptance of Asians from other Asian countries. Several interviewees indicated that there often seemed to be better acceptance of Australian expatriates than Asian staff from other countries. However, despite the difficulties, interviewees indicated that it was imperative that the company Asianised its operations as fully as possible, while at the same time ensuring that BHPs Asian employees were imbued with the BHP company culture, and saw BHPs success as critical to their own, and their country's success.

Case materials are used by permisssion from D A Stace (1997), *Reaching out from Down Under: building competence for global markets*, McGraw Hill, Sydney.

Lend Lease's approach to international staffing

There is less emphasis on policy, formality and structure in Lend Lease than the majority of corporations; active leadership, emphasis on management systems and people seem more crucial aspects. These factors complement Lend Lease's capability in business and industry analysis. Yet the 1990s task of sustaining growth through internationalisation has led to some new and innovative approaches to people and change in the business.

1 Involving the right people

Lend Lease's approach to appointing staff from Australia changed in its recent move into Asia. Where previously Lend Lease Property Services sent relatively young staff offshore, the approach now in both Property and Financial Services is to send or appoint more senior people who can interact with senior counterparts in Asian companies and joint ventures. One of Lend Lease's most senior executives, Lynette Mayne, was responsible for establishing the funds management venture, and has recently been appointed to spearhead retail as well as corporate financial services activities in Asia. It symbolises the level of importance Lend Lease attaches to Asia and to this JV. This has been a deliberate decision to leverage into the top decision makers in Asia. However, the costs of such a strategy are substantial.

Compensation is reported as being very generous to attract the right staff. One executive quoted the cost as 3 times base salary to support a senior expatriate offshore for items like salary, car, driver, club memberships, an apartment, office accommodation costs, travel for employee and family, schooling for children. While the rationale of sending senior staff seems sound, the downside is that older staff (i.e. 40–50s) sometimes find it more difficult to integrate and relocate their families into Asia. Health and social, issues were mentioned frequently as major issues.

While there was a desire to ensure that the 'best 11 were positioned offshore', interviewees, particularly those working offshore, indicated that the best people operating in Australia were not necessarily the best for Asia. The business culture of Asia was different to Australia's, hence the need for an appropriate match of cultural skills.

Hornery's note in 1992, soliciting response from those interested in working in Asia, met with keen interest. Lend Lease now has a substantial list of people wanting to relocate offshore. Opportunities are, however, limited particularly in Financial and Corporate services—the whole Indonesian Sinar Mas JV only has two expatriates, and 200 nationals. Property Services in Singapore has more expatriates, but the numbers overall are in the tens, not the hundreds.

There is no way of measuring the effect of internationalisation on morale in the company. However, a significant number of interviewees said that people are proud that the company is seen to be growing internationally, and individuals can see clearer paths opening where they had become closed in Australia. However, against this, the classic internal labour market philosophy of Lend Lease was now being challenged—with the move to appoint some senior staff from outside appointees with special international skills. This was perceived by some to be undermining some of the previous Australian-based meritocracy approach.

2 Uniformity without centralisation

For a company which avoids policy, the extent of the Asian internationalisation has caused Lend Lease to develop a comprehensive 'Policy on Expatriate Assignments' to ensure a cohesive approach to pay and conditions offshore, and repatriation. There was initially cautious if not negative reception to the development of this document, but its rationale now seems better understood in that it has assisted in minimising widely varying conditions for staff offshore; it is regarded more as a set of guidelines than definitive rules.

Lend Lease works in collaboration with Global Interface, an organisation specialising in expatriate assessment, training and country awareness programs. All Australian staff and their partners about to take up offshore postings must undertake this program. The focus is on intercultural adjustment, partner issues in-country, repatriation and stress management. Unlike several other corporates in this study, Lend Lease at this stage has no other formalised development processes in place such as BHPs Global Leadership programs. It is basically learning by doing. However, there are initial moves being made to investigate the feasibility of Lend Lease Learning, the company's training body, becoming involved in broader business preparation for offshore assignments.

There is no central HR department in Lend Lease, the HR function being carried out by managers, by the Employee Services and Accounting department, the ACTU-Lend Lease Foundation and Lend Lease Learning. In some corporations, the emphasis is on human resource policy development with little day-to-day help for those involved in internationalisation. In Lend Lease, the major emphasis is on practical day-to-day human resource issues with a minimum of policy emphasis.

3 Attracting and retaining national staff

In Jakarta, Lend Lease has relied heavily on its JV partners to provide an initial pool of local appointees, particularly in Financial Services. A key issue has been to create a comprehensive set of employment conditions for the JV itself, so that national staff see themselves as JV staff rather than Sinar Mas staff. The broad aim is to nationalise the majority of staff positions in a 3–5 year period, although the evidence from our interviews was that this may be too ambitious a timeframe to transfer skills, particularly if there is rapid growth in the business. Sinar Mas itself will probably look for a longer time commitment. Said one interviewee '... we are trying to transplant the relevant parts of our business culture in project management, people management and value management. Unless we do this, we will not be successful because they are key components of Lend Lease's competitive edge. Sinar Mas will almost certainly look for continuing Lend Lease assistance as we ourselves keep learning, while we simultaneously develop key local staff'.

Turnover of national, staff is potentially a significant issue. Well trained national staff are at a premium: in Jakarta, many international businesses quote monthly, rather than yearly, staff turnover percentages. Yearly turnover of 30–40 per cent is not uncommon for some companies, and firms report that there is often little loyalty to the firm. Remuneration and pay levels are therefore important. Lend Lease is applying some of its staff ownership and corporate culture building practices from Australia as a hedge against unplanned attrition, particularly of key JV staff.

To ensure the succession of nationals offshore, in 1994 Lend Lease started the recruitment of country nationals while they are studying at Australian tertiary institutions, or at the completion of their studies in Australia. These students, typically from Singapore, Malaysia, Thailand and Indonesia have joined Lend Lease in Australia as trainees/new employees, spending up to 18 months in Australian operations before eventual relocation into one of Lend Lease's Asian operations. The potential downside of this policy was expressed to us by a Trade Commissioner in Jakarta—the policy only works if the national appointee has not become 'too Western' during their tertiary education, otherwise they return to their home countries with greater presumptions than other nationals will, accept, therefore hindering their effectiveness. It is, however, nearly always a case by case matter.

The imperative to nationalise as quickly as possible was aptly summed up by one interviewee '... we need to step up the pace in employing Asians offshore. We have tended up till now to employ white males, aged about 30, who play football. However, in Singapore, if you roll up to a job and you are an expatriate, you are behind the game straight away'.

As part of the development process for national staff, Lend Lease has recently commenced delivering its successful program on project management in offshore locations. The project management approach has been an underlining element of the Lend Lease business culture for over two decades. It will become an important part of the fabric of Lend Lease's international expansion.

Lend Lease has paid close attention to the integration of business and human resource issues. Excerpts from the first Business Plan for the BII Lend Lease Financial Services JV illustrate the sequence of people issues:

Key strategies
1. Complete recruitment phase and formally appoint senior executives. The joint venture intends to appoint a President Director and Operations Manager, both sourced from Lend Lease.
2. Expedite relocation to Jakarta.
3. Establish clear reporting lines and limits of authority. Audit existing employees and establish roles.
4. The President Director will develop an inspiring vision that will be made clear to everyone involved.
5. Encourage full communication, team building and eliminate functional and product barriers from the outset.
6. An exchange program, initially of Indonesians to Australia for skill development purposes, will be established. These programs should be both short term (4–6 weeks) and medium- to long-term (1–2 years).

This is an approach to people management which goes far beyond the 'recruit a warm body' approach. It elaborates an earlier comment that Lend Lease appears to have a more strategic view of its JV relationships than is typical.

Several quotations from our interviews give the flavour of the developing momentum of cultural and people oriented change of Lend Lease.

'APEC happens in our corridors; we are proud to see Indonesians walking down our corridors in Australia'.

'If we are serious about Asia, we will have to think as an international global company and challenge part of our culture regarding our business approaches to HR management, and even not being too proud to look at outside models of internationalisation'.

'We have traditionally been an engineering organisation, very site-based. In going to Asia, we have had to learn the softer side of management—the relational skills'.

'We would like to see Asia as Lend Lease's home, with a very free flow of staff between Australia and Asia'.

Case materials are used by permisssion from D A Stace (1997), *Reaching out from Down Under: building competence for global markets*, McGraw Hill, Sydney.

Telstra's approach to international staffing

The normal HR department relationships are made more complex because of in-country joint venture partnerships. Human resource practices might be driven strongly by joint venture partner, or by a third country alliance. However, the strongest role of Telstra's corporate (Australian based) HR department seems to be in several major areas:
1. in bringing more uniformity to the management of expatriates and their relationships with Telstra as a corporation
2. by offering consultancy advice to country managers and IBU executives where required, and
3. in helping Telstra to address the softer HR issues of country induction; helping with selection processes (e.g. the Overseas Suitability Indicator as a predictor of suitability of staff); re-entry processes; the development of employment conditions in line with international practice of other companies (e.g. the Employment Conditions Abroad connection was extremely important in this); pre-departure training and arrangements for inclusion of partners in induction programs, and partner pre-visits to offshore locations.

The primary reasons for some past failure of expatriate appointments were cited as bad selection; wrong motives for going in the first place (escapism); inadequate expertise, especially in joint venture partnership management; and staff and families not adjusting culturally (this was particularly acute in Moslem countries).

> Anecdotally, there was some evidence from interviewees of a gradual shift under way, in HR practice, and in the model of HR. It was reported that 'there was an attitude in some parts of the business that people who went off shore were opting out, but this now appears to be changing. There is more realisation that these people are Telstra's revenue heroes'. One interviewee continued:
>
> 'We used to select and recruit techo's who wanted to go offshore for any reason, put them on a plane and send them. That has now changed; HR has done some good work in helping us to recruit suitable people'.

Resources
Books
Bartlett, C. A. & Ghoshal, S. (1989), *Managing Across Borders: The Transnational Solution*, Harvard Business School Press, Boston, Mass.

Dowling, P. J., Schuler, R. S. & Welch, D. E. (1994), *International Dimensions of Human Resource Management*, 2nd edition, Wadsworth, Belmont.

Adler, N. J. (1991), *International Dimensions of Organizational Behaviour*, 2nd edition, PWS-Kent, Boston, Mass.

Articles
Black, J. S., & Mendenhall, M. (1991), 'A practical but theory based framework for selecting cross cultural training methods', in M. Mendenhall, & G. Oddou (eds), *International Human Resource Management*, PWS-Kent, Boston, Mass. pp. 177–204.

Mendenhall, M. & Oddou, G. (1995), *Readings and Cases In International Human Resource Management*, 2nd edition, Cincinnati, South Western, OH.

Schuler, R. S., Dowling, P. J. & De Cieri, H. (1993), 'An Integrative Framework of Strategic Integrated Human Resource Management', *The International Journal of Human Resource Management*, vol. 4, pp. 717–64.

Sparrow, P., Schuler, R. & Jackson, S. (1994), 'Convergence or divergence: human resource practices and policies for competitive advantage worldwide', *International Journal of Human Resource Management*, vol. 5, no. 2, pp. 267–99.

Video
'Going International: Managing The Overseas Assignment', Copeland Griggs.

References
Adler, N. (1995), 'Competitive Frontiers: Global management in the 21st Century', *HRMonthly*, March, pp. 10–15.

—— (1987), 'Pacific Basin Managers A Gaijin Not a Woman', *Human Resource Management*, vol. 26, no. 2, pp. 169–91.

—— (1991), *International Dimensions of Organizational Behaviour*, 2nd edition, PWS-Kent, Boston, Mass.

Adler, N. & Bartholomew, B. (1992), 'Managing globally competent people', *Academy of Management Executive*, vol. 6, no. 3, pp. 52–65.

Baker J. C. & Ivancevich, J. M. (1971), 'The Assignment of American Executives Abroad: Systematic, Haphazard or Chaotic?', *California Management Review*, vol. 13, no. 3, pp. 39–44.

Baker, J. C. (1984), 'Foreign language and pre-departure orientation training in U.S. multinational industrial firms', *Personnel Administrator*, vol. 29, pp. 68–70.

Bartlett, C. A. & Ghoshal, S. (1989), *Managing Across Borders: The Transnational Solution*, Harvard Business School Press, Boston, Mass.

—— (1992), 'What Is A Global Manager?', *Harvard Business Review*, vol. 70, no. 5, Sept.–Oct.

Black, J. S. & Mendenhall, M. (1991), 'A practical but theory based framework for selecting cross cultural training methods', in M. Mendenhall & G. Oddou (eds), *International Human Resource Management*, PWS-Kent, Boston, Mass. pp. 177–204.

Boston Consulting Group (1995), 'The Australian Manager of the Twenty-First Century', in Commonwealth of Australia (1995) *Enterprising Nation: Renewing Australia's Managers To Meet The Challenges of The Asia-Pacific Century*, Report of the Industry Task Force on Leadership and Management Skills, Australian Government Publishing Service, Canberra, pp. 1223–88.

Brooks, B. J. (1985), 'Long-Term Incentives for the Foreign-Based Executives', *Compensation and Benefits Review*, vol. 17, no. 3, pp. 46–53.

Cascio, W. F. (1993), 'International human resource management issues for the 1990s', *Asia Pacific Journal of Human Resource Management*, vol. 30, pp. 1–18.

Chong, F. (1992), 'Asia's gain is our loss', *Weekend Australian Magazine*, 8–9 August, p. 19.

Commonwealth of Australia (1995), *Enterprising Nation: Renewing Australia's Managers To Meet The Challenges of The Asia-Pacific Century*, Report of the Industry Task Force on Leadership and Management Skills, Australian Government Publishing Service, Canberra.

Coyle, W. (1995), 'Most companies find dual careers a problem, survey finds', *HRMonthly*, October, pp. 6–7.

De Cieri, H., Dowling, P. J. & Taylor, K. F. (1991), 'The Psychological Impact of Expatriate Relocation on Partners', *The International Journal of Human Resource Management*, vol. 2, no. 3, pp. 377–414.

Desatnick, R. L. & Bennett, M. L. (1978), *Human Resource Management in the Multinational Company*, Nichols, New York.

Domsch, M. & Lichtenberger, B. (1991), 'Managing the global manager: pre-departure training and development for German expatriates in China and Brazil', *Journal of Management Development*, vol. 10, no. 7, pp. 41–52.

Dowling, P. J. (1986), 'Human Resource Issues in International Business', *Syracuse Journal of International Law and Commerce*, vol. 13, no. 2, pp. 255–71.

—— (1988), 'International and Domestic Personnel/Human Resource Management: Similarities and Differences', in R. S. Schuler, S. A. Youngblood & V. L. Huber (eds), *Readings in Personnel and Human Resource Management*, 3rd edition, West Publishing, St. Paul, Minn.

Dowling, P. J. & Welch, D. (1988), 'International Human Resource Management: An Australian Perspective', *Asia-Pacific Journal of Management*, vol. 6, no. 1, pp. 39–65.

Dowling, P. J., Schuler, R. S. & Welch, D. E. (1994) *International Dimensions of Human Resource Management*, 2nd edition, Wadsworth, Belmont.

Duerr, M. G. (1986), 'International Business Management: Its Four Tasks', *Conference Board Record*, vol. 43, October.

Edstrom, A. & Galbraith, J. (1977a), 'Alternative Policies for International Transfers of Managers', *Management International Review*, vol. 17, no. 2, pp. 11–22.

—— (1977b), 'Transfer of managers as a co-ordination and control strategy in mutlinational organizations', *Administrative Science Quarterly*, vol. 22.

Evans, G. (1995), 'The Road to Hell', in *Readings in Cases in International Human Resource Management*, 2nd edition, by M. Mendenhall & G. Oddou, pp. 405–410, Western College Publishing, Cincinatti, OH.

Feldman, D. (1989), 'Relocation Practices', *Personnel*, vol. 66, no. 11, pp. 22–25.

Hamill, J. (1989), 'Expatriate Policies in British Multinationals', *Journal of General Management*, vol. 14, pp. 18–33.

Harris, M. (1994), 'Pearl's lustre lures our industry', *Sydney Morning Herald*, 12 September, p. 7.

Harvey, M. (1985), 'The Executive Family: An Overlooked Variable in International Assignments', *Columbia Journal of World Business*, Spring 84–93, Adler.

Harvey, M. G. (1982), 'The Other Side of Foreign Assignments: Dealing with the Repatriation Dilemma', *Columbia Journal of World Business*, vol. 17, no. 1, pp. 52–59.

—— (1983), 'The Multinational Corporations Expatriate Problem: An Application of Murphy's Law', *Business Horizons*, vol. 26, no. 1, pp. 71–78.

Hays, R. D. (1974), 'Expatriate Selection: Insuring Success and Avoiding Failure', *Journal of International Business Studies*, vol. 5, no. 1, pp. 25–37.

Heenan, D. A. & Perlmutter, H. V. (1979), *Multinational Organization Development*, Addison-Wesley, Reading, Mass.

Heller, J. (1980), 'Criteria for selecting an international manager', *Personnel*, vol. 57, no. 3, p. 48.

Jaeger, A. M. (1986), 'Organization Development and National Culture: Where's the Fit?', *Academy of Management Review*, vol. 11, pp. 178–90.

Kendall, D. W. (1981), 'Repatriation: An Ending and a Beginning', *Business Horizons*, vol. 24, no. 6, pp. 21–25.

Laurent, A. (1986), 'The Cross-Cultural Puzzle of International Human Resource Management', *Human Resource Management*, vol. 25, pp. 91–102.

Leap, T. & Oliva, T. A. (1983), 'General Systems Precursor Theory as a Supplement to Wrens Framework for Studying Management History: The Case of Human Resource/Personnel Management', *Human Relations*, vol. 36, pp. 627–40.

Lorange, P. & Murphy, D. C. (1983), 'Strategy and Human Resources: Concepts and Practice', *Human Resource Management*, vol. 22, pp. 111–35.

McKinsey & Company and Australian Manufacturing Council (1993), 'Emerging Exporter: Australian's High Value-Added Manufacturing Exporter', AMC, Melbourne.

Mendenhall, M. & Oddou, G. (1985), 'The Dimensions of Expatriate Acculturation: A Review', *Academy of Management Review*, vol. 10, pp. 39–47.

Mendenhall, M., Dunbar, E. & Oddou, G. (1987), 'Expatriate Selection, Training and Career-Pathing: A Review and Critique', *Human Resource Management*, vol. 26, pp. 331–45.

Morgan, P. V. (1986), 'International Human Resource Management: Fact or Fiction', *Personnel Administrator*, vol. 31, no. 9.

Murray, F. T. & Murray, A. H. (1986), 'Global Managers for Global Businesses', *Sloan Management Review*, vol. 27, no. 2, pp. 75–80.

Newman, J., Bhatt, B. & Gutteridge, T. (1978), 'Determinants of Expatriate Effectiveness: A Theoretical and Empirical Vacuum', *Academy of Management Review*, vol. 4, pp. 655–61.

Phatak, A. V. (1989), 'International Dimensions of Management', 2nd edition, PWS-Kent, Boston, Mass.

Pinney, D. L. (1982), 'Structuring an Expatriate Tax Reimbursement Program', *Personnel Administrator*, vol. 27, no. 7, pp. 19–25.

Porter, M. (1986), 'Changing Patterns of International Competition', *California Business Review*, vol. 28, no.2, pp. 9–40.

—— (1990), *The Competitive Advantage of Nations*, Free Press, London.

Prahalad, C. K. & Doz, Y. L. (1981), 'An Approach to Strategic Control in MNCs', *Sloan Management Review*, vol. 22, no. 4, pp. 5–13.

Price, V. A. (1982), *Type A Behaviour Pattern: A Model for Research and Practice*, Academic Press, New York.

Pucik, V. (1984), 'The International Management of Human Resources', in C. J. Frombrun, N. M. Tichy & M. A. Devanna (eds), *Strategic Human Resource Management*, John Wiley, New York.

Rahim, A. (1983), 'A Model for Developing Key Expatriate Executives,' *Personnel Journal*, vol. 62, no. 4, pp. 312–17.

Robinson, R. D. (1978), *International Business Management: A Guide to Decision Making*, 2nd edition, Dryden, Hinsdale, Ill.

Robock, S. H. & Simmonds, K. (1983), *International Business and Multinational Enterprises*, 3rd edition, Irwin, Homewood, Ill.

Ronen, S. (1986), *Comparative and Multinational Management*, Wiley, New York.

Ruff, H. J. & Jackson, G. I. (1974), 'Methodological Problems in International Comparisons of the Cost of Living', *Journal of International Business Studies*, vol. 5, no. 2, pp. 57–67.

Schollhammer, H. (1975), 'Current Research on International and Comparative Management Issues', *Management International Review*, vol. 15, no. 2–3, pp. 29–40.

Scullion, H. (1991), 'Why Companies Prefer to use Expatriates', *Personnel Management*, vol. 23, pp. 32–35.

Shenkar, O. (1995), *Global Perspectives on Human Resource Management*, Prentice-Hall, Englewood Cliffs, NJ.

Stace, D. (1996a), 'From Production Push to Market Pull: BHP Steel Goes International: Case Study', Centre for Corporate Change, Paper no. 55, AGSM, Sydney.

—— (1996b), 'Telstra Reaching out Internationally, De-regulating Domestically: Case Study of Telstra's International Business Unit (IBU)', Centre for Corporate Change Paper no. 59, AGSM, Sydney.

—— (1996c), 'Lend Lease's Strategic Shift Into Asia', Centre for Corporate Change Paper no. 57, AGSM, Sydney.

—— (1997), Reaching out from Down Under: building competence for global markets, McGraw-Hill, Sydney.

Stroh L. K. (1995), 'Predicting Turnover Among Repatriates: Can Organisations Affect Retention Rates', *International Journal of Human Resource Management*, vol. 6. no. 2, pp. 443–56.

Teague, B. W. (1972), *Compensating Key Personnel Overseas*, The Conference Board, New York.

Torbiorn, I. (1982), *Living Abroad: Personal Adjustment and Personnel Policy in Overseas Setting*, Wiley, New York.

—— (1985), 'The Structure of Managerial Roles in Cross-Cultural Settings', *International Studies of Management and Organization*, vol. 15, no. 1, pp. 52–74.

Torbiorn, I. & Tung, R. L. (1988), 'Career Issues in International Assignments', *Academy of Management Executive,* vol. 2 , no. 3 pp. 241–44.

Toyne, B. & Kuhne, R. J. (1983), 'The Management of the International Executive Compensation and Benefits Process', *Journal of International Business Studies,* vol. 14, no. 3, pp. 37–50.

Tung, R. (1987), 'Expatriate assignments: Enhancing success and minimising failure', *Academy of Management Executive,* vol. 1, no. 2, pp. 117–26.

Tung, R. L. (1981), 'Selection and Training of Personnel for Overseas Assignments', *Columbia Journal of World Business,* vol. 16, no. 1, pp. 68–78.

—— (1982), 'Selection and Training procedures of US, European and Japanese Multinationals', *California Management Review,* vol. 25, no. 1, pp. 57–71.

—— (1984), 'Strategic Management of Human Resources in the Multinational Enterprise', *Human Resource Management,* vol. 23, pp. 129–43.

Zeira, Y. (1976), 'Management Development in Ethnocentric Multinational Corporations', *California Management Review,* vol. 18, no. 4, pp. 34–42.

Zeira, Y. & Banai, M. (1984), 'Present & Desired Methods of Selecting Expatriate Managers for International Assignments', *Personnel Review,* vol. 13, no. 3, pp. 29–35.

glossary

Absenteeism Time taken off work by employees not approved in advance by management. A proportion of absenteeism will be linked to illness. Other time off will not.

Accord Agreement on economic, industrial relations and social issues made by the Australian Labor Party and the Australian Council of Trade Unions. There were eight Accords issued between 1983 and 1995.

Affirmative action Techniques and methods used to create equal employment opportunity.

Analysers One of four types of organisational strategy identified by Miles & Snow (1978; 1984), in which organisations focus on maintaining some stable product/service lines while searching for related new opportunities in emerging markets.

Anarchic careers A term suggested by Hearn (1980) which refers to a number of types of careers which lack any clear pattern of development or relationship to organisational needs.

Application blank A form seeking information about the applicant's background and present status. Usually this information is used as an initial or pre-employment screen to decide if the candidate meets the minimum job requirements.

Apprenticeship The traditional method of training for skilled workers. Apprentices are 'indentured' to a company that provide them with training. In return, the apprentice works for the company at a lower than normal wage. Apprenticeships in Australia are confined to certain occupations and are governed by the industrial relations system.

Arbitration A method of dispute settlement in which a third party (for instance, the Industrial Relations Commission) makes a ruling binding on the parties in dispute.

Assessment centres A series of activities designed to assess a candidates potential. Usually involving in-basket exercises, leaderless group discussion, various sorts of tests and business games. The composite performance on the exercises and tests is often used to determine an assessment centre attendee's future promotability and the organisation's human resource planning requirements and training needs, as well as to make current selection and placement decisions. This rating is generally given to the attendee, who in turn can use it for his or her own personal career planning purposes. Assessment centres appear to work because they reflect the actual work environment and measure performance on multiple job dimensions. Additionally, more than one trained rater with a common frame of reference evaluates each participant's behaviour. In terms of cost effectiveness, assessment centres are often criticised as being too costly at around $1500 per assessment for a mid-level manager and several thousand dollars for a senior manager. However, annual productivity gains realised by selecting managers via assessment centres have been shown to be on average well above administrative costs.

Award A document setting out the legally enforceable terms and conditions of employment in a firm or industry.

Award restructuring The process by which the industrial awards which have traditionally governed the terms and conditions of Australian workers were reviewed and reformed in the late 1980s. The establishment of new career paths and associated training programs became an important feature of award restructuring.

Base pay or salary The amount of pay or salary that is fixed and constant over a period of time, and is received regardless of performance.

Behaviourally-based recruitment systems Based on the idea that a person's past behaviour is a good predictor of their future behaviour. Consequently, the whole recruitment and selection process is built around the idea that getting an accurate picture of past behaviours will increase the reliability of the process. The first stage in this process is to define the behaviours that lead to success or failure in a given position. These behaviours, sometimes called dimensions, then form the platform for the collection of information in the selection process and the eventual acceptance or rejection of candidates. In many ways this is a comparable process to that of job analysis, which traditionally then leads to the development of a job specification (which defines the job in terms of the attributes required for successful performance) and person specification (which defines the special characteristics required by the ideal candidate for the job). In the behavioural approach, instead of describing a job in terms of the specific knowledge, skills and attributes that the job holder should possess, the job will be described in terms of performance statements. These performance statements can then be specifically tested against the candidates behaviour in the past as ascertained via an interview or their demonstrable competence in terms of a job simulation of some sort.

Behaviour modification A training program of positive reinforcement to reward employees for displaying desirable behaviours.

Benchmark evaluation A sample of jobs selected for detailed analysis and evaluation to establish a basis on which the relative size and worth of other jobs can be determined by comparison.

Benchmarking A process of comparing and measuring an organisation's business processes against business leaders to gain information that will help the organisation take action to improve its performance.

Career anchor Defined by Schein (1978) as a pattern of self-perceived talents, motives, and values that serves to guide, constrain, stabilise and integrate a person's career.

Career development Growth in the individual's work-related knowledge, skills and abilities and thus their potential to contribute to the organisation.

Career ladders Specify movement through a sequence of jobs to reach a higher level position.

Career management The assistance provided by an organisation to aid its employees in their careers.

Career path A logical sequence of positions which typically involves increases in skill and/or responsibility.

Career planning The process of identifying career goals and establishing activities that must be accomplished to attain those goals.

Career plateau A situation in which the career progression is slow or non-existent and the prospects for future promotion appear low.

Career The evolving sequence of a person's work experiences over time.

Centralisation The determination of pay and conditions by 'central' industrial relations tribunals.

Cognitive ability tests Measure the potential of an individual to perform, given the opportunity. These typically will test verbal comprehension, word fluency, numerical aptitude, inductive reasoning and memory. Used in the US and Europe since the turn of the century, these devices are useful and valid.

Combined approach Many organisations also use this approach, in which one or more specific requirements (e.g. qualifications in law or accounting) must be met. Once these hurdles are overcome, performances on the remaining predictors are combined into an overall measure of job suitability. Consider graduate recruiting. Many organisations only interview students with good academic records (first hurdle). The candidate must then pass a campus interview (second hurdle). At corporate headquarters, the applicant may take aptitude tests, participate in an assessment centre, and be interviewed. A composite index that considers performance in all three areas is used to make the final selection (compensatory).

Compa-ratio The salary for an individual or a job expressed as a percentage of the respective grade midpoint salary.

Comparable worth Proponents of this remuneration issue contend that, while the 'true worth' (intrinsic value) of jobs may be similar, some jobs (often held by women) are paid less than others (often held by men). The resulting differences in pay are disproportionate to the differences in 'true worth', and amount to wage discrimination.

Compensable factors Yardsticks of job-related factors that are used to compare or measure the relative worth and size of jobs.

Compensatory approach Because most jobs do not have truly absolute requirements, this is more realistic. It assumes that good performance on one predictor *can* compensate for poor performance on another (e.g. a low score on a written examination can be compensated for by a high score on an interview). With a compensatory approach, no selection decisions are made until the completion of the entire process. Then a composite index is developed that takes into consideration performance on all predictors. The advantage of this approach is that every applicant, regardless of race or ethnic background gets to participate in the *entire* selection process. While more time consuming and costly than a multiple hurdles approach, a compensatory approach is less likely to cause legal problems.

Competency A skill or attribute that is required to perform a certain task. Competencies are specified in terms of performance criteria so that employees can be judged as competent or not competent at a particular task.

Competency-based training (CBT) Training programs that are based on competencies established for a certain job or task. CBT is based on outputs i.e. whether the trainee can perform the task rather than inputs i.e. what the training program should contain. CBT has become the basis for the Australian system under the training reforms.

Conciliation A method of settling disputes in which a third party assists those in dispute. For instance, the industrial relations tribunals act as conciliators where they seek to assist unions and employers in dispute.

Cop-out career A type of career identified by Hearn (1980) in which an employee puts as little energy as possible into their job, searching for satisfaction outside of work hours.

Corporate governance The entire set of incentives, safeguards and dispute resolution processes that orders the activities of the stakeholders.

Cost-of-living allowances Allowances paid under this category include general cost of living, education, housing and tax equalisation. The overall purpose of these allowances is to allow expatriates to maintain their normal pattern or standard of living. With regard to cost-of-living allowance, this reflects market conditions and exchange rate fluctuations in the expatriate's host country. Generally the amount paid is based on spendable income curves and not base salary.

Criterion scores The type of criterion against which a selection device is validated. This can vary greatly. At one end of the spectrum are direct measures of output (e.g. number of items produced, number of trades, number of absences, number of complaints). Unfortunately, for many jobs, direct output measures do not exist. Consequently, performance appraisal ratings become the criterion. Performance ratings need to be based on job related criteria if they are to be useful and valid measures of performance.

Culture Common values, attitudes and behaviours that members of a group or society share and which are expressed, reproduced and communicated partly in symbolic form.

Decentralisation The determination of industrial relations issues by managers, employees and their unions at workplace level, rather than in the 'centralised' industrial relations tribunals.

Defenders One of four types of organisational strategy identified by Miles & Snow (1978; 1984), in which organisations seek to defend a relatively narrow product/market position through stability and efficiency.

Delayering Reducing the number of levels of management in the organisation.

Delphi technique A forecasting technique which uses a group of experts who take turns at presenting their forecasts and assumptions to the others, who then make revisions in their own forecasts until a viable composite forecast emerges.

Demand forecasting The projection of future staffing needs.

Demarcation Demarcation barriers or boundaries identify and separate work tasks. Awards have often indicated which unions should undertake which tasks.

Direct discrimination Exclusion of an individual or group from an employment opportunity or benefit because of a personal characteristic which is irrelevant to the performance of the tasks.

Direct reward, remuneration or **compensation** The cash wage or salary, including any performance related cash payments such as merit pay, bonus or incentive payment.

Downtime Refers, for instance, to machinery available but not in use because of malfunction.

Duty of care The standard of care that a 'reasonable person' in that situation would take.

Employer associations An association whose membership consists mainly of employers.

Enterprise agreement Agreement about the pay and conditions to apply at an enterprise.

Environmental assessment An assessment of the organisation's internal and external environment which will indicate future trends and possible changes in the organisation.

Equal employment opportunity An employment situation in which every individual has access to employment and its benefits.

ESOP Employee share ownership plans that provide opportunity for employees to participate in ownership of the employer.

Estimates or targets Number of women the organisation is aiming to reach in a particular time period as a result of its affirmative action program.

Ethnocentric Approach to staffing results in all key positions in a multinational company being filled by parent country nationals (PCNs).

Expatriate base salary Serves a number of functions in an expatriate manager's remuneration package. First, it represents a home country payroll value for that individual in terms of repatriation upon the expiration of the foreign assignment. This base salary may equal or exceed the host country rate for the position the expatriate will be assuming. While the base salary may be determined using a similar job evaluation plan for domestic and foreign employees, this is frequently problematic because many positions in foreign subsidiaries require considerably more autonomy of action than comparable domestic positions. A second function of the base salary is to provide the basis upon which various allowances and special benefits are calculated.

Expatriate career Where an employee takes up a position in an overseas operation of their organisation.

Expatriate fringe benefits Benefits offered in addition to other components of expatriate salary packages. Three common benefits are home country visits, car allowances and payment of part of base salary in home currency or a third country currency. Depending on local country conditions (i.e. tax laws, exchange-rate fluctuations, currency controls), these benefits can be of significant value to an expatriate.

Expatriate premium Is a general term used to describe payments made to expatriates to increase the attractiveness of foreign posts and to compensate for hardship or danger in the country involved. Two components or allowances are involved: an adjustment allowance to encourage mobility and a hardship allowance. These may be paid as separate allowances or as a single expatriate premium.

External equity Determining wage and salary rates for different jobs on the basis of what other companies pay for similar jobs.

External recruitment Recruiting from outside the organisation. External recruiting sources include walk-in applicants, the Commonwealth Employment Service, private employment agencies, trade unions and schools. In addition to these, organisations use traditional recruitment methods such as advertising in newspapers, on radio and, to a lesser extent, on television. More recent methods of staff recruitment are through acquisitions and mergers and the use of computerised recruiting services.

Extrinsic rewards These are rewards provided by the employer, and include wages and other payments, particularly incentives or bonuses.

Factor-comparison method A method of job evaluation that provides dollar values for specific compensable factors against which the job is rated to determine relative pay.

Flat-rate In reference to pay increases, means specified dollar amounts in contrast to proportional pay increases (e.g. workers receive an extra $10 rather than a 5 per cent increase).

Flexible reward or remuneration An approach to remuneration management that provides employees some degree of choice as to the structure and delivery of their remuneration. This is in contrast to employers that provide a fixed package.

Fringe Benefit Tax (FBT) A tax levied on the employer for the provision of certain non-wage or salary benefits. FBT was introduced in 1986 as a means of recovering tax on a growing number of benefits provided by employers in lieu of cash. FBT is usually costed back into the employee's package when calculating the total reward cost.

Geocentric An approach to staffing whereby the best people are sought for key jobs throughout the organisation, regardless of nationality.

Glass ceiling The invisible barrier which prevents women attaining senior positions in organisations.

Global strategy Followed by organisations pursuing an export oriented strategy based on strong central control, global product lines and classic economies of scale. Such organisations, are typified by very strong control from the centre with very little autonomy at local level.

Golden handcuffs Extremely favourable financial arrangements (cash, shares or a combination) that build up over time and make it very costly for the employee to leave the organisation. These are usually reserved for highly skilled and talented professionals, senior managers and executives.

Golden parachute Contracts with highly skilled and talented professionals, senior managers and executives that provide for large sums of money in the event of job loss due to mergers and acquisitions.

Grade structure An arrangement showing the relationship between the relative value of jobs and pay levels. Typically, this follows a job evaluation process and allows for jobs of similar size to be grouped together within a common pay band.

Guerilla career A type of career identified by Hearn (1980) in which an employee, usually devoted to some external political or social cause, sees their mission as one of trying to change or even revolutionise the organisation from within.

Hay Guide Chart Method A proprietary points-factor method of job evaluation established by Edward Hay in the 1940s. The Hay Guide Chart Method uses three main factors—Know-How, Problem Solving and Accountability—to evaluate jobs, and the points scores that result usually form the basis of a pay grading structure.

Hazard A source of risk to health and safety.

Homosociability The tendency noted in many organisational studies for managers to show preference in selection for socially similar subordinates. Not surprisingly, this is a major source of discrimination in relation to selection. The reasons for homosociability stem mainly from the perceived need of managers to have subordinates that they can trust. This often involves conformity, loyalty and the acceptance of authority which can be shown in part by appearance. Moreover, when managers select people broadly in their own image they reinforce the belief that people of their own kind legitimately deserve authority.

Host Country Nationals Employees from the country of operation.

Human Resource Development (HRD) A broad set of activities concerned with improving the performance of the organisation's human resources as a whole. Thus HRD encompasses not only training and development activities but also career management and organisational development activities also.

Human resource information system (HRIS) A logical and systematic record of information on various aspects of staffing, jobs and productivity.

Human resource planning An activity organisations carry out in an attempt to ensure a match between the knowledge, skills and abilities the organisation will need in the future and those it will have available.

Incentive pay plan Cash or non-cash (e.g. shares) rewards that are directly linked to performance targets, where the targets and rewards are set at the beginning of the performance period.

Indirect discrimination The exclusion of an individual or group from an employment opportunity or benefit because of an apparently neutral condition or requirement, but which incorporates attitudes and assumptions which disadvantage individuals in some groups more than others.

Indirect reward, remuneration or **compensation** Rewards or benefits provided to employees as members of the organisation. Also known as fringe benefits, or supplementary remuneration or compensation.

Industrial relations This refers to issues involved in the formal and informal regulation and control of work. It has often concentrated on the collective relations of employees and employers but it also encompasses the direct relationship of managers and individual workers.

Inter-rater reliability Focuses on the consistency of ratings by different individuals. For example, unstructured interviews tend to be unreliable, with multiple interviewers perceiving the same applicant dissimilarly.

Internal equity The fair and systematic determination of wage rates for different jobs within the organisation on the basis of the internal worth and relativities of the positions to the organisation.

Internal recruitment Using internal resources to recruit. Internal sources include present employees, friends of employees, former employees, and former applicants. Promotions and transfers can also provide applicants for departments or divisions within the organisation. Current employees are a source of job applicants in two respects: they can refer friends to the organisation, and they can also become applicants themselves by potential promotion or transfer.

International strategy Followed primarily by organisations that expanded into international operations in the period of US economic hegemony following the Second World War. According to Bartlett & Ghoshal the strategy of this group is based mainly on transferring and adapting parent country knowledge and expertise into overseas markets thereby following an international product lifecycle.

Intrinsic rewards Those rewards that result from internal feelings of worth and satisfaction, usually related to the nature and design of self-fulfilling work.

Job analysis The process of recording and describing the purpose, characteristics and duties of a given job. The results are used for a variety of human resource activities from recruitment to training and pay determination.

Job burnout Total depletion of physical and mental resources caused by excessive striving to reach some unrealistic goal.

Job classification A system of grouping jobs, on the basis of job classes or grades, reflecting their relative value and worth, and constructed from the results of a job analysis exercise.

Job evaluation A formal and systematic process for objectively comparing the relative size and worth of jobs within an organisation.

Job ranking A hierarchy or ladder of jobs, reflecting the relative value and worth, and constructed from the results of a job analysis exercise.

Judgmental forecasting The use of experts who 'judge' or estimate future conditions such as the demand for or supply of human resources.

Linear career A type of career pattern in which the individual seeks continuing promotions to reach the top rank in an organisation.

Lump sum bonuses A one-off cash payment that does not increase wages or salary.

Management development The process of developing the potential of managers in an organisation. Management development includes a variety of activities such as succession planning, job rotation, mentoring as well as more traditional management training activities.

Managing diversity Valuing differences between stakeholders and developing and implementing policies to manage these differences.

Mentoring programs Use senior level staff to provide one-to-one guidance and support to more junior colleagues.

Merit pay plans A wage and salary management process that provides an increase in fixed pay following assessed performance (or merit).

Midlife transition A period, usually between the ages of 40 and 55, during which an individual re-examines their accomplishments relative to their initial career goals.

Mission Defines the business we are in.

Multidomestic strategy An international strategy whereby an organisation gains its main competitive advantage from sensitivity to local market needs and speed of response to changing circumstances. Each national branch of the company operates with a high degree of independence, which has often led to their being thought of as local companies.

Multiple hurdles approach In such an approach, an applicant must exceed fixed levels of proficiency on all predictors in order to be accepted. A score lower than the cutoff score on one predictor test cannot be compensated for by a higher-than-necessary score on another predictor. Underlying this approach is the assumption that a specific skill or competency is so critical that inadequacy guarantees the person will be unsuccessful on the job. This assumption legitimately applies for some physical ability requirements (e.g. visual acuity for pilots) and for mandated licensing requirements (e.g. registration requirements for nurses).

Multiple linear regression analysis The projection of a future state, such as demand for employees using several variables such as sales, productivity data and turnover rates.

Multiple predictor approach Is taken when more than one selection device is needed to elicit the essence of the various dimensions which are required in successful job performance. The information from multiple predictors can be combined in three ways.

National Training Reform Agenda The name given to the series of reforms to the training system initiated by the federal government in the early 1990s. The reforms included the use of CBT as the basis for training and the Training Guarantee scheme that came into being in 1990.

National Wage Case (NWC) A hearing before the Full Bench of the Industrial Relations Commission usually to determine general wage increases for workers covered by federal awards.

Nominal group technique A forecasting technique in which several people independently list their ideas which are then presented to the group and publicly recorded so that all members can see all the ideas and refer to them in later parts of the session.

Non-career A type of career Identified by Hearn (1980) in which an employee does little real work, with their major focus being on taking advantage of non-work aspects of the workplace.

Objectives Statement of a specific outcome of an affirmative action policy.

Occupational health The maintenance of physical and mental well-being in the work environment.

Occupational safety Protection from the risk of injury or disease in the working environment.

Off-the-job training Training that takes place away from the job situation, often in a classroom or special training facility. Off-the-job training is best used where it is impossible to train in the workplace e.g. flight simulation for aircraft pilots etc.

On-the-job training (OJT) The most usual form of training in organisations, OJT is the process of training an employee at the point of the actual job. This is often the most effective way of training because of its use of the real situation.

Organisational learning The process by which improvements to organisational practice are embedded in the organisation and transmitted from one generation of employees to the next.

Outplacement counselling Employment counselling provided to those who have been, or are about to be made redundant.

Overtime Work performed outside standard hours as specified in an award or agreement, and often paid at a higher ('penalty') rate.

Parent country nationals Employees who are nationals of the country which is the home base for the organisation.

Performance appraisal or performance appraisal system Formal structured system of measuring, evaluating and influencing employee's job related attributes, behaviours and outcomes.

Performance management Series of processes designed to manage employee performance.

Performance-based pay Pay systems that related pay to individual, work team or organisation performance. Incentive and merit pay plans are the most typical examples.

Personality tests Are intended to measure an individual's personality traits or characteristics. Although personality questionnaires are most commonly called 'tests', the term 'inventory' is really more appropriate because, unlike a test, an inventory has no right or wrong answers. Personality questionnaires usually contain statements or questions relating to behaviour, attitudes or beliefs. Subjects are asked to respond to these as they apply to themselves and these responses to individual items are scored on each of several personality dimensions or traits. The best-known personality tests are the Cattell 16PF, the Minnesota Multiphasic Personality Inventory, the California Psychological Inventory and the Myers-Briggs Type Indicator, although the latter should not be used for selection purposes.

Placement Is concerned with matching individual skills, knowledge, abilities, preferences, interests, and personality to the job. Effective selection and placement involve finding the match between organisational needs for qualified individuals and individual needs for jobs in which they are interested.

Polycentric Staffing policy is one where HCNs are recruited to manage subsidiaries in their own country, and PCNs occupy positions in corporate headquarters.

Positive discrimination or reverse discrimination Action taken to overcome or modify the effects of discrimination in the past.

Predictor scores Predict how well applicants will perform. While a wealth of selection devices (background information, paper-and-pencil tests, work simulations, physical tests, interviews) can be used to predict job performance, the usefulness of these depends on their reliability and validity.

Profit sharing plans An organisation-level incentive pay plan involving cash or non-cash (e.g. shares) payments to employees contingent on certain levels of threshold profit.

Prospectors One of four types of organisational strategy identified by Miles & Snow (1978; 1984), in which organisations focus on product/service innovation and the creation of new markets.

Psychomotor tests Tests of dexterity and spatial co-ordination. For example, a bank teller needs the motor skills necessary to operate a computer or a ten-key calculator and the finger dexterity to manipulate currency. There are a variety of psychomotor abilities, each of which is highly specific and shows little relationship to other psychomotor abilities *or* to cognitive ability. For example, control precision involves finely controlled muscular adjustments (e.g. moving a lever to a precise setting), whereas finger dexterity entails skilful manipulation of small objects (e.g. assembling nuts and bolts).

Quality of work life (QWL) The overall impact of work on people as well as on the organisation. Interventions include job enrichment and participation.

Quota Fixed percentage of women to be employed regardless of the number of qualified applicants available.

Reactors One of four types of organisational strategy identified by Miles & Snow (1978; 1984), in which organisations struggle to survive in a reactive manner rather than by anticipating changes.

Realistic job previews The presentation of both positive and negative information about the job and the organisation to applicants for a position.

Recruitment The set of activities and processes used to legally obtain a sufficient number of the right people at the right place and time so that the people and the organisation can select each other in their own best short- and long-term interests.

Redundancy The loss of one or more jobs, often as a result of plant closure or organisational or technological change.

Regiocentric An approach to international staffing which is a mixed policy with regard to executive nationality, allowing for regional considerations to dominate.

Reliability The degree to which a measurement device produces dependable or consistent results indicates its *reliability*. Unreliable measurements produce one set of results at one time and a different set at another. When a selection device yields equivalent results time after time, it is considered reliable. For example, tests of physical attributes (height, weight, hearing) tend to be more reliable than tests of personality characteristics (neuroticism, flexible thinking, emotional stability).

Replacement planning The development of lists of current and potential occupants of positions in an organisation.

Rucker Plan A group-based incentive plan, similar in purpose to the Scanlon Plan, but with a more complex formula for determining payments.

Safety audit A management tool for measuring the standards of safety performance and cost.

Salary compression Relatively small differences in pay, usually between superior and subordinate, or between adjacent pay grades. The differences in pay are said to be compressed.

Scanlon Plan A type of company-wide incentive program that emphasises management–employee relations, especially employee participation and co-operation. Employees share in profits that are attributable to productivity gains above an established historic baseline.

Selection Is the process of gathering legally defensible information about job applicants in order to determine who should be hired for long-or short-term positions.

Self-actualisation An aspect of motivation theory which suggests that all people have a need to develop to their full capacity as a person. It implies that employment will ultimately need to provide challenge, achievement and responsibility if motivation is to be maintained.

Sexual harassment Unlawful behaviour of a sexual nature by a co-worker or employer.

Share (or stock) option An option to buy a share at a later date, but at a price fixed when the option is granted. Share options often form part of management and executive incentive pay plans.

Short-term human resource strategy A short-term approach to human resource planning in which HR-related issues are seen as vital, but the future is too uncertain to place much faith in a detailed long-range human resource plan. Speed of response and flexibility are emphasised and HR issues are identified in reaction to rapidly evolving threats and opportunities.

Simple linear regression analysis The projection of a future state, such as demand for employees, based on a past relationship between two variables such as the organisation's employment level and a variable related to employment such as sales.

Single predictor approach Using only one piece of information or one method for selecting an applicant. Single predictors are used by many organisations to select employees, especially when they can readily be validated. This occurs most frequently when a single predictor captures the essence or the major dimension of the job, thereby making it easy to validate (e.g. requiring a candidate for a keyboard operator's job to pass a typing test).

Skill inventories Information on employee skills collected through a human resource information system includes name, employee, number, job classification, prior jobs, prior experience, specific skills and knowledge, education, licences, publications, and salary levels. The results of formal assessments, such as those obtained in assessment centres, during work-sample tests, and with job interest inventories, are usually included. Skill inventories should also include information regarding the employee's job interests, geographical preferences, and career goals. The inclusion of the latter information ensures that potential job assignments meet individual as well as organisational goals.

Skill-based evaluation, skill-based pay An approach to job evaluation or pay determination, where employees are paid on the basis of their acquisition and application of specific skills required by the enterprise.

Social wage Refers to state provided benefits such as free or subsidised health care, child care, family allowances and unemployment benefits.

Spiral career A type of career pattern in which the individual seeks opportunities to develop and use their various abilities and interests. Spiral careers tend to unfold as the individual's self-concept and interests develop and elaborate.

Staff replacement approach A short-term approach to human resource planning wherein staff are recruited or promoted when a vacancy occurs, unless there are obvious reasons for not doing so, with little if any attempt at long-term or formal human resource planning.

Stakeholder Any group or individual who has a legitimate expectation of the organisation.

Steady state career A type of career pattern in which the individual undergoes a period of study or training prior to entering an occupation, and then spends their working life in this occupation.

Strategy The course of action taken in organisation.

Strengths, weaknesses, opportunities and threats (SWOT) analysis An analysis of both the positive and negative aspects of the organisation's external and internal environments.

Strike Collective withdrawal of labour.

Structured interview An interview where all applicants are asked the same questions in the same order. While structuring the interview restricts the topics that can be covered, it ensures that the same information is collected on all candidates. As a result, managers are less likely to make snap or erroneous judgements.

Succession planning The identification of potential occupants of positions in an organisation along with the provision of suitable developmental experiences.

Superannuation A contributory pension fund, payable on retirement. Such schemes spread to most of the workforce during the late 1980s.

Supply forecasting Projecting the likely availability of staff suitable to meet future staffing needs.

Systems approach to career management Sees the organisation, its environment and the people within the organisation as a complex open system in which all parts are constantly changing and responding to change in other parts of the system. This system must be managed in order to meet the needs of the organisation for staffing and the needs of employees for satisfying careers.

Telecommuting or teleworking An employee using information technology to work from a remote location, often in a home-based office.

Test case A case, for instance before an industrial tribunal, designed to set a precedent for reference in similar cases in the future.

Third country nationals Employees from neither the parent or host country

360 degree feedback Obtaining feedback from a variety of sources including subordinates, peers, boss, self and customers.

Total reward The annual monetary cost of providing total cash (wages and salaries, performance payments) and non-cash (superannuation, benefits) remuneration to an employee.

Traineeship Originally the Australian Traineeship System (ATS), traineeships are a two-year program of structured training based with an employer. Traineeships have been used successfully in those occupations not covered by apprenticeships. Traineeships and apprenticeship are likely to be brought together under a single system in the near future.

Training needs The training requirement of an organisation. These are collected through a process known as Training Needs Analysis (TNA).

Trait-factor approach An approach to career choice which focuses on which worker traits are most usefully measured, which factors in jobs are most relevant, and on what kind of matching processes (tests, interviews, etc.) resulted in the best person-job match.

Transition matrix A chart which traces the flow of human resources from in and out of an organisation and from one job to another.

Transitory career A type of career pattern in which the individual moves from job to job, in reaction to their financial needs, interests and the opportunities available.

Transnational strategy An idealised strategy that combines the advantages of multidomestic, international and global strategies. The need for a transnational solution has emerged according to Bartlett & Ghoshal as the advantages of the previous strategies have declined due to pressure for convergence. Thus even in markets which were previously isolated from one another and suitable for a multidomestic strategy, the forces of globalisation; the increased speed of the diffusion of technology, the reduction of trade barriers and the convergence of consumer preferences has tended to make the industry more global in character.

Turnover The proportion of the workforce that leaves employment during a given period. Turnover may be voluntary (individuals decide to leave their jobs) or forced by management.

Uncareer A type of career identified by Hearn (1980) in which an employee leaves the world of formal organisations behind to develop an alternative careers in the arts or crafts, in small-scale farming or as an entrepreneur or consultant.

Upward or reverse appraisals Subordinates rating their superiors performance.

Validity Refers to how well a measure actually assesses an attribute. The validity of a measure is not absolute; rather, it is relative to the situation in which the selection device is being used. For example, a test of aggression may be a valid predictor of police performance, but it may be useless in predicting job success for machinists.

Vision Forward looking model of the organisation.

Vision-driven human resource development A long-range approach to human resource planning used where there is need for relatively major shifts in employee attitudes, skills and behaviours along with changes in the culture which pervades the organisation. It is driven by vision or a sense of mission and lacks the detail and specific targets characteristic of long-range, detailed human resource planning.

Work sample tests Require applicants to complete verbal or physical activities which are closely related to work tasks under structured 'testing' conditions. Rather than measuring what an individual knows, they assess his or her ability to do. Although they have a high validity as selection devices, work sample tests are somewhat artificial because the selection process itself tends to promote anxiety and tension.

names index

A
Aamolt, M. J. 322
Abbott, J. R. 394
Abraham, M. 218
Abrahamson, E. 487
Acuff, H. A. 312
Adam, E. E. 283
Adams, G. 417
Adelman, A. 287
Adler, N. 543, 546, 560, 562, 564
Alvesson, M. 52
Amrine, H. T. 283
Anderson, G. 221
Andrewartha, G. 238
Argyris, – 16
Armstrong, A. 483
Armstrong, D. 221, 222
Arthur, M. B. 215
Arvey, R. D. 323, 335
Ash, R. A. 292
Asher, – 334
Atchison, T. H. 266
Athanasou, J. A. 228
Aubrey, R. F. 229
Ayres, L. 175

B
Bagnall, D. 147
Bagwell, Sheryle 154
Bailey, C. 267
Baker, J. C. 568
Balgopal, P. R. 199
Balkin, D. 448
Bandura, A. 478
Banai, M. 554
Barlow, M. 71, 72, 74

Bardwick, J. 235
Bartlett, C. A. 548, 549, 550, 553, 570
Barton, P. 239
Barwick, K. D. 192
Bass, B. M. 335
Bavetta, A. G. 472
Baysinger, R. A. 323
Beardwell, I. 295
Beazley, Kim 485
Beer, M. 19, 56, 358, 369, 384, 385, 387, 390
Bennett, G. V. 335
Bennett, M. L. 549, 554
Bennett, N. 292
Bentson, C. 335
Bernstein, A. 278
Betts, Neville 195
Betz, R. E. 228
Bhatt, B. 558
Bishop, R. C. 269
Bittman, M. 72
Black, – 526, 561, 562
Black, J. S. 568
Blake, S. 27, 527
Blenco, A. G. 286
Blinder, A. 448
Blinkhorn, S. 333
Bloom, A. J. 474
Boddy, D. 25
Bond, Michael 511
Boudreau, John 264, 321
Bowen, D. E. 224
Bowey, A. M. 217
Boxall, P. F. 49
Boyatzis, R. E. 483
Boynton, A. C. 225

Braithwaite, J. 170, 175
Brake, T. 513, 521, 522, 525
Brandt, R. 220
Breaugh, J. A. 318
Brewster, – 554
Brickner, M. 335
Brooks, A. 169, 170
Brooks, B. J. 574, 575
Brousseau, K. R. 241, 243, 244
Brown, B. K. 336
Brunswig, Bergen 225
Buchanan, D. 25
Budford, J. R. 358
Burack, E. W. 49
Burch, P. 335
Burgess, K. C. 264
Burak, E. H. 217
Burkhalter, B. B. 358
Burton, Clare 73, 76, 77, 127, 275, 276
Butruille, S, G. 245, 246
Buzzotta V. P. 382
Byrne, J. A. 220

C
Cacioppe, R. 482
Caldwell, D. F. 321
Callendar, J. C. 336
Callus, R. 106, 148
Campbell, D. N. 398
Campbell, I. M. 336
Campion, M. A. 284, 335
Carey, P. 416, 441
Carmean, G. 338
Carmody, H. 245

Carnevale, A. P. 467, 473
Caro, P. C. 236, 237
Carpenter, B. N. 336
Carroll, S. J. 356, 363, 369, 375, 387
Carson, K. P. 295
Carter, C. 71, 72, 74
Cartwright, S. 523
Cascio, W. 153, 279, 445, 546
Casey, A. 177
Champagne, P. J. 470
Chandler, A. D. 49
Chao, G. T. 235
Chia, W. 245
Chong, F. 545
Chorpade, J. 20
Churbuck, D. 79
Cipolla, Larry 400
Clark, K. L. 314
Close, A. 233, 437
Cockburn, C. 127
Cofsky, K. 437
Cohen, M. 516
Cohen, S. A. 472
Cohen, Y. 127
Collins, R. 53, 56, 57, 58, 235, 242, 475, 478, 494
Compton, R. L. 295
Cook, – 17
Cook, F. 416
Cooper, C. L. 197, 523
Cooper, W. H. 383
Cornelius, E. T. 286
Cornford, I. R. 228
Cornish, G. 417
Cousens, Liz 354
Cousens, Ted 354
Cowling, A. 49
Cox, T. H. 27, 527
Coyle, W. 561
Craig, – 550
Crawford, J. 218
Crean, Simon 95
Creighton, W. B. 170
Critchley, R. 238, 239, 248
Crooker, K. J. 245, 246
Cropanzano, R. 338
Cummings, L. L. 358, 358, 363, 394
Curtain, R. 474, 492, 494

D

Dabscheck, B. 105
Daft, – 489
Dalton, G. W. 248
Davidson, P. 247
Davis, E. M. 96, 97, 98, 99, 100
Dawkins, J. S. 482
De Cenzo, D. A. 130
De Cieri, H. 561
Dean, R. A. 318
Delahaye, B. L. 247
Deaming, W. Edwards 195, 401
DeNisi, A. S. 232, 251, 318
Derry, S. 92
Desatnick, Robert L. 31, 549, 554
Devanna, M. A. 56, 57
Deves, L. 244, 245
Dex, S. 130
Dickens, L. 130
DiNisi, A. S. 286
Dolan, S. 335
Donnelly, J. H. 383
Dortch, C. T. 296
Doty, D. 427
Dougherty, T. W. 336
Dowell, B. C. 280
Dowling, P. 49, 56, 59–61, 309, 362, 369, 371, 372, 373, 375, 518, 543, 549, 555, 556, 561
Doz, Y. L. 569
Driver, M. J. 240, 242, 243, 244, 253
Drucker, Peter 34, 64, 68, 72
Duerr, M. G. 542
Dunbar, E. 526, 566
Dunlop, John 93
Dunnette, M. 331
Dunphy, D. C. 18, 25, 56, 61, 215, 488
Dwyer, Paula 527
Dyer, J. 324
Dyer, L. 224, 449

E

Earley, P. C. 389
Ebert, R. J. 283, 336
Edstrom, A. 569
Ehrich, L. 245
Elegant, S. 516
Elman, N. S. 233, 235
Emmett, Ted 163
Engels, F. 104
Erez, M. 388, 389

F

Faley, R. H. 323
Farr, J. L. 361, 373
Farren, C. R. 235
Fastenau, Mauren 124
Favero, J. L. 382
Fay, C. 336
Fear, R. A. 336
Feldman, D. 563, 568
Feldman, J. M. 361
Ferguson, Adele 540
Ferguson, Martin 91, 95
Ferris, G. R. 284
Field, H. S. 278, 295, 323
Field, L. 225, 488, 489
Filipczak, B. 181
Fine, S. A. 279
Fiol, C. 487
Fisher, C. 309
Fitzgerald, L. F. 228, 230
Flanagan, J. C. 287, 368
Fleming, R. L. 398
Fletcher, C. A. 333
Forbes, Ronald 391
Ford, B. 80, 488, 489
Ford, Henry 74
Ford, J. K. 383, 471
Ford, L. 221
Forman, David 62
Fossum, J. 449
Fox, Alan 104
Fox, C. 102
Frandt, P. M. 231
Frantzreb, R. B. 221, 227
Fraser, Malcolm 95, 96
French, J. R. P. 386, 391
Fried, Y. 284
Friedman, F. 286
Friedman, M. 187
Frombrun, C. J. 56, 57

G

Gael, S. 266, 270
Galbraith, J. 569

Garavan, T. N. 490
Gardner, M. 17
Gardener, P. D. 235
Gatewood, R. D. 278, 295, 323
Gaugler, B. B. 335
George, J. 111, 116
Ghiselli, E. E. 332
Ghoshal, S. 548, 549, 550, 553, 570
Gibson, J. L. 383
Gier, J. A. 336
Gilbreth, Frank & Lillian 282
Gilmore, A. 273
Gist, M. E. 472
Gittins, Ross 53
Goldstein, I. 469, 470, 482
Gomez-Mejia, L. 448
Gora, Bronwen 212
Gordon, J. 267
Gottfredson, L. S. 244
Gough, G. 332
Gould, R. 335
Grabosky, P. 170
Grant, P. C. 266
Green, B. 379
Green, G. J. L. 217
Greene, C. N. 445
Greengard, S. 394
Greer, C. R. 221, 222
Gregersen, – 562
Greiner, L. E. 224
Greller, – 390
Griffin, R. 284
Grothe, M. 398
Grote, R. C. 398
Grover, S. L. 245, 246
Guerin, C. D. 245
Guest, D. A. 18, 49
Gun, R. 170
Gunningham, N. 170, 171
Gupta, N. 427
Gutteridge, T. 558

H

Hackman, J. R. 384
Hackman, K. 475, 478
Hakel, M. D. 286, 336
Hall, E. T. 509, 510, 525
Hall, D. T. 215, 386
Hamel, M. 55

Hamill, J. 554
Hammer, M. R. 526
Hancock, Keith 104
Harris, C. 97
Harris, H. 130
Harris, M. 545
Harris, P. R. 519
Hartmann, L. 236
Harvey, M. 562, 563
Harvey, Robert J. 286
Harzing, – 554
Hawke, Bob 95, 96, 99, 103
Haydon, D. 334, 341
Hayes, R. H. 282
Hays, R. D. 557
Hayton, G. 491
Hearn, G. 233, 437
Hearn, J. 240, 241, 242, 244, 253
Hede, A. 244
Heinisch, D. A. 269
Heller, J. 557
Hendry, C. 491
Hennan, D. A. 553
Hequet, M. 267
Herman, Susan 264
Heywood, E. 244
Hill, R. E. 228
Hofstede, G. 509, 511, 512, 516, 517
Holden, L. 295
Hollingworth, S. 178
Holton, E. F. 267
Hong, J. C. 267, 268
Hooper, Narelle 128, 185, 197
Howard, John 90, 91, 114, 264
Howard, W. 102
Huber, V. L. 283, 343
Huczynski, A. A. 16
Hugh, L. 378
Hughes, G. L. 334
Hulin, C. L. 389
Hunt, J. W. 233, 235, 242
Hunter, J. E. 309, 332, 379
Hunter, R. F. 332
Huselid, M. A. 10, 221
Hyatt, J. 185
Hyer, N. L. 283

I

Ilgen, D. R. 361, 382
Ivancevich, J. J. 383
Ivancevich, J. M. 568
Ives, – 24

J

Jackson, G. I. 572
Jackson, S. E. 10, 32, 162, 179, 182, 186, 188
Jackson, S. J. 287
Jacobs, G. T. 358
Jaeger, A. M. 566
Jailkumar, R. 282
James, David 67, 79
James, F. B. 200
James, K. 338
James, S. P. 336
Jarrott, Ken 67
Jeffries, B. J. 217
Jenkins, D. 427, 448
Jerdee, T. H. 236
Johns, G. 111
Johnson, C. 333
Johnson, L. 161
Johnson, S. T. 290
Jones, Barry 237, 238, 240
Jones, M. A. 275

K

Kabanoff, B. 52
Kane, R. L. 218, 224, 225, 226, 237
Kangan, – 17
Kanter, R. M. 23, 49, 343, 431
Karpin, D. S. 238, 485, 506
Karraker, B. L. 382
Kavanagh, M. J. 379, 387
Kay, E. 386, 391
Kaye, B. L. 235
Keast, Roger 264
Keating, Paul 90, 91, 99, 474, 494
Kelly, C. 200
Kelty, Bill 109
Kendall, D. W. 562
Kerr, J. 284
Kiechel, W. 365
Kim, D. 487, 488, 489, 490
Kinzel, E. 247
Kirby, P. 474

Kitay, Jim 54
Kleinman, L. S. 314
Klimoski, R. 335
Kluckhohn, F. R. 509, 512
Kohn, Alfie 447, 448
Komaki, J. 192
Kossek, E. E. 246
Kotter, J. P. 24
Kraigen, K. 383
Kram, K. E. 234, 235, 475
Kramar, R. 78, 150, 228, 361
Krautil, Fiona 380
Kuhne, R. J. 574

L

Lado, A. 218
Lamond, D. A. 266
Lamont, Leonie 151
Lander, D. 422, 426
Landy, F. S. 361, 372, 373
Lang, G. 217
Lansbury, Russell 54, 95, 238, 241
Latham, G. P. 287, 336, 356, 357, 358, 374, 384, 388, 389, 390, 391, 394, 470, 472
Laurent, A. 549
Lawler, E. C. 36
Lawler, E. E. 384, 387, 431, 449
Lawrence, B. S. 215
Lawrence, P. 56
Lawson, Mark 306, 307
Lazer, R. I. 362
Ledford, G. E. 427
Lee, C. 267
Lefton, R. E. 382
Legge, K. 15, 19, 21, 49
Leibowitz, Z. B. 235
Lepani, B. 488
Levine, E. L. 292
Levine, H. Z. 314
Levinson, D. A. 321
Likert, – 16
Lilley, B. 178
Limerick, B. 239, 244
Lin, Y. S. 267, 268
Loar, M. 374
Locke, E. A. 378, 388
London, M. 321
Long, S. 168, 328

Love, K. G. 269
Lovegrove, S. A. 336
Lund, J. 366
Lundy, O. 49
Lyles, M. 487

M

McAfee, B. 379
McAfee, R. B. 470
McCarthy, T. E. 295
McClean, J. 333, 334, 341
McCormick, E. J. 266, 271, 278, 279, 283, 285
McFillen, J. N. 445
McGregor, – 16
McGregor, D. 228
McKenzie, D. 482
Mackey, C. B. 217, 219
McLagan, P. 465, 466
McMahan, G. C. 218
MacRae, J. 178
McWilliams, – 218
Machalaba, D. 278
Mager, R. F. 395, 396
Maglen, L. 467
Maier, N. R. F. 389
Manns, R-A. 136
Manzini, A. O. 222
Margerison, C. 241
Margulies, – 17
Markowitz, J. 279
Marshall, J. 245
Marshall, Ray 112, 113
Martin, R. 95
Marx, Karl 104
Maslow, – 16
Maslow, A. H. 229, 242
Maurer, S. D. 336
Mayo, Elton 16
Mead, R. 510
Meglino, B. M. 232, 251, 318
Mendenhall, M. E. 526, 554, 558, 560, 561, 566, 568, 576
Merrit, A. 170
Meyer, H. H. 386, 391
Michelson, G. 229
Midgley, D. 218
Miles, R. E. 49, 52, 231
Miller, E. L. 49, 217
Miller, H. E. 335
Miller, S. 49

Mills, D. 56
Mills, J. A. 215
Milner, S. 482
Mintzberg, H. 49, 50, 225
Mitchell, T. R. 358, 394
Modrow-Thiel, B. 267
Mohrman, A. M. 374, 387
Montei, M. S. 269
Montminy, P. M. 266
Moore, John 96
Moore, T. 246
Moran, R. T. 519
Morgan, P. V. 542, 543
Morrison, A. 245
Mount, M. K. 390
Mukhi, S. K. 241
Mundey, Jack 98
Murray, A. H. 557
Murray, F. T. 557
Myers, Rupert 96

N

Nadler, L. 465
Nadler, Z. 465
Naisbitt, J. 508
Nankervis, A. R. 295
Nemeroff, – 390
Newman, J. 558
Nichol, V. 246
Nicholson, J. 71, 72, 74
Niland, John 93
Nininger, J. R. 49
Noe, R. A. 471
Novitt, M. S. 338
Nkomo, S. M. 217

O

O'Boyle, T. F. 198
O'Connor, E. J. 384
O'Connor, P. 235, 242
Oddou, G. 526, 554, 558, 560, 561, 566, 576
O'Neal, S. 437
O'Neill, G. 415, 416, 417, 422, 426, 448
O'Reilly, Brian 360
O'Rourke 247
Olian, J. 194, 324
Olivas, L. 376

P

Page, R. 266
Palmer, J. 17

Patcher, M. 199
Patrickson, M. 236, 334, 341
Pearlman, K. 292, 379
Peggins, D. L. 322
Peiperl, M. A. 231
Pelletier, K. R. 185
Perlmutter, H. V. 553
Perrow, C. 179
Peters, L. H. 384
Peters, T. 225
Pettigrew, A. M. 467, 491
Petty, M. M. 335
Pfeffer, Jeffrey 13, 14, 127, 309
Phatak, A. V. 552
Picard, M. 267
Pierce, J. 247
Pinney, D. L. 573
Pinto, P. R. 279
Piore, M. 10
Pipe, P. 395
Piskurich, G. M. 267
Pithers, R. T. 228
Pittard, M. 102
Plowman, D. 92, 95, 100
Plumke, L. P. 333
Podsakoff, P. M. 323, 413, 445
Port, O. 220
Porter, B. 217
Porter, L. W. 384
Porter, Michael 13, 324, 549
Porter, P. 494
Prahalad, C. K. 55, 569
Price, V. A. 561
Prien, E. P. 334
Pringle, J. 245
Pucik, V. 575
Purcell, E. D. 336

R

Rahim, A. 566, 567
Raia, – 17
Ralston, D. 244
Ramanathan, C. 199
Ravlin, E. C. 232, 251
Raza, S. M. 336
Renwick, G. W. 524
Resnick, S. M. 387
Revans R. W. 484
Rimmer, M. 482

Riskind, J. H. 286
Robbins, S. P. 130
Robens, Lord 169, 170
Roberts, Peter 4, 5, 25, 315, 319, 344
Robinson, Peter 4
Robinson, R. D. 547, 553
Robock, S. H. 553, 564, 572
Rodgers, D. D. 336, 346
Ronen, S. 547, 568
Roseman, R. 187
Rosen, B. 236, 244
Rosenthal, D. B. 335
Rossman, G. 267
Ruff, H. J. 572
Russell, Matthew 143, 151
Ruzek, P. 246
Ryall, C. 73, 76, 77
Rynes, S. 244, 321, 324

S

Saari, L. M. 336, 389, 390
Sabel, C. F. 10
Salmon, P. W. 227
Sathe, V. 516
Sauers, D. A. 199, 244
Saul, P. 51, 483
Sayles, L. R. 313
Scanlon, Joe 441
Scerberg, M. 382
Schein, – 16
Schein, E. H. 230, 231
Schmidt, F. L. 309, 310, 379
Schmitt, N. 472
Schneider, J. R. 472
Schneider, S. C. 517
Schneider, T. 70, 310, 375
Schneier, C. E. 356, 363, 369, 387
Schuler, R. S. 9, 10, 12, 32, 49, 56, 59–61, 69, 74, 75, 132, 153, 162, 179, 182, 185, 186, 188, 216, 224, 225, 234, 250, 324, 334, 336, 343, 362, 365, 369, 371, 372, 373, 375, 387, 395, 396, 397, 399, 413, 414, 421, 430, 471, 543
Schuster, J. 431

Schwab, D. P. 358, 363, 449
Schwartz, Adam 524
Schwartz, F. 245
Schweiger, D. M. 324
Sciarrino, – 334
Scott, M. E. 323
Scott, L. 192
Scott, Rebecca 79
Scullion, H. 554
Senge, P. M. 225, 467, 487, 488
Shaker, Ben 328
Sharratt, P. 225
Shaw, J. B. 286
Sheehy, G. 242
Shenkar, O. 543, 544, 545
Shipper, F. C. 153
Shipper, F. M. 153
Shippman, J. S. 334
Shires, David 160
Shore, L. M. 474
Shostak, A. B. 186
Simmonds, K. 553, 564, 572
Sinclair, Amanda 76
Singh, J. P. 390
Slagle, Bob 76
Sloan, Alfred 74
Sloan, S. J. 197
Sloane, M. 244, 245
Smeed, B. 241
Smith, A. 472, 491, 493
Smith, B. 233, 437
Smith, C. R. 245, 246
Snow, C. C. 49, 52, 231
Sonnenfeld, J. A. 231
Southey, G. 233, 437
Sparks, C. P. 266, 270, 285, 286
Sparrow, P. R. 467
Spector, B. 19, 56
Spencer, L. M. 379
Spencer, S. M. 379
Spivey, W. A. 321
Stace, D. 25, 56, 61, 488, 545, 550, 554, 562, 571, 577
Stanton, S. 217, 221, 224, 225, 226
Stening, B. W. 526
Stephens, – 561
Stevens, C. K. 472

Stewart, Cameron 506
Stewart, K. P. 295
Stickels, Georgi 76, 77, 128
Still, L. V. 73, 245
Stock, J. R. 374
Stogdill, R. M. 365
Stone, R. J. 246, 295
Storey, J. 483
Story, J. 19, 20, 21
Stowel, S. J. 474
Stradwick, R. 417
Stratford, D. 216, 247, 248
Strauss G. 313
Strodtbeck, F. L. 509, 512
Stroh, L. K. 563
Stumpf, S. A. 321
Super, D. E. 229, 240, 241, 242, 253
Szilagyi, A. D. 324
Szwejczewski, M. 290

T

Taiichi Ohno 74
Taylor, H. M. 193
Taylor, Frederick W. 15, 265
Taylor, K. F. 561
Thayer, P. W. 284
Thomas, – 563
Thomas, J. 284
Thomas, Ken 79
Thomas, Tony 66
Thornton, G. C. 335
Tichy, N. M. 56, 57
Tiffin, J. 285
Toohey, J. 163, 180, 197
Torbiorn, I. 560, 565
Tornow, W. W. 279

Toyne, B. 574
Trafford, Chris 400
Treadgold, Tim 83
Trompenaars, F. 509, 512
Trumbo, D. A. 372
Tung, R. 555, 556, 557, 558, 559, 561, 562, 566, 567, 568
Tziner, A. 335

U

Ulrich, D. 225

V

Vaill, Peter 23
Van De Voort, D. 266
Van Velsor, E. 245
Vanden Heuval, A. 72
Vasbinder, D. M. 266, 290, 291
Vaughan, E. 333, 334, 341
Verespej, M. A. 266, 290, 291
Victor, B. 225
Villanova, P. 394

W

Wachter, H. 267
Walker, D. 513, 521, 522
Walker, J. W. 63, 64, 65, 66, 216, 222, 224, 225, 295
Wallace, J. 233
Wallace-Bruce, N. L. 181
Walters, P. 130
Walton, R. 56
Walz, P. M. 235
Wanous, J. P. 318

Watson, T. J. 15
Waung, M. 233, 251
Weaver, C. S. 184
Weekley, J. A. 336
Weick, – 489
Weiss, Julian M. 14
Weis, W. L. 185
Welch, D. 543, 556
Wexley, K. N. 280, 287, 356, 357, 374, 384, 390, 470
White, R. P. 245
Wickens, C. D. 199
Wikstrom, W. S. 362
Williams, K. J. 318, 323
Williams, M. 194
Williams, T. 455
Willis, Ralph 95
Wilson, J. A. 233, 235
Wilson, M. C. 218
Woodruffe, C. 483
Wolcot, I. 72
Wright, C. 366
Wright, P. 145
Wright, P. M. 218
Wylie, P. 398

Y

Yager, E. 379
Yetton, – 550
Young, J. 79
Youngblood, S. A. 318
Yukl, G. A. 390, 391

Z

Zedeck, S. 287
Zeira, Y. 551, 554, 566
Zingheim, P. 431

subject index

A
absenteeism 28, 29, 378
accidents *see* occupational accidents
Accord 94, 107
affirmative action 127, 131–33, 137–49, 152–53, 154
    see also Equal Employment Opportunity
Air International 149
alignment and strategic human resource management 53–56
anti-discrimination legislation 130–31, 134–37, 326, 361
ANZ Bank 52
application blanks 326–27
apprenticeship training 473–74
arbitration 102
assessment
    centres 334–35
    framework for Affirmative Action 140–43
attitude surveys 471–72
Australian Business Limited 101, 102
Australian Centre for Industrial Relations Research and Teaching (ACIRRT) 112
Australian Chamber Commerce and Industry (ACCI) 101
Australian Chamber of Manufacturers (ACM) 100
Australian Council of Trade Unions (ACTU) 95, 96, 98, 100, 107, 153, 453
Australian Industrial Relations Commission (AIRC) 72, 143, 153
Australian Labor Party (ALP) 91, 94, 95, 96, 99, 107, 110
Australian National Training Authority (ANTA) 493, 494
Australian Standard Classification of Occupations (ASCO) 279
Australian Traineeship System (ATS) 474
Australian Women's Employment Strategy 131
Australian Workplace Agreements (AWAs) 115
Australian Workplace Industrial Survey (AWIRS) 106
award restructuring 467
awards, industrial 8, 18, 418

B
base pay 416
behaviour
    employee 8, 192–93, 201, 398
    modelling 477–78
    and performance appraisal 373–74, 446
    strategies, negative 398–99
behavioural observation scale (BOS) 374, 375, 446
behaviourally-anchored rating scale (BARS) 373, 446
benchmark evaluations 422
Best Practice 147–52, 199
business
    outcomes, improving 48–49
    strategy 49–50
Business Council of Australia (BCA) 91, 100, 104

C
California Psychological Inventory 332
Caltex 149, 150–52
career(s)

anarchic 240, 253
anchor 230–31
concepts 240–44
cop-out careerists 240
counselling 236–37, 247–48
development 75, 228–32
    individually-orientated models 229, 232
    and organisational strategy 231–32
early career programs 233–35
expatriate 246–47
flexibility 238–40
future 237–42
guerilla 240
ladders 233
late career programs 236
launching your 248–52
linear 241–42, 244, 253
management 227, 232–37
    in Australia 237
    programs 232, 242–48
    systems approach 229–32
mentoring programs 233–35, 474–75
mid career programs 235
mid life transition 235
opportunities 319
organisational entry programs 232–33
paths 233
planning programs 233
plateau 235
self-appraisal 248–50
spiral 242, 253
steady state 241
trait-factor approach 228, 230, 232
transitory 241
Carmichael Report 493
centralisation 34–35
change
    and HRM 22–23
    managing 6, 24–26, 247, 269, 338, 417, 468, 508, 546–47
child-care assistance 246
coaching 474
cognitive ability tests 330
Collins model 57
Comcare Australia 177
communication and culture 508–509
Commonwealth Bank 52
competency-based assessment 379, 472
competition
    domestic and international 70, 269, 359–61
    increased 21–22
competitive advantage 13–14
Computer Assisted Instruction (CAI) 479–80
Computer Managed Instruction (CMI) 479
Computer Managed Learning (CML) 479, 480
computer monitoring 366
computer technology
    and HRIS 30, 296, 345
    and jobs 281
    and selection 345–46
    and training 479–80
    see also technology
Computer-based training 479–80
conciliation 102
Confederation of Australian Industry (CAI) 100
corporate strategy 12, 415–16
cost criteria 29–30
counselling
    career 236–37
    outplacement 247–48
cross-cultural management 6, 506–508, 528
    management problems 517–24
cultural
    change 4
    differences, managing 524–28
    frameworks 508–17
    orientations 513–17, 521, 522
    toughness 560–61
culture
    collegial 52
    and communication 509–510
    defined 51–52
    dimensions of 511
    elite 52
    and internal environment 12
    leader focused 52
    levels of 516
    meritocratic 52
    organisational 51–52, 416–17
    waves of 512
customerisation 31–32

D

decentralisation 34–35
Delphi technique 221
demographic needs analysis 472
demotion 8, 386
development

career 75, 228–32
    individually-orientated models 229, 232
    and organisational strategy 231–32
    centres 484
    international model 567
    management 81, 465, 482–85
    and training 465–82
        international 563–71
        needs 469
        programs 480–82
devolution 34
direct remuneration 411
discrimination
    and employment policies 126–27, 130–31
    legislation 134–37, 326, 361
    resolution of a complaint 135
    see also anti-discrimination legislation
drug and alcohol testing 339

E

economic environment 93–94, 269
Economic Planning Advisory Commission (EPAC) 92
education levels 74
employee(s)
    behaviour 8, 192–93, 201, 373–75, 398, 446, 477–78
    benefits 451–56
    counselling 236–37, 247–48, 398
    empowerment 227, 388
    and HRM 35
    and managers 19
    participation 18, 449–50
    performance 8, 9, 10, 12, 15–16, 267, 356–402
    rights 8, 9, 22
    services and perquisites 453–54
    specifications 274–77
    violence by 181–83
    unsafe 180–81
    welfare 14–15, 17, 18
    see also performance appraisal; performance management
Employee Assistance Programs (EAPs) 194, 398
employee share ownership plans (ESOPs) 454
employers' associations 100–102
enterprise bargaining 94, 107–14, 418
    and equity 110–11

environment
    economic 93–94, 269
    external 9, 11, 13, 67–70, 268–69, 311–12, 314–16, 417–20
    internal 9, 11–13, 268–69, 312–14, 324–39, 415–17
    physical 186–87
    political 269
    workplace 6, 8, 163–68, 197–98
environmental
    assessment 63, 64–65
    change 97–98
equal employment opportunity (EEO) 7, 126–27, 326
    and affirmative action 127, 131–33, 137–43, 148, 149
    Australian developments 130–34
    Australian legislation 134–44
    and Best Practice 147–52
    development 129–34, 152–54
    and discrimination 126–27
    and HRM 145–147
    international standards 129
    interpretation 146–47
    legislation 129–30, 134–44, 137–43
    and sexual harassment 127–28
equity and enterprise bargaining 110–111
ergonomics 191–92, 290–91
expatriates 246–47, 554–61, 564–66
external environment 9, 11, 13, 67–70, 268–69, 311–12, 314–16, 417–20
extrinsic rewards 447

F

factor comparison of job evaluation 426
families and work 74, 77–80, 133–34, 153, 245–46
Finn Review 493
flexible reward 449
forecasting
    demand 219, 220–21
    economic perspective 222
    judgemental 221
    supply 219, 222–23
Fringe Benefits Tax (FBT) 419, 453
future organisational forms *see* organisational

G

gainsharing 441
genetic screening 194
Germany and job training 492–93

glass ceiling 76
globalisation 543–47
goals and internal environment 11–12, 268
golden employment practices 454
government
    and industrial relations 102–103
    legislation and reward management 418–19
group incentive plans 440–42
grievances 8

H

Hancock Committee of Inquiry 104, 105, 107
handwriting analysis 328
Harvard model 21, 56–57
Hay Guide Chart Method 280–81, 324, 424–25, 456
Host Country Nationals (HCNs) 542, 551, 552, 553, 554, 573, 574
human relations theory 16–17
human resource
    analysis 219, 220
    costs 22, 29–30
    demand 219, 220–21
    wheel 466
Human Resource Development (HRD) 465–66
human resource information system (HRIS) 30, 216, 296, 345
human resource management (HRM)
    activities 6, 7–13
    assessment 28–30
    defined 18, 19–21
    department organisation 32–36
    and equal employment opportunity 145–47
    functions 6, 7–13
    hard core 21
    importance 13–14
    importance, events influencing 21–23
    and industrial relations 92
    objectives 9, 10
    and occupational health and safety 195–96
    in the organisation 34
    and personnel management 18–21
    policies 49
    practices 61
    purposes 9, 10–11
    and research 8
    and responsibility 35–36
    soft core 21
    strategic involvement 30–32, 49
    territory map 57
    theory 17
    titles 35–36
    trends 23–32
    see also international human resource management; strategic human resource management
human resource objectives 223
human resource planning 6, 7, 9, 30, 215–16
    assessing supply and demand 219–23
    barriers 226–27
    in a changing environment 224–26
    control and evaluation 223–24
    establishing objectives 223
    evolution 216–18
    and job analysis 325
    phases 219–24
    process 218–19
    programming 223, 227
    and recruitment 312
    and selection 325
    Short-term Human Resource Strategy 224
    staff replacement approach 224, 226
    Vision-driven Human Resource Development 225
human resource roles 32–34
human resource supply 219–20, 222–23

I

ICI Botany 80, 108
incentive pay plans 436, 438–42
indirect rewards 411
industrial
    agreements and awards 8, 18, 418
    disputes 17, 98, 102, 103–104, 105–107, 109
    reforms 465
    tribunals 18, 99, 103–104, 111
industrial psychology movement 15
industrial relations 18, 20, 90–93
    changes 72
    and conflict 104–107
    economic context 93–94
    and employers' associations 100–102
    and enterprise bargaining 107–14
    and environment 97–98
    and government 102–103

and HRM 92
legislation 70, 143–44
and politics 94–95
practices 70
reforms 114–16
and reward management 418
and social change 97
and technological change 96–97
and tribunals 103–104
and unions 98–100
Industrial Relations Commission (IRC) 72, 96, 115, 143, 153, 418
Industry Task Force on Leadership and Management Skills 70, 73, 81, 152
see also Karpin Report
insurance, health and disability 453
interactive video training (IVT) 479
internal environment 9, 11–13, 268–69, 312–14, 324–39, 415–17
internal equity 420
international human resource management (IHRM) 6
  executive national policies 551–53
  expatriate
    careers 246–47
    failure, training to avoid 564–66
    failure rates 554–56
    success predictors 557–61
  introduction 542–43
  and multinational organisations 548–50
  organisational growth 547–48
  pattern of globalisation 543–47
  recruitment and selection 550–63
  remuneration 572–75
  repatriation 562–63
  staffing
    ethnocentric approach 551
    geocentric 552
    policy issues 553–54
    polycentric policy 551–52
    regiocentric 553
  training and development 563–71
international organisations 547–50
international recruitment and selection 550–63
  and cultural toughness 560–61
  ethnocentric approach 551
  executive nationality policies 551–53
  expatriate failure rates 246, 554–56
  expatriate success predictors 557–61
  flow chart 559
  geocentric staffing 552
  policy choice 553–54
  polycentric staffing policy 551–52
  regiocentric staffing 553
  repatriation 562–63
international remuneration 572–75
international training and development 563–71
International Labour Organisation (ILO) 93, 97–98
  conventions 70, 129, 130, 133–34
interviews 251–52, 318, 335–38, 388–93

J

Japan
  cultural orientations 522
  job training 492
job
  analysis and design
    approaches to 278–92
    aspects of 270–77
    assessing methods 292–95
    competency profiling 295
    computer technology and HRIS in 296
    in context 266–69
    Critical Incident Technique 287–89
    external environment 268–69
    flow process charts 282
    functional 278–79
    Guidelines Oriented Job Analysis 289
    internal environment 268–69
    Job Element Inventory 286
    and job relevance 337
    methods analysis 281–83
    needs 470
    organisational development programs 267
    performance management and training 267
    performance appraisal 358
    person-focused techniques 283–89
    Physical Abilities Analysis 286–87
    Position Analysis Questionnaire (PAQ) 285–86
    practical concerns 293–94
    purposes and importance 265–66, 292–93
    recruitment and selection 267, 312, 325

remuneration 267, 420
reward management 413–15
scientific approach 278
team-based approaches 289–90
and technology 268
time and motion study 282–83
trends 294–96
worker-machine charts 282
applicants 312–46
benchmark evaluations 422
burnout 187
classification 423
description 265, 274–77
domains 287
elements 281
enlargement 284
enrichment 284
evaluation 267, 420, 423–28, 430
families 291–92
focused techniques 278–89
information, collecting 270–74
interviews 251, 318, 335–38
managerial 279–80, 335, 337
   Hay Plan 280–81, 324, 424–25, 456
needs analysis 470
opportunities 319
posting 314
promotions 313
ranking 423
realistic job preview 318
relative value 420–28
rotation 290, 473
skills inventories 314
specification 265
training 473, 475–76, 477–82
transfers 313
types 238, 250–51
see also recruitment; selection

K
Karpin Report 23, 152, 354–55, 485–86, 495, 507, 542, 546
Kent Brewery 80

L
labour market and reward management 417–18
law
   common 178
   statute 168–76
Lawrence Livermore Laboratories 236
legal compliance 10, 11
legislation

anti-discrimination 130–3, 134–37, 326, 361
discrimination 134–37, 326, 361
EEO 129–30, 134–44, 137–43
government and reward management 418–19
industrial relations 70, 143–44
occupational health and safety 172–74, 177, 178
Lend Lease Corporation 80
Liberal–National Party Coalition 91, 114
lie detector tests 339
line managers 19, 20, 33, 35, 36, 49, 162, 310, 323

M
management
   action learning 483–84
   cross-cultural 6, 506–508, 517–24, 528
   development 465, 482–85
   development centres 484
   education and development 81
   selection 335
   self-development 484
Management by Objectives (MBO) 363, 374, 375–77, 517
Management Position Description Questionnaire 279–80
managerial incentive plans 440
managers 19, 35, 482–85, 506–508, 517–24
managing diversity 6, 26–28, 74–77, 244–45, 291, 319–20, 422, 476, 524
Mayer Report 493
mentoring 474–75
   programs 233–35
merit pay plans 436, 437–38
Metal Trades Industry Association (MTIA) 101
Michigan University 21
midlife transition 235
Minnesota Multiphasic Personality Inventory 332
Mobil 5
multinational organisations 548–50
   executive nationality policies 551–53
multinational training practices 567–68
multiple linear regression analysis 221
multiple predictors 340
Myers-Briggs Type Indicator 332

N
National Australia Bank 52

National Occupational Health and Safety
    Commission (NOHSC) 165, 168
National Roads and Motorists'
    Association (NRMA) 78, 145, 149, 150
National Training Board (NTB) 493
National Training Reform
    Agenda (NTRA) 493, 494
National Wage Case 100–101, 108–10,
    453, 465
Neo-Human Relations 16, 17, 18
nominal group technique 221
normal time 282
Northern States Power (NSP) 75

O

observed time 282
occupational
    accidents 161, 162–68, 180–81,
        187–201
    diseases 161, 164, 183–85, 193–94
    stress 161, 185–87, 198
occupational health and safety
    (OHS) 160–62
    committees 192
    common law 178
    and employee violence 181–83
    enforcement pyramid 175
    hazards 161, 162–63, 169, 179–83, 187
    and HRM 195–96
    improvement strategies 162–68,
        187–201
    international 198–99
    legal considerations 168–78
    legislation 172–74, 177, 178
    model 179
    and monitoring of foreign firms 198–99
    performance indicators 188–99
    policies 199–200
    and rehabilitation 177, 178
    statute law 168–76, 192
    wellness programs 200
    work environment 163–68
    and workers' compensation 176–78
off-the-job training 475–76
on-the-job training (OJT) 473
organisational
    change 186
    conflict 384–87
    culture 416–17
    design 58
    development programs 267
    fit 49, 52–53
    learning 74, 80, 467, 487–90

life, preparing for 251–52
need analysis 470
rewards 413
stress 185–87
vision 225
organisational forms
    future 6, 436, 484–85
    managing 23–24
organisations
    and career management 237
    and competition 359
    and HRM 34
    international 547–48
    multidivisional 35
    multinational 548–50, 551–53

P

Parent Country Nationals (PCNs) 542,
    551, 552, 553, 554, 566, 573, 574
pay
    grade structure 429–30
    incentive pay plans 436, 438–42
    merit pay plans 436, 437–38
    and performance 411, 436–37, 443,
        446–47, 457
    rates 428–29
    and reward management 428–48
    satisfaction 450–51
    secrecy 450
    structure, establishing 428–31
    see also remuneration; reward
        management; wage determination
performance
    assessment and remuneration 415
    criteria 362–63
    deficiencies 395–96
    identifying gaps in 394–95
    improvement 393–99
    and pay 411, 436–37
    and reward management 431–48
performance appraisal 8, 9, 35, 355
    absolute standards 367–74
    accomplishment records 378
    approaches 366–79
    behavioural observation scale 374, 375,
        446
    behaviourally-anchored rating
        scale 373, 446
    choice of raters 364–66
    comparative standards 366–67
    and computer monitoring 366
    context 382–84
    criteria and standards 361–63, 379

data 384–87
design and use of 379–88
direct index approach 378
by customers 366
and employee empowerment 388
ethical considerations 358
and external environment 359–61
inherent conflicts 384–87
interview 388–93
and job analysis 358
means-based approach 379
objective based approaches 374–78
and organisational conditions 384
and performance improvement 393–99
and positive reinforcement system 397–99
processes and procedures 361–66
qualitative forms 367–69
quantitative forms 369–74
and relationships 358–61
and remuneration 358, 415
roles and purposes 356–58
and selection 325, 326, 358
self-appraisal 364
superior–subordinate relationships 382–83
by superiors 364
system 356, 379, 384, 387–88
team member appraisal 364–65
and training 359
trends 399–401
upward or reversed 365–66
and worker participation 388
performance management 6, 7–8, 267, 355
defined 356
system 379
performance-based pay systems 411, 436–37, 443, 446–47, 457
person needs analysis 470
personal appraisal 248–50
personality tests 332–33
personnel management
historical view 14–18
and human resource management 18–21
industrial relations firefighter role 17
staff forecasting role 17
personnel needs 6, 7
physical environment 186–87
physical examinations 338
point factor of job evaluation 421, 423–25, 426
political
environment 269
security and reward management 419
polygraph test 339
Positive Reinforcement (PR) system 397–99
productivity 10–11, 28, 29
profit-sharing plans 442–43
promotions 313

R
realistic job previews 232
recruitment 75, 267, 309
activity 311
assessing 320–21
behaviourally-based systems 321–22
defined 10
and external environment 311–12, 314–16, 317
and internal environment 312–14, 317
international 550–63
and job applicants 312–19
policies 318–19
procedures, timing of 318
purposes and importance of 310–11
rejection with tact 322
relationships influencing 311–19
and reward management 415
systems, behaviourally-based 321–22
and training 325
trends 319–22
see also international recruitment and selection
redundancy 8, 96
reference verification 330
rehabilitation 177, 178
remuneration 6, 7–8, 9, 267, 358, 412, 415
direct 411
international 572–75
and performance 431–47
planning and management 420–47
see also pay; reward management; wage determination
replacement planning 222
retirement programs 236, 452–53
retrenchment 8, 386, 247–48
reward management
communication and administration 449–51
corporate strategy 415–16
employee benefits 451–56

employee participation 449–50
external environment 417–20
government legislation 418–19
and HRM 413–15
industrial relations system 418
internal environment 414, 415–17
job analysis 413–14, 420
job evaluation 420–28
job value 420–47
labour market 417–18
linking performance to pay 447–51
organisational culture 416–17
pay plans 431–48
pay secrecy 450
pay structure 428–31
performance assessment 415, 431–51
and recruitment 415
relationships of total 413–20
and remuneration 420–47
role of total 411–13
superannuation and retirement benefits 452–53
and social security 419, 452, 453
and taxation 419–20
union–management relations 415
workers' compensation 452
see also remuneration
rewards
    extrinsic 447
    financial 449
    flexible 449
    indirect 411
    organisational 413
role playing 477
Rucker Plan 442

S

Scanlon Plan 441–42
Schuler 5Ps 56, 59, 60
scientific management 15, 17–18
selection 309–10
    application blanks 326–27
    assessment 345–46
        centres 334–35
    biases in 341–44
    cognitive ability tests 330
    of contractors 344–45
    criterion scores 326
    decision aids 343–44
    drug and alcohol testing 339
    education and experience evaluations 327
    handwriting analysis 328
    and human resource planning 325
    and information, methods of using 339–41
    and internal environment 324
    international 550–63
    interviews 335–38
    and job analysis 325
    and job relevance 337
    lie detector tests 339
    managerial 335
    multiple predictor approach 340
    and performance appraisal 325, 326, 358
    personality tests 332–33
    physical examinations 338
    and placement 322–46
    practices, Australian data 340–41
    predictors 325–26, 339–40
    psychomotor tests 330–32
    purposes and importance of 323
    and recruitment 325
    reference verification 330
    ratios 321
    single predictor approach 339–40
    structure 336–37
    techniques 325–29
    and training 325
    trends 344–35
    work simulations 333–34
    written tests 330–32
    see also international recruitment and selection
self-actualisation 229
self-assessed training needs 470–71
self-managing teams 290
self-awareness 251
sexual harassment 127–28
Short-term Human Resource Strategy 224
simple linear regression analysis 221
simulation, job 478
single predictors 339
size, organisational
    and internal environment 13
skill-base evaluation of jobs 426–27
skills inventories 314
social
    change 97
    environment 269
    security and reward management 419, 452, 453
    structure 70–74

society and value orientations 509
Staff Replacement Approach 224
staffing 6, 7, 9
stakeholder 50–51, 57
standard time 282
strategic human resource management
   concepts 49–56
   and diversity 74–77
   future developments 74–81
   models 49, 56–63
   processes 63–67
strategic intent 56
strategy
   corporate and external
     environment 67–69
   corporate and internal environment 12,
     415–16
   corporate and training 490–91
   defined 49–50
   development 63, 65
   formulation 65
   and HRM 49–50
   implementation 63, 66–67
stress *see* occupational stress
structure, organisational
   and internal environment 12–13
success, stakeholders 51
succession planning 222
superannuation 452–53
SWOT analysis 218
systems thinking 487

T

taxation
   Fringe Benefits (FBT) 419, 453
   and reward management 419–20
Taylorism 15, 16
team working 5
technological change
   and industrial relations 96–97
technological environment 268–69
technology 74, 268
   and internal environment 12–13
   see also computer technology
Third Country Nationals (TCNs) 542,
   573, 574
time and motion study 282–83
Total Quality Management (TQM) 195
trade unions *see* unions
traineeship training 473–74
training
   apprenticeship and traineeship 473–74

assessment phase 469
attitude surveys 471–72
and behaviour modelling 477–78
and coaching 474
competency-based assessment 472
Computer-based training 479–80
and corporate strategy 490–91
and development 465–82
   international 563–71
   needs 469
   programs 480–82
evaluation 469, 480–82
and expatriate failure 246, 564–66
formal courses 475–76
implementation phase 469
induction 477
interactive video training (IVT) 479
international comparisons 492–93
international model 567
job instruction 473
location 472–77
and mentoring 474–75
methods 477–79
multinational practices 567–68
needs 7, 267, 312, 325, 469–72
off-the-job 475–76
on-the-job (OJT) 473
outdoor 478–79
and performance appraisal 359
and recruitment 325
policy 493–94
and recruitment 312
reforms 494
and role playing 477
self-assessment
   470–71
simulation technique 478
technologies 479–80
video presentations 479
Training Guarantee Scheme 494
Training Reform Agenda 495
transfers 313

U

union–management relations 8, 9, 17, 415
union(s)
   and industrial relations 98–99
   membership 99–100

V

value
   adding 31, 70

orientations 509
values and internal environment 11–12
Vision-driven Human Resource
    Development 225

W

wage determination 430–31
    see also National Wage Case; pay;
        remuneration
welfare
    officers 14–15
    schemes 14–15, 17, 18, 452
    social 452, 453
wellness programs 200
Westpac 52, 80
women
    in management 73
    in the workforce 71–72, 131–33,
        137–49, 152–54, 214
    see also affirmative action;
        Equal Employment
        Opportunity
work
    and families 74, 77–80, 133–34, 153,
        245–46
flexible arrangements 72–73
life, quality 10, 11, 29, 185
measurement 282
methods 15
pacing 186
sample tests 333–34
sampling 283
workers' compensation 163–68, 176–78,
    452
workforce
    future needs 214
    women 71–72, 131–33, 137–49,
        152–54, 214
workplace
    bargaining 8, 111–14, 115
    and change 22–23
    environment 6, 8, 163–68, 197–98
    hazards 161, 162–63, 169, 179–83,
        187
    practice 111–14
    reform 4, 5, 70, 114–16
    relationships 6, 9
Workplace Relations Act 114–16
Worksafe Australia 168–69, 187, 188, 192
written tests 330–32